VOLKSWAGEN | AIR-COOLED
1949-69 REPAIR MANUAL

CHILTON'S

Covers U.S. and Canadian models of Beetle, Karmann Ghia, Bus, Fastback, Notchback and Squareback

by George B. Heinrich, A.S.C., S.A.E.

CHILTON Automotive Books

PUBLISHED BY **HAYNES NORTH AMERICA**, Inc.

Printed in Malaysia
© 1997, 2007 Haynes North America, Inc.
ISBN-13: 978-0-8019-9073-1
ISBN-10: 0-8019-9073-4
Library of Congress Control Number 97-67981
4567890123 9876543210

Haynes Publishing Group
Sparkford Nr Yeovil
Somerset BA22 7JJ England

Haynes North America, Inc
859 Lawrence Drive
Newbury Park
California 91320 USA

ABCDEF

6K1

Contents

Contents

SAFETY NOTICE

Proper service and repair procedures are vital to the safe, reliable operation of all motor vehicles, as well as the personal safety of those performing repairs. This manual outlines procedures for servicing and repairing vehicles using safe, effective methods. The procedures contain many NOTES, CAUTIONS and WARNINGS which should be followed, along with the standard procedures to eliminate the possibility of personal injury or improper service which could damage the vehicle or compromise its safety.

It is important to note that repair procedures and techniques, tools and parts for servicing motor vehicles, as well as the skill and experience of the individual performing the work may vary widely. It is not possible to anticipate all of the conceivable ways or conditions under which vehicles may be serviced, or to provide cautions as to all possible hazards that may result. Standard and accepted safety precautions and equipment should be used when handling toxic or flammable fluids, and safety goggles or other protection should be used during cutting, grinding, chiseling, prying or any other process that can cause material removal or projectiles.

Some procedures require the use of tools specially designed for a specific purpose. Before substituting another tool or procedure, you must be completely satisfied that neither your personal safety, nor the performance of the vehicle will be endangered.

Although information in this manual is base don industry sources and is as complete as possible at the time of publication, the possibility exists that some car manufacturers made later changes which could not be included here. While striving for total accuracy, the authors or publishers cannot assume responsibility for any errors, changes, or omissions that may occur in the compilation of this data.

PART NUMBERS

Part numbers listed in this reference are not recommended by Haynes North America, Inc. for any product brand name. They are references that can be used with interchange manuals and aftermarket supplier catalogs to locate each brand supplier's discreet part number.

SPECIAL TOOLS

Special tools are recommended by the vehicle manufacturer to perform their specific job. Use has been kept to a minimum, but where absolutely necessary, they are referred to in the text by the part number of the tool manufacturer. These tools can be purchased, under the appropriate part number, from your local dealer or regional distributor, or an equivalent tool can be purchased locally from a tool supplier or parts outlet. Before substituting any tool for the one recommended, read the SAFETY NOTICE at the top of this page.

ACKNOWLEDGEMENTS

The publisher expresses appreciation to Volkswagen of America, Ltd, for their generous assistance.

1

GENERAL INFORMATION AND MAINTENANCE

Chilton's Total Car Care manual is intended to help you learn more about the inner workings of your vehicle while saving you money on its upkeep and operation.

The beginning of the book will likely be referred to the most, since that is where you will find information for maintenance and tune-up. The other sections deal with the more complex systems of your vehicle. Operating systems from engine through brakes are covered to the extent that the average do-it-yourselfer becomes mechanically involved. This book will not explain such things as rebuilding a differential for the simple reason that the expertise required and the investment in special tools make this task uneconomical. It will, however, give you detailed instructions to help you change your own brake pads and shoes, replace spark plugs, and perform many more jobs that can save you money, give you personal satisfaction and help you avoid expensive problems.

A secondary purpose of this book is a reference for owners who want to understand their vehicle and/or their mechanics better. In this case, no tools at all are required.

Where to Begin

Before removing any bolts, read through the entire procedure. This will give you the overall view of what tools and supplies will be required. There is nothing more frustrating than having to walk to the bus stop on Monday morning because you were short one bolt on Sunday afternoon. So read ahead and plan ahead. Each operation should be approached logically and all procedures thoroughly understood before attempting any work.

All sections contain adjustments, maintenance, removal and installation procedures, and in some cases, repair or overhaul procedures. When repair is not considered practical, we tell you how to remove the part and then how to install the new or rebuilt replacement. In this way, you at least save the labor costs. Backyard repair of some components is just not practical.

Avoiding Trouble

Many procedures in this book require you to "label and disconnect . . ." a group of lines, hoses or wires. Don't be lulled into thinking you can remember where everything goes - you won't. If you hook up vacuum or fuel lines incorrectly, the vehicle will run poorly, if at all. If you hook up electrical wiring incorrectly, you may instantly learn a very expensive lesson.

You don't need to know the official or engineering name for each hose or line. A piece of masking tape on the hose and a piece on its fitting will allow you to assign your own label such as the letter A or a short name. As long as you remember your own code, the lines can be reconnected by matching similar letters or names. Do remember that tape will dissolve in gasoline or other fluids; if a component is to be washed or cleaned, use another method of identification. A permanent felt-tipped marker can be very handy for marking metal parts. Remove any tape or paper labels after assembly.

Maintenance or Repair?

It's necessary to mention the difference between maintenance and repair. Maintenance includes routine inspections, adjustments, and replacement of parts which show signs of normal wear. Maintenance compensates for wear or deterioration. Repair implies that something has broken or is not working. A need for repair is often caused by lack of maintenance. Example: draining and refilling the automatic transmission fluid is maintenance recommended by the manufacturer at specific mileage intervals. Failure to do this can ruin the transmission/transaxle, requiring very expensive repairs. While no maintenance program can prevent items from breaking or wearing out, a general rule can be stated: MAINTENANCE IS CHEAPER THAN REPAIR.

Two basic mechanic's rules should be mentioned here. First, whenever the left side of the vehicle or engine is referred to, it is meant to specify the driver's side. Conversely, the right side of the vehicle means the passenger's side. Second, most screws and bolts are removed by turning counterclockwise, and tightened by turning clockwise.

Safety is always the most important rule. Constantly be aware of the dangers involved in working on an automobile and take the proper precautions. See the information in this section regarding SERVICING YOUR VEHICLE SAFELY and the SAFETY NOTICE on the acknowledgment page.

Avoiding the Most Common Mistakes

Pay attention to the instructions provided. There are 3 common mistakes in mechanical work:

1 **Incorrect order of assembly, disassembly or adjustment.** When taking something apart or putting it together, performing steps in the wrong order usually just costs you extra time; however, it CAN break something. Read the entire procedure before beginning disassembly. Perform everything in the order in which the instructions say you should, even if you can't immediately see a reason for it. When you're taking apart something that is very intricate, you might want to draw a picture of how it looks when assembled at one point in order to make sure you get everything back in its proper position. We will supply exploded views whenever possible. When making adjustments, perform them in the proper order; often, one adjustment affects another, and you cannot expect even satisfactory results unless each adjustment is made only when it cannot be changed by any other.

2 **Overtorquing (or undertorquing).** While it is more common for overtorquing to cause damage, undertorquing may allow a fastener to vibrate loose causing serious damage. Especially when dealing with aluminum parts, pay attention to torque specifications and utilize a torque wrench in assembly. If a torque figure is not available, remember that if you are using the right tool to perform the job, you will probably not have to strain yourself to get a fastener tight enough. The pitch of most threads is so slight that the tension you put on the wrench will be multiplied many times in actual force on what you are tightening. A good example of how critical torque is can be seen in the case of spark plug installation, especially where you are putting the plug into an aluminum cylinder head. Too little torque can fail to crush the gasket, causing leakage of combustion gases and consequent overheating of the plug and engine parts. Too much torque can damage the threads or distort the plug, changing the spark gap.

There are many commercial products available for ensuring that fasteners won't come loose, even if they are not torqued just right (a very common brand is Loctite). If you're worried about getting something together tight enough to hold, but loose enough to avoid mechanical damage during assembly, one of these products might offer substantial insurance. Before choosing a threadlocking compound, read the label on the package and make sure the product is compatible with the materials, fluids, etc. involved.

3 **Crossthreading.** This occurs when a part such as a bolt is screwed into a nut or casting at the wrong angle and forced. Cross-threading is more likely to occur if access is difficult. It helps to clean and lubricate fasteners, then to start threading with the part to be installed positioned straight in. Then, start the bolt, spark plug, etc. with your fingers. If you encounter resistance, unscrew the part and start over again at a different angle until it can be inserted and turned several times without much effort. Keep in mind that many parts, especially spark plugs, have tapered threads, so that gentle turning will automatically bring the part you're threading to the proper angle, but only if you don't force it or resist a change in angle. Don't put a wrench on the part until it's been tightened a couple of turns by hand. If you suddenly encounter resistance, and the part has not seated fully, don't force it. Pull it back out to make sure it's clean and threading properly.

Always take your time and be patient; once you have some experience, working on your vehicle may well become an enjoyable hobby.

TOOLS AND EQUIPMENT

Naturally, without the proper tools and equipment it is impossible to properly service your vehicle. It would also be virtually impossible to catalog every tool that you would need to perform all of the operations in this book. Of course, It would be unwise for the amateur to rush out and buy an expensive set of tools on the theory that he/she may need one or more of them at some time.

The best approach is to proceed slowly, gathering a good quality set of those tools that are used most frequently. Don't be misled by the low cost of bargain tools. It is far better to spend a little more for better quality. Forged wrenches, 6 or 12-point sockets and fine tooth ratchets are by far preferable to their less expensive counterparts. As any good mechanic can tell you, there are few worse experiences than trying to work on a vehicle with bad tools. Your monetary savings will be far outweighed by frustration and mangled knuckles.

Begin accumulating those tools that are used most frequently: those associated with routine maintenance and tune-up. In addition to the normal assortment of screwdrivers and pliers, you should have the following tools:

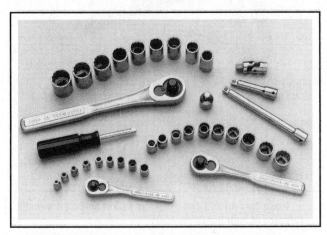

All but the most basic procedures will require an assortment of ratchets and sockets

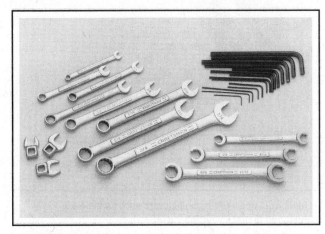

In addition to ratchets, a good set of wrenches and hex keys will be necessary

A hydraulic floor jack and a set of jackstands are essential for lifting and supporting the vehicle

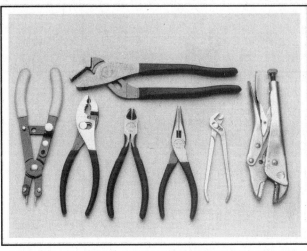

An assortment of pliers, grippers and cutters will be handy for old rusted parts and stripped bolt heads

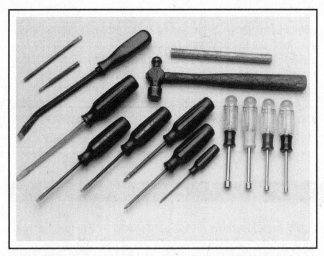

Various drivers, chisels and prybars are great tools to have in your toolbox

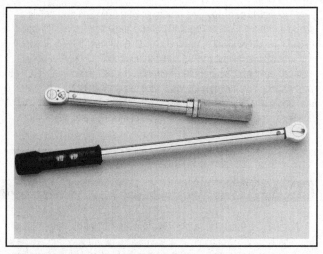

Many repairs will require the use of a torque wrench to assure the components are properly fastened

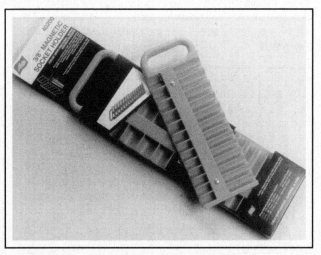

Tools from specialty manufacturers such as Lisle are designed to make your job easier . . .

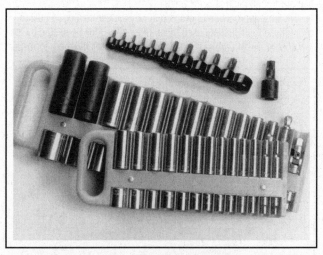

. . . these Torx drivers and magnetic socket holders are just 2 examples of their handy products

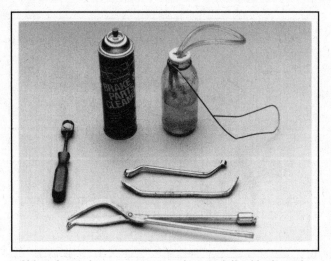

Although not always necessary, using specialized brake tools will save time

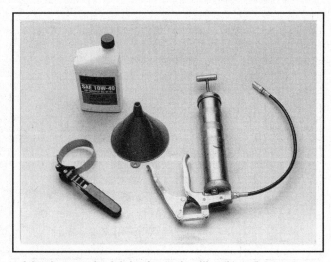

A few inexpensive lubrication tools will make maintenance easier

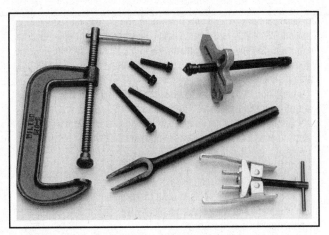

Various pullers, clamps and separator tools are needed for many larger, more complicated repairs

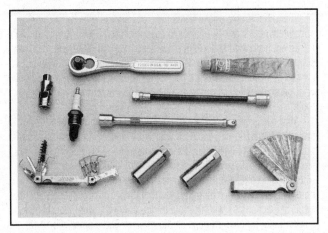

A variety of tools and gauges should be used for spark plug gapping and installation

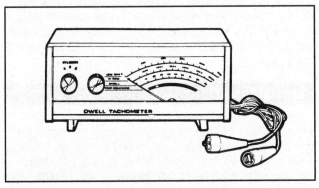

Dwell/tachometer unit (typical)

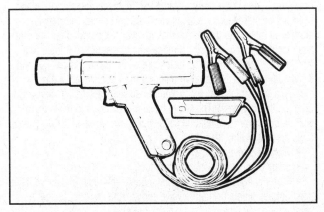

Inductive type timing light

• Wrenches/sockets and combination open end/box end wrenches in sizes from 1/8 - 3/4 in. or 3mm - 19mm (depending on whether your vehicle uses standard or metric fasteners) and a 13/16 in. or 5/8 in. spark plug socket (depending on plug type).

➡**If possible, buy various length socket drive extensions. Universal-joint and wobble extensions can be extremely useful, but be careful when using them, as they can change the amount of torque applied to the socket.**

• Jackstands for support.
• Oil filter wrench.

• Spout or funnel for pouring fluids.
• Grease gun for chassis lubrication (unless your vehicle is not equipped with any grease fittings - for details, please refer to information on Fluids and Lubricants found later in this section).
• Hydrometer for checking the battery (unless equipped with a sealed, maintenance-free battery).
• A container for draining oil and other fluids.
• Rags for wiping up the inevitable mess.

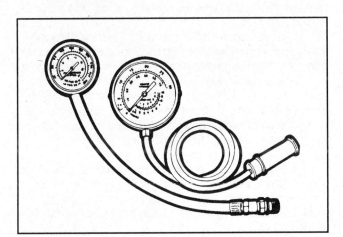

Compression gauge and a combination vacuum/fuel pressure test gauge

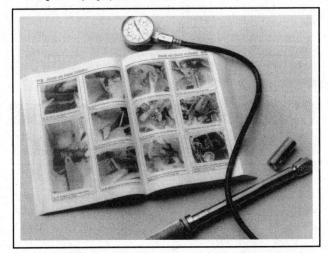

Proper information is vital, so always have a Chilton Total Car Care manual handy

In addition to the above items there are several others that are not absolutely necessary, but handy to have around. These include Oil Dry (or an equivalent oil absorbent gravel - such as cat litter) and the usual supply of lubricants, antifreeze and fluids, although these can be purchased as needed. This is a basic list for routine maintenance, but only your personal needs and desire can accurately determine your list of tools.

After performing a few projects on the vehicle, you'll be amazed at the other tools and non-tools on your workbench. Some useful household items are: a large turkey baster or siphon, empty coffee cans and ice trays (to store parts), ball of twine, electrical tape for wiring, small rolls of colored tape for tagging lines or hoses, markers and pens, a note pad, golf tees (for plugging vacuum lines), metal coat hangers or a roll of mechanics's wire (to hold things out of the way), dental pick or similar long, pointed probe, a strong magnet, and a small mirror (to see into recesses and under manifolds).

A more advanced set of tools, suitable for tune-up work, can be drawn up easily. While the tools are slightly more sophisticated, they need not be outrageously expensive. There are several inexpensive tach/dwell meters on the market that are every bit as good for the average mechanic as a professional model. Just be sure that it goes to a least 1200 - 1500 rpm on the tach scale and that it works on 4, 6 and 8-cylinder engines. (If you own one or more vehicles with a diesel engine, a special tachometer is required since diesels don't use spark plug ignition systems). The key to these purchases is to make them with an eye towards adaptability and wide range. A basic list of tune-up tools could include:

- Tach/dwell meter.
- Spark plug wrench and gapping tool.
- Feeler gauges for valve or point adjustment. (Even if your vehicle does not use points or require valve adjustments, a feeler gauge is helpful for many repair/overhaul procedures).

A tachometer/dwell meter will ensure accurate tune-up work on vehicles without electronic ignition. The choice of a timing light should be made carefully. A light which works on the DC current supplied by the vehicle's battery is the best choice; it should have a xenon tube for brightness. On any vehicle with an electronic ignition system, a timing light with an inductive pickup that clamps around the No. 1 spark plug cable is preferred.

In addition to these basic tools, there are several other tools and gauges you may find useful. These include:

- Compression gauge. The screw-in type is slower to use, but eliminates the possibility of a faulty reading due to escaping pressure.
- Manifold vacuum gauge.
- 12V test light.
- A combination volt/ohmmeter
- Induction Ammeter. This is used for determining whether or not there is current in a wire. These are handy for use if a wire is broken somewhere in a wiring harness.

As a final note, you will probably find a torque wrench necessary for all but the most basic work. The beam type models are perfectly adequate, although the newer click types (breakaway) are easier to use. The click type torque wrenches tend to be more expensive. Also keep in mind that all types of torque wrenches should be periodically checked and/or recalibrated. You will have to decide for yourself which better fits your purpose.

Special Tools

Normally, the use of special factory tools is avoided for repair procedures, since these are not readily available for the do-it-yourself mechanic. When it is possible to perform the job with more commonly available tools, it will be pointed out, but occasionally, a special tool was designed to perform a specific function and should be used. Before substituting another tool, you should be convinced that neither your safety nor the performance of the vehicle will be compromised.

Special tools can usually be purchased from an automotive parts store or from your dealer. In some cases special tools may be available directly from the tool manufacturer.

SERVICING YOUR VEHICLE SAFELY

It is virtually impossible to anticipate all of the hazards involved with automotive maintenance and service, but care and common sense will prevent most accidents.

The rules of safety for mechanics range from "don't smoke around gasoline," to "use the proper tool(s) for the job." The trick to avoiding injuries is to develop safe work habits and to take every possible precaution.

Do's

- Do keep a fire extinguisher and first aid kit handy.
- Do wear safety glasses or goggles when cutting, drilling, grinding or prying, even if you have 20 - 20 vision. If you wear glasses for the sake of vision, wear safety goggles over your regular glasses.
- Do shield your eyes whenever you work around the battery. Batteries contain sulfuric acid. In case of contact with the eyes or skin, flush the area with water or a mixture of water and baking soda, then seek immediate medical attention.
- Do use safety stands (jackstands) for any undervehicle service.

Jacks are for raising vehicles; jackstands are for making sure the vehicle stays raised until you want it to come down. Whenever the vehicle is raised, block the wheels remaining on the ground and set the parking brake.

- Do use adequate ventilation when working with any chemicals or hazardous materials. Like carbon monoxide, the asbestos dust resulting from some brake lining wear can be hazardous in sufficient quantities.
- Do disconnect the negative battery cable when working on the electrical system. The secondary ignition system contains EXTREMELY HIGH VOLTAGE. In some cases it can even exceed 50,000 volts.
- Do follow manufacturer's directions whenever working with potentially hazardous materials. Most chemicals and fluids are poisonous if taken internally.
- Do properly maintain your tools. Loose hammerheads, mushroomed punches and chisels, frayed or poorly grounded electrical cords, excessively worn screwdrivers, spread wrenches (open end), cracked sockets, slipping ratchets, or faulty droplight sockets can cause accidents.

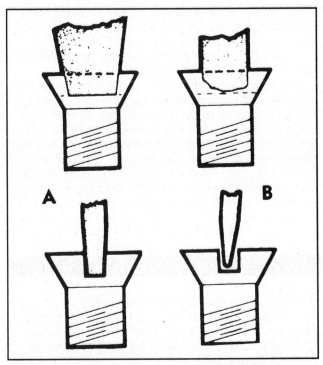

Screwdrivers should be kept in good condition to prevent injury or damage which could result if the blade slips from the screw

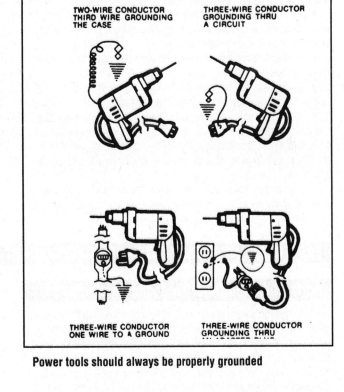

Power tools should always be properly grounded

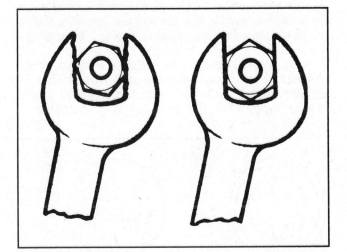

Using the correct size wrench will help prevent the possibility of rounding off a nut

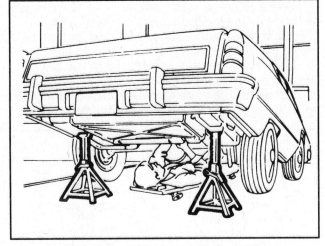

NEVER work under a vehicle unless it is supported using safety stands (jackstands)

• Likewise, keep your tools clean; a greasy wrench can slip off a bolt head, ruining the bolt and often harming your knuckles in the process.

• Do use the proper size and type of tool for the job at hand. Do select a wrench or socket that fits the nut or bolt. The wrench or socket should sit straight, not cocked.

• Do, when possible, pull on a wrench handle rather than push on it, and adjust your stance to prevent a fall.

• Do be sure that adjustable wrenches are tightly closed on the nut or bolt and pulled so that the force is on the side of the fixed jaw.

• Do strike squarely with a hammer; avoid glancing blows.

• Do set the parking brake and block the drive wheels if the work requires a running engine.

Don'ts

• Don't run the engine in a garage or anywhere else without proper ventilation - EVER! Carbon monoxide is poisonous; it takes a long time to leave the human body and you can build up a deadly supply of it in your system by simply breathing in a little every day. You may not realize you are slowly poisoning yourself. Always use power vents, windows, fans and/or open the garage door.

• Don't work around moving parts while wearing loose clothing. Short sleeves are much safer than long, loose sleeves. Hard-toed shoes with neoprene soles protect your toes and give a better grip on slippery surfaces. Jewelry such as watches, fancy belt buckles, beads or body adornment of any kind is not safe working around a vehicle. Long hair should be tied back under a hat or cap.

• Don't use pockets for toolboxes. A fall or bump can drive a screwdriver deep into your body. Even a rag hanging from your back pocket can wrap around a spinning shaft or fan.

• Don't smoke when working around gasoline, cleaning solvent or other flammable material.

• Don't smoke when working around the battery. When the battery is being charged, it gives off explosive hydrogen gas.

• Don't use gasoline to wash your hands; there are excellent soaps available. Gasoline contains dangerous additives which can enter the body through a cut or through your pores. Gasoline also removes all the natural oils from the skin so that bone dry hands will suck up oil and grease.

• Don't service the air conditioning system unless you are equipped with the necessary tools and training. When liquid or compressed gas refrigerant is released to atmospheric pressure it will absorb heat from whatever it contacts. This will chill or freeze anything it touches. Although refrigerant is normally non-toxic, R-12 becomes a deadly poisonous gas in the presence of an open flame. One good whiff of the vapors from burning refrigerant can be fatal.

• Don't use screwdrivers for anything other than driving screws! A screwdriver used as an prying tool can snap when you least expect it, causing injuries. At the very least, you'll ruin a good screwdriver.

• Don't use a bumper or emergency jack (that little ratchet, scissors, or pantograph jack supplied with the vehicle) for anything other than changing a flat! These jacks are only intended for emergency use out on the road; they are NOT designed as a maintenance tool. If you are serious about maintaining your vehicle yourself, invest in a hydraulic floor jack of at least a 1-1/2 ton capacity, and at least two sturdy jackstands.

FASTENERS, MEASUREMENTS AND CONVERSIONS

Bolts, Nuts and Other Threaded Retainers

Although there are a great variety of fasteners found in the modern car or truck, the most commonly used retainer is the threaded fastener (nuts, bolts, screws, studs, etc). Most threaded retainers may be reused, provided that they are not damaged in use or during the repair. Some retainers (such as stretch bolts or torque prevailing nuts) are designed to deform when tightened or in use and should not be reinstalled.

Whenever possible, we will note any special retainers which should be replaced during a procedure. But you should always inspect the condition of a retainer when it is removed and replace any that show signs of damage. Check all threads for rust or corrosion which can increase the torque necessary to achieve the desired clamp load for which that fastener was originally selected. Additionally, be sure that the driver surface of the fastener has not been compromised by rounding or other damage. In some cases a driver surface may become only partially rounded, allowing the driver to catch in only one direction. In many of these occurrences, a fastener may be installed and tightened, but the driver would not be able to grip and loosen the fastener again. (This could lead to frustration down the line should that component ever need to be disassembled again).

If you must replace a fastener, whether due to design or damage, you must ALWAYS be sure to use the proper replacement. In all cases, a retainer of the same design, material and strength should be used. Markings on the heads of most bolts will help determine the proper strength of the fastener. The same material, thread and pitch must be selected to assure proper installation and safe operation of the vehicle afterwards.

Thread gauges are available to help measure a bolt or stud's thread. Most automotive and hardware stores keep gauges available to help you select the proper size. In a pinch, you can use another nut or bolt for a thread gauge. If the bolt you are replacing is not too badly dam-

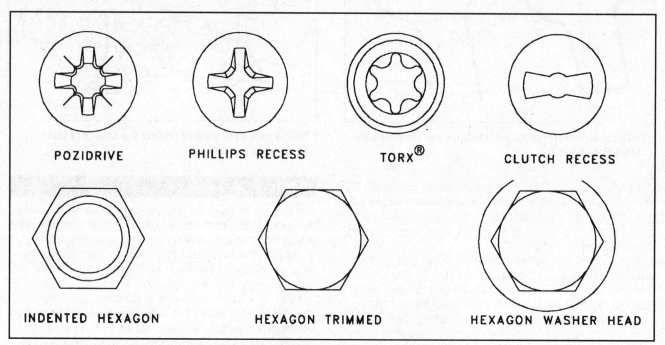

Here are a few of the most common screw/bolt driver styles

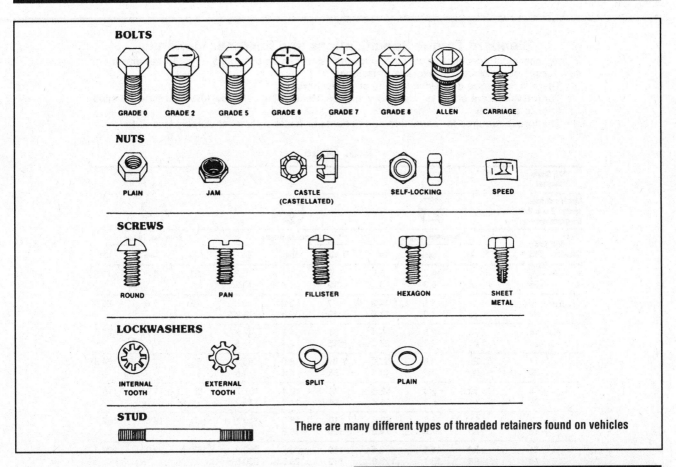

BOLTS

GRADE 0   GRADE 2   GRADE 5   GRADE 6   GRADE 7   GRADE 8   ALLEN   CARRIAGE

NUTS

PLAIN   JAM   CASTLE (CASTELLATED)   SELF-LOCKING   SPEED

SCREWS

ROUND   PAN   FILLISTER   HEXAGON   SHEET METAL

LOCKWASHERS

INTERNAL TOOTH   EXTERNAL TOOTH   SPLIT   PLAIN

STUD

There are many different types of threaded retainers found on vehicles

aged, you can select a match by finding another bolt which will thread in its place. If you find a nut which threads properly onto the damaged bolt, then use that nut to help select the replacement bolt. If however, the bolt you are replacing is so badly damaged (broken or drilled out) that its threads cannot be used as a gauge, you might start by looking for another bolt (from the same assembly or a similar location on your vehicle) which will thread into the damaged bolt's mounting. If so, the other bolt can be used to select a nut; the nut can then be used to select the replacement bolt.

In all cases, be absolutely sure you have selected the proper replacement. Don't be shy, you can always ask the store clerk for help.

✳✳ WARNING:

Be aware that when you find a bolt with damaged threads, you may also find the nut or drilled hole it was threaded into has also been damaged. If this is the case, you may have to drill and tap the hole, replace the nut or otherwise repair the threads. NEVER try to force a replacement bolt to fit into the damaged threads.

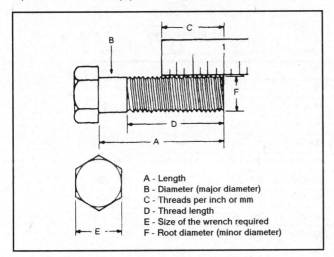

A - Length
B - Diameter (major diameter)
C - Threads per inch or mm
D - Thread length
E - Size of the wrench required
F - Root diameter (minor diameter)

Threaded retainer sizes are determined using these measurements

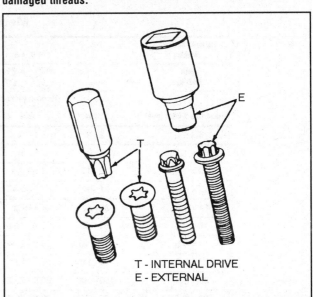

T - INTERNAL DRIVE
E - EXTERNAL

Special fasteners such as these Torx head bolts are used by manufacturers to discourage people from working on vehicles without the proper tools

Standard Torque Specifications and Fastener Markings

In the absence of specific torques, the following chart can be used as a guide to the maximum safe torque of a particular size/grade of fastener.
- There is no torque difference for fine or coarse threads.
- Torque values are based on clean, dry threads. Reduce the value by 10% if threads are oiled prior to assembly.
- The torque required for aluminum components or fasteners is considerably less.

U.S. Bolts

SAE Grade Number	1 or 2			5			6 or 7		
Number of lines always 2 less than the grade number.	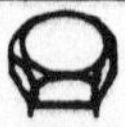			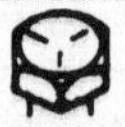			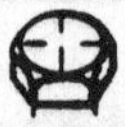		
Bolt Size (Inches)—(Thread)	Ft./Lbs.	Kgm	Nm	Ft./Lbs.	Kgm	Nm	Ft./Lbs.	Kgm	Nm
¼ — 20	5	0.7	6.8	8	1.1	10.8	10	1.4	13.5
— 28	6	0.8	8.1	10	1.4	13.6			
⁵⁄₁₆ — 18	11	1.5	14.9	17	2.3	23.0	19	2.6	25.8
— 24	13	1.8	17.6	19	2.6	25.7			
⅜ — 16	18	2.5	24.4	31	4.3	42.0	34	4.7	46.0
— 24	20	2.75	27.1	35	4.8	47.5			
⁷⁄₁₆ — 14	28	3.8	37.0	49	6.8	66.4	55	7.6	74.5
— 20	30	4.2	40.7	55	7.6	74.5			
½ — 13	39	5.4	52.8	75	10.4	101.7	85	11.75	115.2
— 20	41	5.7	55.6	85	11.7	115.2			
⁹⁄₁₆ — 12	51	7.0	69.2	110	15.2	149.1	120	16.6	162.7
— 18	55	7.6	74.5	120	16.6	162.7			
⅝ — 11	83	11.5	112.5	150	20.7	203.3	167	23.0	226.5
— 18	95	13.1	128.8	170	23.5	230.5			
¾ — 10	105	14.5	142.3	270	37.3	366.0	280	38.7	379.6
— 16	115	15.9	155.9	295	40.8	400.0			
⅞ — 9	160	22.1	216.9	395	54.6	535.5	440	60.9	596.5
— 14	175	24.2	237.2	435	60.1	589.7			
1 — 8	236	32.5	318.6	590	81.6	799.9	660	91.3	894.8
— 14	250	34.6	338.9	660	91.3	849.8			

Metric Bolts

Relative Strength Marking	4.6, 4.8			8.8		
Bolt Markings	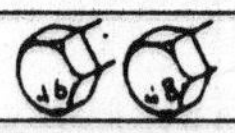			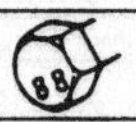		
Bolt Size Thread Size x Pitch (mm)	Ft./Lbs.	Kgm	Nm	Ft./Lbs.	Kgm	Nm
6 x 1.0	2–3	.2–.4	3–4	3–6	4–.8	5–8
8 x 1.25	6–8	.8–1	8–12	9–14	1.2–1.9	13–19
10 x 1.25	12–17	1.5–2.3	16–23	20–29	2.7–4.0	27–39
12 x 1.25	21–32	2.9–4.4	29–43	35–53	4.8–7.3	47–72
14 x 1.5	35–52	4.8–7.1	48–70	57–85	7.8–11.7	77–110
16 x 1.5	51–77	7.0–10.6	67–100	90–120	12.4–16.5	130–160
18 x 1.5	74–110	10.2–15.1	100–150	130–170	17.9–23.4	180–230
20 x 1.5	110–140	15.1–19.3	150–190	190–240	26.2–46.9	160–320
22 x 1.5	150–190	22.0–26.2	200–260	250–320	34.5–44.1	340–430
24 x 1.5	190–240	26.2–46.9	260–320	310–410	42.7–56.5	420–550

Standard and metric bolt torque specifications based on bolt strengths - **WARNING: use only as a guide**

Torque

Torque is defined as the measurement of resistance to turning or rotating. It tends to twist a body about an axis of rotation. A common example of this would be tightening a threaded retainer such as a nut, bolt or screw. Measuring torque is one of the most common ways to help assure that a threaded retainer has been properly fastened.

When tightening a threaded fastener, torque is applied in three distinct areas, the head, the bearing surface and the clamp load. About 50 percent of the measured torque is used in overcoming bearing friction. This is the friction between the bearing surface of the bolt head, screw head or nut face and the base material or washer (the surface on which the fastener is rotating). Approximately 40 percent of the applied torque is used in overcoming thread friction. This leaves only about 10 percent of the applied torque to develop a useful clamp load (the force which holds a joint together). This means that friction can account for as much as 90 percent of the applied torque on a fastener.

TORQUE WRENCHES

In most applications, a torque wrench can be used to assure proper installation of a fastener. Torque wrenches come in various designs and most automotive supply stores will carry a variety to suit your needs. A torque wrench should be used any time we supply a specific torque value for a fastener. A torque wrench can also be used if you are

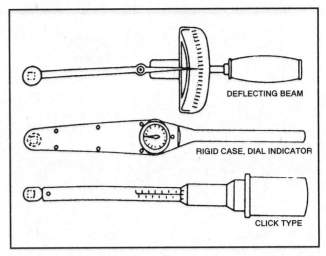

Various styles of torque wrenches are usually available at your local automotive supply store

following the general guidelines in the accompanying charts. Keep in mind that because there is no worldwide standardization of fasteners, the charts are a general guideline and should be used with caution. Again, the general rule of "if you are using the right tool for the job, you should not have to strain to tighten a fastener" applies here.

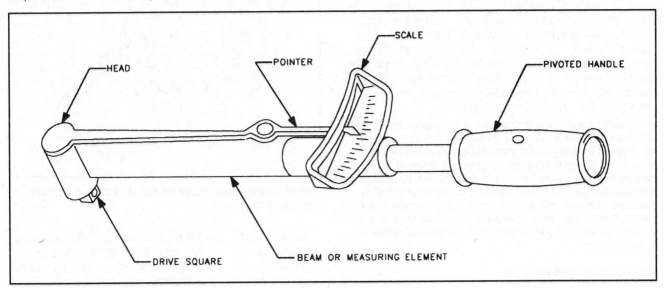

Example of a beam type torque wrench

Beam Type

The beam type torque wrench is one of the most popular types. It consists of a pointer attached to the head that runs the length of the flexible beam (shaft) to a scale located near the handle. As the wrench is pulled, the beam bends and the pointer indicates the torque using the scale.

Click (Breakaway) Type

Another popular design of torque wrench is the click type. To use the click type wrench you pre-adjust it to a torque setting. Once the torque is reached, the wrench has a reflex signalling feature that causes a momentary breakaway of the torque wrench body, sending an impulse to the operator's hand.

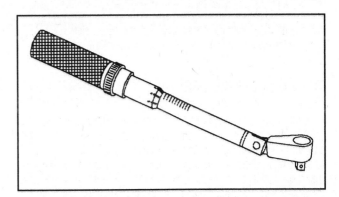

A click type or breakaway torque wrench - note this one has a pivoting head

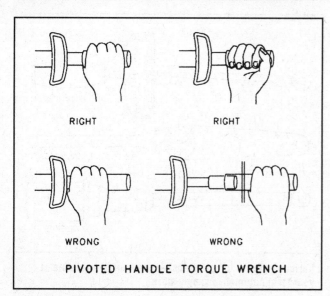

Torque wrenches with pivoting heads must be grasped and used properly to prevent an incorrect reading

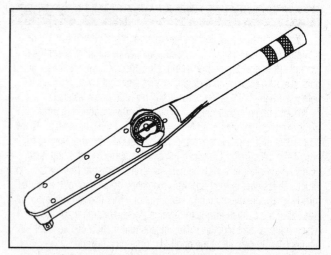

The rigid case (direct reading) torque wrench uses a dial indicator to show torque

Pivot Head Type

Some torque wrenches (usually of the click type) may be equipped with a pivot head which can allow it to be used in areas of limited access. BUT, it must be used properly. To hold a pivot head wrench, grasp the handle lightly, and as you pull on the handle, it should be floated on the pivot point. If the handle comes in contact with the yoke extension during the process of pulling, there is a very good chance the torque readings will be inaccurate because this could alter the wrench loading point. The design of the handle is usually such as to make it inconvenient to deliberately misuse the wrench.

➡It should be mentioned that the use of any U-joint, wobble or extension will have an effect on the torque readings, no matter what type of wrench you are using. For the most accurate readings, install the socket directly on the wrench driver. If necessary, straight extensions (which hold a socket directly under the wrench driver) will have the least effect on the torque reading. Avoid any extension that alters the length of the wrench from the handle to the head/driving point (such as a crow's foot). U-joint or Wobble extensions can greatly affect the readings; avoid their use at all times.

Rigid Case (Direct Reading)

A rigid case or direct reading torque wrench is equipped with a dial indicator to show torque values. One advantage of these wrenches is that they can be held at any position on the wrench without affecting accuracy. These wrenches are often preferred because they tend to be compact, easy to read and have a great degree of accuracy.

TORQUE ANGLE METERS

Because the frictional characteristics of each fastener or threaded hole will vary, clamp loads which are based strictly on torque will vary as well. In most applications, this variance is not significant enough to cause worry. But, in certain applications, a manufacturer's engineers may determine that more precise clamp loads are necessary (such is the case with many aluminum cylinder heads). In these cases, a torque angle method of installation would be specified. When installing fasteners which are torque angle tightened, a predetermined seating

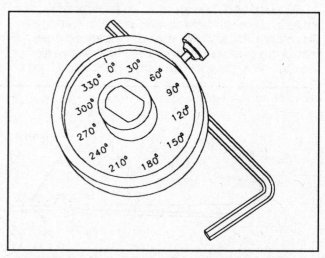

Some specifications require the use of a torque angle meter (mechanical protractor)

torque and standard torque wrench are usually used first to remove any compliance from the joint. The fastener is then tightened the specified additional portion of a turn measured in degrees. A torque angle gauge (mechanical protractor) is used for these applications.

Standard and Metric Measurements

Throughout this manual, specifications are given to help you determine the condition of various components on your vehicle, or to assist you in their installation. Some of the most common measurements include length (in. or cm/mm), torque (ft. lbs., inch lbs. or Nm) and pressure (psi, in. Hg, kPa or mm Hg). In most cases, we strive to provide the proper measurement as determined by the manufacturer's engineers.

Though, in some cases, that value may not be conveniently measured with what is available in your toolbox. Luckily, many of the measuring devices which are available today will have two scales so the Standard or Metric measurements may easily be taken. If any of the various measuring tools which are available to you do not contain the same scale as listed in the specifications, use the accompanying conversion factors to determine the proper value.

CONVERSION FACTORS

LENGTH–DISTANCE

Inches (in.)	x 25.4	= Millimeters (mm)	x .0394	= Inches
Feet (ft.)	x .305	= Meters (m)	x 3.281	= Feet
Miles	x 1.609	= Kilometers (km)	x .0621	= Miles

VOLUME

Cubic Inches (in3)	x 16.387	= Cubic Centimeters	x .061	= in3
IMP Pints (IMP pt.)	x .568	= Liters (L)	x 1.76	= IMP pt.
IMP Quarts (IMP qt.)	x 1.137	= Liters (L)	x .88	= IMP qt.
IMP Gallons (IMP gal.)	x 4.546	= Liters (L)	x .22	= IMP gal.
IMP Quarts (IMP qt.)	x 1.201	= US Quarts (US qt.)	x .833	= IMP qt.
IMP Gallons (IMP gal.)	x 1.201	= US Gallons (US gal.)	x .833	= IMP gal.
Fl. Ounces	x 29.573	= Milliliters	x .034	= Ounces
US Pints (US pt.)	x .473	= Liters (L)	x 2.113	= Pints
US Quarts (US qt.)	x .946	= Liters (L)	x 1.057	= Quarts
US Gallons (US gal.)	x 3.785	= Liters (L)	x .264	= Gallons

MASS–WEIGHT

Ounces (oz.)	x 28.35	= Grams (g)	x .035	= Ounces
Pounds (lb.)	x .454	= Kilograms (kg)	x 2.205	= Pounds

PRESSURE

Pounds Per Sq. In. (psi)	x 6.895	= Kilopascals (kPa)	x .145	= psi
Inches of Mercury (Hg)	x .4912	= psi	x 2.036	= Hg
Inches of Mercury (Hg)	x 3.377	= Kilopascals (kPa)	x .2961	= Hg
Inches of Water (H_2O)	x .07355	= Inches of Mercury	x 13.783	= H_2O
Inches of Water (H_2O)	x .03613	= psi	x 27.684	= H_2O
Inches of Water (H_2O)	x .248	= Kilopascals (kPa)	x 4.026	= H_2O

TORQUE

Pounds–Force Inches (in–lb)	x .113	= Newton Meters (N·m)	x 8.85	= in–lb
Pounds–Force Feet (ft–lb)	x 1.356	= Newton Meters (N·m)	x .738	= ft–lb

VELOCITY

Miles Per Hour (MPH)	x 1.609	= Kilometers Per Hour (KPH)	x .621	= MPH

POWER

Horsepower (Hp)	x .745	= Kilowatts	x 1.34	= Horsepower

FUEL CONSUMPTION*

Miles Per Gallon IMP (MPG)	x .354	= Kilometers Per Liter (Km/L)
Kilometers Per Liter (Km/L)	x 2.352	= IMP MPG
Miles Per Gallon US (MPG)	x .425	= Kilometers Per Liter (Km/L)
Kilometers Per Liter (Km/L)	x 2.352	= US MPG

*It is common to covert from miles per gallon (mpg) to liters/100 kilometers (1/100 km), where mpg (IMP) x 1/100 km = 282 and mpg (US) x 1/100 km = 235.

TEMPERATURE

Degree Fahrenheit (°F)	= (°C x 1.8) + 32
Degree Celsius (°C)	= (°F – 32) x .56

Standard and metric conversion factors chart

The conversion factor chart is used by taking the given specification and multiplying it by the necessary conversion factor. For instance, looking at the first line, if you have a measurement in inches such as "free-play should be 2 in." but your ruler reads only in millimeters, multiply 2 in. by the conversion factor of 25.4 to get the metric equiva-lent of 50.8mm. Likewise, if the specification was given only in a Metric measurement, for example in Newton Meters (Nm), then look at the center column first. If the measurement is 100 Nm, multiply it by the conversion factor of 0.738 to get 73.8 ft. lbs.

HISTORY

In 1932, Ferdinand Porsche produced prototypes for the NSU company of Germany. These led to the design of the Volkswagen. The prototypes had a rear, air-cooled engine, torsion-bar suspension, and the spare tire mounted at an angle in the front luggage compartment. In 1936, Porsche produced three Volkswagen prototypes, one of which was a 995 cc., horizontally-opposed, four-cylinder automobile. In 1945 Volkswagen production began and 1,785 Beetles were built. The Volkswagen convertible was introduced in 1949, the year when only two Volkswagens were sold in the entire U.S.A. The year 1950 marked the beginning of the sunroof models and the transporter series. The Volkswagen Karmann Ghia was introduced in 1956, and is still of the same basic styling format. The "big" Volkswagen, the 1500 Squareback, was introduced in Europe in 1961, and sold in the U.S.A. in 1966 as a member of the new type 3 series (Fastback and Squareback).

MODEL AND SERIAL NUMBER IDENTIFICATION

General Information

To the casual observer, it would appear that the appearance of the Volkswagen Beetle has not changed since the car was first sold in this country in 1949. However, there have been hundreds, if not thousands, of changes made on the inside and outside of this seemingly perpetual automotive design. Because so many changes were made during an actual model run, the only sure way of telling the year of a Volkswagen is by looking at the chassis number of the vehicle.

The accompanying chart gives the yearly chassis numbers, exterior and interior body changes, and the mechanical changes that apply to all Volkswagen Beetle models since the first two were sold here in 1949.

Volkswagen models are further differentiated by type. Type 1 is the Beetle and Karmann Ghia. Type 2 is the transporter, or bus and truck, series. Type 3 is the Fastback and Squareback. The current model numbers are as follows:

Model Number	Description
• 111	1300A sedan
• 115	1300A sedan with folding sunroof
• 113	1500 sedan
• 117	1500 sedan with steel sunroof
• 141	1500 Karmann Ghia convertible
• 143	1500 Karmann Ghia coupe
• 151	500 Convertible (4-seater)
• 211 - 215	Delivery Van
• 221 - 225	Micro Bus
• 231 - 237	Kombi
• 241	Deluxe Micro Bus (9-seater)
• 251	Deluxe Micro Bus (7-seater)
• 261 - 267	Pick-up
• 271 - 273	Ambulance
• 281 - 285	Micro Bus (7-seater)
• 311	1600TL Fastback sedan
• 313	Fastback sedan with steel sunroof
• 315	1600A sedan
• 317	1600A sedan with steel sunroof
• 343	1600L Karmann Ghia coupe
• 345	1600L Karmann Ghia coupe with steel sunroof
• 361	1600L Squareback sedan
• 363	1600L Squareback sedan with steel sunroof
• 365	1600A Squareback sedan
• 367	1600A Squareback sedan with steel sunroof

TYPE 1 SPECIFICATIONS

1200 Engine

➡These specifications apply only to the 1200cc engine manu-factured to July of 1965.

ENGINE

Design: 4 cylinder, 4 cycle, flat, horizontally opposed engine.
Bore: 77mm. (3.03 in.)
Stroke: 64mm. (2.52 in.)
Displacement: 1192 cc. (72.74 cu. in.)
Compression ratio: 7.0 : 1
Performance:
  34 bhp at 3600 RPM (DIN)
  41.5 bhp at 3900 RPM (SAE)
  61 ft. lbs. at 2000 RPM (DIN)
  65 ft. lbs. at 2400 RPM (SAE)
Engine weight, dry: 238 lbs.
Crankcase: magnesium alloy, two-piece.
Cylinders: individually cast; of special gray iron, finned.
Cylinder heads: one for each pair of cylinders, sintered steel valve seat inserts shrunk in; 14mm. spark plug thread cut into cylinder head.
Crankshaft: steel forging, hardened journals. Four main bearings, aluminum-alloy bearing shells. Main bearings 1, 2 and 3 are sleeve-type. Numbers 1, 2 and 3 are 55mm. diameter. Number 4 (at rear of engine) is 40mm. diameter.
Flywheel: steel forging, integral starter ring.
Connecting rods: H-section, steel forgings. Connecting rod bearing 3-layer steel-backed. Pressed-in wrist pin bushing of bronze.
Pistons: aluminum alloy with steel inserts, 2 compression rings, 1 oil control ring. Fully floating wrist pin.
Camshaft: situated below crankshaft; gray cast-iron, running in three bearings. Gear driven.

Valves: one intake and one exhaust per cylinder. Exhaust valve has special heat-resistant seating surface.

Valve clearances: .004". Cold when indicated by sticker. Older engines: .008" intake and .012" exhaust. (Engines without sticker on fan housing.)

Valve springs: one per valve.

Valve timing: with clearance for checking, .040".

Intake opens: 6 degrees before TDC

Intake closes: 35-degrees 30;pr after BDC

Exhaust opens: 42-degrees 30;pr before BDC

Exhaust closes: 3-degrees after TDC

Cooling: by forced air. Belt-driven fan on generator shaft. Drive ratio approximately 1 : 1.8, crankshaft/generator. Thermostatically controlled cooling. Capacity approximately 500 liters (19 cubic feet) per second at 3600 RPM.

Lubrication: wet sump, full pressure type with gear pump. Oil cooler in path of cooling air.

Ignition system: battery ignition with conventional distributor and coil.

Spark timing: 10-degrees before top dead center.

Firing order: 1-4-3-2

Spark advance: under full vacuum control

Breaker point gap: .016"

Spark plugs: Bosch W 175 T 1 and other good quality plugs of same heat range.

FUEL SYSTEM

Carburetor: Solex, single throat down-draft type. 28 PICT-1 with accelerator and automatic choke.

Venturi: 22.5mm. diameter

Main jet: 122.5

Air correction jet: 130 y with emulsion tube 145 y Karmann Ghia (sedan and convertible)

Pilot jet: g 55

Pilot jet air bleed: 2.0mm. diameter

Pump jet: 0.5

Power fuel jet: 1.0mm. diameter

Float needle valve: 1.5mm. diameter

Float weight: 5.7 gram, plastic material

Pump feed: approx. 1.1 - 1.4 cc/stroke

Air cleaner: oil bath type with air preheater.

Fuel pump: diaphragm type, mechanical.

Fuel filter: filter in fuel pump.

Fuel gauge: float type, mechanical sender.

CLUTCH

Design: single dry plate.

Lining area: 41.6 square inches.

Free play: .4 to .8 in. at pedal

TRANSMISSION AND FINAL DRIVE

Design: transmission and final drive integral with four speeds forward, all fully synchronized.

Gear ratios: 1st 3.80:1   2nd: 2.06:1   3rd: 1.32:1   4th: .89:1 reverse 3.88:1   final drive: 4.375:1

CHASSIS

Frame design: flat platform with tubular backbone. Forked at rear to accommodate engine and trans-axle unit.

Front suspension: two trailing links at each wheel. Two torsion bar springs consisting of 8 leaves each. Anti-sway bar.

Rear suspension: trailing links, swing axles independently suspended.

Shock absorbers: front and rear are hydraulic, telescopic, double-acting.

Steering: worm and roller with divided tie rods and steering damper.

Steering ratio: 14.3:1   2.6 turns lock to lock.

Wheel angle at full lock: inside wheel: 34-degrees + or - 2-degrees. Outside wheel 28-degrees - 1-degrees.

Camber: 0-degrees 40;pr + or - 30;pr with wheels straight ahead.

Toe-in: 2 to 4.5mm.

Axle beam angle: 2-degrees + or - 15;pr

King pin inclination: 4-degrees 20;pr at maximum permissible weight.

Rear wheel camber: 3-degrees + or - 30;pr

Wheels: 4J x 15 steel discs.

Tires: tubeless, 5.60 x 29> 15 inch.

Rolling radius: 309mm. + or - 3mm.

BRAKES

Foot brake: hydraulic, acting on all four wheels.

Hand brake: cable operating, rear wheels.

Brake lining area: 96 square inches.

4>1300 Engine

➡**Only the differences from the 1200cc engine are presented here; all other specifications are the same.**

ENGINE

Stroke: 69mm. (2.72 in.)

Displacement: 1285 cc. (78.3 cu. in.)

Performance:
  40 bhp at 4000 RPM (DIN)
  50 bhp at 4600 RPM (SAE)
  63 ft. lbs. at 2000 RPM (DIN)
  69 ft. LBS. at 2600 RPM (SAE)

Engine weight, dry: 244 lbs.

Camshaft bearings: replaceable steel-backed lead-coated shells.

Valve timing: with checking clearance of .040 in.

Intake opens: 7-degrees 30;pr before TDC

Intake closes: 37-degrees after BDC

Exhaust opens: 44-degrees 30;pr before BDC

Exhaust closes: 4-degrees after TDC

Cooling air delivery: approximately 556 liters per second (20 cubic feet per second) at 4000 RPM.

Ignition timing: basic ignition timing of 7.5-degrees before TDC.

FUEL SYSTEM

Carburetor: Solex 30 PICT-1

Venturi: 24mm. in diameter

Main jet: 125

Air correction jet:
  125 z for sedans and convertibles
  170 z for Karmann Ghia

Pilot jet: g 55 (with electromagnetic shut-off valve).

Pilot jet air bleed: 150

Pump jet: 50

Power fuel jet: 75mm. diameter, for Karmann Ghia models only.

Float needle valve: 1.5mm. diameter

Float weight: 5.7 grams (plastic material)

Pump delivery: 1.3 - 1.6 cc/stroke

Fuel pump: diaphragm, mechanical, with cut-off valve in upper part.

CHASSIS

Steering ratio: 15:1
Wheels: perforated steel disc, 4J x 15.

1500 Engine

➡Only the differences from the 1300cc engine are presented here; all other data is the same.

ENGINE

Bore: 83mm. (3.27 in.)
Stroke: 69mm. (2.72 in.)
Displacement: 1493 cc. (91.1 cu. in.)
Compression ratio: 7.5:1
Performance:
   44 bhp at 4000 RPM (DIN)
   53 bhp at 4200 RPM (SAE)
   10.2 mkg at 2000 RPM (DIN)
   78.1 ft. lbs. at 2600 RPM (SAE)
Engine weight, dry: 250 lbs.
Cooling fan drive ratio: 1.9:1 approximately
Air cleaner: oil bath with two intakes
Transmission and final drive: 3rd gear ratio 1.26:1   final drive ratio 4.125:1

CHASSIS

Rear suspension: equipped with overload compensator spring.
Rear radius arm setting: 20-degrees + 50;pr.
Rear track: 1358mm. (53.4")

General Data

Top speed:
   78 mph (53 bhp engine) (3950 RPM)
   75 mph (50 bhp engine) (4010 RPM)
   72 mph (41.5 bhp engine) (3870 RPM)
   68 mph (36 bhp engine) (3400 RPM)
Hill climbing ability, with two occupants:

	53 bhp engine	36 bhp engine
1st gear	46%	40.0%
2nd gear	24%	20.5%
3rd gear	13%	12.0%
4th gear	7.5%	6.5%

Acceleration:
   from 0 to 100 kph (0 to 62 mph):
      53 bhp 23 sec.
      50 bhp 26 sec.
      41.5 bhp 37 sec.
      36 bhp 50 sec.
   from 80 to 100 kph (50 to 62 mph):
      53 bhp 10 sec.
      50 bhp 12 sec.
      41.5 bhp 19 sec.
      36 bhp 29 sec.
Fuel consumption:
   53 bhp 26.7 mpg.
   50 bhp 27.7 mpg.
   41.5 bhp 30.4 mpg.
   36 bhp 32.2 mpg.

CAPACITIES

Fuel tank: 10.5 U.S. gallons
Crankcase: 5.3 U.S. pints

Transmission and final drive: 6.3 pints
Reduction gears (Transporter models): 1/2 pint each.
Steering: sector type .26 pint
roller type .4 pint
ross type .5 pint (transporters)
Brake fluid: .5 pint
Oil bath air cleaner: .5 pint

DIMENSIONS, VW SEDAN

Wheelbase: 94.5 in.
Track: front 51.4 in.
Track: rear 53.4 in.
Length: 160.6 in.
Width: 60.6 in.
Height: unladen 59.1 in.
Ground clearance: 6.0 in.

1968 MODELS, TYPE 1

Length: 158.6 in.
Width: 61.0 in.
Height: 59.1 in.
Ground clearance: 5.9 in.
Unladen weight: 1807 lbs.
Permissible total weight: 2645 lbs.

TYPE 2 SPECIFICATIONS

Engine

Bore: 3.36 in.
Stroke: 2.72 in.
Displacement: 96.6 cubic inches.
Compression ratio: 7.7:1
Output: 57 bhp at 4400 RPM (SAE)
Torque: 81.7 ft. lbs. at 3000 RPM (SAE)
Weight, with oil: 253 lbs.
Ignition timing: 0-degrees (TDC)

Fuel System

Carburetor: downdraft Solex 30 PICT-2
Venturi: 24mm.
Main jet: x 116
Air correction jet: 125 z with emusion tube
Pilot jet: 55 with electromagnetic cut-off valve
Pilot air jet: 130
Pump jet: 50
Power fuel jet: 60
Float needle valve: 1.5mm. dia.
Float weight: 8.5 grams

Rear Axle and Transmission

Hypoid gear differential with bevel gearing; ratio, 5.375:1.

Front End

Wheel alignment: (vehicle unladen) track - 5;pr to +10;pr with wheels not pressed together.
Camber: +40;pr + or - 15;pr
Axle beam angle: 3-degrees. Caster: 3-degrees + or - 40;pr

Steering

Ratio: 14.7:1, 2.8 turns lock to lock. Angles at maximum wheel lock, inner wheel, 32-degrees; outer wheel, 24-degrees.

Wheels and Tires

Steel disc wheels, 5 JK x 29> 14.7.00 x 14 6 PR tires on Station Wagon, 7.00 x 14 8 PR on all other models.

Tire Pressures

Front: 28 psi. **Rear:** 36 psi up to 3/4 load, 41 psi with full load.
Spare wheel: 44 psi.

Weights and Dimensions

Wheelbase: 94.5 in.
Track: front 54.5 in.
       rear 46.1 in.
Overhang: front 42.3 in.
         rear 37.2 in.
Overhang angle: front 19-degrees
             rear 21-degrees
Turning circle: between walls 40.4 feet
           between curbs 37.1 feet
Length: 174 in.
Width: 69.5 in.
Height: 77.0 in. (unladen)
Load compartment volume:

Van, Kombi	177 cubic feet
Pick-up	166 cubic feet
Double Cab Pick-up	113 cubic feet

Load compartment length: Van, Kombi, 110.2 in.
Pick-up 106.3 in., Double-Cab Pick-up 73.0 in.

Weights

➡**All weights are shown in lbs.**

	Unladen Weight	Payload	Gross Weight
Station Wagon	2723	1962	4685
Kombi	2624	2171	4795
Van	2425	2370	4795
Pick-up (with tarp.)	2503	2292	4795
Double Cab (with tarp.)	2591	2204	4795

Capacities

Fuel: 15.8 U.S. gallons
Crankcase: 5.3 U.S. pints
Transmission and final drive: 7.4 pints
Steering gear: 160 cc
Brake fluid reservoir: .63 pint
Air cleaner: .95 pint
Windshield washer: 1.45 quarts, approx.

Performance

Maximum speed: 65 mph at 3900 RPM
Average piston speed at maximum speed: 1764 ft./min.
Road Speeds at 4000 RPM and Hill Climbing Ability

14.5 mph	1st gear	27%
27	2nd gear	14%
43.5	3rd gear	7%
65.5	4th gear	4%

Fuel Consumption

Approx. 22.6 miles per gallon (DIN 70 030)
Octane requirement: 91 octane (regular)

TYPE 3 SPECIFICATIONS

➡**Only the major deviations from Type 1 models are presented here.**

Engine

Design: cooling fan is mounted directly on end of crankshaft.
Bore: 85.5mm. (3.37 in.)
Stroke: 69mm. (2.72 in.)
Displacement: 1584 cc. (96.7 cu. in.)
Compression ratio: 7.7:1
Performance:
    54 bhp at 4000 RPM (DIN)
    65 bhp at 4600 RPM (SAE)
    81 ft. lbs. at 2200 RPM (DIN)
    87 ft. lbs. at 2800 RPM (DIN)
Engine weight, dry: 276 lbs.
Cooling air delivery: 565 liters/second (20 cubic feet/second) at 4000 RPM.

Clutch

Lining area: 52 square inches.

Fuel System

Carburetion: Two Solex 32 PDSIT-2/3 carburetors with accelerator pumps and automatic chokes. Carburetor specifications, 1600 models to August 1967, when electronic fuel injection was introduced.
Venturi: dia. (mm.) 24
Main jet: X 132.5 (l. carb.)   X 130 (r. carb.)
Air correction jet: 150 (l. carb.)   120 (r. carb.)
Pilot jet: 50
Float needle valve: dia. 1.2
Float weight: 7.3 gr.
Pump capacity: .35 - .55 cc/stroke
Power fuel system: none

Chassis

Front torsion bar setting: 39-degrees 10;pr + 50;pr
Rear torsion bar setting, unloaded:
    Fastback Sedan: 20-degrees 30;pr + 50;pr
    Squareback Sedan: 21-degrees 30;pr + 50;pr
Front wheel toe-in: 3.6 to 6mm. toe-in wheels not pressed together.
Front wheel camber: wheels straight ahead: 1-degrees 20;pr + or - 10;pr
Axle beam angle: 11-degrees 50;pr
King pin inclination: 5-degrees 15;pr
Rear wheel track: 0-degrees + or - 5;pr
Rear wheel camber: 3-degrees + or - 30;pr
Wheels: Perforated steel disc, 4-1/2 J x 15
Tires: tubeless, 600 x 15, with dynamic rolling radius of 12.2 in.
Tire pressures:
    Fastback Sedan with:
        1 or 2 occupants 16 front/24 rear (psi)
        3 to 5 occupants 18 front/27 rear (psi)
    Squareback Sedan with:
        half payload   17 front/26 rear (psi)
        full payload   18 front/37 rear (psi)

Steering: overall ratio 14.8:1 with 2.8 turns lock to lock.
Brakes: disc front, drum rear. Lining area of discs:
12.5 square inches; lining area of drum brakes:
70 square inches.

General Data

Top speed: 84 mph (4250 RPM)
Hill climbing ability:

	Squareback*	Fastback
1st gear	39.5%	46.0%
2nd gear	20.5%	24.0%
3rd gear	12.0%	14.0%
4th gear	7.0%	8.0%

*with half payload

Acceleration:
from 0 to 100 kph (0 to 62 mph): 20.0 sec.
from 80 to 100 kph (50 5o 62 mph): 7.5 sec.

Fuel consumption:
28.6 miles per gallon
Capacities:
Fuel tank: 10.5 U.S. gallons
Crankcase: 5.3 U.S. pints
Transmission and differential: 6.3 U.S. pints
Brake fluid: .53 pint
Oil bath air cleaner: .84 pint
Dimensions and weights:

	Fastback	Squareback
Length, in.	166.3	166.3
Width	63.2	63.2
Height	57.9	57.9
Ground clearance	5.9	5.9
Unladen weight	2116 lbs.	2116 lbs.
Permissible total weight	2998 lbs.	3108 lbs.

Chassis Number

The chassis number is on the frame tunnel under the back seat in the type 1 and 3. In the type 2, the chassis number is on the right engine cover plate in the engine compartment.

Beginning with the 1965 model year, a nine-digit serial number system was instituted. In this system, the first two numbers are the first two digits of the car's model number and the third digit stands for the car's model year - "5" stands for 1965, "8" stands for 1968, etc. A tenth digit was added when production passed one million.

Identification Plate

The identification plate carries the vehicle serial number and paint, body, and assembly codes. It is behind the spare tire in the luggage compartment on type 1 models, and on the right side of the overhead air duct in early type 2 vehicles. The type 3 identification plate is next to the hood latch, in front of the spare tire in the luggage compartment.

Engine Number

On type 1 and 2 vehicles, which have the upright engine fan housing, the engine number is on the crankcase flange for the generator support. The number can readily be seen by looking through the center of the fan belt. On type 3 engines, which have the fan on the end of the crankshaft, the number is along the crankcase joint between the oil cooler and the air cleaner. The engine can be identified by the letter preceding the serial number. Refer to the Engine Identification Chart.

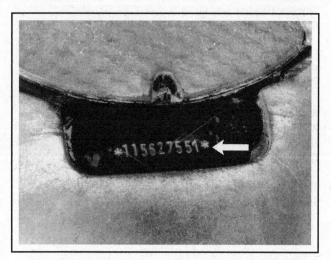

The chassis number (arrow) can be found under the rear seat, stamped into the center tunnel

The engine identification number (arrow) on "upright engines" is stamped into the case below the generator stand

Engine Identification

Common Designation	Number Of Cylinders	C.C. Displacement (cu. in.)	Type Engine	Type Vehicle	Engine Code Letter	Year
–	4	1,131 (69.02)	Upright fan	1	–	To December, 1953
1,200	4	1,192 (72.74)	Upright fan	1,2	A	To July, 1960
1,200	4	1,192 (72.74)	Upright fan	1,2	D	From August, 1960
1,300	4	1,285 (78.4)	Upright fan	1,2	F	From August, 1965
1,500	4	1,493 (91.1)	Upright fan	1,2	H	From August, 1967 ①
1,600	4	1,584 (96.6)	Upright fan	1,2	B	From August, 1969 ②
1,500	4	1,493 (91.1)	Upright fan	2	G	To July, 1965
1,500	4	1,493 (91.1)	Suitcase engine	3	K	To July, 1965 ③ From August, 1965 ④
1,500S	4	1,493 (91.1)	Suitcase engine	3 1500S	R	To July, 1965
1,600	4	1,584 (96.6)	Suitcase engine	3	T	From August, 1965
1,600	4	1,584 (96.6)	Suitcase engine	3 injected	U	From August, 1967

① Type 2 from August, 1965
② Type 2 from August, 1967
③ High compression
④ Low compression

Type 1 Model Changes

Year	Chassis Numbers	Major Body Changes	Major Mechanical Changes
1969	119,000,001–119,1,093,704	Electric rear window defroster; ignition lock combined with steering lock. Locking gas flap.	Double-jointed rear axle standard.
1968	118,000,000–118,1,016,098	Raised bumpers, front and rear; vertical bumper guards eliminated. Built-in headrest in front seats; extensive padding in front compartment and dashboard. Seat belts in rear standard; external gas filler.	Exhaust emission control; collapsible steering column; optional automatic stick shift.
1967	117,000,001–118,000,000	Back-up lights. Retractable seat belts. Armrest for driver. Locking buttons on doors. Parking light built into turn signals. Narrower chrome trim. Volkswagen nameplate on engine lid. Two-speed windshield wipers. Headlights now vertical in indented fenders.	Dual brake system. Increased horsepower, from 50 to 53. (SAE) Larger engine, from 1300 cc. to 1500 cc. 12-volt electrical system. Number of fuses increased from 8 to 10. More powerful starter motor. Equalizer spring rear axle.
1966	116,000,0001–116,1,021,298	Number "1300" on engine lid. Flat hub caps; ventilated wheel discs. Four-way flasher system. Dimmer switch on turn signal. Defroster outlet in center of dash. Front seat backs equipped with safety locks.	Increased engine size, from 1200 cc. to 1300 cc. Increased engine output, from 40 hp. to 50 hp. (SAE)
1965	115,000,0001–115,979,200	Larger windows, narrower window and door posts. Heater control levers now mounted on tunnel, formerly a twisting knob. Push-button handle on engine lid. Back of rear seat convertible to a flat platform.	No major changes.
1964	5,677,119–6,502,399	Steel sliding sunroof; crank operated. Wider license plate light. Non-porous leatherette upholstery replaced by porous vinyl material.	No major changes.
1963	4,846,836–5,677,118	Sunroof equipped with folding handle. Fresh air heating system. Nylon window guides. Introduction of leatherette headliner; formerly "mouse fuzz". Wolfsburg hood crest eliminated from front hood.	No major changes.
1962	4,010,995–4,846,835	Spring-loaded hood. Addition of seat belt mounting points. Gasoline gauge on dashboard; formerly only a reserve fuel tap. Size of tail lights increased. Sliding covers for front floor heating outlets. Windshield washer added; compressed air type.	Worm and roller steering; formerly worm and sector. Tie rod ends permanently lubricated.
1961	3,192,507–4,010,994	Flatter gasoline tank. Increased front luggage space. Windshield washer; pump-type. Key slot in doors now vertical; formerly horizontal. Starter switch now non-repeat.	Increased engine output, from 36 hp. to 40 hp. (SAE). Automatic choke. Push-on electrical connectors. First gear now synchromesh; all forward speeds now synchromesh.
1960	2,528,668–3,192,506	"Dished" steering wheel. Push-button door handles; formerly lever-type. Foot rest for passenger. Padded sunvisor.	Front anti-sway bar added. Generator output increased to 180 watts, formerly 160. Steering damper added.

Type 1 Model Changes (Cont.)

Year	Chassis Numbers	Major Body Changes	Major Mechanical Changes
1959	2,007,616– 2,528,667	No major changes.	Stronger clutch springs. Fan belt improved. Frame given additional reinforcement.
1958	1,600,440– 2,007,615	Larger rear window and windshield. Front turn signal lights moved to top of fenders. Radio grill moved to far left of dashboard.	Wider brake drums and shoes.
1957	1,246,619– 1,600,439	Doors fitted with adjustable striker plates. Front heater outlets moved rearward, to within five inches of door. Tubeless tires used; formerly tube-type.	No major changes.
1956	929,746– 1,246,618	Tail light housings raised two inches. Steering wheel spoke moved lower and off-center. Heater knob moved forward. Adjustable front seat backs; formerly non-adjustable. Increased front luggage space.	Dual tail pipe; formerly single tail pipe.
1955	722,935– 929,745	Flashing turn signal lights replace "semaphore"-type flappers. Indicators mounted near outside bottom of front fenders.	No major changes.
1954	575,415– 722,934	Starter switch combined with ignition switch; formerly a separate button on dashboard. Interior courtesy light added.	Increased engine size, from 1131 cc. to 1192 cc. Addition of oil-bath air cleaner.
1953	428,157– 575,414	Oval rear window replaces two-piece split rear window. Vent window handles now provided with a lock button.	No major changes.
1952	313,830– 428,156	Vent windows added. Body vent flaps eliminated. Window crank geared down from 10½ to 3½ turns. Door added to glove compartment. Turn signal control to steering wheel; formerly on dashboard. 5.60 x 15 tires. Formerly 5.00 x16.	Top three gears synchromesh; formerly crashbox.
1951	220,472– 313,829	Vent flaps in front quarter-panel of body. Wolfsburg crest above front hood handle.	No major changes.
1950	138,555– 220,471	Ash tray added to dashboard.	Hydraulic brakes; formerly mechanical.
1949	91,922– 138,554	Pull release for front hood; formerly locking handle.	Solex carburetor now standard equipment.

Vehicle Identification—Types 1, 2 and 3

Model	SAE Output	from Chassis No.	Date	to Chassis No.	Date
Vehicle, Type 1					
Standard Sedan	36bhp.	1-0575 415	December 1953	6 502 399	July 1964
Standard Sedan, Sedan A	36bhp.	115 000 001	August 1964	115 979 202	July 1965
Deluxe Sedan Karmann Ghia Models VW Convertible	36bhp.	1-0575 415	December 1953	3192 506	July 1960
	42bhp.	3192 507	August 1960	6 502 399	July 1964
		115 000 001	August 1964	115 979 202	July 1965
1200A	42bhp.	116 000 001	August 1965	1161 021 297	July 1966
VW 1200	42bhp.	117 483 306	January 1967	117 844 900	July 1967
		118 000 001	August 1967	1181 016 095	July 1968
		119 000 001	August 1968	1191 093 701	July 1969
		110 2000 001	August 1969		
VW 1300 Sedan Karmann Ghia Models VW Convertible	50bhp.	116 000 001	August 1965	1161 021 298	July 1966
VW 1300 A	50bhp.	117 000 001	August 1966	117 403 305	Jan. 1967
VW 1300 Sedan	50bhp.	117 000 001	August 1966	117 844 901	July 1967
		118 000 001	August 1967	1181 016 096	July 1968
		119 000 002	August 1968	1191 093 702	July 1969
		110 2000 002	August 1969		
VW 1500 Sedan Karmann Ghia Models VW Convertible	53bhp.	117 000 001	August 1966	117 844 902	July 1967
		118 000 001	August 1967	118 1016 097	July 1968
		119 000 003	August 1968	119 1093 703	July 1969
		110 2000 003	August 1969		
	57bhp.	110 2000 004	August 1969		
VW 1600 Sedan Karmann Ghia Models VW Convertible	57bhp.		1970		
VW 1600 Sedan Super Beetle Karmann Ghia Models VW Convertible	60bhp.		1971		

Vehicle Identification (Cont.)

Model	SAE Output	from Chassis No.	Date	to Chassis No.	Date
Vehicle, type 2					
	1200	36bhp.			
		20-069 409	December 1953	614 455	May 1960
		42bhp.			
		614 456	June 1960	1 328 271	July 1964
		215 000 001	August 1964	215 036 378	Sept. 1964
Transporter	1500	51bhp.			
		1041 014	January 1963	1 328 271	July 1964
		215 000 001	August 1964	215 176 339	July 1965
		53bhp.			
		216 000 001	August 1965	216 179 668	July 1966
		217 000 001	August 1966	217 148 459	July 1967
	1600	57bhp.			
		218 000 001	August 1967	218 202 251	July 1968
		219 000 001	August 1968	219 238 131	July 1969
		210 2000 001	August 1969		
		60bhp.	1971		
Vehicle, type 3					
Volkswagen 1500		54bhp.			
		0 000 001	April 1961	0 483 592	July 1964
		315 000 001	August 1964	315 220 883	July 1965
		316 000 001	August 1965	316 316 237	July 1966
		317 000 001	August 1966	317 283 852	July 1967
		318 000 001	August 1967	318 235 386	July 1968
		319 000 001	August 1968	319 264 031	July 1969
		310 2000 002	August 1969		
Volkswagen 1600		66bhp.			
		0 221975	August 1963	0 483 592	July 1964
		315 000 001	August 1964	315 220 883	July 1965
		316 000 001	August 1965	316 316 238	July 1966
		317 000 001	August 1966	317 233 853	July 1967
		318 000 002	August 1967	318 235 387	July 1968
		319 000 002	August 1968	319 264 032	July 1969
		310 2000 002	August 1969		

ROUTINE MAINTENANCE

ENGINE COMPARTMENT MAINTENANCE COMPONENTS – TYPE 1 AND 2 ENGINES

1. Generator drive belt
2. Engine oil dipstick
3. Fuel filter (located inside the fuel pump)
4. Engine oil fill cap
5. Air filter assembly
6. No. 1 cylinder spark plug
7. No. 2 cylinder spark plug
8. No. 3 cylinder spark plug
9. No. 4 cylinder spark plug

GENERAL MAINTENANCE ITEMS – MANUAL TRANSAXLE MODELS

1. Transmission case drain plug
2. Transmission case fill plug
3. Differential case drain plug
4. Differential case fill plug

5. CV-boot
6. Oil drain plug
7. Oil strainer plate

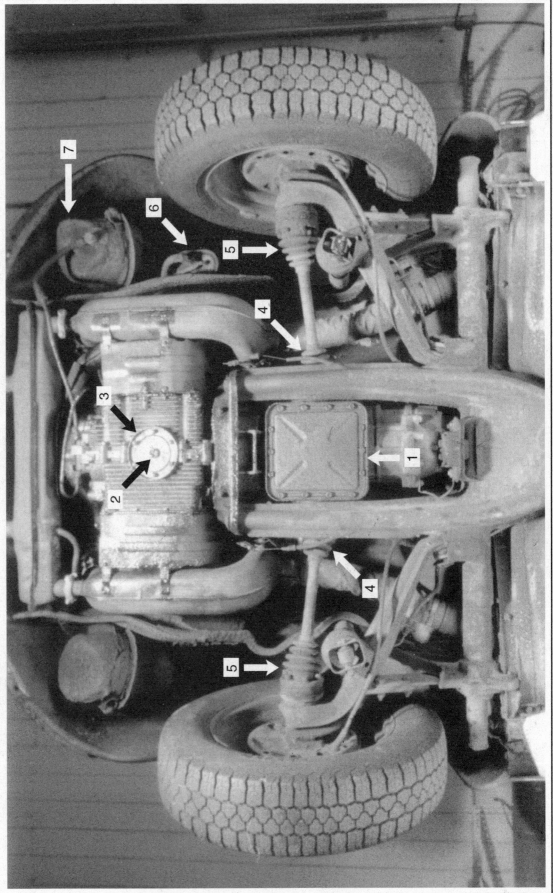

GENERAL MAINTENANCE ITEMS (CONTINUED) – AUTOMATIC STICK-SHIFT MODELS

1. Automatic stick-shift fluid cover
2. Engine oil drain plug
3. Engine oil strainer plate
4. Inner CV boots
5. Outer CV boots
6. Charcoal (EVAP) canister
7. Automatic stick-shift fluid reservoir

Air Cleaner

DESCRIPTION

Volkswagen carburetors are equipped with the very efficient oil bath type of air cleaner. In this type of cleaner, the incoming air is directed over the surface of the oil bath, causing a large portion of the dust contained to be retained in the oil bath.

Type 1 and 2 models have had numerous variations on the basic oil bath air cleaner. Most have some sort of an intake pipe or pipes, equipped with one or two warm air hoses. At low speeds, a weighted flap in the intake portion of the air cleaner is closed, causing pre-heated air from the cylinder head to enter the carburetor. At higher speeds, the flap is forced open by the force of the air, and pre-heated air is kept from entering. This arrangement makes it possible to have smoother idling and faster warm-up in extremely cold temperatures while at the same time allowing all of the needed air to enter the air cleaner at higher speeds. For summertime or higher-temperature operation, it is recommended that the flaps be held open by clipping their weight levers to the side of the intake pipe. In wintertime it is necessary that these flaps be allowed to rotate freely, because this helps to prevent the formation of carburetor icing.

Labels providing information for the upkeep of your vehicle can be found in several places

On later models, the adjustable flap is replaced by a thermostatically controlled flap. On some units, the flap is regulated through a Bowden cable by a thermostatic unit mounted on the engine. On others, the

To remove the oil bath air cleaner assembly . . .

. . . first detach the breather hose from it . . .

. . . then loosen the clamp screw . . .

. . . and lift the air cleaner off of the carburetor

To change the air cleaner oil, remove the lid and pour out the old oil . . .

. . . then add clean engine oil until the level reaches the mark inside the air cleaner

thermostatic unit is located on the body of the air cleaner.

The oil bath air cleaner on type 3 models is similar to that of type 1 models, except for the presence of more extensive ductwork, needed because the same air cleaner serves both of the 32PDSIT carburetors of this engine. Also, the type 3 air cleaner is equipped with a second flap which allows air from the engine compartment to enter the air cleaner. Otherwise, air comes in from the slits on each side of the rear fender position. The fuel injected type 3 has a similar air cleaner.

REMOVAL & INSTALLATION

Carbureted Engines

On type 1 and 2 models, the air cleaner is removed by taking the preheater pipe(s) from the intake tube of the air cleaner, disconnecting the thermostatic flap control wire, pulling the crankcase breather hose from the cleaner, and loosening the clamp screw that holds the cleaner onto the carburetor throat. After the air cleaner has been removed, the top part can be separated from the lower part by removing the clips that hold the halves together.

When the cleaner has been taken apart, the dirty oil should be poured out and the lower part cleaned. The upper part does not generally require cleaning. The bottom part of the air cleaner should then be filled to the mark with new engine oil of the same viscosity as that used in the engine. If there is no mark, refill with the quantity of oil specified in the Capacities and Pressures Chart.

Removal of the air cleaner in the type 3 dual carburetor engine is slightly more complex, but accomplished in much the same manner. The right-hand connecting rod must be removed from between the rotating lever and the carburetor, the cables removed from the automatic choke and electromagnetic pilot jet, the crankcase ventilation hose taken off the air cleaner, and the three wing nuts unscrewed. The center wing nut is removed before removing the air cleaner; those at each of the carburetors remain in place. After the center wing nut is removed, the air cleaner can be lifted from its position and the upper and lower parts separated.

When installing the air cleaner of the type 3 engine, care should be taken to see that the oil is up to the mark, that the rubber sealing ring on each carburetor is secure, that the water drain hole is free in the lower part of the air cleaner, and that the marks are lined up when the upper and lower halves are put back together. If the marks do not line up exactly, the intake pipe will point in the wrong direction and be

either difficult or impossible to connect to the intake extension. When tightening the wing nuts of the air cleaner, it is very important that the outer wing nuts are tightened down first. There is an expansion-contraction joint between the left outer wing nut and the center wing nut which makes these not quite so critical. However, there is no such joint between the center and right-hand wing nuts. Subsequently, if the center nut is tightened first, then the right-hand nut, the result could be a slight movement on the part of the right-hand carburetor, thus causing an alteration in a very sensitive adjustment. Tighten down the center wing nut only after the two outer wing nuts have been fully tightened.

Fuel Injected Engines

To remove:

1 Detach the crankcase and the auxiliary air regulator hoses.

2 Loosen the hose clamps at either end of the air cleaner. Pull off the rubber hoses.

3 Remove the wingnut and the air cleaner.

To clean, refill, and replace the air cleaner:

4 Release the three clips. Remove the top section.

5 Clean the filter assembly and refill it with SAE 30 oil to the red mark; SAE 10 may be used in arctic climates.

6 Be sure that the red arrows on the top and bottom sections are aligned when reassembling.

7 Reconnect the hoses, tighten the clamps and the wingnut.

Fuel Filter

REMOVAL & INSTALLATION

Carbureted Engines

On carbureted models, the fuel filter is located in the mechanical fuel pump. There are three types of fuel pumps. Two types have a single screw holding a cover on the top of the pump. To remove the filter screen, undo the screw and carefully lift the cover off the pump. Remove the cover gasket and filter screen taking careful note of the position of the screen. Blow the screen out with air and replace the screen and cover using a new gasket if necessary.

The third type of fuel pump has four screws securing the top cover to the pump. This type of pump has a large plug with a hexagonal head. Remove this plug and washer (gasket) to gain access to the cylindrical

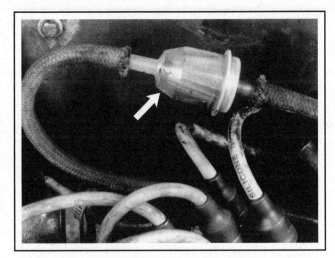

An aftermarket filter (arrow) is often installed in the hose running from the fuel pump to the carburetor

filter screen located beneath the plug. Blow the screen out with air and replace it in its bore with the open end facing into the pump. Install the washer and plug. Do not overtighten the plug.

Fuel Injected Engines

The fuel filter is in the pump suction line, either near, or mounted on the fuel pump. It should be replaced every 6,000 miles. To replace the filter:

1   Pinch clamp the fuel lines shut on either side of the filter.
2   Remove the pin holding the filter bracket to the pump. Remove the filter.
3   Install the new filter making sure that the arrow points to the pump. Replace the bracket and pin.
4   Install screw type hose clamps on the fuel lines.
5   Remove the pinch clamps.

Battery

GENERAL MAINTENANCE

All batteries, regardless of type, should be carefully secured by a battery hold-down device. If this is not done, the battery terminals or casing may crack from stress applied to the battery during vehicle operation. A battery which is not secured may allow acid to leak out, making it discharge faster; such leaking corrosive acid can also eat

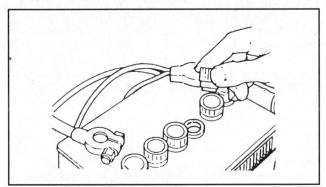

On non-maintenance free batteries, the level can be checked through the case on translucent batteries; the cell caps must be removed on other models

away components under the hood. A battery that is not sealed must be checked periodically for electrolyte level. You cannot add water to a sealed maintenance-free battery (though not all maintenance-free batteries are sealed), but a sealed battery must also be checked for proper electrolyte level as indicated by the color of the built-in hydrometer "eye."

Keep the top of the battery clean, as a film of dirt can help completely discharge a battery that is not used for long periods. A solution of baking soda and water may be used for cleaning, but be careful to flush this off with clear water. DO NOT let any of the solution into the filler holes. Baking soda neutralizes battery acid and will de-activate a battery cell.

❋ CAUTION:

Always use caution when working on or near the battery. Never allow a tool to bridge the gap between the negative and positive battery terminals. Also, be careful not to allow a tool to provide a ground between the positive cable/terminal and any metal component on the vehicle. Either of these conditions will cause a short circuit leading to sparks and possible personal injury.

Batteries in vehicles which are not operated on a regular basis can fall victim to parasitic loads (small current drains which are constantly drawing current from the battery). Normal parasitic loads may drain a battery on a vehicle that is in storage and not used for 6 - 8 weeks. Vehicles that have additional accessories such as a cellular phone, an alarm system or other devices that increase parasitic load may discharge a battery sooner. If the vehicle is to be stored for 6 - 8 weeks in a secure area and the alarm system, if present, is not necessary, the negative battery cable should be disconnected at the onset of storage to protect the battery charge.

Remember that constantly discharging and recharging will shorten battery life. Take care not to allow a battery to be needlessly discharged.

BATTERY FLUID

❋ CAUTION:

Battery electrolyte contains sulfuric acid. If you should splash any on your skin or in your eyes, flush the affected area with plenty of clear water. If it lands in your eyes, get medical help immediately.

Check the specific gravity of the battery's electrolyte with a hydrometer

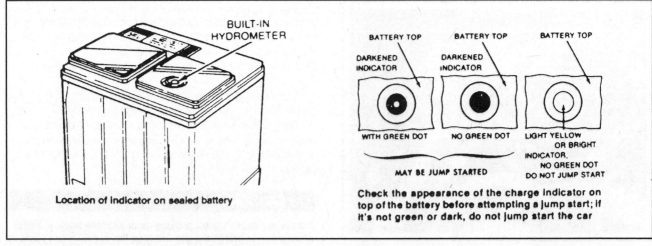

A typical sealed (maintenance-free) battery with a built-in hydrometer - NOTE that the hydrometer eye may vary between battery manufacturers; always refer to the battery's label

The fluid (sulfuric acid solution) contained in the battery cells will tell you many things about the condition of the battery. Because the cell plates must be kept submerged below the fluid level in order to operate, maintaining the fluid level is extremely important. And, because the specific gravity of the acid is an indication of electrical charge, testing the fluid can be an aid in determining if the battery must be replaced. A battery in a vehicle with a properly operating charging system should require little maintenance, but careful, periodic inspection should reveal problems before they leave you stranded.

Fluid Level

Check the battery electrolyte level at least once a month, or more often in hot weather or during periods of extended vehicle operation. On non-sealed batteries, the level can be checked either through the case on translucent batteries or by removing the cell caps on opaque-cased types. The electrolyte level in each cell should be kept filled to the split ring inside each cell, or the line marked on the outside of the case.

If the level is low, add only distilled water through the opening until the level is correct. Each cell is separate from the others, so each must be checked and filled individually. Distilled water should be used, because the chemicals and minerals found in most drinking water are harmful to the battery and could significantly shorten its life.

If water is added in freezing weather, the vehicle should be driven several miles to allow the water to mix with the electrolyte. Otherwise, the battery could freeze.

Although some maintenance-free batteries have removable cell caps for access to the electrolyte, the electrolyte condition and level on all sealed maintenance-free batteries must be checked using the built-in hydrometer "eye." The exact type of eye varies between battery manufacturers, but most apply a sticker to the battery itself explaining the possible readings. When in doubt, refer to the battery manufacturer's instructions to interpret battery condition using the built-in hydrometer.

➡**Although the readings from built-in hydrometers found in sealed batteries may vary, a green eye usually indicates a properly charged battery with sufficient fluid level. A dark eye is normally an indicator of a battery with sufficient fluid, but one which may be low in charge. And a light or yellow eye is usually an indication that electrolyte supply has dropped below the necessary level for battery (and hydrometer) operation. In this last case, sealed batteries with an insufficient electrolyte level must usually be discarded.**

Specific Gravity

As stated earlier, the specific gravity of a battery's electrolyte level can be used as an indication of battery charge. At least once a year, check the specific gravity of the battery. It should be between 1.20 and 1.26 on the gravity scale. Most auto supply stores carry a variety of inexpensive battery testing hydrometers. These can be used on any non-sealed battery to test the specific gravity in each cell.

The battery testing hydrometer has a squeeze bulb at one end and a nozzle at the other. Battery electrolyte is sucked into the hydrometer until the float is lifted from its seat. The specific gravity is then read by noting the position of the float. If gravity is low in one or more cells, the battery should be slowly charged and checked again to see if the gravity has come up. Generally, if after charging, the specific gravity between any two cells varies more than 50 points (0.50), the battery should be replaced as it can no longer produce sufficient voltage to guarantee proper operation.

On sealed batteries, the built-in hydrometer is the only way of checking specific gravity. Again, check with your battery's manufacturer for proper interpretation of its built-in hydrometer readings.

CABLES

Once a year (or as necessary), the battery terminals and the cable clamps should be cleaned. Loosen the clamps and remove the cables, negative cable first. On batteries with posts on top, the use of a puller specially made for this purpose is recommended. These are inexpensive and available in most auto parts stores. Side terminal battery cables are secured with a small bolt.

Clean the cable clamps and the battery terminal with a wire brush, until all corrosion, grease, etc., is removed and the metal is shiny. It is especially important to clean the inside of the clamp (an old knife is useful here) thoroughly, since a small deposit of foreign material or oxidation there will prevent a sound electrical connection and inhibit either starting or charging. Special tools are available for cleaning these parts, one type for conventional top post batteries and another type for side terminal batteries.

Before installing the cables, loosen the battery hold-down clamp or strap, remove the battery and check the battery tray. Clear it of any debris, and check it for soundness (the battery tray can be cleaned with a baking soda and water solution). Rust should be wire brushed away,

Maintenance is performed with household items and with special tools like this post cleaner

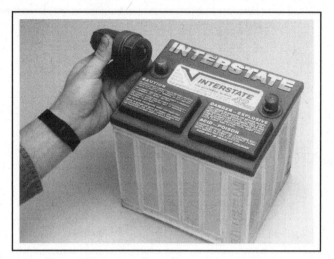

The underside of this special battery tool has a wire brush to clean post terminals

teries. Tighten the clamps securely, but do not distort them. Give the clamps and terminals a thin external coating of grease after installation, to retard corrosion.

Check the cables at the same time that the terminals are cleaned. If the cable insulation is cracked or broken, or if the ends are frayed, the cable should be replaced with a new cable of the same length and gauge.

CHARGING

> ✳✳ **CAUTION:**
>
> The chemical reaction which takes place in all batteries generates explosive hydrogen gas. A spark can cause the battery to explode and splash acid. To avoid serious personal injury, be sure there is proper ventilation and take appropriate fire safety precautions when connecting, disconnecting, or charging a battery and when using jumper cables.

A battery should be charged at a slow rate to keep the plates inside from getting too hot. However, if some maintenance-free batteries are allowed to discharge until they are almost "dead," they may have to be charged at a high rate to bring them back to "life." Always follow the charger manufacturer's instructions on charging the battery.

Place the tool over the terminals and twist to clean the post

and the metal given a couple coats of anti-rust paint. Install the battery and tighten the hold-down clamp or strap securely. Do not overtighten, as this can crack the battery case.

After the clamps and terminals are clean, reinstall the cables, negative cable last; DO NOT hammer the clamps onto post bat-

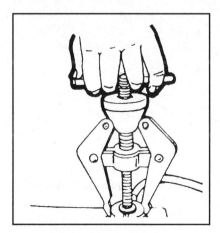

A special tool is available to pull the clamp from the post

Clean the battery terminals until the metal is shiny

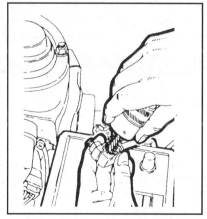

The cable ends should be cleaned as well

The battery is located under the rear seat on type 1 and 3 models

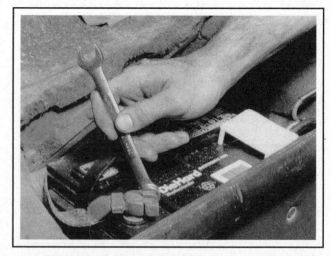

Loosen the battery cable clamp bolt . . .

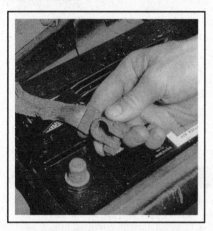

. . . then separate the cable from the battery terminal post

A plastic cover helps prevent the metal seat springs from contacting the battery post

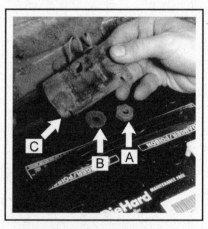

Remove the hold-down nut (A), washer (B) and bracket (C), then lift the battery out of the car

REPLACEMENT

When it becomes necessary to replace the battery, select one with a rating equal to or greater than the battery originally installed. Deterioration and just plain aging of the battery cables, starter motor, and associated wires makes the battery's job harder in successive years. The slow increase in electrical resistance over time makes it prudent to install a new battery with a greater capacity than the old.

Belts

INSPECTION

Inspect the belts for signs of glazing or cracking. A glazed belt will be perfectly smooth from slippage, while a good belt will have a slight texture of fabric visible. Cracks will usually start at the inner edge of the belt and run outward. All worn or damaged drive belts should be replaced immediately. It is best to replace all drive belts at one time, as a preventive maintenance measure, during this service operation.

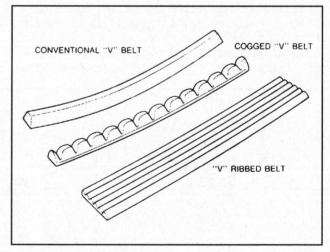

There are typically 3 types of accessory drive belts found on vehicles today

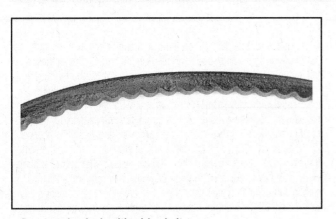

An example of a healthy drive belt

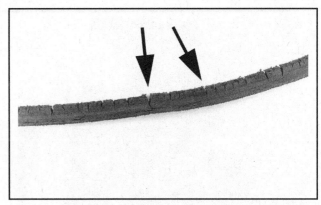

Deep cracks in this belt will cause flex, building up heat that will eventually lead to belt failure

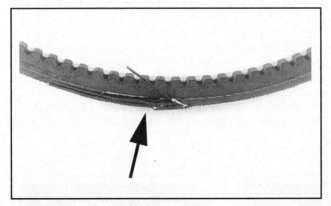

The cover of this belt is worn, exposing the critical reinforcing cords to excessive wear

Installing too wide a belt can result in serious belt wear and/ or breakage

ADJUSTMENT, REMOVAL & INSTALLATION

Generator/Drive Belt

Improper fan belt adjustment can lead to either overheating of the engine or to loss in generating power, or both. In the Type 1 or Type 2 a loose fan belt can cause both, while the slipping of the generator or alternator belt of the Type 3 engine will cause loss of generator efficiency only. In any case, it is important that the fan belt adjustment be checked and, if necessary, corrected at periodic intervals. When adjusted properly, the belt of any Volkswagen engine should deflect approximately 1/2 in. when pressed firmly in the center with the thumb. Check the tension at 6,000 mile intervals.

TYPE 1 and 2 MODELS

Adjustment of the type 1 and 2 fan belt is made as follows: loosen the fan pulley by unscrewing the nut while at the same time holding the pulley from rotating by using a prytool inserted into the slot cut into the inner half of the generator pulley and supported against the upper generator bolt to cause a counter-torque. Remove the nut from the generator shaft pulley and remove the outer half of the pulley. The spacer washers must then be arranged so as to make the fan belt tension either greater or lower. The greater the number of washers between the pulley halves, the smaller the effective diameter of the pulley, and the less the fan belt tension will be. Conversely, the subtraction of washers from between the pulley halves will lead to a larger effective diameter and to a greater degree of fan belt tension. If it is impossible to achieve proper adjustment with all the washers removed, then the fan belt is exces-

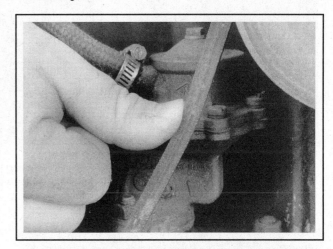

Check the tension of the drive belt with your thumb, as shown

sively stretched, and must be replaced. If it is impossible to adjust a new belt properly by using some combination of the available washers, the belt is the wrong size and must not be used. After the correct number of washers has been applied between the pulley halves, install the outer pulley half and place all surplus washers between the outer pulley half and the pulley nut so that they will be available if needed in a subsequent adjustment. Tighten the pulley nut and recheck the adjustment. If incorrect, add or subtract washers between the pulley halves until the proper amount of deflection is achieved. If the belt is too tight, the generator bearings will be subjected to undue stress and to very early

To remove the generator pulley, use a prybar to hold the pulley while loosening the nut . . .

failure. On the other hand, if the belt is too loose, it will slip and cause overheating. Cracked or frayed belts should be replaced. There is no comparison between the cost of a fan belt and that of repairing a badly overheated engine. If it is necessary to replace the belt, remove the three sheet metal screws and the crankshaft pulley cover plate to gain access to the pulley.

TYPE 3 MODELS

Adjustment of the fan belt on the type 3 engine is much the same as that of the upright Volkswagen engines. On the type 3 engine, the fan belt is subject to a great deal less stress because it has no fan to turn. Therefore, a loose adjustment is not quite so critical as on the type 1 and 2 models. However, the 1/2 in. deflection should nevertheless be maintained, because a loose fan belt could possibly climb over the pulley and foul the fan. In addition, loose fan belts have a shorter service life. In adjusting the type 3 fan belt, the first step is to remove the cover of the air intake housing. Next, hold the generator pulley with a suitable wrench, and unscrew the retaining nut. (Note: a 27mm and a 21mm wrench will come in handy here. Also, be careful that no adjusting washers fall off the shaft into the air intake housing, for they could be quite difficult to remove.) Loosen the generator strap and push the generator slightly forward. Remove the outer pulley half, sleeve and washers included. Arrange the spacer washers as was described in the type 1 and 2 procedure belt adjustment; i.e., more washers between halves mean a looser belt, and fewer washers mean a tighter belt. Install the outer half of the pulley. Install the unused washers on the outside of the outer pulley half so that the total number of washers on the shaft will remain the same. Fit the nut into place and tighten down the generator strap after pulling the generator back to the rear. Tighten the retaining nut and make sure that the generator belt is parallel to the air intake housing and at least 4mm away from it at all points. Install the housing cover.

. . . then remove the nut, spacer and washers from the pulley

Remove the outer half of the generator pulley and the generator belt

Belt tension is controlled by the number of washers used between the two pulley halves

Boots

INSPECTION

The CV (Constant Velocity) boots should be checked for damage each time the oil is changed and any other time the vehicle is raised for service. These boots keep water, grime, dirt and other damaging matter from entering the CV-joints. Any of these could cause early CV-joint failure which can be expensive to repair. Heavy grease thrown around the inside of the front wheel(s) and on the brake caliper/drum can be an indication of a torn boot. Thoroughly check the boots for missing clamps and tears. If the boot is damaged, it should be replaced immediately.

Windshield Wipers

ELEMENT (REFILL) CARE & REPLACEMENT

For maximum effectiveness and longest element life, the windshield and wiper blades should be kept clean. Dirt, tree sap, road tar and so on will cause streaking, smearing and blade deterioration if left on the glass. It is advisable to wash the windshield carefully with a commercial glass cleaner at least once a month. Wipe off the rubber blades with the wet rag afterwards. Do not attempt to move wipers across the windshield by hand; damage to the motor and drive mechanism will result.

To inspect and/or replace the wiper blade elements, place the wiper switch in the LOW speed position and the ignition switch in the ACC

CV-boots must be inspected periodically for damage

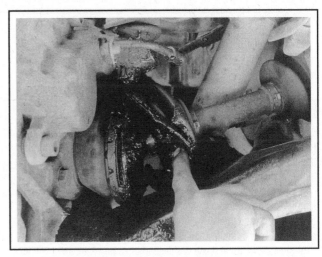

A torn boot should be replaced immediately

position. When the wiper blades are approximately vertical on the windshield, turn the ignition switch to OFF.

Examine the wiper blade elements. If they are found to be cracked, broken or torn, they should be replaced immediately. Replacement intervals will vary with usage, although ozone deterioration usually limits element life to about one year. If the wiper pattern is smeared or streaked, or if the blade chatters across the glass, the elements should be replaced. It is easiest and most sensible to replace the

elements in pairs.

If your vehicle is equipped with aftermarket blades, there are several different types of refills and your vehicle might have any kind. Aftermarket blades and arms rarely use the exact same type blade or refill as the original equipment. Here are some typical aftermarket blades; not all may be available for your vehicle:

The Anco type uses a release button that is pushed down to allow the refill to slide out of the yoke jaws. The new refill slides back into the

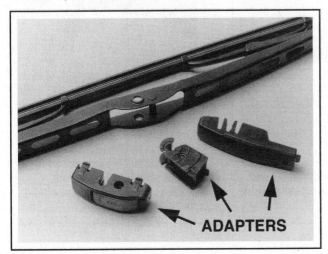

Bosch wiper blade and fit kit

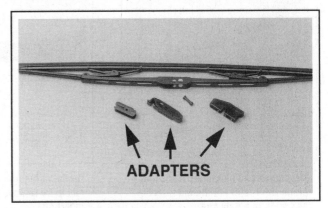

Lexor wiper blade and fit kit

Pylon wiper blade and adaptor

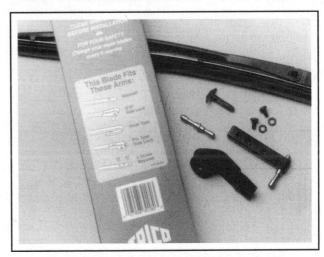

Trico wiper blade and fit kit

frame and locks in place.

Some Trico refills are removed by locating where the metal backing strip or the refill is wider. Insert a small screwdriver blade between the frame and metal backing strip. Press down to release the refill from the retaining tab.

Other types of Trico refills have two metal tabs which are unlocked by squeezing them together. The rubber filler can then be withdrawn from the frame jaws. A new refill is installed by inserting the refill into the front frame jaws and sliding it rearward to engage the remaining frame jaws. There are usually four jaws; be certain when installing that the refill is engaged in all of them. At the end of its travel, the tabs will lock into place on the front jaws of the wiper blade frame.

Another type of refill is made from polycarbonate. The refill has a simple locking device at one end which flexes downward out of the groove into which the jaws of the holder fit, allowing easy release. By sliding the new refill through all the jaws and pushing through the slight resistance when it reaches the end of its travel, the refill will lock into position.

To replace the Tridon refill, it is necessary to remove the wiper blade. This refill has a plastic backing strip with a notch about 1 in. (25mm) from the end. Hold the blade (frame) on a hard surface so that the frame is tightly bowed. Grip the tip of the backing strip and pull up while twisting counterclockwise. The backing strip will snap out of the

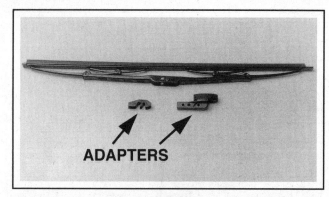

Tripledge wiper blade and fit kit

retaining tab. Do this for the remaining tabs until the refill is free of the blade. The length of these refills is molded into the end and they should be replaced with identical types.

Regardless of the type of refill used, be sure to follow the part manufacturer's instructions closely. Make sure that all of the frame jaws are engaged as the refill is pushed into place and locked. If the metal blade holder and frame are allowed to touch the glass during wiper operation, the glass will be scratched.

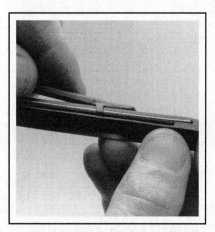

To remove and install a Lexor wiper blade refill, slip out the old insert and slide in a new one

On Pylon inserts, the clip at the end has to be removed prior to sliding the insert off

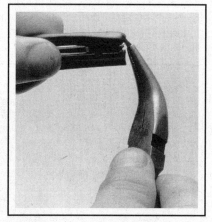

On Trico wiper blades, the tab at the end of the blade must be turned up . . .

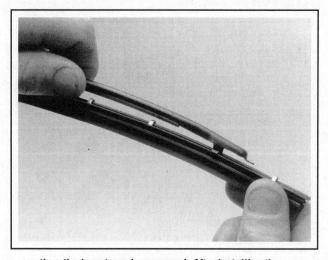

. . . then the insert can be removed. After installing the replacement insert, bend the tab back

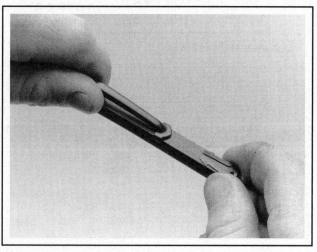

The Tripledge wiper blade insert is removed and installed using a securing clip

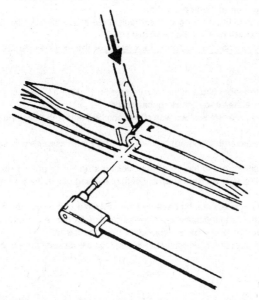

BLADE REPLACEMENT

1. CYCLE ARM AND BLADE ASSEMBLY TO UP POSITION ON THE WINDSHIELD WHERE REMOVAL OF BLADE ASSEMBLY CAN BE PERFORMED WITHOUT DIFFICULTY. TURN IGNITION KEY OFF AT DESIRED POSITION.

2. TO REMOVE BLADE ASSEMBLY, INSERT SCREWDRIVER IN SLOT, PUSH DOWN ON SPRING LOCK AND PULL BLADE ASSEMBLY FROM PIN (VIEW A)

3. TO INSTALL, PUSH THE BLADE ASSEMBLY ON THE PIN SO THAT THE SPRING LOCK ENGAGES THE PIN (VIEW A). BE SURE THE BLADE ASSEMBLY IS SECURELY ATTACHED TO PIN

VIEW A

NOTE INSERT SCREWDRIVER 3 2 mm (1/8 INCH) OR LESS PAST THIS EDGE

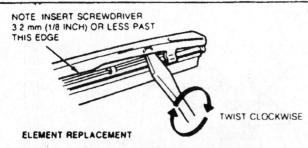

TWIST CLOCKWISE

ELEMENT REPLACEMENT

1 INSERT SCREWDRIVER BETWEEN THE EDGE OF THE SUPER STRUCTURE AND THE BLADE BACKING DRIP (VIEW B) TWIST SCREWDRIVER SLOWLY UNTIL ELEMENT CLEARS ONE SIDE OF THE SUPER STRUCTURE CLAW

2 SLIDE THE ELEMENT INTO THE SUPER STRUCTURE CLAWS

VIEW B

4 INSERT ELEMENT INTO ONE SIDE OF THE END CLAWS (VIEW D) AND WITH A ROCKING MOTION PUSH ELEMENT UPWARD UNTIL IT SNAPS IN (VIEW E)

VIEW D

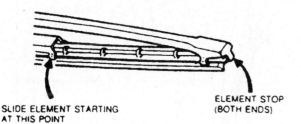

SLIDE ELEMENT STARTING AT THIS POINT

ELEMENT STOP (BOTH ENDS)

3. SLIDE THE ELEMENT INTO THE SUPER STRUCTURE CLAWS, STARTING WITH SECOND SET FROM EITHER END (VIEW C) AND CONTINUE TO SLIDE THE BLADE ELEMENT INTO ALL THE SUPER STRUCTURE CLAWS TO THE ELEMENT STOP (VIEW C)

VIEW C

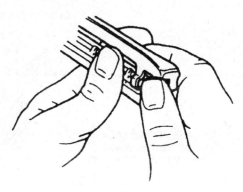

VIEW E

Trico wiper blade insert (element) replacement

BLADE REPLACEMENT

1. Cycle arm and blade assembly to a position on the windshield where removal of blade assembly can be performed without difficulty. Turn ignition key off at desired position.
2. To remove blade assembly from wiper arm, pull up on spring lock and pull blade assembly from pin (View A). Be sure spring lock is not pulled excessively or it will become distorted.
3. To install, push the blade assembly onto the pin so that the spring lock engages the pin (View A). Be sure the blade assembly is securely attached to pin.

ELEMENT REPLACEMENT

1. In the plastic backing strip which is part of the rubber blade assembly, there is an 11.11mm (7/16 inch) long notch located approximately one inch from either end. Locate either notch.
2. Place the frame of the wiper blade assembly on a firm surface with either notched end of the backing strip visible.
3. Grasp the frame portion of the wiper blade assembly and push down until the blade assembly is tightly bowed.
4. With the blade assembly in the bowed position, grasp the tip of the backing strip firmly, pulling up and twisting C.C.W. at the same time. The backing strip will then snap out of the retaining tab on the end of the frame.
5. Lift the wiper blade assembly from the surface and slide the backing strip down the frame until the notch lines up with the next retaining tab, twist slightly, and the backing strip will snap out. Continue this operation with the remaining tabs until the blade element is completely detached from the frame.
6. To install blade element, reverse the above procedure, making sure all six (6) tabs are locked to the backing strip before installing blade to wiper arm.

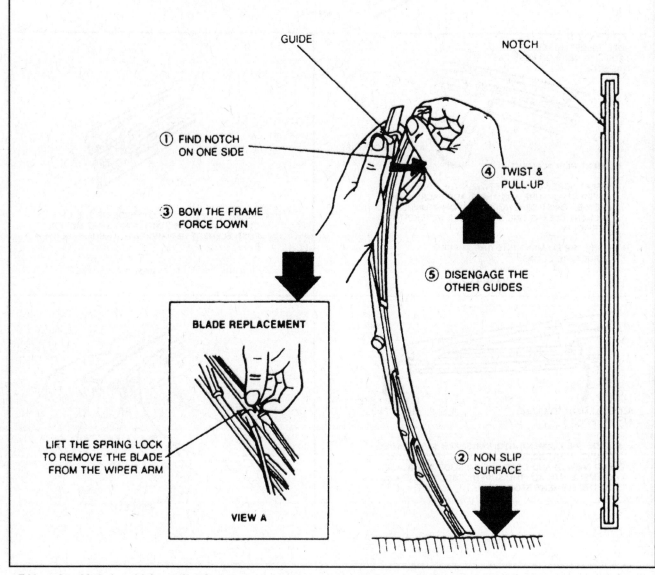

Tridon wiper blade insert (element) replacement

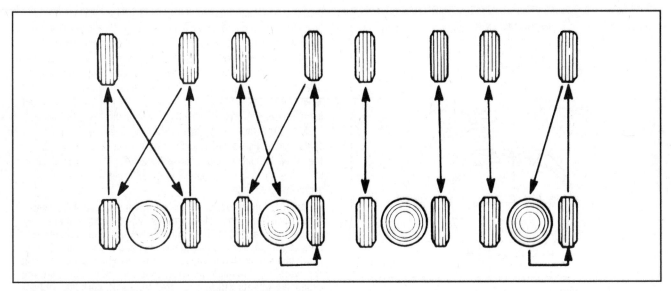

Common tire rotation patterns for 4 and 5-wheel rotations

Tires and Wheels

Common sense and good driving habits will afford maximum tire life. Fast starts, sudden stops and hard cornering are hard on tires and will shorten their useful life span. Make sure that you don't overload the vehicle or run with incorrect pressure in the tires. Both of these practices will increase tread wear.

➡**For optimum tire life, keep the tires properly inflated, rotate them often and have the wheel alignment checked periodically.**

Inspect your tires frequently. Be especially careful to watch for bubbles in the tread or sidewall, deep cuts or underinflation. Replace any tires with bubbles in the sidewall. If cuts are so deep that they penetrate to the cords, discard the tire. Any cut in the sidewall of a radial tire renders it unsafe. Also look for uneven tread wear patterns that may indicate the front end is out of alignment or that the tires are out of balance.

TIRE ROTATION

Tires must be rotated periodically to equalize wear patterns that vary with a tire's position on the vehicle. Tires will also wear in an uneven way as the front steering/suspension system wears to the point where the alignment should be reset.

Rotating the tires will ensure maximum life for the tires as a set, so you will not have to discard a tire early due to wear on only part of the tread. Regular rotation is required to equalize wear.

When rotating "unidirectional tires," make sure that they always roll in the same direction. This means that a tire used on the left side of the vehicle must not be switched to the right side and vice-versa. Such tires should only be rotated front-to-rear or rear-to-front, while always remaining on the same side of the vehicle. These tires are marked on the sidewall as to the direction of rotation; observe the marks when reinstalling the tire(s).

Some styled or "mag" wheels may have different offsets front to rear. In these cases, the rear wheels must not be used up front and vice-versa. Furthermore, if these wheels are equipped with unidirectional tires, they cannot be rotated unless the tire is remounted for the proper

direction of rotation.

➡**The compact or space-saver spare is strictly for emergency use. It must never be included in the tire rotation or placed on the vehicle for everyday use.**

TIRE DESIGN

For maximum satisfaction, tires should be used in sets of four. Mixing of different types (radial, bias-belted, fiberglass belted) must be avoided. In most cases, the vehicle manufacturer has designated a type of tire on which the vehicle will perform best. Your first choice when replacing tires should be to use the same type of tire that the manufacturer recommends.

When radial tires are used, tire sizes and wheel diameters should be selected to maintain ground clearance and tire load capacity equivalent to the original specified tire. Radial tires should always be used in sets of four.

Unidirectional tires are identifiable by sidewall arrows and/ or the word "rotation"

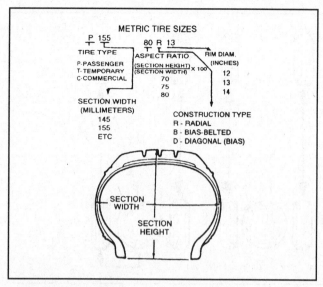

P-Metric tire coding

✳✳ CAUTION:

Radial tires should never be used on only the front axle.

When selecting tires, pay attention to the original size as marked on the tire. Most tires are described using an industry size code sometimes referred to as P-Metric. This allows the exact identification of the tire specifications, regardless of the manufacturer. If selecting a different tire size or brand, remember to check the installed tire for any sign of interference with the body or suspension while the vehicle is stopping, turning sharply or heavily loaded.

Snow Tires

Good radial tires can produce a big advantage in slippery weather, but in snow, a street radial tire does not have sufficient tread to provide traction and control. The small grooves of a street tire quickly pack with snow and the tire behaves like a billiard ball on a marble floor. The more open, chunky tread of a snow tire will self-clean as the tire turns, providing much better grip on snowy surfaces.

To satisfy municipalities requiring snow tires during weather emer-gencies, most snow tires carry either an M + S designation after the tire size stamped on the sidewall, or the designation "all-season." In general, no change in tire size is necessary when buying snow tires.

Most manufacturers strongly recommend the use of 4 snow tires on their vehicles for reasons of stability. If snow tires are fitted only to the drive wheels, the opposite end of the vehicle may become very unstable when braking or turning on slippery surfaces. This instability can lead to unpleasant endings if the driver can't counteract the slide in time.

Note that snow tires, whether 2 or 4, will affect vehicle handling in all non-snow situations. The stiffer, heavier snow tires will noticeably change the turning and braking characteristics of the vehicle. Once the snow tires are installed, you must re-learn the behavior of the vehicle and drive accordingly.

➡**Consider buying extra wheels on which to mount the snow tires. Once done, the "snow wheels" can be installed and removed as needed. This eliminates the potential damage to tires or wheels from seasonal removal and installation. Even if your vehicle has styled wheels, see if inexpensive steel wheels are available. Although the look of the vehicle will change, the expensive wheels will be protected from salt, curb hits and pothole damage.**

TIRE STORAGE

If they are mounted on wheels, store the tires at proper inflation pressure. All tires should be kept in a cool, dry place. If they are stored in the garage or basement, do not let them stand on a concrete floor; set them on strips of wood, a mat or a large stack of newspaper. Keeping them away from direct moisture is of paramount importance. Tires should not be stored upright, but in a flat position.

INFLATION & INSPECTION

The importance of proper tire inflation cannot be overemphasized. A tire employs air as part of its structure. It is designed around the supporting strength of the air at a specified pressure. For this reason, improper inflation drastically reduces the tires's ability to perform as intended. A tire will lose some air in day-to-day use; having to add a few pounds of air periodically is not necessarily a sign of a leaking tire.

Two items should be a permanent fixture in every glove compartment: an accurate tire pressure gauge and a tread depth gauge. Check the tire pressure (including the spare) regularly with a pocket type

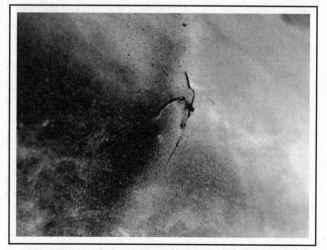

Tires should be checked frequently for any sign of puncture or damage

Tires with deep cuts, or cuts which show bulging should be replaced immediately

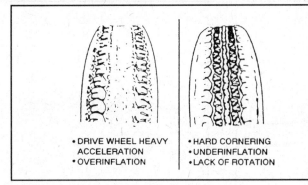

Examples of inflation-related tire wear patterns

- DRIVE WHEEL HEAVY ACCELERATION
- OVERINFLATION

- HARD CORNERING
- UNDERINFLATION
- LACK OF ROTATION

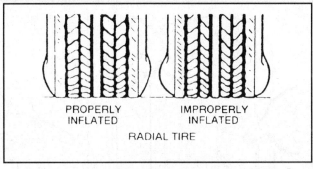

PROPERLY INFLATED   IMPROPERLY INFLATED

RADIAL TIRE

Radial tires have a characteristic sidewall bulge; don't try to measure pressure by looking at the tire. Use a quality air pressure gauge

gauge. Too often, the gauge on the end of the air hose at your corner garage is not accurate because it suffers too much abuse. Always check tire pressure when the tires are cold, as pressure increases with temperature. If you must move the vehicle to check the tire inflation, do not drive more than a mile before checking. A cold tire is generally one that has not been driven for more than three hours.

A plate or sticker is normally provided somewhere in the vehicle (door post, hood, tailgate or trunk lid) which shows the proper pressure for the tires. Never counteract excessive pressure build-up by bleeding off air pressure (letting some air out). This will cause the tire to run hotter and wear quicker.

✳✳ CAUTION:

Never exceed the maximum tire pressure embossed on the tire! This is the pressure to be used when the tire is at maximum loading, but it is rarely the correct pressure for everyday driving. Consult the owner's manual or the tire pressure sticker for the correct tire pressure.

Once you've maintained the correct tire pressures for several weeks, you'll be familiar with the vehicle's braking and handling personality. Slight adjustments in tire pressures can fine-tune these characteristics, but never change the cold pressure specification by more than 2 psi. A

slightly softer tire pressure will give a softer ride but also yield lower fuel mileage. A slightly harder tire will give crisper dry road handling but can cause skidding on wet surfaces. Unless you're fully attuned to the vehicle, stick to the recommended inflation pressures.

All tires made since 1968 have built-in tread wear indicator bars that show up as 1/2 in. (13mm) wide smooth bands across the tire when 1/16 in. (1.5mm) of tread remains. The appearance of tread wear indicators means that the tires should be replaced. In fact, many states have laws prohibiting the use of tires with less than this amount of tread.

You can check your own tread depth with an inexpensive gauge or by using a Lincoln head penny. Slip the Lincoln penny (with Lincoln's head upside-down) into several tread grooves. If you can see the top of Lincoln's head in 2 adjacent grooves, the tire has less than 1/16 in. (1.5mm) tread left and should be replaced. You can measure snow tires in the same manner by using the "tails" side of the Lincoln penny. If you can see the top of the Lincoln memorial, it's time to replace the snow tire(s).

CARE OF SPECIAL WHEELS

If you have invested money in magnesium, aluminum alloy or sport wheels, special precautions should be taken to make sure your investment is not wasted and that your special wheels look good for the life of the vehicle.

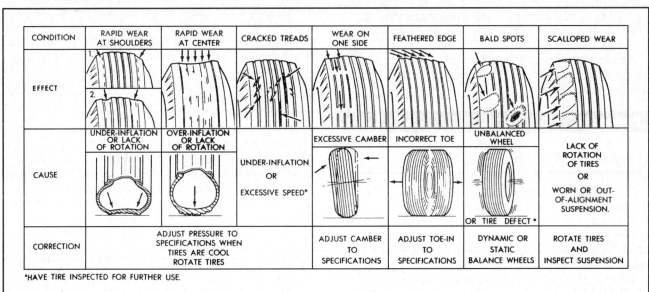

CONDITION	RAPID WEAR AT SHOULDERS	RAPID WEAR AT CENTER	CRACKED TREADS	WEAR ON ONE SIDE	FEATHERED EDGE	BALD SPOTS	SCALLOPED WEAR
EFFECT							
CAUSE	UNDER-INFLATION OR LACK OF ROTATION	OVER-INFLATION OR LACK OF ROTATION	UNDER-INFLATION OR EXCESSIVE SPEED*	EXCESSIVE CAMBER	INCORRECT TOE	UNBALANCED WHEEL / OR TIRE DEFECT*	LACK OF ROTATION OF TIRES OR WORN OR OUT-OF-ALIGNMENT SUSPENSION.
CORRECTION	ADJUST PRESSURE TO SPECIFICATIONS WHEN TIRES ARE COOL ROTATE TIRES			ADJUST CAMBER TO SPECIFICATIONS	ADJUST TOE-IN TO SPECIFICATIONS	DYNAMIC OR STATIC BALANCE WHEELS	ROTATE TIRES AND INSPECT SUSPENSION

*HAVE TIRE INSPECTED FOR FURTHER USE.

Common tire wear patterns and causes

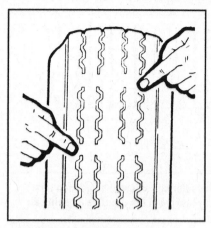

Tread wear indicators will appear when the tire is worn

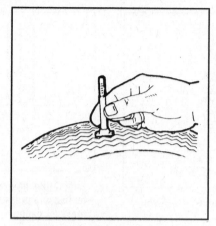

Accurate tread depth indicators are inexpensive and handy

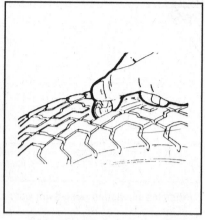

A penny works well for a quick check of tread depth

Special wheels are easily damaged and/or scratched. Occasionally check the rims for cracking, impact damage or air leaks. If any of these are found, replace the wheel. But in order to prevent this type of damage and the costly replacement of a special wheel, observe the following precautions:

• Use extra care not to damage the wheels during removal, installation, balancing, etc. After removal of the wheels from the vehicle, place them on a mat or other protective surface. If they are to be stored for any length of time, support them on strips of wood. Never store tires and wheels upright; the tread may develop flat spots.

• When driving, watch for hazards; it doesn't take much to crack a wheel.

• When washing, use a mild soap or non-abrasive dish detergent (keeping in mind that detergent tends to remove wax). Avoid cleansers with abrasives or the use of hard brushes. There are many cleaners and polishes for special wheels.

• If possible, remove the wheels during the winter. Salt and sand used for snow removal can severely damage the finish of a wheel.

• Make certain the recommended lug nut torque is never exceeded or the wheel may crack. Never use snow chains on special wheels; severe scratching will occur.

FLUIDS AND LUBRICANTS

FLUID DISPOSAL

Used fluids such as engine oil, transmission fluid, antifreeze and brake fluid are hazardous wastes and must be disposed of properly. Before draining fluids, consult with the local authorities: in many areas, waste oil, etc. is being accepted as a part of recycling programs. A number of service stations and auto parts stores are also accepting waste fluids for recycling.

Be sure of the recycling center's policies before draining any fluids, as many will not accept different fluids that have been mixed together, such as oil and antifreeze.

Engine Oil

LUBRICATION SYSTEM DESCRIPTION

The flow diagram represents the flow of lubricating oil through the Volkswagen engine. After being sucked up through the suction tube at the bottom of the crankcase, oil flows through the oil pump to either the oil cooler or the oil pressure relief valve, depending on whether the oil is under high or low pressure. When the engine is cold, and the oil thick, the oil cooler is bypassed and the cold, high pressure, oil flows through the relief valve to the engine passageways. However, when the engine is warm and the oil thinner, oil travels through the oil cooler, which is directly in the path of the cooling air from the cool-

ing fan. In this way, the oil is able to act as an even greater medium of engine cooling. After leaving the cooler or relief valve, the engine oil makes its way to critical lubrication points in the Volkswagen powerplant. The first route is to the crankshaft main bearings, where the oil is transferred to the crankshaft by means of drilled passageways. From the crankshaft, oil then flows to the connecting rod bearings, and is splashed onto the cylinder walls, pistons and piston rings. The force of oil hurled from the rotating parts to the cylinder walls is considerable. It is for this reason that the oil does a proper job of lubricating the cylinder walls and pistons.

A second route of the engine oil is to the camshaft bearings, while a third is through the hollow pushrods to the rocker arm bearings and the valve stems.

The Volkswagen engine uses a gear type pump. In this method, two gears are enclosed in a snug housing - the driven gear and the idler gear. The driven gear is turned by the camshaft, and the idler gear is mounted to turn freely on a stub shaft. The turning of the gears creates the oil-pumping action. The pump creates considerable suction at the suction pipe located inside the wire mesh oil strainer at the bottom of the crankcase.

FLUID RECOMMENDATIONS

The theory involved in the lubrication of any internal combustion engine is to place a substance between two objects in relative motion so as to lessen friction and make their movement easier. The substance must be both adhesive and cohesive - adhesive so that it clings to each of the moving surfaces, cohesive so that it does not separate and be driven out of the space it must occupy. An engine which would last practically forever would be possible if a lubricant could be found which would fully separate all moving surfaces so that there would be no contact whatsoever between them. Full lubrication is the goal of all engine lubrication systems, and the choice of the proper type and weight of engine oil can mean a great deal. In addition to reducing friction between moving parts, the oil in the Volkswagen engine also serves the following purposes: (1) it dissipates heat and helps parts to run more coolly, especially with the help of the oil cooler; (2) it acts as a seal for the pistons, rings, and cylinder walls; (3) it helps to reduce engine noises; (4) it helps to keep surfaces from rusting or corroding; (5) it acts as a cleaning agent, especially if it is of the high-detergent type commonly used today; (6) it removes foreign substances with the help of the wire mesh oil strainer.

Types of Engine Oil

In addition to detergent versus nondetergent oils, there are three major categories of oil designed for use in automobile engines. The following classifications have been set up by the American Petroleum Institute:

Service MS (Severe). When the letters MS appear on an oil container, they mean that the oil is refined and reinforced with additives so that it will satisfy the most severe demands made on it by a gasoline engine. Service MS oils are able to stand up to the especially hard demands imposed by start-stop driving in which condensation tends to build up on cylinder walls and in the crankcase. It is in this type of service that crankcase dilution takes place most readily and sludge and varnish are most rapidly formed. Therefore, if you drive your Volkswagen at low speeds and for short distances (and, of course, at turnpike speeds), you should especially be sure that the crankcase contains oil meeting the MS classification requirements.

Service MM (Medium). This classification indicates that the oil is meant for engines that receive only moderate demands and service. This type of oil is not recommended for the Volkswagen unless it also exceeds the requirements of the MS class. Engines using oil for service MM are generally not called upon to perform under severe conditions for any significant length of time, although there may be brief periods of severe operation.

Service ML (Light). This oil is designed for use in engines operating under light and favorable conditions, and which present no problems in the way of sludge deposits, bearing corrosion, or otherwise have no special requirements.

➡**Only oils displaying the ratings HD (high-detergency) and MS (motor severe) should be used in the Volkswagen engine. Ratings exceeded by the engine oil must include these two classifications.**

On some early engines (prior to 1954), a fiber camshaft timing gear was used. High-detergency oil is not recommended for these engines.

In 1970, new categories were set up for oil designations by the American Petroleum Institute. The new designations replaced the old. The new designations are:

SD. This type oil is required for warranty service on 1968 and later gasoline engines. It resists formation of deposits at both high and low temperatures and prevents rust and corrosion.

SC. This is the minimum requirement for 1964 - 67 automobiles and light trucks. It is also rust and corrosion resistant.

SB. SB oil is suitable for light duty engine operation only. This is not to be used in any Volkswagen or other air cooled engine.

SA. SA should be used for mild duty only. It has no special protec-

tion capabilities. This oil is not to be used in any Volkswagen or other air cooled engine.

Viscosity Requirements

In addition to meeting the HD and MS classifications of the American Petroleum Institute, oils for the Volkswagen engine must also be of a certain viscosity, depending upon the outside temperature in which the car is operated. Viscosity is defined as resistance to flow, and oils with higher viscosity numbers (e.g. 30) are thicker than those of lower viscosity numbers (e.g. 10W). The "W" after the lower viscosity indices means that the oils are desirable for use in cold weather or winter periods.

SAE viscosity ratings presently run from 5 to 50, and reflect the flow ability of the oil at a definite temperature. It is most important that the correct viscosity oil be used in the Volkswagen engine. If the viscosity is too low, moving parts will tend to come into contact, thereby causing high friction and wear, and possible bearing failures. Just as oils must be able to separate moving parts properly, they must be thin enough to get between the parts in the first place. If an oil is too thick it will not be able to flow properly into tight and critical bearing areas, with the result that incomplete separation of moving parts leads to bearing failure or a high rate of wear. If an oil is either too thick or too thin it cannot provide full lubrication and separation of close-tolerance moving parts in the engine. In order to underscore the importance of the proper engine oil, consider the following example: the Volkswagen Squareback Sedan, while cruising at 70 miles per hour, will have its engine turning at approximately 3,000 revolutions per minute. This means that the crankshaft will turn 3,000 times each minute. Each point on the crankshaft number one main bearing surface is traveling in the same 2.16 in. circle at a frequency of 58 times each **second!** The engine oil has only 0.00033 second to get from the main bearing drilling into the crankshaft drilling; obviously not time enough for oil that flows too slowly. At this same time, the four pistons are sliding along the cylinder walls at a speed of 18 miles per hour. The choice of engine oil can mean the difference between sliding, gliding, rubbing, or galling in all of these parts. With the closely-

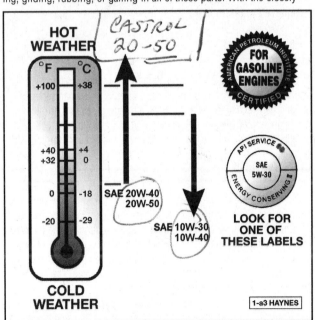

Make sure to add the proper viscosity oil to your engine, depending on the temperature range expected until the next oil change

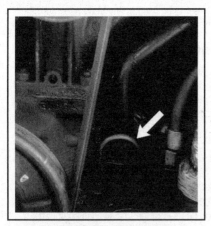

The oil dipstick (arrow) is located near the right-hand side of the crankshaft pulley

The oil dipstick on older models is mounted in the same position as on newer engines

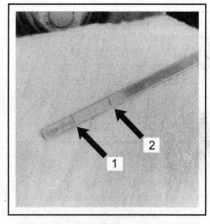

The oil level in the engine should fall between the two marks

1   Add   2   Fulll

Remove the oil fill cap . . .

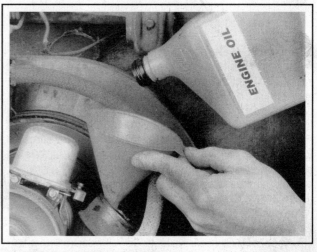

. . . then fill the engine with the proper type and amount of clean engine oil

machined surfaces and clearances in the Volkswagen engine, it is important that lubricating oil be of such a weight that it can separate moving parts effectively and still be able to flow at the proper rate. For maximum engine life and efficiency, the Volkswagen factory recommends the following selection process in choosing the oil for your car:

LEVEL CHECK

To check the engine oil level, park the car on level ground and wait 5 minutes to allow all the oil in the engine to drain into the crankcase.

Check the oil level by withdrawing the dipstick and wiping it clean. Insert the dipstick into its hole and note the position of the oil level on the bottom of the stick. The level should be between the two marks on the bottom of the stick, preferably closer to the top mark. The distance between the two marks represents one quart of oil.

On upright fan engines, the dipstick is located directly beneath the generator; oil is added through the capped opening beside the generator support post. On the type 3 the dipstick and filler are located in the lower door jamb of the rear compartment lid.

DRAIN & REFILL

The engine oil should be changed only after the engine has been warmed up to operating temperature. In this way, the oil holds in suspension many of the contaminants that would otherwise remain in the engine. As the oil drains, it carries dirt and sludge from the engine. After the initial oil change at 600 miles, the oil should be changed regularly at a period not to exceed 3,000 miles. If a Volkswagen is being operated mainly for short, slow-speed trips it may be advisable to change oil more often, say 1,500 or 2,000 miles, especially if cold temperatures prevail. In arctic climates, it is recommended that engine oil be changed every 750 miles.

When changing the oil, first unscrew the drain plug in the center of the crankcase and allow the dirty oil to drain into a suitable receptacle. During every oil change, the oil strainer should also be cleaned. This wire mesh strainer is held in place by six cap nuts, and should be cleaned thoroughly with a safe solvent. The strainer plate should also be cleaned. This lowest part of the crankcase collects a great deal of sludge in the course of 3,000 miles. Install the assembly, using new

After raising and safely supporting the vehicle, loosen and remove the oil drain plug . . .

. . . and allow the oil to drain into an aptly-sized catch pan

To clean the oil strainer, remove the 6 capnuts . . .

. . . then remove the strainer plate from the crankcase

gaskets (2) and the copper washers on the cap nuts in order to prevent leaking at the strainer plate. Before refilling the engine with oil, install the drain plug and tighten to a torque not to exceed 22 ft. lbs. (3mkg).

The proper amount of oil to put into the crankcase of any Volkswa-

gen is 5.3 U.S. pints (2.5 liters). This quantity should be measured, possibly through use of a pint jar. Under no circumstances should a full 3 quarts be put into the engine. Overfilling will probably result in failure of various engine oil seals and severe leakage. It is not harmful if,

Make certain to thoroughly clean off all dirt and grime, as seen on this oil strainer plate (arrow)

Remove the lower oil strainer gasket . . .

. . . pull the oil strainer out of its hole . . .

. . . then remove the upper oil strainer gasket from the crankcase

When installing the cover plate, make sure to tighten the cap nuts in the sequence shown

upon refilling with this quantity, the oil level is either a few millimeters above or below the full mark on the dipstick. As long as the oil level is between the two marks, there is no danger of the oil level being too low. However, should the level fall below the lower mark at any time, approximately one quart should be added to the crankcase as soon as possible to assure proper lubrication.

It is recommended that the Volkswagen owner stay with the same brand of oil, because mixing different types of oils could possibly be detrimental to proper lubrication of the engine. If a Volkswagen has been run for many thousands of miles on a non-detergent oil (not recommended), it is advisable to be careful in switching to a high-detergency brand. When such a change is made, it is possible that the detergent oil will do its cleaning job too well, and clog up narrow oil passages with dirt or other foreign matter that has accumulated over the miles.

After the oil has been changed, the air cleaner should be inspected for possible cleaning and/or topping up with fresh oil. The refill requirement for the oil bath air cleaner is given in the Capacities and Pressures Chart. It is a welcome convenience that the total of the crankcase requirement and the oil cleaner requirement is approximately three quarts. In this way, there is no leftover or wasted oil. The air cleaner oil bath uses the same oil.

Transaxle

FLUID RECOMMENDATIONS

Manual Transaxle

The Volkswagen transmission and differential are combined in a single case, and lubricated by a common oil. The differential gears are of the hypoid (technically, a special type of skew bevel gearing) variety. Extreme-pressure hypoid gear lubricants must be used because of the high tooth pressures and high rubbing velocities encountered in this type of gearing. Care must be taken to see that straight mineral oil is not used in the Volkswagen transaxle assembly. Such a lubricant would lead to metal-to-metal contact, scoring, galling, and seizure of the gear teeth.

In the Volkswagen transaxle unit, use only good quality SAE 90 hypoid oil all year. In countries with arctic climates, the thinner SAE 80

hypoid oil may be used.

Because hypoid oil can cause corrosion and premature hardening of the main driveshaft oil seal in a car that is stored for a long period, drain the transaxle fluid and refill with an anti-corrosion oil before storing a car for the winter.

Automatic Transaxle

➡**This procedure covers both the automatic stick-shift and fully automatic transaxles.**

Automatic Transmission Fluid (ATF), such as Dexron should be used in both of the automatic transaxles. Unlike the manual transaxles, the transmission case and differential case do not use separate fluid reservoirs. Therefore, when the differential is drained, the entire transaxle is drained.

LEVEL CHECK

Manual Transaxle

The oil level is checked by removing the 17mm socket head plug located on the driver's side of the transaxle. The oil level should be even with the hole when the vehicle is level. Check it with your finger.

✳✳ CAUTION:

Do not fill the transaxle too quickly because it may overflow from the filler hole and give the impression that the unit has been filled when it has not.

Top up as necessary with SAE 90 gear oil.

Automatic Stick Shift Transaxle

TYPE 1

The automatic Stick Shift transaxle is checked by means of a dipstick. The oil level should be between two marks at the bottom of the stick. The engine should be warm when the transmission oil level is checked. Top up as necessary with DEXRON.

➡**The engine must be turned OFF when checking the transaxle oil level.**

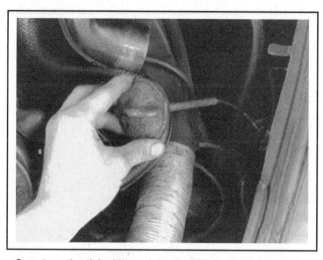

On automatic stick-shift models, the ATF dipstick and fill tube are located on the right inner fender

TYPES 2 AND 3

Automatic transaxles are checked in the same manner as Automatic Stick Shift transaxles, except that the engine should be running at an idle, transaxle in Neutral, and parking brake firmly applied. Top up as necessary with DEXRON through the transaxle dipstick tube located above the distributor (Type 2) or above the air manifold pipes (Type 3). The difference between the two marks on the dipstick is less than one pint. On all Type 2 models and on Squareback Type 3 models, the dipstick is accessible through the hatch in the luggage compartment. On Fastback Type 3 models, the dipstick is reached through the rear engine lid.

DRAIN & REFILL

Manual Transaxle

The oil in the transaxle unit should be changed approximately every 30,000 miles. As with the engine oil, the transaxle lubricant should be changed only after it has reached operating temperature and carries in suspension the maximum quantity of unwanted particles of dirt and other matter. When draining the transaxle oil, both magnetic drain plugs should be removed and cleaned. Because the magnetic tips of the drain plugs are little larger than a 1/4 in., they can hold only a limited

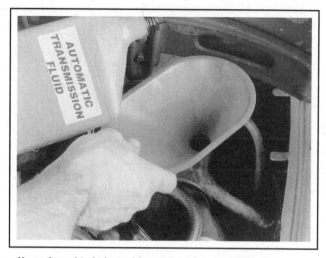

Use a funnel to help avoid messy spills when filling an automatic stick-shift transaxle

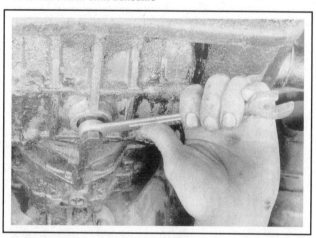

To drain the manual transaxle, first loosen the differential drain plug . . .

quantity of iron-based particles. If the oil is drained while the rear end is in an unloaded condition, it is possible that some oil will remain in the half axles. This may change the refill requirement slightly. However, the oil can be drained and renewed regardless of whether the rear end is loaded or unloaded.

. . . and allow the oil to drain from the case

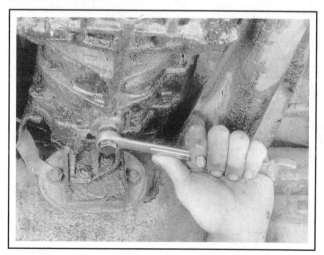

Then loosen the transmission case drain plug . . .

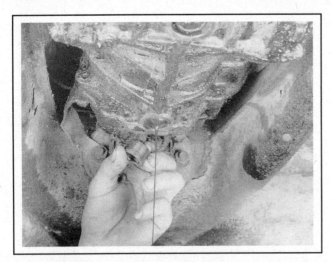

. . . and allow all of the oil to drain

. . . then fill the two cases with the proper type and amount of lubricant

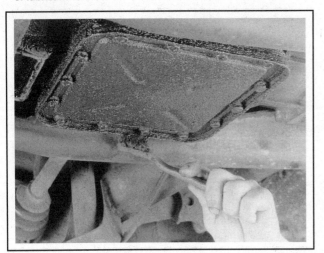

Clean the ATF cover bolt heads . . .

Remove the fill plugs from the side of the transmission and differential cases . . .

There is one very important point of caution in refilling the Volkswagen transaxle unit with oil: if the oil has been put in too quickly it may overflow from the filler hole and give the impression that the unit has been filled when, in fact, it has not. The

Volkswagenwerke, therefore, suggests that it is good practice to pour in two or three pints, wait a few minutes, and then pour the rest in.

Automatic Transaxle

On automatic models, draining the transaxle oil requires removing, cleaning, and replacing the transaxle oil pan. The refill capacity of each model is given in the Capacities and Pressures Chart.

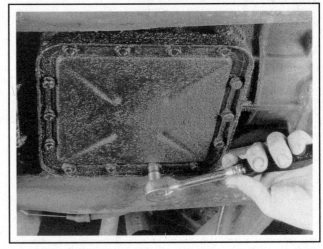

. . . then remove the bolts

Separate the cover from the transaxle and allow the oil to drain

Make certain not to forget to install the cover hold-down strips

The master brake fluid reservoir (A) is mounted under the luggage compartment lid

Once the fluid cover is removed, the differential gears (arrows) can be seen

Master Cylinder

FLUID RECOMMENDATIONS & FILL

The fluid level in all vehicles should be above the upper seam of the reservoir. Fill the reservoir only with the new, clean heavy-duty brake fluid. If the vehicle is equipped with disc brakes make sure the fluid is marked for use with disc brakes. All fluid used should meet DOT 3, DOT 4, or SAE J1703 specifications.

Steering Gear

FLUID RECOMMENDATIONS & FILL

The Volkswagen steering gear is filled with transaxle oil and does not need topping up or regular changing. However, on earlier models, it had been recommended that the level of oil in the steering gearbox be kept slightly below the filler plug hole. While periodic topping up and

Add new brake fluid if the level is not within 1/4 in. of the top of the reservoir

changing are not necessary, the steering gearbox should be checked for the proper oil level at intervals of 3,000 miles in order to ensure that there has been no extensive leakage which might otherwise be overlooked. The steering gear should be lubricated only with SAE 90 hypoid oil and under no circumstance should any other lubricant be used.

Chassis Greasing

GREASE RECOMMENDATIONS

Grease is a mineral oil thickened by compounding with soap and containing alkalis or metals such as calcium, sodium, lithium, barium and others to acquire various qualities. Because there are so many different varieties of grease, Volkswagen specifies them by chemical make-up and also by specifying the ASTM dropping point or melting point. Volkswagen transmission grease should be saponified with sodium and have a drip point above 284 degrees F.

The multi-purpose greases specified for the lubrication of the front end, the front wheel bearings, and the breaker arm fiber block in the distributor are of the lithium base variety, and are to have a melting point of at least 330-degrees F. With the temperatures generated and the shocks absorbed by the front wheel bearings, it is not surprising that the grease used must be of the highest quality.

High-pressure universal grease is specified for the door and hood locks of the Volkswagen. This grease must be both cold-resistant and water-repellent and have a drip point above 230-degreesF.

Lithium grease (multi-purpose)
• Front end, front wheel bearings, breaker arm fiber block in distributor.

Universal grease
• Door and hood locks.

GREASING DOOR HINGES & HOOD LOCKS

The door hold-open rods and hood locks should be greased lightly with universal grease. Hinges of the doors and hoods should be oiled at each lubrication service after they have been cleaned. Late type 1 models have a plastic plug in each external door hinge. To lubricate the hinge, pry out the plug and insert two or three drops of engine oil. Molybdenum disulphide-based paste should be used in lightly greasing the striker plates on their friction surfaces. Excess grease in this area should always be cleaned off. A graphite lubricant should be used for the door lock cylinders. It is especially advisable to lubricate the door lock cylinders in the winter months to help prevent moisture from accumulating and freezing the mechanism. Dip the key in graphite, insert in the lock and turn several times to ensure full lubrication.

GREASING CARBURETOR LINKAGES

Ball joints on the carburetors (type 3 dual carburetors) should be lubricated with a molybdenum disulphide-based paste. In the type 3, three ball joints are on each of the two carburetors, and two additional ball joints on the center three-arm lever. While the molybdenum-based paste is desirable, chassis grease can also be used on these ball joints if the molybdenum variety is not available.

Other parts of the carburetor(s) that should be given periodic lubrication are the choke valve shaft, the throttle valve shaft, the accelerator cable swivel pin, and the connecting rod and lever that operate the accelerator pump. Use a few drops of oil in each location.

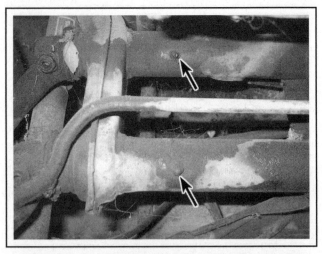

Using a general purpose chassis grease, lubricate all of the grease fittings on the suspension and steering components, such as those shown by the arrows

GREASING THE FRONT AXLE

It is important to the proper functioning of the front end that all moving parts be thoroughly lubricated at the correct intervals. Most important, the front axle should be raised during the entire operation. This will ensure that grease will be able to reach all points requiring service.

On 1966 and later models, it is recommended that the front axle be greased only every 6,000 miles. However, on models preceding 1966, service should be carried out more frequently; the torsion bar nipples should be greased at least once every 3,000 miles and preferably every 1,500 miles to eliminate any doubt.

Before lubricating the front end, all grease nipples should be wiped clean with a suitable rag, and the nipples should be inspected for damage. If a body-point high lift is not used, the car may be jacked up one side at a time so that the fittings on that side can be lubricated. Raising the car in this manner should be done on a level surface, with the wheels chocked on the side not being raised and using jackstands to safely support the vehicle. After letting the car down, the handbrake should be released and reset before raising the other side. This is a good way to keep the car from moving in the fore-and-aft direction while you are jacking up the second side. Because the Volkswagen jack is applied to the midpoint of the car's weight at the side supports, it is relatively easy for the car to move slightly and twist the jacking support if care is not taken to avoid this.

➡**Never do any work on or under a jacked-up car unless the weight of the vehicle is supported by jackstands.**

Owners of 1962 and earlier models must ensure that the tie rod ends are lubricated via the grease nipples provided for this purpose. Owners of 1965 and earlier models should lubricate the four grease nipples that serve the king pins and the torsion arm link pins.

When greasing, continue to apply grease until fresh grease can be seen emerging from the extremities of the lubrication points. Care should be taken to see that no grease or oil comes into contact with rubber parts, especially the tires and brake hoses. If grease should accidentally contact these parts it should be wiped off immediately.

Wheel Bearings

REMOVAL, PACKING & INSTALLATION

Beginning with 1966 models, tapered roller bearings were used in the front wheels of all model Volkswagens. Previously, all models were equipped with ball bearings in the front wheels. The front wheel bearings should be cleaned and repacked with grease at intervals of 30,000 miles. In servicing the front wheel bearings, the following procedures should be followed:

Ball-Bearing Equipped Models

1 Jack up the side of the car, remove the hub cap from the wheel, then remove the wheel.

2 Remove the small dust cap that covers the locking nuts at the tip of the axle.

3 Unscrew the hexagonal locknut, remove the locking plate, inner hexagonal nut, and the thrust washer. Nuts on the left axle have left-hand thread; those on the right have right-hand threads.

4 Pull the brake drum off the axle stub, while at the same time being careful to keep the inner raceway and the cage of the outer bearing from falling on the ground. If the brake drum resists being removed, it may be necessary to back off the brake adjustment slightly and also bolt the wheel back onto the brake drum so as to have more leverage in pulling on the drum.

5 Remove the plastic grease seal from the hub and take out the cage of the inner bearing.

6 Leaving the inner raceway in place on the axle, and the outer raceway in place in the hub, clean all components in solvent and also clean the inside of the brake drum, being careful to keep any grease or oil from touching the interior surface of the drum. Caution should also be exercised in order that the brake shoes themselves remain free of grease.

7 Repack the inner bearing cage with grease and place it within the hub. Now the plastic seal can be reinstalled by tapping it in lightly until it achieves a flush position. A flat piece of wood placed atop the seal may prove helpful in this operation.

8 The inner raceway on the axle should now be greased and the wheel replaced. After repacking the outer bearing cage, this part can now be inserted in the hub. Bearing installation is completed with the installation of the inner race, thrust washer and hexagonal nut.

9 Tighten the hexagonal nut until the thrust washer can just be moved sideways with a prytool. Install the locking plate (replace it with a new one, if unusable) and the locknut. The locking plate tabs should be bent over, and the hexagonal nut tightened down.

➡It is always a good idea to use new plastic seals and locking plates. When working on the left front wheel, take note that this wheel drives the speedometer cable. After removing the cotter pin and the dirving end of the cable, proceed normally.

Roller-Bearing Equipped Models

Roller-bearing equipped models include the type 3 and the type 1 Karmann Ghia and beetle models of 1966 and later.

On beetle models, equipped with drum brakes, the procedure is much the same as that listed for roller-bearing equipped models except that the final adjustment is more exact. Adjustment requires that the following procedure be followed:

1 Loosen the clamp nut screw.

2 Tighten the clamp nut to a torque of 11 ft. lbs. while at the same time turning the wheel.

3 Loosen the clamp nut until the axial play of the wheel is between 0.001 - 0.005 in. (0.03 - 0.12mm.).

4 Tighten the clamp nut screw to a torque of 7 ft. lbs. and recheck the axial play.

5 Install the hub cap.

The following directions apply to type 3 and the 1500 and 1600 Karmann Ghia, supplied with disc brakes:

6 After removing the front wheel and disc cap, bend up the lock plates on the caliper securing screws and remove both the screws and the caliper assembly.

7 Secure the caliper to the brake hose bracket by means of a piece of wire or rope. The caliper should not be allowed to hang by the brake hose.

8 Loosen the socket head screw of the clamp nut. Unscrew the clamp nut.

9 Remove the wheel bearing thrust washer.

10 Remove the disc.

11 The parts removed should be cleaned thoroughly in a cleaning solvent solution. Because dirt and lining dust can act as abrasives, these particles should be kept out of the bearings for obvious reasons. Check all parts for wear, damage, and proper size.

12 Lubricate the bearings with a lithium grease of the proper type, pressing grease into the cages and fill the grease cavity of the disc. Grease should not be put into the disc cap.

13 Press in the outer race of the inner bearing.

14 Fit the inner race and cage and insert the grease seal. When fitting the grease seal, drive it in by tapping it lightly with a rubber hammer; avoid tilting seal.

15 Press in the outer race of the outer bearing.

16 Install the thrust washer and ensure that it is not tilted.

17 Adjust the bearings so that the axial play is between 0.001 - 0.005 in. (0.03 - 0.12mm.). The adjustment process is as described in the preceding section on adjusting front wheel bearings on beetle models equipped with roller bearings.

TRAILER TOWING

General Recommendations

Your vehicle was primarily designed to carry passengers and cargo. It is important to remember that towing a trailer will place additional loads on your vehicles engine, drivetrain, steering, braking and other systems. However, if you decide to tow a trailer, using the prior equipment is a must.

Local laws may require specific equipment such as trailer brakes or fender mounted mirrors. Check your local laws.

Trailer Weight

The weight of the trailer is the most important factor. A good weight-to-horsepower ratio is about 35:1, 35 lbs. of Gross Combined Weight (GCW) for every horsepower your engine develops. Multiply the engine's rated horsepower by 35 and subtract the weight of the vehicle passengers and luggage. The number remaining is the approximate ideal maximum weight you should tow, although a numerically higher axle ratio can help compensate for heavier weight.

Hitch (Tongue) Weight

Calculate the hitch weight in order to select a proper hitch. The weight of the hitch is usually 9 - 11% of the trailer gross weight and should be measured with the trailer loaded. Hitches fall into various categories: those that mount on the frame and rear bumper, the bolt-on type, or the weld-on distribution type used for larger trailers. Axle mounted or clamp-on bumper hitches should never be used.

Check the gross weight rating of your trailer. Tongue weight is usually figured as 10% of gross trailer weight. Therefore, a trailer with a maximum gross weight of 2000 lbs. will have a maximum tongue weight of 200 lbs. Class I trailers fall into this category. Class II trailers are those with a gross weight rating of 2000 - 3000 lbs., while Class III trailers fall into the 3500 - 6000 lbs. category. Class IV trailers are those over 6000 lbs. and are for use with fifth wheel trucks, only.

When you've determined the hitch that you'll need, follow the manufacturer's installation instructions, exactly, especially when it comes

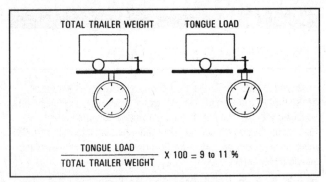

Calculating proper tongue weight for your trailer

to fastener torques. The hitch will subjected to a lot of stress and good hitches come with hardened bolts. Never substitute an inferior bolt for a hardened bolt.

Handling A Trailer

Towing a trailer with ease and safety requires a certain amount of experience. It's a good idea to learn the feel of a trailer by practicing turning, stopping and backing in an open area such as an empty parking lot.

JUMP STARTING A DEAD BATTERY

Whenever a vehicle is jump started, precautions must be followed in order to prevent the possibility of personal injury. Remember that batteries contain a small amount of explosive hydrogen gas which is a by-product of battery charging. Sparks should always be avoided when working around batteries, especially when attaching jumper cables. To minimize the possibility of accidental sparks, follow the procedure carefully.

✳✳ CAUTION:

NEVER hook the batteries up in a series circuit or the entire electrical system will go up in smoke, including the starter!

Vehicles equipped with a diesel engine may utilize two 12 volt batteries. If so, the batteries are connected in a parallel circuit (positive terminal to positive terminal, negative terminal to negative terminal). Hooking the batteries up in parallel circuit increases battery cranking power without increasing total battery voltage output. Output remains at 12 volts. On the other hand, hooking two 12 volt batteries up in a series circuit (positive terminal to negative terminal, positive terminal to negative terminal) increases total battery output to 24 volts (12 volts plus 12 volts).

Jump Starting Precautions

- Be sure that both batteries are of the same voltage. Vehicles covered by this manual and most vehicles on the road today utilize a 12 volt charging system.
- Be sure that both batteries are of the same polarity (have the same terminal, in most cases NEGATIVE grounded).
- Be sure that the vehicles are not touching or a short could occur.
- On serviceable batteries, be sure the vent cap holes are not obstructed.
- Do not smoke or allow sparks anywhere near the batteries.
- In cold weather, make sure the battery electrolyte is not frozen.

This can occur more readily in a battery that has been in a state of discharge.

- Do not allow electrolyte to contact your skin or clothing.

Jump Starting Procedure

1. Make sure that the voltages of the 2 batteries are the same. Most batteries and charging systems are of the 12 volt variety.

2. Pull the jumping vehicle (with the good battery) into a position so the jumper cables can reach the dead battery and that vehicle's engine. Make sure that the vehicles do NOT touch.

3. Place the transmissions/transaxles of both vehicles in **Neutral** (MT) or **P** (AT), as applicable, then firmly set their parking brakes.

➡**If necessary for safety reasons, the hazard lights on both vehicles may be operated throughout the entire procedure without significantly increasing the difficulty of jumping the dead battery.**

4. Turn all lights and accessories OFF on both vehicles. Make sure the ignition switches on both vehicles are turned to the OFF position.

5. Cover the battery cell caps with a rag, but do not cover the terminals.

6. Make sure the terminals on both batteries are clean and free of

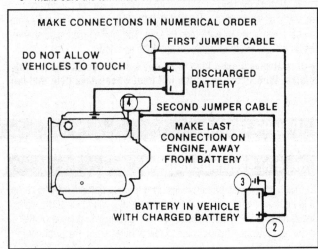

Connect the jumper cables to the batteries and engine in the order shown

corrosion or proper electrical connection will be impeded. If necessary, clean the battery terminals before proceeding.

7 Identify the positive (+) and negative (-) terminals on both batteries.

8 Connect the first jumper cable to the positive (+) terminal of the dead battery, then connect the other end of that cable to the positive (+) terminal of the booster (good) battery.

9 Connect one end of the other jumper cable to the negative (-) terminal on the booster battery and the final cable clamp to an engine bolt head, alternator bracket or other solid, metallic point on the engine with the dead battery. Try to pick a ground on the engine that is positioned away from the battery in order to minimize the possibility of the 2 clamps touching should one loosen during the procedure. DO NOT connect this clamp to the negative (-) terminal of the bad battery.

✳✳ CAUTION:

Be very careful to keep the jumper cables away from moving parts (cooling fan, belts, etc.) on both engines.

10 Check to make sure that the cables are routed away from any moving parts, then start the donor vehicle's engine. Run the engine at moderate speed for several minutes to allow the dead battery a chance to receive some initial charge.

11 With the donor vehicle's engine still running slightly above idle, try to start the vehicle with the dead battery. Crank the engine for no more than 10 seconds at a time and let the starter cool for at least 20 seconds between tries. If the vehicle does not start in 3 tries, it is likely that something else is also wrong or that the battery needs additional time to charge.

13 Once the vehicle is started, allow it to run at idle for a few seconds to make sure that it is operating properly.

14 Turn ON the headlights, heater blower and, if equipped, the rear defroster of both vehicles in order to reduce the severity of voltage spikes and subsequent risk of damage to the vehicles' electrical systems when the cables are disconnected. This step is especially important to any vehicle equipped with computer control modules.

15 Carefully disconnect the cables in the reverse order of connection. Start with the negative cable that is attached to the engine ground, then the negative cable on the donor battery. Disconnect the positive cable from the donor battery and finally, disconnect the positive cable from the formerly dead battery. Be careful when disconnecting the cables from the positive terminals not to allow the alligator clips to touch any metal on either vehicle or a short and sparks will occur.

JACKING

The factory jack is designed to be used only with the jack fittings on the underside of the vehicle

Position the floor jack under the jacking point (arrow) when lifting the rear of the vehicle

Jacking points are provided at the sides of all models for the standard equipment jack. The jack supplied with the car should never be used for any service operation other than tire changing. NEVER get under the car while it is supported by just a jack. If the jack should slip or tip over, as jacks often do, it would be exceedingly difficult to raise the car again while pinned underneath. Always block the wheels when changing tires.

The service operations in this book often require that one end or the other, or both, of the car be raised and supported safely. The best arrangement is a grease pit or a vehicle hoist. It is realized that these items are not often found in the home garage, but there are reasonable and safe substitutes. Small hydraulic, screw, or scissors jacks are satisfactory for raising the car. Heavy wooden blocks or adjustable jackstands should be used to support the car while it is being worked on.

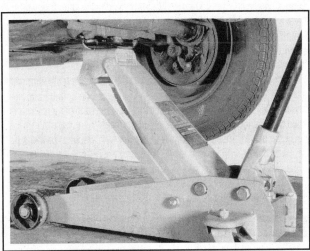

Raise the front of the vehicle by positioning the jack beneath the front axle assembly . . .

Drive-on trestles, or ramps, are a handy and safe way to raise the car. These can be bought or constructed from suitable heavy boards or steel.

When raising the car with a floor, screw or scissors jack, or when supporting the car with jackstands, care should be taken in the placement of this equipment. The front of the car may be supported beneath the axle tube on Type 1 Beetles, all Karmann Ghias, Type 2 models through 1969, and all Type 3 models.

In any case, it is always best to spend a little extra time to make sure that the car is lifted and supported safely.

➡**Concrete blocks are not recommended. They may break if the load is not evenly distributed.**

Jacking Precautions

The following safety points cannot be overemphasized:
- Always block the opposite wheel or wheels to keep the vehicle from rolling off the jack.
- When raising the front of the vehicle, firmly apply the parking brake.
- When the drive wheels are to remain on the ground, leave the vehicle in gear to help prevent it from rolling.
- Always use jackstands to support the vehicle when you are working underneath. Place the stands beneath the vehicle's jacking brackets. Before climbing underneath, rock the vehicle a bit to make sure it is firmly supported.

. . . then secure the vehicle in this position with a jackstand

CARE OF THE BODY

Besides being a constant source of pride for the owner, a well-preserved Volkswagen will be worth many more dollars at trade-in time.

Washing

A new Volkswagen should be washed frequently during the first weeks of ownership. This will contribute to the best possible final drying of the paint. The paint on a new Volkswagen is not really **wet,** but it is still relatively soft and has not yet hardened to the point where it should be waxed or polished. In washing the Volkswagen, it is well to have a soft sponge for the body, a soft brush for the wheels, a long-handled brush for the underside of the chassis, and a good supply of clean water. A chamois leather will be desirable for drying the car after it has been washed.

Dirt on the exterior of the body should be sprayed evenly with water, after which it can be removed with a soft sponge. The sponge should be cleaned at short intervals in order that abrasive dirt particles will not have the chance to scratch the polished surfaces. After washing, the body should be rinsed thoroughly and dried. The washing process may be made easier with various auto soaps and wash-and-wax preparations. After using any such detergent, it is very important to rinse the body thoroughly with clean water. A powerful jet of water should never be allowed to hit the painted surface of the car.

Waxing

The paint of a new Volkswagen should not be waxed until after the first 8 - 10 weeks. Before applying a coat of wax preservative, the car must be washed and completely dried with a chamois. When water on the painted surfaces tends to remain in large patches instead of forming small beads and running off, it is time for an application of wax. Wax can be applied in the form of wash-and-wax preparations if the interval between washings is not too great. This method is not nearly as long-lasting as those involving the harder-to-apply paste waxes. In general, it can be stated that the harder a wax is to apply, the longer it will protect the finish. While there are exceptions to every rule, this is a good one to remember. The car should never be waxed in open sunshine. A preservative specially produced for the paint of the Volkswagen is available at Volkswagen dealers and is known as "L 190" preservative. When applying the L 190, one spreads a thin film on the finish and then rubs it down when it is dry, using a soft polishing cloth.

Polishing

After years of exposure to the elements, any paint will have its appearance adversely affected by dust, sunlight and rain. In this event, it is possible to renew much of the original luster of the paint with the use of a polishing compound. One made especially for the synthetic-resin enamel finish of the Volkswagen is available at most Volkswagen dealerships, and is known by the designation "L 170". This specially-formulated polish seems to be one of the best possible compounds for restoring both the original color and brightness of the Volkswagen finish. It is recommended that the paint be waxed after every application of polish so that the renewed luster can be maintained for as long as possible. When polishing the Volkswagen, one should be careful not to polish too large an area at one time, and, in any event, to observe the instructions given on the label by the manufacturer.

Chrome Care

Chrome parts can be best preserved by being periodically washed, dried, and treated with a chrome preservative such as that available at Volkswagen dealers - "VW Chromlin."

Removing Spots

Because water alone will not always be able to remove tar, oil, insects, etc., this type of foreign matter must be removed as soon as possible by other means. Tar splashes in particular have a tendency to corrode the finish in a short time, and should be removed with a soft cloth soaked with turpentine oil. After removing the tar spots, the treated areas must be washed with a mild, lukewarm soap solution, and the area rinsed in order to remove the cleansing agent. Preservatives such as the VW L 190 and L 170 can also be used for this purpose. Baked-on insects can be removed with either a soap solution or with the previously-mentioned preservatives. Tree droppings and industrial dirt should, like all foreign matter on the paint, be removed as soon as possible. Special cleaners containing acid can be used for the purpose of removing industrial grime that adheres to the paint, and can be obtained from automobile accessory dealers.

Care of Windows

Windows are best cleaned with an ammonia solution in which ammonia is combined with luke-warm water. Because silicone is pres-ent in many liquid and paste cleaners, the windshield should not be exposed to any such preparations. When silicone comes into contact with the windshield, the result is severe streaking by the wiper blades and subsequent poor visibility and danger. When cleaning the windshield with ammonia, the blades should also be wiped off with the same solution. It is advisable to move the wiper arms forward where they will be out of the way and less likely to become bent or otherwise abused. Care should be taken to see that ammonia solutions do not come into contact with the paint.

Weatherstripping

Doors and windows will not seal properly if weatherstripping becomes brittle or damaged. For this reason, all weatherstripping on the Volkswagen should be given a light treatment with talcum powder from time to time. If the movement of rubber weatherstripping causes squeaking or groaning noises, apply talcum powder or glycerine to the surface of the rubber. If the weatherstripping around the windshield or rear window is not leakproof, apply a good quality window cement between the rubber seal and the metal frame.

Upholstery

The leatherette upholstery of U.S. Volkswagens is cleaned by means of either a mild soap solution or a solution of water and leatherette cleaner. The use of a soft brush will facilitate the cleaning process. After the leatherette is cleaned, it should be rubbed with a soft rag until dry.

HOW TO BUY A USED VEHICLE

Many people believe that a two or three year old used car or truck is a better buy than a new vehicle. This may be true as most new vehicles suffer the heaviest depreciation in the first two years and, at three years old, a vehicle is usually not old enough to present a lot of costly repair problems. But keep in mind, when buying a non-warranted automobile, there are no guarantees. Whatever the age of the used vehicle you might want to purchase, this section and a little patience should increase your chances of selecting one that is safe and dependable.

Tips

1   First decide what model you want, and how much you want to spend.
2   Check the used car lots and your local newspaper ads. Privately owned vehicles are usually less expensive, however, you may not get a warranty that, in many cases, comes with a used vehicle purchased from a lot. Of course, some aftermarket warranties may not be worth the extra money, so this is a point you will have to debate and consider based on your priorities.
3   Never shop at night. The glare of the lights make it easy to miss faults on the body caused by accident or rust repair.
4   Try to get the name and phone number of the previous owner. Contact him/her and ask about the vehicle. If the owner of a lot refuses this information, look for a vehicle somewhere else.
    A private seller can tell you about the vehicle and maintenance. But remember, there's no law requiring honesty from private citizens selling used vehicles. There is a law that forbids tampering with or turning back the odometer mileage. This includes both the private citizen and the lot owner. The law also requires that the seller or anyone transferring ownership of the vehicle must provide the buyer with a signed statement indicating the mileage on the odometer at the time of transfer.

5   You may wish to contact the National Highway Traffic Safety Administration (NHTSA) to find out if the vehicle has ever been included in a manufacturer's recall. Write down the year, model and serial number before you buy the vehicle, then contact NHTSA (there should be a 1-800 number that your phone company's information line can supply). If the vehicle was listed for a recall, make sure the needed repairs were made.
6   Refer to the Used Vehicle Checklist in this section and check all the items on the vehicle you are considering. Some items are more important than others. Only you know how much money you can afford for repairs, and depending on the price of the vehicle, may consider performing any needed work yourself. Beware, however, of trouble in areas that will affect operation, safety or emission. Problems in the Used Vehicle Checklist break down as follows:
    • Numbers 1 - 8: Two or more problems in these areas indicate a lack of maintenance. You should beware.
    • Numbers 9 - 13: Problems here tend to indicate a lack of proper care, however, these can usually be corrected with a tune-up or relatively simple parts replacement.
    • Numbers 14 - 17: Problems in the engine or transmission can be very expensive. Unless you are looking for a project, walk away from any vehicle with problems in 2 or more of these areas.
7   If you are satisfied with the apparent condition of the vehicle, take it to an independent diagnostic center or mechanic for a complete check. If you have a state inspection program, have it inspected immediately before purchase, or specify on the bill of sale that the sale is conditional on passing state inspection.
8   Road test the vehicle - refer to the Road Test Checklist in this section. If your original evaluation and the road test agree - the rest is up to you.

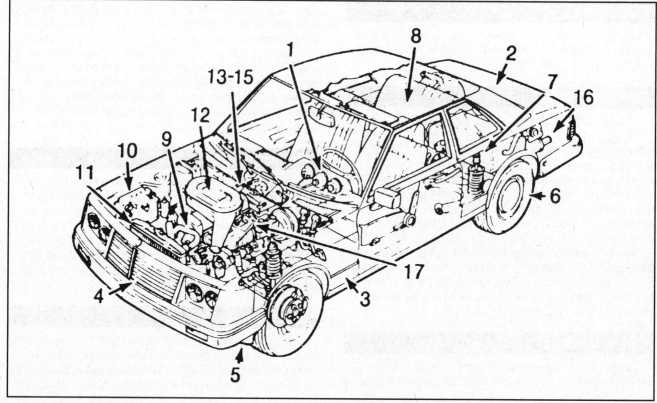

Each of the numbered items should be checked when purchasing a used vehicle

USED VEHICLE CHECKLIST

➡**The numbers on the illustrations refer to the numbers on this checklist.**

1 Mileage: Average mileage is about 12,000 - 15,000 miles per year. More than average mileage may indicate hard usage or could indicate many highway miles (which could be less detrimental than half as many tough around town miles).

2 Paint: Check around the tailpipe, molding and windows for overspray indicating that the vehicle has been repainted.

3 Rust: Check fenders, doors, rocker panels, window moldings, wheelwells, floorboards, under floormats, and in the trunk for signs of rust. Any rust at all will be a problem. There is no way to permanently stop the spread of rust, except to replace the part or panel.

➡**If rust repair is suspected, try using a magnet to check for body filler. A magnet should stick to the sheet metal parts of the body, but will not adhere to areas with large amounts of filler.**

4 Body appearance: Check the moldings, bumpers, grille, vinyl roof, glass, doors, trunk lid and body panels for general overall condition. Check for misalignment, loose hold-down clips, ripples, scratches in glass, welding in the trunk, severe misalignment of body panels or ripples, any of which may indicate crash work.

5 Leaks: Get down and look under the vehicle. There are no normal leaks, other than water from the air conditioner evaporator.

6 Tires: Check the tire air pressure. One old trick is to pump the tire pressure up to make the vehicle roll easier. Check the tread wear, then open the trunk and check the spare too. Uneven wear is a clue that the front end may need an alignment.

7 Shock absorbers: Check the shock absorbers by forcing downward sharply on each corner of the vehicle. Good shocks will not allow

the vehicle to bounce more than once after you let go.

8 Interior: Check the entire interior. You're looking for an interior condition that agrees with the overall condition of the vehicle. Reasonable wear is expected, but be suspicious of new seat covers on sagging seats, new pedal pads, and worn armrests. These indicate an attempt to cover up hard use. Pull back the carpets and look for evidence of water leaks or flooding. Look for missing hardware, door handles, control knobs, etc. Check lights and signal operations. Make sure all accessories (air conditioner, heater, radio, etc.) work. Check windshield wiper operation.

9 Belts and Hoses: Open the hood, then check all belts and hoses for wear, cracks or weak spots.

10 Battery: Low electrolyte level, corroded terminals and/or cracked case indicate a lack of maintenance.

11 Radiator: Look for corrosion or rust in the coolant indicating a lack of maintenance.

12 Air filter: A severely dirty air filter would indicate a lack of maintenance.

13 Ignition wires: Check the ignition wires for cracks, burned spots, or wear. Worn wires will have to be replaced.

14 Oil level: If the oil level is low, chances are the engine uses oil or leaks. Beware of water in the oil (there is probably a cracked block or bad head gasket), excessively thick oil (which is often used to quiet a noisy engine), or thin, dirty oil with a distinct gasoline smell (this may indicate internal engine problems).

15 Automatic Transmission: Pull the transmission dipstick out when the engine is running. The level should read FULL, and the fluid should be clear or bright red. Dark brown or black fluid that has distinct burnt odor, indicates a transmission in need of repair or overhaul.

16 Exhaust: Check the color of the exhaust smoke. Blue smoke indicates, among other problems, worn rings. Black smoke can indicate

burnt valves or carburetor problems. Check the exhaust system for leaks; it can be expensive to replace.

17 Spark Plugs: Remove one or all of the spark plugs (the most accessible will do, though all are preferable). An engine in good condition will show plugs with a light tan or gray deposit on the firing tip.

ROAD TEST CHECKLIST

1 Engine Performance: The vehicle should be peppy whether cold or warm, with adequate power and good pickup. It should respond smoothly through the gears.

2 Brakes: They should provide quick, firm stops with no noise, pulling or brake fade.

3 Steering: Sure control with no binding harshness, or looseness and no shimmy in the wheel should be expected. Noise or vibration from the steering wheel when turning the vehicle means trouble.

4 Clutch (Manual Transmission/Transaxle): Clutch action should give quick, smooth response with easy shifting. The clutch pedal should have free-play before it disengages the clutch. Start the engine,

set the parking brake, put the transmission in first gear and slowly release the clutch pedal. The engine should begin to stall when the pedal is 1/2 - 3/4 of the way up.

5 Automatic Transmission/Transaxle: The transmission should shift rapidly and smoothly, with no noise, hesitation, or slipping.

6 Differential: No noise or thumps should be present. Differentials have no normal leaks.

7 Driveshaft/Universal Joints: Vibration and noise could mean driveshaft problems. Clicking at low speed or coast conditions means worn U-joints.

8 Suspension: Try hitting bumps at different speeds. A vehicle that bounces excessively has weak shock absorbers or struts. Clunks mean worn bushings or ball joints.

9 Frame/Body: Wet the tires and drive in a straight line. Tracks should show two straight lines, not four. Four tire tracks indicate a frame/body bent by collision damage. If the tires can't be wet for this purpose, have a friend drive along behind you and see if the vehicle appears to be traveling in a straight line.

ROUTINE MAINTENANCE INTERVALS

Every 600 Miles

- Check tire pressure and tightness of wheel bolts.

Every 1,500 Miles

- Lubricate tie rod ends on front end of 1961 and earlier models.
- Lubricate front axle tubes, king pins on 1965 and earlier models.

Every 3,000 Miles

- Change engine oil, clean strainer.
- Check for leaks from engine and transaxle.
- Lubricate carburetor controls and linkages.
- Check battery, clean and grease terminals.
- Examine the level of electrolyte in the cells and, if necessary, add distilled water via the plugs on top of the battery to bring the electrolyte level up to the top of the vertical separators.
- Lubricate door and hood locks with cold-resistant, water-repellent universal grease.
- Lubricate rear brake cable conduit tubes on earlier models which have fittings provided for this purpose. Universal grease should be applied to these fittings if they are present.
- Lubricate pedal cluster grease nipple on earlier models having such a fitting.

Every 6,000 Miles

- Check V-belt for tightness. Clean fuel pump filter.
- Check breaker points and replace, if necessary.
- Lubricate distributor cam with lithium grease. Check point gap and ignition timing. (refer to Section 2.)
- Adjust valve clearances. (refer to Section 2.)
- Clean and gap spark plugs.
- Check compression pressures.

- Check exhaust system for damage.
- Check water drain flaps and cooling bellows on 1600 Fastback and Squareback models.
- Adjust clutch pedal free-play.
- Check dust seals on steering joints and tie rod ends.
- Check tightness of tie rods.
- Check axial play of upper torsion arms; and camber and toe-in.
- Check steering gear and, if necessary, adjust play between roller and worm.
- Check for tire wear and damage.
- Check braking system for leaks or damage.
- Check brake fluid level; top up if necessary with Genuine VW • Brake Fluid or Lockheed brake fluid. Do not use mineral oil.
- Check for defective light bulbs and other possible defects in the electrical system.
- Check and clean air cleaner, top up with oil if necessary.
- Check rear axle oil level and inspect for leaks.
- Lubricate front end.
- Check automatic transaxle level, fill up if necessary.
- On automatic stick-shift, check clutch servo rod clearance, clean control valve air filter, and clean and adjust shift lever contacts.

Every 12,000 Miles

- Transporter - change oil in reduction gear cases.
- Replace spark plugs and points.
- Lubricate felt above cam bearing in distributor, earlier models.

Every 30,000 Miles

- Clean, grease, and adjust front wheel bearings.
- Renew transaxle lubricant, clean two magnetic drain plugs, check for leaks.
- On automatic stick-shift, clean and lubricate rear wheel bearings.

Capacities and Pressures

| Model | Crankcase Refill After Draining (pts.) | Transmission Refill After Draining (pts.) | | | | Final Drive (pts.) | Air Cleaner (pts.) [8] | Fuel Tank (gals.) | Normal Fuel Pressure (psi) |
		Standard	Auto. Stick Shift	Fully Auto.	Reduction Gears				
Type 1	5.3	6.3	6.3 [1]	N/A	N/A	[2]	.5 [3]	10.5 [9]	[10]
Type 2	5.3	7.4	N/A	N/A	.5 each	[2]	.63 [4]	15.8	[10]
Type 3	5.3	6.3	N/A	6.3-8.4 [6]	N/A	2.1 [7]	.85 [5]	10.5	[10]

(handwritten: 2.65 qts.)

(handwritten: 1/4 qt.)

N/A - Not applicable to this vehicle.

[1] The total capacity of the Automatic Stickshift torque converter circuit is 7.6 pts. ATF. The refill capacity is somewhat less.

[2] in unit with transmission

[3] 1,300 cc. Karmann Ghia - .63 pts., 1,500 cc. Karmann Ghia - .96 pts., 1,500 cc. sedan and convertible - .85 pts.

[4] 1,200 cc. - .44 pts., Late 1,500 and 1,600 cc. - .95 pts.

[5] Single carburetor engine; .44 pts, fuel injected engine .53 pts.

[6] Total capacity - 12.6 pts. ATF.

[7] Only with automatic transmission; otherwise, note [2] applies.

[8] Since so many different air cleaners have been used in production, it is best to rely on the full mark on the air cleaner body. If there is no such mark, these figures may be used.

[9] Super Beetle - 11.1 gals.

[10]

Pump Marking	Pressure @ RPM
Unmarked (36 hp and earlier)	1.3-1.8 @ 1,000 - 3.000
Unmarked	2.5 @ 3,000 - 3,400
VW 2	5.0 @ 3,800
VW 3	3.5 @ 3,400-3,800
VW 4	3.5 @ 3,800
VW 6	5.0 @ 3,800
VW 7	3.5 @ 3,800
VW 8	3.5 @ 3,800

ENGLISH TO METRIC CONVERSION: MASS (WEIGHT)

Current **mass** measurement is expressed in pounds and ounces (lbs. & ozs.). The metric unit of mass (or weight) is the kilogram (kg). Even although this table does not show conversion of masses (weights) larger than 15 lbs, it is easy to calculate larger units by following the data immediately below.

To convert ounces (oz.) to grams (g): multiply th number of ozs. by 28
To convert grams (g) to ounces (oz.): multiply the number of grams by .035

To convert pounds (lbs.) to kilograms (kg): multiply the number of lbs. by .45
To convert kilograms (kg) to pounds (lbs.): multiply the number of kilograms by 2.2

lbs	kg	lbs	kg	oz	kg	oz	kg
0.1	0.04	0.9	0.41	0.1	0.003	0.9	0.024
0.2	0.09	1	0.4	0.2	0.005	1	0.03
0.3	0.14	2	0.9	0.3	0.008	2	0.06
0.4	0.18	3	1.4	0.4	0.011	3	0.08
0.5	0.23	4	1.8	0.5	0.014	4	0.11
0.6	0.27	5	2.3	0.6	0.017	5	0.14
0.7	0.32	10	4.5	0.7	0.020	10	0.28
0.8	0.36	15	6.8	0.8	0.023	15	0.42

ENGLISH TO METRIC CONVERSION: TEMPERATURE

To convert Fahrenheit (°F) to Celsius (°C): take number of °F and subtract 32; multiply result by 5; divide result by 9

To convert Celsius (°C) to Fahrenheit (°F): take number of °C and multiply by 9; divide result by 5; add 32 to total

Fahrenheit (F)	Celsius (C)			Fahrenheit (F)	Celsius (C)			Fahrenheit (F)	Celsius (C)		
°F	°C	°C	°F	°F	°C	°C	°F	°F	°C	°C	°F
−40	−40	−38	−36.4	80	26.7	18	64.4	215	101.7	80	176
−35	−37.2	−36	−32.8	85	29.4	20	68	220	104.4	85	185
−30	−34.4	−34	−29.2	90	32.2	22	71.6	225	107.2	90	194
−25	−31.7	−32	−25.6	95	35.0	24	75.2	230	110.0	95	202
−20	−28.9	−30	−22	100	37.8	26	78.8	235	112.8	100	212
−15	−26.1	−28	−18.4	105	40.6	28	82.4	240	115.6	105	221
−10	−23.3	−26	−14.8	110	43.3	30	86	245	118.3	110	230
−5	−20.6	−24	−11.2	115	46.1	32	89.6	250	121.1	115	239
0	−17.8	−22	−7.6	120	48.9	34	93.2	255	123.9	120	248
1	−17.2	−20	−4	125	51.7	36	96.8	260	126.6	125	257
2	−16.7	−18	−0.4	130	54.4	38	100.4	265	129.4	130	266
3	−16.1	−16	3.2	135	57.2	40	104	270	132.2	135	275
4	−15.6	−14	6.8	140	60.0	42	107.6	275	135.0	140	284
5	−15.0	−12	10.4	145	62.8	44	112.2	280	137.8	145	293
10	−12.2	−10	14	150	65.6	46	114.8	285	140.6	150	302
15	−9.4	−8	17.6	155	68.3	48	118.4	290	143.3	155	311
20	−6.7	−6	21.2	160	71.1	50	122	295	146.1	160	320
25	−3.9	−4	24.8	165	73.9	52	125.6	300	148.9	165	329
30	−1.1	−2	28.4	170	76.7	54	129.2	305	151.7	170	338
35	1.7	0	32	175	79.4	56	132.8	310	154.4	175	347
40	4.4	2	35.6	180	82.2	58	136.4	315	157.2	180	356
45	7.2	4	39.2	185	85.0	60	140	320	160.0	185	365
50	10.0	6	42.8	190	87.8	62	143.6	325	162.8	190	374
55	12.8	8	46.4	195	90.6	64	147.2	330	165.6	195	383
60	15.6	10	50	200	93.3	66	150.8	335	168.3	200	392
65	18.3	12	53.6	205	96.1	68	154.4	340	171.1	205	401
70	21.1	14	57.2	210	98.9	70	158	345	173.9	210	410
75	23.9	16	60.8	212	100.0	75	167	350	176.7	215	414

ENGLISH TO METRIC CONVERSION: LENGTH

To convert inches (ins.) to millimeters (mm): multiply number of inches by 25.4

To convert millimeters (mm) to inches (ins.): multiply number of millimeters by .04

Inches		Decimals	Milli-meters	Inches to millimeters inches	mm	Inches		Decimals	Milli-meters	Inches to millimeters inches	mm
	1/64	0.051625	0.3969	0.0001	0.00254		33/64	0.515625	13.0969	0.6	15.24
1/32		0.03125	0.7937	0.0002	0.00508	17/32		0.53125	13.4937	0.7	17.78
	3/64	0.046875	1.1906	0.0003	0.00762		35/64	0.546875	13.8906	0.8	20.32
1/16		0.0625	1.5875	0.0004	0.01016	9/16		0.5625	14.2875	0.9	22.86
	5/64	0.078125	1.9844	0.0005	0.01270		37/64	0.578125	14.6844	1	25.4
3/32		0.09375	2.3812	0.0006	0.01524	19/32		0.59375	15.0812	2	50.8
	7/64	0.109375	2.7781	0.0007	0.01778		39/64	0.609375	15.4781	3	76.2
1/8		0.125	3.1750	0.0008	0.02032	5/8		0.625	15.8750	4	101.6
	9/64	0.140625	3.5719	0.0009	0.02286		41/64	0.640625	16.2719	5	127.0
5/32		0.15625	3.9687	0.001	0.0254	21/32		0.65625	16.6687	6	152.4
	11/64	0.171875	4.3656	0.002	0.0508		43/64	0.671875	17.0656	7	177.8
3/16		0.1875	4.7625	0.003	0.0762	11/16		0.6875	17.4625	8	203.2
	13/64	0.203125	5.1594	0.004	0.1016		45/64	0.703125	17.8594	9	228.6
7/32		0.21875	5.5562	0.005	0.1270	23/32		0.71875	18.2562	10	254.0
	15/64	0.234375	5.9531	0.006	0.1524		47/64	0.734375	18.6531	11	279.4
1/4		0.25	6.3500	0.007	0.1778	3/4		0.75	19.0500	12	304.8
	17/64	0.265625	6.7469	0.008	0.2032		49/64	0.765625	19.4469	13	330.2
9/32		0.28125	7.1437	0.009	0.2286	25/32		0.78125	19.8437	14	355.6
	19/64	0.296875	7.5406	0.01	0.254		51/64	0.796875	20.2406	15	381.0
5/16		0.3125	7.9375	0.02	0.508	13/16		0.8125	20.6375	16	406.4
	21/64	0.328125	8.3344	0.03	0.762		53/64	0.828125	21.0344	17	431.8
11/32		0.34375	8.7312	0.04	1.016	27/32		0.84375	21.4312	18	457.2
	23/64	0.359375	9.1281	0.05	1.270		55/64	0.859375	21.8281	19	482.6
3/8		0.375	9.5250	0.06	1.524	7/8		0.875	22.2250	20	508.0
	25/64	0.390625	9.9219	0.07	1.778		57/64	0.890625	22.6219	21	533.4
13/32		0.40625	10.3187	0.08	2.032	29/32		0.90625	23.0187	22	558.8
	27/64	0.421875	10.7156	0.09	2.286		59/64	0.921875	23.4156	23	584.2
7/16		0.4375	11.1125	0.1	2.54	15/16		0.9375	23.8125	24	609.6
	29/64	0.453125	11.5094	0.2	5.08		61/64	0.953125	24.2094	25	635.0
15/32		0.46875	11.9062	0.3	7.62	31/32		0.96875	24.6062	26	660.4
	31/64	0.484375	12.3031	0.4	10.16		63/64	0.984375	25.0031	27	690.6
1/2		0.5	12.7000	0.5	12.70						

ENGLISH TO METRIC CONVERSION: TORQUE

To convert foot-pounds (ft. lbs.) to Newton-meters: multiply the number of ft. lbs. by 1.3

To convert inch-pounds (in. lbs.) to Newton-meters: multiply the number of in. lbs. by .11

in lbs	N-m	in lbs	N-m	in lbs	N-m	in lbs	N-m	in lbs	N-m
0.1	0.01	1	0.11	10	1.13	19	2.15	28	3.16
0.2	0.02	2	0.23	11	1.24	20	2.26	29	3.28
0.3	0.03	3	0.34	12	1.36	21	2.37	30	3.39
0.4	0.04	4	0.45	13	1.47	22	2.49	31	3.50
0.5	0.06	5	0.56	14	1.58	23	2.60	32	3.62
0.6	0.07	6	0.68	15	1.70	24	2.71	33	3.73
0.7	0.08	7	0.78	16	1.81	25	2.82	34	3.84
0.8	0.09	8	0.90	17	1.92	26	2.94	35	3.95
0.9	0.10	9	1.02	18	2.03	27	3.05	36	4.0

ENGLISH TO METRIC CONVERSION: TORQUE

Torque is now expressed as either foot-pounds (ft./lbs.) or inch-pounds (in./lbs.). The metric measurement unit for torque is the Newton-meter (Nm). This unit—the Nm—will be used for all SI metric torque references, both the present ft./lbs. and in./lbs.

ft lbs	N-m	ft lbs	N-m	ft lbs	N-m	ft lbs	N-m
0.1	0.1	33	44.7	74	100.3	115	155.9
0.2	0.3	34	46.1	75	101.7	116	157.3
0.3	0.4	35	47.4	76	103.0	117	158.6
0.4	0.5	36	48.8	77	104.4	118	160.0
0.5	0.7	37	50.7	78	105.8	119	161.3
0.6	0.8	38	51.5	79	107.1	120	162.7
0.7	1.0	39	52.9	80	108.5	121	164.0
0.8	1.1	40	54.2	81	109.8	122	165.4
0.9	1.2	41	55.6	82	111.2	123	166.8
1	1.3	42	56.9	83	112.5	124	168.1
2	2.7	43	58.3	84	113.9	125	169.5
3	4.1	44	59.7	85	115.2	126	170.8
4	5.4	45	61.0	86	116.6	127	172.2
5	6.8	46	62.4	87	118.0	128	173.5
6	8.1	47	63.7	88	119.3	129	174.9
7	9.5	48	65.1	89	120.7	130	176.2
8	10.8	49	66.4	90	122.0	131	177.6
9	12.2	50	67.8	91	123.4	132	179.0
10	13.6	51	69.2	92	124.7	133	180.3
11	14.9	52	70.5	93	126.1	134	181.7
12	16.3	53	71.9	94	127.4	135	183.0
13	17.6	54	73.2	95	128.8	136	184.4
14	18.9	55	74.6	96	130.2	137	185.7
15	20.3	56	75.9	97	131.5	138	187.1
16	21.7	57	77.3	98	132.9	139	188.5
17	23.0	58	78.6	99	134.2	140	189.8
18	24.4	59	80.0	100	135.6	141	191.2
19	25.8	60	81.4	101	136.9	142	192.5
20	27.1	61	82.7	102	138.3	143	193.9
21	28.5	62	84.1	103	139.6	144	195.2
22	29.8	63	85.4	104	141.0	145	196.6
23	31.2	64	86.8	105	142.4	146	198.0
24	32.5	65	88.1	106	143.7	147	199.3
25	33.9	66	89.5	107	145.1	148	200.7
26	35.2	67	90.8	108	146.4	149	202.0
27	36.6	68	92.2	109	147.8	150	203.4
28	38.0	69	93.6	110	149.1	151	204.7
29	39.3	70	94.9	111	150.5	152	206.1
30	40.7	71	96.3	112	151.8	153	207.4
31	42.0	72	97.6	113	153.2	154	208.8
32	43.4	73	99.0	114	154.6	155	210.2

ENGLISH TO METRIC CONVERSION: FORCE

Force is presently measured in pounds (lbs.). This type of measurement is used to measure spring pressure, specifically how many pounds it takes to compress a spring. Our present force unit (the pound) will be replaced in SI metric measurements by the Newton (N). This term will eventually see use in specifications for electric motor brush spring pressures, valve spring pressures, etc.

To convert pounds (lbs.) to Newton (N): multiply the number of lbs. by 4.45

lbs	N	lbs	N	lbs	N	oz	N
0.01	0.04	21	93.4	59	262.4	1	0.3
0.02	0.09	22	97.9	60	266.9	2	0.6
0.03	0.13	23	102.3	61	271.3	3	0.8
0.04	0.18	24	106.8	62	275.8	4	1.1
0.05	0.22	25	111.2	63	280.2	5	1.4
0.06	0.27	26	115.6	64	284.6	6	1.7
0.07	0.31	27	120.1	65	289.1	7	2.0
0.08	0.36	28	124.6	66	293.6	8	2.2
0.09	0.40	29	129.0	67	298.0	9	2.5
0.1	0.4	30	133.4	68	302.5	10	2.8
0.2	0.9	31	137.9	69	306.9	11	3.1
0.3	1.3	32	142.3	70	311.4	12	3.3
0.4	1.8	33	146.8	71	315.8	13	3.6
0.5	2.2	34	151.2	72	320.3	14	3.9
0.6	2.7	35	155.7	73	324.7	15	4.2
0.7	3.1	36	160.1	74	329.2	16	4.4
0.8	3.6	37	164.6	75	333.6	17	4.7
0.9	4.0	38	169.0	76	338.1	18	5.0
1	4.4	39	173.5	77	342.5	19	5.3
2	8.9	40	177.9	78	347.0	20	5.6
3	13.4	41	182.4	79	351.4	21	5.8
4	17.8	42	186.8	80	355.9	22	6.1
5	22.2	43	191.3	81	360.3	23	6.4
6	26.7	44	195.7	82	364.8	24	6.7
7	31.1	45	200.2	83	369.2	25	7.0
8	35.6	46	204.6	84	373.6	26	7.2
9	40.0	47	209.1	85	378.1	27	7.5
10	44.5	48	213.5	86	382.6	28	7.8
11	48.9	49	218.0	87	387.0	29	8.1
12	53.4	50	224.4	88	391.4	30	8.3
13	57.8	51	226.9	89	395.9	31	8.6
14	62.3	52	231.3	90	400.3	32	8.9
15	66.7	53	235.8	91	404.8	33	9.2
16	71.2	54	240.2	92	409.2	34	9.4
17	75.6	55	244.6	93	413.7	35	9.7
18	80.1	56	249.1	94	418.1	36	10.0
19	84.5	57	253.6	95	422.6	37	10.3
20	89.0	58	258.0	96	427.0	38	10.6

ENGLISH TO METRIC CONVERSION: LIQUID CAPACITY

Liquid or fluid capacity is presently expressed as pints, quarts or gallons, or a combination of all of these. In the metric system the liter (l) will become the basic unit. Fractions of a liter would be expressed as deciliters, centiliters, or most frequently (and commonly) as milliliters.

To convert pints (pts.) to liters (l): multiply the number of pints by .47
To convert liters (l) to pints (pts.): multiply the number of liters by 2.1
To convert quarts (qts.) to liters (l): multiply the number of quarts by .95

To convert liters (l) to quarts (qts.): multiply the number of liters by 1.06
To convert gallons (gals.) to liters (l): multiply the number of gallons by 3.8
To convert liters (l) to gallons (gals.): multiply the number of liters by .26

gals	liters	qts	liters	pts	liters
0.1	0.38	0.1	0.10	0.1	0.05
0.2	0.76	0.2	0.19	0.2	0.10
0.3	1.1	0.3	0.28	0.3	0.14
0.4	1.5	0.4	0.38	0.4	0.19
0.5	1.9	0.5	0.47	0.5	0.24
0.6	2.3	0.6	0.57	0.6	0.28
0.7	2.6	0.7	0.66	0.7	0.33
0.8	3.0	0.8	0.76	0.8	0.38
0.9	3.4	0.9	0.85	0.9	0.43
1	3.8	1	1.0	1	0.5
2	7.6	2	1.9	2	1.0
3	11.4	3	2.8	3	1.4
4	15.1	4	3.8	4	1.9
5	18.9	5	4.7	5	2.4
6	22.7	6	5.7	6	2.8
7	26.5	7	6.6	7	3.3
8	30.3	8	7.6	8	3.8
9	34.1	9	8.5	9	4.3
10	37.8	10	9.5	10	4.7
11	41.6	11	10.4	11	5.2
12	45.4	12	11.4	12	5.7
13	49.2	13	12.3	13	6.2
14	53.0	14	13.2	14	6.6
15	56.8	15	14.2	15	7.1
16	60.6	16	15.1	16	7.6
17	64.3	17	16.1	17	8.0
18	68.1	18	17.0	18	8.5
19	71.9	19	18.0	19	9.0
20	75.7	20	18.9	20	9.5
21	79.5	21	19.9	21	9.9
22	83.2	22	20.8	22	10.4
23	87.0	23	21.8	23	10.9
24	90.8	24	22.7	24	11.4
25	94.6	25	23.6	25	11.8
26	98.4	26	24.6	26	12.3
27	102.2	27	25.5	27	12.8
28	106.0	28	26.5	28	13.2
29	110.0	29	27.4	29	13.7
30	113.5	30	28.4	30	14.2

ENGLISH TO METRIC CONVERSION: PRESSURE

The basic unit of pressure measurement used today is expressed as pounds per square inch (psi). The metric unit for psi will be the kilopascal (kPa). This will apply to either fluid pressure or air pressure, and will be frequently seen in tire pressure readings, oil pressure specifications, fuel pump pressure, etc.

To convert pounds per square inch (psi) to kilopascals (kPa): multiply the number of psi by 6.89

Psi	kPa	Psi	kPa	Psi	kPa	Psi	kPa
0.1	0.7	37	255.1	82	565.4	127	875.6
0.2	1.4	38	262.0	83	572.3	128	882.5
0.3	2.1	39	268.9	84	579.2	129	889.4
0.4	2.8	40	275.8	85	586.0	130	896.3
0.5	3.4	41	282.7	86	592.9	131	903.2
0.6	4.1	42	289.6	87	599.8	132	910.1
0.7	4.8	43	296.5	88	606.7	133	917.0
0.8	5.5	44	303.4	89	613.6	134	923.9
0.9	6.2	45	310.3	90	620.5	135	930.8
1	6.9	46	317.2	91	627.4	136	937.7
2	13.8	47	324.0	92	634.3	137	944.6
3	20.7	48	331.0	93	641.2	138	951.5
4	27.6	49	337.8	94	648.1	139	958.4
5	34.5	50	344.7	95	655.0	140	965.2
6	41.4	51	351.6	96	661.9	141	972.2
7	48.3	52	358.5	97	668.8	142	979.0
8	55.2	53	365.4	98	675.7	143	985.9
9	62.1	54	372.3	99	682.6	144	992.8
10	69.0	55	379.2	100	689.5	145	999.7
11	75.8	56	386.1	101	696.4	146	1006.6
12	82.7	57	393.0	102	703.3	147	1013.5
13	89.6	58	399.9	103	710.2	148	1020.4
14	96.5	59	406.8	104	717.0	149	1027.3
15	103.4	60	413.7	105	723.9	150	1034.2
16	110.3	61	420.6	106	730.8	151	1041.1
17	117.2	62	427.5	107	737.7	152	1048.0
18	124.1	63	434.4	108	744.6	153	1054.9
19	131.0	64	441.3	109	751.5	154	1061.8
20	137.9	65	448.2	110	758.4	155	1068.7
21	144.8	66	455.0	111	765.3	156	1075.6
22	151.7	67	461.9	112	772.2	157	1082.5
23	158.6	68	468.8	113	779.1	158	1089.4
24	165.5	69	475.7	114	786.0	159	1096.3
25	172.4	70	482.6	115	792.9	160	1103.2
26	179.3	71	489.5	116	799.8	161	1110.0
27	186.2	72	496.4	117	806.7	162	1116.9
28	193.0	73	503.3	118	813.6	163	1123.8
29	200.0	74	510.2	119	820.5	164	1130.7
30	206.8	75	517.1	120	827.4	165	1137.6
31	213.7	76	524.0	121	834.3	166	1144.5
32	220.6	77	530.9	122	841.2	167	1151.4
33	227.5	78	537.8	123	848.0	168	1158.3
34	234.4	79	544.7	124	854.9	169	1165.2
35	241.3	80	551.6	125	861.8	170	1172.1
36	248.2	81	558.5	126	868.7	171	1179.0

ENGLISH TO METRIC CONVERSION: PRESSURE

The basic unit of pressure measurement used today is expressed as pounds per square inch (psi). The metric unit for psi will be the kilopascal (kPa). This will apply to either fluid pressure or air pressure, and will be frequently seen in tire pressure readings, oil pressure specifications, fuel pump pressure, etc.

To convert pounds per square inch (psi) to kilopascals (kPa): multiply the number of psi by 6.89

Psi	kPa	Psi	kPa	Psi	kPa	Psi	kPa
172	1185.9	216	1489.3	260	1792.6	304	2096.0
173	1192.8	217	1496.2	261	1799.5	305	2102.9
174	1199.7	218	1503.1	262	1806.4	306	2109.8
175	1206.6	219	1510.0	263	1813.3	307	2116.7
176	1213.5	220	1516.8	264	1820.2	308	2123.6
177	1220.4	221	1523.7	265	1827.1	309	2130.5
178	1227.3	222	1530.6	266	1834.0	310	2137.4
179	1234.2	223	1537.5	267	1840.9	311	2144.3
180	1241.0	224	1544.4	268	1847.8	312	2151.2
181	1247.9	225	1551.3	269	1854.7	313	2158.1
182	1254.8	226	1558.2	270	1861.6	314	2164.9
183	1261.7	227	1565.1	271	1868.5	315	2171.8
184	1268.6	228	1572.0	272	1875.4	316	2178.7
185	1275.5	229	1578.9	273	1882.3	317	2185.6
186	1282.4	230	1585.8	274	1889.2	318	2192.5
187	1289.3	231	1592.7	275	1896.1	319	2199.4
188	1296.2	232	1599.6	276	1903.0	320	2206.3
189	1303.1	233	1606.5	277	1909.8	321	2213.2
190	1310.0	234	1613.4	278	1916.7	322	2220.1
191	1316.9	235	1620.3	279	1923.6	323	2227.0
192	1323.8	236	1627.2	280	1930.5	324	2233.9
193	1330.7	237	1634.1	281	1937.4	325	2240.8
194	1337.6	238	1641.0	282	1944.3	326	2247.7
195	1344.5	239	1647.8	283	1951.2	327	2254.6
196	1351.4	240	1654.7	284	1958.1	328	2261.5
197	1358.3	241	1661.6	285	1965.0	329	2268.4
198	1365.2	242	1668.5	286	1971.9	330	2275.3
199	1372.0	243	1675.4	287	1978.8	331	2282.2
200	1378.9	244	1682.3	288	1985.7	332	2289.1
201	1385.8	245	1689.2	289	1992.6	333	2295.9
202	1392.7	246	1696.1	290	1999.5	334	2302.8
203	1399.6	247	1703.0	291	2006.4	335	2309.7
204	1406.5	248	1709.9	292	2013.3	336	2316.6
205	1413.4	249	1716.8	293	2020.2	337	2323.5
206	1420.3	250	1723.7	294	2027.1	338	2330.4
207	1427.2	251	1730.6	295	2034.0	339	2337.3
208	1434.1	252	1737.5	296	2040.8	240	2344.2
209	1441.0	253	1744.4	297	2047.7	341	2351.1
210	1447.9	254	1751.3	298	2054.6	342	2358.0
211	1454.8	255	1758.2	299	2061.5	343	2364.9
212	1461.7	256	1765.1	300	2068.4	344	2371.8
213	1468.7	257	1772.0	301	2075.3	345	2378.7
214	1475.5	258	1778.8	302	2082.2	346	2385.6
215	1482.4	259	1785.7	303	2089.1	347	2392.5

NOTES

2

ENGINE PERFORMANCE AND TUNE-UP

Tune-Up Specifications

Year	Engine Code, ⑨ SAE HP Rating Displacement	Spark Plugs Make, Type ⑧	Gap (in.)	Distributor Approx. Point Dwell (deg.)	Point Gap (in.)	Basic Ignition Timing (deg.)	Cranking Comp. Pressure (psi)	Valves Clearance (in.) Intake	Exhaust	Intake Opens (deg.) ①	Idle Speed (rpm)
To December, 1953	25 hp, 1,100	Bosch W 175 T1, Champion L-10	.026	50	.016	5 BTDC	85-107	.004	.004	2½ BTDC	550
To July 1960	A, 36 hp, 1,200	Bosch W175T1, Champion L-10	.026	50	.016	7.5 BTDC	100-114	.004	.004	2½ BTDC	550
From August, 1960	D, 42 hp, 1,200	Bosch W175T1, Champion L87Y	.026	50	.016	10 BTDC	100-128	.004 ②	.004 ⑤	6 BTDC	550
From August 1965	F, 50 hp, 1,300	Bosch W175T1, Champion L-87Y	.028	50	.016	7.5 BTDC	107-135	.004	.004	7½ BTDC	550
From August, 1965-Type 2, From August 1967- Type 1	H, 53 hp, 1,500	Bosch ③ W175T1, Champion L-87Y	.028	42-58	.016	7.5 ④ BTDC	114-142	.004	.004	7½ BTDC	550 ⑤
From August, 1969-Type 1, From August 1967-Type 2	B, 57 hp, 1,600	Bosch W145T1	.026	47-53	.016	0 ATDC	114-142	.004	.004	7½ BTDC	850
To July 1963	G, 51 hp, 1,500	Bosch W145T1	.028	42-58	.016	10 BTDC	121-142	.004 ②	.004 ②	7½ BTDC	550

Tune-Up Specifications

Year	Engine Code, ⑨ SAE HP Rating Displacement	Spark Plugs Make, Type ⑧	Spark Plugs Gap (in.)	Distributor Approx. Point Dwell (deg.)	Distributor Point Gap (in.)	Basic Ignition Timing (deg.)	Cranking Comp. Pressure (psi)	Valves Clearance (in.) Intake	Valves Clearance (in.) Exhaust	Intake Opens (deg.) ①	Idle Speed (rpm)
To July 1965 ⑥ From August, 1965 ⑦	K, 54 hp, 1,500	Bosch W175T1	.026	50	.016	10 BTDC ⑥ 7.5 BTDC ⑦	121-142 ⑥ 114-142 ⑦	.004 ②	.004 ②	7½ BTDC	550
To July 1965	R, 66 hp, 1,500S	Bosch W175T1	.026	50	.016	10 BTDC	135-164	.004 ②	.004 ②	7½ BTDC	750
From August, 1965	T, 65 hp, 1,600	Bosch W175T1	.028	50	.016	7.5 BTDC	114-142	.004	.004	7½ BTDC	750
From August, 1967, Injected	U, 65 hp, 1,600	Bosch W175T1	.028	47-53	.016	0 ATDC	114-142	.004	.004	7½ BTDC	850

① With valve clearance of .04 in. (This clearance is used for checking valve timing only.)

② Before 1965, some 1,200 and 1,500 cc engines which used long rocker arm mounting studs which pass through the full thickness of the cylinder head. Valve clearances on engines with long studs must be set at .008 in. (intake), and .012 in. (exhaust). These engines are:

Engine Code	Up to Engine No.
D	9205699
G	0710799
K	0672748
R	0672297

Some of these engines have had short studs installed in one or both heads. In this case, the valves are set at .004 in. (intake and exhaust); The only sure way to determine what clearance to use on these engines is by a sticker on the engine, or by feeling the stud ends between the pushrod tubes under the engine.

③ Type 1 - Bosch W145T1
④ Type 1 with throttle positioner - 0° ATDC
⑤ Type 1 - 850 rpm
⑥ High compression
⑦ Low compression
⑧ The Bosch W175T1 plug can be used to replace the W145T1 for sustained high speeds

⑨ See Engine Identification Chart in Chapter 1 for explanation of codes
NOTE: If any of this tune-up information conflicts with the information on the engine sticker(s), use the sticker figures

TUNE-UP PROCEDURES

As any car, including the Volkswagen, covers the miles between tune-ups, changes occur in the engine and elsewhere. The clearances between engine parts and the adjustments in other systems of the car become slowly less efficient. Mechanical wear, high temperatures and engine vibration all play a part in causing engine performance to fall off. Loss of power becomes almost impossible for the driver to notice.

One reason why the VW engine should be tuned at periodic intervals is that a small, four-cylinder engine really can't afford to be running inefficiently. Unlike big American cars, the Volkswagen is designed to operate with a small, economical engine and give reasonable performance. However, when the engine is out of tune, it can't do either. While an American V-8, with 300-plus horsepower, can afford to have 100 of these horses sleeping, the Volkswagen can ill afford to have even 20 horsepower going to waste. When a V-8 is running on only seven cylinders, it's only a 12 percent drop. However, when one cylinder in a Volkswagen fails to produce, the drop is twice as great - 25 percent.

Apart from power and efficiency considerations, there is one other major reason for giving the Volkswagen engine periodic tuning attention - money. This is one incentive that should appeal to practically everyone. An engine that is kept in perfect tune will last longer because it's running exactly the way its manufacturers intended it to. And the Volkswagenwerke are by no means going to ruin their reputation of Teutonic efficiency by recommending tuning specs which do not contribute to the maximum life of their engines. Besides lasting longer, a consistently-tuned engine will get more miles per gallon over its entire life. Tuning is not expensive, either. The most expensive component of a tune-up, new spark plugs, will pay for itself in gas mileage alone even if replaced every 10,000 miles. So there you have it: more miles per gallon, more miles per engine, and most important, more miles per dollar.

Tune-Up Steps

➡**Perform the engine tune-up in the order presented here to obtain optimum engine performance.**

1 Battery service
2 Compression check
3 Electrical and mechanical checks
4 Air cleaner and fuel filter service
5 Fan belt deflection check
6 Spark plug service
7 Point adjustment and ignition timing
8 Carburetor or fuel injection adjustment
9 Valve clearance adjustment
10 Throttle regulator adjustment

With these steps accomplished, the Volkswagen engine will have been given a very thorough tuning. If, after tuning, the engine should still not perform up to par, consult Section 4.

Battery

SERVICE

Without a battery strong enough to crank it, even the best of engines can't go anywhere. Make sure that the battery is filled to the level of the plates with electrolyte. If it is not up to the proper level (just above the vertical plates) add distilled water, which is available at any auto supply store. The average battery lasts between 2 - 5 years, but with periodic attention to the electrolyte level most would last much longer.

➡**For more information on battery service, please refer to Section 1.**

Cylinder Compression

TESTING

Before going to the trouble of trying to tune an engine, it is good idea to first check and see if it is possible to tune the engine satisfactorily. If compression is much below par in any or all of the cylinders it will be impossible to tune the engine without first having the cause of the low compression remedied. If any Volkswagen is found to have a compression lower than 65 pounds per square inch (psi) in one or more cylinders, it will be difficult to put the engine in proper running condition through tuning alone.

✳✳ WARNING:

Be very careful when removing spark plugs from Volkswagen engines. The soft aluminum cylinder head spark plug threads have a nasty tendency to strip when removing spark plugs, on which no anti-seizing compound has been used. If uncertain whether the spark plugs in your engine have anti-seizing compound applied to them, remove the plugs when the engine is completely cold to check them. If necessary, apply the anti-seizing compound to the threads of the plugs, then reinstall them into the cylinder heads and commence with the service procedure. This is extremely important when directed to remove the plugs when the engine is at normal operating temperature (hot).

A noticeable lack of engine power, excessive oil consumption and/or poor fuel mileage measured over an extended period are all indicators of internal engine wear. Worn piston rings, scored or worn cylinder bores, blown head gaskets, sticking or burnt valves and worn valve seats are all possible culprits here. A check of each cylinder's compression will help you locate the problems.

As mentioned in the Tools and Equipment section of Section 1, a screw-in type compression gauge is more accurate then the type you simply hold against the spark plug hole, although it takes slightly longer to use. It's worth it to obtain a more accurate reading. Follow the procedures below.

1 Warm up the engine to normal operating temperature.
2 Remove all the spark plugs.
3 Disconnect the high tension lead from the ignition coil.
4 Fully open the throttle, either by operating the carburetor throttle linkage by hand or by having an assistant hold the accelerator pedal to the floor.
5 Screw the compression gauge into the No. 1 spark plug hole until the fitting is snug.

✳✳ WARNING:

Be careful not to crossthread the plug hole. On aluminum cylinder heads use extra care, as the threads in these heads are easily damaged.

6   Ask an assistant to depress the accelerator pedal fully on both carbureted and fuel injected vehicles. Then, while you read the compression gauge, ask the assistant to crank the engine 4 to 6 revolutions using the ignition switch. Repeat the test two or three times until a consistent reading is obtained.

7   Read the compression gauge at the end of each series of cranks, and record the highest of these readings. Repeat this procedure for each of the engine's cylinders.

The resulting compression pressure should be in the neighborhood of that specified for each of the Volkswagen engines. Compression differences between cylinders should be no greater than 15 psi, and any cylinder that is even 10 pounds less than the others should be given particularly close attention during subsequent compression checks.

When compression is low in one cylinder, it is due either to worn piston rings or to valve leakage in that cylinder. Squirting about a tablespoon of heavy lubricating oil into the spark plug hole will reveal the cause of the low compression. If, after squirting the oil into the cylinder, compression increases, the low compression is due to worn piston rings. If, on the other hand, squirting the oil does not result in a higher compression reading, the problem is most likely to be leaking valves. With regard to leaking valves, a valve may leak slightly in a compression test due to the presence of a particle of dirt on the seat of that valve. In this case, subsequent compression checks will probably reveal that the reading involving the dirt particle was unusually low.

It is an excellent idea to check and record compression readings in all cylinders at periodic intervals, especially if one is interested in keeping a close eye on engine wear and also wants to be forewarned of problems which might otherwise come as a surprise at an inconvenient time. Although compression readings on any particular engine will vary widely from one compression check to the next (due to oil temperature, viscosity, outside temperature, method of measurement, etc.) cylinders will generally show the same relative readings. For example cylinder number one may always be 3 - 4 lbs. higher than cylinder two, and cylinder three may usually be 5 - 6 lbs. higher than number four.

Electrical and Mechanical Checks

VISUAL INSPECTION

Every engine tune-up should include a visual check of major electrical and mechanical systems, including the following: (1) coil primary wiring and connections, (2) battery connections, (3) starter, generator, and voltage regulator connections. Electrical connections must be tight to ensure trouble-free operation. Wiring that is frayed or cracked should be replaced.

Visual checking of mechanical components should include inspection of the following: fuel-line and vacuum-line connections, tightness of carburetor attaching nuts, and freedom of operation of the choke and carburetor linkages.

Air Cleaner and Fuel Filter

SERVICE

The air cleaner should be serviced as described in Section 1, and the fuel filter (built into the fuel pump) should be cleaned and reinstalled. The fuel pump filter on some Volkswagen models is removed by unscrewing the hexagonal head plug from the side of the fuel pump assembly. For more information on fuel filters, please refer to Section 1.

Fan Belt

TENSION & ADJUSTMENT

On all Volkswagens except the type 3, the V-belt drives both the generator and the fan which cools the engine. On the type 3 the V-belt drives the generator only; the blower fan being mounted directly on the crankshaft of the engine, thereby rotating at the same speed as the engine. In all Volkswagen models, the fan belt should deflect approximately 3/5 in. (15mm) when pressed firmly at its midpoint with one's thumb. The quality and adjustment of the fan belt is especially important on the smaller Volkswagens, in which it drives the cooling fan. If the fan belt goes bad in one of the type 1 or 2 models, the car can be driven no further without causing severe damage to the engine. However, in type 3 and 4 models, it is possible to drive without the fan belt for fairly long distances, especially in the daytime. An average battery will power a car's ignition for some distance before running out of energy. However, if the headlights must also be used, the distance that can be covered will be much shorter. In short, if the fan belt fails in a VW, stop right then and there without further delay. (When you see the red light in the speedometer dial, the generator is no longer charging.) But if the belt fails in a Squareback, Fastback, or Notchback, you can drive to the nearest service area. Regardless of the model you drive, it is a good idea to carry an extra V-belt.

If belt tension is too great, the result will be a shortening of the life of the generator bearings due to unnecessary stress. If the belt is too loose, the result will be a loss of cooling efficiency in beetles and a loss of generating power in both the small and large Volkswagens. The following steps should be followed in adting the fan belt tension on all Volkswagens, regardless of year:

1   Remove the holding nut from the generator pulley shaft. In type 3 models, the pulley must be held from turning by using a suitable wrench. In the smaller Volkswagens the pulley is held by a screwdriver wedged between the notch in the generator pulley and the upper generator housing bolt.

2   Remove the outer half of the generator pulley and adjust the fan belt tension by fitting the proper number of spacer washers between the halves of the pulley. Each washer added or removed changes the play in the belt about 1/4".

3   If the fan belt is too loose, one or more spacer washers will have to be removed from between the pulley halves. If the belt is too tight one or more washers will have to be added between the pulley halves.

4   When correct adjustment has been achieved, the belt will deflect approximately 3/5 in. (15mm) when pressed by thumb pressure at its midpoint.

5   When adjustment is correct, install the outer half of the generator pulley, and insert all left-over washers between the pulley nut and the outer pulley half. In this way, all spacer washers will remain on the pulley shaft and will be readily available whenever subsequent belt adjustments are required.

6   Tighten pulley nut.

If the belt has stretched to the extent that correct adjustment can no longer be achieved by removing spacers from between the pulley halves, the belt should be replaced. Also, if a belt has frayed edges or cracks, it should be replaced. Fan belts should be kept free from grease and oil.

It is recommended that a new belt be inspected regularly during the first several hundred miles of use, since new belts have a tendency to stretch slightly.

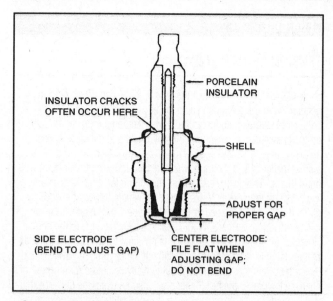

Cross-section of a spark plug

Spark Plugs

A typical spark plug consists of a metal shell surrounding a ceramic insulator. A metal electrode extends downward through the center of the insulator and protrudes a small distance. Located at the end of the plug and attached to the side of the outer metal shell is the side electrode. The side electrode bends in at a 90-degree angle so that its tip is just past and parallel to the tip of the center electrode. The distance between these two electrodes (measured in thousandths of an inch or hundredths of a millimeter) is called the spark plug gap.

The spark plug does not produce a spark but instead provides a gap across which the current can arc. The coil produces anywhere from 20,000 to 50,000 volts (depending on the type and application) which travels through the wires to the spark plugs. The current passes along the center electrode and jumps the gap to the side electrode, and in doing so, ignites the air/fuel mixture in the combustion chamber.

SPARK PLUG HEAT RANGE

Spark plug heat range is the ability of the plug to dissipate heat. The longer the insulator (or the farther it extends into the engine), the hotter the plug will operate; the shorter the insulator (the closer the electrode is to the block's cooling passages) the cooler it will operate. A plug that absorbs little heat and remains too cool will quickly accumulate deposits of oil and carbon since it is not hot enough to burn them off. This leads to plug fouling and consequently to misfiring. A plug that absorbs too much heat will have no deposits but, due to the excessive heat, the electrodes will burn away quickly and might possibly lead to preignition or other ignition problems. Preignition takes place when plug tips get so hot that they glow sufficiently to ignite the air/fuel mixture before the actual spark occurs. This early ignition will usually cause a pinging during low speeds and heavy loads.

The general rule of thumb for choosing the correct heat range when picking a spark plug is: if most of your driving is long distance, high speed travel, use a colder plug; if most of your driving is stop and go, use a hotter plug. Original equipment plugs are generally a good compromise between the 2 styles and most people never have the need to change their plugs from the factory-recommended heat range.

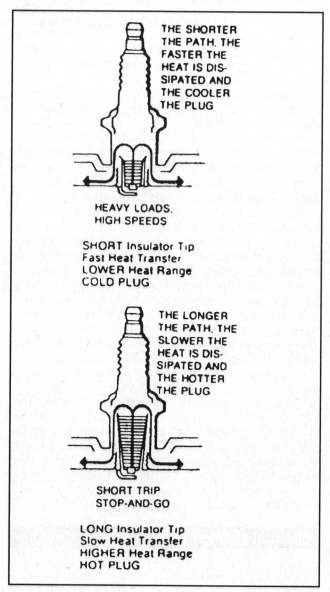

Spark plug heat range

REMOVAL & INSTALLATION

Spark plugs should be cleaned and gapped at 6,000 mile intervals and replaced every 12,000 miles.

In normal operation plug gap increases about 0.001 in. (0.025mm) for every 2500 miles (4000 km). As the gap increases, the plug's voltage requirement also increases. It requires a greater voltage to jump the wider gap and about two to three times as much voltage to fire the plug at high speeds than at idle. The improved air/fuel ratio control of modern fuel injection combined with the higher voltage output of modern ignition systems will often allow an engine to run significantly longer on a set of standard spark plugs, but keep in mind that efficiency will drop as the gap widens (along with fuel economy and power).

When you're removing spark plugs, work on one at a time. Don't start by removing the plug wires all at once, because, unless you number them, they may become mixed up. Take a minute before you begin and number the wires with tape.

1 Disconnect the negative battery cable, and if the vehicle has been

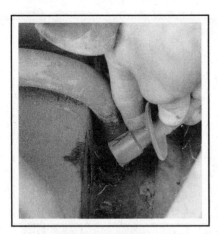

To remove the spark plugs, detach the cables from the plugs . . .

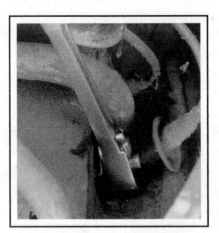

. . . then use a socket and ratchet to loosen the plug

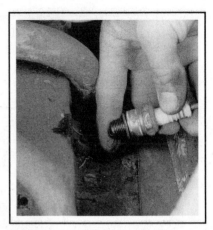

Once the plug is loose, unthread it by hand to prevent damage to the threads in the cylinder head

run recently, allow the engine to thoroughly cool.

2   Carefully twist the spark plug wire boot to loosen it, then pull upward and remove the boot from the plug. Be sure to pull on the boot and not on the wire, otherwise the connector located inside the boot may become separated.

3   Using compressed air, blow any water or debris from the spark plug well to assure that no harmful contaminants are allowed to enter the combustion chamber when the spark plug is removed. If compressed air is not available, use a rag or a brush to clean the area.

➡Remove the spark plugs when the engine is cold, if possible, to prevent damage to the threads. If removal of the plugs is difficult, apply a few drops of penetrating oil or silicone spray to the area around the base of the plug, and allow it a few minutes to work.

4   Using a spark plug socket that is equipped with a rubber insert to properly hold the plug, turn the spark plug counterclockwise to loosen and remove the spark plug from the bore.

❋❋ WARNING:

Be careful when using a flexible extension on the socket. Use of a flexible extension may allow a shear force to be applied to the plug. A shear force could break the plug off in the cylinder head, leading to costly and frustrating repairs.

To install:

5   Inspect the spark plug boot for tears or damage. If a damaged boot is found, the spark plug wire must be replaced.

6   Using a wire feeler gauge, check and adjust the spark plug gap. When using a gauge, the proper size should pass between the electrodes with a slight drag. The next larger size should not be able to pass while the next smaller size should pass freely.

7   When installing spark plugs, care should be taken not to overtighten them. The Volkswagen cylinder heads are made of a relatively light alloy and can be cross-threaded more easily than the more common cast iron heads in domestic automobiles. For this reason, a few drops of light oil or anti-seizing compound should be placed on each plug before it is inserted by hand (using the extension holder supplied with the VW tool kit) and turned cautiously for several turns before tightening down to a torque of roughly 22 - 29 ft. lbs. New gaskets should be used. When the proper torque is used in tightening the

plugs, only the compression ring of the new gaskets will be crushed - this is the desirable condition

❋❋ WARNING:

Do not use the spark plug socket to thread the plugs. Always carefully thread the plug by hand or using an old plug wire to prevent the possibility of crossthreading and damaging the cylinder head bore.

8   Apply a small amount of silicone dielectric compound to the end of the spark plug lead or inside the spark plug boot to prevent sticking, then install the boot to the spark plug and push until it clicks into place. The click may be felt or heard, then gently pull back on the boot to assure proper contact.

INSPECTION & GAPPING

After the spark plugs are removed from the engine, they should be inspected for outside appearance which gives valuable information on the running condition and mixture adjustment of the engine. If they are not going to be replaced, clean the plugs thoroughly. Remember that any kind of deposit will decrease the efficiency of the plug. Plugs can be cleaned on a spark plug cleaning machine, which can sometimes be found in service stations, or you can do an acceptable job of cleaning with a stiff brush. If the plugs are cleaned, the electrodes must be filed flat. Use an ignition points file, not an emery board or the like, which will leave deposits. The electrodes must be filed perfectly flat with sharp edges; rounded edges reduce the spark plug voltage by as much as 50%.

In the dual-carburetor type 3 engine, each carburetor feeds two cylinders. It is not unusual to discover that one bank of cylinders is running either richer or leaner than the other bank. When this situation occurs, the carburetors should be adjusted properly.

The spark plugs in the Volkswagen should be gapped to between 0.024 - 0.028 in. (0.6 - 0.7mm). In general, the best idling will result from a wide spacing of the spark plug gap, but a wide gap will also cause starting to be slightly harder. A wide gap at high speeds will also lead to missing. On the other hand, a plug with a smaller gap will miss less at high speeds, give easier starting, but will cause poor idling. In order to improve starting ability when outside temperatures are very low, the plug gap may **temporarily** be reduced to 0.020 in. (0.5mm).

Be sure the rubbing block is positioned on the high point of the lobe (arrows)

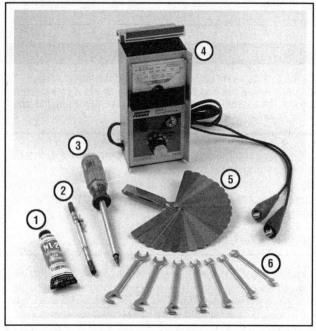

Tools and materials needed for contact point replacement and dwell angle adjustment

1 *Distributor cam lube* - *Sometimes this special lubricant comes with the new points, however, it's a good idea to buy a new tube and have it on hand.*
2 *Screw starter* - *This tool has special claws which hold the screw securely as it's started, which helps prevent accidental dropping of the screw*
3 *Magnetic screwdriver* - *Serves the same purpose as 2 above. If you don't have one of these special screwdrivers, you risk dropping the point mounting screws down into the distributor body*
4 *Dwell meter* - *A dwell meter is the only accurate way to determine the point setting (gap). Connect the meter according to the instructions supplied with it*
5 *Blade-type feeler gauges* - *These are required to set the initial point gap (space between the points when they are open*
6 *Ignition wrenches* - *These special wrenches are made to work within the tight confines of the distributor. Specifically, they are needed to loosen the nut/bolt which secures the leads to the points*

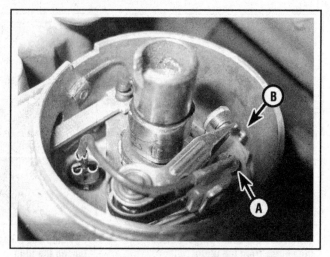

First loosen the adjusting screw (A) and use the tip of the screwdriver to adjust the points at the adjusting tabs (B)

Because of the wide range of conditions under which the Volkswagen operates, it is probably best to gap plugs in the middle of the 0.024 - 0.028 in. range, in other words 0.026 in. However, if one places more emphasis on good idling than on good high-speed performance, or vice-versa, one may wish to choose gaps in either the higher or the lower portion of the recommended range. The Volkswagen will operate equally well at any setting in the recommended range, and any differences would probably be so slight as to be unnoticeable.

It is advisable to adjust only the side electrode by bending it either toward or away from the center electrode with a special spark plug gapping tool. In the normal operation of the engine, spark plug gaps increase due to natural burning, so used plugs must have their gaps reduced in order to achieve the correct adjustment.

Breaker Points

REPLACEMENT AND ADJUSTMENT

▶ See Figures 1 and 2

The breaker points are the heart of the Volkswagen ignition system, and must be given their share of attention. All Volkswagens ever made

Disconnect the wire from the points at the terminal

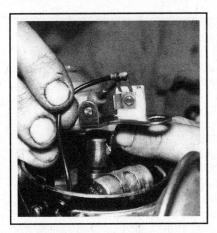

On some early models, the wire connector is attached with a screw

Remove the hold-down screw

If the points are mounted externally like this, remove the screw (arrow) and pull the connector block out of the housing

require a breaker point gap of 0.016 in. (COLD) and a dwell angle of 50 degrees. It is best if the engine is cold from sitting overnight or for several hours. If you are not able to rest your hand comfortably on any part of the engine, it is too warm to set the breaker point gap and the ignition timing. In adjusting the contact points, the following steps are taken:

1 Remove the distributor cap and rotor.

2 Turn the engine by hand until the fiber block on the movable breaker point rests on a high point of the cam lobe.

3 With a screwdriver, loosen the locking screw of the stationary breaker points.

4 Manipulate the stationary point plate so that the clearance between the points is 0.016 in.

5 Tighten the locking screw of the stationary point.

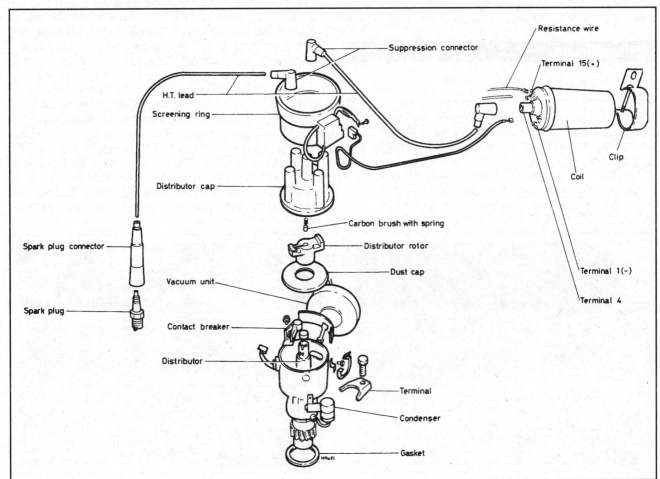

Fig. 1 Exploded view of a common Bosch distributor used on many Volkswagen models

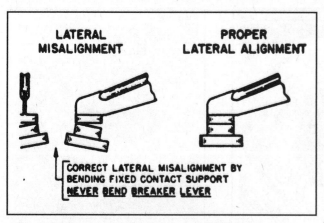

Fig. 2 Ensure that the surfaces of the breaker point contact faces are properly aligned to avoid premature wear

6   Recheck the point gap, correct if it has changed from Step 4 due to the tightening of the locking screw.

When replacing points, the same steps are followed, as with adjusting except that in between Steps 3 and 4, the old points are taken out and the new points inserted. Points should be replaced when they have been badly burned or have been in use so long that correct adjustment is no longer possible. When checking the gap of points which have been in use for some time, it is advisable to use a round gauge rather than a flat feeler gauge. In the case of points that have a peak in one point and a valley in the other, the flat-type gauge will result in a reading which is smaller than the actual gap between the two points.

Ignition Timing

DESCRIPTION

Ignition timing is the measurement, in degrees of crankshaft rotation, of the point at which the spark plugs fire in each of the cylinders. It is measured in degrees before or after Top Dead Center (TDC) of the compression stroke.

Because it takes a fraction of a second for the spark plug to ignite the mixture in the cylinder, the spark plug must fire a little before the piston reaches TDC. Otherwise, the mixture will not be completely ignited as the piston passes TDC and the full power of the explosion will not be used by the engine.

The timing measurement is given in degrees of crankshaft rotation before the piston reaches TDC (BTDC). If the setting for the ignition timing is 5-degrees BTDC, the spark plug must fire 5-degrees before each piston reaches TDC. This only holds true, however, when the engine is at idle speed.

As the engine speed increases, the pistons go faster. The spark plugs have to ignite the fuel even sooner if it is to be completely ignited when the piston reaches TDC.

If the ignition is set too far advanced (BTDC), the ignition and expansion of the fuel in the cylinder will occur too soon and tend to force the piston down while it is still traveling up. This causes engine ping. If the ignition spark is set too far retarded, after TDC (ATDC), the piston will have already passed TDC and started on its way down when the fuel is ignited. This will cause the piston to be forced down for only a portion of its travel. This will result in poor engine performance and lack of power.

ADJUSTMENT

It is only after adjusting the breaker points properly that the ignition timing should be adjusted. It is most important that the ignition timing adjustment be carried out only when the engine is dead cold, because rising engine temperature causes the setting to change.

If, in exceptional cases, it is necessary to adjust the timing with a warm engine, not exceeding 122-degrees F, the timing should be advanced about 2.5-degrees beyond the normal setting. The timing must then be rechecked at the first opportunity with the engine cold.

VW engines have had several different arrangements of crankshaft pulley timing marks. On early type 1 engines, the pulley bore two timing marks, 7.5-degrees Before Top Dead Center (BTDC) and 10-degrees BTDC, reading clockwise. Later, with the introduction of emission controls, a 0-degree TDC mark was added. The 7.5-degrees and 10-degrees marks were subsequently removed, leaving only the 0-degree mark. Newer engines have only a 5-degrees After Top Dead Center (ATDC) mark. Type 2 engines are generally the same as type 1 models. Early type 3 engines have marks at 7.5-degrees and 10-degrees BTDC; later engines have marks at 7.5-degrees, 10-degrees, and 12.5-degrees BTDC. Fuel injected type 3 engines have marks corresponding to 0-degrees, 7.5-degrees, 10-degrees, and 12.5-degrees BTDC. Refer to the Tune-Up Specifications Chart and the sticker on your particular engine for the correct timing setting.

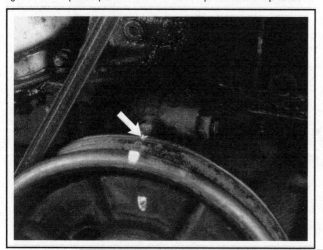

On upright engines the TDC timing mark is stamped into an edge of the crankshaft pulley

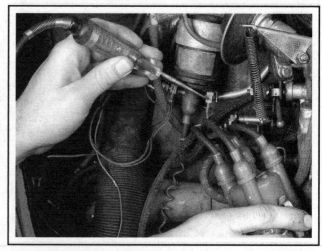

Connect a test light and turn the distributor until you find the point where the light just comes on and off

Distributor Advance Characteristics

Vehicle	Engine	Distributor	Centrifugal Advance (deg. @ rpm.)				Vacuum Advance (deg. @ mm. hg.)			
			Start	Intermed-iate	Intermed-iate	End	Start	Intermed-iate	Intermed-iate	End
Type 1	25 hp.	Bosch VE 4 BRS 383	5@ O rpm	5-9 @ 600	15-20 @ 1,400	32-37 @ 2800	–	–	–	–
Type 1	36 hp. 1,200	Bosch VJU 4BR 3 mk	7.5@ O rpm	8-13 @ 1,200	13.5-16.5@ 2,000	31.5-34.5@ 3,300	0 @ 80	8.0-11.5 @200	17.5-19.5 @300	18-22 @ 370
Type 1	36 hp. 1,200	Bosch VJU 4BR 8 mk	7.5@ O rpm	10-14 @ 1,800	–	23-27 @ 3,400	0 @ 100	5-7.5 @200	11-14.5 @300	13-17 @ 350
Type 1	40 hp. 1,200	VW 113 905 205H	NA	NA	NA	NA	0 @ 140	7-13 @ 300	15-21 @ 400	19-25 @ 450
Type 1	50 hp. 1,300	Bosch 113 905 205K or VW113 905 2051	NA	NA	NA	NA	0 @ 40-110	5-11 @ 200	14-20 @ 400	23-28 @ 620-650
Type 1	53 hp. 1,500	Bosch 113905 205M	–	–	–	–	@ 40-80	17-19 @300	–	32-35 @ 800
Type 1	53 hp. 1,500, 57 hp. 1,600	Bosch 113 905 205T								
Type 1	53 hp. 1,500 Auto-matic	Bosch 113 905 205P	14-23 @ 1,500	19-23 @ 1,600	19-23 @ 2,100	30-33 @ 3,750	@ 50-100	14-20 @ 300	–	8-12 @ 230
Type 1	53 hp. 1,500 Auto-matic	Bosch 113 905 205AA	14-23 @ 1,500	19-23 @ 1,600	19-23 @ 2,100	30 -33@ 3,750	@ 50-100	3-7 @ 150	–	8-12 @ 230
Type 1	57 hp. 1,600 Auto-matic	Bosch 113 905 205AD	@ 1,050-1,200	13-15 @ 1,700	13-16 @ 2,200	25-28@ 3,900	@ 70-120 @ 60-100	– –	–	8-12@ 240 6-8(retard) @170
Type 2	57 hp. 1,600	Bosch 113 905 205M	–	–	–	–	@ 40-80	17-19 @ 300	–	32-35 @ 800
Type 2	57 hp. 1,600	Bosch 113 905 205T	–	–	–	–	@ 40-80	17-19 @ 300	–	32-35@ 800
Type 3	65 hp. 1,600	Bosch 311 905 205F	–	–	–	–	@ 10-70	–	–	23-28 @ 310-340
Type 3	65 hp. 1,600	Bosch 311 905 205G	–	–	–	–	@ 10-70	17-19 @ 300	–	23-28 @ 310-340

Distributor Advance Characteristics

Vehicle	Engine	Distributor	Centrifugal Advance (deg. @ rpm.)				Vacuum Advance (deg. @ mm. hg.)			
			Start	Intermediate	Intermediate	End	Start	Intermediate	Intermediate	End
Type 3	65 hp. 1,600	Bosch 311 905 205L	@ 900 1,100	6-12 @ 1,350	10-14 @ 1,500	26-30 @ 2,600	@ 50-100	10-16 @ 300	—	8-12 @ 200
Type 3	65 hp. 1,600	Bosch 311 905 205AB	@ 900- 1,100	10-14 @ 1,500	20-23 @ 2,300	27-30 @ 2,800	@ 60-100	2-8 @ 150	—	8-12 @ 200
Type 3	65 hp. 1,600	Bosch 311 905 205M	@ 900 1,050	19-22 @ 1,600	19-22 @ 2,100	27-30 @ 2,700	@ 60- 100	17-19 @ 300	—	8-12 @ 200

NOTE: Figures given are for crankshaft degrees and rpm. To obtain distributor degrees and rpm, divide crankshaft figures by two.

NA - Not available.

1 Turn the engine by hand until the appropriate mark on the crankshaft pulley is lined up with the crankcase dividing line. (On type 3 models, the mark is to be lined up with the timing setting surface, or pointer, on the fan housing. At the same time that the appropriate mark is opposite the dividing line the rotor must be pointing to the spark plug wire of cylinder No. 1 (the cylinder toward the front of the car on the passenger side). No. 1 position is indicated by a mark on the rim of the distributor. If the rotor is not pointing toward the No. 1 cylinder, the crankshaft must be turned one more revolution clockwise until it is. On recent models, No. 3 cylinder is retarded about 4-degrees compared with No. 1 cylinder and only No. 1 cylinder is to be used in setting the ignition timing.

2 Loosen the clamp screw at the base of the distributor.

3 Attach the lead of a test lamp (6 volt for 1966 and earlier models, 12 volt for 1967 and later) to terminal 1 of the ignition coil and ground the test lamp.

4 With the ignition switched **ON**, rotate the distributor body clockwise until the contact points close and the test lamp illuminates, then rotate it slowly counterclockwise until the points begin to open and the test light turns off.

5 Without moving the distributor body, tighten the clamp screw at the base of the distributor.

6 Recheck the timing setting by turning the crankshaft pulley counterclockwise one-half turn, then engine block timing turning clockwise until the timing mark is within 1 in. of the line. At this point, proceed more slowly by tapping the right side of the fan belt with your hand. Such tapping will cause the fan belt to move in either moderate or very small jumps, depending on the strength of the tap. Slight taps toward the end of the check will ensure the finest possible check on the accuracy of the adjustment. If, upon rechecking, the lamp lights before the mark gets to the dividing line, the timing will have to be retarded slightly by loosening the clamp screw and rotating the distributor body in the clockwise direction. Rotating the distributor clockwise retards the timing, while rotation in the counterclockwise direction advances the timing.

➡Adjustment of ignition timing on 1967 and earlier engines must always be done with a test lamp. A stroboscopic timing light should not be used, as it will alter the entire setting range.

However, it is recommended that exhaust emission controlled engines (1968 and later) and type 3 fuel injected engines be timed with a stroboscopic light. These engines should be timed at idle speed, with the distributor vacuum line disconnected and the engine at normal operating temperature.

Idle Speed and Mixture

ADJUSTMENT

Single Carburetor System

As a part of a routine tune-up it is necessary only to adjust the idle speed and mixture screws on the carburetors of most single carburetor Volkswagens. Before adjustment is begun, the engine should be at normal operating temperature and the idle adjusting screw must not be

Idle speed and mixture adjustment screws found on 30 PICT-3 carburetors used on some 1968 - 69 models

1 Throttle valve adjustment
2 By-pass (idle speed) screw
3 Volume control (mixture) screw

Location of the idle speed (A) and mixture (B) screws on early carburetors

resting on the fast idle cam of the automatic choke. The following steps should be followed in setting the idle speed and mixture adjustments on single-carburetor Volkswagen engines:

1 With the engine warm and running, turn the idle speed adjusting screw in or out until the proper idle speed is attained. The correct speed can be found in the Tune-Up Specifications Chart or on the sticker on the engine. If the Tune-up Specifications Chart valve differs from that given on the engine sticker, use the engine sticker valve.

2 With the engine running at the proper idle speed, turn the idle mixture control screw slowly clockwise until the engine speed begins to drop, then turn slowly counterclockwise until the engine is running smoothly again. Now turn the mixture control screw another 1/4 turn counterclockwise.

3 If necessary, readjust the idle speed. With the clutch pedal depressed, the engine should continue to run after the accelerator has been quickly depressed and released. If the engine stalls, either the mixture adjustment or the idle speed adjustment is incorrect and should be remedied.

➡**The setting of the slow-speed (idle) mixture will have a great influence on the performance and economy of the Volkswagen at speeds as great as 50 or 60 miles per hour. If the mixture is too rich, the result will be excess fuel consumption, stalling when the accelerator pedal is suddenly released, and possible "running on" when the ignition switch is turned OFF. If the mixture is too lean (too much air, not enough gasoline), the result will be better fuel consumption, but exhaust valves may suffer burning or warping. The previously-given method for adjusting the slow-speed adjustment will give the proper mixture setting. Turning the mixture screw clockwise will lean the mixture, while turning counterclockwise will enrich it.**

Dual Carburetor System

On certain type 3 models, there are two carburetors - one for each bank of two cylinders. While the current models are equipped with a fuel injection system, type 3 vehicles sold in the U.S.A. in 1966 and 1967 have dual carburetors and require slightly more sophistication in the tune-up operation. Adjusting the carburetors on the dual-carb models requires the use of a special instrument to measure air flow. This device measures the vacuum created by carburetor suction by means of a red piston which rides up and down inside a graded glass tube. The higher the vacuum, the higher the piston is raised.

Besides the synchronizing device mentioned above, a small frozen

juice can will also be required in order that the device will fit on the air horns of the carburetors. Because of the screws that stick straight up from the air horn for the purpose of holding the air cleaner, the small can (open on both ends) is needed. By mounting it on top of the can, the test device will clear the screws without losing vacuum. Before attempting adjustment, the engine must be at operating temperature.

1 Remove the right-hand connecting rod of the carburetor linkage system. This is the rod which connects the center bell crank with the right-hand carburetor throttle.

2 Remove the air cleaner. It is held on by two wing nuts on each carburetor and one wing nut in the center. The connections to the air intake and to the crankcase ventilation system must also be removed.

3 With the engine running, adjust the idle speed screw of each carburetor until the correct idle speed is attained. Each carburetor should then be flowing the same amount of air. When the synchronizer is moved from one carburetor to the other, the height of the red piston should not change more than 1 in., preferably less. Because of the fine adjustment possible with the use of the idle speed adjusting screws, there is no excuse for not being able to adjust the carburetor idle speeds so that the maximum variation is less than 1/4 of an inch. When checking the air flow through each carburetor, the disc on the device should be turned clockwise or counterclockwise until the piston rides approximately in the center of the range.

4 In adjusting the volume control screw of each carburetor, slowly turn the screw clockwise until the engine speed begins to drop, then turn counterclockwise until the engine runs smoothly once again, then a further 1/4 of a turn counterclockwise.

5 Recheck the idle speed adjustment, and, if necessary, increase or decrease the idle speed of each carburetor so that the correct speed is maintained. Make sure the synchronizer shows the same reading when it is moved from one carburetor to the other without moving the disc on the device.

6 Recheck the adjustment on the mixture control screws. On 1600 engines, there is present, on each screw, a raised portion on the outside perimeter. This will enable one to feel the position of the screw when it cannot be seen. The correct position for the mixture control screw will be approximately 1-1/2 turns from the screwed-in position. When turning the screw fully to the closed position, care should be taken not to apply too much torque, because the seat or needle of the screw could be damaged.

7 After the mixture adjustment has been rechecked, the idle speed and balance should also be checked again and corrected, if necessary.

8 In checking the balance of the carburetors at an increased speed, it is necessary to once again install the right-hand connecting rod which was removed in Step 1. Block the front wheels, apply the parking brake and make certain the transmission is in Neutral. Then, have an assistant sit in the vehicle and, using the accelerator pedal, keep the engine running at between 1,200 - 1,500 rpm. With the engine running at this speed, check the carburetors for high speed balance.

9 Install the synchronizer onto the left-hand carburetor and adjust the disc until the red piston rides in the center of the range. Now move the device over to the right-hand carburetor and, without moving the disc, compare the height of the piston here with the height achieved at the left carburetor. If the height of the piston is higher on the right side, the length of the right-hand connecting rod must be increased slightly. If the height of the piston is lower on the right side, the length of the right-hand connecting rod will have to be decreased. Changing the length of the right-hand control rod is accomplished by loosening the nuts on both ends and twisting the rod while leaving the ends stationary. The opposite ends have threads which tighten in opposite directions. The length of the right control rod must be adjusted until there is

little or no difference between the readings of the test device when it is moved from one carburetor to the other.

For a really fine adjustment, it is possible to loosen only one of the control rod ends and turn it slightly in the desired direction. If loosening and moving this end is not sufficient to effect the adjustment needed, then the opposite end must also be loosened and moved slightly after the first end has been tightened. This is a step-by-step method which is guaranteed to be more accurate than simply loosening both ends and tightening them up again at the same time. It is quite impossible to avoid changing the setting when tightening the ends. Ordinarily the ends are offset by 90 degrees, but the step-by-step method takes into consideration that the ends may be offset slightly more or less if it will contribute to a more accurate balance.

10 After low-speed and high-speed balance has been checked, the connecting rods should be lubricated at their ends with lithium grease and the carburetor's moving parts lubricated with a light oil.

11 Reinstall the oil bath air cleaner, being careful to tighten the two outer wing nuts first, then the center wing nut. If the center wing nut is tightened first, it is possible that the adjustment of the right-hand carburetor will be altered when the air cleaner is fastened tightly to the screw protruding from its air horn. Replace the crankcase ventilation hose and air intake connections. In order to install the air cleaner it will be necessary to remove the right-hand carburetor connecting rod temporarily. Take care not to bend this rod.

Fuel Injection System

The only tune-up adjustment possible on the Bosch electronic fuel injection system is that for idle speed. The adjusting screw is located on the left side of the intake air distributor. Early models have a knurled screw with a lockspring; newer models have a locknut on the adjusting screw. After adjusting idle speed to specifications, make sure that the throttle valve is completely closed at idle. See Section 5 for further information on fuel injection.

Valve Lash

ADJUSTMENT

If valve clearances in the Volkswagen engine are too small, the valves can be seriously damaged by warping or burning, and compression will eventually suffer from lack of proper valve sealing. Valves

are cooled by resting against the valve seat - if the valves are opened for too long, they have insufficient time to rest against their seats, and hence to transfer their heat to the cylinder head. On the other hand, if the valve clearance is too great, the result will be rough running, loss of power, and excessive wear of the valve train components. However, if error is necessary, it is best to err in the direction of too large a clearance. A few thousandths of an inch of excess clearance will be much less harmful than the same error in the opposite direction. As long as you can hear the valves clicking, you are at least assured that they are not burning.

Before the valves can be adjusted in any Volkswagen, the engine must be cold, preferably after sitting overnight. Volkswagen valve clearances vary somewhat between models of different years. To determine the correct setting, refer to both the Tune-Up Specifications Chart and the engine sticker.

Preference is to be given to the valve clearance specified on the engine fan housing sticker, if one is present. On models built after late 1964, such a sticker will be on the fan housing. Such stickers will also be present on all factory rebuilt engines, regardless of horsepower output, and the clearances specified should be followed closely.

1 Remove the distributor cap and turn the engine until the rotor points to the notch in the distributor rim and the crankshaft pulley timing mark is aligned with the crankcase split or pointer. No. 1 cylinder is now at top dead center of its compression stroke. In type 3 engines, the belt housing cover must be removed so that the engine can be turned by hand.

2 Remove the rocker arm cover of cylinders No. 1 and No. 2.

3 With the proper feeler gauge, check the clearance between the adjusting screw and the valve stem of both valves for the No. 1 cylinder. If the feeler gauge slides in snugly without being forced, the clearance is correct. It would be well to use the "go, no go" gauge system in which the proper leaf slides in but one which is 0.002 in. thicker will not.

4 If the clearance is incorrect, the locknut must be loosened and the adjusting screw turned until the proper clearance is obtained. After tightening down the locknut, it is then advisable to recheck the clearance, because it is possible that the adjustment was altered when tightening the locknut.

5 Turn the engine one-half revolution counterclockwise. This will turn the distributor rotor 90 degrees counterclockwise so that it will now point to the spark plug wire for cylinder No. 2. No. 2 cylinder is now at top dead center.

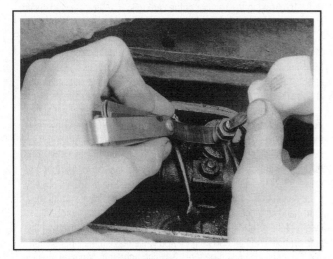

Use a screwdriver and feeler gauge to adjust the valve lash . . .

. . . then hold the adjusting screw steady while tightening the locknut

6 Repeat adjustment process for cylinder No. 2.

7 Replace valve rocker arm cover on cylinders Nos. 1 and 2, using a new gasket and cleaning off the seating surfaces to guard against leakage.

8 Remove the valve rocker arm cover on cylinders Nos. 3 and 4.

9 Turn the engine another one-half turn counterclockwise so that the distributor rotor now points to the spark plug wire of cylinder No. 3. No. 3 cylinder is now at top dead center.

10 Adjust the clearances on cylinder No. 3.

➡**On type 1 and 2 engines, No. 3 cylinder runs hotter than the other three cylinders because its cooling air flow is partially blocked by the oil cooler. To counter a tendency for this cylinder to burn exhaust valves, some mechanics set the No. 3 exhaust valve clearance 0.001 - 0.002 in. bigger than specified.**

11 Turn the engine a further one-half turn counterclockwise and adjust the clearances of the valves in cylinder No. 4.

12 Replace the rocker arm cover of cylinders Nos. 3 and 4, cleaning the sealing surfaces and using a new gasket.

13 Replace the distributor cap. Replace the belt housing cover in type 3 models.

While correct valve clearance is important to all Volkswagen engines, it is especially important in those having a specified clearance of 0.008 and 0.012 in. (intake and exhaust respectively). In these engines the valve clearance actually decreases as the engine warms up, so too little initial clearance, or a clearance obtained with a warm engine, can lead to trouble within a short time. On engines with 0.004 in. clearance, the clearance increases as the engine temperature increases.

It is also possible to adjust valves in normal firing order sequence, 1-4-3-2, rotating the engine clockwise. It is helpful to mark the crankshaft pulley directly opposite the 0-degree mark in order to determine precisely when the engine is turned one-half revolution.

Throttle Regulator

ADJUSTMENT

The exhaust emission control device used on 1968 - 69 type 1 and 2 vehicles is the throttle valve regulator. This device holds the throttle open slightly on deceleration to prevent an excessively rich mixture.

The throttle regulator unit is of a one piece design, and mounted on the carburetor.

1 The engine must be at operating temperature with the automatic choke fully open.

2 Start the engine. Turn the regulator adjusting screw clockwise until the control rod just starts to move the throttle valve lever. The stop collar on the control rod will be against the regulator body. Engine speed should be 1,700 - 1,800 rpm.

3 If the speed is too high, shorten the control rod.

4 After adjustment, tighten the locknuts on the control rod.

5 Turn the regulator adjusting screw counterclockwise until an idle speed of 850 rpm is obtained.

6 Increase engine speed to 3,000 rpm, then release the throttle valve lever. The engine should take 3 - 4 seconds to return to idle.

Incorrect throttle regulator adjustment may cause erratic idle, excessively high idle speed, and backfiring on deceleration.

FIRING ORDERS

▶ **See Figure 10**

➡**To avoid confusion, remove and tag the spark plug wires one at a time, for replacement.**

If a distributor is not keyed for installation with only one orientation, it could have been removed previously and rewired. The resultant wiring would hold the correct firing order, but could change the relative placement of the plug towers in relation to the engine. For this reason it is imperative that you label all wires before disconnecting any of them. Also, before removal, compare the current wiring with the accompanying illustrations. If the current wiring does not match, make notes in your book to reflect how your engine is wired.

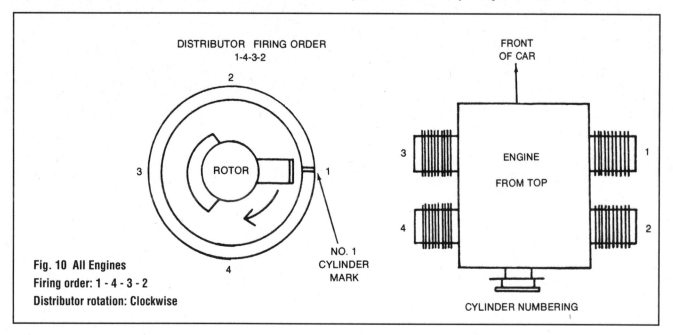

DISTRIBUTOR FIRING ORDER
1-4-3-2

ROTOR

NO. 1 CYLINDER MARK

Fig. 10 All Engines
Firing order: 1 - 4 - 3 - 2
Distributor rotation: Clockwise

FRONT OF CAR

ENGINE
FROM TOP

CYLINDER NUMBERING

NOTES

3

ENGINE AND ENGINE OVERHAUL

ENGINE ELECTRICAL

Understanding Electricity

For any electrical system to operate, there must be a complete circuit. This simply means that the power flow from the battery must make a full circle. When an electrical component is operating, power flows from the battery to the components, passes through the component (load) causing it to function, and returns to the battery through the ground path of the circuit. This ground may be either another wire or a metal part of the vehicle (depending upon how the component is designed).

BASIC CIRCUITS

Perhaps the easiest way to visualize a circuit is to think of connecting a light bulb (with two wires attached to it) to the battery. If one of the two wires was attached to the negative post (-) of the battery and the other wire to the positive post (+), the circuit would be complete and the light bulb would illuminate. Electricity could follow a path from the battery to the bulb and back to the battery. It's not hard to see that with longer wires on our light bulb, it could be mounted anywhere on the vehicle. Further, one wire could be fitted with a switch so that the light could be turned on and off. Various other items could be added to our primitive circuit to make the light flash, become brighter or dimmer under certain conditions, or advise the user that it's burned out.

Ground

Some automotive components are grounded through their mounting points. The electrical current runs through the chassis of the vehicle and returns to the battery through the ground (-) cable; if you look, you'll see that the battery ground cable connects between the battery and the body of the vehicle.

Load

Every complete circuit must include a "load" (something to use the electricity coming from the source). If you were to connect a wire between the two terminals of the battery (DON'T do this, but take our word for it) without the light bulb, the battery would attempt to deliver its entire power supply from one pole to another almost instantly. This is a short circuit. The electricity is taking a short cut to get to ground and is not being used by any load in the circuit. This sudden and uncontrolled electrical flow can cause great damage to other components in the circuit and can develop a tremendous amount of heat. A short in an automotive wiring harness can develop sufficient heat to melt the insulation on all the surrounding wires and reduce a multiple wire cable to one sad lump of plastic and copper. Two common causes of shorts are broken insulation (thereby exposing the wire to contact with surrounding metal surfaces or other wires) or a failed switch (the pins inside the switch come out of place and touch each other).

Switches and Relays

Some electrical components which require a large amount of current to operate also have a relay in their circuit. Since these circuits carry a large amount of current (amperage or amps), the thickness of the wire in the circuit (wire gauge) is also greater. If this large wire were connected from the load to the control switch on the dash, the switch would have to carry the high amperage load and the dash would be twice as large to accommodate wiring harnesses as thick as your wrist. To prevent these problems, a relay is used. The large wires in the circuit are connected from the battery to one side of the relay and from

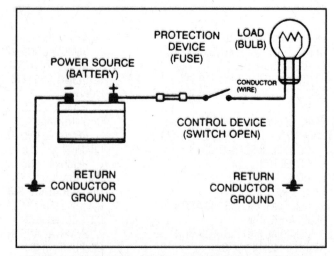

Here is an example of a simple automotive circuit. When the switch is closed, power from the positive battery terminal flows through the fuse, the switch and then the load (light bulb). The light illuminates and the circuit is completed through the return conductor and the vehicle ground. If the light did not work, the tests could be made with a voltmeter or test light at the battery, fuse, switch or bulb socket

the opposite side of the relay to the load. The relay is normally open, preventing current from passing through the circuit. An additional, smaller wire is connected from the relay to the control switch for the circuit. When the control switch is turned on, it grounds the smaller wire to the relay and completes its circuit. The main switch inside the relay closes, sending power to the component without routing the main power through the inside of the vehicle. Some common circuits which may use relays are the horn, headlights, starter and rear window defogger systems.

Protective Devices

It is possible for larger surges of current to pass through the electrical system of your vehicle. If this surge of current were to reach the load in the circuit, it could burn it out or severely damage it. To prevent this, fuses, circuit breakers and/or fusible links are connected into the supply wires of the electrical system. These items are nothing more than a built-in weak spot in the system. It's much easier to go to a known location (the fusebox) to see why a circuit is inoperative than to dissect 15 feet of wiring under the dashboard, looking for what happened.

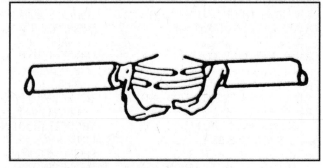

Damaged insulation can allow wires to break (causing an open circuit) or touch (causing a short circuit)

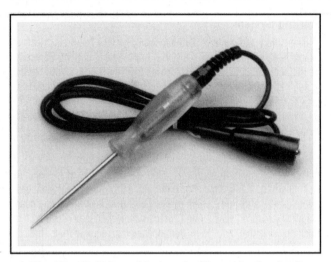

A 12 volt test light is useful when checking parts of a circuit for power

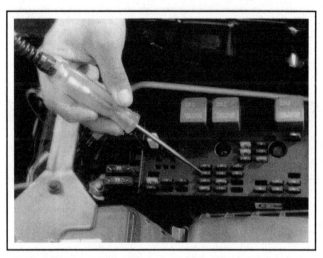

Here, someone is checking a circuit by making sure there is power to the component's fuse

When an electrical current of excessive power passes through the fuse, the fuse blows (the conductor melts) and breaks the circuit, preventing the passage of current and protecting the components.

A circuit breaker is basically a self repairing fuse. It will open the circuit in the same fashion as a fuse, but when either the short is removed or the surge subsides, the circuit breaker resets itself and does not need replacement.

A fuse link (fusible link or main link) is a wire that acts as a fuse. One of these is normally connected between the starter relay and the main wiring harness under the hood. Since the starter is usually the highest electrical draw on the vehicle, an internal short during starting could direct about 130 amps into the wrong places. Consider the damage potential of introducing this current into a system whose wiring is rated at 15 amps and you'll understand the need for protection. Since this link is very early in the electrical path, it's the first place to look if nothing on the vehicle works, but the battery seems to be charged and is properly connected.

TROUBLESHOOTING

Electrical problems generally fall into one of three areas:
• The component that is not functioning is not receiving current.
• The component is receiving power but is not using it or is using it incorrectly (component failure).
• The component is improperly grounded.

The circuit can be can be checked with a test light and a jumper wire. The test light is a device that looks like a pointed screwdriver with a wire on one end and a bulb in its handle. A jumper wire is simply a piece of wire with alligator clips or special terminals on each end. If a component is not working, you must follow a systematic plan to determine which of the three causes is the villain.

1   Turn ON the switch that controls the item not working.

➡**Some items only work when the ignition switch is turned ON.**

2   Disconnect the power supply wire from the component.

3   Attach the ground wire of a test light or a voltmeter to a good metal ground.

4   Touch the end probe of the test light (or the positive lead of the voltmeter) to the power wire; if there is current in the wire, the light in the test light will come on (or the voltmeter will indicate the amount of voltage). You have now established that current is getting to the component.

5   Turn the ignition or dash switch **OFF** and reconnect the wire to the component.

If there was no power, then the problem is between the battery and the component. This includes all the switches, fuses, relays and the battery itself. The next place to look is the fusebox; check carefully either by eye or by using the test light across the fuse clips. The easiest way to check is to simply replace the fuse. If the fuse is blown, and upon replacement, immediately blows again, there is a short between the fuse and the component. This is generally (not always) a sign of an internal short in the component. Disconnect the power wire at the component again and replace the fuse; if the fuse holds, the component is the problem.

✳ WARNING:

DO NOT test a component by running a jumper wire from the battery UNLESS you are certain that it operates on 12 volts. Many electronic components are designed to operate with less voltage and connecting them to 12 volts could destroy them. Jumper wires are best used to bypass a portion of the circuit (such as a stretch of wire or a switch) that DOES NOT contain a resistor and is suspected to be bad.

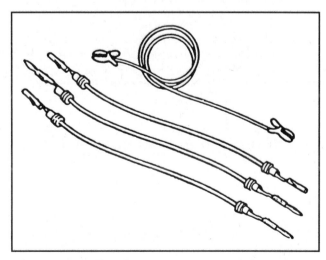

Jumper wires with various connectors are handy for quick electrical testing

If all the fuses are good and the component is not receiving power, find the switch for the circuit. Bypass the switch with the jumper wire. This is done by connecting one end of the jumper to the power wire coming into the switch and the other end to the wire leaving the switch. If the component comes to life, the switch has failed.

✳✳ WARNING:

Never substitute the jumper for the component. The circuit needs the electrical load of the component. If you bypass it, you will cause a short circuit.

Checking the ground for any circuit can mean tracing wires to the body, cleaning connections or tightening mounting bolts for the component itself. If the jumper wire can be connected to the case of the component or the ground connector, you can ground the other end to a piece of clean, solid metal on the vehicle. Again, if the component starts working, you've found the problem.

A systematic search through the fuse, connectors, switches and the component itself will almost always yield an answer. Loose and/or corroded connectors, particularly in ground circuits, are becoming a larger problem in modern vehicles. The computers and on-board electronic (solid state) systems are highly sensitive to improper grounds and will change their function drastically if one occurs.

Remember that for any electrical circuit to work, ALL the connections must be clean and tight.

➡For more information on Understanding and Troubleshooting Electrical Systems, please refer to Section 6 of this manual.

Battery, Starting and Charging Systems

BASIC OPERATING PRINCIPLES

Battery

The battery is the first link in the chain of mechanisms which work together to provide cranking of the automobile engine. In most modern vehicles, the battery is a lead/acid electrochemical device consisting of six 2v subsections (cells) connected in series so the unit is capable of producing approximately 12v of electrical pressure. Each subsection consists of a series of positive and negative plates held a short distance apart in a solution of sulfuric acid and water.

The two types of plates are of dissimilar metals. This sets-up a chemical reaction, and it is this reaction which produces current flow from the battery when its positive and negative terminals are connected to an electrical accessory such as a lamp or motor. The continued transfer of electrons would eventually convert the sulfuric acid to water, and make the two plates identical in chemical composition. As electrical energy is removed from the battery, its voltage output tends to drop. Thus, measuring battery voltage and battery electrolyte composition are two ways of checking the ability of the unit to supply power. During engine cranking, electrical energy is removed from the battery. However, if the charging circuit is in good condition and the operating conditions are normal, the power removed from the battery will be replaced by the alternator which will force electrons back through the battery, reversing the normal flow, and restoring the battery to its original chemical state.

Starting System

The battery and starting motor are linked by very heavy electrical cables designed to minimize resistance to the flow of current. Generally, the major power supply cable that leaves the battery goes directly to the starter, while other electrical system needs are supplied by a smaller cable. During starter operation, power flows from the battery to the starter and is grounded through the vehicle's frame/body or engine and the battery's negative ground strap.

The starter is a specially designed, direct current electric motor capable of producing a great amount of power for its size. One thing that allows the motor to produce a great deal of power is its tremendous rotating speed. It drives the engine through a tiny pinion gear (attached to the starter's armature), which drives the very large flywheel ring gear at a greatly reduced speed. Another factor allowing it to produce so much power is that only intermittent operation is required of it. Thus, little allowance for air circulation is necessary, and the windings can be built into a very small space.

The starter solenoid is a magnetic device which employs the small current supplied by the start circuit of the ignition switch. This magnetic action moves a plunger which mechanically engages the starter and closes the heavy switch connecting it to the battery. The starting switch circuit usually consists of the starting switch contained within the ignition switch, a neutral safety switch or clutch pedal switch, and the wiring necessary to connect these in series with the starter solenoid or relay.

The pinion, a small gear, is mounted to a one way drive clutch. This clutch is splined to the starter armature shaft. When the ignition switch is moved to the **START** position, the solenoid plunger slides the pinion toward the flywheel ring gear via a collar and spring. If the teeth on the pinion and flywheel match properly, the pinion will engage the flywheel immediately. If the gear teeth butt one another, the spring will be compressed and will force the gears to mesh as soon as the starter turns far enough to allow them to do so. As the solenoid plunger reaches the end of its travel, it closes the contacts that connect the battery and starter, then the engine is cranked.

As soon as the engine starts, the flywheel ring gear begins turning fast enough to drive the pinion at an extremely high rate of speed. At this point, the one-way clutch begins allowing the pinion to spin faster than the starter shaft so that the starter will not operate at excessive speed. When the ignition switch is released from the starter position, the solenoid is de-energized, and a spring pulls the gear out of mesh interrupting the current flow to the starter.

Some starters employ a separate relay, mounted away from the starter, to switch the motor and solenoid current on and off. The relay replaces the solenoid electrical switch, but does not eliminate the need for a solenoid mounted on the starter used to mechanically engage the starter drive gears. The relay is used to reduce the amount of current the starting switch must carry.

Charging System

The automobile charging system provides electrical power for operation of the vehicle's ignition system, starting system and all electrical accessories. The battery serves as an electrical surge or storage tank, storing (in chemical form) the energy originally produced by the engine driven generator. The system also provides a means of regulating output to protect the battery from being overcharged and to avoid excessive voltage to the accessories.

The storage battery is a chemical device incorporating parallel lead plates in a tank containing a sulfuric acid/water solution. Adjacent plates are slightly dissimilar, and the chemical reaction of the two dissimilar plates produces electrical energy when the battery is connected to a load such as the starter motor. The chemical reaction is reversible, so that when the generator is producing a voltage (electrical pressure) greater than that produced by the battery, electricity is forced into the battery, and the battery is returned to its fully charged state.

Newer automobiles use alternating current generators or alternators, because they are more efficient, can be rotated at higher speeds, and have fewer brush problems. In an alternator, the field usually rotates while all the current produced passes only through the stator winding. The brushes bear against continuous slip rings. This causes the current produced to periodically reverse the direction of its flow. Diodes (electrical one way valves) block the flow of current from traveling in the wrong direction. A series of diodes is wired together to permit the alternating flow of the stator to be rectified back to 12 volts DC for use by the vehicle's electrical system.

The voltage regulating function is performed by a regulator. The regulator is often built in to the alternator; this system is termed an integrated or internal regulator.

Volkswagen Electrical System

GENERAL INFORMATION

The six-volt electrical system was standard on all Volkswagens through the 1966 models. Beginning with the 1967 models - August 1966 - the change was made to the 12-volt system.

The Volkswagen electrical system is fairly conventional, consisting of generator, starter, battery, ignition and lighting systems and electrical accessories. Most of the electrical equipment is supplied by Bosch, although VW also produces some of its own components. The output of the generator is, as in most systems, controlled by a voltage regulator. In case of belt failure or other generator problems, a warning light in the speedometer dial lights.

The starter motor produces about 1/2 horsepower and is of the overrunning-clutch type. It is actuated by the ignition key and incorporates a solenoid, which engages the pinion of the starter.

The electrical system of the Volkswagen is of the negative-ground type, the negative terminal of the battery being grounded. In most VW models, the battery is located under the right-hand side of the rear seat. In the Karmann Ghia and Transporter models it is in the engine compartment.

Generator

DESCRIPTION

Different types of generators have been used throughout the years and models. Refer to the Generator and Regulator Electrical Equipment Specifications Chart for details.

The generator warning light in the speedometer housing connects to the voltage regulator by means of terminals in the ignition switch. The warning lamp lights as soon as the ignition is turned **ON,** and goes out when the voltage of the generator approaches that of the battery. The warning lamp simply gives a yes-no answer to the question of whether the generator is charging or not. As such, it is potentially useful in detecting broken fan belts, because when a fan belt is broken,

the generator is no longer being turned and will not charge. In type 1 or 2 models, a broken belt means that the car must not be driven until a new belt is installed. With type 3 models the fan is mounted directly on the crankshaft and the car can be driven until the battery runs out of electricity.

The generator is equipped with ball bearings that are packed with special high-temperature grease. Lubrication of the generator is not necessary under normal conditions. However, if the unit has been disassembled and/or overhauled, it is necessary to provide new lubricant for the bearings. Under no circumstances should ordinary grease be used, for it will not hold up under operating conditions.

TESTING

No-Load Voltage
▶ **See Figure 1**

In testing the no-load voltage of the generator, the cable from terminal **B+** (51) at the regulator must first be disconnected. The positive lead of the voltmeter being used should be attached to terminal **B+** (51) of the regulator and the negative lead of the meter grounded. With the engine running, the speed should be increased gradually until the reading of the voltmeter reaches its highest reading. If the regulator is functioning properly, the high point of the no-load voltage should be _12v_ approximately 7.4 to 8.1 volts for the 6-volt system and 13.6 to 14.4 for the 12-volt system. When the engine is turned **OFF**, the needle of the voltmeter should drop from 6 volts (12 volts) to zero just before the engine stops.

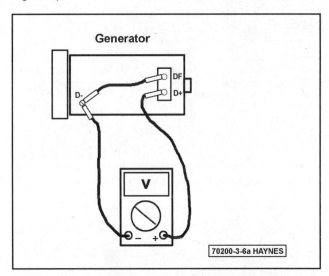

Fig. 1 Schematic for diagnosing the generator with a no-load test

Testing Without Regulator
▶ **See Figure 2**

The generator can be given a very quick check without the regulator. It is most important that the duration of the test be very brief (only a few seconds) in order that the generator field windings will not be overloaded during the test.

Disconnect the two leads from the generator. Connect terminal **DF** of the generator to ground. Connect the positive terminal of the voltmeter to terminal **D+** and the negative terminal to the generator ground. For 6 volt systems, approximately 6 volts should be generated at 1500

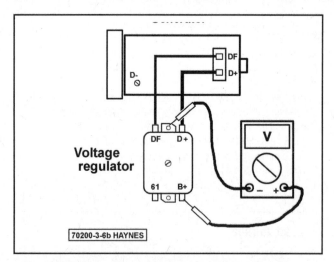

Fig. 2 Connect a voltmeter to the generator as shown to perform a generator test without the regulator

rpm and about 15 volts at 3000 rpm.

Installation of the regulator is the reverse of the preceding procedure, but it should be noted that the thicker cable (coming from the positive brush of the generator) must be attached at the regulator bottom to terminal **+** (D+). The thin cable coming from the generator field windings should be attached to the **F** (DF) terminal at the bottom of the regulator. If the replacement of the regulator does not correct a deficiency in the charging system, chances are that the generator itself is defective.

Inspecting the Brushes

The generator brushes should be examined periodically for wear. If they are worn to the point where they no longer extend from their holders, they should be replaced.

REMOVAL & INSTALLATION

▶ **See Figure 3**

Disconnect the negative battery cable and the leads from the regulator. Remove the air cleaner and the carburetor, then take off the fan belt. Remove the retaining strap from the generator. Remove the cooling air thermostat. Remove hot air hoses from the fan housing, take out the fan

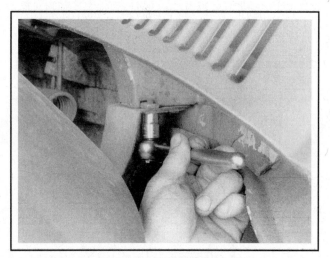

To remove the generator, first remove the deck lid . . .

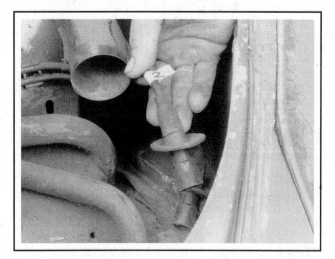

Detach all wiring from the fan housing, including the spark plug cables . . .

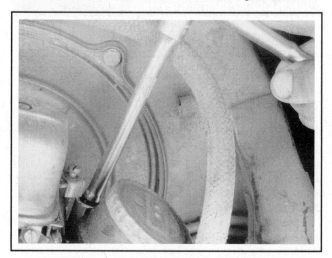

. . . then loosen the generator strap retaining bolt

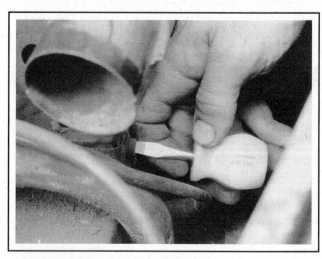

. . . and remove all fan housing to cylinder head cooling tin screws

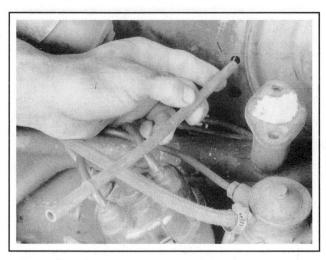

Remove the accelerator cable and guide tube from the fan housing

Lift the fan housing, generator and ignition coil off of the engine as a unit

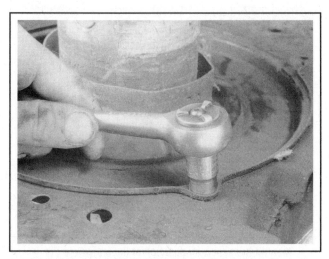

Once removed from the engine, remove the fan tin-to-housing bolts . . .

. . . and separate the generator from the fan housing

If the engine is removed from the car, remove the generator mounting strap adjusting bolt . . .

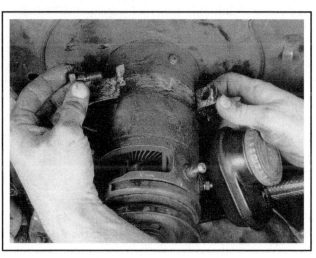

. . . then remove the generator mounting strap

Loosen the generator-to-fan housing bolts with a 10mm wrench . . .

. . . then remove the 4 bolts

Lift the generator out of the fan housing

The generator stand may now be removed from the engine - remove the 4 mounting nuts . . .

. . . then lift the generator stand off of the crankcase . .

. . . and remove the oil baffle - make sure to install the new one with the louvers pointing downward

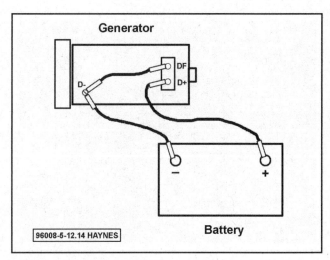

96008-5-12.14 HAYNES

Fig. 3 To polarize the generator, connect a 12-volt battery momentarily as shown

Older models use a voltage regulator (A) which is mounted on the generator housing (B)

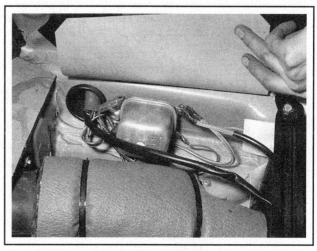

On later Beetle models the voltage regulator is mounted under the rear seat

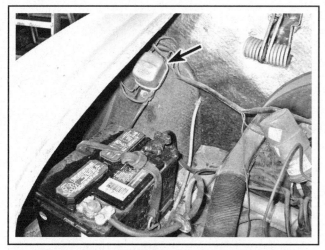

On Karmann Ghias, the voltage regulator is mounted in the left side of the engine compartment

housing screws and lift it off the housing. After removing the fan housing screws, the generator can be lifted off along with the fan.

Installation is the reverse of the removal procedure. If a new, rebuilt or used generator was installed, it must be polarized. To polarize the generator refer to the accompanying illustration.

✲✲ WARNING:

Connect the polarizing wires to the battery first, then momentarily touch them to the generator terminals. If you connect them to the battery, you will create a spark near the battery that could ignite the hydrogen gas created in the battery and cause an explosion.

Regulator

REMOVAL & INSTALLATION

Take off the connections from terminals **B+ (51)** and **61** at the regulator. Remove the screws and remove the regulator. Disconnect the electrical cables from the bottom of the regulator. These are marked **+** (D+) and **F** (DF).

To remove the regulator, detach the electrical wiring from it . . .

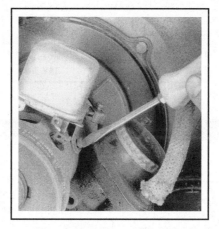

. . . then remove the mounting screws . . .

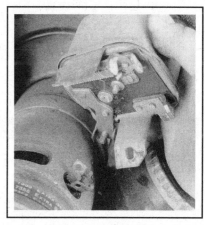

. . . and lift the regulator off of the generator

Electrical Specifications—Generator and Regulator

| Part Number | Generator | | | Regulator | | |
	Brush Spring Pressure (oz.)	Field Resistance (ohms.)	Max. Output	Part Number	Cut-in Voltage	Voltage Setting (No Load)
25 hp.-Bosch RED 130/6-2600 AL 16	16-21	1.20-1.32	NA	Bosch RS/G130/6/11 (on generator)	NA	7.3-8.6
36 hp. 1,200 cc. Bosch LJ/REF 160/-2500 L4	16-21	1.20-1.32	NA	Bosch RS/TA 160/6/Al (on generator)	5.5-6.3	7.3-8.6
36 hp. 1,200 cc. Bosch LJ/REF 160/6/2500 L17	16-21	1.20-1.32	NA	Bosch RS/TAA 160/6/1 (on generator)	6.4-6.7	7.4-8.1
40 hp. 1,200 cc. Bosch 111 903 021 G	16-21	1.20-1.32	270 WATTS	Bosch RS/TAA 180/6/A4	6.2-6.8	7.3-8.0
40 hp. 1,200 cc. -VW 113 903 021 C	16-21	1.20-1.32	270 WATTS	VW 113 903 801 C	6.4-6.7	7.4-8.1
Late 1,200 and 1,300 cc.-Bosch 113 903 021 H	16-21	1.20-1.32	NA	Bosch 113 903 801F	6.2-6.8	7.4-8.1
Late 1,200 and 1,300 cc.-VW 111 903 021 J	16-21	1.20-1.32	NA	VW 113 903 801G	6.4-6.7	7.4-8.1
Karmann Ghia 1,300 and Type 1 1,500-Bosch 131 903 021	16-21	NA	30 AMPS	Bosch 131 903 801	6.2-6.8	7.3-8.0
Bosch 450 M 12/3700-14 38A 32 (12 Volt)	16-21	NA	38 AMPS	Bosch UA 14 V 38A	12.5-13.2	13.5-14.5
Bosch E(L) 14V 38A 32, EG (R) 14V 38A 32 (12 Volt)	16-21	NA	38 AMPS	Bosch RS/VA 14V 38A	12.4-13.1	13.6-14.4
Bosch G(L) 14 V 30A 20	16-21	NA	30 AMPS	Bosch RS/VA 14V 30A	12.4-13.1	13.6-14.4

NA - Information not available.

Starter Motor

DESCRIPTION

The starter motor of the Volkswagen is of the sliding gear type and is rated at about 1/2 horsepower. The motor used in the starter is a series wound type and draws a heavy current in order to provide the high torque needed to crank the engine during starting. The starter cannot be switched on accidently while the engine is still running - the device responsible for this safeguard is a non-repeat switch in the ignition switch. If the engine should stall for any reason, the ignition key must be turned to the **OFF** position before it is possible to re-start the engine.

The starter is flange-mounted on the right-hand side of the transaxle housing. Attached to the starter motor housing is a solenoid which

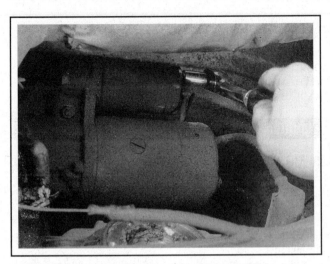

Before disconnecting the wiring from the starter motor, disconnect the negative battery cable

engages the pinion and connects the starting motor to the battery when the ignition key is turned **ON**. When the engine starts, and the key is released from the **START** position, the solenoid circuit is opened and the pinion is returned to its original position by the return spring. However, if for any reason the starter is not switched off immediately after the engine starts, a pinion freewheeling device stops the armature from being driven so that the starter will not be damaged.

REMOVAL & INSTALLATION

Disconnect the negative battery cable and remove it from terminal **30** and the lead from terminal **50** of the solenoid. After removal of the two retaining screws, the starter can be separated from the transaxle housing.

Prior to installation, the outboard bushing should be lubricated with special lithium grease, and sealing compound should be applied to the mating surfaces between the starter and the transaxle. After putting the long screw into the hole in the flange, locate the starter on the transaxle housing. Be sure that the cables are tightly connected to the terminals, and that the contact points between the cables and terminals are clean.

Electrical Specifications—Battery and Starter

Model	Battery Capacity (Amp Hours)	Volts	Grounded Terminal	Model	Starter Lock Test Amps	Volts	Torque (ft.lbs.)	No Load Test Amps	Volts	RPM
Type 1 up to Chassis No. 929745	70	6	Neg.	25, 36 hp. Bosch EED 0.4/6L/4	500	3.5	NA	80	5.5	5,400
Type 1 from Chassis No. 929746	66	6	Neg.	40 hp. 1,200cc. Bosch EEF 0.5/ 6L/1	450-520	3.5	8	60-80	5.5	5,500-7,300
Type 1 from Chassis No. 118000001 ①	36	12	Neg.	40 hp. 1,200 and 1,300cc.- VW 113 911 021 A	450-520	3.5	8	60-80	5.5	5,500-7,300
Type 2 up to Chassis No. 117901	84	6	Neg.	40 hp. 1,200 and 1,300 cc. -Bosch 113 911 021 B	450-520	3.5	8	60-80	5.5	5,500-7,300
Type 2 from chassis No.117902	77	6	Neg.	Bosch AL/EEF 0.8/12L1 (12 Volt)	250-285	6.0	6.5 8.2	38-45	12	6,400-7,900
Type 2 from chassis No.217000001	45	12	Neg.	1,500cc.- 111 911 021 G (12 Volt) ②	250-285	NA	NA	38-45	12	7,150
Type 3 from chassis No.0000001	77	6	Neg.	—	—	—	—	—	—	—
Type 3 from chassis No. 317000001	36	12	Neg.	—	—	—	—	—	—	—

① *Excluding VW 1,200, Type 1.*
② *Test figures for 6 Volt units on 1,500 cc. engines should be the same as for previous 6 volt units.*

NA - Not Available

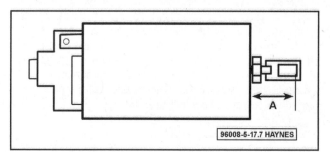

Fig. 4 When installing a new solenoid onto the starter motor, distance (A) should be 18.9 - 19.1mm

SOLENOID REPLACEMENT

▶ **See Figure 4**

Unthread the nut and remove the connector strip. Take out the two retaining screws on the mounting bracket and withdraw the solenoid after it has been unhooked from its actuating lever. When replacing a defective solenoid with a new one, care should be taken to ensure that the distance **A** in the accompanying diagram is 0.74 - 0.75 in. (18.9 - 19.1mm) when the magnet is drawn in. The actuating rod can be adjusted after loosening the locknut.

To remove the ignition coil, label all of the ignition coil wires . . .

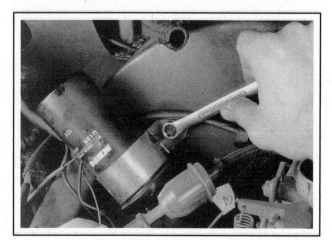

Using a 10mm wrench, remove the ignition coil bracket attaching bolts . . .

Installation of the solenoid is the reverse of the removal procedure. Be certain that the rubber seal on the starter mounting bracket is properly seated. A small strip of VW Sealing Compound D 14 should be placed on the outside of the switch. In order to facilitate engagement of the actuating rod, the pinion should be pulled out as far as possible when the solenoid is inserted.

Ignition Coil

REMOVAL & INSTALLATION

1 Disconnect the negative battery cable.
2 Label and detach the wiring from the ignition coil.
3 Remove the ignition coil bracket mounting bolts, then remove the ignition coil from the engine.
To install:
4 Situate the ignition coil on the engine in its original position, then install the ignition coil bracket mounting bolts. Tighten them until snug.
5 Attach the wiring to the ignition coil. Make certain to connect the wiring to the appropriate terminals of the ignition coil, otherwise the polarity of the ignition system will be reversed. Refer to Section 4 for the procedure to check the system for reversed polarity, if necessary.
6 Connect the negative battery cable.

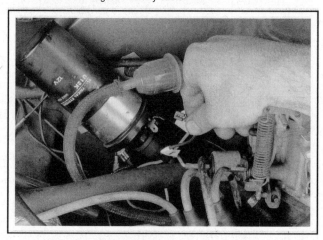

. . . then detach the wires from the coil terminals

. . . and lift the coil off of the fan housing

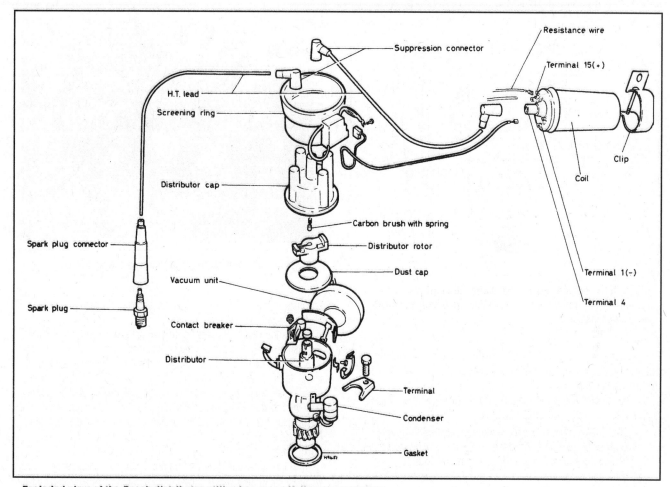

Exploded view of the Bosch distributor utilized on many Volkswagen engines

Distributor

GENERAL INFORMATION

▶ See Figure 5

The Volkswagen is equipped with a 6 or 12-volt battery-operated ignition system. The major parts of the system are the battery, coil, distributor, spark plugs and wiring. The job of the ignition system is to convert the 6 or 12 volts of the battery into voltage large enough to force a spark to jump across the 0.025-0.028 in. (0.6 - 0.7mm) gap of the spark plug.

The ignition coil has two circuits - a primary circuit and a secondary circuit. The primary circuit consists of heavy wire wrapped around the iron core of the coil, while the secondary circuit is made up of similar windings of fine wire. The separating of the contact points causes the current through the primary winding to cease, which in turn causes the magnetic field to collapse and induce a high-voltage surge to flow through the rotor to a spark plug. The condenser serves to help increase the surge in the circuit. Maintenance of the coil is limited to keeping the insulating cap clean and dry so that short circuits and carbon tracking do not occur.

The distributor is of the four-cam type, with a single set of breaker points. The distributor camshaft rotates at a speed of one-half that of the crankshaft. The fiber block of the moveable breaker point should be

lubricated periodically with lithium grease. In using the lubricant, care should be taken to ensure that no grease gets onto the contact points - only a small amount of grease should be used. The vacuum advance mechanism requires no maintenance, but should be checked periodically for leakage of the diaphragm. Sucking air from the vacuum tube should cause the interior of the distributor to rotate slightly. When air is sucked out and the tube blocked off, the interior plate of the distributor should not move from its advanced position until the air passage is opened.

The contact breaker points are adjusted as described in Section 2, and should have a clearance of 0.016 in. (0.41mm).

REMOVAL & INSTALLATION

▶ See Figure 6

1 Disconnect the negative battery cable.

2 Trace the No. 1 spark plug from the front right-hand cylinder (clinder No. 1) back to the distributor. Mark the position of the No. 1 cylinder spark plug cable terminal tower of the distributor cap on the distributor housing, so that when the cap is removed from the distributor the position of this terminal can be seen.

➡**Some distributors are equipped with a notch in the housing corresponding to the No. 1 cylinder terminal tower position, so a mark is not needed on these distributors.**

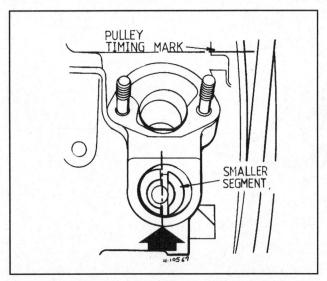

Fig. 6 If the engine was rotated while the distributor was removed, position the distributor shaft drive cam as shown for proper installation

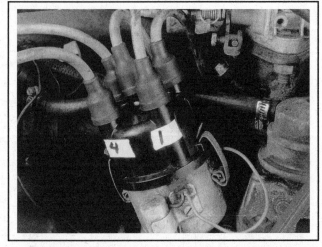

To remove the distributor, label the spark plug towers . . .

3   Label and disconnect all of the spark plug cables from the distributor cap. Disengage the retaining clamps and lift the cap off of the distributor housing.

4   Position the engine at Top Dead Center (TDC) on the compression stroke of the No. 1 cylinder, as follows:

   a   *Using a wrench on the drive belt pulley center bolt, turn the crankshaft until the TDC mark on the pulley is aligned with the timing mark on the engine (as explained in Section 2).*

   b   *Once the marks are aligned, look at the distributor rotor and determine if the contact end of the rotor is pointing toward the No. 1 terminal tower mark on the distributor housing. If the contact end of the rotor is aligned with the mark, the engine is at TDC, otherwise the crankshaft should be rotated an additional complete revolution (360 degrees) until the TDC pulley mark aligns with the engine timing mark again.*

5   Matchmark the distributor housing with the engine block. Now the rotor-to-distributor housing and the distributor-to-engine relationships are marked for installation.

6   If equipped, label and disconnect the vacuum hose from the advance mechanism on the distributor. Label and detach the breaker point lead wire from the ignition coil.

7   Remove the distributor hold-down bracket nut or bolt, then lift the distributor up and out of the engine block.

8   Before doing anything else, look down into the distributor hole and note the orientation of the distributor drive slot. Note that the two areas separated by the drive slot are not equal: one is smaller in size than the other. Marking the direction of the slot on the engine block will greatly help installation if the crankshaft is turned while the distributor is removed.

To install:

9   If the crankshaft position was not disturbed (rotated or removed) while the distributor was removed, skip to Step 10, otherwise perform the following. Look down into the distributor hole and rotate the crankshaft until the drive slot is oriented in the same direction as indicated in Step 8. Once again, make sure that the small and large halves of the drive gear are positioned correctly.

10 Align the rotor and the No. 1 cylinder mark on the distributor housing, then slide the distributor into the engine block with the distributor-to-engine matchmarks also aligned. The distributor should slide completely into the engine block. If it does not, slightly turn the distributor rotor from side-to-side until the distributor settles completely into the engine. If the rotor requires a 180 degree rotation before

. . . and detach the spark plug wires from the cap

Unfasten the retaining clamps, then lift the distributor cap off of the distributor housing . . .

. . . and matchmark the rotor tip to the housing

Matchmark the distributor housing to the crankcase for proper positioning during installation

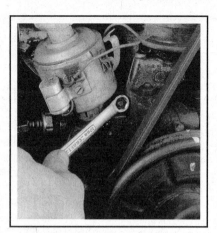

Loosen the distributor retaining clamp nut . . .

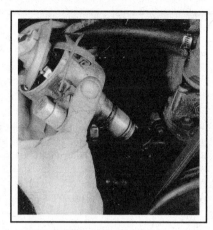

. . . then lift the distributor out of the engine

the distributor will settle completely into the engine, the distributor should be removed and the crankshaft turned 360 degrees. The distributor should now fit into the engine correctly.

11 Install and tighten the hold-down nut or bolt and tighten it securely.

12 Attach the vacuum advance hose to the distributor.

13 Set the distributor cap onto the distributor housing and secure it in place with the two hold-down clamps.

14 Attach the spark plug cables to the distributor cap.

15 Attach the breaker point lead to the ignition coil.

16 Connect the negative battery cable.

17 Adjust the ignition timing as described in Section 2 of this manual.

DRIVE PINION REPLACEMENT

To remove the distributor driveshaft, loosen the distributor clamp bolt, turn the engine so that the rotor is pointing to the No. 1 cylinder (the notch on the distributor housing), lift out the distributor. Remove the fuel pump and the intermediate flange, gaskets, and fuel pump pushrod. Remove the distance spring on the distributor drive shaft. Be sure that the No. 1 cylinder is at its firing point, and withdraw the driveshaft via a removal tool by pulling with the extractor and turning the driveshaft to the left at the same time.

Remove the washer(s) under the driveshaft, being careful not to drop a washer into the crankcase. When the engine is installed, a mag-

net is handy for removing these washers.

When installing, the reverse of the previous procedure applies. The fuel pump pushrod drive eccentric and the pinion teeth should be checked for wear. If the teeth are badly worn, the teeth on the crankshaft should also be examined. Check the washer under the driveshaft for wear and replace them, if necessary. Position the No. 1 cylinder at its firing point and insert the distributor driveshaft.

The slot in the top of the distributor driveshaft has an offset slot which divides the top of the driveshaft into two unequal segments.

The driveshaft is installed as follows:

Engine	Distributor Driveshaft Installation (No. 1 Cylinder in Firing Position)
Type 1 and 2 (except early 1968 models with throttle positioner)	Slot at right angles to crankcase split, small segment toward the crankshaft pulley.
Type 3	Slot at about 60-degrees to crankcase split, small segment toward oil cooler.

Insert the distance spring, install the distributor, set the ignition timing, and install the fuel pump.

➡**When the engine has been completely disassembled, it is necessary that the oil pump, the fan housing, the fan, and the crankshaft pulley be installed before the distributor drive shaft is inserted.**

ENGINE MECHANICAL

Engine Design

GENERAL INFORMATION

The Volkswagen engine's flat four (opposing) design has proven itself in automotive, industrial and aerial applications as one of the most rugged and reliable made in the world today. The four-cycle, overhead valve engine has two pairs of cylinders horizontally opposed; it is attached to the transmission case by four bolts, and is easily removed for service.

The engine in the smaller (beetle) Volkswagens is capable of 60 hp. output, while that used in the larger (Fastback and Squareback) cars is

rated at 65 hp. on the SAE scale. Both engines are of the same basic design as that of the original prototypes but are much more highly developed.

Because it is air-cooled, the VW engine is slightly noisier than a water-cooled power-plant of the same size due to the lack of a water jacket to provide a silencing function. In addition, air-cooled engines tend to be somewhat noisier because of clearances between parts. Higher operating temperatures of air-cooled engines require more room for expansion of parts. However, noise in the Volkswagen is damped by good insulation and the little that is present should serve to remind the Volkswagen driver that he has one of the most reliable and trouble-free engines made anywhere, anytime.

Type 1 and 2 (Upright) Engine

The engines used in the type 1 and type 2 vehicles are known as "upright" engines, because of the configuration of the cooling system tins. Since the cooling fan, on these engines, is mounted on the generator shaft, the cooling system sheet metal is arranged in an upright fashion (most of it is above the engine and stands taller than the carburetor and generator).

➡**Although the pancake and upright engines differ in the arrangement of their cooling systems, the engine block, the internal components and many of the external engine components are the same.**

Type 3 (Suitcase) Engine

The engine in the type 3 (Fastback and Squareback) series is similar to the type 1 and 2 engines, the main exception being the location of the cooling fan on the crankshaft rather than on the generator shaft. With the type 3 engine, there is no chance of cooling fan failure due to fan belt breakage, because there is no fan belt. If the generator belt should fail, the driver could drive some distance in daylight before running out of electricity for the ignition. In addition, the type 3 engine is slightly different in the location of the oil cooler and, of course, in the layout of the cooling ductwork.

Engine Overhaul Tips

Most engine overhaul procedures are fairly standard. In addition to specific parts replacement procedures and specifications for your individual engine, this section is also a guide to acceptable rebuilding procedures. Examples of standard rebuilding practice are given and should be used along with specific details concerning your particular engine.

Competent and accurate machine shop services will ensure maximum performance, reliability and engine life. In most instances it is more profitable for the do-it-yourself mechanic to remove, clean and inspect the component, buy the necessary parts and deliver these to a shop for actual machine work.

On the other hand, much of the rebuilding work (crankshaft, block, bearings, piston rods, and other components) is well within the scope of the do-it-yourself mechanic's tools and abilities. You will have to decide for yourself the depth of involvement you desire in an engine repair or rebuild.

TOOLS

The tools required for an engine overhaul or parts replacement will depend on the depth of your involvement. With a few exceptions, they will be the tools found in a mechanic's tool kit (see Section 1 of this manual). More in-depth work will require some or all of the following:
  • A dial indicator (reading in thousandths) mounted on a universal base
  • Micrometers and telescope gauges
  • Jaw and screw-type pullers
  • Scraper
  • Valve spring compressor
  • Ring groove cleaner
  • Piston ring expander and compressor
  • Ridge reamer
  • Cylinder hone or glaze breaker
  • Plastigage
  • Engine stand

The use of most of these tools is illustrated in this chapter. Many can be rented for a one-time use from a local parts jobber or tool supply house specializing in automotive work.

Occasionally, the use of special tools is called for. See the information on Special Tools and the Safety Notice in the front of this book before substituting another tool.

INSPECTION TECHNIQUES

Procedures and specifications are given in this chapter for inspecting, cleaning and assessing the wear limits of most major components. Other procedures such as Magnaflux and Zyglo can be used to locate material flaws and stress cracks. Magnaflux is a magnetic process applicable only to ferrous materials. The Zyglo process coats the material with a fluorescent dye penetrant and can be used on any material.

Checking for suspected surface cracks can be more readily made using spot check dye. The dye is sprayed onto the suspected area, wiped off and the area sprayed with a developer. Cracks will show up brightly.

OVERHAUL TIPS

Aluminum has become extremely popular for use in engines, due to its low weight. Observe the following precautions when handling aluminum parts:
  • Never hot tank aluminum parts (the caustic hot tank solution will eat the aluminum.
  • Remove all aluminum parts (identification tag, etc.) from engine parts prior to the tanking.
  • Always coat threads lightly with engine oil or anti-seize compounds before installation, to prevent seizure.
  • Never overtorque bolts or spark plugs especially in aluminum threads.

Stripped threads in any component can be repaired using any of several commercial repair kits (Heli-Coil, Microdot, Keenserts, etc.).

When assembling the engine, any parts that will be exposed to frictional contact must be prelubed to provide lubrication at initial start-up. Any product specifically formulated for this purpose can be used, but engine oil is not recommended as a prelube in most cases.

When semi-permanent (locked, but removable) installation of bolts or nuts is desired, threads should be cleaned and coated with Loctite or another similar, commercial non-hardening sealant.

REPAIRING DAMAGED THREADS

Several methods of repairing damaged threads are available. Heli-Coil (shown here), Keenserts and Microdot are among the most widely used. All involve basically the same principle - drilling out stripped threads, tapping the hole and installing a prewound insert - making welding, plugging and oversize fasteners unnecessary.

Two types of thread repair inserts are usually supplied: a standard type for most inch coarse, inch fine, metric course and metric fine thread sizes and a spark lug type to fit most spark plug port sizes. Consult the individual tool manufacturer's catalog to determine exact applications. Typical thread repair kits will contain a selection of prewound threaded inserts, a tap (corresponding to the outside diameter threads of the insert) and an installation tool. Spark plug inserts usually differ because they require a tap equipped with pilot threads and a combined reamer/tap section. Most manufacturers also supply blister-packed thread repair inserts separately in addition to a master kit containing a variety of taps and inserts plus installation tools.

Before attempting to repair a threaded hole, remove any snapped, broken or damaged bolts or studs. Penetrating oil can be used to free

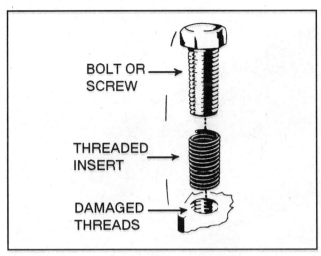

Damaged bolt hole threads can be replaced with thread repair inserts

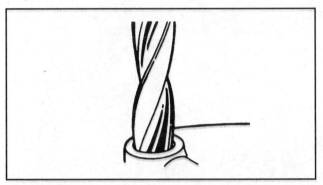

Drill out the damaged threads with the specified size bit. Be sure to drill completely through the hole or to the bottom of a blind hole

frozen threads. The offending item can usually be removed with locking pliers or using a screw/stud extractor. After the hole is clear, the thread can be repaired, as shown in the series of accompanying illustrations and in the kit manufacturer's instructions.

Engine Components

DESCRIPTION

Crankcase

The crankshaft of all Volkswagen engines is mounted in a two-piece crankcase. The halves of the crankcase are machined to very close tolerances, and should be replaced only in pairs. When fitting them, it is necessary to coat the mating surfaces only with sealing compound and tighten down to the correct torque - no gasket is used.

Crankshaft

The crankshaft rests in four main bearings, and is heat-treated at all bearing points. The main bearings are of light alloy and are lead coated. The end-thrust of the crankshaft is taken up by the No. 1 main bearing (as seen from the clutch). No. 2 main bearing is of the split type - the other 3 bearings are of the one-piece type. In the engine of the beetle, the generator-fan pulley is bolted onto the crankshaft, while in the type 3 "suitcase" engine, the cooling fan is attached directly to the crankshaft. The clutch side of the crankshaft is provided with an oil seal, the

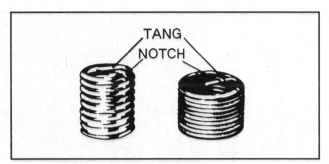

Standard thread repair insert (left), and spark plug thread insert

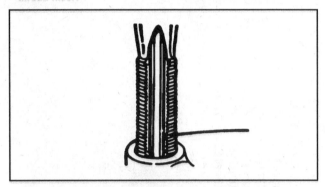

Using the kit, tap the hole in order to receive the thread insert. Keep the tap well oiled and back it out frequently to avoid clogging the threads

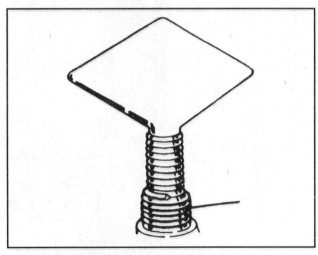

Screw the insert onto the installer tool until the tang engages the slot. Thread the insert into the hole until it is 1/4 - 1/2 turn below the top surface, then remove the tool and break off the tang using a punch

fan side with an oil thrower and oil return thread. Drive gears for the camshaft and the distributor are secured to the crankshaft by means of woodruff keys.

Pistons and Cylinders

The four pistons are made of light alloy and have three rings: two compression and one oil-scraping. Each piston is provided with a fully-floating piston pin secured by means of circlips. The cylinders in the Volkswagen engine are interchangeable, and can be easily replaced along with their corresponding pistons. Fins on the cylinders ensure efficient cooling of the engine.

COMMON ENGINE COMPONENTS – TYPE 1 AND 2 ENGINES

1. Fan housing
2. Cylinder head
3. Heater air hose
4. Exhaust crossover pipe
5. Breather hose
6. Regulator
7. Oil fill/generator stand
8. Rear engine cover plate
9. Engine case
10. Fuel pump
11. Generator
12. Carburetor
13. Air cleaner
14. Ignition coil
15. Pre-heated air hose
16. Vacuum advance canister
17. Distributor
18. Oil pump (located behind the crankshaft pulley)
19. Crankshaft pulley

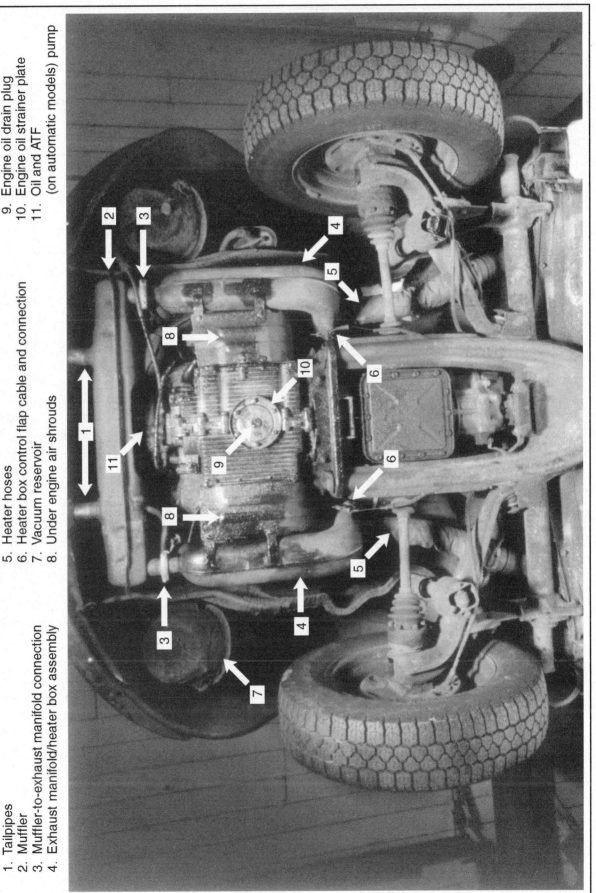

ENGINE COMPONENTS – UNDERSIDE OF VEHICLE

1. Tailpipes
2. Muffler
3. Muffler-to-exhaust manifold connection
4. Exhaust manifold/heater box assembly
5. Heater hoses
6. Heater box control flap cable and connection
7. Vacuum reservoir
8. Under engine air shrouds
9. Engine oil drain plug
10. Engine oil strainer plate
11. Oil and ATF (on automatic models) pump

General Engine Specifications

Engine Code ①	CC Displacement (cu. in.)	Carburetor	Developed Horsepower (SAE) @ rpm	Developed Torque (ft. lbs.) @ rpm	Bore x Stroke (in.)	Compression Ratio	Normal Oil Pressure (P.S.I.) @ 2,500 rpm
—	1,131 (69.02)	Single barrel downdraft	25@ 3,300	51@ 2,000	2.953 x 2.520	5.8:1	42 ⑤
A	1,192 (72.74)	Single barrel downdraft	36@ 3,700	60@ 2,400	3.03 x 2.52	6.6:1	42 ⑤
D	1,192 (72.74)	Single barrel downdraft	41.5@ 3,900	65@ 2,400	3.03 x 2.52	7.0:1	42 ⑤
F	1,285 (78.4)	Single barrel downdraft	50@ 4,600	69@ 2,600	3.03 x 2.72	7.3:1	42 ⑤
H	1,493 (91.1)	Single barrel downdraft	53@ 4,200	78@ 2,600	3.27 x 2.72	7.5:1	42 ⑤
B	1,584 (96.6)	Single barrel downdraft	57@ 4,400	113@ 3,000 ②	3.36 x 2.72	7.5:1 ③	42 ⑤
G	1,493 (91.1)	Single barrel downdraft	51@ 4,000	74@ 2,600	3.27 x 2.72	7.8:1	42 ⑤
K	1,493 (91.1)	Single barrel downdraft	54@ 4,200	84@ 2,800	3.27 x 2.72	7.8:1 ④	42 ⑤
R	1,493 (91.1)	Two single barrel downdraft	66@ 4,800	84@ 3,000	3.27 x 2.72	8.5:1	42 ⑤
T	1,584 (96.6)	Two single barrel downdraft	65@ 4,600	87@ 2,800	3.36 x 2.72	7.5:1	42 ⑤
U	1,584 (96.6)	Electronic fuel injection	65@ 4,600	87@ 2,800	3.36 x 2.72	7.7:1	42 ⑤
AD, AE	1,584 (96.6)	Single barrel downdraft	60@ 4,400	81.6@ 3,000	3.36 x 2.72	7.5:1	42 ⑤

① See Engine Identification Chart in Chapter 1 for explanation of codes.
② Type 2 - 82@ 3,000
③ Type 2 - 7.7:1
④ To July 1965; 7.5:1 from August 1965.
⑤ Minimum - 28@ 2,500 rpm, 7@ idle rpm.

Torque Specifications—Engine

Fastener	Thread Size	Torque (ft. lbs.)
All Engines		
1-Nuts for crankcase halves	M12x1.5	25 ①
2-Screws and nuts for crankcase halves	M8	14
3-Cylinder head nuts ②	M10	23
4-Rocker shaft nuts	M8	14-18
5-Flywheel gland nut	M 28x1.5	217
6-Connecting rod bolts and nuts	M9x1	22-25 ④
7-Special nut for fan	M12x1.5	40-47
8-Generator pulley nut	M12x1.5	40-47
9-Crankshaft pulley bolt	M20x1.5	29-36
10-Spark plugs	M14x1.25	22-29
11-Oil drain plug	M14x1.5	25
12-Clutch to flywheel	M8x1.5	18
13-Self-locking nuts for engine carrier to the crankcase	M8	18 ⑤
14-Nuts for oil pump	M8	14
15-Cap nut for oil filter cover	M6	5
16-Nuts for engine mounting	M10	22
17-Screws for converter to drive plate	M8	18
25 and 36 hp. - exceptions		
1-Nuts for crankcase halves	M10	22
3-Cylinder head nuts ② ③	M10	26-27
11-Oil drain plug	M18x1.5	22-29
13-Insert for spark plug	M18x1.5	50-54
Type 3 - exceptions		
8-Generator pulley nut	M12x1.5	40-47
9-Special bolt for fan and crankshaft pulley	M20x1.5	94-108
17-Screws for converter to drive plate	M8	14
19-Self locking nuts for engine carrier to body	M8	18 ⑤

① For cap nuts: 18 ft. lbs.

② Tightening sequences are given in Chapter 4.

③ As above from August 1959.

④ Contact surfaces oiled.
1,300 cc. and earlier
- 28 - 36 ft. lbs.

⑤ Renew.

Engine Rebuilding Specifications—Valves

Engine	Seat Angle Deg.	Valve Seat Width (in.)		Spring Pressure (lbs. @ in.)	Stem (in.) Diameter		Stem to Guide Rock (in.)		Valve Guide Removeable
		Intake	Exhaust		Intake	Exhaust	Intake	Exhaust	
25 hp., 36 hp., A engine - Type 1, and Type 2 engine before May, 1959	45	.05 -.09	.05- .09	73.5± 3.7@ 1.1	.2739- .2736	.2736- .2732	.011- .012	.011- .012	With Special Equipment
All Later Engines	45	.05- .09	.05- :09	①	.3130- .3126	.3118- .3114	.008- .009	.011- .012	With Special Equipment

① Engine Code | To Engine No. | Spring Pressure
G	0627578	96.4± 6.6 @
K, R, T	0663330	1.32 in.
D	6805938 (type 2)	102.0± 5.0 @
	6850939 (type 1)	1.35 in.
K	0042987	

Engines with progressively wound springs   126.0± 8.8 @ 1.22 in.

NOTE: Cylinder head combustion chamber volumes are are as follows:

Engine	Volume (cc.)
A	45.5 - 47.0
D	43.0 - 45.0
F	44.0 - 46.0
All 1,500 and 1,600 cc.	48.0 - 50.0

Engine Rebuilding Specifications—Pistons, Cylinders and Rings

Engine	Cylinders — Cylinder Diameter (mm)									Pistons — Piston Diameter (mm)									Wrist Pin ② Diameter (in.)		Rings — Side Clearance (in.)			End Gap (in.)	
	Std			1st O/S			2nd O/S			Std			1st O/S			2nd O/S			No Mark	Green	Top	2nd	Oil Scraper	Top 2nd	Oil Scraper
	B	P	G	B	P	G	B	P	G	B	P	G	B	P	G	B	P	G							
1,131, 1,200, and 1,300 cc.	76.99	77.00	77.01	77.49	77.50	77.51	77.99	78.00	78.01	76.95	76.96	76.97	77.45	77.46	77.47	77.95	77.96	77.97	19.996-20.00①	20.001-20.004 ①	.002-.0027	.002-.0027	.001-.002	.012-.018	.010-.016
1,500 cc.	82.99	83.00	83.01	83.49	83.50	83.51	83.99	84.00	84.01	82.96	82.96	82.97	83.45	83.46	83.47	83.95	83.96	83.97	21.996-22.000	22.001-22.004	.0027-.0035	.002-.0027	.001-.002	.012-.018	.010-.016
1,600 cc.	85.49	85.50	85.51	85.99	86.00	86.01	86.49	86.50	86.51	85.45	85.46	85.47	85.95	85.96	85.97	86.45	86.46	86.47	21.996-22.000	22.001-22.004	.0027-.0035	.002-.0027	.001-.002	.012-.018	.010-.016

O/S - Oversize

Color coding of cylinders and matching pistons: B - blue
P - pink
G - green

① Pin diameter given applies to 1,131 and 1,200 cc. engines only. Pins for the 1,300 cc. engine are the same as for the 1,500 and 1,600.

② Pin should be light push fit in piston. Piston pin to connecting rod clearance: .0004-.001 in. - maximum -.002 in.

Engine Rebuilding Specifications—Crankshaft

Engine	Main Bearing Journals (in.)												Connecting Rod Journals (in.)						Max. Journal Out-of-Round (in.)
	Journal Diameter								Oil Clearance		Shaft End-Play	Thrust On No.	Journal Diameter				Oil Clearance	End-Play	
	Journal 1, 2, 3				Journal 4				Journal 1, 2, 3	Journal 4			Std.	1st U/S	2nd U/S	3rd U/S			
	Std.	1st U/S	2nd U/S	3rd U/S	Std.	1st U/S	2nd U/S	3rd U/S											
36 hp, A engine -type 1, and Type 2 Engine before May, 1959 ③	1.9681, 1.9675	1.9583, 1.9577	1.9484, 1.9478	1.9386, 1.9380	1.5748, 1.5742	1.5650, 1.5643	1.5551, 1.5545	1.5453, 1.5446	.002-.004	.002-.004	.0027-.005	1 (at flywheel)	1.9861, 1.9675	1.9583. 1.9577	1.9484, 1.9478	1.9386, 1.9380	.0008-.0024	.0067-.016	.001
All later engines ①	2.1648, 2.1642	2.1551, 2.1544	2.1453, 2.1445	2.1353, 2.1347	1.5748, 1.5742	1.5650, 1.5643	1.5551, 1.5545	1.5452, 1.5446	②	.002-.004	.0027-.005	1 (at flywheel)	2.1650, 2.1645	2.1553, 2.1544	2.1455, 2.1448	2.1355, 2.1350	.0008-.003 ④	.004-.016	.001

NOTE: The crankshaft of type 1/1,200 cc, engines may be reground only twice.

U/S - undersize

① Including modified 36 hp. type 2 engine from May, 1959 (chassis 469477, engine 3400000)

② Bearings No. 1 and 3 from August, 1965: .0016 - .004 in.
Bearings No. 1, 2, 3: to engine 3520332: .0016 - .0035 in. ① to engine 3472699: .001 - .0035 in. ①
Steel backed bearing No. 2 from August, 1965 and all other steel backed bearings (used in cold countries): .001 - .0035 in.

③ Also 25 hp.

④ All 1,500 and 1,600 cc : .0008 in.

Cylinder Heads

Each pair of cylinders shares a detachable cylinder head made of light alloy casting. The cylinder head contains the overhead valves of both cylinders, and is also provided with cooling fins to further improve cooling efficiency. Shrunk-in valve guides and inserts are used. No. gasket is used between the cylinders and the cylinder head on 1963 and later engines.

Connecting Rods

The four connecting rods are steel forgings and have lead-bronze bearings at the crankshaft end, while the piston pin ends are equipped with bronze bushes. The connecting rod caps are held to the rods by bolts which screw directly into the lower caps, eliminating the need for separate bolt nuts.

Camshaft

Beginning with the 1966 model year, Volkswagen engines were equipped with camshafts running in three replaceable steel-backed bearings. Prior to this time, the camshaft ran in three bearings which were built into the crankcase. Because of the four-cylinder horizontally-opposed design of the engine, each of the four camlobes drives two valves, one on each side of the crankshaft. It is necessary to separate the crankcase halves in order to replace the camshaft, which is driven from the crankshaft by means of helical gears. The end-thrust of the camshaft is taken up by a special shoulder on the left-hand side of the crankcase.

Valves

The overhead valves are operated by pushrods and rocker arms actuated by flat base camshaft followers.

Cooling System

The air cooling system includes an oil cooler situated directly in the path of the cooling air. The presence of the oil cooler helps the Volkswagen engine to protect itself against excessively high temperatures of the internal engine parts served by the lubricating oil. The cooling fan moves a very large quantity of air in performing its very important function. For example, the cooling fan of a typical type 3 moves approximately 20 cubic feet of air each second when operating at 4000 engine rpm. When operating at cruising speed, the fan forces the equivalent of a roomful of cooling air through the engine each minute. This flow is regulated by a thermostat in order to ensure a quick warm-up, as well as efficient high-speed cooling.

Engine

REMOVAL & INSTALLATION

The Volkswagen engine is mounted on the transaxle, which in turn is attached to the frame. In Type 1 models, there are four attaching points - two bolts and two studs - -while on the type 3 there is an extra mounting point at the rear of the engine. Type 3 vehicles with automatic transaxles have front and rear engine and transaxle mounts. At the front, the gearbox is supported by the rear tubular crossmember; at the rear, a crossmember is bolted to the crankcase and mounted to the body at either end. When removing the engine from the car, it is recommended that the rear of the car be approximately three feet off the ground. The engine is removed by bringing it out from underneath the car. However, before raising the car, the following steps should be followed:

1 Disconnect the negative cable from the battery and the cables from the generator. Disconnect the wiring from the regulator on type 1 models.

2 Remove the air cleaner from the engine, and the rear engine cover plate on type 1 models. Remove the throttle positioner.

3 Rotate the distributor (type 1 models) so that this part will be able to clear the rear cover plate.

➡**On 1967 and later models, the rear cover plate need not be removed, since the redesigned rear deck and compartment allow sufficient room for engine withdrawal from the car.**

4 Disconnect the throttle cable from the carburetor(s), and remove the electrical connections from the automatic choke, coil, electromagnetic cut-off jet, and oil pressure sending unit.

5 Disconnect the fuel hose at the front engine cover plate and seal it to prevent leakage.

6 On type 3 models, remove the oil dipstick and the rubber boot between the oil filler and body.

7 Remove the cooling air intake bellows on type 3 models after loosening the clip that secures the unit.

8 Remove the warm air hose on type 3 models.

9 After disconnecting the appropriate electrical and control cables, remove the rear engine support (type 3 models) and raise the car off the ground.

10 After removing the flexible air hoses between the engine and heat exchangers, disconnect the heater flap cables, unscrew the two lower engine mounting nuts and slide a jack under the engine. Be sure that it is suitable for supporting the weight of the engine without placing undue strain on the components.

11 On type 1 automatic stick-shift models, disconnect the control valve cable and manifold vacuum hoses. Disconnect the ATF suction line and plug it with a 16\#29>1.5mm cap.

12 On type 3 fully automatic models, disconnect the vacuum hose and kickdown cable.

13 On either model, remove the four 8mm bolts from the converter drive plate through the holes in the transaxle case. After removing the engine, hold the torque converter in place on the transaxle with a strap or a plastic wire tie.

14 On fuel injected type 3 models, the fuel pressure and return lines must be clamped off and disconnected, and the injection unit wiring disconnected.

15 Raise the jack until it just contacts the engine, and have an assistant hold the bolts of the two upper engine mounts so that you will be able to unscrew the nuts. If an assistant is not available at this stage, it is possible to wedge sockets into the proper places so that one man can do the job without having four hands.

16 When the engine mounts are disconnected and there are no remaining cables or controls linking the engine with the car, roll the engine backwards slightly so that the release plate will be able to clear the main drive shaft.

17 Lower the engine very slowly, and be sure that the clutch release plate does not contact the main drive shaft of the transmission.

To install:

18 Roughly speaking, engine installation is the reverse of the preceding operation, although it is important that some special precautions be taken:

• Before replacing the engine, the clutch plate must be centered, the clutch release bearing and release plate checked for wear, and a number of components greased or cleaned.

• The starter shaft bush should be lubricated with lithium grease, the needle bearing in the gland nut supplied with 1 gram of universal grease, and the main drive shaft splines lubricated with molydenum-disulphide powder applied with a clean cloth or brush.

The VW upright engine is compact and easy to remove as a complete unit

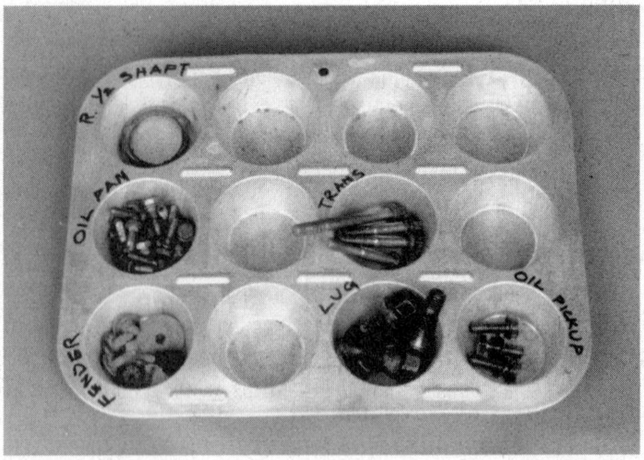

When removing nuts, bolts and other parts, place them in a tray or other container

• Before installing the engine, care must also be taken to ensure that the mating surfaces of the engine and transaxle are cleaned thoroughly.

19 The engine is then lifted into position and the engine rotated via the generator pulley so that the clutch plate hub will engage the transaxle shaft splines. In pushing the engine home, care must be taken to see that the gland nut needle bearing, clutch release bearing, and main drive shaft are not damaged.

20 After the engine is in position, put the lower engine mounting bolts through the holes in the flange of the transaxle case and press the engine against the flange so that proper and even contact is made.

21 Tighten the upper nuts first, then the lower ones. After this initial tightening, tighten all nuts evenly in this same sequence.

22 To avoid interference with the function of the automatic stick-shift clutch, take care to route the connecting hoses so that they are not kinked or jammed when installing the engine. This applies particularly to the small diameter pipe from the control valve to the carburetor venturi, which will work properly only if routed in the original production manner.

23 On the type 3 reinstallation, synthetic washers are used to raise the engine about 2 - 3mm when the rear engine mounting is attached and tightened. Use only enough washers in the rear mount so that the engine is lifted no more than 3mm when the mounting is tightened down. Care should be used when installing the rear air intake housing bellows of the type 3 engine, for this unit can be easily damaged through careless handling.

24 Reconnect cables and controls. Attach the thick lead to terminal D+ of the generator.

25 Adjust the accelerator cable with the engine at full throttle, and set the ignition timing.

DISASSEMBLY & ASSEMBLY

⁂ CAUTION:

The EPA warns that prolonged contact with used engine oil may cause a number of skin disorders, including cancer! You should make every effort to minimize your exposure to used engine oil. Protective gloves should be worn when changing the oil. Wash your hands and any other exposed skin areas as soon as possible after exposure to used engine oil. Soap and water, or waterless hand cleaner should be used.

The disassembly of the type 3 engine is different from that of the other VW engines mainly in the removal of the engine cover plates and cooling ductwork. In tearing down a Volkswagen engine, the following is the recommended sequence of operations:

1 Drain the engine oil.
2 Remove the hoses between the engine and the heat exchangers.
3 Remove the front engine cover plate.
4 Remove the muffler and the intake manifold, including the carburetor(s).
5 Remove the fan belt, the cooling air intake housing, the generator and the crankshaft pulley.
6 Remove the rear half of the fan housing, the fan, and the front half of the fan housing.
7 Remove the distributor and the fuel pump and take out the distributor drive pinion.
8 Remove the cooling air ductwork from the cylinder area.
9 Remove the oil cooler.
10 Remove the rocker arm shaft and the cylinder heads.
11 Remove the cylinders and pistons.
12 Remove the clutch assembly and flywheel.
13 Remove the oil pump and oil strainer.
14 Disassemble the crankcase and remove the camshaft, the crankshaft and the connecting rods.

Assembly, generally speaking, is the reverse of the foregoing procedure. Detailed Removal and installation instructions follow.

➡The torque, capacity, tune-up, and clearance figures given in the text apply, generally, to the most common engines. However, since there are so many variations in production, it is always best to consult the applicable chart for the figure in question.

Cylinder Head

REMOVAL & INSTALLATION

➧ **See Figure 7**

⁂ CAUTION:

The EPA warns that prolonged contact with used engine oil may cause a number of skin disorders, including cancer! You should make every effort to minimize your exposure to used engine

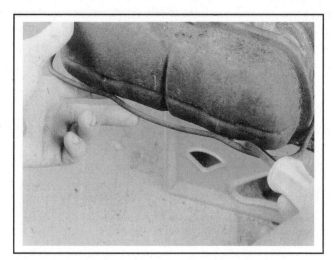

To remove the cylinder head, first pry the retaining wire down and off of the cover . . .

. . . then remove the rocker arm cover from the cylinder head

oil. Protective gloves should be worn when changing the oil. Wash your hands and any other exposed skin areas as soon as possible after exposure to used engine oil. Soap and water, or waterless hand cleaner should be used.

In order to remove the cylinder head of either pair of cylinders, it is first necessary that the rocker arm and shaft assembly be removed. The cylinder head is held in place by eight studs. Since the cylinder head also holds the cylinders in place in the VW engine, if it is not desired that the cylinders be removed, they should be held in place with an appropriate holding clamp. After the rocker arm cover, the rocker arm retaining nuts and rocker arm and shaft assembly have been removed, the cylinder head nuts can be removed and the cylinder head lifted off.

When reinstalling the cylinder head, several points must be remembered. The cylinder head should be checked for cracks both in the combustion chamber and in the intake and exhaust ports. Cracked cylinder heads should be replaced. Spark plug threads should be checked at this time for tightness. If the threads are stripped, they can be corrected by means of Heli-coil threaded inserts. On 1963 and later engines, no gasket is necessary between the cylinder head and the cylinders. However, on earlier models, which do not have a fresh air heating system, a

Make sure to discard the old gasket - a new gasket will be needed upon assembly

gasket should be fitted. New seals should be used on the pushrod tube ends, and should be checked for proper seating.

The pushrod tubes should be turned so that the seam faces

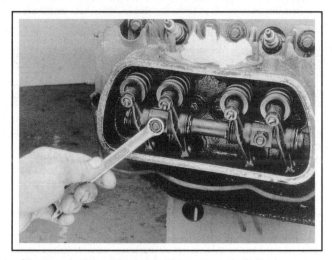

Slowly and alternately remove the rocker arm shaft mounting nuts . . .

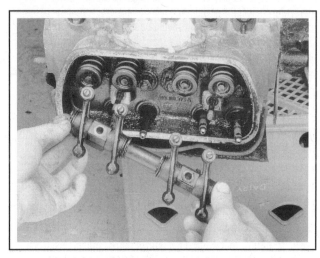

. . . then remove the shaft from the cylinder head

Once the rocker arm shaft is removed, the pushrods can be pulled out of their tubes

Loosen the cylinder head nuts . . .

. . . and slowly slide the cylinder head off of the mounting studs

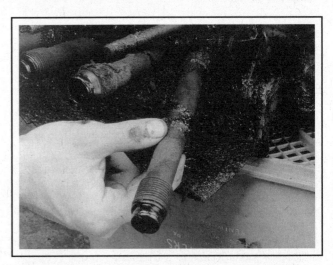

Remove the pushrod tubes from either the cylinder head or the crankcase

upwards. In order to ensure perfect sealing, used tubes should be stretched to the correct length of 190 - 191mm before they are installed. (Note: in the 40 hp engine, the correct length is 180.5 - 181.5mm. On the 40 hp engine, the sealing ring between the outer shoulder of the cylinder and the cylinder head should be renewed, placing the slotted side of the ring toward the cylinder head. On the 50 hp engine of 1966 and subsequent engines, no sealing ring is needed.)

After inserting the cylinder head nut washers, the cylinder head nuts

should be tightened slightly, then to a torque of 7 ft. lbs. before fully tightening them to the value of 23 ft. lbs. (27 ft. lbs. in 1959 and earlier models). The sequences of tightening shown in the accompanying diagram should be followed. (Note the different sequences for the initial and final tightening procedures.)

Cylinders

❊❊ CAUTION:

The EPA warns that prolonged contact with used engine oil may cause a number of skin disorders, including cancer! You should make every effort to minimize your exposure to used engine oil. Protective gloves should be worn when changing the oil. Wash your hands and any other exposed skin areas as soon as possible after exposure to used engine oil. Soap and water, or waterless hand cleaner should be used.

Before removing the cylinders, the cylinder head, valve pushrods, pushrod tubes, and deflector plate below the cylinders must be removed. The cylinders may then be pulled off.

Reinstall the cylinders as follows:

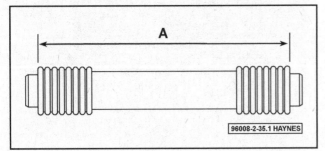

96008-2-35.1 HAYNES

Fig. 7 Before installing the pushrod tubes, make sure that distance (A) is 7.48 - 7.52 in. (190 - 191mm) to ensure enough compression for sealing

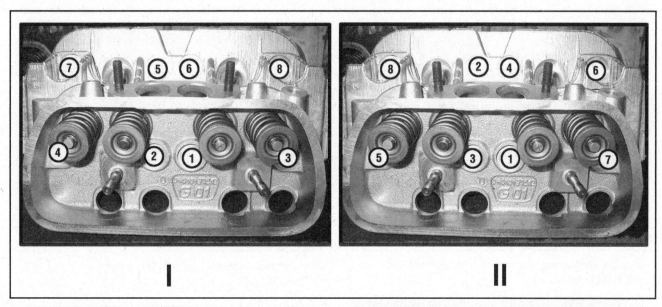

I

II

To install the cylinder heads, first tighten the cylinder head nuts to 7 ft. lbs. (following sequence I), then tighten the nuts to 15 ft. lbs. (following sequence II) and finally to 23 ft. lbs. (also sequence II)

Cylinders should be checked for wear, and if necessary replaced with another matched cylinder and piston assembly of the same size. Also check the cylinder seating surface on the crankcase, cylinder shoulder, and gasket, for cleanliness. Foreign matter here could cause leaks due to distortion of the mating parts. When reinstalling the cylinders, a new gasket should be used between each cylinder and the crankcase.

The piston rings, and piston pin should be liberally oiled (a MoS_2 based lubricant is suitable). Compress the rings with a compression tool. Be sure that ring gaps are adequate and staggered on the piston with the oil ring inserted into the cylinder so that its gap is positioned UP when the pistons are in their horizontal position in the engine.

Lubricate the cylinder wall and slide the cylinder over the piston. Crankcase studs should not contact the cylinder cooling fins. Install the deflector plates under the cylinders, bending slightly if necessary to make them seat tightly on the cylinder head studs.

Install the pushrod tubes and pushrods, ensuring that the tubes are inserted with the seam facing upwards and are of the proper length.

Make certain to tighten the cylinder heads to the proper value with a torque wrench

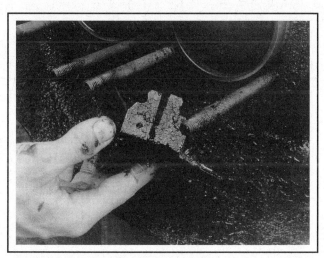

To remove the cylinders, slide the cooling air shield out from between the lower, middle two studs

Slide the cylinder jug off of the mounting studs and the piston

To remove the pistons, first remove the circlip from both ends of the piston pin bore . . .

Pistons

REMOVAL & INSTALLATION

Following the removal of the cylinder head and the cylinder, the pistons should be marked with a number (cylinder number) and an arrow (pointing to the clutch side of engine) if they are to be reinstalled in the engine. The pistons are removed as follows:

Using piston circlip pliers, remove the circlips used to retain the piston wrist pin. Heat the piston to 80-degreesC. (176-degreesF.), remove the piston pin and take the piston off the end of the connecting rod. If it is necessary to remove the piston rings, use piston ring pliers in order to avoid damage.

Install the piston as follows: First, clean the piston and the ring grooves, taking care to see that the ring grooves are not scratched or otherwise damaged. The piston should then be checked for wear and, if necessary, replaced by one of corresponding size and weight. Weight between pistons must not be greater than 10 grams. If the running clearance between the piston and cylinder is 0.2mm (0.008 in.) or more, the piston and cylinder should be replaced by a set of the same size grading. If, however, the cylinder of a worn or damaged piston shows no signs of wear, it is permissible to install a new piston of

. . . then slide the wrist pin out of the piston and connecting rod

Remove the piston from the connecting rod

appropriate size. See accompanying diagram for piston markings.

After making a decision concerning the piston to be used, select piston rings of the correct size. After the ring has been inserted in the cylinder and pushed down about 0.2 in. by the piston, check the gap

Use a ring expander tool to remove the piston rings

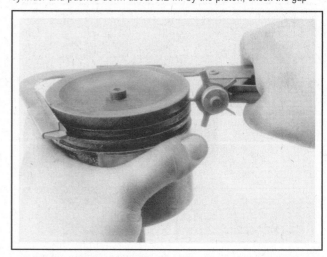

Clean the piston grooves using a ring groove cleaner

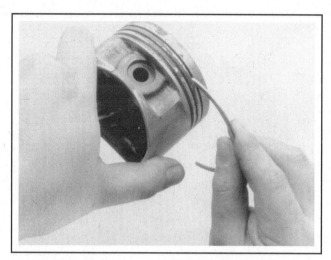

You can use a piece of an old ring to clean the piston grooves, BUT be careful, the ring is sharp

Measure the piston's outer diameter using a micrometer

Checking the ring-to-ring groove clearance

Checking piston ring end gap

with a feeler gauge. After using a piston ring tool to install the rings, check the side-clearance of the rings in their grooves with a feeler gauge. Ring side-clearance and end-gap should be as specified in the

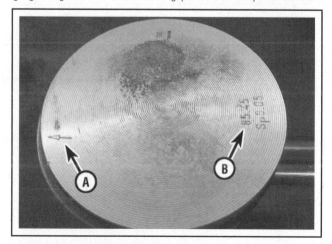

Piston crown markings (typical, may differ by model, year, and part manufacturer). The arrow must face the flywheel end of the engine when installed

Engine Rebuilding Specifications Chart for Pistons, Cylinders, and Rings in this section.

Because the compression rings are slightly tapered, they should be installed with the marking "Top" or "Oben" toward the top of the piston. Insert the piston pin circlip which faces toward the flywheel. Because piston pin holes are offset, make sure that the arrow (or word "vorn") points toward the flywheel. This offset is to help accommodate thrust loads which amplify and lead to objectionable piston slap.

Check and fit the piston pin. The pin may be found to be a light finger-push fit in the piston, even when the piston is cold. However, this condition is normal, even to the extent of the pin sliding out of the piston under its own weight. Clearance between the piston pin and the connecting rod bushing should be as specified in the Engine Rebuilding Specifications Chart. If the clearance is near the wear limit, renew the piston pin and the rod bushing. It is not advisable to install an oversize pin in this case. In all cases where the pin is not a light finger push fit in the cold piston, heat the piston in oil to about 176-degreesF. Insert the second circlip and make sure that the circlips fit perfectly in their grooves. A good barometer in deciding whether or not a new cylinder and piston should be installed is oil consumption. If the engine uses more than one quart of oil each 600 miles, it is quite likely that the engine is in need of reconditioning.

Align the main bearing shell with the dowel

Crankcase

DISASSEMBLY & ASSEMBLY

※ WARNING:

The EPA warns that prolonged contact with used engine oil may cause a number of skin disorders, including cancer! You should make every effort to minimize your exposure to used engine oil. Protective gloves should be worn when changing the oil. Wash your hands and any other exposed skin areas as soon as possible after exposure to used engine oil. Soap and water, or waterless hand cleaner should be used.

With the cylinders, pistons, and other outer parts removed, the crankcase is split as follows:

1 Remove the oil strainer, oil pressure switch, and crankcase nuts.

2 Keep the cam followers of the right crankcase half in position by using the retaining springs.

3 Use a rubber hammer to break the seal between the crankcase halves. Under no circumstances insert sharp tools, wedges, etc. between the crankcase halves, for this will lead to damage of the engine case mounting surfaces, which will cause oil leakage when reassembled.

4 After the seal between the mating surfaces has been broken, remove the righthand crankcase half, the crankshaft oil seal and camshaft end plug, and lift out the camshaft and the crankshaft.

5 Remove the camshaft followers, bearing shells and oil pressure relief valve.

Assembly is generally the reverse of the foregoing procedure, but includes the following:

6 Before reassembling the crankcase, check it for damage and cracks after thorough cleaning. Mating and sealing surfaces should be cleaned especially well. A solvent should be used to remove traces of the old sealant from mating surfaces.

7 Flush and blow out all ducts and oil passages.

8 Check the oil suction pipe for leaks.

9 Check the studs for tightness. If the tapped holes are worn, correction involves the installation of Helicoil inserts.

10 Insert the camshaft followers after checking both the followers and their bores in the crankcase.

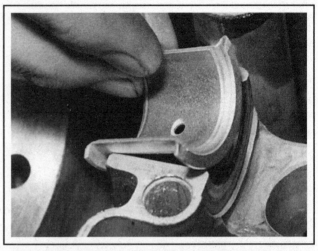

The camshaft thrust bearing (with flanges) fits in the crankcase at the end opposite from the flywheel

11 Install crankshaft bearing dowel pins and bearing shells for the crankshaft and camshaft.

12 Install the crankshaft and camshaft after the bearings have been well lubricated. (When installing the crankshaft, note the position of the timing marks on the timing gears.)

13 Install the camshaft end plug, using a sealing compound.

14 Install the thrust washers and the crankshaft oil seal. The oil seal must rest squarely on the bottom of its recess in the crankcase.

15 Check and install the oil pressure switch.

16 Spread a thin film of sealing compound on the crankcase joining faces. Use care so that no sealing compound enters the oil passages of the crankshaft or the camshaft bearings.

17 Keep the camshaft followers of the right crankcase half in place by using retaining springs.

18 Join the crankcase halves and evenly tighten the fasteners to the torque specified in the Engine Torque Specifications Chart.

➡**First tighten the 8mm nut which is beside the 12mm stud of the No. 1 crankshaft bearing. Only then should the 12mm nuts be tightened fully.**

19 Turn the crankshaft to check for ease of movement, and check the end-play of the crankshaft. The crankshaft end-play is measured with the engine assembled and the flywheel installed.

Tighten this nut first

Camshaft

REMOVAL & INSTALLATION

❊❊ CAUTION:

The EPA warns that prolonged contact with used engine oil may cause a number of skin disorders, including cancer! You should make every effort to minimize your exposure to used engine oil. Protective gloves should be worn when changing the oil. Wash your hands and any other exposed skin areas as soon as possible after exposure to used engine oil. Soap and water, or waterless hand cleaner should be used.

Removal of the camshaft requires that the crankcase be split. The camshaft and camshaft bearing shells are then easily removed.

Before reinstalling the camshaft, it should be checked for wear of the bearing faces and bearing points. In addition, the riveted joint between the camshaft timing gear and the camshaft should be examined for security. If there is slight damage to the camshaft, it may be smoothed with a silicon carbide oilstone. A 100 - 120 grit stone is first used to smooth the damaged area, then a 280 - 320 stone may be used for final polishing. The camshaft should be checked for run-out, which should not exceed 0.0008 in. (0.02mm). The timing gear should be checked for correct tooth contact and for wear, and the edges of the camshaft bearing bores lightly chamfered to avoid seizure. If the camshaft shells removed are either worn or damaged, new shells should be installed. The camshaft bearing shells should be installed with the tabs engaging the notches in the crankcase. Before installing the camshaft, the bearing journals and camshaft lobes should be generously coated with oil. When the camshaft is installed, care should be taken to ensure that the timing gear tooth marked "O," or with a punch mark, is located between the two teeth of the crankshaft timing gear marked by a center punch. The end-play at the thrust bearing (bearing number 3) should be 0.0024 - 0.0043 in. (0.06 - 0.11mm) and the wear limit is 0.006 in. (0.14mm).

Crankshaft and Connecting Rods

❊❊ CAUTION:

The EPA warns that prolonged contact with used engine oil may cause a number of skin disorders, including cancer! You should make every effort to minimize your exposure to used engine oil. Protective gloves should be worn when changing the oil. Wash your hands and any other exposed skin areas as soon as possible after exposure to used engine oil. Soap and water, or waterless hand cleaner should be used.

Removal of the crankshaft requires the removal of the cylinder heads, cylinders, pistons, the splitting of the crankcase halves, and the withdrawal of the camshaft. When installing the crankshaft, check to see that the crankcase does not have sharp edges at points of junction. If foreign matter has become lodged in the main bearings, it will be necessary to remove it with a scraper, taking care not to remove material from the bearing shell itself. Check the dowel pins for tightness. Place one half of the No. 2 crankshaft bearing in the crankcase. Slide on crankshaft bearing No. 1 so that the dowel pin hole is toward the flywheel. Install the crankshaft, making sure that the dowel pins are correctly seated in the crankshaft bearings. When installing the camshaft, note the marks on the timing gears.

The marks on the teeth must mesh like this

After the crankshaft has been removed and clamped into position, remove the connecting rod clamping bolts and the connecting rods and caps.

When installing, check the connecting rods for external damage and for weight. The difference in weight of the connecting rods in an engine must not be in excess of 0.35 oz. (10g) in order that proper engine balance can be maintained. If necessary, metal should be removed from the heavier connecting rods at the points indicated on the accompanying illustration.

Inspect the piston pin bushing. With a new bushing, the correct clearance is indicated by a light finger push fit of the pin at room temperature. Check and, if necessary, correct the connecting rod alignment. Reinsert the connecting rod bearing shells after all parts have been thoroughly cleaned and the connecting rods have been assembled onto the crankshaft. The identification numbers stamped on the connecting rods and bearing caps must both be on one side.

Crankshaft components

1	Crankshaft	9	Main bearing No. 3
2	Woodruff key	10	Nut for connecting
3	Oil slinger		rod bolt (8)
4	Main bearing No. 4	11	Connecting rod
5	Circlip	12	Casting mark (must
6	Distributor drive gear		face UP when the rod
7	Spacer		is pointing toward its
8	Crankshaft gear		cylinder)

➥**New connecting rod screws should always be used, and the wax removed from the screws before they are installed.**

Tighten the connecting rod bolts to the specified torque. A slight pretension between the bearing halves, which is likely to occur when tightening connecting rod bolts, can be eliminated by light hammer taps. The connecting rods, lubricated with engine oil prior to assembly, must slide on the crank pin by their own weight. The connecting rod bushings must not be scraped, reamed or filed during assembly. Using a peening chisel, secure the connecting rod bolts in place.

CRANKSHAFT END-PLAY INSPECTION

With the engine installed, the crankshaft end-play can be read with a dial indicator mounted at the pulley side of the engine. End-play should be as specified with an upper wear limit of 0.006 in. (0.15mm). When the engine is not installed, crankshaft end-play can be measured at the flywheel end with an indicator mounted on the flywheel. Desirable end-play is obtained by adding or subtracting shims at the outer end of the main bearings. Shims for this purpose are available in various thicknesses. Never use more than three shims. Install the paper or metal gasket, or the oil seal, depending on your model-year endine.

Flywheel

REMOVAL & INSTALLATION

The flywheel is attached to the crankshaft with a gland nut, and is located by 4 dowels. Some models have a paper gasket between the flywheel and the crankshaft; others have a metal gasket. Beginning with the 1967 model year, a metal sealing gasket is no longer present between the flywheel and crankshaft. An oil seal is recessed in the crankcase casting the No. 1 main bearing. A needle bearing, which supports the main drive shaft, is located in the gland nut. Prior to removing the flywheel, it is necessary to remove the clutch pressure plate and the clutch driven plate. Loosen the gland nut and remove it, using a 36mm socket, a long breaker bar and a flywheel retainer. Remove the guide plate of the special wrench. Remove the gland nut and withdraw the flywheel.

Installation is the reverse of the foregoing procedure, plus the following: check flywheel teeth for wear and damage. Check the dowel

Three shims are used to control crankshaft endplay

holes in the flywheel and the crankshaft and renew the dowels, if necessary. Adjust the crankshaft end-play and check the needle bearing in the gland nut for wear. Lubricate the needle bearing with about 1 gram of universal grease. Insert the flywheel gasket, if one is used in the engine. (Note: to minimize engine imbalance, the crankshaft, flywheel, and clutch are marked at their heaviest points. Upon assembly, be sure that the marks on these units are offset by 120-degrees. If but two of these parts are marked, the marks should be offset by 180-degrees. Tighten the flywheel gland nut to 217 ft. lbs. torque and check flywheel run-out, which should be a maximum of 0.012 in. (0.3mm).

Crankshaft Oil Seal

✷✷ CAUTION:

The EPA warns that prolonged contact with used engine oil may cause a number of skin disorders, including cancer! You should make every effort to minimize your exposure to used engine oil. Protective gloves should be worn when changing the oil. Wash your hands and any other exposed skin areas as soon as possible after exposure to used engine oil. Soap and water, or waterless hand cleaner should be used.

A length of angle iron and two of the clutch pressure plate bolts can be used to immobilize the flywheel

The flywheel gland nut houses a set of needle bearings (arrow) for the transaxle input shaft

REMOVAL & INSTALLATION

Oil losses at the flywheel could well be the result of a leaky crankshaft oil seal. This seal is removed after removing the flywheel. After the flywheel is removed, inspect the surface on the flywheel joining flange where the oil seal makes contact. Remove old oil seal by prying it out of its counterbore. Before installing new crankshaft oil seal, clean the crankcase oil seal recess and coat it thinly with sealing compound. The sharp edges should be slightly chamfered so that the outer edge of the seal is not damaged. Using VW tool 204b, press in the new seal, being sure that it rests squarely on the bottom of its recess. Remove the tool and reinstall the flywheel after coating the oil seal contact surface with oil.

VALVE SYSTEM

Rocker Arm and Shaft

REMOVAL & INSTALLATION

Before the valve rocker assembly can be reached, it is necessary to undo the clip that retains the cover plate. Prior to removing the cover plate, however, it is advisable to dust off and clean the cylinder head and cover plate; this will prevent dirt from entering the assembly.

Remove the cover plate after taking off the retaining clip with a prytool. Remove the rocker arm retaining nuts, the rocker arm shaft and the rocker arms. Remove the stud seals.

Before installing the rocker arm mechanism, be sure that the parts are as clean as possible, including the inside of the cover plate. Install the stud seals and the rocker shaft, making sure that the chamfered edges of the supports are pointing outward and the slots, upward. Tighten the retaining nuts to a torque of 14 - 18 ft. lbs. The only type of retaining nuts which should be used are 8mm nuts of the 8G grade.

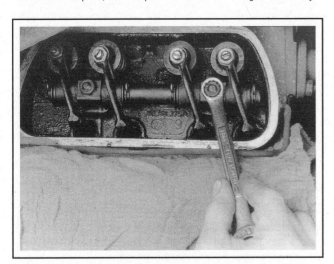

After removing the rocker arm cover, slowly and alternately remove the rocker arm shaft nuts . . .

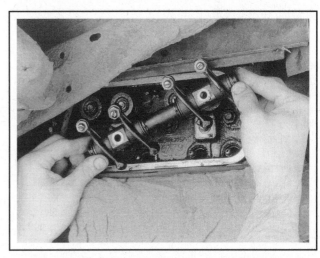

. . . then lift the rocker arm shaft off of the mounting studs

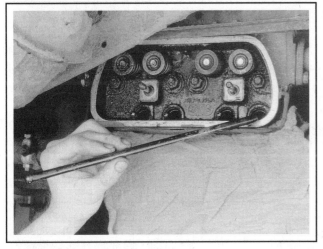

At this point the pushrods can be removed from the pushrod tubes

Install the rocker arm assemblies with the slots (A) facing UP and the chamfered edges (B) facing out

These nuts are distinguishable by their copper color. Ball ends of the pushrods must be centered in the sockets of the rocker arms. In addition, to help the valves rotate during operation, the rocker arm adjusting screws should contact the tip of the valve slightly off center. After adjusting valves to their proper clearance, reinstall the cover plate with a new gasket. Be sure that the proper cover plate gasket is used. There are two types of gaskets, early and late. The late type is straight across the top edge, while the early type has a tab in the center of the top edge. After the engine has been run for a brief period, check the cover plates for oil leakage.

DISASSEMBLY AND ASSEMBLY

Remove the spring clips from the rocker arm shaft. Remove the washers, rocker arms, and bearing supports. Before installation, check the rocker arm shaft, the seats, and ball sockets (of the rocker arm adjusting screws), for wear. Loosen the adjusting screws before installing the rocker arms. Otherwise, installation is the reverse of the disassembly procedure.

Valves

REMOVAL & INSTALLATION

In order to remove the valves, the cylinder head must first be removed. With the cylinder head removed, compress the valve springs with a special tool and remove the valve keys, valve spring caps, valve springs, and oil deflector rings. Remove the valves from the cylinder head after removing any burrs that may be present near the seating surface of the keys on the valve stem. While the valve springs are out, they should be tested. Proper valve spring pressures are given in the Engine Rebuilding Specifications Chart for Valves. Valve keys should be checked prior to installation, and new and worn keys ground at the joining faces until it is still possible to turn the valve when the key halves are pressed together. Valve stems should be checked for run-out and valve guides for wear. Because exhaust valves generally do heavy-duty work in the air-cooled engine of a Volkswagen, it is good practice to replace them since their cost is not great and the cylinder head is already dismantled. If the stems of the valves are hammered in,

When disassembling the rocker arm shafts, lay the parts out in order of removal to avoid confusion

A small plastic bag, with an appropriate label, can be used to store the valve train components so they can be kept together and reinstalled in the original position

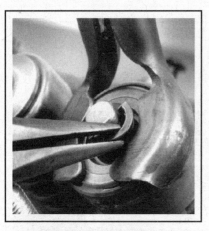

Compress the spring until the keepers can be removed with a small magnetic screwdriver or needle-nose pliers

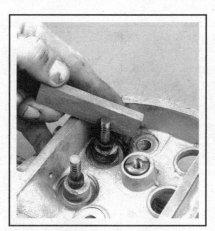

If the valve binds in the guide when trying to remove it, deburr the area around the tip with a fine file or whetstone

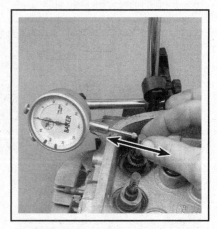

A dial indicator can be used to determine the valve stem-to-guide clearance - move the valve stem as indicated by the arrows

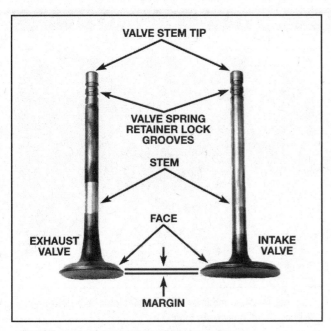

Check for valve wear at the points shown here

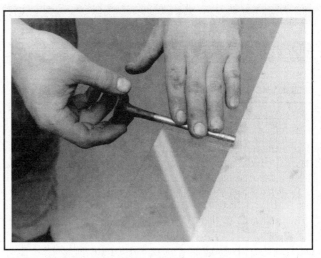

Valve stems may be rolled on a flat surface to check for bends

the valves can still be used again after valve caps have been installed. Polish rough valve stems carefully with emery cloth. After coating the valve stems with a moly paste, insert them into their guides and fit oil deflector rings. Install valve springs with the close-wound coils facing the cylinder head. Used valves must be refaced before being reinstalled. Damaged seats must also be reconditioned.

ADJUSTMENT

Valve clearances must be adjusted with the engine **cold**, and adjustment is carried out in accordance with the method described in Section 2.

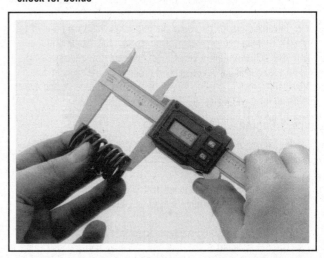

Use a caliper gauge to check the valve spring free-length

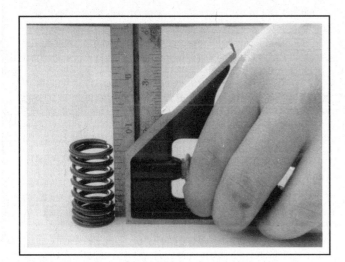

Check the valve spring for squareness on a flat service; a carpenter's square can be used

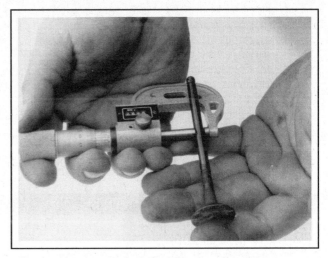

Use a micrometer to check the valve stem diameter

COOLING SYSTEM

Fan Housing

REMOVAL & INSTALLATION

1 Remove the two heater hoses and the generator strap.
2 Pull out the lead wire of the ignition coil.
3 Remove the distributor cap and take off the spark plug connectors.
4 Remove the retaining screws on both sides of the fan housing.
5 Remove the outer half of the generator pulley and remove the fan belt.
6 Remove the thermostat securing screw and take out the thermostat.
7 Remove the lower part of the carburetor preheater duct.
8 The fan housing can now be removed with the generator. After removal, check the fan housing for damage and for loose air-deflector plates. Accumulated dirt should be removed at this time.
9 Installation is the reverse of the removal sequence, and involves installation of fan housing flap assemblies, and the insertion of the thermostat actuating rod in the cylinder head and lower fan housing. It is necessary that the fan housing fit properly on the cylinder cover plates so that loss of cooling air will be avoided. In order to achieve proper fit, the cover plates may have to be bent slightly.

Type 3 Engine

The removal of the fan housing on the type 3 engine is accomplished in a slightly different manner due to the layout of the cooling system of this engine.

1· Remove the crankshaft pulley, rear fan housing half and fan.
S0>Unhook the linkage and the spring at the right-hand air control flap.
2 Remove the attaching screws of the front half of the fan housing.
3 Prior to installation, the front half of the fan housing should be checked for damage.

To install:

4 Install the front half of the fan housing, ensuring correct sealing with the cylinder cover plates.
5 Replace and tighten the two lower mounting screws slightly.
6 Turn the two halves of the fan housing to the left until the left crankcase half is contacted by the front lug.
7 Tighten fully the two lower mounting screws.
8 Loosen the nuts at the breather support until it can be moved.
9 Insert and tighten the mounting screws of the upper fan housing half.
10 Tighten the breather support nuts fully. Connect the linkage and spring to the right-hand air control flap.
11 Install the fan and rear half of the fan housing.

Cooling Fan

REMOVAL & INSTALLATION

Type 1 and 2 Engines

Using a T-wrench, remove the four retaining screws on the fan cover. Remove the generator and fan. While holding fan from rotating, unscrew the fan retaining nut and take off the fan, spacer washers, and hub.

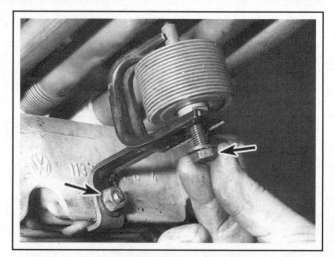

The thermostat is mounted on a bracket under the right-hand cylinder head on upright engines

Installation of the fan is as follows: place the hub on the generator shaft, making sure that the woodruff key is securely positioned. Insert the spacer washers. (Note: the distance between the fan and the fan cover should be between 0.06 - 0.07 in. (1.5 - 1.8mm). Place the fan into position and tighten its retaining nut with a torque wrench and socket to 40 - 47 ft. lbs. Check the distance from the fan to the cover. Correct spacing is achieved by inserting the proper number of spacer washers between the hub and the thrust washer. When only one washer is used, the other two should be positioned between the lockwasher and the fan. Insert the generator in the fan housing and tighten the retaining screws on the fan housing cover. (With 1967 and more recent models, be sure that the cooling air intake slot is at the bottom when the retaining plate is screwed onto the fan housing.)

Type 3 Engine

Fan removal begins with the removal of the crankshaft pulley, coil, and the rear half of the fan housing. The fan can then be removed.

During installation of the fan, check the condition of the oil return thread on the fan hub, and install the rear half of the fan housing, coil and crankshaft pulley.

Crankshaft Pulley

REMOVAL & INSTALLATION

Type 1 and 2 Engines

The crankshaft pulley can be removed while the engine is still in the car. However, in this instance it is necessary for the rear cover plate of the engine to be removed. Remove the cover plate after taking out the screws in the cover plate below the crankshaft pulley. Remove the fan belt, and crankshaft pulley securing screw. Using a puller tool, remove the crankshaft pulley. The crankshaft pulley should be checked for proper seating and for proper belt contact surface. The oil return thread should be cleaned and lubricated with a molybdenum-disulphide based oil. The crankshaft pulley should be installed in the reverse sequence, and should have no run-out.

Type 3 Engine

The crankshaft pulley can be removed only when the engine is out of the car and the muffler, generator, and cooling air intake housing are removed. After these parts have been removed, take out the plastic cap from the pulley. This can be done easily with a prytool. Remove the crankshaft pulley retaining bolt and remove the pulley.

Installation is the reverse of the foregoing but the following should be noted:

• When installing use a new paper gasket between the fan and the crankshaft pulley. If shims are used, do not forget them. No more than two shims may be used.

• When inserting the pulley, make sure that the pin engages the hole in the fan.

• The crankshaft pulley retaining bolt should be tightened to a torque of 94 - 108 ft. lbs.

• Ensure that the clearance between the generator belt and the intake housing is at least 0.16 in. (4mm) and that the belt is parallel to the housing.

• Check the seal on the cooling air intake housing and if damaged, cement a new seal into place.

LUBRICATING SYSTEM

Oil Strainer

REMOVAL & INSTALLATION

✳✳ WARNING:

The EPA warns that prolonged contact with used engine oil may cause a number of skin disorders, including cancer! You should make every effort to minimize your exposure to used engine oil. Protective gloves should be worn when changing the oil. Wash your hands and any other exposed skin areas as soon as possible after exposure to used engine oil. Soap and water, or waterless hand cleaner should be used.

All Volkswagen models are equipped with the same type of oil strainer. The oil strainer can be easily removed simply by removing the restraining nuts, washers, oil strainer plate, strainer and gaskets. Once taken out, the strainer must be thoroughly cleaned and all traces of old gaskets removed prior to fitting new ones. The suction pipe should be checked for tightness and proper position. When the strainer is installed, be sure that the suction pipe is correctly seated in the strainer. If necessary, the strainer may be bent slightly. The measurement from the strainer flange to the tip of the suction pipe should be 0.35 - 0.43 in. (9 - 11mm). The measurement from the flange to the bottom of the strainer should be 0.20 - 0.28 in. (5 - 7mm). The cap nuts at the bottom of the strainer should not be overtightened, for the bottom plate may become distorted and lead to leakage of engine lubricant. If it is desired, the strainer can be equipped with a permanent magnet designed to retain metal particles that are circulating in the oil. This magnet is held in place by means of a spring clip, and should be removed and cleaned whenever the strainer is removed for the same purpose. Magnetic drain plugs are also available.

Oil Cooler

REMOVAL & INSTALLATION

✳✳ CAUTION:

The EPA warns that prolonged contact with used engine oil may cause a number of skin disorders, including cancer! You should make every effort to minimize your exposure to used engine oil. Protective gloves should be worn when changing the oil. Wash your hands and any other exposed skin areas as soon as possible after exposure to used engine oil. Soap and water, or waterless hand cleaner should be used.

The Volkswagen oil cooler is mounted on the crankcase and is positioned in the path of the cooling air. The oil cooler in the type 1 engine can be removed with the engine in the car, but it is first necessary that the fan housing be removed. The oil cooler can be removed after the three oil cooler retaining nuts have been taken off. The gaskets

Oil cooler mounting nuts (third nut, on the other side of the cooler, not visible in this photo)

Remove the adapter from the engine (1971 and later models)

Remove the bracket (1971 and later models)

Some engines have flat seals . . .

. . . and others have stepped seals

should be removed along with the oil cooler and replaced with new ones when the cooler in installed. Before installation, the oil cooler should be checked for leaks at a pressure of 85 psi. If the cooler is found to leak, the oil pressure relief valve should also be checked. The studs and bracket on the cooler should be checked for tightness. See that the hollow ribs of the oil cooler do not touch one another. Clean the contact surfaces on the crankcase, install new gaskets, and attach the oil cooler. Tighten the retaining nuts. On the type 3 engine, be sure that a spacer ring is present between the crankcase and the cooler at each securing screw. If these rings are omitted, the seals may be squeezed too tightly, resulting in a stoppage of oil flow and consequent damage to the engine. The type 3 oil cooler is similar in design to that of the type 1 and 2, except that it lies horizontally cross-wise in the path of the air, while that of the other models is in a vertical position.

Oil Pump

REMOVAL & INSTALLATION

✳✳ WARNING:

The EPA warns that prolonged contact with used engine oil may cause a number of skin disorders, including cancer! You should make every effort to minimize your exposure to used engine oil. Protective gloves should be worn when changing the oil. Wash your hands and any other exposed skin areas as soon as possible after exposure to used engine oil. Soap and water, or waterless hand cleaner should be used.

In the type 3 engine, the oil pump can be removed only after the engine is removed from the car and the air intake housing, the belt pulley fan housing, and the fan are dismantled. On type 1 and 2 engines, the pump can be removed with the engine in the car, but it is first necessary to remove the cover plate, the crankshaft pulley, and the cover plate under the pulley. Removal on all model Volkswagens is similar. On Automatic Stickshift models, the torque converter oil pump is driven by the engine oil pump.

Remove the nuts from the oil pump cover and remove the cover and its gasket. Remove the gears and take out the pump body with a special extractor. Care should be taken not to damage the inside of the pump housing.

Prior to assembly, check the oil pump body for wear, especially the gear seating surface. If the pump body is worn, the result will be loss of oil pressure and possible damage to the engine. Check driven gear shaft for tightness, and if necessary peen it tightly into place or replace the pump housing. The gears should be checked for wear, backlash and end-play. Backlash may be from 0.0012 - 0.0031 in. (0.03-0.08mm) and the maximum end-play, without gasket, 0.004 in. (0.1mm). The end-play can be checked using a T-square and a feeler gauge. Check the mating surfaces of the pump body and the crankcase for damage and clean them. Install the pump body with a gasket, but without sealing compound. Insert the oil pump pilot instead of the oil pump drive shaft into the pump body. Then turn the camshaft by 360-degrees (one complete turn of the camshaft requires two complete turns of the crankshaft.) This will ensure the centering of the pump body opposite to the slot in the camshaft. Mark the pump body so that the correct fit of the oil pump can be checked after the cover has been installed. Remove the oil pump pilot and install the gears. Check the cover for wear - worn covers should be either machined or replaced. Before installing the cover, new gaskets should be fitted and secured with sealing compound. Install the cover and tighten the nuts without disturbing the position of the pump housing.

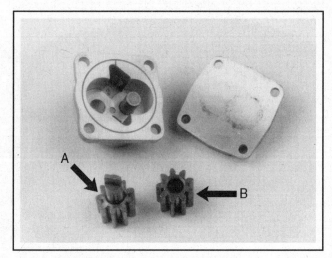

The oil pump houses both a drive gear (A) and a driven gear (B)

After removing the crankshaft pulley, remove the two screws and lift off the shroud for access to the oil pump

After removing the oil pump cover, measure the oil pump gear backlash

When installing the pump, position a new gasket over the pump without using sealant . . .

. . . then slip the pump over the studs

Install the upper gear first, turn it until the tang meshes with the slot in the camshaft . . .

. . . then install the lower gear

Oil Breather

REMOVAL & INSTALLATION

The Volkswagen crankcase is ventilated by a hose which carries oil fumes from the crankcase into the air cleaner where they are burned with the fuel air mixture. In order to remove the oil breather, the connecting hose must be pulled off, the threaded ring removed, and the oil filler and drain pipe extracted.

Installation involves putting a rubber cap on the water drain pipe and sliding the rubber valve properly onto the drain pipe (until the button on the valve engages the hole in the pipe). When installing the oil filler, do not omit the gasket between the generator support and the oil filler.

On the pre-1968 type 3 engine, the oil breather serves the same function as in the other models, and the procedure is much the same. However, since the oil filler tube serves as the dipstick tube, it is necessary to use a setting jig to ensure dipstick accuracy if the filler pipe is removed and then replaced. Otherwise, the procedure is similar to that just described. After 1968, type 3 engines have a closed ventilation system with a separate dipstick tube.

Before attempting to remove the relief valve, spray it with penetrating oil . . .

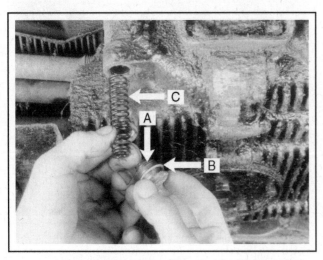

. . . remove the cap (A), gasket (B) and spring (C) from the bore in the engine case

Oil Pressure Relief Valve

REMOVAL & INSTALLATION

✳✳ CAUTION:

The EPA warns that prolonged contact with used engine oil may cause a number of skin disorders, including cancer! You should make every effort to minimize your exposure to used engine oil. Protective gloves should be worn when changing the oil. Wash your hands and any other exposed skin areas as soon as possible after exposure to used engine oil. Soap and water, or waterless hand cleaner should be used.

When the oil is cold and thick, and oil pressure is very high, the plunger is in its lowest position and oil flows directly to the lubrication points and some of it back to the crankcase. When the oil warms up and thins out, the oil pressure drops, the plunger covers the bypass port and oil flows to the lubrication points both directly and via the oil cooler. After the oil has warmed up to normal operating temperature and is thin, oil pressure is low, the plunger of the relief valve is in its highest position, and the oil is routed to the lubrication points only after it has passed through the oil cooler.

The oil pressure relief valve should be checked whenever there is any disturbance in oil circulation, and especially when the oil cooler is found to be leaky. If the plunger should stick at its highest point when the oil is thick, there is danger of the oil cooler leaking from excess pressure. If, on the other hand, the plunger sticks in the bottom of its

. . . then loosen the screw cap with a screwdriver socket and . . .

Pull the relief valve cylinder out of the bore

travel, the oil will tend to flow directly back to the sump and lubrication will be lacking when the engine is warm.

The oil pressure relief valve is removed by unscrewing the end plug and removing the gasket ring, spring and plunger. If the plunger is stuck, it can be removed by screwing a 10mm tap into it. Prior to installation, check the plunger and the bore in the crankcase for signs of seizure. If necessary, the plunger should be renewed. The spring should be checked to assure that it conforms to the following specifications:

Condition	Length	Load in lbs.
Unloaded	2.44 - 2.52 in.	0
Loaded	0.93 in.	17.1 lbs.

When installing the relief valve, care should be taken to ensure that the upper end of the spring does not scratch the wall of the bore. The gasket should be removed and the end-plug tightened securely.

There are two types of oil pressure relief valve plungers available. The first is the plain type normally found in type 1 and 2 engines. The second type is longer and has an annular groove. This is used in some type 3 engines. It has been found that, if the grooved plunger is substituted for the plain plunger, the result will be more oil flow through the cooler and a drop in oil temperature of about 15-degreesF. This, as all other engine modifications, is discouraged by the VW factory.

EXHAUST SYSTEM

General Information

➡**Safety glasses should be worn at all times when working on or near the exhaust system. Older exhaust systems will almost always be covered with loose rust particles which will shower you when disturbed. These particles are more than a nuisance and could injure your eye.**

Whenever working on the exhaust system always keep the following in mind:

• Check the complete exhaust system for open seams, holes loose connections, or other deterioration which could permit exhaust fumes to seep into the passenger compartment.

• The exhaust system is usually supported by free-hanging rubber mountings which permit some movement of the exhaust system, but does not permit transfer of noise and vibration into the passenger compartment. Do not replace the rubber mounts with solid ones.

• Before removing any component of the exhaust system, ALWAYS squirt a liquid rust dissolving agent onto the fasteners for ease of removal. A lot of knuckle skin will be saved by following this rule. It may even be wise to spray the fasteners and allow them to sit overnight.

⁂ CAUTION:

Allow the exhaust system to cool sufficiently before spraying a solvent exhaust fasteners. Some solvents are highly flammable and could ignite when sprayed on hot exhaust components.

• Annoying rattles and noise vibrations in the exhaust system are usually caused by misalignment of the parts. When aligning the system, leave all bolts and nuts loose until all parts are properly aligned, then tighten, working from front to rear.

• When installing exhaust system parts, make sure there is enough clearance between the hot exhaust parts and pipes and hoses that would be adversely affected by excessive heat. Also make sure there is adequate clearance from the floor pan to avoid possible overheating of the floor.

Muffler

REMOVAL & INSTALLATION

To remove the muffler from all Volkswagen models, first remove the clamps from the muffler and heat exchangers. (Early 1963 and earlier models do not have exchangers.) Remove the clips connecting the warm air channels. Loosen the clamps on the tail pipe(s) and remove the tail pipe(s). Remove the nuts from the muffler flange and remove the pre-heater adaptor pipe. Remove the four screws from the manifold preheater pipe and take the muffler off, including gaskets. Check the muffler to be installed and the exhaust pipes for leaks or damage. If necessary, the exhaust pipes can be re-used. However, in practice it is often difficult to remove the tail pipes from the old muffler without damaging them extensively. This generally occurs with old mufflers that have become rusty, and in such cases it is advisable to install new tail pipes. Type 1 tail pipes should protrude about 7.5 in. on pre-1968 models; 8.3 in. on later models. New gaskets should be used when installing the muffler.

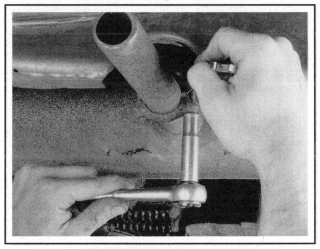

If necessary, remove the tail pipe clamp bolts and pull the tail pipe out of the muffler

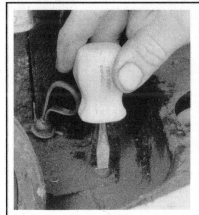

To remove the muffler, first remove the rear sheet metal cover retaining screws . . .

. . . then lift the cover off of the engine

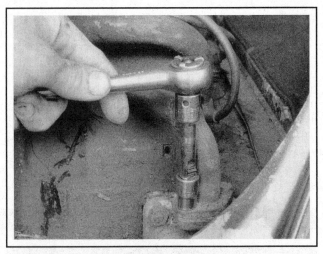

Remove the exhaust gas crossover retaining bolts . . .

. . . and the muffler-to-cylinder head bolts

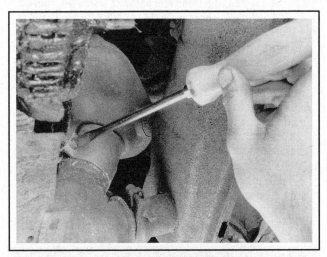

Loosen the hot air channel connector clamp screws . . .

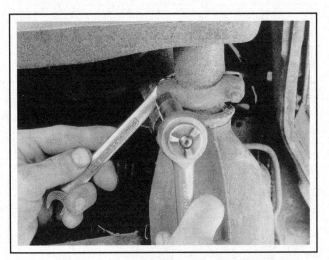

. . . and remove the muffler-to-heat exchanger retaining clamp bolts . . .

. . . then remove the muffler from the engine

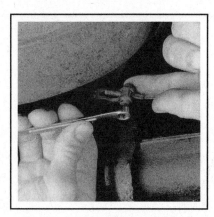

To remove the heater boxes, loosen the heater control flap cable retaining bolt . . .

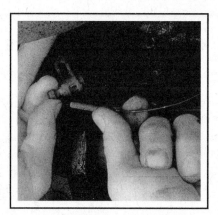

. . . then slide the flap cable out of the retaining fixture

Remove the rubber heater hose clamps and slide the hoses off of the heater boxes

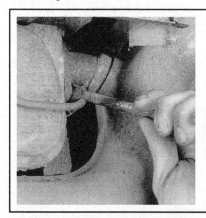

After disconnecting the heater boxes from the muffler, disconnect them from the cylinder head

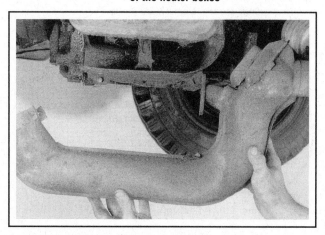

Lower the heater box down and out of the engine compartment

Heat Exchangers

REMOVAL & INSTALLATION

To remove the heat exchangers, remove the exhaust pipe clamps, the clamps between the heat exchanger and the exhaust pipe, and the rear engine cover plate (type 1 and 2). Remove the nuts on the cylinder head and warm air pipe connecting clips. The heat exchanger can now be removed. Check the outer shell and exhaust pipes for damage and leakage. If the heat exchangers leak, there could be a possibility of poisonous gases entering the heating system. The sealing surfaces must be clean and smooth, and flanges that are distorted or bent through excessive tightening should be straightened or machined. Use new gaskets and ensure that all connections are gastight. Heat exchangers must be attached at the cylinder heads with self-locking 8mm nuts. It is not permissible for any other type of nut to be used, even with lockwashers.

Accessory Exhaust Systems

GENERAL INFORMATION

Accessory exhaust systems are not approved by the VW factory and are not generally sold by dealers. Further, some states with outdated inspection codes disapprove of any exhaust system that is not an original factory equipment type. However, accessory systems do usually give a power boost (up to 10%) and a satisfying sound.

There are two basic types of accessory exhaust systems currently available. The first, the header type, has a separate muffler on each side, one for cylinders 1 and 2, and one for cylinders 3 and 4. This type of system does not allow the use of the heater and will not fit on sedans and buses, unless the rear body panels have been cut away. The header system is rather loud and rough sounding, because it is actually two completely separate two cylinder systems. It is most often seen on dune buggies, where a large ground clearance is necessary.

The second type of accessory exhaust system is known as the 180-degrees tuned, or extractor system. In most such systems, equal length pipes are run from each cylinder, the pipes from each cylinder 180-degrees apart in the firing order are run together, then both pipes are run together into a single outlet. The effect is a small horsepower boost and a smooth exhaust note. These systems are installed in much the same way as the stock muffler, and are available in models which utilize the original heater. Some extractor exhaust kits furnish canvas tubing to connect the heat exchangers to the fan housing tubing. The canvas tubing will rot out quickly, and should be replaced with stanless steel flexible tubing held with screw type hose clamps.

When fitting any low restriction exhaust system, it is advisable to rejet the carburetor to prevent an excessively lean mixture and resultant valve burning. Normally a main jet one or two sizes larger will be sufficient. It may also be necessary to replace the air correction, or air bleed, jet. The spark plugs and the inside of the tail pipe will give evidence of changes in mixture.

➡**The results of rejetting, or of any other engine modifications, must be checked with suitable testing equipment to ensure that exhaust emissions remain within legal limits.**

USING A VACUUM GAUGE

White needle = steady needle   *Dark needle = drifting needle*

The vacuum gauge is one of the most useful and easy-to-use diagnostic tools. It is inexpensive, easy to hook up, and provides valuable information about the condition of your engine.

Indication: Normal engine in good condition

Gauge reading: Steady, from 17–22 in./Hg.

Indication: Sticking valve or ignition miss

Gauge reading: Needle fluctuates from 15–20 in./Hg. at idle

Indication: Late ignition or valve timing, low compression, stuck throttle valve, leaking carburetor or manifold gasket.

Gauge reading: Low (15–20 in./Hg.) but steady

Indication: Improper carburetor adjustment, or minor intake leak at carburetor or manifold

NOTE: Bad fuel injector O-rings may also cause this reading.

Gauge reading: Drifting needle

Indication: Weak valve springs, worn valve stem guides, or leaky cylinder head gasket (vibrating excessively at all speeds).

NOTE: A plugged catalytic converter may also cause this reading.

Gauge reading: Needle fluctuates as engine speed increases

Indication: Burnt valve or improper valve clearance. The needle will drop when the defective valve operates.

Gauge reading: Steady needle, but drops regularly

Indication: Choked muffler or obstruction in system. Speed up the engine. Choked muffler will exhibit a slow drop of vacuum to zero.

Gauge reading: Gradual drop in reading at idle

Indication: Worn valve guides

Gauge reading: Needle vibrates excessively at idle, but steadies as engine speed increases

Troubleshooting Engine Mechanical Problems

Problem	Cause	Solution
External oil leaks	• Cylinder head cover RTV sealant broken or improperly seated	• Replace sealant; inspect cylinder head cover sealant flange and cylinder head sealant surface for distortion and cracks
	• Oil filler cap leaking or missing	• Replace cap
	• Oil filter gasket broken or improperly seated	• Replace oil filter
	• Oil pan side gasket broken, improperly seated or opening in RTV sealant	• Replace gasket or repair opening in sealant; inspect oil pan gasket flange for distortion
	• Oil pan front oil seal broken or improperly seated	• Replace seal; inspect timing case cover and oil pan seal flange for distortion
	• Oil pan rear oil seal broken or improperly seated	• Replace seal; inspect oil pan rear oil seal flange; inspect rear main bearing cap for cracks, plugged oil return channels, or distortion in seal groove
	• Timing case cover oil seal broken or improperly seated	• Replace seal
	• Excess oil pressure because of restricted PCV valve	• Replace PCV valve
	• Oil pan drain plug loose or has stripped threads	• Repair as necessary and tighten
	• Rear oil gallery plug loose	• Use appropriate sealant on gallery plug and tighten
	• Rear camshaft plug loose or improperly seated	• Seat camshaft plug or replace and seal, as necessary
Excessive oil consumption	• Oil level too high	• Drain oil to specified level
	• Oil with wrong viscosity being used	• Replace with specified oil
	• PCV valve stuck closed	• Replace PCV valve
	• Valve stem oil deflectors (or seals) are damaged, missing, or incorrect type	• Replace valve stem oil deflectors
	• Valve stems or valve guides worn	• Measure stem-to-guide clearance and repair as necessary
	• Poorly fitted or missing valve cover baffles	• Replace valve cover
	• Piston rings broken or missing	• Replace broken or missing rings
	• Scuffed piston	• Replace piston
	• Incorrect piston ring gap	• Measure ring gap, repair as necessary
	• Piston rings sticking or excessively loose in grooves	• Measure ring side clearance, repair as necessary
	• Compression rings installed upside down	• Repair as necessary
	• Cylinder walls worn, scored, or glazed	• Repair as necessary

Troubleshooting Engine Mechanical Problems

Problem	Cause	Solution
Excessive oil consumption (cont.)	• Piston ring gaps not properly staggered • Excessive main or connecting rod bearing clearance	• Repair as necessary • Measure bearing clearance, repair as necessary
No oil pressure	• Low oil level • Oil pressure gauge, warning lamp or sending unit inaccurate • Oil pump malfunction • Oil pressure relief valve sticking • Oil passages on pressure side of pump obstructed • Oil pickup screen or tube obstructed • Loose oil inlet tube	• Add oil to correct level • Replace oil pressure gauge or warning lamp • Replace oil pump • Remove and inspect oil pressure relief valve assembly • Inspect oil passages for obstruction • Inspect oil pickup for obstruction • Tighten or seal inlet tube
Low oil pressure	• Low oil level • Inaccurate gauge, warning lamp or sending unit • Oil excessively thin because of dilution, poor quality, or improper grade • Excessive oil temperature • Oil pressure relief spring weak or sticking • Oil inlet tube and screen assembly has restriction or air leak • Excessive oil pump clearance • Excessive main, rod, or camshaft bearing clearance	• Add oil to correct level • Replace oil pressure gauge or warning lamp • Drain and refill crankcase with recommended oil • Correct cause of overheating engine • Remove and inspect oil pressure relief valve assembly • Remove and inspect oil inlet tube and screen assembly. (Fill inlet tube with lacquer thinner to locate leaks.) • Measure clearances • Measure bearing clearances, repair as necessary
High oil pressure	• Improper oil viscosity • Oil pressure gauge or sending unit inaccurate • Oil pressure relief valve sticking closed	• Drain and refill crankcase with correct viscosity oil • Replace oil pressure gauge • Remove and inspect oil pressure relief valve assembly
Main bearing noise	• Insufficient oil supply • Main bearing clearance excessive • Bearing insert missing • Crankshaft end-play excessive • Improperly tightened main bearing cap bolts • Loose flywheel or drive plate • Loose or damaged vibration damper	• Inspect for low oil level and low oil pressure • Measure main bearing clearance, repair as necessary • Replace missing insert • Measure end-play, repair as necessary • Tighten bolts with specified torque • Tighten flywheel or drive plate attaching bolts • Repair as necessary

Troubleshooting Engine Mechanical Problems

Problem	Cause	Solution
Connecting rod bearing noise	· Insufficient oil supply	· Inspect for low oil level and low oil pressure
	· Carbon build-up on piston	· Remove carbon from piston crown
	· Bearing clearance excessive or bearing missing	· Measure clearance, repair as necessary
	· Crankshaft connecting rod journal out-of-round	· Measure journal dimensions, repair or replace as necessary
	· Misaligned connecting rod or cap	· Repair as necessary
	· Connecting rod bolts tightened improperly	· Tighten bolts with specified torque
Piston noise	· Piston-to-cylinder wall clearance excessive (scuffed piston)	· Measure clearance and examine piston
	· Cylinder walls excessively tapered or out-of-round	· Measure cylinder wall dimensions, rebore cylinder
	· Piston ring broken	· Replace all rings on piston
	· Loose or seized piston pin	· Measure piston-to-pin clearance, repair as necessary
	· Connecting rods misaligned	· Measure rod alignment, straighten or replace
	· Piston ring side clearance excessively loose or tight	· Measure ring side clearance, repair as necessary
	· Carbon build-up on piston is excessive	· Remove carbon from piston
Valve actuating component noise	· Insufficient oil supply	· Check for: (a) Low oil level (b) Low oil pressure (c) Wrong hydraulic tappets (d) Restricted oil gallery (e) Excessive tappet to bore clearance
	· Rocker arms or pivots worn	· Replace worn rocker arms or pivots
	· Foreign objects or chips in hydraulic tappets	· Clean tappets
	· Excessive tappet leak-down	· Replace valve tappet
	· Tappet face worn	· Replace tappet; inspect corresponding cam lobe for wear
	· Broken or cocked valve springs	· Properly seat cocked springs; replace broken springs
	· Stem-to-guide clearance excessive	· Measure stem-to-guide clearance, repair as required
	· Valve bent	· Replace valve
	· Loose rocker arms	· Check and repair as necessary
	· Valve seat runout excessive	· Regrind valve seat/valves
	· Missing valve lock	· Install valve lock
	· Excessive engine oil	· Correct oil level

Troubleshooting Engine Performance

Problem	Cause	Solution
Hard starting (engine cranks normally)	• Faulty engine control system component	• Repair or replace as necessary
	• Faulty fuel pump	• Replace fuel pump
	• Faulty fuel system component	• Repair or replace as necessary
	• Faulty ignition coil	• Test and replace as necessary
	• Improper spark plug gap	• Adjust gap
	• Incorrect ignition timing	• Adjust timing
	• Incorrect valve timing	• Check valve timing; repair as necessary
Rough idle or stalling	• Incorrect curb or fast idle speed	• Adjust curb or fast idle speed (If possible)
	• Incorrect ignition timing	• Adjust timing to specification
	• Improper feedback system operation	• Refer to Chapter 4
	• Faulty EGR valve operation	• Test EGR system and replace as necessary
	• Faulty PCV valve air flow	• Test PCV valve and replace as necessary
	• Faulty TAC vacuum motor or valve	• Repair as necessary
	• Air leak into manifold vacuum	• Inspect manifold vacuum connections and repair as necessary
	• Faulty distributor rotor or cap	• Replace rotor or cap (Distributor systems only)
	• Improperly seated valves	• Test cylinder compression, repair as necessary
	• Incorrect ignition wiring	• Inspect wiring and correct as necessary
	• Faulty ignition coil	• Test coil and replace as necessary
	• Restricted air vent or idle passages	• Clean passages
	• Restricted air cleaner	• Clean or replace air cleaner filter element
Faulty low-speed operation	• Restricted idle air vents and passages	• Clean air vents and passages
	• Restricted air cleaner	• Clean or replace air cleaner filter element
	• Faulty spark plugs	• Clean or replace spark plugs
	• Dirty, corroded, or loose ignition secondary circuit wire connections	• Clean or tighten secondary circuit wire connections
	• Improper feedback system operation	• Refer to Chapter 4
	• Faulty ignition coil high voltage wire	• Replace ignition coil high voltage wire (Distributor systems only)
	• Faulty distributor cap	• Replace cap (Distributor systems only)
Faulty acceleration	• Incorrect ignition timing	• Adjust timing
	• Faulty fuel system component	• Repair or replace as necessary
	• Faulty spark plug(s)	• Clean or replace spark plug(s)
	• Improperly seated valves	• Test cylinder compression, repair as necessary
	• Faulty ignition coil	• Test coil and replace as necessary

Troubleshooting Engine Performance

Problem	Cause	Solution
Faulty acceleration (cont.)	• Improper feedback system operation	• Refer to Chapter 4
Faulty high speed operation	• Incorrect ignition timing • Faulty advance mechanism	• Adjust timing (if possible) • Check advance mechanism and repair as necessary (Distributor systems only)
	• Low fuel pump volume • Wrong spark plug air gap or wrong plug • Partially restricted exhaust manifold, exhaust pipe, catalytic converter, muffler, or tailpipe • Restricted vacuum passages • Restricted air cleaner • Faulty distributor rotor or cap • Faulty ignition coil • Improperly seated valve(s) • Faulty valve spring(s) • Incorrect valve timing • Intake manifold restricted • Worn distributor shaft • Improper feedback system operation	• Replace fuel pump • Adjust air gap or install correct plug • Eliminate restriction • Clean passages • Cleaner or replace filter element as necessary • Replace rotor or cap (Distributor systems only) • Test coil and replace as necessary • Test cylinder compression, repair as necessary • Inspect and test valve spring tension, replace as necessary • Check valve timing and repair as necessary • Remove restriction or replace manifold • Replace shaft (Distributor systems only) • Refer to Chapter 4
Misfire at all speeds	• Faulty spark plug(s) • Faulty spark plug wire(s) • Faulty distributor cap or rotor • Faulty ignition coil • Primary ignition circuit shorted or open intermittently • Improperly seated valve(s) • Faulty hydraulic tappet(s) • Improper feedback system operation • Faulty valve spring(s) • Worn camshaft lobes • Air leak into manifold • Fuel pump volume or pressure low • Blown cylinder head gasket • Intake or exhaust manifold passage(s) restricted	• Clean or relace spark plug(s) • Replace as necessary • Replace cap or rotor (Distributor systems only) • Test coil and replace as necessary • Troubleshoot primary circuit and repair as necessary • Test cylinder compression, repair as necessary • Clean or replace tappet(s) • Refer to Chapter 4 • Inspect and test valve spring tension, repair as necessary • Replace camshaft • Check manifold vacuum and repair as necessary • Replace fuel pump • Replace gasket • Pass chain through passage(s) and repair as necessary
Power not up to normal	• Incorrect ignition timing • Faulty distributor rotor	• Adjust timing • Replace rotor (Distributor systems only)

Troubleshooting Engine Performance

Problem	Cause	Solution
Power not up to normal (cont.)	• Incorrect spark plug gap	• Adjust gap
	• Faulty fuel pump	• Replace fuel pump
	• Faulty fuel pump	• Replace fuel pump
	• Incorrect valve timing	• Check valve timing and repair as necessary
	• Faulty ignition coil	• Test coil and replace as necessary
	• Faulty ignition wires	• Test wires and replace as necessary
	• Improperly seated valves	• Test cylinder compression and repair as necessary
	• Blown cylinder head gasket	• Replace gasket
	• Leaking piston rings	• Test compression and repair as necessary
	• Improper feedback system operation	• Refer to Chapter 4
Intake backfire	• Improper ignition timing	• Adjust timing
	• Defective EGR component	• Repair as necessary
	• Defective TAC vacuum motor or valve	• Repair as necessary
Exhaust backfire	• Air leak into manifold vacuum	• Check manifold vacuum and repair as necessary
	• Faulty air injection diverter valve	• Test diverter valve and replace as necessary
	• Exhaust leak	• Locate and eliminate leak
Ping or spark knock	• Incorrect ignition timing	• Adjust timing
	• Distributor advance malfunction	• Inspect advance mechanism and repair as necessary (Distributor systems only)
	• Excessive combustion chamber deposits	• Remove with combustion chamber cleaner
	• Air leak into manifold vacuum	• Check manifold vacuum and repair as necessary
	• Excessively high compression	• Test compression and repair as necessary
	• Fuel octane rating excessively low	• Try alternate fuel source
	• Sharp edges in combustion chamber	• Grind smooth
	• EGR valve not functioning properly	• Test EGR system and replace as necessary
Surging (at cruising to top speeds)	• Low fuel pump pressure or volume	• Replace fuel pump
	• Improper PCV valve air flow	• Test PCV valve and replace as necessary
	• Air leak into manifold vacuum	• Check manifold vacuum and repair as necessary
	• Incorrect spark advance	• Test and replace as necessary
	• Restricted fuel filter	• Replace fuel filter
	• Restricted air cleaner	• Clean or replace air cleaner filter element
	• EGR valve not functioning properly	• Test EGR system and replace as necessary
	• Improper feedback system operation	• Refer to Chapter 4

ENGINE REBUILDING

This section describes, in detail, the procedures involved in rebuilding a horizontally opposed, air-cooled Volkswagen/Porsche four cylinder engine. It is divided into two sections. The first section, Cylinder Head Reconditioning, assumes that the cylinder head is removed from the engine, all manifolds and sheet metal shrouding is removed, and the cylinder head is on a workbench. The second section, Crankcase Reconditioning, covers the crankcase halves, the connecting rods, crankshaft, camshaft and lifters. It is assumed that the engine is mounted on a work stand (which can be rented), with the cylinder heads, cylinders, pistons, and all accessories removed.

In some cases, a choice of methods is provided. The choice of a method for a procedure is at the discretion of the user. It may be limited by the tools available to a user, or the proximity of a local engine rebuilding or machine shop.

The tools required for the basic rebuilding procedures should, with minor exceptions, be those included in a mechanic's tool kit: An accurate torque wrench (preferably a preset, click type), inside and outside micrometers, electric drill with grinding attachment, valve spring com-

Metric

Bolt Diameter (mm)	Bolt Grade				Wrench Size (mm) Bolt and Nut
	5D	8G	10K	12K	
6	5	6	8	10	10
8	10	16	22	27	14
10	19	31	40	49	17
12	34	54	70	86	19
14	55	89	117	137	22
16	83	132	175	208	24
18	111	182	236	283	27
22	182	284	394	464	32
24	261	419	570	689	36

*—Torque values are for lightly oiled bolts.
CAUTION: Bolts threaded into aluminum require much less torque.

If no specific torque value is given in the text, tighten the bolts according to the bolt grade of the particular fastener - bolts threaded into aluminum require much less torque

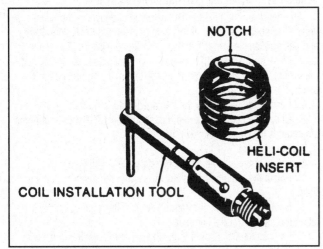

The tool, included in the Heli-Coil kit, is used to thread the Heli-Coil into the damaged hole, after the hole is drilled oversize

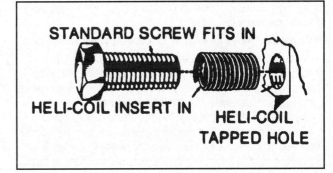

Once the Heli-Coil is installed in the hole a normal bolt can be used again

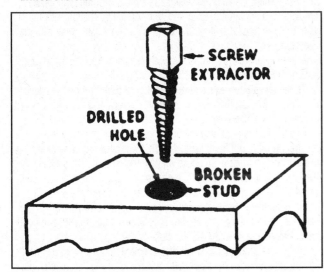

A broken stud can be removed with a screw extractor after a hole is drilled down the center of the stud

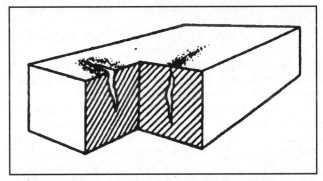

Magnafluxing an engine component shows surface and sub-surface cracks - Magnflux only works on ferrous (iron or steel) components

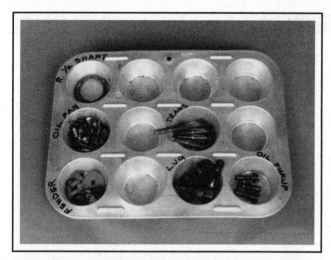

When removing nuts, bolts and other parts, place them in a tray or other container

pressor, a set of taps and reamers, a valve lapping tool, and a dial indicator (reading in thousandths of an inch). Special tools, where required, are available from the major tool suppliers (i.e. Zelenda, Craftsman, K-D, Snap-On). The services of a competent automotive or aviation machine shop must also be readily available.

When assembling the engine, bolts and nuts with no torque specification should be tightened according to size and marking (see chart).

Any parts that will be in frictional contact must be pre-lubricated before assembly to provide protection on initial start-up. Many different pre-lubes are available and each mechanic has his own favorite. However, any product specifically formulated for this purpose, such as Vortex Pre-Lube, STP, Wynn's Friction Proofing, or even a good grade of white grease may be used.

➡**Do not use engine oil only, as its viscosity is not sufficient.**

Where semi-permanent (locked but removable) installation of nuts or bolts is required, the threads should be cleaned and coated with locking compound. Studs may be permanently installed using a special compound such as Loctite Stud and Bearing Mount.

Aluminum is used liberally in VW and Porsche engines due to its low weight and excellent heat transfer characteristics. Both the cylinder heads and the crankcase are aluminum alloy castings. However, a few precautions must be observed when handling aluminum engine parts:

• Never hot-tank aluminum parts, unless the hot-tanking solution is specified for aluminum application (i.e. Oakite Aluminum Cleaner 164, or ZEP Hot Vat Aluminum Cleaner). Most hot-tanking solutions are used for ferrous metals only, and "cook" at much higher temperatures than the 175-degreesF used for aluminum cleaners. The result would be a dissolved head or crankcase.

• Always coat threads lightly with engine oil or anti-seize compound before installation, to prevent seizure.

• Never overtorque bolts or spark plugs in aluminum threads. Should stripping occur, threads can be restored using inserts such as the Heli-Coil, K-D Insert for Keenserts kits.

To install a Heli-Coil insert, tap drill the hole with the stripped threads to the specified size (see chart). If you are performing this operation on a spark plug hole with the head installed, coat the tap with wheel bearing grease to prevent aluminum shavings from falling into the combustion chamber (it will also help if the engine is rotated so that the exhaust valve of the subject cylinder is open, so that when the engine is initially started, if any chips did fall into the engine, they will be blown out the exhaust instead of scoring the cylinder walls, and, if

compressed air is available, it may be applied through the spark plug hole and the chips blown out the exhaust port).

➡**Heli-Coil tap sizes refer to the size thread being replaced, rather than the actual tap size.**

Using the specified tap, tap the hole for the Heli-Coil. Place the insert on the proper installation tool (see chart). Apply pressure on the insert while winding it clockwise into the hole, until the top of the insert is one turn below the surface. Remove the installation tool and break the installation tang from the bottom of the insert by moving it up and down. If, for some reason, the Heli-Coil must be removed, tap the removal tool firmly into the hole, so that it engages the top thread, and turn the tool counterclockwise to extract the insert.

K-D makes an insert specifically designed for the 14mm spark plugs used in all VW's. The steel insert is 3/8 in. deep and has a lip which will seat the insert automatically to the correct depth. To install the K-D insert, screw the combination reamer and tap into the damaged hole to ream the hole to the proper size and cut new threads for the insert. Then, screw the insert onto a spark plug, and torque the plug to 15 - 18 ft. lbs. to seat the insert.

➡**Apply locking compound to the threads of the insert (cylinder head side) to make the installation permanent.**

Another spark plug insert that has come into favor is the Keenserts insert. The special features of this type of insert are the locking keys and gas tight sealing ring. The Keenserts kit consists of a ream and countersink tool, a tap with pilot point, an installation tool (drift), and the inserts. To install a Keenserts insert, the following procedure is used:

1 Ream and countersink the damaged spark plug hole.

2 Check the countersink depth. It should be 13/16 tool in until the stop comes into full contact with the head.

3 Tap the hole.

4 Select an insert. Mount the insert on the installation tool.

5 Rotate the tool and insert clockwise until the insert bottoms in the hole.

6 Drive the special anti-rotation keys into the head using the installation tool, sleeve, and a hammer.

7 Remove the installation tool. Check that the insert is flush with the cylinder head surface and that all keys have seated at the undercut portion of the insert.

8 To install the sealing ring, place it squarely around the top of the insert. Then, install a flat seated spark plug, with the plug gasket removed, and tighten it to 35 ft. lbs. Remove the plug and check the seating of the ring. This should provide a gas tight seal, flush with the insert top.

9 Finally, install the spark plug with its gasket into the insert, and tighten it to its normal 18 ft. lbs.

To remove a Keenserts insert, use a 21/32 drill through the center of the insert to a depth of 1/4 in. Remove the locking keys with a punch and remove the insert with an E-Z out tool.

Snapped bolts or studs may be removed using Vise-Grip pliers. Penetrating oil (e.g. Liquid Wrench, CRC) will often aid in breaking the torque of frozen threads. In cases where the stud or bolt is broken off flush with, or below the surface, the following procedure may be used: Drill a hole (using a hardened bit) in the broken stud or bolt, about 1/2 of its diameter. Select a screw extractor (e.g. E-Z Out) of the proper diameter, and tap it into the stud or bolt. Slowly turn the extractor counterclockwise to remove the stud or bolt.

One of the problems of small displacement, high-revving engines is that they are prone to developing fatigue cracks and other material flaws because they are highly stressed. One of the more popular procedures for checking metal fatigue and stress is Magnafluxing. Magnafluxing

Engine Identification

Common Designation	Number Of Cylinders	C.C. Displacement (cu. in.)	Type Engine	Type Vehicle	Engine Code Letter	Year
–	4	1,131 (69.02)	Upright fan	1	–	To December, 1953
1,200	4	1,192 (72.74)	Upright fan	1,2	A	To July, 1960
1,200	4	1,192 (72.74)	Upright fan	1,2	D	From August, 1960
1,300	4	1,285 (78.4)	Upright fan	1,2	F	From August, 1965
1,500	4	1,493 (91.1)	Upright fan	1,2	H	From August, 1967 ①
1,600	4	1,584 (96.6)	Upright fan	1,2	B	From August, 1969 ②
1,500	4	1,493 (91.1)	Upright fan	2	G	To July, 1965
1,500	4	1,493 (91.1)	Suitcase engine	3	K	To July, 1965 ③ From August, 1965 ④
1,500S	4	1,493 (91.1)	Suitcase engine	3 1500S	R	To July, 1965
1,600	4	1,584 (96.6)	Suitcase engine	3	T	From August, 1965
1,600	4	1,584 (96.6)	Suitcase engine	3 injected	U	From August, 1967

① Type 2 from August, 1965
② Type 2 from August, 1967
③ High compression
④ Low compression

coats the part with fine magnetic particles, and subjects the part to a magnetic field. Cracks cause breaks in the magnetic field (even cracks below the surface not visible to the eye), which are outlined by the particles. However, since Magnafluxing is a magnetic process, it applies only to ferrous metals (crankshafts, flywheels, connecting rods, etc.) It will not work with the aluminum heads and crankcases of these engines which are most prone to cracking.

Another process of checking for cracks is the Zyglo process. This process does work with aluminum alloy. First the part is coated with a flourescent dye penetrant. Then the part is subjected to a blacklight inspection, under which cracks glow brightly, both at or below the surface.

A third method of checking for suspected cracks is the use of spot check dye. This method is quicker, and cheaper to perform, although hidden cracks beneath the surface may escape detection. First, the dye is sprayed onto the suspected area and wiped off. Then, the area is sprayed with a developer. The cracks will show up brightly.

If any of the threaded studs for the rocker arms or manifolds become damaged, and they are not broken off below the surface, they may be removed easily using the following procedure. Lock two nuts on the stud and unscrew the stud using the lower nut. It's as easy as that. Then, to make sure that the new stud remains in place, use locking compound on the threads.

Cylinder Head

RECONDITIONING

Identifying the Valves

Keep the valves in order, so that you know which valve (intake and exhaust) goes in which combustion chamber. If the valve faces are not full of carbon, you may number them, front to rear, with a permanent felt tip marker.

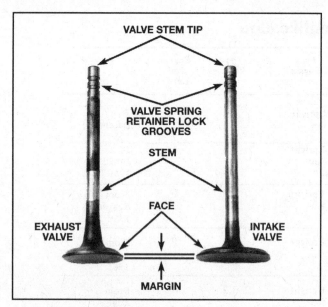

Check for valve wear at the points shown here

Removing the Valves and Springs

Using an appropriate valve spring compressor, compress the valve springs and lift out the keepers with needlenose pliers. Then, slowly release the compressor, and remove the valve, spring and spring retainer. A valve stem seal is used beneath the keepers which can be discarded. Check the keeper seating surfaces on the valve stem for burrs which may scratch the valve guide during installation of the valve. Remove any burrs with a fine file.

This section assumes that the cylinder head is removed for this operation. However, if it is desired to remove the valve springs with the head installed, it will be necessary to screw a compressed air adaptor into the subject spark plug hole and maintain a pressure of 85 psi to keep the valve from dropping down.

Inspect the exhaust valves closely. More often than not, the cause of low compression is a burned exhaust valve. The classic burned valve is cracked on the valve face from the edge of the seat to the stem the way you could cut a pie. Remove all carbon, gum and varnish from the valve stem with a hardwood chisel, or with a wire brush and solvent (i.e. carburetor cleaner, lacquer thinner).

Hot-Tanking the Cylinder Head

Take the head(s) to an engine rebuilding or machine shop and have it (them) hot-tanked to remove grease, corrosion, carbon deposits and scale.

➡ **Make sure that the hot tanking solution is designed to clean aluminum, not to dissolve it.**

After hot-tanking, inspect the combustion chambers (around the spark plug hole) and the exhaust ports for cracks. Also, check the plug threads, manifold studs, and rocker arm studs for damage and looseness.

Degreasing the Remaining Cylinder Head Parts

Using solvent (i.e. Gunk or Zep carburetor cleaner), clean the rockers, rocker shafts, valve springs, spring retainers, keepers and the pushrods. You may also use solvent to clean the cylinder head although it will not clean as well as hot-tanking. Also clean the sheet metal shrouding at this time. Do not clean the pushrod tubes in solvent.

Cleaning the Cylinder Head

Chip carbon away from the combustion chambers and exhaust ports using a chisel made of hardwood. Remove the remaining deposits with a stiff wire brush. You may also use a power brush (drill with wire attachment if you use a very light touch). Remember that you are working with a relatively soft metal (aluminum), and you do not want to grind into the metal. If you have access to a machine shop that works on aluminum heads, ask them about glass-beading the cylinder head.

Checking the Valve Stem-to-Guide Clearance

(Valve Rock)

Clean the valve stem with lacquer thinner or carburetor cleaner to remove all gum and varnish. Clean the valve guides using solvent and an expanding wire-type valve guide cleaner or brass bristle brush. Mount a dial indicator to the head so that the gauge pin is at a 90-degrees angle to the valve stem, up against the edge of the stem. Move the valve off its seat, and measure the clearance by rocking the stem back and forth to actuate the dial indicator. Check the figure against specifications. Maximum rock should not exceed the wear limit.

To check whether excessive rock is due to worn valve stems or guides (or both), one of two methods may be used. If a new valve is available, you may recheck the valve rock. If rock is still excessive

A wire wheel may be used to clean the combustion chambers of carbon deposits

A dial indicator can be used to determine the valve stem-to-guide clearance - move the valve stem as indicated by the arrows

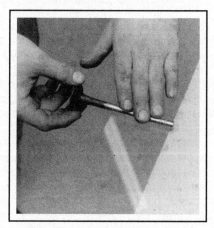

Valve stems may be rolled on a flat surface to check for bends

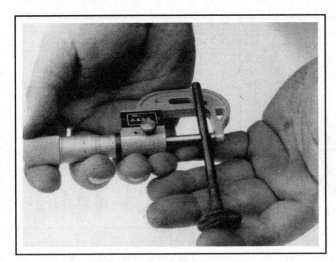

Use a micrometer to check the valve stem diameter

the guide is at fault. Or, you may measure the old valve stem with a micrometer, and determine if it has passed its wear limit.

In any case, most VW and Porsche mechanics will replace the exhaust valve and guides anyway, since they often wear out inside of 50,000 miles.

VW does not make available oversize valve stems to clean up excessive valve rock. Therefore, if excessive clearance is evident, replace the guides.

Knurling the Valve Guides

Knurling is a process whereby metal is displaced and raised, thereby reducing clearance. It is a procedure used in engines where the guides are shrunk in making replacement a costly procedure. Although this operation can be performed on VW and Porsche engines, it is not recommended, since the exhaust guides will eventually need replacement anyway.

Replacing the Valve Guides

The valve guides are a press fit into the head.

➡**If your replacement valve guides do not have a collar at the top, measure the distance the old guides protrude above the head.**

Several different methods may be used to remove worn valve guides. One method is to press or tap the guides out of the head using a stepped drift. The problem with this method is the risk of cracking the head. Another method, which reduces this risk, is to first drill out the guide about 2/3 of the length of the guide so that the walls of the guide at the top are paper thin (1/32 in. or so). This relieves most of the tension from the cylinder head guide bore, but still provides a solid base at the bottom of the guide to drift out the guide from the top. A third method of removing guides is to tap threads into the guide and pull it out from the top. After tapping the guide, place an old wrist pin (or some other type of sleeve) over the guide, so that the wrist pin rests squarely on the boss on the cylinder head around the guide. Then, take a long bolt (about 4 or 5 inches long with threads running all the way up to the bolt head) and thread a nut about halfway up the bolt. Place a washer on top of the wrist pin (see illustration) and thread the bolt into the valve guide until the nut contacts the washer and wrist pin. Finally, screw the nut down against the washer and wrist pin to pull out the guide.

If you are installing the guides without the aid of a press, using only

hand tools, it will help to place the new valve guides in the freezer for an hour or so, and the clean, bare cylinder head in the oven at 350 - 400-degrees F for 1/2 hour to 45 minutes. Controlling the temperature of the metals in this manner will slightly shrink the valve guides and slightly expand the guide bore in the cylinder head, allowing easier installation and lessening the risk of cracking the head in the process.

Most replacement valve guides, other than those manufactured by VW, have a collar at the top which provides a positive stop to seat the guides in the head. However, VW guides have no such collar. Therefore, on these guides, you will have to determine the height above the cylinder head boss that the guide must extend (about 1/4 in.). Then, obtain a stack of washers, their inner diameter slightly larger than the outer diameter of the guide at the top of the guide. If the guide should extend 1/4 in., use a 1/4 in. thick stack of washers around the guide.

To install the valve guides in the head, use a collared drift, or a special valve guide installation tool of the proper outer diameter (see illustration).

✲✲ CAUTION:

If you have heated the head in the oven to aid installation, be extremely careful handling metal of this temperature. Use pot holders, or gloves with thick insulation. Do not set the head down on any surface that may be affected by the heat.

If the replacement guide is collared, drive in the guide until it seats against the boss on the cylinder head. If the guide is not collared, drive in the guide until the installation tool butts against the stack of washers (approx. 1/4 in. thick) on the head.

➡**If you do not heat the head to aid installation, use penetrating lubricant in the guide bore, instead.**

Resurfacing (Grinding) the Valve Face

Using a valve grinding machine, have the valves resurfaced according to specifications. The valve stem tip should also be squared and resurfaced, by placing the stem in the V-block of the grinder, and turning it while pressing lightly against the grinding wheel.

➡**After grinding, the minimum valve head margin must be 0.50mm (.020 in.). The valve head margin is the straight surface on the edge of the valve head, parallel with the valve stem.**

Replacing Valve Seat Inserts

This operation is not normally performed on VW and Porsche engines due to its expense and special shrink fit of the insert in the head. Usually, if the seat is destroyed, the head is also in bad shape (i.e. cracked, or hammered from a broken valve or piston). Some high-performance engine builders will replace the inserts to accommodate larger diameter valve heads. Otherwise, the operation will usually cost more than replacement of the head. Also, a replacement insert, if not installed correctly, could come out of the head, damaging the engine.

Resurfacing the Valve Seats

Most valve seats can be reconditioned by resurfacing. This is done with a reamer or grinder. First, a pilot is installed in the valve guide (a worn valve guide will allow the pilot to wobble, causing an inaccurate seat cut). When using a reamer, apply steady pressure while rotating clockwise. The seat should clean up in about four complete turns, taking care to remove only as much metal as necessary.

➡**Never rotate a reamer counterclockwise.**

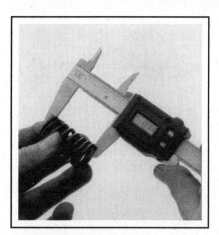

Use a caliper gauge to check the valve spring free-length

Check the valve spring for squareness on a flat service; a carpenter's square can be used

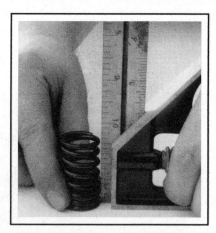

The valve spring should be straight up and down when placed like this

When using a grinder, lift the cutting stone on and off the seat at approximately two cycles per second, until all flaws are removed.

It takes three separate cuts to recondition a VW or Porsche valve seat. After each cut, check the position of the valve seat using Prussian blue dye. First, you cut the center of the seat using a 45-degrees cutter. Then, you cut the bottom of the seat with a 75-degrees cutter and narrow the top of the seat with a 15-degrees stone. Equally as important as the width of the seat is its location in relation to the valve. Using a caliper, measure the distance between the center of the valve face on both sides of a valve. Then, place the caliper on the valve seat, and check that the pointers of the caliper locate in the center of the seat.

Checking Valve Seat Concentricity

In order for the valve to seat perfectly in its seat, providing a gas tight seal, the valve seat must be concentric with the valve guide. To check concentricity, coat the valve face with Prussian blue dye and install the valve in its guide. Applying light pressure, rotate the valve 1/4 turn in its valve seat. If the entire valve seat face becomes coated, and the valve is known to be concentric, the seat is concentric.

Lapping the Valves

With accurately refaced valve seat inserts and new valves, it is not usually necessary to lap the valves. Valve lapping alone is not recommended for use as a resurfacing procedure.

Prior to lapping, invert the cylinder head, lightly lubricate the valve stem and install the valves in their respective guides. Coat the valve seats with fine Carborundum grinding compound, and attach the lapping tool suction cup (moistened for adhesion) to the valve head. Then, rotate the tool between your palms, changing direction and lifting the tool often to prevent grooving. Lap the valve until a smooth, polished seat is evident. Finally, remove the tool and thoroughly wash away all traces of grinding compound. Make sure that no compound accumulates in the guides as rapid wear would result.

Checking the Valve Springs

Place the spring on a flat surface next to a square. Measure the height of the spring and compare that value to that of the other 7 springs. All springs should be the same height. Rotate the spring against the edge of the square to measure distortion. Replace any spring that varies (in both height and distortion) more than 1/16 in.

If you have access to a valve spring tester, you may use the following specifications to check the springs under a load

(which is the only specification VW gives).

If any doubt exists as to the condition of the springs, and a spring tester is not available, replace them, they're cheap.

Installing the Valves

Lubricate the valve stems with white grease (molybdenum-disulphide), and install the valves in their respective guides. Lubricate and install the valve stem seals.

Position the valve springs on the head. The spring is positioned with the closely coiled end facing the head.

Check the valve stem keys (keepers) for burrs or scoring. The keys should be machined so that the valve may still rotate with the keys held together. Finally, install the spring retainers, compress the springs (using a valve spring compressor), and insert the keys using needle-nose pliers or a special tool designed for this purpose.

➡**You can retain the keys with wheel bearing grease during installation.**

Inspecting the Rocker Shafts and Rocker Arms

Remove the rocker arms, springs and washers from the rocker shaft.

➡**Lay out the parts in the order they are removed.**

Inspect the rocker arms for pitting or wear on the valve stem contact point, and check for excessive rocker arm bushing wear where the arm rides on the shaft. If the shaft is grooved noticeably, replace it. Use the following chart to check the rocker arm inner diameter and the rocker shaft outer diameter.

Minor scoring may be removed with an emery cloth. If the valve

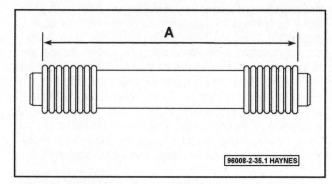

96008-2-35.1 HAYNES

Measure dimension "A" to determine pushrod tube length

stem contact point of the rocker arm is worn, grind it smooth, removing as little metal as necessary. If it is noticed at this point that the valve stem is worn concave where it contacts the rocker arm, and it is not desired to disassemble the valve from the head, a cap (see illustration) may be installed over the stem prior to installing the rocker shaft assembly.

Inspecting the Pushrods and Pushrod Tubes

After soaking the pushrods in solvent, clean out the oil passages using fine wire, then blow through them to make sure there are no obstructions. Roll each pushrod over a piece of clean, flat glass. Check for run-out. If a distinct, clicking sound is heard as the pushrod rolls, the rod is bent, necessitating replacement. All pushrods must be of equal length.

Inspect the pushrod tubes for cracks or other damage to the tube that would let oil out and dirt into the engine. The tubes are particularly susceptible to damage at the stretchable bellows. Also, the tubes must be maintained at length "A" (see illustration) which is 190 - 191mm or 7.4 - 7.52 in. If a tube is too short, it may be carefully stretched, taking care to avoid cracking. However, if the bellows are damaged or if a gritty, rusty sound occurs when stretching the tube, replace it. Always use new seals. When installing tubes rotate the tubes so that the seams face upwards.

If, on an assembled engine, it is desired to replace a damaged or leaky pushrod tube without pulling the engine, it may be accomplished using a "quick-change" pushrod tube available from several different specialty manufacturers. The special two-piece aluminum replacement tube is installed after removing the valve cover, rocker arm assembly and pushrod of the subject cylinder. The old tube is then pried loose with a screwdriver. Using new seals, the replacement tube is positioned between the head and crankcase, and expanded into place, via a pair of threaded, locking nuts.

Crankcase

RECONDITIONING

Disassembling Crankcase

See "Crankcase Disassembly & Assembly" earlier in this section.

Hot Tanking the Crankcase

Using only a hot-tanking solution formulated for aluminum or magnesium alloy, clean the crankcase to remove all sludge, scale, or foreign particles. You may also cold-tank the case, using a strong degreasing solvent, but you will have to use a brush and a lot of elbow grease to get the same results.

After cleaning, blow out all oil passages with compressed air. Remove all old gasket sealing compound from the mating surfaces.

Inspecting the Crankcase

Check the case for cracks using the Zyglo or spot-check method described earlier in this section.

Inspect all sealing or mating surfaces, especially along the crankcase seam, as the crankcase halves are machined in pairs and use no gasket.

Check the tightness of the oil suction pipe. The pipe must be centered over the strainer opening. On 1600 engines, peen over the crankcase where the suction pipe enters the camshaft bearing web.

Check all studs for tightness. Replace any defective studs as mentioned earlier in this section. Check all bearing bores for nicks and

scratches. Remove light marks with a file. Deeper scratches and scoring must be removed by align boring the crankshaft bearing bores.

Align-boring the Crankcase

There are two surfaces on a VW crankcase that take quite a hammering in normal service. One is the main bearing saddles and the other the thrust flange of #1 bearing (at the flywheel end). Because the case is constructed of softer metal than the bearings, it is more malleable. The main bearing saddles are slowly hammered in by the rotation of the heavy crankshaft working against the bearings. This is especially true for an out-of-round crankshaft. The thrust flange of #1 main bearing receives its beating trying to control the end-play of the crankshaft. This beating is more severe in cases of a driver with a heavy clutch foot. Popping the clutch bangs the pressure plate against the clutch disc, against the flywheel, against the crankcase flange, and finally against the thrust flange. All of this hammering leaves its mark on the case, but can be cleaned up by align boring.

Most VW engine rebuilders who want their engines to stay together will align bore the case. This assures proper bearing bore alignment. Then, main bearings with the correct oversize outer diameter (and oversize thrust shoulder on #1) are installed.

Also, as the split crankcase is constructed of light aluminum and magnesium alloy, it is particularly susceptible to warpage due to overheating. Align boring the case will clean up any bearing saddle misalignment due to warpage.

Checking Connecting Rod Side Clearance and Straightness

Before removing the connecting rods from the crankshaft, check the clearance between the rod and the crank throw using a feeler gauge. Replace any rod exceeding the wear limit. Proper side clearance (also known as end-play or axial play) is .004-.016 in. (0.10 - 0.40mm).

Also, prior to removing the rods from the crankshaft, check them for straightness. This is accomplished easily using an old wrist pin, and sliding the wrist pin through each connecting rod (small end) in succession. Position each rod, in turn, so that as the pin begins to leave one rod, it is entering the next rod. Any binding indicates a scored wrist pin bushing or misaligned (bent) connecting rod. If the wrist pin absolutely will not slide from one adjacent rod to another, then you've got a really bent rod. Be ready for bent rods on any engine which has dropped a valve and damaged a piston.

Checking connecting rod side clearance with a feeler gauge

Crankshaft components

1	Crankshaft	9	Main bearing No. 3
2	Woodruff key	10	Nut for connecting rod
3	Oil slinger		bolt (8)
4	Main bearing No. 4	11	Connecting rod
5	Circlip	12	Casting mark (must
6	Distributor drive gear		face UP when the rod
7	Spacer		is pointing toward its
8	Crankshaft gear		cylinder)

Remove the circlip

The rods have numbers such as this on them - be sure they are kept together

Carefully remove the Woodruff key

Disassembling the Crankshaft

Number the connecting rods (1 through 4 from the flywheel side) and matchmark their bearing halves. Remove the connecting rod retaining nuts (do not remove the bolts) from the bit end and remove the rods. Slide off the oil thrower and #4 main bearing. Slide off #1 main bearing from the flywheel end. Remove the snapring (circlip) using snapring pliers. #2 main bearing is the split type, each half of which should remain in its respective crankcase half. Using a large gear puller, or an arbor or hydraulic press, remove the distributor drive gear and crankshaft timing gear and spacer. Don't lose the woodruff keys.

Mark the cylinder number on the rods with a sharp punch - two dots for number two cylinder, etc.

Use a puller to remove the gears

➡️**The engines have two woodruff keys.**

Finally, slide off #3 main bearing.

Inspecting the Crankshaft

Clean the crankshaft with solvent. Run all oil holes through with a brass bristle brush. Blow them through with compressed air. Lightly oil the crankshaft to prevent rusting.

Using a micrometer of known accuracy, measure the crankshaft journals for wear. The maximum wear limit for all journals is .0012 in. (0.03mm). Check the micrometer reading against those specifications listed under "Crankshaft & Connecting Rod Specifications" which appears earlier in this section.

Check the crankshaft run-out. With main bearing journals #1 and #3 supported on V-blocks and a dial gauge set up perpendicular to the crankshaft, measure the run-out at #2 and #4 main bearing journals. Maximum permissable run-out is .0008 in. (0.02mm).

Inspect the crankshaft journals for scratches, ridges, scoring and nicks. All small nicks and scratches necessitate regrinding of the crankshaft at a machine shop. Journals worn to a taper or slightly out-of-round must also be reground. Standard undersizes are .010, .020, .030 in. (0.25, 0.50, 0.75mm).

Inspecting the Connecting Rods

Check the connecting rods for cracks, bends and burns. Check the rod bolts for damage; replace any rod with a damaged bolt. If possible, take the rods to a machine shop and have them checked for twists and magnafluxed for hidden stress cracks. Also, the rods must be checked for straightness, using the wrist pin method described earlier. If you did not perform this check before removing the rods from the crankshaft, definitely do so before dropping the assembled crankshaft into the case.

Weigh the rods on a gram scale. On all engines, the rods should weigh within 10 grams (lightest to heaviest). All rods should ideally weigh the same. If not, find the lightest rod and lighten the others to match. Up to 8 grams of metal can be removed from a rod by filing or grinding at the low stress points shown in the illustration.

Check the fit of the wrist pin bushing. At 72-degrees F, the pin should slide through the bushing with only light thumb pressure.

Checking Connecting Rod Bearing (Oil) Clearance

It is always good practice to replace the connecting rod bearings at every teardown. The bearing size is stamped on the back of the inserts. However, if it is desired to reuse the bearings, two methods may be used to determine bearing clearance.

One tedious method is to measure the crankshaft journals using a micrometer to determine what size bearing inserts to use on reassembly (see Crankshaft and Connecting Rod Specifications) to obtain the required 0.0008 - 0.0027 in. oil clearance.

Another method of checking bearing clearance is the Plastigage method. This method can only be used on the split-type bearings and not on the ring-type bearings used to support the crankshaft. First, clean all oil from the bearing surface and crankshaft journal being checked. Plastigage is soluble in oil. Then, cut a piece of Plastigage the width of the rod bearing and insert it between the journal and bearing insert.

➡️**Do not rotate the rod on the crankshaft.**

Tighten the rod cap nuts to 22 - 25 ft. lbs. Remove the bearing insert and check the thickness of the flattened Plastigage using the Plastigage scale. Journal taper is determined by comparing the width of the Plastigage strip near its ends. To check for journal eccentricity, rotate the crankshaft 90-degrees and retest. After checking all four connecting rod bearings in this manner, remove all traces of Plastigage

from the journal and bearing. Oil the crankshaft to prevent rusting.

If the oil clearance is .006 in. (0.15mm) or greater, it will be necessary to have the crankshaft ground to the nearest undersize (.010 in.) and use oversize connecting rod bearings.

Checking Main Bearing (Oil) Clearance

It is also good practice to replace the main bearings at every engine teardown as their replacement cost is minimal compared to the replacement cost of a crankshaft or short block. However, if it becomes necessary to reuse the bearings, you may do so after checking the bearing clearance.

Main bearings #1, 3 and 4 are ring-type bearings that slip over the crankshaft. These bearings cannot be checked using the Plastigage method. Only the split-type #2 main bearing can be checked using Plastigage. However, since this involves bolting together and unbolting the crankcase halves several times, it is not recommended. Therefore, the main bearings are checked using a micrometer.

Never reuse a bearing that shows signs of wear, scoring or blueing. If the bearing clearance exceeds its wear limit, it will be necessary to regrind the crankshaft to the nearest undersize and use oversize main bearings.

Cleaning and Inspecting the Camshaft

Degrease the camshaft using solvent. Clean out all oil holes and blow through with compressed air. Visually inspect the cam lobes and bearing journals for excessive wear. The edges of the camshaft lobes should be square. Slight damage can be removed with silicone carbide oilstone. To check for lobe wear not visible to the eye, measure the camshaft diameter from the tip of the lobe to base (distance A) and then mike the diameter of the camshaft at a 90-degrees angle to the previous measurement (distance B). This will give you camshaft lift. Measure lift for each lobe. If any lobe differs more than .025 in., replace the camshaft.

Check the camshaft for run-out. Place the #1 and #3 journals in V-blocks and rest a dial indicator on #2 journal. Rotate the camshaft and check the reading. Run-out must not exceed 0.0015 in. (0.04mm). Repair is by replacement.

Check the camshaft timing gear rivets for tightness. If any of the gear rivets are loose, or if the gear teeth show a poor contact pattern, replace the camshaft and timing gear assembly. Check the axial (end) play of the timing gear. Place the camshaft in the left crankcase half. The wear limit is .0063 in. (0.16mm). If the end-play is excessive, the thrust shoulder of #3 camshaft bearing is probably worn, necessitating replacement of the cam bearings.

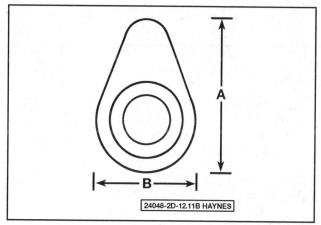

24048-2D-12.11B HAYNES

To compute camshaft lobe lift, subtract measurement (B) from measurement (A)

Lubricate the journal and slip the bearing into place with the offset hole toward the flywheel end

Install the camshaft drive gear with the chamfer facing the flywheel end

Slip the spacer in place

Carefully guide the distributor drive gear onto the crankshaft

Install the circlip in the groove next to the distributor drive gear

Checking the Camshaft Bearings

The camshaft bearings are the split-type. #3 camshaft bearing has shoulders on it to control axial play. Since there is no load on the camshaft, the bearings are not normally replaced. However, if the bearings are scored or imbedded with dirt, if the camshaft itself is being replaced, or if the thrust shoulders of #3 bearing are worn (permitting excessive axial play), the bearings should be replaced.

In all cases, clean the bearing saddles and check the oil feed holes for cleanliness. Make sure that the oil holes for the bearing inserts align with those in the crankcase. Coat the bearing surfaces with prelube.

Install the number four bearing with the offset hole toward the flywheel end

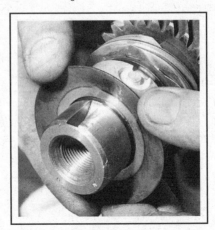

Place the oil slinger on the crankshaft with the concave face out

Gently tap the Woodruff key into the keyway

The marks on the teeth must mesh like this

Install the circular camshaft plug

Checking the Lifters (Tappets)

Remove all gum and varnish from the lifters using a toothbrush and carburetor cleaner. The cam following surface of the lifters is slightly convex when new. In service, this surface will wear flat which is OK to reinstall. However, if the cam following surface of the lifter is worn concave, the lifter should be replaced. To check this, place the cam following surface of one lifter against the side of another, using the one lifter as a straightedge. After checking, coat the lifters with oil to prevent rusting.

Assembling the Crankshaft

➡All dowel pin holes in the main bearings must locate to the flywheel end of the bearing saddles.

Coat #3 main bearing journal with assembly lubricant. Slide the #3 bearing onto the pulley side of the crankshaft and install the large woodruff key in its recess (the hole in the bearing should be nearest to the flywheel end of the crankshaft). In the meantime, heat both the crankshaft timing gear and distributor drive gears to 176-degrees F in an oil bath. If a hydraulic or an arbor press is available, press on the timing gear, taking care to keep the slot for the woodruff key aligned, the timing marks facing away from the flywheel, and the chamfer in the gear bore facing #3 main bearing journal.

✳✳ CAUTION:

Use protective gloves when handling the heated gears.

➡Be careful not to scratch the crankshaft journals.

Or, if a press is not available, you may drive on the gear using a 2 in. diameter length of pipe and a hammer, taking care to protect the flywheel end of the crankshaft with a piece of wood. The woodruff key must lie flat in its recess. Then, slide on the spacer ring and align it with the woodruff key. Install the smaller woodruff key. Now, press or drive on the distributor drive gear in the same manner as the crankshaft timing gear. Make sure it seats against the spacer ring. Install the snap-ring (circlip) using snapring pliers. Take care not to scratch #4 main bearing journal. Prelube main bearings #1 and #4 and slide them on the crankshaft. Install the oil slinger, concave side out.

➡Make sure crankshaft timing gear and distributor drive gear fit snugly on the crankshaft once they return to room temperature.

Install the bearing inserts for the connecting rods and rod caps by

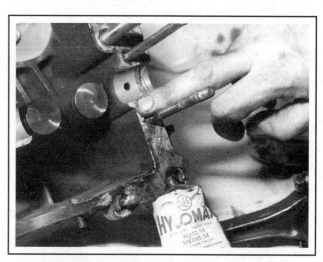

Apply sealant to the mating surfaces of the crankcase

pressing in on bearing ends with both thumbs. Make sure the tangs fit in the notches. Don't press in the middle as the inserts may soil or crack. Prelube the connecting rod bearings and journals. Then, install the connecting rods on the crankshaft, making sure the forge marks are up (as they would be installed in the crankcase [3, 1, 4, 2 from flywheel end]), and the rod and bearing cap matchmarks align. Use new connecting rod nuts. After tightening the nuts, make sure that each rod swings freely 180-degrees on the crankshaft by its own weight.

➡A slight pretension (binding) of the rod on the crankshaft may be relieved by lightly rapping on the flat side of the big end of the rod with a hammer.

If the connecting rod nuts are not of the self-locking type (very rare), peen the nuts into the slot on the rods to lock them in place and prevent the possibility of throwing a rod.

Installing the Crankshaft and Camshaft

Pencil mark a line on the edge of each ring-type main bearing to indicate the location of the dowel pin hole. Install the lower half of #2 main bearing in the left side of the crankcase so that the shell fits securely over its dowel pin. Prelube the bearing surface.

Lift the crankshaft by two of the connecting rods and lower the assembly into the left crankcase halve. Make sure the other connecting rods protrude through their corresponding cylinder openings. Then,

ENGINE BEARING ANALYSIS

Debris

Babbitt bearing embedded with debris from machinings

Microscopic detail of debris

Microscopic detail of gouges

Overplated copper alloy bearing gouged by cast iron debris

Aluminum bearing embedded with glass beads

Microscopic detail of glass beads

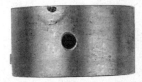 

Damaged lining caused by dirt left on the bearing back

Misassembly

Result of a lower half assembled as an upper - blocking the oil flow

Excessive oil clearance is indicated by a short contact arc

Polished and oil-stained backs are a result of a poor fit in the housing bore

Result of a wrong, reversed, or shifted cap

Overloading

Damage from excessive idling which resulted in an oil film unable to support the load imposed

Damaged upper connecting rod bearings caused by engine lugging; the lower main bearings (not shown) were similarly affected

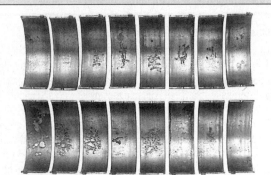

The damage shown in these upper and lower connecting rod bearings was caused by engine operation at a higher-than-rated speed under load

Misalignment

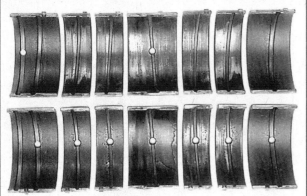

A warped crankshaft caused this pattern of severe wear in the center, diminishing toward the ends

A poorly finished crankshaft caused the equally spaced scoring shown

A tapered housing bore caused the damage along one edge of this pair

A bent connecting rod led to the damage in the "V" pattern

Lubrication

Result of dry start: The bearings on the left, farthest from the oil pump, show more damage

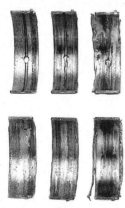

Result of a low oil supply or oil starvation

Severe wear as a result of inadequate oil clearance

Corrosion

Microscopic detail of corrosion

Corrosion is an acid attack on the bearing lining generally caused by inadequate maintenance, extremely hot or cold operation, or interior oils or fuels

Microscopic detail of cavitation

Example of cavitation - a surface erosion caused by pressure changes in the oil film

Damage from excessive thrust or insufficient axial clearance

Bearing affected by oil dilution caused by excessive blow-by or a rich mixture

rotate each ring-type main bearing (#1, then #3, then #4) until the pencil marks made previously align with the center of the bearing bore. As each bearing is aligned with its dowel pin, a distinctive click should be heard and the crankshaft should be felt dropping into position. After each bearing is seated, you should not be able to rock any of the main bearings or the crankshaft in the case. Just to be sure, check the bearing installation by placing the other half of #2 main bearing over the top of its crankshaft journal. If the upper half rocks, the bearing or bearings are not seated properly on their dowels. Then, install the other half of #2 main bearing in the right crankcase halve. Prelube the bearing surface.

Rotate the crankshaft until the timing marks (twin punch marks on two adjacent teeth) on the timing gear point towards the camshaft side of the case. Lubricate and install the lifters. Coat the lifters for the right half of the case with grease to keep them from falling out during assembly. Coat the camshaft journals and bearing surfaces with assembly lubricant. Install the camshaft so that the single timing mark (0) or punch mark on the camshaft timing gear aligns (lies between) with the two on the crankshaft timing gear. This is critical as it establishes valve timing.

Install the camshaft end plug using oil-resistant sealer. On cars with manual transmission, the hollow end of the plug faces in towards the engine. On cars equipped with automatic or automatic stick shift transmission, the hollow end faces out towards the front of the car to provide clearance for the torque converter drive plate retaining bolts.

The timing gear mesh is correct if the camshaft does not lift from its bearings when the crankshaft is rotated backwards (opposite normal direction of rotation).

Checking Timing Gear Backlash

Mount a dial indicator to the crankcase with its stem resting on a tooth of the camshaft gear. Rotate the gear until all slack is removed, and zero the indicator. Then, rotate the gear in the opposite direction until all slack is removed and record gear backlash. The reading should be between .000 and .002 in. (0.00 and 0.05mm).

Assembling the Crankcase

See "Crankcase Assembly & Disassembly" earlier in this section. Use the following installation notes;
1   Make sure all bearing surfaces are prelubed.
2   Always install new crankcase stud seals.
3   Apply only non-hardening oil resistant sealer to all crankcase mating surfaces.
4   Always use new case nuts. Self-sealing nuts must be installed with the red coated side down.
5   All small crankcase retaining nuts are first torqued to 10 ft. lbs., then 14 ft. lbs. All large crankcase retaining nuts are torqued to 20 ft.

Three shims are used to control crankshaft endplay

lbs., then 25 ft. lbs. (except self-sealing large nuts [red plastic insert], which are torqued to a single figure of 18 ft. lbs.). Use a crisscross torque sequence.

6   While assembling the crankcase halves, always rotate the crankshaft periodically to check for binding. If any binding occurs, immediately disassemble and investigate the case. Usually, a main bearing has come off its dowel pin, or maybe you forgot to align bore that warped crankcase.

Checking Crankshaft End-Play

After assembling the case, crankshaft end-play can be checked. End-play is controlled by the thickness of 3 shims located between the flywheel and #1 main bearing flange. End-play is checked with the flywheel installed as follows. Attach a dial indicator to the crankcase with the stem positioned on the face of the flywheel. Move the flywheel in and out and check the reading. End-play should be between .003-.005 in. (0.07 - 0.13mm). The wear limit is .006 in. (0.15mm).

To adjust end-play, remove the flywheel and reinstall, this time using only two shims. Remeasure the end-play. The difference between the second reading and the .003-.005 in. figure is the required thickness of the third shim. Shims come in the following sizes:

0.24mm - .0095 in.
0.30mm - .0118 in.
0.32mm - .0126 in.
0.34mm - .0134 in.
0.36mm - .0142 in.

4

DRIVEABILITY AND TROUBLESHOOTING

TROUBLESHOOTING

General Information

Troubleshooting is an orderly procedure in which possible causes of trouble are eliminated one by one until the fault is found.

Troubleshooting of the engine entails investigation of parts of four different subsystems: fuel, air, spark, and compression. Troubleshooting other parts of the car also includes basic mechanical logic applied to known symptoms, and, if done methodically, should prove successful for the troubleshooter.

Troubleshooting Instruments

HYDROMETER

▶ See Figure 1

A specific gravity test is a practical indicator of the state of charge of the battery. As a battery is discharged, a chemical change takes place within each cell. The sulfate of the electrolyte combines chemically with the battery plates, thus reducing the weight of the electrolyte. For this reason the specific gravity of the acid, or electrolyte, of a partially charged battery will be less than that of one that is fully charged. The electrolyte in a fully charged battery is usually about 1.285 times as heavy as pure water at the same temperature. The accompanying chart gives an indication of specific gravity value and how it relates to battery charge condition.

The battery hydrometer consists simply of a glass cylinder, a moving float, and a calibrated scale. When acid is drawn into the glass cylinder, the calibrated float displaces its weight in acid, and thereby reveals the specific gravity of the battery acid and the condition of the battery. Hydrometers are available at auto supply houses at a fairly low price. It is often possible to have the specific gravity checked at a service station.

VACUUM GAUGE

Another useful instrument in troubleshooting and tuning the Volkswagen is the vacuum gauge, which can be applied with the use of a T-connection to the vacuum take-off from the carburetor to the distributor advance mechanism. On engines with a throttle regulator, the vacuum gauge should be T-connected to the regulator hose which comes from the intake manifold. An adapter for a vacuum fitting is available for engines which do not have any vacuum connection to the distributor. This adapter mounts under the carburetor. Because of atmospheric variables, engine design, and many other factors, it is not practical to establish a fixed vacuum gauge reading for any engine, even engines of the same basic series. Nevertheless, a vacuum gauge reading, in inches of mercury (in. Hg), is a very reliable index of performance value for comparison purposes.

Before taking vacuum gauge readings, the engine should be warmed up to operating temperature and allowed to idle. At a normal idle, the typical engine will show a reading of about 18 in. Hg with the pointer steady. Gauge readings indicate various conditions, as follows:

1   If the reading is low, but steady, the trouble indicates a condition that affects all of the cylinders, such as, late valve timing, late ignition timing, or an intake manifold leak. Any of the above conditions can result in a reduction of up to 2 in. Hg in vacuum gauge reading. A more severe condition (cracked intake manifold, warped intake manifold, or

Specific Gravity Reading	Charge Condtion
1.260–1.280	Fully charged
1.230–1.250	¾ charged
1.200–1.220	½ charged
1.170–1.190	¼ charged
1.140–1.160	Almost flat
1.110–1.130	Nil

The specific gravity of the electrolyte mixture indicates the amount of battery charge

very bad carburetor-to-manifold gasket, depending upon cases) can result in an intake manifold vacuum reading drop of up to 15 in. Hg.

2   If the reading fluctuates, with rhythm (needle continues to waver in a regular pattern) it indicates trouble in one area. This may be a fouled spark plug, a burned valve seat, a cracked distributor cap, or any number of things that would upset normal combustion in only one cylinder.

3   A wavering and BOLD irregular BOLD gauge reading may be caused by the conditions listed in Step 2, but with the conditions existing in more than one cylinder. Possible causes here are a poorly adjusted carburetor, a high float level, excess wear in the distributor shaft or bushing, poorly adjusted ignition timing, too-wide spark plug gaps or poorly seating intake valves.

4   If the pointer wavers, with irregularity, as in Step 3 and the range of the needle becomes greater with an increase in speed, weak or broken valve springs are a strong possibility. However, if the range of

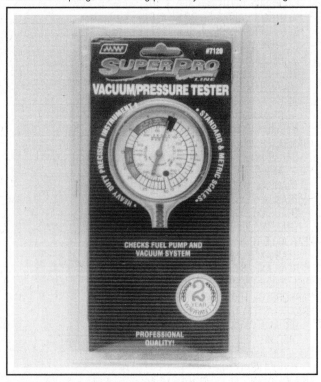

There are many aftermarket vacuum gauges available, such as this one from Make Waves

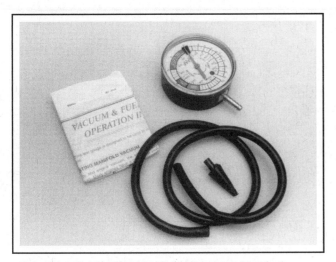

The vacuum gauge should come with vacuum hose and instructions on its use

Instead of using a separate voltmeter, ohmmeter and ammeter . . .

fluctuation of the needle decreases but the needle wavers more rapidly with increased engine speed, the trouble more than likely lies in an intake manifold leak. If the pointer tends to become more stable as the engine speed is increased, the indication would be toward trouble in the carburetor or the ignition system.

5 If the gauge needle wavers through a wide range, the trouble could lie with a gasket leakage between two adjacent cylinders. Another possibility is ignition crossfire, caused by poor plug wire insulation or by induction firing of cylinders which are adjacent to each other in the firing order. The distributor cap should also be checked for cracks. Spark plugs that are damaged or oil-fouled can cause a wide sweeping range of the needle, as can plugs which are fouled from over-rich running or gapped to the wrong specifications. In order to isolate the troubles indicated by an unsteady gauge reading, it will be necessary to use instruments that are more precise and related to more specific functions.

6 If the gauge needle registers a very low reading, it may be possible to effect a correction by changing the ignition timing to the proper specification. If this does not correct the situation, the possibilities of a leak in the intake system should be explored by the following procedure:

a) *Remove the carburetor air cleaner.*

b) *Crank the engine for about 10 revolutions while holding a hand tightly over the air horn of the carburetor. A vacuum gauge reading during this cranking period should be roughly 2/3 of the reading obtained at a normal engine idle. If the reading is low, it will be necessary to proceed further in order to narrow down the source of the leak.*

c) *Remove the carburetor and seal off the carburetor opening to the intake manifold very tightly. Repeat the cranking test and watch the gauge reading. If the reading is higher than in the previous test, the leak is in the carburetor, or at the carburetor to manifold mounting flange. Carburetor vacuum leaks could be in the distributor vacuum control line, the throttle shaft, or the result of a cracked or broken carburetor body. A method of locating leaks is to squirt oil at a suspected point and watch the vacuum gauge needle at the same time. When oil is applied to the trouble spot, the vacuum gauge needle should rise significantly.*

It is possible that exhaust restrictions can cause a low vacuum reading. Restrictions anywhere in the exhaust system (tail pipe, muffler, resonator, exhaust pipe, exhaust manifold or exhaust valve ports) can

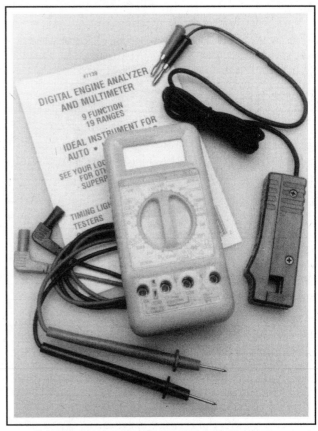

. . . purchase a digital multimeter, which combines all features of the other three

cause back pressure, especially at higher engine speeds. Such restrictions will cause the vacuum gauge reading at approximately 2,000 RPM to be only slightly, if any, higher than the reading at idle. Also, the needle may tend to hesitate in returning to the idle reading when the throttle is returned to the idle position.

VOLTMETER

A voltmeter is an instrument used to measure the voltage (electrical pressure) which tends to push electrical current through a unit or circuit. The voltmeter is connected across the terminals of the unit or circuit being tested, and the meter reading is the difference in pressure (voltage drop) between the two sides of the unit.

A compression tester provides an accurate way of troubleshooting many engine problems

AMMETER

An ammeter is an instrument used to measure the amount of electrical current flowing through a circuit or a unit. Ammeters are always connected in series with the unit or circuit being tested.

OHMMETER

The ohmmeter is used to measure the amount of electrical resistance in a unit or circuit. The ohmmeter has a self-contained power supply and is always connected across (in parallel with) the terminals of the unit being tested.

COMPRESSION GAUGE

The compression gauge is an instrument used to measure pressure in a cylinder or cylinders. With experience and skill, it is possible to combine the compression gauge with other tests in order to narrow down the source of trouble to specific problems such as poor valve

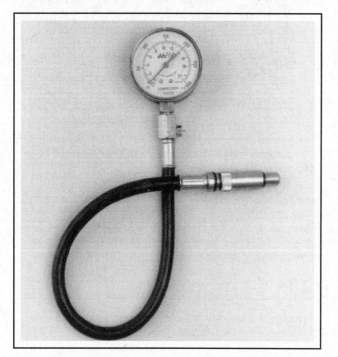

The compression tester should come with a spark plug hole adapter to fit many different engines

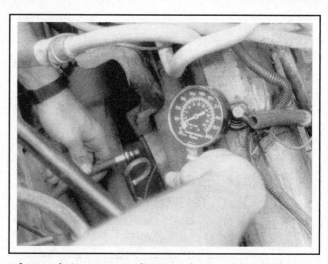

A screw-in type compression gauge is more accurate and easier to use without an assistant

seating, worn piston rings, broken pistons, or blown cylinder head gaskets. In addition, when used and the readings recorded on a periodic basis, it is possible for the compression gauge to tell a mechanical history of the comparative wear on individual cylinders.

OSCILLOSCOPE

Because it is time consuming to check individually all the possible sources of engine trouble, it may be advisable to have a troublesome engine put under the watchful screen of an oscilloscope. These instruments are widely used in engine diagnosis, and are even available in kits or fully built for the home mechanic or do-it-yourselfer. However, the cost places them out of the reach of the average home mechanic. With the oscilloscope, it is possible to test engine components while they are actually in operation. The oscilloscope, when connected to the proper wires of the engine, presents a television screen-type picture of the situation within the running engine.

By looking at this picture, a competent mechanic can translate the lines into engine functions which, though critical, mean little to the average driver. In addition, when an oscilloscope is used in conjunction with other pieces of test equipment, most engine problems can be brought to light and subsequently corrected quickly. A good oscil-

Although not as extensive as an oscilloscope, an engine analyzer can perform many functions

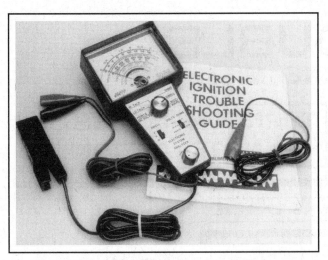

The engine analyzer booklet should provide detailed instructions on its use

loscope in the hands of an average mechanic can determine conditions such as the following:

- Compression balance.
- Condition of spark plugs.
- Condition of distributor points.
- Ignition coil or condenser problems.
- Bad ignition wiring.
- Distributor point dwell measurement.
- Cracked distributor cap.
- Worn or broken rotor.
- Worn distributor points.
- Bad secondary wires and terminals.
- Reversed coil polarity.
- Distributor shaft "wobble."

Many other items, depending on the scope of the instrument and the experience of the mechanic.

Engine Mechanical Troubleshooting

The accompanying engine diagnosis chart, is a flow diagram presentation of the logic involved in tracking down problems within the engine and narrowing down the field of possible engine ailments. The following engine conditions and possible causes should also prove helpful to the troubleshooter:

ENGINE WILL NOT START

The following are possible reasons why the engine will not start. Eliminate them one at a time.
1 Battery is weak.
2 Coil or condenser is faulty.
3 Cracked or shorted ignition cables.
4 Defective starter motor.
5 Starter solenoid defective.
6 Moisture contained in distributor cap.
7 Battery connections loose or corroded.
8 Blockage of fuel line.
9 Carburetor float setting incorrect.
10 Fuel pump inoperative.
11 Dirt in carburetor, blocking needle valve or jet.
12 Carburetor flooded due to extended starting attempts.

13 Distributor contact points dirty.
14 Ignition timing incorrect.
15 Spark plugs improperly gapped.

ENGINE MISSES DURING ACCELERATION

The following are possible reasons why the engine misses during acceleration. Eliminate them one at a time until the problem is discovered.
1 Ignition timing incorrect.
2 Spark plugs dirty or improperly gapped.
3 Faulty carburetor accelerator pump.
4 Distributor contact points dirty or burned.
5 Engine valves burned or warped.
6 Carburetor improperly adjusted.
7 Ignition coil or condenser faulty.
8 Distributor advance mechanism inoperative.

ENGINE MISSES AT HIGH SPEEDS

The following are possible reasons why the engine misses at high speeds. Eliminate them one at a time until the problem is discovered.
1 Dirt in fuel line or carburetor.
2 Ignition timing incorrect.
3 Excessive play in distributor shaft.
4 Distributor cam or rotor burned or worn.
5 Ignition points incorrectly gapped.
6 Inoperative ignition coil or condenser.

ENGINE EXHIBITS POOR PERFORMANCE AT ALL SPEEDS

The following are possible reasons why the engine exhibits poor performance at all speeds. Eliminate them one at a time until the problem is discovered.
1 Ignition timing incorrect.
2 Ignition coil or condenser faulty.
3 Excessive play in distributor shaft.
4 Distributor shaft cam worn.
5 Malfunctioning of distributor advance mechanism.
6 Spark plugs dirty or incorrectly gapped.
7 Compression low or unbalanced in different cylinders.
8 Ignition cables cracked and shorting out.
9 Engine valves burned, warped, or pitted.
10 Carburetor float setting incorrect.
11 Fuel line or carburetor blocked by dirt.
12 Excessive back pressure in exhaust system due to clogged muffler or tail pipe.
13 Valve timing incorrect.
14 Leaky intake manifold or carburetor gasket.
15 Carburetor out of adjustment or broken.

ENGINE STALLS

The following are possible reasons why the engine stalls. Eliminate them one at a time until the problem is discovered.
1 Incorrect idle speed setting.
2 Choke adjustment incorrect.
3 Improper slow-speed mixture setting in carburetor.
4 Coil or condenser faulty.
5 Distributor points dirty or incorrectly gapped.

TROUBLE
ENGINE MISFIRING

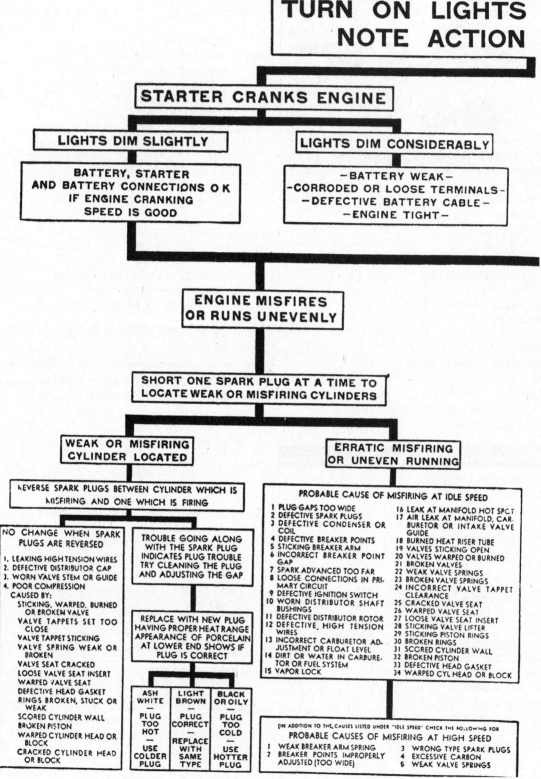

TURN ON LIGHTS NOTE ACTION

STARTER CRANKS ENGINE

LIGHTS DIM SLIGHTLY

BATTERY, STARTER
AND BATTERY CONNECTIONS O K
IF ENGINE CRANKING
SPEED IS GOOD

LIGHTS DIM CONSIDERABLY

—BATTERY WEAK—
—CORRODED OR LOOSE TERMINALS—
—DEFECTIVE BATTERY CABLE—
—ENGINE TIGHT—

ENGINE MISFIRES OR RUNS UNEVENLY

SHORT ONE SPARK PLUG AT A TIME TO LOCATE WEAK OR MISFIRING CYLINDERS

WEAK OR MISFIRING CYLINDER LOCATED

REVERSE SPARK PLUGS BETWEEN CYLINDER WHICH IS MISFIRING AND ONE WHICH IS FIRING

NO CHANGE WHEN SPARK PLUGS ARE REVERSED

1. LEAKING HIGH TENSION WIRES
2. DEFECTIVE DISTRIBUTOR CAP
3. WORN VALVE STEM OR GUIDE
4. POOR COMPRESSION
   CAUSED BY:
   STICKING, WARPED, BURNED OR BROKEN VALVE
   VALVE TAPPETS SET TOO CLOSE
   VALVE TAPPET STICKING
   VALVE SPRING WEAK OR BROKEN
   VALVE SEAT CRACKED
   LOOSE VALVE SEAT INSERT
   WARPED VALVE SEAT
   DEFECTIVE HEAD GASKET
   RINGS BROKEN, STUCK OR WEAK
   SCORED CYLINDER WALL
   BROKEN PISTON
   WARPED CYLINDER HEAD OR BLOCK
   CRACKED CYLINDER HEAD OR BLOCK

TROUBLE GOING ALONG WITH THE SPARK PLUG INDICATES PLUG TROUBLE TRY CLEANING THE PLUG AND ADJUSTING THE GAP

REPLACE WITH NEW PLUG HAVING PROPER HEAT RANGE APPEARANCE OF PORCELAIN AT LOWER END SHOWS IF PLUG IS CORRECT

ASH WHITE — PLUG TOO HOT — USE COLDER PLUG	LIGHT BROWN — PLUG CORRECT — REPLACE WITH SAME TYPE	BLACK OR OILY — PLUG TOO COLD — USE HOTTER PLUG

ERRATIC MISFIRING OR UNEVEN RUNNING

PROBABLE CAUSE OF MISFIRING AT IDLE SPEED

1 PLUG GAPS TOO WIDE
2 DEFECTIVE SPARK PLUGS
3 DEFECTIVE CONDENSER OR COIL
4 DEFECTIVE BREAKER POINTS
5 STICKING BREAKER ARM
6 INCORRECT BREAKER POINT GAP
7 SPARK ADVANCED TOO FAR
8 LOOSE CONNECTIONS IN PRIMARY CIRCUIT
9 DEFECTIVE IGNITION SWITCH
10 WORN DISTRIBUTOR SHAFT BUSHINGS
11 DEFECTIVE DISTRIBUTOR ROTOR
12 DEFECTIVE, HIGH TENSION WIRES
13 INCORRECT CARBURETOR ADJUSTMENT OR FLOAT LEVEL
14 DIRT OR WATER IN CARBURETOR OR FUEL SYSTEM
15 VAPOR LOCK
16 LEAK AT MANIFOLD HOT SPOT
17 AIR LEAK AT MANIFOLD, CARBURETOR OR INTAKE VALVE GUIDE
18 BURNED HEAT RISER TUBE
19 VALVES STICKING OPEN
20 VALVES WARPED OR BURNED
21 BROKEN VALVES
22 WEAK VALVE SPRINGS
23 BROKEN VALVE SPRINGS
24 INCORRECT VALVE TAPPET CLEARANCE
25 CRACKED VALVE SEAT
26 WARPED VALVE SEAT
27 LOOSE VALVE SEAT INSERT
28 STICKING VALVE LIFTER
29 STICKING PISTON RINGS
30 BROKEN RINGS
31 SCORED CYLINDER WALL
32 BROKEN PISTON
33 DEFECTIVE HEAD GASKET
34 WARPED CYL HEAD OR BLOCK

[IN ADDITION TO THE CAUSES LISTED UNDER "IDLE SPEED" CHECK THE FOLLOWING FOR]
PROBABLE CAUSES OF MISFIRING AT HIGH SPEED

1 WEAK BREAKER ARM SPRING
2 BREAKER POINTS IMPROPERLY ADJUSTED (TOO WIDE)
3 WRONG TYPE SPARK PLUGS
4 EXCESSIVE CARBON
5 WEAK VALVE SPRINGS

SHOOTING
LACK OF POWER

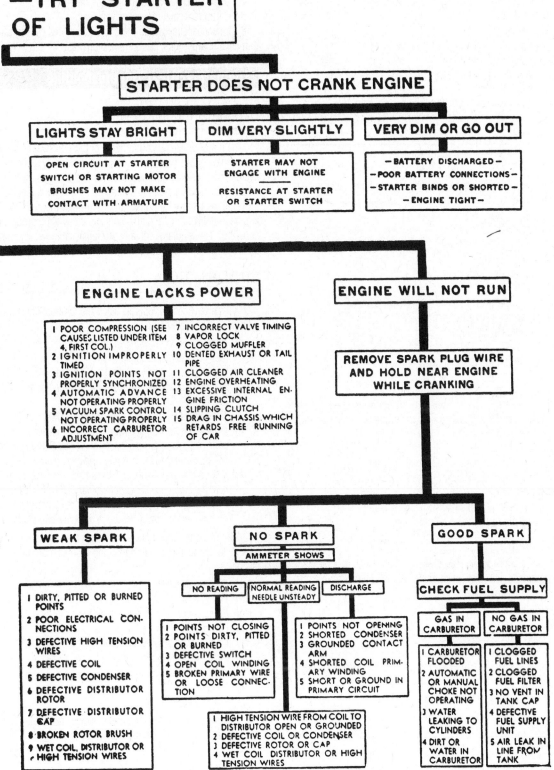

6 Carburetor float setting incorrect.
7 Leaky intake manifold or carburetor gasket.
8 Ignition wiring faulty.

LOW OIL PRESSURE

The following are possible reasons why the engine exhibits low oil pressure. Eliminate them one at a time until the problem is discovered.
1 Oil thin or diluted.
2 Oil level too low.
3 Oil pump worn or not operating properly.
4 Bearing clearances excessive.
5 Oil pressure sending unit inoperative.
6 Oil pressure relief valve sticking.
7 Obstruction in oil pump suction tube.

ENGINE NOISES

Valve

The following are possible reasons why the engine is making valve noises. Eliminate them one at a time until the problem is discovered.
1 Sticky valves.
2 Bent valve stem.
3 Warped or burned valve head.
4 Valve spring broken.
5 Valve tappets out of adjustment.
6 Loose rocker arms.
7 Bent or worn pushrod.
8 Worn or loose rocker arm shaft.
9 Worn valve or tappet guides.
10 Tappets dirty.
11 Valve springs of wrong specifications.

Piston

The following are possible reasons why the engine is making piston noises. Eliminate them one at a time until the problem is discovered.
1 Piston collapsed or broken.
2 Piston pin too tight.
3 Excessive clearance between piston and cylinder.
4 Piston or cylinder wall scored.
5 Broken piston rings.
6 Loose or broken piston pin.
7 Misalignment of piston and cylinder bore.

Crankshaft Bearing

The following are possible reasons why the engine is making crankshaft bearing noises. Eliminate them one at a time until the problem is discovered.
1 Loose connecting rod bearing.
2 Main bearing loose.
3 Connecting rod bent.
4 Flywheel loose.
5 Excessive crankshaft end-play (noticeable when engaging clutch).
6 Loose crankshaft pulley. (Sounds like bearing.)
7 Crankshaft misalignment.

DETONATION

The following are possible reasons why the engine is producing detonation noises. Eliminate them one at a time until the problem is discovered.

Detonation is a spontaneous combustion within the cylinder. It is caused by an imbalance of compression ratio, heat, fuel value, and timing. Detonation can be annoying, wasteful and also destructive to engine parts.
1 Excessively high engine temperature.
2 Spark plugs that are too hot for their intended use.
3 Improper ignition timing.
4 Use of a fuel of a too low octane rating.
5 Carburetor mixture excessively lean.
6 Incandescence within the combustion area caused by carbon particles, sharp edges, burnt spark plugs, etc.

Engine Electrical Troubleshooting

GENERAL INFORMATION

The major electrical components of the Volkswagen are the generator, the starter motor, the battery, the ignition system, the lighting system, and the electrical accessories. The electrical system is of the negative-ground type and is controlled by a voltage regulator which prevents the battery from discharging through the generator when the engine is not running and also controls the voltage produced by the generator. The regulator contains no replaceable wearing parts, and for this reason cannot be repaired in a normal workshop.

STARTER MOTOR

1 If starter does not operate when the ignition key is turned (switch on lights when testing):
   a) *If the lights do not burn, the battery is run down or the cables are loose or poorly grounded.*
   b) *If the lights go out when the key is turned to the **START** position, the terminals are corroded or the connections are loose.*
   c) *If the lights go dim, the battery is run down.*
   d) *If the lights stay bright when the key is turned, make a jumper contact between terminals **30** and **50** at the starter motor. If the starter operates, there is an open circuit.*
   e) *If the lights stay bright and the solenoid switch operates, disconnect the battery cable from terminal **30** at the starter motor and attach it to the connector strip terminal. If the starter motor operates, the solenoid is defective and should be replaced.*

2 If the starter does not operate when the battery cable is attached directly to connector strip terminal, the problem could be any of the following.
   a) *Sticking brushes.*
   b) *Worn brushes.*
   c) *Brushes not making contact, weak spring tension.*
   d) *Commutator dirty.*
   e) *Commutator grooved or burned.*
   f) *Defective armature or field coils.*
   g) *Jammed armature end bearings.*
   h) *Bent shaft.*
   i) *Broken starter housing.*

3 If the starter turns the engine slowly or not at all, the problem could be any of the following.
   a) *Run down battery.*
   b) *Loose connections.*
   c) *Sticking or worn starter motor brushes.*

d) *Commutator dirty, grooved, or burned.*
e) *Defective armature or field coils.*
f) *Broken or seized engine parts, such as crankshaft seized in bearings, bent or broken connecting rod, or seized connecting rod bearing.*

4   If the starter engages, but cranks the engine erratically, the problem could be any of the following.

a) *Defective drive pinion.*
b) *Defective flywheel gear ring.*

5   If the starter drive pinion does not disengage:

a) *Dirty or damaged drive pinion or armature shaft.*
b) *Defective solenoid switch.*

GENERATOR

1   Generator light does not light up when ignition switch is turned BOLD ON BOLD with the engine not running:

a) *Bulb burned out.*
b) *Ignition switch defective.*
c) *Battery terminals loose or corroded.*
d) *Battery discharged or defective.*
e) *Defective voltage regulator.*
f) *Generator brushes not making contact with commutator.*

2   Generator charging lamp remains on or comes on occasionally when the engine is accelerated:

a) *Generator belt slipping.*
b) *Defective voltage regulator.*
c) *Commutator dirty.*

3   Generator lamp goes out only at high speed:

a) *Defective generator or voltage regulator.*

4   Generator lamp remains on when ignition switch is turned BOLD OFF: BOLD

a) *Voltage regulator contact points sticking.*

IGNITION SYSTEM

The ignition system is divided into two circuits: a low voltage or PRIMARY circuit, and a high voltage or SECONDARY circuit. The purpose of the primary circuit is to carry current at battery voltage. It includes the battery, ignition-starter switch, starter solenoid, primary winding of the coil, condenser, contact points, and ground. The secondary circuit begins with the ignition coil. The secondary voltage is a product of the coil and emerges from the secondary terminal of the coil and flows through a cable to the distributor cap. From the distributor cap, it flows through the rotor, through the distributor cables, to the spark plugs, and ultimately to the ground. The secondary circuit must be handled with a great deal of caution, as the electrical pressure (voltage) in this circuit can reach as high as 30,000 volts.

1   Burned or pitted distributor contact points:

a) *Dirt or oil on contact point surfaces.*
b) *Voltage regulator setting too high.*
c) *Contact points misaligned, or point gap too small.*
d) *Defective coil.*
e) *Defective condenser or condenser of wrong capacity.*
f) *"Wobble" in distributor cam shaft.*

2   Failure of ignition coil:

a) *Carbon tracking in coil tower.*
b) *Voltage regulator setting too high.*

3   Failure of condenser:

a) *Normal fatigue or damage due to heat or moisture.*

Testing Coil Polarity

See Figure 2

The polarity of the coil is predetermined, and designed to suit the rest of the ignition circuit. Electron flow through the spark plug is generally better from the hotter center plug electrode-to-ground than by the opposite route, i.e. from ground-to-center electrode. It is for this reason that negative to ground polarity is the most popular set-up. There is said to be about a 14;pc difference in required voltage of the two polarity systems at idle speed, with the differential increasing with increasing engine speed.

Correct coil polarity can be checked by the use of a voltmeter, in which case the voltmeter negative lead is connected to the secondary wire of the coil, and the positive voltmeter lead to the engine ground. If the voltmeter reading is up-scale, polarity is correct; if, however, the voltmeter reading is down-scale, the coil polarity is reversed. Another method of checking for correct coil polarity is to hold a regular carbon pencil in the gap between a disconnected spark plug wire and ground (or the plug). It is possible to observe the direction of spark flow from wire-to-pencil-to-ground when polarity is correct (see accompanying diagram). Although terminal sizes and cable lengths discourage improper battery installation, improper attachment of the battery and distributor terminals of the coil can still result in reversed polarity.

Testing Condenser

The condenser helps the ignition system attain the high voltage necessary for plug sparking, and also serves to prevent the points from burning prematurely by reducing spark formation when the points are breaking. It is rare that a condenser will give trouble, but if one is suspected to be defective, and no condenser tester is available, the following procedure should be followed:

1   Remove the distributor cap and turn the engine until the contact points are fully open.

2   Disconnect cable No. 1 at the ignition coil.

3   Using a 6- or 12-volt test lamp, connect one lead of the lamp to terminal No. 15 of the ignition coil as shown in the wiring diagram, and connect the other lamp lead to the distributor cable which was removed from the coil in Step 2.

4   Turn on the ignition and note whether the test lamp lights. If it

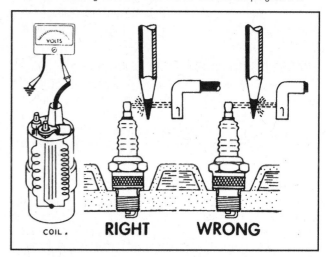

A carbon pencil can be used to determine whether or not the polarity in your ignition system is correct

does, the condenser is grounded and must be replaced.

5   Reconnect cable No. 1 to the ignition coil.

6   Test for a suitable spark by removing the main high tension cable from the distributor cap and holding it about 1/4 in. (6mm) from a suitable ground. With the engine turned over with the ignition BOLD ON, BOLD the spark should be able to jump the 1/4 in. (6mm) distance. If the spark is not able to jump the gap, the test should be repeated with a condenser known to be non-defective.

Clutch Troubleshooting

While nothing can substitute perfectly for a careful examination and experience, it is nevertheless helpful to be aware of the symptoms which may accompany clutch problems so that they may be attacked in an orderly fashion. Some of these symptoms are:

- Excessive noise
- Clutch chatter or grab
- Clutch slipping
- Clutch drag or failure to release
- Pulsation of the clutch pedal
- Low life of clutch facing
- Gear lockup or hard shifting
- Hard pedal

For each of these symptoms, there is a logical sequence of possible causes and remedies. Once the causes are known, the remedies should be relatively obvious. It is for this reason that in the troubleshooting portion of this book only the causes are discussed in any detail.

EXCESSIVE CLUTCH NOISE

RELEASE BEARING

When the engine is idling and the foot is resting on the clutch pedal, there will be a high-pitched rubbing noise. Usual causes of release bearing failure are age of bearing, riding the clutch, insufficient pedal free-play, lack of lubricant in the bearing, and worn or out-of-true clutch release fingers.

PILOT BEARING

Clutch shaft pilot bearing noises are heard only when the bearing is in operation; in other words, when the crankshaft speed is different from the speed of the clutch shaft - when the clutch is disengaged and the transmission is in gear. The noise made by the pilot bearing is a high-pitched squeal and the bearing, which is probably dry, should be replaced.

TRANSMISSION PINION SHAFT BEARING

A rough or damaged input shaft bearing noise will be heard only when the clutch is engaged and the transmission is in any position. The noise is generally most noticeable when the transmission is in Neutral. The noise should diminish and completely disappear when the clutch is disengaged and the pinion gear of the transmission slows down and stops.

TRANSMITTED ENGINE NOISES

When the correct amount of free-play is present in the clutch pedal, there should not be an unreasonable amount of noise transmitted to the passenger area via the clutch. Such noises, if they exist, are generally modified through a manipulation of the clutch pedal. Such problems rarely exist in the Volkswagen because of the relatively great distance between the clutch pedal and the engine compartment.

CLUTCH LINKAGE NOISE

Noise in the clutch linkage is generally a clicking or snapping sound heard or felt in the pedal itself when the pedal is moved completely up or down. If the noise is heard to occur within the center tunnel of the passenger compartment, there is a strong possibility that lubrication is needed at the pivot point just inside the tunnel. In this case, the pedal cluster (throttle, brake and clutch) must be removed by means of the two mounting bolts, and the pivot point lubricated with a high quality grease such as lithium-base type. If such grease is not used to lubricate this point, it will be a matter of only a few weeks before lubrication is again required.

CLUTCH CHATTER OR GRAB

The cause of clutch chatter or grab is generally located within the clutch assembly and can be corrected only by removal of the engine and the clutch from the vehicle. To diagnose, perform the following procedure:

1   Check to ensure that the clutch linkage is in adjustment and not grinding. If necessary, the linkage should be adjusted, aligned and lubricated.

2   Check for defective, worn, or loose engine and/or transmission mounts. If necessary, such mounts must be tightened or replaced.

3   Check the attaching bolts on the clutch pressure plate for looseness. Also tighten or replace loose bolts on the transmission and clutch housings.

4   Check freedom of movement of the clutch release bearing. Free it up or replace it as necessary.

5   Check the clutch and flywheel for oil or grease. The trouble may also be caused by oil or grease on the friction disc or pressure plate.

6   Check the friction disc for warpage, and ensure that the disc hub is not binding on the splines of the transmission input shaft.

7   Check the disc and pressure plate for breakage.

8   Examine the pressure plate and cover plate assembly for cracks or heat discoloration.

CLUTCH SLIPPAGE

This condition is generally most noticeable when the car is started from a standing stop or when the gears are shifted quickly and the clutch disengaged quickly for fast acceleration. This treatment of the clutch may well be the cause of clutch slippage sooner or later, for no clutch is designed to withstand such mistreatment for long. One way of testing for clutch slippage is to apply the parking brake with the car on a level surface, start the engine and put the transmission into second gear. With the foot brake also applied, accelerate the engine slightly and release the clutch pedal. If the clutch is in good condition, it will grip and the engine will stall. If, however, the clutch is heard to slip, the cause may be one or more of the following:

- Insufficient free-play at the clutch pedal.
- Broken or disconnected parts in the clutch.
- Clutch linkage binding and not allowing full-pressure application of the clutch.
- Oil or grease on the friction disc. Also a worn friction disc.
- Worn pressure plate or weak springs from temper loss or failure. Such damaging heat as results in temper loss will usually cause the afflicted parts to appear blue.

In applying the clutch slippage test, it should be remembered that this test is most severe. In other words, one should not apply this test every other day in order to determine whether one's clutch is slipping.

After not too many of these tests, it is practically guaranteed that the clutch will slip if it wasn't slipping before.

CLUTCH DRAG OR FAILURE TO RELEASE

Clutch drag is the condition that takes place when the clutch pedal is fully depressed and the clutch disc is not completely released. The clutch disc does not come fully to rest, but continues to be rotated due to the rotation of the engine. Dragging of the clutch generally causes difficult shifting and clashing of the gears, especially when shifting in the lower gears. Possible causes of clutch drag are:

- Insufficient pedal free-play
- Clutch plate binding on the transmission input shaft
- Pressure plate or friction disc warped or bent
- Misalignment, engine to transmission
- Transmission lubricant too thick

CLUTCH PEDAL PULSATION

This condition is evident when, with a slight pressure applied to the pedal, and the engine running, the pedal is felt to vibrate or pulsate with every revolution of the engine. When the pedal is pushed down further, the pulsation is no longer evident. Clutch pedal pulsation may be caused by any of the following:

- Clutch release fingers bent or uneven
- Flywheel run-out excessive due to bent flywheel or crankshaft flange
- Release bearing cocked on transmission bearing retainer
- Poor alignment of engine and transmission

LOW CLUTCH-FACING LIFE

When low clutch-facing life is experienced, the first thing to look for is the presence of improper driving habits on the part of the operator(s) of the vehicle. These are the most likely reasons why the lining is not lasting as long as it should. The possible causes of low clutch facing life are:

- Riding the clutch, i.e. driving with the left foot constantly on the clutch pedal, or slipping the clutch instead of shifting to a lower gear.
- Jack-rabbit type starts from stop lights, etc.
- Continuous overloading of the car, or the excessive hauling of heavy trailers or other equipment.
- Using the clutch to keep from drifting backward while stopped on a grade. When stopped on a grade, the handbrake should be applied rather than holding position by slipping the clutch.
- Improper amount of clutch pedal free-play.
- The presence of a rough surface on the flywheel or the pressure plate.
- The presence of oil or water on the clutch facing material.
- Clutch creep or slip caused by weak pressure plate springs.

GEAR LOCK UP OR HARD SHIFTING

The causes of this condition are similar to those that cause the Clutch Drag or Failure to Release condition, and should be diagnosed in the same manner. If, however, the elimination of all possible causes as listed in this section does not serve to locate the cause of the problem, it is most likely that the problem lies in the shifting assembly, the transaxle cover, or in the transaxle itself. In the latter case, it will be necessary to dismantle the transaxle and correct the cause of the trouble.

A HARD CLUTCH PEDAL

The presence of this condition is evidenced by a clutch pedal that requires an abnormal amount of pedal pressure in order to disengage the clutch. Possible causes are:

- Dry or binding linkage
- Clutch linkage out of alignment
- Release bearing sleeve dry or binding
- Use of the wrong type of clutch assembly, especially one of the heavier duty than is required

Transaxle Troubleshooting

It is generally acknowledged that the Volkswagen transaxle is one of the most durable parts of the automobile. Any well-treated VW transaxle is capable of well over 100,000 trouble-free miles. In the event, however, that an owner should have transaxle problems, here are some problems along with their possible causes:

CAR IS NOISY WHILE MOVING IN ANY GEAR

- Insufficient lubrication
- One or more worn bearings in the transaxle
- Mainshaft end-play excessive
- Sliding gears worn or broken
- Misalignment of transaxle case or clutch housing

TRANSAXLE SLIPS OUT OF GEAR

- Improper shifting procedure
- Worn shift detent parts
- Shift linkage improperly adjusted
- Misalignment between the transaxle and the engine

TRANSAXLE NOISY IN NEUTRAL

- Insufficient lubrication
- One or more worn gears or bearings

TRANSAXLE DIFFICULT TO SHIFT

- Shift linkage improperly adjusted
- Clutch not releasing properly
- Improper lubricant in transaxle
- Binding of shift linkage due to worn or damaged parts

TRANSAXLE LEAKS LUBRICANT

- Axle boot not sealing properly due to looseness, crack, or other damage.
- Oil seals damaged.
- Transaxle axle retainer nuts loose. (Do not overtighten because the retainer will then be slightly distorted and may leak more than before.)
- Transaxle housing nuts loose.
- Transaxle filler and/or drain plugs loose or stripped of thread.
- Use of a lubricant that tends to foam excessively.
- Excessively high transaxle oil level.

Rear Axle Troubleshooting

The Volkswagen rear axle and transaxle are combined in a single unit. Therefore, some of the possible problems may be hard to attribute to one assembly or the other, especially in the event of lubricant leakage. When lubricant leaks from one part of the unit, it may be blown onto another section or carried there by gravity while the car is in motion. However, like the transaxle, the Volkswagen rear axle is a very sturdy piece of equipment, and not likely to give any trouble for a very long time. In the event of trouble, here are possible problems and causes:

REAR AXLE LEAKS LUBRICANT

- Excess level of lubricant in unit.
- Leakage at rear axle boots, caused by improper sealing or damaged boots.
- Oil is too light or of poor quality.
- Axle retainer not tightened down properly. Improper sealing of seals or gaskets.

REAR AXLE NOISES

Because of the close proximity of the rear axle to the transaxle and the engine, it should be ascertained that the rear axle is in fact making whatever noise is being heard. The following are possible causes of noise in the vicinity of the rear axle:

Tire noise - driving the car over various types of road surfaces will reveal the extent of tire noise. If tire noise is to be minimized for noise detection purposes, it is advisable to drive on a smooth asphalt or black top road while trying to pinpoint noise causes.

Rear wheel bearing noise can be checked by jacking up the car and rotating the rear wheels, by coasting at a low speed, or by driving at low speed and applying the brakes after disengaging the clutch. If, in the latter test, the noise diminishes, defective wheel bearings are a definite possibility.

Noise when accelerating in a straight line is generally caused by heavy heel contact on the gear teeth. It is necessary to move the ring gear nearer to the drive pinion.

If noise is most evident when coasting with the car in gear and the throttle closed, it is most likely that there is heavy toe contact on the gear teeth, in which case the ring gear must be moved away from the drive pinion.

➡**The toe end of the gear tooth is the smaller of the two circles formed by the ends of the gear teeth, while the heel is the larger circle.**

If the noise is present only when the car is driven around a curve, the cause of the noise is probably excessive backlash between gears, damaged gears or thrust washers, differential side gears that are tight in the case, or differential-pinion gears that are tight on the pinion shaft.

The cause of a knocking noise in the rear axle may be bearings or gears that are either damaged or badly worn.

The presence of a constant humming noise may indicate that the drive pinion or ring gear is out of adjustment. Such a condition should be remedied before gear-tooth wear becomes significant and the noise changes from a hum to a growl.

Excessive end-play in the shafts of the rear axles will result in a thumping sound being heard when the car is driven around a corner on a rough road.

Fuel Pump Troubleshooting

Problems in the fuel system are generally of two different types: fuel pump troubles and carburetor troubles.

Following are some of the problems and possible causes within the mechanically operated diaphragm fuel pump:

1 Pump leaking at joining faces and losing fuel.
   a) *Screws insufficiently tightened.*
   b) *Torn fuel pump diaphragm.*
2 Diaphragm leaking at rivets and losing fuel.
   a) *Diaphragm is damaged and must be replaced.*
3 Diaphragm material leaky.
   a) *Diaphragm material is damaged by solvent substance in fuel, and must be replaced.*
4 Excessive pump stroke overstraining diaphragm.
   a) *Pump not installed correctly; gasket too thin.*
5 Pump pressure low
   a) *Pump incorrectly installed; gasket too thick.*
   b) *Spring pressure low.*
6 Pump pressure excessive; float needle valve forced down.
   a) *Pump installed incorrectly; gasket too thin.*
   b) *Spring pressure excessive.*
7 Fuel pump inoperative or insufficient fuel delivery.
   a) *Valves leaky or sticking; top half of pump must be renewed.*

Carburetor Troubleshooting

The following are some of the problems and possible causes within the carburetor:

1 Engine will not start (ignition system working properly and fuel in tank.)
   a) *Automatic choke not working properly.*
   b) *Choke valve sticking.*
   c) *Bi-metallic spring broken or unhooked.*
   d) *Ceramic plate broken.*
   e) *Float needle valve sticking, causing flooding of carburetor.*
2 Engine runs at a fast idle.
   a) *Automatic choke not switching off.*
   b) *Defective heater element.*
   c) *Throttle positioner incorrectly adjusted.*
3 Engine runs unevenly, with tendency to stall.
   a) *Incorrect idle speed adjustment.*
   b) *Carburetor pilot jet blocked.*
   c) *Incorrect idle mixture adjustment.*
   d) *Throttle positioner incorrectly adjusted.*
4 Engine diesels (runs on) after ignition is turned BOLD OFF. BOLD
   a) *Idling mixture too lean.*
   b) *Idle speed too fast.*
   c) *Electro-magnetic cut-off jet inoperative.*
5 Banging in the exhaust when the engine is revved.
   a) *Idle mixture too weak.*
   b) *Throttle positioner incorrectly adjusted.*
6 Poor transfer from idle speed to normal running.
   a) *Defective accelerator pump system; sticking ball or blocked passages.*

b) Accelerator pump diaphragm torn.

c) Incorrect idle adjustment.

d) Accelerator pump system injecting too much or too little fuel.

7   Engine stalls when accelerator is suddenly released.

a) Idle mixture too rich.

8   Engine runs unevenly at low idle speed; exhaust soots excessively at high idle speed; spark plugs tend to soot up. (i.e. the mixture is too rich.)

a) Excessive fuel pump pressure causing needle valve to remain open.

b) Float leaking.

c) Float needle valve defective, not closing.

9   Engine runs unevenly, misfires at high speeds.

a) Fuel starvation, due to dirty main jet, needle valve, fuel tank, or insufficient fuel pump pressure.

10 Excessive fuel consumption.

a) Incorrect jet sizes.

b) Excessive fuel pump pressure causing float level to be too high.

c) Float leaking, causing high float level.

d) Float needle valve does not close.

e) Improper operation of automatic choke.

➡**When checking and adjusting the carburetors one should keep in mind that the engine will respond to fine carburetor adjustments only after the electrical and mechanical parts of the engine are set to the proper specifications. If such things as the ignition timing, valve clearance, compression balance, and point gap are not in order, fine carburetor tuning will be of little or no avail.**

Brake System Troubleshooting

DRUM BRAKES

1   Pedal goes to floorboard.

a) Normal lining wear. Adjust or renew shoes.

2   Spongy response at brake pedal.

a) Air present in the hydraulic system.

b) Lack of fluid in the master cylinder reservoir. Top up.

3   Without braking action, pedal goes to floorboard although system has been bled and adjusted.

a) Defective valve in master cylinder.

b) Dirty valve seat. Clean or renew.

4   Braking action is obtained only after pumping pedal several times.

a) Air is present in the system.

b) Piston return-spring weak.

5   Although brakes have been adjusted, brake action decreases and pedal goes to floorboard.

a) Fluid leak in the braking system.

b) Damaged or unserviceable cups in master or wheel cylinder.

6   Brakes drag and overheat.

a) Clogging of by-pass port in master cylinder.

b) Insufficient clearance between piston pushrod and master cylinder piston.

c) Shoe return-springs broken or weak.

d) Rubber parts swollen because of improper brake fluid being used.

7   Poor stopping accompanied by excessive pressure required on pedal.

a) Oil on brake shoe lining.

b) Improper brake shoe lining.

8   Brakes bind while driving.

a) By-pass port in master cylinder not free, possibly as the result of a swollen or deformed cup.

b) Improper brake fluid in use.

c) Incorrect position of brake pedal stop plate.

9   Brakes uneven in operation (car tends to pull to left or right when brakes are applied.)

a) Oil or grease on brake shoe linings.

b) Brake drums out of round or scored.

c) Different types of linings on opposite sides of car.

d) Incorrect and/or uneven tire pressures.

e) Brake drums distorted due to uneven tightening of wheel bolts.

f) Dirt in brake lines or hoses.

g) Different types of tires (especially new versus badly worn) on opposite sides of vehicle.

h) Natural causes, such as when the right track is through snow, while the left side is on dry road. Such conditions occur often during winter on narrow snow-covered roads.

10 Brakes chatter.

a) Brake shoe lining not chamfered at ends.

b) Brake shoe lining worn; rivets making contact with drum.

c) Brake drum eccentric (out of round).

11 Brakes noisy.

a) Improper brake shoe lining.

b) Lining not chamfered at ends.

c) Brake lining loose on shoe.

d) Brakes dirty.

➡**Often brakes will squeak after the car has been in a damp atmosphere for some time. Such squeaking will occur only during the first few brake applications, and will then disappear. Sometimes brake squeaking can be stopped by inserting a high pressure air hose through the brake adjusting or inspection hole and blowing out the accumulation of dirt and brake dust. However, if such squeaking continues, other possible causes should be investigated.**

DISC BRAKES

Beginning in 1967, the Karmann Ghia models were equipped with front disc brakes, which had been standard on type 3 models since the 1966 model year. 1949 - 69 Type 1 and 2 vehicles were not available with disc brakes. The following symptoms and possible causes relate to problems that sometimes develop in disc braking systems.

1   Excessive Pedal Travel

a) Excessive disc runout.

b) Air leak or insufficient fluid in system or in caliper.

c) Improper fluid (boils).

d) Damaged caliper piston seal.

e) Piston and/or lining not properly seated.

2   Brake roughness or chatter

a) Excessive disc runout.

b) Excessive thickness variation of disc.

c) Excessive thickness variation of lining.

3   Excessive pedal effort

a) Brake fluid, oil or grease on lining.
b) Incorrect lining.
c) Seized or frozen piston.
d) Excessively worn lining.

4 Brakes pull to one side

a) Brake fluid, grease or oil on lining.
b) Caliper out of proper alignment to disc.
c) Pistons frozen or seized.
d) Improper tire pressures.
e) Restricted hose or line.

5 Noises

a) Groaning noises: too slow brake release.
b) Rattles: excessive clearance between disc and caliper.
c) Scraping noises: mounting bolts too long, loose wheel bearings, or brake disc rubbing housing.

6 Brakes heat up and fail to release

a) Piston seized or frozen.
b) Residual pressure in master cylinder.

7 Leaky wheel cylinder

a) Caliper seals damaged or worn.
b) Cylinder bore corroded or scored.
c) Scored or corroded piston surface.

8 No braking action when pedal is depressed

a) Leak in system or caliper.
b) Leaks at rear brake system.
c) Improper rear brake adjustment.
d) Air in hydraulic system.

➡**On Volkswagens, adjusting the rear brakes automatically compensates for excessive movement of the handbrake lever. However, in the event that the handbrake operating cable has stretched, an adjustment is possible at the lever itself.**

Steering and Suspension Troubleshooting

1 Steering is stiff from lock-to-lock and front wheels do not automatically return to the straight-ahead position after a turn.

a) Inadequate lubrication of front axle.
b) Seizing or stiffening of king pins or ball joints.
c) Tight adjustment of steering gear.
d) Low level of lubricant in steering gear box.
e) Wheels out of alignment.
f) Tire pressure too low.

2 Hard steering accompanied by squeaking noise.

a) Steering wheel binding in steering column.
b) Steering column is not correctly centered in the steering column tube.

3 Although there is no binding in system, front wheels do not automatically seek the straight-ahead position after a turn.

a) Improper front alignment: caster, camber, or toe-in.
b) Steering arms of stub axles bent or twisted.

4 Excessive play in steering system.

a) Improper adjustment of steering gear.
b) Looseness in steering gear mounting.
c) Steering linkage worn excessively.

5 Car steers to one side at all times.

a) Incorrect alignment: caster, camber or king pin angle.
b) Unequal air pressure in tires or unequal tread on tires.
c) Unequal shock absorber control.
d) Bent or damaged steering components.

6 Excessive play in front suspension.

a) Worn bearing points: torsion arm link pins, front wheel bearings, stub axle.

7 Car wanders - steers erratically.

a) Front wheel bearings loose.
b) Improper tire pressure.
c) Incorrect caster.
d) Steering linkage loose.
e) Excessive wear or damaged suspension components.

8 Steering wheel spoke is at an angle when driving straight ahead.

a) Depending on which way the spoke is off the horizontal, one tie rod must be lengthened and the other shortened by the same amount in order that the toe-in is not changed. The steering wheel should not be removed, nor its position changed on the column.

Tire Wear Troubleshooting

1 Tires wear at both sides of tread.

a) Under inflation for loads carried.

2 Tires wear at center of tread.

a) Over inflation.

3 Spotty or irregular wear at one side of the tread (gouges and/or waves).

a) Wheel assembly out of balance statically and dynamically.
b) Excessive lateral wheel runout.
c) Excessive play in wheel bearings or at king pins.

4 Lightly worn spots at the center of the tread.

a) Static unbalance of wheel and tire.
b) Excessive radial run-out.

5 Isolated flat spots at center of tread.

a) Brakes binding in panic application, or brake drums out of round. Check brakes.

6 Stepped tread wear. (One end of each tread block worn more than the other.)

a) Overloading. Inside of casing should be checked for cracks.

7 Side wear.

a) Incorrect camber.
b) Continual driving on steeply cambered roads.
c) Fast cornering.

➡**For best total tire life, it is advisable to rotate all five tires, including the spare, at periodic intervals, say 5,000 miles.**

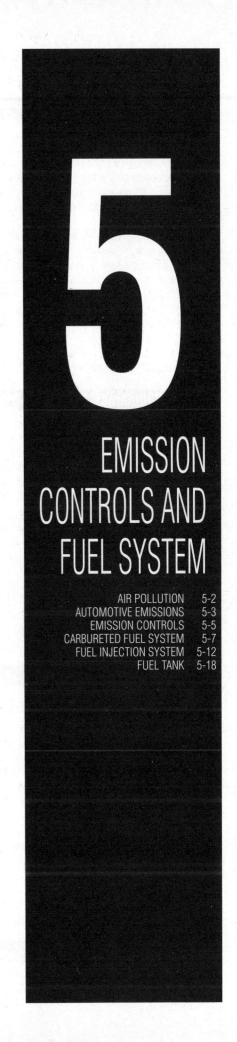

5

EMISSION CONTROLS AND FUEL SYSTEM

AIR POLLUTION

The earth's atmosphere, at or near sea level, consists approximately of 78 percent nitrogen, 21 percent oxygen and 1 percent other gases. If it were possible to remain in this state, 100 percent clean air would result. However, many varied sources allow other gases and particulates to mix with the clean air, causing our atmosphere to become unclean or polluted.

Some of these pollutants are visible while others are invisible, with each having the capability of causing distress to the eyes, ears, throat, skin and respiratory system. Should these pollutants become concentrated in a specific area and under certain conditions, death could result due to the displacement or chemical change of the oxygen content in the air. These pollutants can also cause great damage to the environment and to the many man made objects that are exposed to the elements.

To better understand the causes of air pollution, the pollutants can be categorized into 3 separate types, natural, industrial and automotive.

Natural Pollutants

Natural pollution has been present on earth since before man appeared and continues to be a factor when discussing air pollution, although it causes only a small percentage of the overall pollution problem. It is the direct result of decaying organic matter, wind born smoke and particulates from such natural events as plain and forest fires (ignited by heat or lightning), volcanic ash, sand and dust which can spread over a large area of the countryside.

Such a phenomenon of natural pollution has been seen in the form of volcanic eruptions, with the resulting plume of smoke, steam and volcanic ash blotting out the sun's rays as it spreads and rises higher into the atmosphere. As it travels into the atmosphere the upper air currents catch and carry the smoke and ash, while condensing the steam back into water vapor. As the water vapor, smoke and ash travel on their journey, the smoke dissipates into the atmosphere while the ash and moisture settle back to earth in a trail hundreds of miles long. In some cases, lives are lost and millions of dollars of property damage result.

Industrial Pollutants

Industrial pollution is caused primarily by industrial processes, the burning of coal, oil and natural gas, which in turn produce smoke and fumes. Because the burning fuels contain large amounts of sulfur, the principal ingredients of smoke and fumes are sulfur dioxide and particulate matter. This type of pollutant occurs most severely during still, damp and cool weather, such as at night. Even in its less severe form, this pollutant is not confined to just cities. Because of air movements, the pollutants move for miles over the surrounding countryside, leaving in its path a barren and unhealthy environment for all living things.

Working with Federal, State and Local mandated regulations and by carefully monitoring emissions, big business has greatly reduced the amount of pollutant introduced from its industrial sources, striving to obtain an acceptable level. Because of the mandated industrial emission clean up, many land areas and streams in and around the cities that were formerly barren of vegetation and life, have now begun to move back in the direction of nature's intended balance.

Automotive Pollutants

The third major source of air pollution is automotive emissions. The emissions from the internal combustion engines were not an appre-

ciable problem years ago because of the small number of registered vehicles and the nation's small highway system. However, during the early 1950's, the trend of the American people was to move from the cities to the surrounding suburbs. This caused an immediate problem in transportation because the majority of suburbs were not afforded mass transit conveniences. This lack of transportation created an attractive market for the automobile manufacturers, which resulted in a dramatic increase in the number of vehicles produced and sold, along with a marked increase in highway construction between cities and the suburbs. Multi-vehicle families emerged with a growing emphasis placed on an individual vehicle per family member. As the increase in vehicle ownership and usage occurred, so did pollutant levels in and around the cities, as suburbanites drove daily to their businesses and employment, returning at the end of the day to their homes in the suburbs.

It was noted that a smoke and fog type haze was being formed and at times, remained in suspension over the cities, taking time to dissipate. At first this "smog," derived from the words "smoke" and "fog," was thought to result from industrial pollution but it was determined that automobile emissions shared the blame. It was discovered that when normal automobile emissions were exposed to sunlight for a period of time, complex chemical reactions would take place.

It is now known that smog is a photo chemical layer which develops when certain oxides of nitrogen (NOx) and unburned hydrocarbons (HC) from automobile emissions are exposed to sunlight. Pollution was more severe when smog would become stagnant over an area in which a warm layer of air settled over the top of the cooler air mass, trapping and holding the cooler mass at ground level. The trapped cooler air would keep the emissions from being dispersed and diluted through normal air flows. This type of air stagnation was given the name "Temperature Inversion."

TEMPERATURE INVERSION

In normal weather situations, surface air is warmed by heat radiating from the earth's surface and the sun's rays. This causes it to rise upward, into the atmosphere. Upon rising it will cool through a convection type heat exchange with the cooler upper air. As warm air rises, the surface pollutants are carried upward and dissipated into the atmosphere.

When a temperature inversion occurs, we find the higher air is no longer cooler, but is warmer than the surface air, causing the cooler surface air to become trapped. This warm air blanket can extend from above ground level to a few hundred or even a few thousand feet into the air. As the surface air is trapped, so are the pollutants, causing a severe smog condition. Should this stagnant air mass extend to a few thousand feet high, enough air movement with the inversion takes place to allow the smog layer to rise above ground level but the pollutants still cannot dissipate. This inversion can remain for days over an area, with the smog level only rising or lowering from ground level to a few hundred feet high. Meanwhile, the pollutant levels increase, causing eye irritation, respiratory problems, reduced visibility, plant damage and in some cases, even disease.

This inversion phenomenon was first noted in the Los Angeles, California area. The city lies in terrain resembling a basin and with certain weather conditions, a cold air mass is held in the basin while a warmer air mass covers it like a lid.

Because this type of condition was first documented as prevalent in the Los Angeles area, this type of trapped pollution was named Los

Angeles Smog, although it occurs in other areas where a large concentration of automobiles are used and the air remains stagnant for any length of time.

HEAT TRANSFER

Consider the internal combustion engine as a machine in which raw materials must be placed so a finished product comes out. As in any machine operation, a certain amount of wasted material is formed. When we relate this to the internal combustion engine, we find that through the input of air and fuel, we obtain power during the combustion process to drive the vehicle. The by-product or waste of this power is, in part, heat and exhaust gases with which we must dispose.

The heat from the combustion process can rise to over 4000-degrees F (2204-degrees C). The dissipation of this heat is controlled by a ram air effect, the use of cooling fans to cause air flow and a liquid coolant solution surrounding the combustion area to transfer the heat of combustion through the cylinder walls and into the coolant. The coolant is then directed to a thin-finned, multi-tubed radiator, from which the excess heat is transferred to the atmosphere by 1 of the 3 heat transfer methods, conduction, convection or radiation.

The cooling of the combustion area is an important part in the control of exhaust emissions. To understand the behavior of the combustion and transfer of its heat, consider the air/fuel charge. It is ignited and the flame front burns progressively across the combustion chamber until the burning charge reaches the cylinder walls. Some of the fuel in contact with the walls is not hot enough to burn, thereby snuffing out or quenching the combustion process. This leaves unburned fuel in the combustion chamber. This unburned fuel is then forced out of the cylinder and into the exhaust system, along with the exhaust gases.

Many attempts have been made to minimize the amount of unburned fuel in the combustion chambers due to quenching, by increasing the coolant temperature and lessening the contact area of the coolant around the combustion area. However, design limitations within the combustion chambers prevent the complete burning of the air/fuel charge, so a certain amount of the unburned fuel is still expelled into the exhaust system, regardless of modifications to the engine.

AUTOMOTIVE EMISSIONS

Before emission controls were mandated on internal combustion engines, other sources of engine pollutants were discovered along with the exhaust emissions. It was determined that engine combustion exhaust produced approximately 60 percent of the total emission pollutants, fuel evaporation from the fuel tank and carburetor vents produced 20 percent, with the final 20 percent being produced through the crankcase as a by-product of the combustion process.

Exhaust Gases

The exhaust gases emitted into the atmosphere are a combination of burned and unburned fuel. To understand the exhaust emission and its composition, we must review some basic chemistry.

When the air/fuel mixture is introduced into the engine, we are mixing air, composed of nitrogen (78 percent), oxygen (21 percent) and other gases (1 percent) with the fuel, which is 100 percent hydrocarbons (HC), in a semi-controlled ratio. As the combustion process is accomplished, power is produced to move the vehicle while the heat of combustion is transferred to the cooling system. The exhaust gases are then composed of nitrogen, a diatomic gas (N_2), the same as was introduced in the engine, carbon dioxide (CO_2), the same gas that is used in beverage carbonation, and water vapor (H_2O). The nitrogen (N_2), for the most part, passes through the engine unchanged, while the oxygen (O_2) reacts (burns) with the hydrocarbons (HC) and produces the carbon dioxide (CO_2) and the water vapors (H_2O). If this chemical process would be the only process to take place, the exhaust emissions would be harmless. However, during the combustion process, other compounds are formed which are considered dangerous. These pollutants are hydrocarbons (HC), carbon monoxide (CO), oxides of nitrogen (NOx) oxides of sulfur (SOx) and engine particulates.

HYDROCARBONS

Hydrocarbons (HC) are essentially fuel which was not burned during the combustion process or which has escaped into the atmosphere through fuel evaporation. The main sources of incomplete combustion are rich air/fuel mixtures, low engine temperatures and improper spark timing. The main sources of hydrocarbon emission through fuel evaporation on most vehicles used to be the vehicle's fuel tank and carburetor float bowl.

To reduce combustion hydrocarbon emission, engine modifications were made to minimize dead space and surface area in the combustion chamber. In addition, the air/fuel mixture was made more lean through the improved control which feedback carburetion and fuel injection offers and by the addition of external controls to aid in further combustion of the hydrocarbons outside the engine. Two such methods were the addition of air injection systems, to inject fresh air into the exhaust manifolds and the installation of catalytic converters, units that are able to burn traces of hydrocarbons without affecting the internal combustion process or fuel economy.

To control hydrocarbon emissions through fuel evaporation, modifications were made to the fuel tank to allow storage of the fuel vapors during periods of engine shut-down. Modifications were also made to the air intake system so that at specific times during engine operation, these vapors may be purged and burned by blending them with the air/fuel mixture.

CARBON MONOXIDE

Carbon monoxide is formed when not enough oxygen is present during the combustion process to convert carbon (C) to carbon dioxide (CO_2). An increase in the carbon monoxide (CO) emission is normally accompanied by an increase in the hydrocarbon (HC) emission because of the lack of oxygen to completely burn all of the fuel mixture.

Carbon monoxide (CO) also increases the rate at which the photo chemical smog is formed by speeding up the conversion of nitric oxide (NO) to nitrogen dioxide (NO_2). To accomplish this, carbon monoxide (CO) combines with oxygen (O_2) and nitric oxide (NO) to produce carbon dioxide (CO_2) and nitrogen dioxide (NO_2). ($CO + O_2 + NO \; CO_2 + NO_2$).

The dangers of carbon monoxide, which is an odorless and colorless toxic gas are many. When carbon monoxide is inhaled into the lungs and passed into the blood stream, oxygen is replaced by the carbon monoxide in the red blood cells, causing a reduction in the amount of oxygen supplied to the many parts of the body. This lack of oxygen causes headaches, lack of coordination, reduced mental alertness and, should the carbon monoxide concentration be high enough, death could result.

NITROGEN

Normally, nitrogen is an inert gas. When heated to approximately 2500-degrees F (1371-degrees C) through the combustion process, this gas becomes active and causes an increase in the nitric oxide (NO) emission.

Oxides of nitrogen (NOx) are composed of approximately 97 - 98 percent nitric oxide (NO). Nitric oxide is a colorless gas but when it is passed into the atmosphere, it combines with oxygen and forms nitrogen dioxide (NO_2). The nitrogen dioxide then combines with chemically active hydrocarbons (HC) and when in the presence of sunlight, causes the formation of photo-chemical smog.

Ozone

To further complicate matters, some of the nitrogen dioxide (NO_2) is broken apart by the sunlight to form nitric oxide and oxygen. (NO_2 + sunlight NO + O). This single atom of oxygen then combines with diatomic (meaning 2 atoms) oxygen (O_2) to form ozone (O_3). Ozone is one of the smells associated with smog. It has a pungent and offensive odor, irritates the eyes and lung tissues, affects the growth of plant life and causes rapid deterioration of rubber products. Ozone can be formed by sunlight as well as electrical discharge into the air.

The most common discharge area on the automobile engine is the secondary ignition electrical system, especially when inferior quality spark plug cables are used. As the surge of high voltage is routed through the secondary cable, the circuit builds up an electrical field around the wire, which acts upon the oxygen in the surrounding air to form the ozone. The faint glow along the cable with the engine running that may be visible on a dark night, is called the "corona discharge." It is the result of the electrical field passing from a high along the cable, to a low in the surrounding air, which forms the ozone gas. The combination of corona and ozone has been a major cause of cable deterioration. Recently, different and better quality insulating materials have lengthened the life of the electrical cables.

Although ozone at ground level can be harmful, ozone is beneficial to the earth's inhabitants. By having a concentrated ozone layer called the "ozonosphere," between 10 and 20 miles (16 - 32 km) up in the atmosphere, much of the ultra violet radiation from the sun's rays are absorbed and screened. If this ozone layer were not present, much of the earth's surface would be burned, dried and unfit for human life.

OXIDES OF SULFUR

Oxides of sulfur (SOx) were initially ignored in the exhaust system emissions, since the sulfur content of gasoline as a fuel is less than 1/10 of 1 percent. Because of this small amount, it was felt that it contributed very little to the overall pollution problem. However, because of the difficulty in solving the sulfur emissions in industrial pollutions and the introduction of catalytic converter to the automobile exhaust systems, a change was mandated. The automobile exhaust system, when equipped with a catalytic converter, changes the sulfur dioxide (SO_2) into sulfur trioxide (SO_3).

When this combines with water vapors (H_2O), a sulfuric acid mist (H_2O_4) is formed and is a very difficult pollutant to handle since it is extremely corrosive. This sulfuric acid mist that is formed, is the same mist that rises from the vents of an automobile battery when an active chemical reaction takes place within the battery cells.

When a large concentration of vehicles equipped with catalytic converters are operating in an area, this acid mist may rise and be distributed over a large ground area causing land, plant, crop, paint and building damage.

PARTICULATE MATTER

A certain amount of particulate matter is present in the burning of any fuel, with carbon constituting the largest percentage of the particulates. In gasoline, the remaining particulates are the burned remains of the various other compounds used in its manufacture. When a gasoline engine is in good internal condition, the particulate emissions are low but as the engine wears internally, the particulate emissions increase. By visually inspecting the tail pipe emissions, a determination can be made as to where an engine defect may exist. An engine with light gray or blue smoke emitting from the tail pipe normally indicates an increase in the oil consumption through burning due to internal engine wear. Black smoke would indicate a defective fuel delivery system, causing the engine to operate in a rich mode. Regardless of the color of the smoke, the internal part of the engine or the fuel delivery system should be repaired to prevent excess particulate emissions.

Diesel and turbine engines emit a darkened plume of smoke from the exhaust system because of the type of fuel used. Emission control regulations are mandated for this type of emission and more stringent measures are being used to prevent excess emission of the particulate matter. Electronic components are being introduced to control the injection of the fuel at precisely the proper time of piston travel, to achieve the optimum in fuel ignition and fuel usage. Other particulate afterburning components are being tested to achieve a cleaner emission.

Good grades of engine lubricating oils should be used, which meet the manufacturers specification. Cut-rate oils can contribute to the particulate emission problem because of their low flash or ignition temperature point. Such oils burn prematurely during the combustion process causing emission of particulate matter.

The cooling system is an important factor in the reduction of particulate matter. The optimum combustion will occur, with the cooling system operating at a temperature specified by the manufacturer. The cooling system must be maintained in the same manner as the engine oiling system, as each system is required to perform properly in order for the engine to operate efficiently for a long time.

Crankcase Emissions

Crankcase emissions are made up of water, acids, unburned fuel, oil fumes and particulates. These emissions are classified as hydrocarbons (HC) and are formed by the small amount of unburned, compressed air/fuel mixture entering the crankcase from the combustion area (between the cylinder walls and piston rings) during the compression and power strokes. The head of the compression and combustion help to form the remaining crankcase emissions.

Since the first engines, crankcase emissions were allowed into the atmosphere through a road draft tube, mounted on the lower side of the engine block. Fresh air came in through an open oil filler cap or breather. The air passed through the crankcase mixing with blow-by gases. The motion of the vehicle and the air blowing past the open end of the road draft tube caused a low pressure area (vacuum) at the end of the tube. Crankcase emissions were simply drawn out of the road draft tube into the air.

To control the crankcase emission, the road draft tube was deleted. A hose and/or tubing was routed from the crankcase to the intake manifold so the blow-by emission could be burned with the air/fuel mixture. However, it was found that intake manifold vacuum, used to draw the crankcase emissions into the manifold, would vary in strength at the wrong time and not allow the proper emission flow. A regulating valve was needed to control the flow of air through the crankcase.

Testing, showed the removal of the blow-by gases from the crankcase as quickly as possible, was most important to the longevity of the engine. Should large accumulations of blow-by gases remain and condense, dilution of the engine oil would occur to form water, soots, resins, acids and lead salts, resulting in the formation of sludge and varnishes. This condensation of the blow-by gases occurs more frequently on vehicles used in numerous starting and stopping conditions, excessive idling and when the engine is not allowed to attain normal operating temperature through short runs.

Evaporative Emissions

Gasoline fuel is a major source of pollution, before and after it is burned in the automobile engine. From the time the fuel is refined, stored, pumped and transported, again stored until it is pumped into the fuel tank of the vehicle, the gasoline gives off unburned hydrocarbons (HC) into the atmosphere. Through the redesign of storage areas and venting systems, the pollution factor was diminished, but not eliminated, from the refinery standpoint. However, the automobile still remained the primary source of vaporized, unburned hydrocarbon (HC) emissions.

Fuel pumped from an underground storage tank is cool but when exposed to a warmer ambient temperature, will expand. Before controls were mandated, an owner might fill the fuel tank with fuel from an underground storage tank and park the vehicle for some time in warm area, such as a parking lot. As the fuel would warm, it would expand and should no provisions or area be provided for the expansion, the fuel would spill out of the filler neck and onto the ground, causing hydrocarbon (HC) pollution and creating a severe fire hazard. To correct this condition, the vehicle manufacturers added overflow plumbing and/or gasoline tanks with built in expansion areas or domes.

However, this did not control the fuel vapor emission from the fuel tank. It was determined that most of the fuel evaporation occurred when the vehicle was stationary and the engine not operating. Most vehicles carry 5 - 25 gallons (19 - 95 liters) of gasoline. Should a large concentration of vehicles be parked in one area, such as a large parking lot, excessive fuel vapor emissions would take place, increasing as the temperature increases.

To prevent the vapor emission from escaping into the atmosphere, the fuel systems were designed to trap the vapors while the vehicle is stationary, by sealing the system from the atmosphere. A storage system is used to collect and hold the fuel vapors from the carburetor (if equipped) and the fuel tank when the engine is not operating. When the engine is started, the storage system is then purged of the fuel vapors, which are drawn into the engine and burned with the air/fuel mixture.

EMISSION CONTROLS

Exhaust Emission Controls

GENERAL INFORMATION

Exhaust emission control systems try to prevent excessive pollutants from escaping into the atmosphere from the vehicle's exhaust output. Many of the 1949 - 69 models do not utilize any emission control devices or systems at all. On these vehicles, as well as on vehicles equipped with emission controls, one of the best methods for preventing your vehicle from polluting excessively is to keep the engine running as efficiently as possible. Performing the maintenance and tune-up procedures in Section 1 and 2 regularly will help your engine to run as efficient and cleanly as possible.

1949 to Early 1967 Models

With the exception of the thermostatic air cleaner, these vehicles were not available with any exhaust emission control systems or devices.

Late 1967 to 1969 Models

Along with the fuel injection system available on some of the type 3 models, which is designed to reduce exhaust gas emissions, only some carbureted models manufactured from August 1967 to 1969 (engine No. H 5 000 001 and newer) were equipped with an additional control system. This system, which is referred to by Volkswagen as the Exhaust Emission Control System (EECS), is comprised of a specially tuned carburetor, a throttle (valve) positioner and a vacuum advance/retard canister attached to the distributor.

THROTTLE (VALVE) POSITIONER

Carbureted Volkswagen models equipped with the EECS utilize a throttle valve positioner. This device attempted to reduce exhaust emissions by automatically adjusting the throttle closing rate. By controlling the rate the throttle closed, the positioner avoided an over-rich condition in the engine, which causes a large amount of unburned fuel (hydrocarbons) to exit into the atmosphere through the exhaust system. Some models also came equipped with a dashpot to supplement this positioner.

VACUUM ADVANCE/RETARD CANISTER

A vacuum advance/retard canister was used on models equipped with the EECS. This mechanism was designed to advance or retard the ignition timing depending on the engine vacuum, which changed according to engine speed and load. Changing the ignition timing affects exhaust gas emissions; therefore, by changing the timing according to engine speed and load the exhaust emission output could be fine tuned.

1970 - 81 Models

While Volkswagen vehicles manufactured from 1970 - 72 were equipped with the Throttle (Valve) Positioner, 1973 - 81 models were equipped with a different system designed to limit the amount of harmful exhaust gases from the engine. This system is described here to further general automotive understanding of emission systems.

EXHAUST GAS RECIRCULATION (EGR) SYSTEM

Instead of utilizing a throttle valve positioner, some 1972 - 73 models and all 1974 - 81 models use an Exhaust Gas Recirculation (EGR) system to lower exhaust gas emissions. The EGR system lowers the emissions by diverting a portion of the exhaust gases back into the intake manifold below the carburetor. This dilutes the incoming charge of fuel and air. Since the recirculated exhaust gases are largely non-combustible, and since these gases dilute the incoming air/fuel charge, the exhaust gases restrict the amount of burnable intake charge allowed into the cylinder for combustion. Also, since the incoming exhaust gases are noncombustible, the exhaust gas does not appreciably affect the air/fuel mixture. Since the incoming air/fuel charge is diluted, combustion is maintained at a lower temperature, which reduces the formation of oxides of nitrogen.

➡**None of the 1949 - 69 Volkswagen vehicles are equipped with this system; this description is only for general information on exhaust emission controls used on 1973 - 81 models.**

Crankcase Emission Controls

GENERAL INFORMATION

To vent the crankcase vapors from the engine, 1949 - 69 Volkswagen vehicles utilize a simple road-draft tube. The road-draft tube is connected to the oil filler/generator stand and allows the engine crankcase vapors to vent out below the engine as the vehicle drives down the road.

This system is designed only to vent the vapors; the road-draft tube does nothing to prevent the release of these crankcase vapors into the atmosphere. Newer Volkswagen models still use a road-draft tube, but also have a hose attaching the upper end of the road-draft tube to the air cleaner. The incoming air charge passing through the air cleaner creates a vacuum in the road-draft tube so that the crankcase vapors are routed up and into the air cleaner. Once in the air cleaner, the crankcase vapors pass through the carburetor to be burned along with the incoming air/fuel mixture.

Most newer vehicles utilize a Positive Crankcase Ventilation (PCV) system to combat the release of crankcase vapors into the atmosphere.

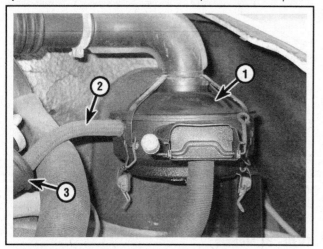

The PCV hose runs from the oil filler housing to the air cleaner

1	Air cleaner	3	Oil filler housing
2	PCV hose		

This system is described here to further general automotive understanding of emission systems.

Positive Crankcase Ventilation (PCV) System

The PCV system used on most newer vehicles is designed to prevent the crankcase vapors from entering the atmosphere by burning them along with the incoming air/fuel charge. The PCV system is usually composed of a PCV valve, vacuum hoses and a fresh air breather hose. The PCV system vents the crankcase vapors in the following manner:

Fresh air is introduced into the engine crankcase through a fresh air breather hose, which is connected to the air cleaner or a similar air filter element. This prevents dirt and other contaminants from entering the engine, which would accelerate engine wear. The fresh air enters the crankcase and sweeps the blow-by gases along with it. The gases pass through the cylinder head cover through the PCV valve, which is controlled by engine vacuum. Once through the PCV valve, the gases are routed through a vacuum hose to the carburetor. The gases enter the incoming air/fuel charge to be burned in the combustion chambers.

The PCV system only functions when engine vacuum is high (idle and high-way cruising). Carbureted vehicles with PCV systems utilize carburetors that are specially calibrated.

➡**None of the 1949 - 69 Volkswagen vehicles are equipped with this system; this description is only for general information on crankshaft emission controls used on newer vehicles.**

Evaporative Emission Controls

GENERAL INFORMATION

The 1949 - 69 Volkswagen models do not utilize an evaporative emission control system. 1970 - 81 models do utilize this system. A description of the 1970 - 81 evaporation emission control system will be presented here to provide further general automotive understanding of emission systems.

The evaporative emission control system prevents fuel vapors from escaping into the atmosphere from the fuel tank. The fuel tank is vented to a system which contains fuel vapors until they can be burned by the engine.

The fuel tank is attached to an overflow chamber via a fuel hose. Liquid gasoline can be temporarily stored in this chamber when the fuel

On Beetles, the canister is located under the right rear fender (on other models it's located in the engine compartment)

level in the fuel tank rises due to expansion. When the gasoline level in the fuel tank decreases, the gasoline stored in the overflow chamber can drain back into the fuel tank.

Fuel vapors can escape from the overflow chamber through a fuel hose to an activated charcoal (EVAP) canister located under one of the rear fenders. The charcoal in the EVAP canister absorbs the fuel vapors so that they do not vent into the atmosphere. When the engine

is started, air is forced through the EVAP canister by the engine cooling fan. The fuel vapor from the canister passes through a hose into the air cleaner, where it mixes with the incoming air charge to be burned in the engine.

➡**None of the 1949 - 69 Volkswagen vehicles are equipped with this system; this description is only for general information on exhaust emission controls used on 1970 - 81 models.**

CARBURETED FUEL SYSTEM

Fuel System Description

The fuel system of the Volkswagen begins at the front of the automobile, where the fuel tank is situated behind the spare tire. On type 2 vehicles, the tank is at the rear, ahead of the engine. From the tank the fuel is drawn through fuel lines to the mechanically-operated fuel pump located on the crankcase of the engine. From the pump, fuel goes to either a single down-draft Solex carburetor (type 1 and 2) or to a pair of Solex down-draft carburetors (type 3).

Since 1968, the type 3 has used an electronic fuel injection system. This system is discussed at the end of this section.

Carburetor

GENERAL INFORMATION

Volkswagens have used a variety of carburetors over the years, but all have a great deal in common. First, all are Solex; second, all operate under the same conditions in practically identical ways. Tuning of Volkswagen carburetors is found in Section 2.

Choke System

Every carburetor must have a way of enriching the mixture in order that a cold engine can be easily started. On Volkswagens produced through the 1960 model year, the choke was of the manual variety. In this setup the butterfly valve in the carburetor horn was turned to restrict incoming air as the knob on the dashboard was pulled out. As the engine warmed up and ran smoother, thoughtful drivers gradually pushed the choke home again.

The Volkswagen automatic choke is a simple, trouble-free unit. All the driver must do is fully depress the accelerator pedal and let it up again before starting a cold engine, even on the coldest mornings.

The automatic choke is located at the upper half of the carburetor on most Volkswagen models. Inside the cover of the choke control housing is a bi-metallic spring which is curled up with a slight hook at its outer end. When the temperature is low, the coil tends to uncurl, thereby causing the butterfly valve to close off the air horn from incoming air. When the temperature is high, or the engine warm, the bi-metal coil tends to coil up tighter, and the hooked end acts upon the intermediate lever and butterfly valve shaft to open the valve fully. Also, a fast-idle cam makes the engine idle more quickly when it is cold, thereby avoiding stalling the engine. There are several "steps" on the fast idle cam. As the engine warms up, and the bi-metallic spring curls up, the fast-idle cam is turned so that the throttle stop screw or lever rests on a lower step. When the engine is completely warm, the cam will be turned

to its lowest step and idle speed will be normal. For this reason, idle speed should not be adjusted unless the engine is warm.

Because the choke valve is off-center (i.e. the shaft does not run through the center of the valve), incoming air tends to open the butterfly and make the mixture less rich. Opposing the force of the incoming air is the tension of the bi-metal spring. However, as the spring heats up, it loses its closing power and even ends up holding the butterfly valve wide open.

The heating of the coil is accomplished both through the heating of the engine and through electricity supplied to the choke heating element when the ignition is turned **ON.** The current to the heating coil is supplied by a wire from terminal **15** of the ignition coil. After only a few minutes, the heating coil will cause the bi-metallic spring to curl up and release its closing force on the choke valve. Because most of the warming-up is the result of the current to the heating element of the choke, it is wise to start the engine as soon as the ignition switch is turned **ON.** If the key is turned **ON** and the engine is not started until minutes later, the choke will be "warm", but the engine will still be cold, hence difficult starting.

On the 32PDSIT carburetors used on the type 3, there is a vacuum piston which automatically modifies the choke valve position to better suit engine operating conditions. When the throttle is slightly open, a vacuum is set up in the vacuum cylinder, causing the piston to move and transmit a rotational force to the operating lever which in turn weakens the mixture by opening the choke valve.

The Solex carburetors used in Volkswagen models meet the engine's differing requirements under different conditions by utilizing four systems: (1) idling, or low speed, (2) normal operating, (3) accelerating, and (4) the power fuel system. The type 1 1200A and the Karmann Ghia 1300 and 1500 models have the power fuel system. In addition, the 1966 1600 type 3 also incorporated it, along with the 1500 type 3 "notch-back" and other 1500 type 3 models which were never officially imported and sold by Volkswagen of America. The presence of four different systems tends to make the Volkswagen carburetor similar to four carburetors in one. Each system operates under its own conditions, as well as overlapping with other systems as the need arises.

Idling (Low-Speed) System

When the engine is idling or running at a very slow speed, the formation of the air/fuel mixture takes place mainly through the idling system. At idle speed, the throttle valve is practically closed, so there is not enough vacuum in the venturi to cause the fuel to be drawn out of the discharge arm. In this case the fuel coming from the float chamber passes through the main jet and is mixed with air which has been drawn in by the pilot air bleed jet (above the pilot jet in the 32PDSIT). The combination of air and fuel flows through a drilling slightly below the nearly-horizontal throttle valve. The degree of opening of the end of this drilling is controlled by the volume (mixture) control screw. If the screw is turned in the clockwise direction, the idle mixture will be lean because the air coming past the slightly-open throttle valve will have less fuel to mix with. On the other hand, if the volume control screw is turned counterclockwise, the result will be a richer mixture, for the incoming air in the air horn will have more fuel to mix with.

For the engine to make a smooth transition from idle speed to normal running, it is necessary to incorporate what are known as "bypass ports." These are small drillings near the throttle valve, and they may have different positions in different engines. If a new carburetor has a flat spot in acceleration (transfer from slow speed to normal), the cause may be the lack of a bypass drilling or the presence of a bypass drilling which is in the wrong position.

Normal Operating System

When the car is running normally, under partial load, the mixture for the combustion chamber is supplied by the discharge arm. The vacuum in the venturi area of the carburetor is great enough so that fuel is forced from the float bowl, through the main jet, to the emulsion (mixing) tube, and finally to the discharge arm. As the fuel first enters the discharge arm, it is mixed with air which has come in through the air correction jet.

The nozzle of the discharge arm is placed in the narrowest part of the venturi (the constricted section of the carburetor "pipe"), where the incoming air suddenly accelerates on its way to the engine. As a result of this air acceleration, the discharge nozzle, depending on the position of the throttle valve, is in the center of a varying amount of vacuum. The more open the throttle valve, the higher the vacuum will be at the center of the venturi. The normal running circuit is set up so that the air correction jet acts to weaken the mixture as the engine speed increases, thereby eliminating a tendency toward rich mixtures at these speeds. In the Volkswagen carburetor, there are two sources of air for the air/fuel mixture: (1) the so-called "primary" air which flows directly from the air horn to the engine, and (2) the air which goes to the engine only after it has passed through the air correction jet.

Accelerating System

The accelerating system of the Volkswagen is centered around a mechanical accelerator pump positioned at the side of the carburetor body. When the throttle is suddenly opened, motion is transmitted via the throttle shaft to a connecting rod, pump lever and a diaphragm which pumps additional fuel into the mixing chamber.

The presence of ball check valves in the accelerating system serves to help regulate the quantity of raw fuel which is squirted into the mixing chamber. As the throttle is first pushed open, the diaphragm moves forward and fuel is forced out of a calibrated drilling into the accelerator pump discharge arm. When the fuel is forced out, the upper ball check valve is pushed upward toward the outlet of the drilling. When the upper ball reaches the outlet, fuel flow is cut off. When the throttle is once again closed, the diaphragm relaxes and the lower ball check valve is drawn inward, allowing more fuel to enter the diaphragm chamber for use the next time the throttle is opened.

The accelerator pump system operates only in the lower and medium speed ranges. When the throttle is almost open, the diaphragm is already fully depressed and therefore has no movement left when the throttle is opened further. The injection of fuel begins when the throttle first begins to open and ends when the throttle valve reaches an angle of about 30 degrees.

During normal running, every downward movement of the accelerator pedal tends to cause enriching of the mixture via the accelerator pump. Therefore, it is advantageous not to move the accelerator up and down more than necessary if maximum fuel economy is desired. With the excellent economy capability of the Volkswagen, it is a shame to see so many drivers unwittingly motoring along using the accelerator as a foot-exerciser and wasting gasoline through needless acceleration and deceleration. Constant, slowly-changed, speeds are best both for the life of the engine and for economy.

Power Fuel Circuit System

The power fuel system is present on 1966 and earlier type 3 models, as well as on the type 1 1200A and Karmann Ghia 1300 models. This system comes into play in the upper speed ranges and when the engine is pulling at full load. Under conditions of high RPM and large throttle openings, a high vacuum is present near the outlet of the power fuel discharge tube. This causes additional fuel to be drawn out of the tube under the vacuum present at higher speeds. When the engine is operating at maximum speed, fuel is also drawn through the accelerator pump, thereby enriching the mixture further.

REMOVAL & INSTALLATION

Type 1 and 2 Engine

1 Remove the pre-heat hose from the air cleaner intake pipe.
2 Disconnect the thermostatic flap control wire. Disconnect the crankcase breather hose from the air cleaner intake.
3 Loosen the air cleaner holding clamp and remove the air cleaner.
4 Disconnect the fuel and vacuum hoses from the carburetor. Disconnect the wires from the automatic choke and the electromagnetic pilot jet.
5 Disconnect the throttle cable at the carburetor and take off the spring, pin and spring retaining plate.
6 Take off the two carburetor retaining nuts and remove the carburetor from the intake manifold. The throttle positioner may be removed in unit with the carburetor.
7 It would, at this point, be a good idea to stuff part of a clean rag into the intake manifold hole in order to ensure that dirt and other foreign matter will not find its way into the manifold and cause damage to the engine.
8 Installation of the carburetor is the reverse of the removal operation. When installing the carburetor, it is advisable that a new intake

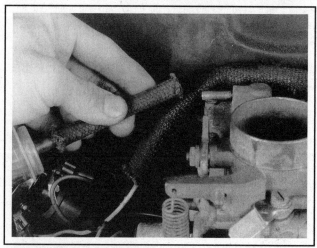

To remove the single carburetor on upright engines, disconnect and plug the fuel line . . .

. . . and disconnect all vacuum lines from the carburetor housing

Label and detach all wiring from the automatic choke assembly and the cut-off solenoid

manifold gasket be used. The retaining nuts should be tightened evenly, but not too tightly. The accelerator cable should be adjusted so that there is very little play (about 1mm) between the throttle lever and the

stop point on the carburetor body when the pedal is fully depressed. The idle speed should be checked with the engine at operating temperature.

Type 3 Engine

1 Remove the air cleaner as described earlier.

2 Be sure that the electrical connections are removed from the automatic chokes and the electromagnetic pilot jets.

3 Remove the connecting rods from between the center lever and the left- and right-hand carburetors.

4 Disconnect the carburetor return springs and pull off the spark plug connecting caps.

5 Remove the balance tube from between the carburetors by pulling it out of the connecting hoses on either side.

6 Remove the nuts that hold the intake manifolds to the cylinder heads.

7 Remove intake pipes, cylinder head gaskets, and take carburetors off of intake pipes.

8 Installation of the type 3 carburetors is the reverse of the removal procedure. New gaskets should be used on the cylinder head intake, and the carburetor gaskets should be inspected for damage and replaced if need be.

Loosen the accelerator cable retaining setscrew . . .

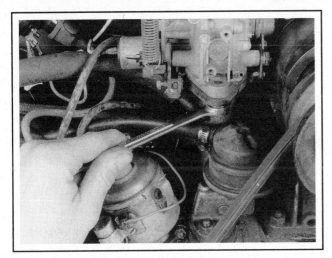

. . . then remove the 2 carburetor mounting nuts

Remove the carburetor and allow the cable to slide out of the accelerator lever

30 - PICT-1

DISASSEMBLY & ASSEMBLY

> **CAUTION:**
>
> Gasoline vapors are EXTREMELY volatile. To prevent the potential danger of spilled gasoline, drain the fuel tank with a hand pump siphon prior to removal. When servicing the fuel system: extinguish all open flames, do not smoke, have a fire extinguisher handy at all times, and always ensure proper ventilation of fresh air in the service area.

Disassembly of all Volkswagen carburetors is covered by the same procedure.

1 After removing the five upper carburetor housing mounting screws, lift the upper housing off of the carburetor.

2 Remove the float, needle valve and needle valve gasket from the float bowl.

3 Remove the automatic choke housing, retaining ring and bi-metallic spring from the side of the carburetor body. The choke unit is mounted onto the carburetor by 3 machine screws.

4 Remove the accelerator pump cotter pin (fastens the pump level to the connecting rod).

5 Remove the four screws from the pump housing, then remove the pump diaphragm and spring.

6 The main jet and the volume control screws should be removed along with the main jet access plug.

After disassembly, clean all parts in a suitable solvent, except for the cover of the automatic choke unit. After cleaning through soaking and rubbing with a soft cloth, all jets, valves and drillings should be blown out with compressed air. Mouth pressure or the pressure from a simple tire pump is not enough. If necessary, pack the pieces into a box and head for the place where you usually buy gasoline. It is highly probable that the attendant will be glad to lend you the use of his compressed air hose. Especially important in the compressed air cleaning process is the cleaning of the needle valve. When cleaning the carburetor passageways and jets, do not use pins, pipe cleaners, or other pieces of wire. The drillings are finely calibrated and might be damaged or enlarged through such mistreatment.

When taking the carburetor apart for cleaning, it is not necessary that every single part be dismantled. It is sufficient for most purposes to remove only the major components, along with the needle valve, float, main jet and accelerator pump diaphragm. The most important part of the entire operation is probably the blowing out with compressed air of all passageways.

On reassembly, check the needle valve for proper operation. On the type 3, the height of the accelerator pump injector tube opening should be 0.47 in. (12mm) from the upper part of the carburetor (9mm. for engine nos. T0244544 and onward). When the carburetor is assembled, the injector tube should squirt gasoline directly into the gap between the throttle valve and the carburetor throat when the accelerator pump is displaced. The power fuel tube opening of the type 3 dual carburetor models should be 0.59 in. (15mm) from the upper part of the carburetor. When the carburetor is assembled this tube should point roughly in the center of the gap between the discharge arm and the venturi. When replacing the cover of the automatic choke, be sure that the hooked end of the bi-metallic spring engages the operating lever. The mark on the cover of the choke should line up with the center lug on the upper part of the carburetor. When fastening down the automatic choke cover, care should be taken not to over-tighten the retaining screws. Be sure to put the proper choke on the proper carburetor. They are not interchangeable.

The model of the carburetor is stamped onto the side of the float bowl (arrow)

The diaphragm of the accelerator pump should be checked for leakage, and replaced if defective. The diaphragm should be tightened down while pressed in the pressure stroke position. On the type 3, the length of the operating rod should be adjusted so that a gap of 0.024 - 0.026 in. (0.60-0.65mm) exists at the throttle valve when the choke valve is closed. This gap should be measured with a wire feeler gauge while the throttle valve is pushed lightly in the closing direction. After tightening the two nuts on the operating rod, be sure that the parts have sufficient freedom of movement.

Rebuild Kits

Carburetor and fuel pump repair and rebuilding kits are available at authorized Volkswagen dealers and various other sources. These kits contain the critical parts of the units to be rebuilt or repaired, and are well worth the money compared to the trading in of the old unit on a new one. Such kits are also handy to have on hand during long trips through low-population areas, because even the ultra-reliable Volkswagen sometimes (though rarely) becomes incapacitated due to unexpected failures in these two most important elements of the fuel system.

TESTING

Electromagnetic Pilot Jet

If the engine is equipped with an electromagnetic pilot jet in the carburetor, and still shows a tendency to "run-on" after being shut off, chances are that the electromagnetic jet is defective. Operation can be checked by turning on the ignition and touching the slip-on connector against the terminal of the jet. If the jet is operating properly, a clicking sound will be heard each time the connector touches the terminal. When the current is off, the needle of this jet moves so as to block off the fuel supply, so when the connector is removed while the engine is running, it should stop the engine.

ADJUSTMENTS

After reassembly, the carburetor should be adjusted as described in Section 2. If the car is equipped with dual carburetors, these should be synchronized at idle and at 1,500 RPM by the method shown in the same section.

Accelerator Pump Injection

On type 3 models, the amount of fuel injected by the accelerator pump can be adjusted by altering the position of the cotter pin on the connecting rod. Moving the cotter pin from the center to either the outer or the inner hole of the connecting rod will result in either less or more fuel injected when the throttle valve is moved from the fully closed to the fully opened position:

Hole in Rod	Quantity of Fuel
Inner	larger (by .3cc)
center	normal (.35-.55cc)
outer	smaller (by .3cc)

Accelerator Cable

REMOVAL & INSTALLATION

The Volkswagen accelerator cable runs from the accelerator pedal to the carburetor by means of the central tunnel, the fan housing and the throttle valve lever. Guide tubes are used in both the central frame tunnel and the fan housing, while a plastic hose is present between the tunnel and the front engine cover plate.

To remove the accelerator cable, disconnect the cable from the throttle lever pin, raise the rear of the car, and pull the cable through from the front of the car after disconnecting the rod from the accelerator pedal.

Installation is the reverse of the removal. Grease the cable well before inserting from the front of the car. Be sure that the rear rubber boot and hose are properly seated, so that water will not enter the guide tubes. In order to avoid excessive strain of the throttle cable and assembly, there should be about 0.04 in. (1mm) clearance between the throttle stop and the carburetor body when the throttle is in the wide-open position. For this reason, it is advisable that the cable be tightened down at the carburetor end only when the accelerator pedal is at the fully-floored position.

Fuel Pump

GENERAL INFORMATION

The Volkswagen fuel pump, except on fuel injected engines, is mechanical, and of the diaphragm type, being pushrod operated from a cam on the distributor drive gear. The fuel flow is regulated automatically as the fuel is used up from the float bowl. The fuel pump consists of the top cover, containing the suction valve and the delivery valve, and the lower half, which contains the rocker mechanism.

As the distributor shaft turns, the cam on the distributor drive gear pushes the pushrod against the rocker arm, which in turn pulls the diaphragm downward against the diaphragm spring. In this way a vacuum is created above the diaphragm, causing the lifting of the suction valve off its seat so that fuel can be drawn in. After the pushrod moves away, the loaded diaphragm spring pushes the diaphragm upward, forcing the fuel in the pump through the delivery valve and to the carburetor. This process is repeated each time the distributor drive gear turns, which is once every two turns of the engine.

The pump pressure is determined by the amount the diaphragm spring is compressed during the suction stroke of the pump. The pressure of the spring is balanced by the upward force of the carburetor float on the needle valve. The higher the fuel level in the carburetor, the greater is the upward force on the needle valve. Under normal engine

operation, the diaphragm of the fuel pump is moved only a fraction of an inch.

Other than cleaning the filter of the pump at regular intervals, no other maintenance is necessary. The pushrod and pump rocker arm are lubricated by the lubricant in the lower part of the pump.

REMOVAL & INSTALLATION

The fuel pump is removed by taking off the fuel line, disconnecting the hose from the pump, and removing the retaining nuts from the mounting studs. After the pump has been removed, the intermediate flange, pushrod and gaskets can be removed. Be careful in handling the pushrod, as it could be inconvenient to have to fish it out of the crankcase.

Once removed, the stroke of the fuel pump is adjusted by the insertion or removal of the proper number of flange gaskets. Adjustment is checked after installing the intermediate flange with two gaskets and pushrod, and nuts are tightened to the same tightness as if the entire pump were being installed. Normal full-stroke is approximately 4mm. The length of the pushrod stroke is measured from the pump contact surface on the intermediate flange, including gaskets.

When installing the fuel pump, care must be taken to install the

To remove the fuel pump, detach the fuel lines from the pump . . .

. . . then remove the fuel pump mounting nuts

Lift the pump and old gasket off of the fuel pump spacer

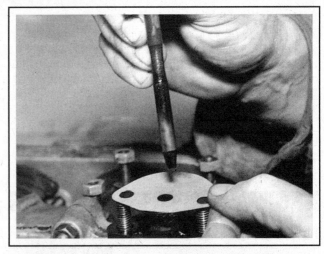

Install the pushrod with the tapered end pointing downward

intermediate flange before the pushrod, otherwise the rod may fall through into the crankcase. Before installing the fuel pump, the lower chamber should be filled with universal grease. Tighten nuts to mounting studs, taking care not to overtighten. (Nuts should be retightened when the engine has reached operating temperature.) Connect the fuel line and hose, and check for correct seating of the fuel line rubber grommet in the panel of the engine compartment.

Fuel pump pressure can be checked by the insertion of a suitable gauge between the pump and the carburetor. Correct fuel pump pressure for various models is given in the Capacities and Pressures Chart.

Rebuild Kits

Carburetor and fuel pump repair and rebuilding kits are available at authorized Volkswagen dealers and various other sources. These kits contain the critical parts of the units to be rebuilt or repaired, and are well worth the money compared to the trading in of the old unit on a new one. Such kits are also handy to have on hand during long trips through low-population areas, because even the ultra-reliable Volkswagen sometimes (though rarely) becomes incapacitated due to unexpected failures in these two most important elements of the fuel system.

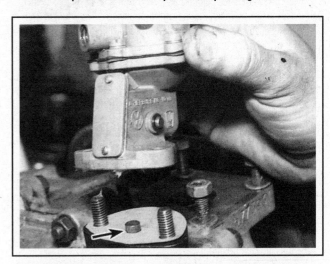

Install the fuel pump with the pushrod in its lowest position (rotate the engine using a wrench on the crank pulley bolt, if necessary)

FUEL INJECTION SYSTEM

General Information

One advantage of the Volkswagen fuel injection system is the reduction of unburned fuel, carbon monoxide and hydrocarbons in the exhaust gas. The engine receives the proper air/fuel mixture under all conditions as the result of the sophisticated controls designed into the system. The fuel injection system is made up of three sub-systems - the fuel system, the air system and the control unit.

FUEL SYSTEM

Fuel is drawn from the front-mounted tank through a filter by an electric fuel pump. The pump pushes the fuel through the pressure line into the fuel loop line, to which the electro-magnetic injectors are connected by distributor pipes. A pressure regulator is present to keep the fuel at a constant pressure of 28 psi. Excess fuel flows back to the tank via a return line.

AIR SYSTEM

Four pipes are used to transfer air into the four cylinders. Connected to the pipes is the intake air distributor, which is in turn connected to the pressure switch and pressure sensor. The intake side of the air distributor contains a throttle valve attached to the accelerator pedal via a cable. When the engine is idling, the throttle valve is fully closed and the air must pass through an idling air circuit. An idling air screw controls the amount of air for idling. An auxiliary air regulator is used to vary the quantity of air to suit the engine temperature when the engine is idling.

Carburetor Specifications—Types 1 and 2

Vehicle	Engine	Carburetor	Venturi (mm dia.)	Main Jet	Air Correction Jet	Pilot Jet	Pilot Jet Air Bleed or Pilot Air Jet (mm. dia.)	Pump Fuel Jet	Pump Air Correction Jet	Power Fuel Jet (mm.dia.)	Emulsion Tube	Emulsion Tube Carrier (mm.dia.)	Float Needle Valve (mm.dia.)	Float Needle Valve Washer (mm.)	Float Weight (gms.)	Accel. Pump Cap. (cc./Stroke)	By Pass Mixture Cutoff Valve
Type 1	1,131 cc. 25 hp.	Solex 28 PCI	20	105	190	50	.8	50	2.0	–	10	–	1.5	–	12.5	–	–
Type 1	1,200 cc. 36 hp. from No. 695282	Solex 28 PCI	21.5	122.5	200	g50	.8	50	2.0	–	29	5.0	1.5	–	5.7	.4-.6	–
Type 1	1,200 cc. 36 hp. from No. 849905	Solex 28 PCI	21.5	117.5	195	g50	.8	50	2.0	–	29	5.0	1.5	–	5.7	.4-.6	–
Karmann Ghia-Type 1	1,200 cc. 36 hp. from No. 1118403	Solex 28 PCI	21.5	117.5	180	g50	.8	50	2.0	–	29	5.0	1.5	–	5.7	.4-.6	–
Type 2	1,200 cc. 36 hp. from No. 991590	Solex 28 PCI															
Type 1 & 2	1,200 cc. 42 hp. from No. 5000 001	Solex 28 PICT(1)	22.5	122.5	130Y/ 140Z/ 135Z/	g55	2.0	.5	–	1.0/75	①	–	1.5	–	5.7	1.1- 1.4/ .8-1.0	–
Type 2	1,500 cc. 51 hp. from No. 0143543	Solex 28 PICT-2	22.5	115	145Y/ 150Z/	g45	1.55	.5	–	.7	①	–	1.5	–	5.7	1.1-1.4/ 1.2-1.3	–
Type 1	1,300 cc. 50 hp. from No. F0 000 001	Solex 30 PICT-1	24.0	125	125Z ②	g55	150	50	–	③	①	–	1.5	–	5.7	1.3- 1.6	–

Carburetor Specifications—Types 1 and 2

Vehicle	Engine	Carburetor	Venturi (mm. dia.)	Main Jet	Air Correction Jet	Pilot Jet	Pilot Jet Air Bleed or Pilot Air Jet (mm. dia.)	Pump Fuel Jet	Pump Air Correction Jet	Power Fuel Jet (mm. dia.)	Emulsion Tube	Emulsion Tube Carrier (mm.dia.)	Float Needle Valve (mm.dia.)	Float Needle Valve Washer (mm.)	Float Weight (gms.)	Accel. Pump Cap. (cc./Stroke)	By Pass Mixture Cutoff Valve
Type 1	1,600 cc. 57 hp. from No. B6000001	Solex 30 PICT-3	24.0	x122.5	125Z	65	135	-	-	100	①	-	1.5	1.5	8.5	1.2-1.35	-
Type 1	1,600 cc. 57 hp. Automatic from No. B6000002	Solex 30 PICT-3	24.0	x112.5	125Z	65	135	-	-	100	①	-	1.5	1.5	8.5	1.2-1.35	-
Type 2	1,600 cc. 57 hp. from No. B5116437	Solex 30 PICT-3															
Type 1 & 2	1,600 cc. 60 hp. 1971 Models	Solex 34 PICT-3	26	130	75Z	60	147.5	-	-	100	-	-	1.5	.5	8.5	-	-

① Fixed to air correction jet. ④ Karmann Ghia - 135Z. ⑦ With emission control.
② Karmann Ghia - 170Z. ⑤ From engine No. H0874200 - 140.
③ Karmann Ghia - 75. ⑥ From No. H0874200 - 8.5.

Carburetor Specifications—Type 3

Vehicle Engine	Carburetor	Venturi (mm.dia.)	Main Jet	Air Correction Jet	Pilot Jet	Idling Air Drilling	Pump Injector Tube (mm. dia.)	Pump Air Correction Tube Jet	Power Fuel Jet (mm. dia.)	Emulsion Tube (No.)	Emulsion Tube Carrier (mm. dia.)	Float Needle Valve (mm. dia.)	Float Needle Valve Washer (mm.)	Float Weight (gms.)	Accel. Pump Cap. (cc./Stroke)	Throttle Valve Gap (mm.)
Type 3 Single Carburetor																
From No. 0 000 001	Solex 32 PHN	23.5	137.5	125	g45 g50	–	.8	–	1.05	48	–	1.5	–	12.5	.9-1.2 /1.2-1.5	.8-.9
From No. 0 084 752	Solex 32 PHN -1	23.5	132.5	115	g45	–	.8	–	.7	48	–	1.5	–	12.5	.9-1.2	.8-.9
From No. 0220137	Solex 32 PHN -1	23.5	127.5	115	g45	–	.8	–	.7	48	–	1.5	–	12.5	.9-1.2	.8-.9
From No. 0319841	Solex 32 PHN	23.5	130.0	115	g50	–	.7	–	.7	48	–	1.5	–	12.5	.8-1.0	.8-.9
From No. K0150001	Solex 32 PHN	23.5	01300	115	–	1.4	.7	–	.7	48	–	1.5	–	12.5	.8-1.0	.8
Type 3 Dual Carburetors																
1,500cc. From No. 0255001	Solex ① 32 PDSIT-2(-3)	21.5	x125	180	g45	–	.5 (12 mm.)	–	.9 (9.5 mm.)	–	–	1.2	–	7.3	.35-.55	.60-.65
1,500cc. From No. 0633331	Solex 32 PDSIT 2(-3) ①	23	x135	180	g45	–	.5 (15 mm.)	–	.8 (10.5mm.)	–	–	1.2	1.5	7.3	.35-.55	.60-.65
1,600cc. From No. T0000001	Solex ① 32 PDSIT -2(-3)	23	x130	240	g45	–	50 (12 mm.)	–	80 (15 mm.)	–	–	1.2	1.5	7.3	.35-.55	.60-.65
1,600cc. From No. T0244544	Solex 32 PDSIT-2 (Left)	24	x132.5	150 ~	g50	–	.5 (9 mm.)	–	–	–	–	1.2	.5	7.3	.35-.55	.60-.65

Carburetor Specifications—Type 3

Vehicle	Engine	Carburetor	Venturi (mm.dia.)	Main Jet	Air Correction Jet	Pilot Jet	Idling Air Drilling	Pump Injector Tube (mm. dia.)	Pump Air Correction Jet	Power Fuel Jet (mm. dia.)	Emulsion Tube (No.)	Emulsion Tube Carrier (mm. dia.)	Float Needle Valve (mm. dia.)	Float Needle Valve Washer (mm.)	Float Weight (gms.)	Accel. Pump Cap. (cc./ Stroke)	Throttle Valve Gap (mm.)
		Solex 32 PDSIT-3 (Right)	24	x130	120	g50	-	.5 (9 mm.)	-	-	-	-	1.2	.5	7.3	.35-.55	.60-.65
	1,600cc. From No. T0576724	Solex 32 PDSIT-2 (Left)	24	x132.5	150	50	-	.5	-	-	-	-	1.2	.5	7.0	.35-.55	.60-.65
		Solex 32 PDSIT-3 (Right)	24	x130	120	50	-	.5	-	-	-	-	1.2	.5	7.0	.35-.55	.60-.65
Type 3 Dual Carburetors —Automatic	1,600cc. From No. T0690001	Solex 32 PDSIT-2 (Left)	24	x130	155	-	135	-	-	-	-	-	1.2	.5	7.0	.3-.45	.7
		Solex 32 PDSIT-3 Right	24	x127.5	120	-	135	-	-	-	-	-	1.2	.5	7.0	.3-.45	.7
	1,600cc. From No. T0463930	Solex 32 PDSIT-2 (Left)	24	130	155	50	-	.5 (9 mm.)	-	-	-	-	1.2	.5	7.0	.25-.4	.60-.65
		Solex 32 PDSIT-3 (Right)	24	127.5	120	50	-	.5 (9 mm.)	-	-	-	-	1.2	.5	7.0	.25-.4	.60-.65
	1,600cc. From No. T069000	Solex 32 PDSIT-2 (Left)	24	130	155	-	135	-	-	-	-	-	1.2	.5	7.0	.23-.4 ②	.9
		Solex 32 PDSIT-3 (Right)	24	127.5	120	-	135	-	-	-	-	-	1.2	.5	7.0	.25-.4 ②	.9

① 2 - Left carburetor, with distributor vacuum connection
3- Right carburetor
② Return valve for accelerator pump - .3

CONTROL SYSTEM

The central brain of the fuel injection system is the control unit which controls the amount of fuel injected according to various inputs, such as the engine speed, the intake manifold pressure, and the engine temperature. The main relay supplies current to the control unit when the ignition is turned BOLD ON. BOLD The control unit controls the fuel pump via the pump relay.

The control unit "masterminds" the operation by electrically opening the injector valves in pairs. Nos. 1 and 4, and 2 and 3 injector valves open simultaneously. It keeps the injector valves open for exactly the right length of time to suit the requirements of the engine. Because the fuel is under constant pressure (28 psi), the amount of fuel injected into the cylinders is directly proportional to the length of time that the injectors are held open by the control unit. In "deciding" how long to keep the injectors open, the control unit processes information received from the following sources: pressure sensor, pressure switch, two temperature sensors, trigger contacts in the distributor, and the throttle valve switch. The pressure sensor senses the load condition of the engine by measuring the pressure in the intake manifold. The pressure switch controls fuel enriching at full load, and is actuated by the difference in pressure between the air in the intake manifold and the air in the surrounding atmosphere. Two temperature sensors in the crankcase and cylinder head control the mixture enrichment both during starting and warming up of the engine. On later units, one sensor is fitted in the intake air distributor and the other to the cylinder head. Trigger contacts in the distributor "tell" the control unit into which set of cylinders to inject the fuel. The contacts also regulate injection timing. The function of the throttle valve switch is to cut off the supply of fuel when the engine is decelerating. In later models, the throttle valve switch also controls mixture enrichment on acceleration.

A cold starting device is present in later units. This device consists of a fuel jet fitted to the intake air distributor and a thermostatic switch. The switch actuates at 55-degrees F. The cold starting device is available as a kit for installation in earlier models. In current production, a new cold starting device is used, consisting of a thermostatic switch, which operates between 32-degrees F and 50-degrees F and a fuel jet combined into a single unit, fitted under and between the intake manifolds on the right side. The new cold starting device cannot be used to replace the earlier unit.

TESTING & TROUBLESHOOTING

Testing and troubleshooting of the fuel injection system requires special Bosch electronic testing apparatus. For this reason, these operations are best left to qualified personnel at an authorized dealer's shop. Removal and replacement of components, and adjustments that can be made without special equipment are covered in this section. Refer to Section 2 for ignition timing and idle speed adjustments.

Throttle Valve Switch

ADJUSTMENT

The throttle valve switch is mounted to a base plate with graduated markings secured to the intake air distributor inlet. An alignment mark is located on the air distributor housing. The switch is affixed by two mounting screws and an electrical plug. To adjust the switch:
1   Remove the air cleaner for access.
2   Close the throttle valve completely.

3   Loosen the base plate mounting screws. Slowly rotate the switch and plate assembly counterclockwise until a click is heard.
4   Continue rotating the switch and plate assembly counterclockwise one more graduation. (Each graduation indicates 2-degrees.)
5   Tighten the base plate mounting screw.
6   Throttle valve switch should come into operation when the throttle has moved 4-degrees from the closed position. Unhook the throttle return spring and check that the throttle is not binding.
7   Replace the throttle spring and air cleaner.

Pressure Regulator

The pressure regulator is located on the front engine cover plate beneath the right side of the intake manifold. It is fitted with an adjusting nut and a locknut. There is a T-fitting for a pressure gauge in the fuel loop line between the take off points for the right side injector units. This fitting is normally plugged with a stop screw.

➡ **Before making any adjustment, be absolutely certain that the pressure gauge being used is accurate.**

To adjust the pressure regulator:
1   Remove the air cleaner for access.
2   Attach the pressure gauge securely to the T-fitting.
3   Start the engine and allow it to idle. Make sure that the idle speed is correct. Adjustment of idling speed is explained in Section 2.
4   If the pressure reading is not 28 psi, loosen the locknut and regulate the pressure with the adjusting nut.
5   Tighten the locknut. Check that the pressure is still correct.
6   Stop the engine. Disconnect the pressure gauge and plug the T-fitting with the stop screw. Replace the air cleaner.

Injectors

REMOVAL & INSTALLATION

To remove the injectors on either side of the engine:
1   Remove both cable plugs.
2   Unscrew both retainer plate nuts.
3   Pull out both injectors with the retainer plate, centering bushings, base plate, and stud sleeves. Be sure to remove the inner bushings from the intake manifold base.
4   Loosen the hose clamps and pull out the injectors. Be careful not to damage the needles.
5   Reverse the procedure to replace the injectors. Use lockwashers under the retaining nuts. Tighten them to 52 inch lbs. Install cable plug with gray protective cap toward rear of car, and plug with black cap at front.

Fuel Pump

REMOVAL & INSTALLATION

✷✷ WARNING:

Gasoline is extremely flammable, so take extra precautions when you work on any part of the fuel system. Don't smoke or allow open flames or bare light bulbs near the work area, and don't work in a garage where a gas-type appliance (such as a water heater or a clothes dryer) is present. Since gasoline is carcinogenic, wear fuel-resistant gloves when there's a possibility of being exposed to fuel, and, if you spill any fuel on

your skin, rinse it off immediately with soap and water. Mop up any spills immediately and do not store fuel-soaked rags where they could ignite. When you perform any kind of work on the fuel system, wear safety glasses and have a Class B type fire extinguisher on hand.

The electric fuel pump is mounted at the front of the chassis. There are three fuel lines: suction, pressure, and return.

To remove the pump:

1 Pinch clamp the fuel lines shut to prevent leakage.
2 Unplug the electrical cable plug.
3 Cut off the original hose clamps. Pull off the hoses and catch the fuel which drains out.
4 Raise the pressure hose to prevent draining the fuel loop line.
5 Unbolt and remove the pump.

To install:

6 Connect the three fuel hoses. Install screw type hose clamps at all three connections.
7 Bolt the pump to the mounting supports.
8 Remove the pinch clamps from the hoses.
9 Install the cable plug. The brown negative ground wire must be

to the bottom and the half circular cavity toward the right. Install the protective plug cap.

Distributor Trigger Contact

REMOVAL & INSTALLATION

The distributor on fuel injected engines has two breaker plates. The first is the normal breaker point plate for the ignition system. The second plate, mounted in the base of the distributor head, carries two similar breaker assemblies which regulate fuel injection. There is no adjustment provided for the injection trigger contact breakers. To replace the trigger contacts:

1 Remove the distributor cap. Pull out the triple plug and disconnect the flat plug at terminal 1 of the coil. Loosen the clamp and remove the distributor after noting the rotor position and marking the relationship between the engine block and the distributor body.
2 Remove the two contact plate holding screws.
3 Pull out the plate holder.
4 Reverse the procedure to install the new plate holder. If ignition timing is correct, the injection timing will also be correct.

FUEL TANK

Tank Assembly

REMOVAL & INSTALLATION

Type 1 and 3 Models

✳✳ CAUTION:

Gasoline vapors are EXTREMELY volatile. To prevent the potential danger of spilled gasoline, drain the fuel tank with a hand pump siphon prior to removal. When servicing the fuel system: extinguish all open flames, do not smoke, have a fire extinguisher handy at all times, and always ensure proper ventilation of fresh air in the service area.

---

1 Disconnect the negative battery cable.
2 Using a small hose clamp, squeeze the rubber fuel line shut

To remove the fuel tank, detach any hoses from the tank . . .

. . . then remove the fuel gauge cable/sending unit cover

Detach the cable from the sender by sliding the ball (arrow) out of the lever housing

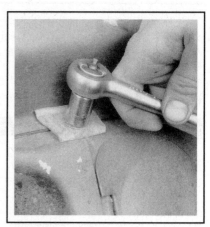

Remove the four hold-down bolts and brackets . . .

. . . then lift the tank up and out of its recess

between the fuel tank and the metal fuel line. Detach the rubber fuel line from the metal one.

3   If equipped, remove the luggage compartment fiberboard liner.

4   Label and detach all wires from the fuel gauge sending unit.

5   Disengage the fuel vapor ventilation hose from the fuel tank connection.

6   Detach the fuel filler hose from the fuel tank neck by loosening the metal hose clamp.

7   Remove the four fuel tank retaining plate mounting bolts, remove the retaining plates, then lift the fuel tank out of the vehicle. It is good idea to have an assistant help lift the tank to prevent personal injury or fuel spillage.

✳✳ WARNING:

When lifting the fuel tank out of its recess, take care not to damage the rubber sealing strip.

8   Installation is the reverse of the removal procedure. New hose clamps should be used on the ventilation hose and the hoses should not be bent, twisted or kinked during installation.

➡**The newer type fuel tank can be installed in earlier models.**

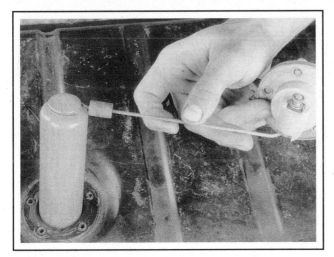

. . . and lift the unit out of the tank

To remove the sending unit, detach the cable and remove the 5 retaining screws . . .

Type 2 Models

✳✳ CAUTION:

Gasoline vapors are EXTREMELY volatile. To prevent the potential danger of spilled gasoline, drain the fuel tank with a hand pump siphon prior to removal. When servicing the fuel system: extinguish all open flames, do not smoke, have a fire extinguisher handy at all times, and always ensure proper ventilation of fresh air in the service area.

1   Disconnect the negative battery cable.

2   Except on pick-up truck models, remove the engine from the vehicle as described in Section 3 of this manual.

3   On fully-enclosed models manufactured after May of 1968, remove the engine compartment front panel retaining screws, then lift the panel out of the vehicle.

4   On pick-up truck models, remove the retaining screws from the two tank compartment cover panels. Remove the panels from the side of the truck.

5   Using a small hose clamp, squeeze the rubber fuel supply line shut, then detach it from the metal fuel line.

Make certain to replace the old gasket with a new one prior to installation

6   Label and detach all wires from the fuel gauge sending unit.

7   If equipped, disengage the fuel vapor ventilation hose from the fuel tank connection.

8   Detach the fuel filler hose from the fuel tank neck by loosening the metal hose clamp.

9   Remove the fuel tank retaining strap mounting bolts, remove the retaining straps, then lift the fuel tank out of the vehicle. It is a good idea to have an assistant help lift the tank to prevent personal injury or fuel spillage. On pick-up truck models, remove the tank toward the cargo area, and on fully-enclosed models, remove the tank toward the engine compartment.

✳✳ WARNING:

When lifting the fuel tank out of its recess, take care not to damage the foam rubber tank seal.

10   Installation is the reverse of the removal procedure. New hose clamps should be used on the ventilation hose and the hoses should not be bent, twisted or kinked during installation. If the foam rubber seal was damaged during removal, replace it with a new one.

Sending Unit

TESTING & REPLACEMENT

✳✳ WARNING:

Gasoline vapors are EXTREMELY volatile. To prevent the potential danger of spilled gasoline, drain the fuel tank with a hand pump siphon prior to removal. When servicing the fuel system: extinguish all open flames, do not smoke, have a fire extinguisher handy at all times, and always ensure proper ventilation of fresh air in the service area.

1   Disconnect the negative battery cable.

2   On type 2 models, remove the fuel tank from the vehicle.

3   Label and detach all electrical wiring from the sending unit.

4   To test the sending unit while it is installed in the vehicle (on type 2 models this is impossible), perform the following:

   a) *Connect an ohmmeter to the sending unit. Connect the negative lead from the ohmmeter to the sending unit metal housing and the positive lead to the lead wire terminal connector on the top of the sending unit.*

   b) *If the sending unit displays infinite resistance, the sending unit is bad and must be replaced with a new one.*

   c) *If the fuel tank is partially empty, the sending unit can be further tested while installed by slowly filling the fuel tank with gasoline until full. While filling the tank, watch the ohmmeter value. The resistance value should change smoothly. If the reading does not change or changes erratically, replace the sending unit with a new one.*

5   Remove the five sending unit mounting bolts, then carefully lift the unit up and out of the fuel tank. Remove the old sending unit gasket.

6   If not already done, test the sending unit as follows:

   a) *Connect an ohmmeter to the sending unit. Connect the negative lead from the ohmmeter to the sending unit metal housing and the positive lead to the lead wire terminal connector on the top of the sending unit.*

   b) *If the sending unit displays infinite resistance, the sending unit is bad and must be replaced with a new one.*

   c) *If the sending unit shows anything but infinite resistance, slowly tilt the sending unit upside-down and watch the ohmmeter reading. (Tilting the sending unit upside-down moves the float arm) The resistance value should change smoothly. If the reading does not change or changes erratically, replace the sending unit with a new one.*

7   Installation is the reverse of the removal procedure. Be sure that the rubber gasket is positioned correctly. The ground lug on the sending unit must be able to slip through the cut out in the gasket and make contact with the fuel tank. The fuel tank should be clean and bright where the ground lug contacts it.

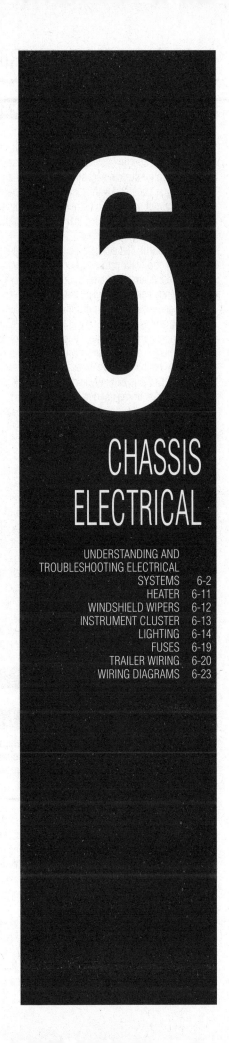

6

CHASSIS ELECTRICAL

UNDERSTANDING AND TROUBLESHOOTING ELECTRICAL SYSTEMS

Over the years import and domestic manufacturers have incorporated electronic control systems into their production lines. In fact, electronic control systems are so prevalent that all new cars and trucks built today are equipped with at least one on-board computer. These electronic components (with no moving parts) should theoretically last the life of the vehicle, provided that nothing external happens to damage the circuits or memory chips.

While it is true that electronic components should never wear out, in the real world malfunctions do occur. It is also true that any computer-based system is extremely sensitive to electrical voltages and cannot tolerate careless or haphazard testing/service procedures. An inexperienced individual can literally cause major damage looking for a minor problem by using the wrong kind of test equipment or connecting test leads/connectors with the ignition switch **ON**. When selecting test equipment, make sure the manufacturer's instructions state that the tester is compatible with whatever type of system is being serviced. Read all instructions carefully and double check all test points before installing probes or making any test connections.

The following section outlines basic diagnosis techniques for dealing with automotive electrical systems. Along with a general explanation of the various types of test equipment available to aid in servicing modern automotive systems, basic repair techniques for wiring harnesses and connectors are also given. Read the basic information before attempting any repairs or testing. This will provide the background of information necessary to avoid the most common and obvious mistakes that can cost both time and money. Although the replacement and testing procedures are simple in themselves, the systems are not, and unless one has a thorough understanding of all components and their function within a particular system, the logical test sequence these systems demand cannot be followed. Minor malfunctions can make a big difference, so it is important to know how each component affects the operation of the overall system in order to find the ultimate cause of a problem without replacing good components unnecessarily. It is not enough to use the correct test equipment; the test equipment must be used correctly.

Safety Precautions

✳✳ CAUTION:

Whenever working on or around any electrical or electronic systems, always observe these general precautions to prevent the possibility of personal injury or damage to electronic components.

• Never install or remove battery cables with the key **ON** or the engine running. Jumper cables should be connected with the key **OFF** to avoid power surges that can damage electronic control units. Engines equipped with computer controlled systems should avoid both giving and getting jump starts due to the possibility of serious damage to components from arcing in the engine compartment if connections are made with the ignition **ON**.

• Always remove the battery cables before charging the battery. Never use a high output charger on an installed battery or attempt to use any type of "hot shot" (24 volt) starting aid.

• Exercise care when inserting test probes into connectors to insure good contact without damaging the connector or spreading the pins. Always probe connectors from the rear (wire) side, NOT the pin side, to avoid accidental shorting of terminals during test procedures.

• Never remove or attach wiring harness connectors with the ignition switch **ON**, especially to an electronic control unit.

• Do not drop any components during service procedures and never apply 12 volts directly to any component (like a solenoid or relay) unless instructed specifically to do so. Some component electrical windings are designed to safely handle only 4 or 5 volts and can be destroyed in seconds if 12 volts are applied directly to the connector.

• Remove the electronic control unit if the vehicle is to be placed in an environment where temperatures exceed approximately 176-degrees F (80-degrees C), such as a paint spray booth or when arc/gas welding near the control unit location.

Understanding Basic Electricity

Understanding the basic theory of electricity makes electrical troubleshooting much easier. Several gauges are used in electrical troubleshooting to see inside the circuit being tested. Without a basic understanding, it will be difficult to understand testing procedures.

THE WATER ANALOGY

Electricity is the flow of electrons - hypothetical particles thought to constitute the basic stuff of electricity. Many people have been taught electrical theory using an analogy with water. In a comparison with water flowing in a pipe, the electrons would be the water. As the flow of water can be measured, the flow of electricity can be measured. The unit of measurement is amperes, frequently abbreviated amps. An ammeter will measure the actual amount of current flowing in the circuit.

Just as the water pressure is measured in units such as pounds per square inch, electrical pressure is measured in volts. When a voltmeter's two probes are placed on two live portions of an electrical circuit with different electrical pressures, current will flow through the voltmeter and produce a reading which indicates the difference in electrical pressure between the two parts of the circuit.

While increasing the voltage in a circuit will increase the flow of current, the actual flow depends not only on voltage, but on the resistance of the circuit. The standard unit for measuring circuit resistance is an ohm, measured by an ohmmeter. The ohmmeter is somewhat similar to an ammeter, but incorporates its own source of power so that a standard voltage is always present.

CIRCUITS

An actual electric circuit consists of four basic parts. These are: the power source, such as a generator or battery; a hot wire, which conducts the electricity under a relatively high voltage to the component supplied by the circuit; the load, such as a lamp, motor, resistor or relay coil; and the ground wire, which carries the current back to the source under very low voltage. In such a circuit the bulk of the resistance exists between the point where the hot wire is connected to the load, and the point where the load is grounded. In an automobile, the vehicle's frame or body, which is made of steel, is used as a part of the ground circuit for many of the electrical devices.

Remember that, in electrical testing, the voltmeter is connected in parallel with the circuit being tested (without disconnecting any wires) and measures the difference in voltage between the locations of the two probes; that the ammeter is connected in series with the load (the circuit is separated at one point and the ammeter inserted so it becomes a part of the circuit); and the ohmmeter is self-powered, so that all the power in the circuit should be off and the portion of the circuit to be measured contacted at either end by one of the probes of the meter.

For any electrical system to operate, it must make a complete circuit. This simply means that the power flow from the battery must make a complete circle. When an electrical component is operating, power flows from the battery to the component, passes through the component causing it to perform it to function (such as lighting a light bulb) and then returns to the battery through the ground of the circuit. This ground is usually (but not always) the metal part of the vehicle on which the electrical component is mounted.

Perhaps the easiest way to visualize this is to think of connecting a light bulb with two wires attached to it to your vehicle's battery. The battery in your vehicle has two posts (negative and positive). If one of the two wires attached to the light bulb was attached to the negative post of the battery and the other wire was attached to the positive post of the battery, you would have a complete circuit. Current from the battery would flow out one post, through the wire attached to it and then to the light bulb, where it would pass through causing it to light. It would then leave the light bulb, travel through the other wire, and return to the other post of the battery.

AUTOMOTIVE CIRCUITS

The normal automotive circuit differs from this simple example in two ways. First, instead of having a return wire from the bulb to the battery, the light bulb return the current to the battery through the chassis of the vehicle. Since the negative battery cable is attached to the chassis and the chassis is made of electrically conductive metal, the chassis of the vehicle can serve as a ground wire to complete the circuit. Secondly, most automotive circuits contain switches to turn components on and off.

Some electrical components which require a large amount of current to operate also have a relay in their circuit. Since these circuits carry a large amount of current, the thickness of the wire in the circuit (gauge size) is also greater. If this large wire were connected from the component to the control switch on the instrument panel, and then back to the component, a voltage drop would occur in the circuit. To prevent this potential drop in voltage, an electromagnetic switch (relay) is used. The large wires in the circuit are connected from the vehicle battery to one side of the relay, and from the opposite side of the relay to the component. The relay is normally open, preventing current from passing through the circuit. An additional, smaller wire is connected from the relay to the control switch for the circuit. When the control switch is turned on, it grounds the smaller wire from the relay and completes the circuit.

SHORT CIRCUITS

If you were to disconnect the light bulb (from the previous example of a light-bulb being connected to the battery by two wires) from the wires and touch the two wires together (please take our word for this; don't try it), the result will be a shower of sparks. A similar thing happens (on a smaller scale) when the power supply wire to a component or the electrical component itself becomes grounded before the normal ground connection for the circuit. To prevent damage to the system, the fuse for the circuit blows to interrupt the circuit - protecting the components from damage. Because grounding a wire from a power source

makes a complete circuit - less the required component to use the power - the phenomenon is called a short circuit. The most common causes of short circuits are: the rubber insulation on a wire breaking or rubbing through to expose the current carrying core of the wire to a metal part of the car, or a shorted switch.

Some electrical systems on the vehicle are protected by a circuit breaker which is, basically, a self-repairing fuse. When either of the described events takes place in a system which is protected by a circuit breaker, the circuit breaker opens the circuit the same way a fuse does. However, when either the short is removed from the circuit or the surge subsides, the circuit breaker resets itself and does not have to be replaced as a fuse does.

Troubleshooting

When diagnosing a specific problem, organized troubleshooting is a must. The complexity of a modern automobile demands that you approach any problem in a logical, organized manner. There are certain troubleshooting techniques that are standard:

1   Establish when the problem occurs. Does the problem appear only under certain conditions? Were there any noises, odors, or other unusual symptoms?

2   Isolate the problem area. To do this, make some simple tests and observations; then eliminate the systems that are working properly. Check for obvious problems such as broken wires, dirty connections or split/disconnected vacuum hoses. Always check the obvious before assuming something complicated is the cause.

3   Test for problems systematically to determine the cause once the problem area is isolated. Are all the components functioning properly? Is there power going to electrical switches and motors? Is there vacuum at vacuum switches and/or actuators? Is there a mechanical problem such as bent linkage or loose mounting screws? Performing careful, systematic checks will often turn up most causes on the first inspection without wasting time checking components that have little or no relationship to the problem.

4   Test all repairs after the work is done to make sure that the problem is fixed. Some causes can be traced to more than one component, so a careful verification of repair work is important in order to pick up additional malfunctions that may cause a problem to reappear or a different problem to arise. A blown fuse, for example, is a simple problem that may require more than another fuse to repair. If you don't look for a problem that caused a fuse to blow, a shorted wire (for example) may go undetected.

Experience has shown that most problems tend to be the result of a fairly simple and obvious cause, such as loose or corroded connectors or air leaks in the intake system. This makes careful inspection of components during testing essential to quick and accurate troubleshooting.

BASIC TROUBLESHOOTING THEORY

Electrical problems generally fall into one of three areas:

- The component that is not functioning is not receiving current.
- The component itself is not functioning.
- The component is not properly grounded.

Problems that fall into the first category are by far the most complicated. It is the current supply system to the component which contains all the switches, relay, fuses, etc.

The electrical system can be checked with a test light and a jumper wire. A test light is a device that looks like a pointed screwdriver with a wire attached to it. It has a light bulb in its handle. A jumper wire is a piece of insulated wire with an alligator clip attached to each end.

If a light bulb is not working, you must follow a systematic plan to determine which of the three causes is the villain.

1 Turn on the switch that controls the inoperable bulb.

2 Disconnect the power supply wire from the bulb.

3 Attach the ground wire to the test light to a good metal ground.

4 Touch the probe end of the test light to the end of the power supply wire that was disconnected from the bulb. If the bulb is receiving current, the test light will go on.

➡**If the bulb is one which works only when the ignition key is turned on (turn signal), make sure the key is turned on.**

If the test light does not go on, then the problem is in the circuit between the battery and the bulb. As mentioned before, this includes all the switches, fuses, and relays in the system. Turn to a wiring diagram and find the bulb on the diagram. Follow the wire that runs back to the battery. The problem is an open circuit between the battery and the bulb. If the fuse is blown and, when replaced, immediately blows again, there is a short circuit in the system which must be located and repaired. If there is a switch in the system, bypass it with a jumper wire. This is done by connecting one end of the jumper wire to the power supply wire into the switch and the other end of the jumper wire to the wire coming out of the switch. If the test light illuminates with the jumper wire installed, the switch or whatever was bypassed is defective.

➡**Never substitute the jumper wire for the bulb, as the bulb is the component required to use the power from the power source.**

5 If the bulb in the test light goes on, then the current is getting to the bulb that is not working in the car. This eliminates the first of the three possible causes. Connect the power supply wire and connect a jumper wire from the bulb to a good metal ground. Do this with the switch which controls the bulb works with jumper wire installed, then it has a bad ground. This is usually caused by the metal area on which the bulb mounts to the vehicle being coated with some type of foreign matter.

6 If neither test located the source of the trouble, then the light bulb itself is defective.

The above test procedure can be applied to any of the components of the chassis electrical system by substituting the component that is not working for the light bulb. Remember that for any electrical system to work, all connections must be clean and tight.

TEST EQUIPMENT

➡**Pinpointing the exact cause of trouble in an electrical system can sometimes only be accomplished by the use of special test equipment. The following describes different types of commonly used test equipment and explains how to use them in diagnosis. In addition to the information covered below, the tool manufacturer's instructions booklet (provided with the tester) should be read and clearly understood before attempting any test procedures.**

Jumper Wires

Jumper wires are simple, yet extremely valuable, pieces of test equipment. They are basically test wires which are used to bypass sections of a circuit. The simplest type of jumper wire is a length of multi-strand wire with an alligator clip at each end. Jumper wires are usually fabricated from lengths of standard automotive wire and whatever type of connector (alligator clip, spade connector or pin connector) that is required for the particular vehicle being tested. The well equipped tool box will have several different styles of jumper wires in several different lengths. Some jumper wires are made with three or more terminals

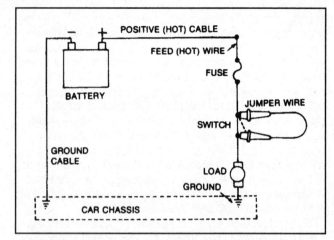

Example of using a jumper wire to bypass a switch during a diagnostic test

coming from a common splice for special purpose testing. In cramped, hard-to-reach areas it is advisable to have insulated boots over the jumper wire terminals in order to prevent accidental grounding, sparks, and possible fire, especially when testing fuel system components.

Jumper wires are used primarily to locate open electrical circuits, on either the ground (-) side of the circuit or on the hot (+) side. If an electrical component fails to operate, connect the jumper wire between the component and a good ground. If the component operates only with the jumper installed, the ground circuit is open. If the ground circuit is good, but the component does not operate, the circuit between the power feed and component may be open. By moving the jumper wire successively back from the lamp toward the power source, you can isolate the area of the circuit where the open is located. When the component stops functioning, or the power is cut off, the open is in the segment of wire between the jumper and the point previously tested.

You can sometimes connect the jumper wire directly from the battery to the hot terminal of the component, but first make sure the component uses 12 volts in operation. Some electrical components, such as fuel injectors, are designed to operate on about 4 volts and running 12 volts directly to the injector terminals can cause damage.

By inserting an in-line fuse holder between a set of test leads, a fused jumper wire can be used for bypassing open circuits. Use a 5 amp fuse to provide protection against voltage spikes. When in doubt, use a voltmeter to check the voltage input to the component and measure how much voltage is normally being applied.

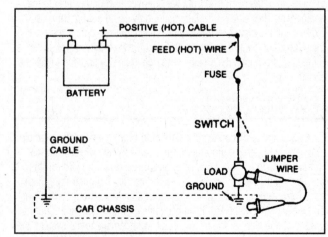

Checking for a bad ground connection with a jumper wire

Unpowered Test Lights

The 12 volt test light is used to check circuits and components while electrical current is flowing through them. It is used for voltage and ground tests. Twelve volt test lights come in different styles but all have three main parts; a ground clip, a probe, and a light. The most commonly used 12 volt test lights have pick-type probes. To use a 12 volt test light, connect the ground clip to a good ground and probe wherever necessary with the pick. The pick should be sharp so that it can be probed into tight spaces.

Like the jumper wire, the 12 volt test light is used to isolate opens in circuits. But, whereas the jumper wire is used to bypass the open to operate the load, the 12 volt test light is used to locate the presence of voltage in a circuit. If the test light glows, you know that there is power up to that point; if the 12 volt test light does not glow when its probe is inserted into the wire or connector, you know that there is an open circuit (no power). Move the test light in successive steps back toward the power source until the light in the handle does glow. When it glows, the open is between the probe and point which was probed previously.

➡ **The test light does not detect that 12 volts (or any particular amount of voltage) is present; it only detects that some voltage is present. It is advisable before using the test light to touch its terminals across the battery posts to make sure the light is operating properly.**

Self-Powered Test Lights

The self-powered test light usually contains a 1.5 volt penlight battery. One type of self-powered test light is similar in design to the 12 volt unit. This type has both the battery and the light in the handle, along with a pick-type probe tip. The second type has the light toward the open tip, so that the light illuminates the contact point. The self-powered test light is a dual purpose piece of test equipment. It can be used to test for either open or short circuits when power is isolated from the circuit (continuity test). A powered test light should not be used on any computer controlled system or component unless specifically instructed to do so. Many engine sensors can be destroyed by even this small amount of voltage applied directly to the terminals.

Voltmeters

A voltmeter is used to measure voltage at any point in a circuit, or to measure the voltage drop across any part of a circuit. It can also be used to check continuity in a wire or circuit by indicating current flow from one end to the other. Analog voltmeters usually have various scales on the meter dial and a selector switch to allow the selection of different voltages. The voltmeter has a positive and a negative lead. To avoid damage to the meter, always connect the negative lead to the negative (-) side of the circuit (to ground or nearest the ground side of the circuit) and connect the positive lead to the positive (+) side of the circuit (to the power source or the nearest power source). Note that the negative voltmeter lead will always be black and that the positive voltmeter will always be some color other than black (usually red).

Depending on how the voltmeter is connected into the circuit, it has several uses. A voltmeter can be connected either in parallel or in series with a circuit and it has a very high resistance to current flow. When connected in parallel, only a small amount of current will flow through the voltmeter current path; the rest will flow through the normal circuit current path and the circuit will work normally. When the voltmeter is connected in series with a circuit, only a small amount of current can flow through the circuit. The circuit will not work properly, but the voltmeter reading will show if the circuit is complete or not.

Ohmmeters

The ohmmeter is designed to read resistance (which is measured in ohms or in a circuit or component. Although there are several different styles of ohmmeters, all analog meters will usually have a selector switch which permits the measurement of different ranges of resistance (usually the selector switch allows the multiplication of the meter reading by 10, 100, 1000, and 10,000). A calibration knob allows the meter to be set at zero for accurate measurement. Since all ohmmeters are powered by an internal battery, the ohmmeter can be used as a self-powered test light. When the ohmmeter is connected, current from the ohmmeter flows through the circuit or component being tested. Since the ohmmeter's internal resistance and voltage are known values, the amount of current flow through the meter depends on the resistance of the circuit or component being tested.

The ohmmeter can be used to perform a continuity test for opens or shorts (either by observation of the meter needle or as a self-powered test light), and to read actual resistance in a circuit. It should be noted that the ohmmeter is used to check the resistance of a component or wire while there is no voltage applied to the circuit. Current flow from an outside voltage source (such as the vehicle battery) can damage the ohmmeter, so the circuit or component should be isolated from the vehicle electrical system before any testing is done. Since the ohmmeter uses its own voltage source, either lead can be connected to any test point.

➡ **When checking diodes or other solid state components, the ohmmeter leads can only be connected one way in order to measure current flow in a single direction. Make sure the positive (+) and negative (-) terminal connections are as described in the test procedures to verify the one-way diode operation.**

In using the meter for making continuity checks, do not be concerned with the actual resistance readings. Zero resistance, or any ohm reading, indicates continuity in the circuit. Infinite resistance indicates an open in the circuit. A high resistance reading where there should be none indicates a problem in the circuit. Checks for short circuits are made in the same manner as checks for open circuits except that the circuit must be isolated from both power and normal ground. Infinite resistance indicates no continuity to ground, while zero resistance indicates a dead short to ground.

Ammeters

An ammeter measures the amount of current flowing through a circuit in units called amperes or amps. Amperes are units of electron flow which indicate how fast the electrons are flowing through the circuit.

Since Ohms Law dictates that current flow in a circuit is equal to the circuit voltage divided by the total circuit resistance, increasing voltage also increases the current level (amps). Likewise, any decrease in resistance will increase the amount of amps in a circuit. At normal operating voltage, most circuits have a characteristic amount of amperes, called "current draw" which can be measured using an ammeter. By referring to a specified current draw rating, measuring the amperes, and comparing the two values, one can determine what is happening within the circuit to aid in diagnosis. An open circuit, for example, will not allow any current to flow so the ammeter reading will be zero. More current flows through a heavily loaded circuit or when the charging system is operating.

An ammeter is always connected in series with the circuit being tested. All of the current that normally flows through the circuit must also flow through the ammeter; if there is any other path for the current to follow, the ammeter reading will not be accurate. The ammeter itself has very little resistance to current flow and therefore will not affect the circuit, but it will measure current draw only when the circuit is closed and electricity is flowing. Excessive current draw can blow fuses and drain the battery, while a reduced current draw can cause motors to run slowly, lights to dim and other components to not operate properly. The ammeter can help diagnose these conditions by locating the cause of the high or low reading.

Multimeters

Different combinations of test meters can be built into a single unit designed for specific tests. Some of the more common combination test devices are known as Volt/Amp testers, Tach/Dwell meters, or Digital Multimeters. The Volt/Amp tester is used for charging system, starting system or battery tests and consists of a voltmeter, an ammeter and a variable resistance carbon pile. The voltmeter will usually have at least two ranges for use with 6, 12 and/or 24 volt systems. The ammeter also has more than one range for testing various levels of battery loads and starter current draw. The carbon pile can be adjusted to offer different amounts of resistance. The Volt/Amp tester has heavy leads to carry large amounts of current and many later models have an inductive ammeter pickup that clamps around the wire to simplify test connections. On some models, the ammeter also has a zero-center scale to allow testing of charging and starting systems without switching leads or polarity. A digital multimeter is a voltmeter, ammeter and ohmmeter combined in an instrument which gives a digital readout. These are often used when testing solid state circuits because of their high input impedance (usually 10 megohms or more).

The tach/dwell meter that combines a tachometer and a dwell (cam angle) meter is a specialized kind of voltmeter. The tachometer scale is marked to show engine speed in rpm and the dwell scale is marked to show degrees of distributor shaft rotation. In most electronic ignition systems, dwell is determined by the control unit, but the dwell meter can also be used to check the duty cycle (operation) of some electronic engine control systems. Some tach/dwell meters are powered by an internal battery, while others take their power from the vehicle battery in use. The battery powered testers usually require calibration (much like an ohmmeter) before testing.

TESTING

Open Circuits

To use the self-powered test light or a multimeter to check for open circuits, first isolate the circuit from the vehicle's 12 volt power source by disconnecting the battery or wiring harness connector. Connect the test light or ohmmeter ground clip to a good ground and probe sec-

tions of the circuit sequentially with the test light. (start from either end of the circuit). If the light is out/or there is infinite resistance, the open is between the probe and the circuit ground. If the light is on/or the meter shows continuity, the open is between the probe and end of the circuit toward the power source.

Short Circuits

By isolating the circuit both from power and from ground, and using a self-powered test light or multimeter, you can check for shorts to ground in the circuit. Isolate the circuit from power and ground. Connect the test light or ohmmeter ground clip to a good ground and probe any easy-to-reach test point in the circuit. If the light comes on or there is continuity, there is a short somewhere in the circuit. To isolate the short, probe a test point at either end of the isolated circuit (the light should be on/there should be continuity). Leave the test light probe engaged and open connectors, switches, remove parts, etc., sequentially, until the light goes out/continuity is broken. When the light goes out, the short is between the last circuit component opened and the previous circuit opened.

➡The battery in the test light and does not provide much current. A weak battery may not provide enough power to illuminate the test light even when a complete circuit is made (especially if there are high resistances in the circuit). Always make sure that the test battery is strong. To check the battery, briefly touch the ground clip to the probe; if the light glows brightly the battery is strong enough for testing. Never use a self-powered test light to perform checks for opens or shorts when power is applied to the electrical system under test. The 12 volt vehicle power will quickly burn out the light bulb in the test light.

Available Voltage Measurement

Set the voltmeter selector switch to the 20V position and connect the meter negative lead to the negative post of the battery. Connect the positive meter lead to the positive post of the battery and turn the ignition switch **ON** to provide a load. Read the voltage on the meter or digital display. A well charged battery should register over 12 volts. If the meter reads below 11.5 volts, the battery power may be insufficient to operate the electrical system properly. This test determines voltage available from the battery and should be the first step in any electrical trouble diagnosis procedure. Many electrical problems, especially on computer controlled systems, can be caused by a low state of charge in the battery. Excessive corrosion at the battery cable terminals can cause a poor contact that will prevent proper charging and full battery current flow.

Normal battery voltage is 12 volts when fully charged. When the battery is supplying current to one or more circuits it is said to be "under load." When everything is off the electrical system is under a "no-load" condition. A fully charged battery may show about 12.5 volts at no load; will drop to 12 volts under medium load; and will drop even lower under heavy load. If the battery is partially discharged the voltage decrease under heavy load may be excessive, even though the battery shows 12 volts or more at no load. When allowed to discharge further, the battery's available voltage under load will decrease more severely. For this reason, it is important that the battery be fully charged during all testing procedures to avoid errors in diagnosis and incorrect test results.

Voltage Drop

When current flows through a resistance, the voltage beyond the resistance is reduced (the larger the current, the greater the reduction in voltage). When no current is flowing, there is no voltage drop because there is no current flow. All points in the circuit which are connected to the power source are at the same voltage as the power source. The total voltage drop always equals the total source voltage. In a long circuit with many connectors, a series of small, unwanted voltage drops due to corrosion at the connectors can add up to a total loss of voltage which impairs the operation of the normal loads in the circuit. The maximum allowable voltage drop under load is critical, especially if there is more than one high resistance problem in a circuit because all voltage drops are cumulative. A small drop is normal due to the resistance of the conductors.

INDIRECT COMPUTATION OF VOLTAGE DROPS

1 Set the voltmeter selector switch to the 20 volt position.
2 Connect the meter negative lead to a good ground.
3 While operating the circuit, probe all loads in the circuit with the positive meter lead and observe the voltage readings. A drop should be noticed after the first load. But, there should be little or no voltage drop before the first load.

DIRECT MEASUREMENT OF VOLTAGE DROPS

1 Set the voltmeter switch to the 20 volt position.
2 Connect the voltmeter negative lead to the ground side of the load to be measured.
3 Connect the positive lead to the positive side of the resistance or load to be measured.
4 Read the voltage drop directly on the 20 volt scale.

Too high a voltage indicates too high a resistance. If, for example, a blower motor runs too slowly, you can determine if perhaps there is too high a resistance in the resistor pack. By taking voltage drop readings in all parts of the circuit, you can isolate the problem. Too low a voltage drop indicates too low a resistance. Take the blower motor for example again. If a blower motor runs too fast in the MED and/or LOW position, the problem might be isolated in the resistor pack by taking voltage drop readings in all parts of the circuit to locate a possibly shorted resistor.

HIGH RESISTANCE TESTING

1 Set the voltmeter selector switch to the 4 volt position.
2 Connect the voltmeter positive lead to the positive post of the battery.
3 Turn on the headlights and heater blower to provide a load.
4 Probe various points in the circuit with the negative voltmeter lead.
5 Read the voltage drop on the 4 volt scale. Some average maximum allowable voltage drops are:

• FUSE PANEL: 0.7 volts
• IGNITION SWITCH: 0.5 volts
• HEADLIGHT SWITCH: 0.7 volts
• IGNITION COIL (+): 0.5 volts
• ANY OTHER LOAD: 1.3 volts

➡**Voltage drops are all measured while a load is operating; without current flow, there will be no voltage drop.**

Resistance Measurement

The batteries in an ohmmeter will weaken with age and temperature, so the ohmmeter must be calibrated or "zeroed" before taking measurements. To zero the meter, place the selector switch in its lowest range and touch the two ohmmeter leads together. Turn the calibration knob until the meter needle is exactly on zero.

➡**All analog (needle) type ohmmeters must be zeroed before use, but some digital ohmmeter models are automatically**

calibrated when the switch is turned on. Self-calibrating digital ohmmeters do not have an adjusting knob, but its a good idea to check for a zero readout before use by touching the leads together. All computer controlled systems require the use of a digital ohmmeter with at least 10 megohms impedance for testing. Before any test procedures are attempted, make sure the ohmmeter used is compatible with the electrical system or damage to the on-board computer could result.

To measure resistance, first isolate the circuit from the vehicle power source by disconnecting the battery cables or the harness connector. Make sure the key is **OFF** when disconnecting any components or the battery. Where necessary, also isolate at least one side of the circuit to be checked in order to avoid reading parallel resistances. Parallel circuit resistances will always give a lower reading than the actual resistance of either of the branches. When measuring the resistance of parallel circuits, the total resistance will always be lower than the smallest resistance in the circuit. Connect the meter leads to both sides of the circuit (wire or component) and read the actual measured ohms on the meter scale. Make sure the selector switch is set to the proper ohm scale for the circuit being tested to avoid misreading the ohmmeter test value.

❋❋ WARNING:

Never use an ohmmeter with power applied to the circuit. Like the self-powered test light, the ohmmeter is designed to operate on its own power supply. The normal 12 volt automotive electrical system current could damage the meter!

Wiring Harnesses

The average automobile contains about 1/2 mile of wiring, with hundreds of individual connections. To protect the many wires from damage and to keep them from becoming a confusing tangle, they are organized into bundles, enclosed in plastic or taped together and called wiring harnesses. Different harnesses serve different parts of the vehicle. Individual wires are color coded to help trace them through a harness where sections are hidden from view.

Automotive wiring or circuit conductors can be in any one of three forms:

1 Single strand wire
2 Multi-strand wire
3 Printed circuitry

Single strand wire has a solid metal core and is usually used inside such components as alternators, motors, relays and other devices. Multi-strand wire has a core made of many small strands of wire twisted together into a single conductor. Most of the wiring in an automotive electrical system is made up of multi-strand wire, either as a single conductor or grouped together in a harness. All wiring is color coded on the insulator, either as a solid color or as a colored wire with an identification stripe. A printed circuit is a thin film of copper or other conductor that is printed on an insulator backing. Occasionally, a printed circuit is sandwiched between two sheets of plastic for more protection and flexibility. A complete printed circuit, consisting of conductors, insulating material and connectors for lamps or other components is called a printed circuit board. Printed circuitry is used in place of individual wires or harnesses in places where space is limited, such as behind instrument panels.

Since automotive electrical systems are very sensitive to changes in resistance, the selection of properly sized wires is critical when systems are repaired. A loose or corroded connection or a replacement wire that is too small for the circuit will add extra resistance and an additional voltage drop to the circuit. A ten percent voltage drop can result in slow or erratic motor operation, for example, even though the circuit is complete. The wire gauge number is an expression of the cross-section area of the conductor. The most common system for expressing wire size is the American Wire Gauge (AWG) system.

Gauge numbers are assigned to conductors of various cross-section areas. As gauge number increases, area decreases and the conductor becomes smaller. A 5 gauge conductor is smaller than a 1 gauge conductor and a 10 gauge is smaller than a 5 gauge. As the cross-section area of a conductor decreases, resistance increases and so does the gauge number. A conductor with a higher gauge number will carry less current than a conductor with a lower gauge number.

➡**Gauge wire size refers to the size of the conductor, not the size of the complete wire. It is possible to have two wires of the same gauge with different diameters because one may have thicker insulation than the other.**

12 volt automotive electrical systems generally use 10, 12, 14, 16 and 18 gauge wire. Main power distribution circuits and larger accessories usually use 10 and 12 gauge wire. Battery cables are usually 4 or 6 gauge, although 1 and 2 gauge wires are occasionally used. Wire length must also be considered when making repairs to a circuit. As conductor length increases, so does resistance. An 18 gauge wire, for example, can carry a 10 amp load for 10 feet without excessive voltage drop; however if a 15 foot wire is required for the same 10 amp load, it must be a 16 gauge wire.

An electrical schematic shows the electrical current paths when a circuit is operating properly. It is essential to understand how a circuit works before trying to figure out why it doesn't. Schematics break the entire electrical system down into individual circuits and show only one particular circuit. In a schematic, no attempt is made to represent wiring and components as they physically appear on the vehicle; switches and other components are shown as simply as possible. Face views of harness connectors show the cavity or terminal locations in all multi-pin connectors to help locate test points.

If you need to backprobe a connector while it is on the component, the order of the terminals must be mentally reversed. The wire color code can help in this situation, as well as a keyway, lock tab or other reference mark.

WIRING REPAIR

Soldering is a quick, efficient method of joining metals permanently. Everyone who has the occasion to make wiring repairs should know how to solder. Electrical connections that are soldered are far less likely to come apart and will conduct electricity much better than connections that are only "pig-tailed" together. The most popular (and preferred) method of soldering is with an electrical soldering gun. Soldering irons are available in many sizes and wattage ratings. Irons with higher wattage ratings deliver higher temperatures and recover lost heat faster. A small soldering iron rated for no more than 50 watts is recommended, especially on electrical systems where excess heat can damage the components being soldered.

There are three ingredients necessary for successful soldering; proper flux, good solder and sufficient heat. A soldering flux is necessary to clean the metal of tarnish, prepare it for soldering and to enable the solder to spread into tiny crevices. When soldering, always use a rosin core solder which is non-corrosive and will not attract moisture once the job is finished. Other types of flux (acid core) will leave a residue that will attract moisture and cause the wires to corrode. Tin is a unique metal with a low melting point. In a molten state, it dissolves

and alloys easily with many metals. Solder is made by mixing tin with lead. The most common proportions are 40/60, 50/50 and 60/40, with the percentage of tin listed first. Low priced solders usually contain less tin, making them very difficult for a beginner to use because more heat is required to melt the solder. A common solder is 40/60 which is well suited for all-around general use, but 60/40 melts easier and is preferred for electrical work.

Soldering Techniques

Successful soldering requires that the metals to be joined be heated to a temperature that will melt the solder, usually 360 - 460-degrees F (182 - 238-degrees C). Contrary to popular belief, the purpose of the soldering iron is not to melt the solder itself, but to heat the parts being soldered to a temperature high enough to melt the solder when it is touched to the work. Melting flux-cored solder on the soldering iron will usually destroy the effectiveness of the flux.

➡**Soldering tips are made of copper for good heat conductivity, but must be "tinned" regularly for quick transference of heat to the project and to prevent the solder from sticking to the iron. To "tin" the iron, simply heat it and touch the flux-cored solder to the tip; the solder will flow over the hot tip. Wipe the excess off with a clean rag, but be careful as the iron will be hot.**

After some use, the tip may become pitted. If so, simply dress the tip smooth with a smooth file and "tin" the tip again. Flux-cored solder will remove oxides but rust, bits of insulation and oil or grease must be removed with a wire brush or emery cloth. For maximum strength in soldered parts, the joint must start off clean and tight. Weak joints will result in gaps too wide for the solder to bridge.

If a separate soldering flux is used, it should be brushed or swabbed on only those areas that are to be soldered. Most solders contain a core of flux and separate fluxing is unnecessary. Hold the work to be soldered firmly. It is best to solder on a wooden board, because a metal vise will only rob the piece to be soldered of heat and make it difficult to melt the solder. Hold the soldering tip with the broadest face against the work to be soldered. Apply solder under the tip close to the work, using enough solder to give a heavy film between the iron and the piece being soldered, while moving slowly and making sure the solder melts properly. Keep the work level or the solder will run to the lowest part and favor the thicker parts, because these require more heat to melt the solder. If the soldering tip overheats (the solder coating on the face of the tip burns up), it should be retinned. Once the soldering is completed, let the soldered joint stand until cool. Tape and seal all soldered wire splices after the repair has cooled.

Wire Harness Connectors

Most connectors in the engine compartment or that are otherwise exposed to the elements are protected against moisture and dirt which could create oxidation and deposits on the terminals.

These special connectors are weather-proof. All repairs require the use of a special terminal and the tool required to service it. This tool is used to remove the pin and sleeve terminals. If removal is attempted with an ordinary pick, there is a good chance that the terminal will be bent or deformed. Unlike standard blade type terminals, these weather-proof terminals cannot be straightened once they are bent. Make certain that the connectors are properly seated and all of the sealing rings are in place when connecting leads. On some models, a hinge-type flap provides a backup or secondary locking feature for the terminals. Most secondary locks are used to improve connector reliability by retaining the terminals if the small terminal lock tangs are not positioned properly.

Molded-on connectors require complete replacement of the connection. This means splicing a new connector assembly into the harness. All splices should be soldered to insure proper contact. Use care when

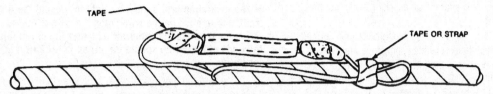

REMOVE EXISTING VINYL TUBE SHIELDING
REINSTALL OVER FUSE LINK BEFORE CRIMPING
FUSE LINK TO WIRE ENDS

TAPE

TAPE OR STRAP

TYPICAL REPAIR USING THE SPECIAL #17 GA. (9.00" LONG-YELLOW) FUSE LINK REQUIRED FOR THE AIR/COND.
CIRCUITS (2) #687E and #261A LOCATED IN THE ENGINE COMPARTMENT

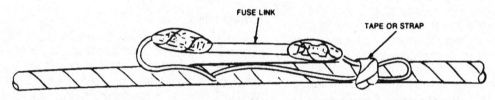

FUSE LINK

TAPE OR STRAP

TYPICAL REPAIR FOR ANY IN-LINE FUSE LINK USING THE SPECIFIED GAUGE FUSE LINK FOR THE SPECIFIC CIRCUIT

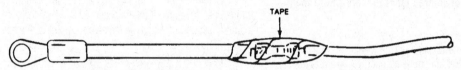

TAPE

TYPICAL REPAIR USING THE EYELET TERMINAL FUSE LINK OF THE SPECIFIED GAUGE FOR ATTACHMENT TO A CIRCUIT WIRE END

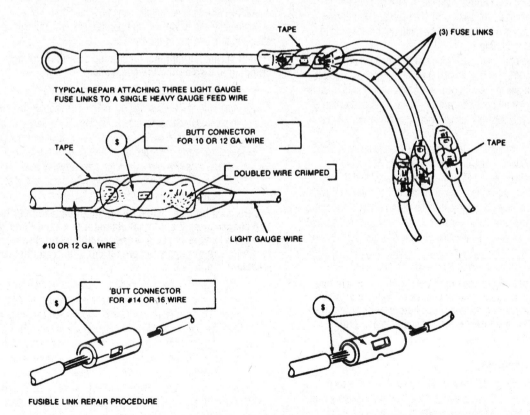

TAPE

(3) FUSE LINKS

TYPICAL REPAIR ATTACHING THREE LIGHT GAUGE
FUSE LINKS TO A SINGLE HEAVY GAUGE FEED WIRE

TAPE

BUTT CONNECTOR
FOR 10 OR 12 GA. WIRE

TAPE

DOUBLED WIRE CRIMPED

#10 OR 12 GA. WIRE

LIGHT GAUGE WIRE

'BUTT CONNECTOR
FOR #14 OR 16 WIRE

FUSIBLE LINK REPAIR PROCEDURE

General fusible link repair - never replace a fusible link with regular wire or a fusible link rated at a higher amperage than the one being replaced

probing the connections or replacing terminals in them as it is possible to short between opposite terminals. If this happens to the wrong terminal pair, it is possible to damage certain components. Always use jumper wires between connectors for circuit checking and never probe through weatherproof seals.

Open circuits are often difficult to locate by sight because corrosion or terminal misalignment are hidden by the connectors. Merely wiggling a connector on a sensor or in the wiring harness may correct the open circuit condition. This should always be considered when an open circuit or a failed sensor is indicated. Intermittent problems may also be caused by oxidized or loose connections. When using a circuit tester for diagnosis, always probe connections from the wire side. Be careful not to damage sealed connectors with test probes.

All wiring harnesses should be replaced with identical parts, using the same gauge wire and connectors. When signal wires are spliced into a harness, use wire with high temperature insulation only. It is seldom necessary to replace a complete harness. If replacement is necessary, pay close attention to insure proper harness routing. Secure the harness with suitable plastic wire clamps to prevent vibrations from causing the harness to wear in spots or contact any hot components.

➡**Weatherproof connectors cannot be replaced with standard connectors. Instructions are provided with replacement connector and terminal packages. Some wire harnesses have mounting indicators (usually pieces of colored tape) to mark where the harness is to be secured.**

In making wiring repairs, its important that you always replace damaged wires with wiring of the same gauge as the wire being replaced. The heavier the wire, the smaller the gauge number. Wires are color-coded to aid in identification and whenever possible the same color coded wire should be used for replacement. A wire stripping and crimping tool is necessary to install solderless terminal connectors. Test all crimps by pulling on the wires; it should not be possible to pull the wires out of a good crimp.

Wires which are open, exposed or otherwise damaged are repaired by simple splicing. Where possible, if the wiring harness is accessible and the damaged place in the wire can be located, it is best to open the harness and check for all possible damage. In an inaccessible harness, the wire must be bypassed with a new insert, usually taped to the outside of the old harness.

When replacing fusible links, be sure to use fusible link wire, NOT ordinary automotive wire. Make sure the fusible segment is of the same gauge and construction as the one being replaced and double the stripped end when crimping the terminal connector for a good contact. The melted (open) fusible link segment of the wiring harness should be cut off as close to the harness as possible, then a new segment spliced in as described. In the case of a damaged fusible link that feeds two harness wires, the harness connections should be replaced with two fusible link wires so that each circuit will have its own separate protection.

➡**Most of the problems caused in the wiring harness are due to bad ground connections. Always check all vehicle ground connections for corrosion or looseness before performing any power feed checks to eliminate the chance of a bad ground affecting the circuit.**

Hard-Shell Connectors

Unlike molded connectors, the terminal contacts in hard-shell connectors can be replaced. Weatherproof hard-shell connectors with the leads molded into the shell have non-replaceable terminal ends. Replacement usually involves the use of a special terminal removal tool that depresses the locking tangs (barbs) on the connector terminal and allows the connector to be removed from the rear of the shell. The

connector shell should be replaced if it shows any evidence of burning, melting, cracks, or breaks. Replace individual terminals that are burnt, corroded, distorted or loose.

➡**The insulation crimp must be tight to prevent the insulation from sliding back on the wire when the wire is pulled. The insulation must be visibly compressed under the crimp tabs, and the ends of the crimp should be turned in for a firm grip on the insulation.**

The wire crimp must be made with all wire strands inside the crimp. The terminal must be fully compressed on the wire strands with the ends of the crimp tabs turned in to make a firm grip on the wire. Check all connections with an ohmmeter to insure a good contact. There should be no measurable resistance between the wire and the terminal when connected.

Fusible Links

The fuse link is a short length of special, Hypalon (high temperature) insulated wire, integral with the engine compartment wiring harness and should not be confused with standard wire. It is several wire gauges smaller than the circuit which it protects. Under no circumstances should a fuse link replacement repair be made using a length of standard wire cut from bulk stock or from another wiring harness.

To repair any blown fuse link use the following procedure:

1 Determine which circuit is damaged, its location and the cause of the open fuse link. If the damaged fuse link is one of three fed by a common No. 10 or 12 gauge feed wire, determine the specific affected circuit.

2 Disconnect the negative battery cable.

3 Cut the damaged fuse link from the wiring harness and discard it. If the fuse link is one of three circuits fed by a single feed wire, cut it out of the harness at each splice end and discard it.

4 Identify and procure the proper fuse link with butt connectors for attaching the fuse link to the harness.

➡**Heat shrink tubing must be slipped over the wire before crimping and soldering the connection.**

5 To repair any fuse link in a 3-link group with one feed:

   a) *After cutting the open link out of the harness, cut each of the remaining undamaged fuse links close to the feed wire weld.*

   b) *Strip approximately 1/2-in. (13mm) of insulation from the detached ends of the two good fuse links. Insert two wire ends into one end of a butt connector, then carefully push one stripped end of the replacement fuse link into the same end of the butt connector and crimp all three firmly together.*

➡**Care must be taken when fitting the three fuse links into the butt connector as the internal diameter is a snug fit for three wires. Make sure to use a proper crimping tool. Pliers, side cutters, etc. will not apply the proper crimp to retain the wires and withstand a pull test.**

   c) *After crimping the butt connector to the three fuse links, cut the weld portion from the feed wire and strip approximately 1/2-in. (13mm) of insulation from the cut end. Insert the stripped end into the open end of the butt connector and crimp very firmly.*

   d) *To attach the remaining end of the replacement fuse link, strip approximately 1/2-in. (13mm) of insulation from the wire end of the circuit from which the blown fuse link was removed, and firmly crimp a butt connector or equivalent to the stripped wire. Then, insert the end of the replacement link into the other end of the butt connector and crimp firmly.*

   e) *Using rosin core solder with a consistency of 60 percent tin and 40 percent lead, solder the connectors and the wires at the repairs then insulate with electrical tape or heat shrink tubing.*

6   To replace any fuse link on a single circuit in a harness, cut out the damaged portion, strip approximately 1/2-in. (13mm) of insulation from the two wire ends and attach the appropriate replacement fuse link to the stripped wire ends with two proper size butt connectors. Solder the connectors and wires, then insulate.

7   To repair any fuse link which has an eyelet terminal on one end such as the charging circuit, cut off the open fuse link behind the weld, strip approximately 1/2-in. (13mm) of insulation from the cut end and attach the appropriate new eyelet fuse link to the cut stripped wire with an appropriate size butt connector. Solder the connectors and wires at the repair, then insulate.

8   Connect the negative battery cable to the battery and test the system for proper operation.

➡**Do not mistake a resistor wire for a fuse link. The resistor wire is generally longer and has print stating, "Resistor-don't cut or splice."**

When attaching a single No. 16, 17, 18 or 20 gauge fuse link to a heavy gauge wire, always double the stripped wire end of the fuse link before inserting and crimping it into the butt connector for positive wire retention.

Add-On Electrical Equipment

The electrical system in your vehicle is designed to perform under reasonable operating conditions without interference between components. Before any additional electrical equipment is installed, it is recommended that you consult your dealer or a reputable repair facility that is familiar with the vehicle and its systems.

If the vehicle is equipped with mobile radio equipment and/or mobile telephone, it may have an effect upon the operation of any on-board computer control modules. Radio Frequency Interference (RFI) from the communications system can be picked up by the vehicle's wiring harnesses and conducted into the control module, giving it the wrong messages at the wrong time. Although well shielded against RFI, the computer should be further protected by taking the following measures:

• Install the antenna as far as possible from the control module. For instance, if the module is located behind the center console area, then the antenna should be mounted at the rear of the vehicle.

• Keep the antenna wiring a minimum of eight inches away from any wiring running to control modules and from the module itself. NEVER wind the antenna wire around any other wiring.

• Mount the equipment as far from the control module as possible. Be very careful during installation not to drill through any wires or short a wire harness with a mounting screw.

• Insure that the electrical feed wire(s) to the equipment are properly and tightly connected. Loose connectors can cause interference.

• Make certain that the equipment is properly grounded to the vehicle. Poor grounding can damage expensive equipment.

HEATER

General Information

The heating system on air-cooled Volkswagen vehicles includes the heater boxes (part of the exhaust manifolds), the heater control cables, the heater channels (or center tube on type 2 models) and the cooling fan. The heating system is ingenious in its design and functions as follows:

The cooling fan not only blows air over the engine to cool it down, but also blows air through hoses into the back end of the heater boxes. The bosses are designed to allow the incoming air to pass over the hot exhaust pipes, thereby absorbing heat. The heated air then exits out the front of the heater boxes, through connecting hoses to the heater channels or center tube. The heater channels, found on type 1 and 3 models, run along the rocker panel of the vehicle, whereas the center tube on type 2 models is routed up the center of the Transporter body. The heated air travels up the heater channels/center tube and can exit at a number of openings (at the rear seat, the front seat or up at the windshield for defrosting purposes). The control flaps, which dictate at which opening the air exists, are controlled by cables and knobs.

For the removal and installation of the heater boxes or the cooling fan, refer to the exhaust system or cooling system portions of Section 3.

The heater channels are often a problem spot in the heating system, because they rust and become obstructed. Welding is required for heater channel installation and is better left to a professional automotive body technician.

For the removal and installation of the heater control cables, refer to the following procedure.

Heater Cables

REMOVAL & INSTALLATION

1   Disconnect the cables at the heat exchangers. The cables are usually held in the flap levers at the heat exchangers with sleeve bolts with 10mm heads and locked with 9mm head nuts.

2   Remove the cable ends from the sleeve bolts and pull the rubber boots off the cable guide tubes and off the disconnected cables.

3   Disconnect the cables at the heater controls. They are usually held by pins with cotter pin retainers. You will have to unbolt and pull out the temperature control lever to unfasten the cables on Types 1 and 3 models. On type 2 models, disconnect the cables from the heater control knob, located on the floor for 1949 - 67 vehicles, or on the dashboard for 1968 - 69 transporters.

4   Remove the cables by pulling them out from the heater control side.

5   Feed new cables into the guide tubes at the heater controls after you have sprayed them completely with silicone to prevent rust and wear.

WINDSHIELD WIPERS

Wiper Blade and Arm

REMOVAL & INSTALLATION

To remove the wiper blade element, refer to Section 1. To remove the wiper blade and arm together as a unit, perform the following:

1 Ensure that the wiper motor is in the Park position.
2 Remove the cap nut where the arm attaches to the windshield wiper driveshaft.
3 Lift the arm and blade off of the driveshaft.

To install:

4 Ensure that the wiper motor is in the Park position.
5 Slide the wiper arm down onto the driveshaft so that the splines are correctly engaged. The wiper arms should be positioned so that the wiper blades are approximately 1 in. (25mm) from the bottom of the windshield.
6 Install and tighten the wiper arm retaining cap nut until secure.
7 Turn the wiper motor ON and ensure that the wiper arms sweep the windshield correctly and do not contact each other.

Wiper Motor

REMOVAL & INSTALLATION

Type 1 Models

1 Disconnect the negative battery cable.
2 Remove the wiper arms.
3 Remove the wiper bearing nuts as well as the washers. Take off the outer bearing seals.
4 Remove the back of the instrument panel from the luggage compartment.
5 Remove the fresh air box/rain drain by removing the three screws at the top and the nut at the bottom; next remove the glove box and the right side air vent.
6 Disconnect the wiper motor wiring harness and remove the screw which secures the wiper frame to the body.
7 Remove the frame and motor with the linkage.

➡The ball joints at the ends of the linkage may be slipped apart by gently popping the ball and socket apart with a small prytool. Always lubricate the joints upon reassembly.

8 Remove the lock and spring washers from the motor driveshaft and remove the connecting rod. Matchmark the motor and frame to ensure proper realignment when the motor is reinstalled.
9 Remove the nut located at the base of the motor driveshaft, and remove the motor from the frame.
10 To install, reverse the removal procedure and heed the following reminders:
• The pressed lug on the wiper frame must engage the groove in the wiper bearing. Make sure that the wiper spindles are perpendicular to the plane of the windshield.
• Check the linkage bushings for wear.
• The hollow side of the links must face toward the frame with the angled end of the driving link toward the right bearing.
• The inner bearing seal should be placed so that the shoulder of the rubber molding faces the wiper arm.

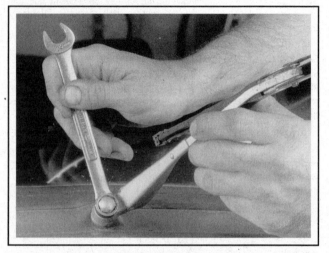

Remove the windshield wiper arm hold-down nut . . .

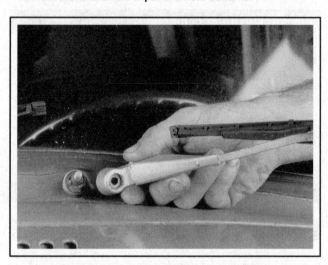

. . . then lift the arm up and off of the arm drive shaft

Type 2 Models

1949 - 67 VEHICLES

1 Disconnect the negative battery cable.
2 Remove the wiper arms as described earlier in this section.
3 Remove the nuts securing the wiper arm shafts.
4 From inside of the Transporter, remove the mounting fasteners and lower the right-hand side of the parcel tray, located under the dashboard.
5 Disconnect the wire from the wiper motor, then remove the motor mounting fasteners and pull it out from the body until the wiper linkage can be accessed.
6 Detach the linkage from the wiper motor, then remove the motor from the vehicle by sliding it out to the right (to clear the linkage arm).
7 Installation is the reverse of the removal procedure.

1968 - 69 VEHICLES

1 Disconnect the negative wire from the battery.
2 Remove both wiper arms.
3 Remove the bearing cover and nut.

4   Remove the heater branch connections under the instrument panel.

5   Disconnect the wiper motor wiring.

6   Remove the wiper motor securing screw and remove the motor.

7   Reverse the removal procedure to install.

Type 3 Models

1   Disconnect the negative battery cable.

2   Remove the ashtray and glove compartment.

3   Remove the fresh air controls.

4   Remove the cover for the heater and water drainage hoses.

5   Disconnect the motor wiring.

6   Remove the wiper arms.

7   Remove the bearing covers and nuts, washers, and outer bearing seals.

8   Remove the wiper motor securing screws and remove the motor.

9   Reverse the removal procedure to install.

REMOVAL & INSTALLATION

The windshield wiper linkage is secured at the ends by a ball and socket type joint. The ball and joint may be gently pried apart with the aid of a small prytool. Always lubricate the joints with grease before assembly.

Wiper Arm Shaft

1   Remove the wiper arm.

2   Remove the bearing cover or the shaft seal, depending on the type.

3   Remove the large wiper shaft bearing securing nut and remove the accompanying washer and rubber seal.

4   Disconnect the wiper linkage from the wiper arm shaft.

5   Working from inside the car, slide the shaft out of its bearing.

➡**It may be necessary to lightly tap the shaft out of its bearing. Use a soft-faced hammer.**

6   Installation is the reverse of the removal procedure.

INSTRUMENT CLUSTER

Speedometer

REMOVAL & INSTALLATION

Except 1968 - 69 Type 2 Models

➡**On type 2 models, the parcel tray must be lowered to access the back of the speedometer.**

1   Disconnect the negative battery cable.

➡**On the Type 3, it is necessary to remove the fuse panel to gain access to the speedometer.**

2   Disconnect the speedometer light bulb wires.

3   Unscrew the knurled nut which secures the speedometer cable to the back of the speedometer. Pull the cable from the back of the speedometer.

4   Remove the two knurled nuts which secure the speedometer brackets. Remove the brackets.

5   Remove the speedometer from the dashboard by sliding it out toward the steering wheel.

6   Reverse the above steps to install. Before fully tightening the nuts for the speedometer brackets, make sure the speedometer is correctly positioned in the dash.

1968 - 69 Type 2 Models

1   Disconnect the negative battery cable.

2   Remove the fresh air control lever knobs.

3   Remove the Phillips head screws at the four corners of the instrument panel.

4   Disconnect the speedometer cable.

5   Lift the instrument panel out of the dash far enough to disconnect the wiring, then remove the instrument panel. Remove the two long screws, separate the panel halves, then remove the screws and remove the speedometer. Installation is the reverse of removal.

Speedometer Cable

REMOVAL & INSTALLATION

1   Unscrew the cable from the back of the speedometer.

2   At the left front wheel, pry off the circlip retaining the square end of the speedometer shaft to the wheel bearing dust cap.

3   Pull the cable out of the back of the steering knuckle from under the car. With the circlip removed, the cable should pull right out. Pull the cable out of its holding grommets and remove.

4   Installation is the reverse of removal.

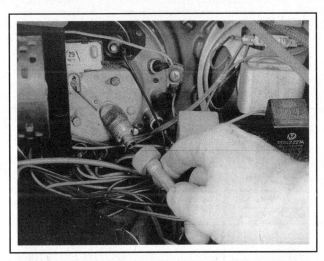

The speedometer cable attaches to the speedometer with a threaded collar

Fuel Gauge and Clock Assembly

REMOVAL & INSTALLATION

1 Disconnect the negative battery cable.
2 Disconnect the wiring from the back of the assembly.

➡**On the Type 3 it is necessary to remove the fuse panel to gain access to this assembly.**

3 Remove the knurled nuts and brackets which secure the assembly in the dash. Use a 4mm allen wrench.

LIGHTING

Headlights

REMOVAL & INSTALLATION

1949 - 66 Models

1 Disconnect the negative battery cable.
2 Loosen the front rim retaining screw and pull out the complete headlight unit.

4 Remove the assembly by gently sliding it toward the steering wheel and out of the dash.
5 The fuel gauge is secured into the base of the clock by two screws. Remove the screws and slip the fuel gauge out of the clock.
6 Installation is the reverse of the removal procedure. Make sure the clock and fuel gauge assembly is properly centered in the dash before fully tightening the nuts.

Ignition Switch

Ignition switch removal and installation is covered in Section 8.

3 Separate the wiring connector from the sealed beam unit.
4 Disconnect the two wires from the parking light bulb socket.
5 Remove the parking light bulb by unscrewing it from the housing.

❊❊ WARNING:

The lens retaining springs are under heavy tension. To prevent accidental component damage, be cautious when removing them.

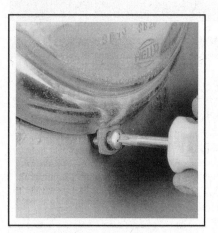

To remove the headlight on 1949 - 66 models, unscrew the lower retaining bolt . . .

. . . and lift the headlight assembly out of the fender

Remove the retaining springs . . .

. . . then separate the bulb and ring from the headlight housing

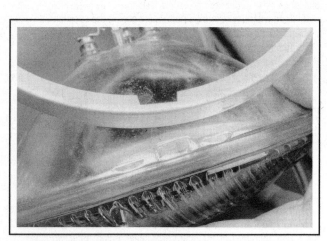

Remove the retaining ring from the bulb

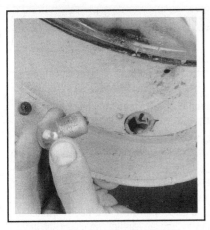

If necessary the front parking light bulb may be replaced as well

On 1949 - 66 models, use the two diagonally-located screws to aim the headlight assembly

To remove a 1967 - 69 headlight bulb, first remove the trim ring retaining screw(s) . . .

. . . then pull the trim ring away from the headlight assembly

6 Remove the lens retaining springs. Hold the lamp unit with one thumb controlling the spring while the other thumb pulls the springs out of their seats.

7 Withdraw the retaining ring and sealed beam unit.

To install:

8 Install the sealed unit and the parking light bulb into the housing. If replacement bulbs are needed, install the following depending on the voltage system:

- Headlight for the 6-volt system - 161 A (VW part number)
- Headlight for the 12-volt system - 6012 (standard replacement0 or 111 941 261 A (VW part number)
- Parking bulb for the 6-volt system - 719 1 (VW part number)
- Parking bulb for the 12-volt system - 1034 standard replacement) or N 17 738 2 (VW part number)

9 Use the tabs and slots of the retaining ring as a guide for correct positioning of the sealed beam unit.

10 Attach all of the wiring to the light bulbs.

11 Inspect the rubber seal between the front rim and the vehicle fender for proper mounting.

12 Adjust the headlight aiming, if necessary.

1967 - 69 Models

1 Remove the screws which secures the headlight ring and remove the ring.

2 The sealed beam is held in place by a ring secured by three screws. Remove the screws and the ring. Do not confuse the headlight aiming screws with the screws for the ring. There are only two screws used for aiming.

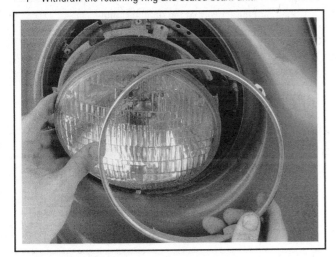

Once all trim ring screws are removed, pull the ring and headlight out of the mounting bracket . . .

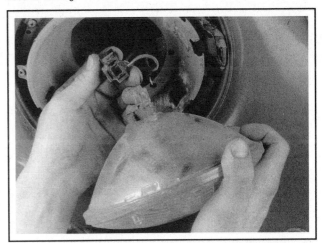

. . . then detach the wiring from the back of the headlight

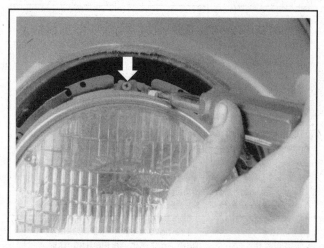

On 1967 - 69 models, the aiming screws (arrow) are located under the trim ring

3   Pull the wiring off the back of the sealed beam and remove the beam.

4   Installation is the reverse of the removal procedure.

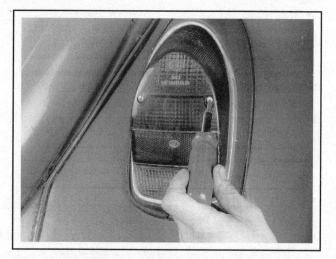

To remove the rear brake/turn signal/back-up light bulbs, first remove the lens retaining screws . . .

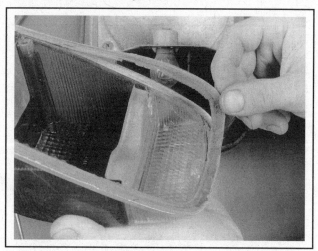

Be certain to inspect the sealing gasket for damage, such as dry rot or excessive cracking

Rear Brake/Turn Signal/Back-up Lights

REMOVAL & INSTALLATION

➡This is a general procedure and applies to all models and types covered by this manual. A few steps may need to be slightly altered to comply with your particular vehicle.

1   Disconnect the negative battery cable.

2   Using a Phillips screwdriver, remove the rear light assembly lens retaining screws.

3   Pull the lens and gasket off of the rear fender.

4   Inspect the lens gasket for tearing or crumbling. If any such damage is evident, replace the old gasket with a new one upon installation.

5   Once the lens is removed from the rear light assembly, the individual light bulbs can be removed. To remove the light bulbs:

   a) Grasp the light bulb to be removed and gently press it in toward its socket.

   b) While pressing the bulb in, turn the bulb counterclockwise until the two little pins on the bulb base clear the channels in the socket.

   c) Pull the bulb up and out of its socket.

6   Installation is the reverse of the removal procedure. During installation, make sure that the light bulb contacts are clean and free of corrosion.

. . . then pull the lens off of the light assembly

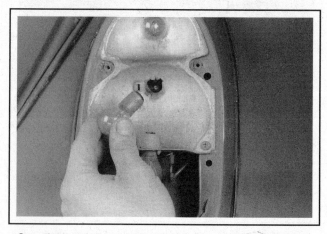

Once the lens is removed the light bulbs may be inspected and replaced

Light Bulbs

Model	Usage	U.S. Replacement Bulbs	VW Part No.	Wattage
36 hp. 1,200 Type 1 (6 Volt) January, 1954-August 1955	Headlights	—	—	35/35
	Parking lights	—	—	1.5
	Stoplights	—	—	15
	Taillights	—	—	5
	License plate light	—	—	5
	Interior light	—	—	10
	All warning lights	—	—	1.2
	Instrument lighting	—	—	1.2
	Turn signals	—	—	3
36 hp. 1,200 Type 1 (6 Volt) from August, 1955	Headlights	—	—	35/35
	Parking lights	—	—	2
	Stoplights	—	—	20
	Taillights	—	—	5
	License plate light (tubular bulb)	—	—	5
	Interior light	—	—	10
	Semaphore-type	—	—	3
	Turn signals (tubular bulbs)	—	—	1.2
	All warning lights	—	—	1.2
	Instrument lighting			
36 hp. 1,200 Type 1 (6 Volt) Karmann Ghia, from August, 1955	Headlights	—	—	35/35
	Parking lights	—	—	3
	Taillights	—	—	5
	Rear stop/turn signal	—	—	15
	License plate lights	—	—	5
	Interior light	—	—	5
	Front turn signals	—	—	15
42 hp. 1,200 and 1,300 Type 1 (6 Volt) Sedan and Convertible	Headlights	—	N177051	45/40
	Parking lights	—	N177171	4
	Stoplight/taillight	—	N177371	18/5
	Turn signals	—	N177311	18
	License plate light	—	N177191	10 ①
	Interior light	—	N177231	10
	Warning and instrument lights	—	N177221	1.2
42 hp. 1,200 and 1,300 Type 1 (6 Volt) Karmann Ghia	Headlights	—	—	45/40
	Parking lights	—	—	4
	Taillights	—	—	5
	Stoplights	—	—	18
	Turn signals	—	—	18
	License plate lights	—	—	5
	Interior light	—	—	10
	Warning, instrument lights, clock	—	—	1.2
1,300 Type 1 (12 Volt)	Headlights	6012	11194126A	45/40
	License plate light	—	—	10
	Interior light	—	—	10
	Instrument and warning lights	—	—	2
	Parking lights	—	—	4
	Turn signals	—	—	18
	Stoplight/taillight	—	—	18/5
1,500 and 1,600 Type 1 (12 Volt) Sedan and Convertible	Headlights	6012	111941261A	—
	Parking/turn signal, taillight/stoplight	1034	N177382	—
	Rear turn signal	1073	N177322	—
	License plate light	89	N177192	—
	Backup lights	1073	N177332	—
	Instrument and warning lights	—	N177222	—
	Sedan interior light	—	N177232	—
	Convertible interior light	—	N177252	—
	Warning lights for emergency flasher, brake, rear window defroster	—	N177512	—
1,500 Type 2 (6 Volt)	Headlights	—	N177051	45/40
	Parking lights	—	N177171	4
	Turn signals	—	N177311	18
	Taillights/stoplights	—	N177371	5/18
	License plate light	—	N177191	10
	Warning lights, Instrument lights	—	N177221	1.2
	Dome light	—	N177251	5
	Clock	—	N177221	1.2
1,600 Type 3 (6 Volt)	Headlights	6006, Type 2	N177051	—
	Front parking/turn signal	1154	N177171	5/18
	Rear turn signal, stoplight	1129	N177311	18
	Taillight	81	N177181	5
	License plate light	81	N177191	10
	Warning, instrument lights	—	N177221	1.2
	Interior and luggage compartment lights	—	N177231	10

① 1,200 uses 5 watt bulb after August, 1965.

Front Turn Signal/Side Marker Lights

REMOVAL & INSTALLATION

➡️**This is a general procedure and applies to all models and types covered by this manual. A few steps may need to be slightly altered to comply with your particular vehicle.**

1 Disconnect the negative battery cable.

2 Using a Phillips screwdriver, remove the front light assembly lens retaining screws.

3 Pull the lens and gasket off of the front fender.

4 Inspect the lens gasket for tearing or crumbling. If any such damage is evident, replace the old gasket with a new one upon installation.

5 Once the lens is removed from the light assembly, the individual light bulbs can be removed. To remove the light bulbs:

  a) *Grasp the light bulb to be removed and gently press it in toward its socket.*

  b) *While pressing the bulb in, turn the bulb counterclockwise until the two little pins on the bulb base clear the channels in the socket.*

  c) *Pull the bulb up and out of its socket.*

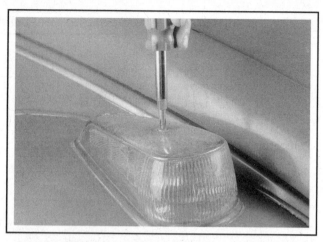

On newer models, remove the front turn signal/side marker light assembly lens retaining screws . . .

6 Installation is the reverse of the removal procedure. During installation, make sure that the light bulb contacts are clean and free of corrosion.

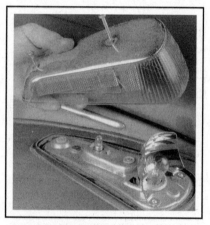

. . . then lift the lens off of the light assembly

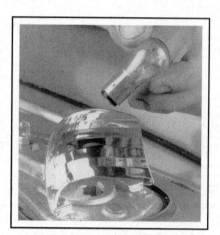

Once the lens is removed either the front turn signal bulb . . .

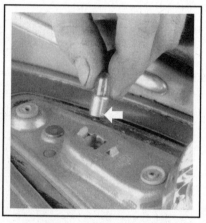

. . . or the side marker bulb can be removed - note the small retaining knob on the bulb

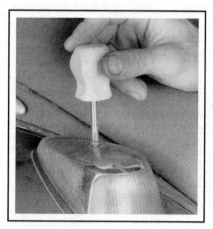

The removal for older models is essentially the same - remove the screw . . .

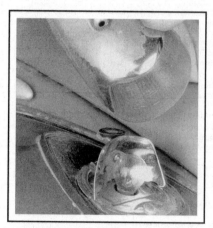

. . . and lift the lens off of the fender . . .

. . . then remove the bulb from the socket

License Plate Light

REMOVAL & INSTALLATION

→This is a general procedure and applies to all models and types covered by this manual. A few steps may need to be slightly altered to comply with your particular vehicle.

1 Disconnect the negative battery cable.

2 If necessary for easier access to the light assembly lens retaining screws, open the rear hood.

3 Using a Phillips screwdriver, remove the light assembly lens retaining screws.

4 Pull the lens and gasket, if equipped, off of the license plate light assembly.

5 If applicable, inspect the lens gasket for tearing or crumbling. If any such damage is evident, replace the old gasket with a new one upon installation.

6 Once the lens is removed from the light assembly, the light bulb can be removed. To remove the light bulb:

a) *Grasp the light bulb and gently press it in toward its socket.*

b) *While pressing the bulb in, turn the bulb counterclockwise until the two little pins on the bulb base clear the channels in the socket.*

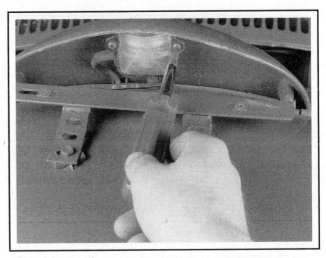

Remove the 2 license plate lens retaining screws to gain access to the bulb

c) *Pull the bulb up and out of its socket.*

7 Installation is the reverse of the removal procedure. During installation, make sure that the light bulb contacts are clean and free of corrosion.

FUSES

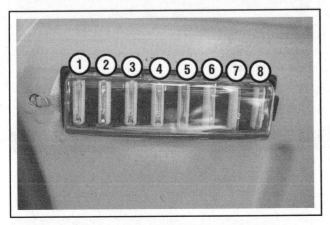

Typical fuse box layout on pre-1967 (six-volt) models

1 *Brake lights, turn signals, windshield wipers and horn (except 1961) (16-amp)*
2 *Left high beam and high beam warning light (8-amp)*
3 *Right high beam (8-amp)*
4 *Left low beam (8-amp)*
5 *Right low beam (8-amp)*
6 *Left tail light and left front parking brake (8-amp)*
7 *Right tail light, license plate light and right front parking light (except 1966) (8-amp)*
8 *Radio, interior light, horn (1961 only) and emergency flasher (1966 only) (8-amp, through 1965; 16 amp, 1966 only)*

All major circuits are protected from overloading or short circuiting by fuses. A 12 position fusebox is located beneath the dashboard near the steering column, or located in the luggage compartment on some air conditioned models.

When a fuse blows, the cause should be investigated. Never install a fuse of a larger capacity than specified, and never use foil, a bolt or a nail in place of a fuse. Make sure to always carry a few spares in case of an emergency. There are 8 amp (white) fuses and 16 amp (red) fuses in a typical VW fusebox. To replace a fuse, pry off the clear plastic cover for the fusebox and depress a contact at either end of the subject fuse.

Typical fuse box layout on 1967 and later Beetles

1   Horn (except 1968), turn signals, brake lights (except 1969), fuel gauge (except 1967), Automatic Stick Shift warning lights (except 1967) and rear window defroster switch (1969 only) (8-amp)
2   Windshield wipers, brake lights (1969 only) and horn (1967 only) (8-amp)
3   Left high beam and high beam warning light (8-amp)
4   Right high beam (8-amp)
5   Left low beam (8-amp)
6   Right low beam (8-amp)
7   Right tail light (1967 and 1968 only), left tail light (1969 only), license plate light (1967 only) and left front parking light (except 1967) (8-amp)
8   Left tail light (1967 only), right tail light (except 1967), right front parking light (except 1967) and license plate light (except 1967) (8-amp)
9   Radio (1967 only), dome light (except 1967), emergency flasher (except 1967) and ignition warning light (1969) (8-amp, 1967; 16-amp, 1968 and 1969)
10 Dome light (1967 only), emergency flasher (1967 only) and radio (except 1967) (8-amp, 1968 and 1969); 16-amp, 1967 only)

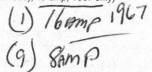

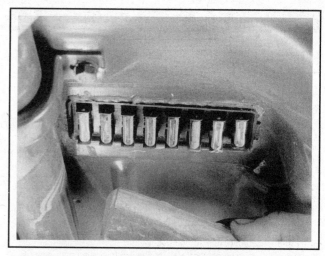

The fuse block is located under the dashboard

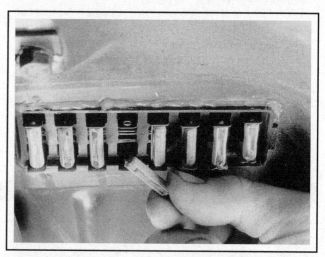

The fuses can be removed from the block by pulling them out carefully

TRAILER WIRING

Wiring the vehicle for towing is fairly easy. There are a number of good wiring kits available and these should be used, rather than trying to design your own.

All trailers will need brake lights and turn signals as well as tail lights and side marker lights. Most areas require extra marker lights for over-wide trailers. Also, most areas have recently required back-up lights for trailers, and most trailer manufacturers have been building trailers with back-up lights for several years.

Additionally, some Class I, most Class II and just about all Class III trailers will have electric brakes. Add to this number an accessories wire, to operate trailer internal equipment or to charge the trailer's battery, and you can have as many as seven wires in the harness.

Determine the equipment on your trailer and buy the wiring kit necessary. The kit will contain all the wires needed, plus a plug adapter set which includes the female plug, mounted on the bumper or hitch, and the male plug, wired into, or plugged into the trailer harness.

When installing the kit, follow the manufacturer's instructions. The color coding of the wires is usually standard throughout the industry. One point to note: some domestic vehicles, and most imported vehicles, have separate turn signals. On most domestic vehicles, the brake lights and rear turn signals operate with the same bulb. For those vehicles with separate turn signals, you can purchase an isolation unit so that the brake lights won't blink whenever the turn signals are operated, or, you can go to your local electronics supply house and buy four diodes to wire in series with the brake and turn signal bulbs. Diodes will isolate the brake and turn signals. The choice is yours. The isolation units are simple and quick to install, but far more expensive than the diodes. The diodes, however, require more work to install properly, since they require the cutting of each bulb's wire and soldering in place of the diode.

One, final point, the best kits are those with a spring loaded cover on the vehicle mounted socket. This cover prevents dirt and moisture from corroding the terminals. Never let the vehicle socket hang loosely; always mount it securely to the bumper or hitch.

Fuse Applications

Model	System Voltage	Circuit Description	Fuse Amperage
Type 1	6 Volt	Horn, flashers, brake lights, wipers, high beam warning light, left high beam	16
		Right high beam	8
		Left low beam	8
		Right low beam	8
		Left parking light, left taillight	8
		Right parking light, right taillight, license plate light	8
		Headlight dimmer switch, radio, interior light	16
	12 Volt	Turn signals, horn, brake lights, brake warning light, Automatic Stick-shift, rear window defroster and switch	16
		Wipers	8
		High beam warning light, left high beam	8
		Right high beam	8
		Left low beam	8
		Right low beam	8
		Left parking light, left taillight	8
		License plate light, right parking light, right taillight	8
		Interior light, emergency blinkers	8
		Spare fuse	8
		Rear window defroster main current (under rear seat, left side)	8
		Back up lights (right side of engine fan housing)	8
		Automatic Stick-shift control valve (left side of engine fan housing)	8
Type 2	6 Volt	Left low beam	8
		Right low beam	8
		Left high beam, high beam warning light	8
		Right high beam	8
		Left taillight	8
		Right taillight, license plate light, parking lights	8
		Brake lights, turn signals	16
		Horn, interior lights, wipers, headlight dimmer switch	16
	12 Volt	Emergency flashers, interior lights	16
		Left high beam, high beam indicator light	8
		Right high beam	8
		Horn, brake lights, turn signals, brake warning light	8
		License plate light, parking brake lights, right taillight	8
		Left low beam	8
		Right low beam	8
		Rear window defroster switch, windshield wipers	8
		Left taillight	8
		Unassigned (accessory)	8

Fuse Applications (cont.)

Model	System Voltage	Circuit Description	Fuse Amperage
Type 3	6 Volt	Right parking light, left parking light, left taillight, luggage compartment light	8
		Right taillight, license plate light	8
		Left low beam	8
		Right low beam	8
		Left high beam, high beam warning light	8
		Right high beam	8
		Spare fuse	8
		Emergency flashers, interior light, horn, clock, radio	16
		Brake lights, turn signals	8
		Windshield wipers, fuel gauge, warning lights	16
	12 Volt	Right taillight, license plate light, luggage compartment light, rear window defroster switch, parking lights	8
		Left taillight	8
		Left low beam	8
		Right low beam	8
		Left high beam, high beam warning light	8
		Right high beam	8
		Unassigned (accessory)	8
		Windshield wipers	16
		Brake lights, turn signals, horn, brake warning light	8
		Interior light, emergency flashers	8
		Electric fuel pump for fuel injection (no other equipment may be attached here)	8
		Unassigned (accessory)	16

WIRING DIAGRAMS

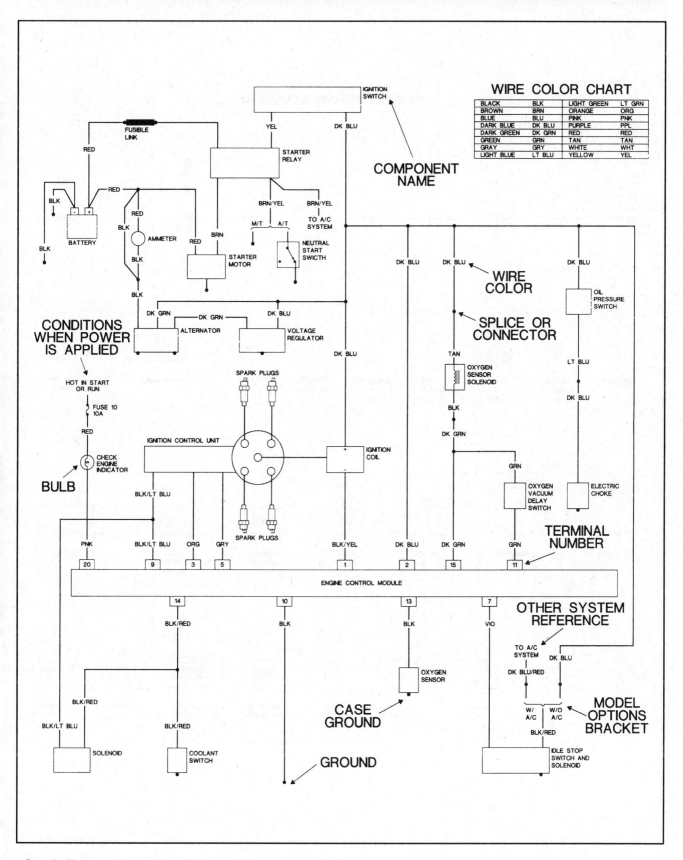

WIRE COLOR CHART

BLACK	BLK	LIGHT GREEN	LT GRN
BROWN	BRN	ORANGE	ORG
BLUE	BLU	PINK	PNK
DARK BLUE	DK BLU	PURPLE	PPL
DARK GREEN	DK GRN	RED	RED
GREEN	GRN	TAN	TAN
GRAY	GRY	WHITE	WHT
LIGHT BLUE	LT BLU	YELLOW	YEL

Sample diagram - how to read and interpret wiring

WIRING DIAGRAM SYMBOLS

BATTERY	CONNECTOR OR SPLICE	CIRCUIT BREAKER	CAPACITOR	COIL	DIODE	FUSE	FUSIBLE LINK	GROUND	LED

RESISTOR	SINGLE FILAMENT BULB	DUAL FILAMENT BULB	HEATING ELEMENT	SOLENOID OR COIL	VARIABLE RESISTOR	CRYSTAL	POTENTIOMETER	HORN OR SPEAKER

ALTERNATOR	DISTRIBUTOR ASSEMBLY	IGNITION COIL	SPARK PLUG	STEPPER MOTOR	HEAT ACTIVATED SWITCH	RELAY

NORMALLY OPEN SWITCH	NORMALLY CLOSED SWITCH	GANGED SWITCH	3-POSITION SWITCH	REED SWITCH	MOTOR OR ACTUATOR	SPEED SENSOR	JUNCTION BLOCK	MODEL OPTIONS BRACKET

Common wiring diagram symbols

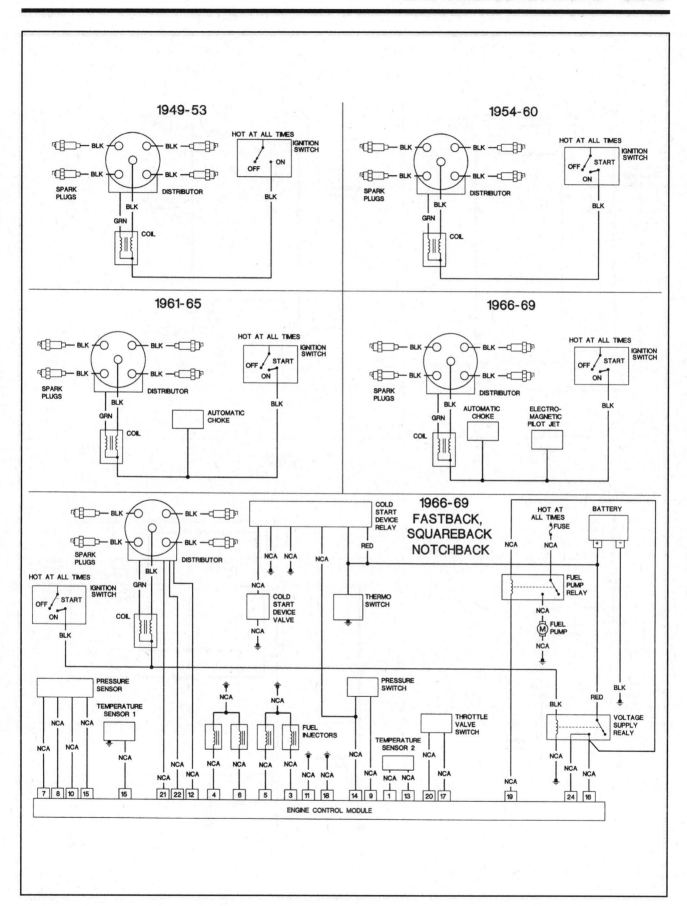

Engine control wiring schematic - all models

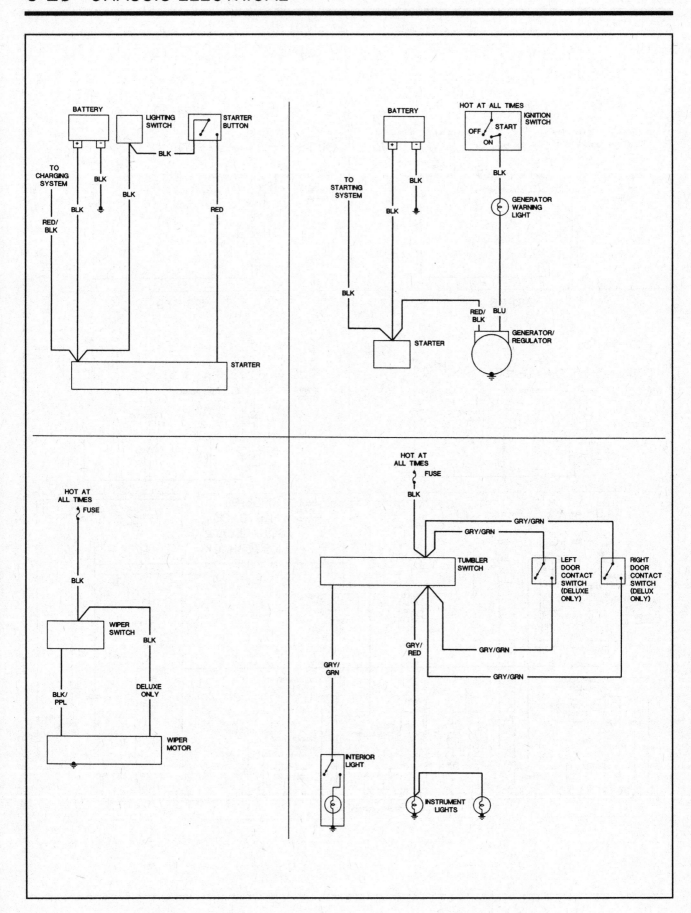

Chassis wiring schematic - 1949 - 53 models

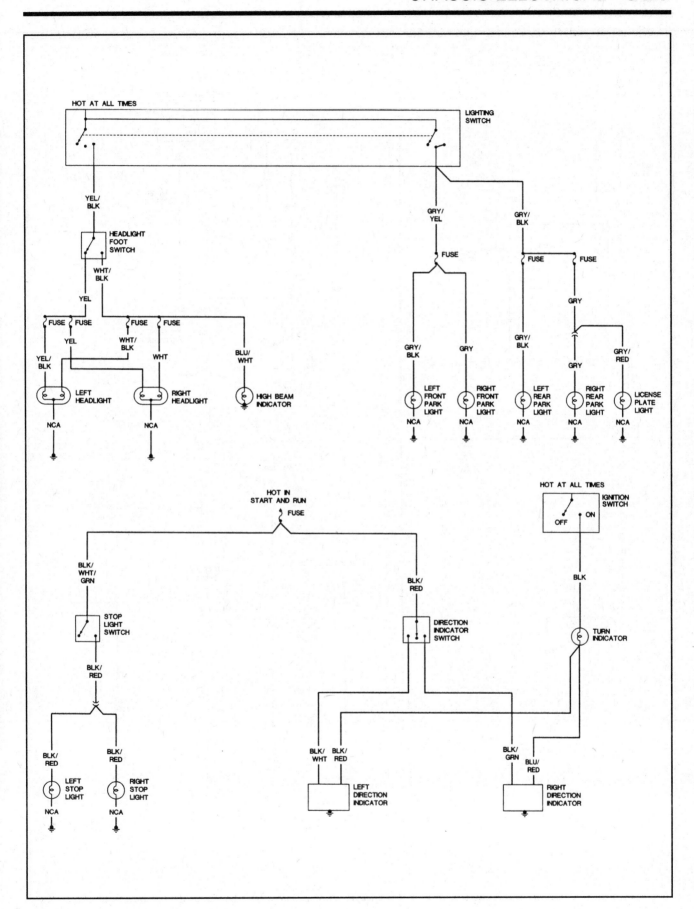

Chassis wiring schematic (continued) - 1949 - 53 models

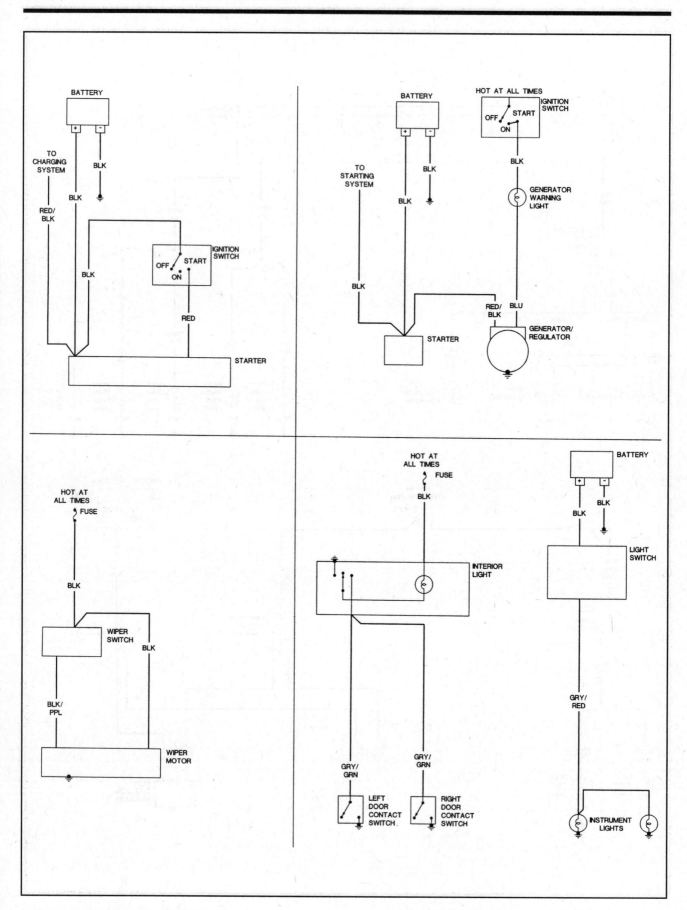

Chassis wiring schematic - 1954 - 57 models

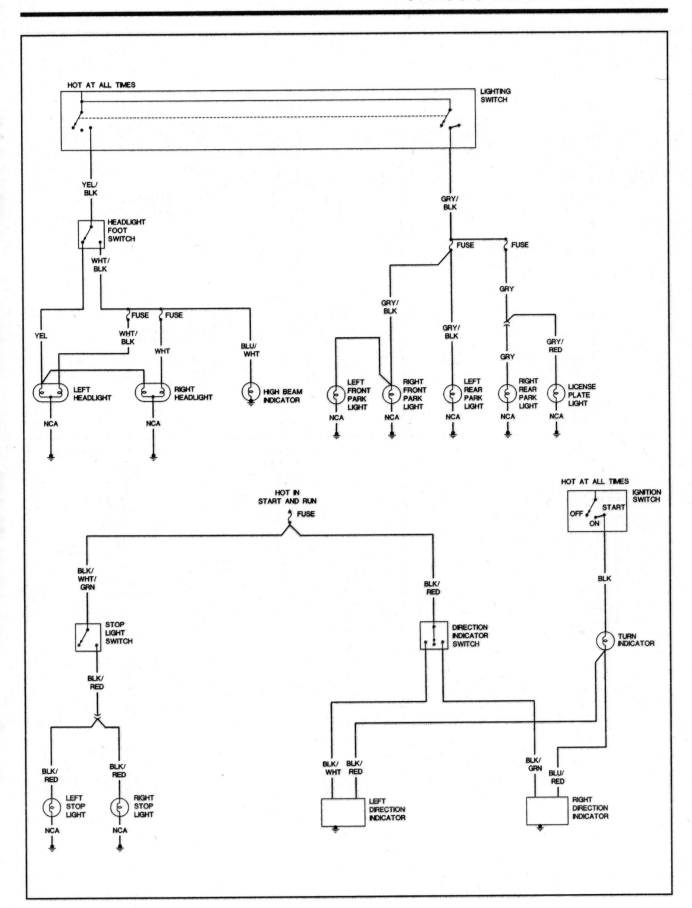

Chassis wiring schematic (continued) - 1954 - 57 models

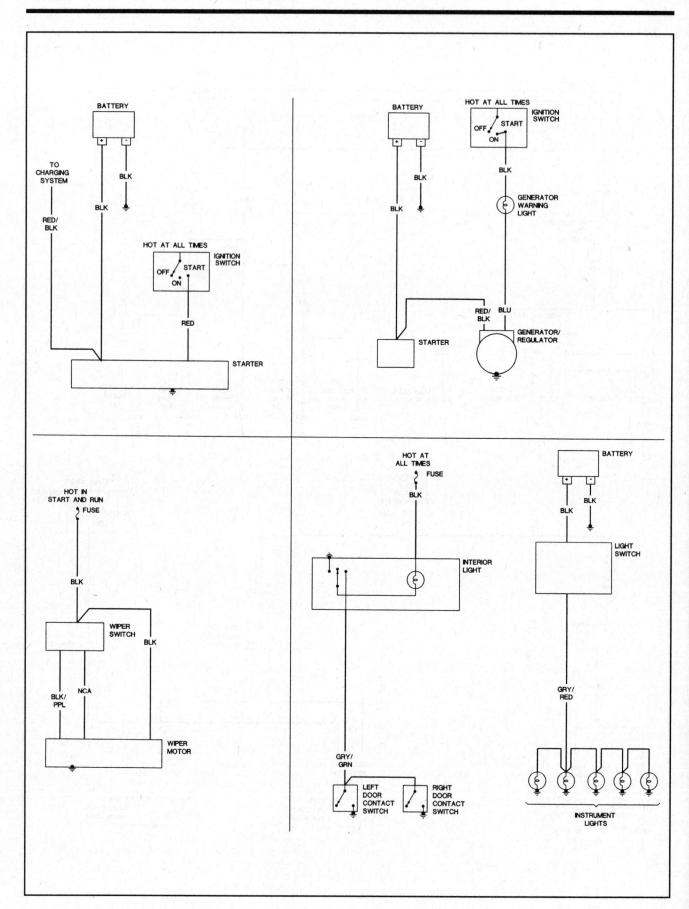

Chassis wiring schematic - 1958 - 65 models

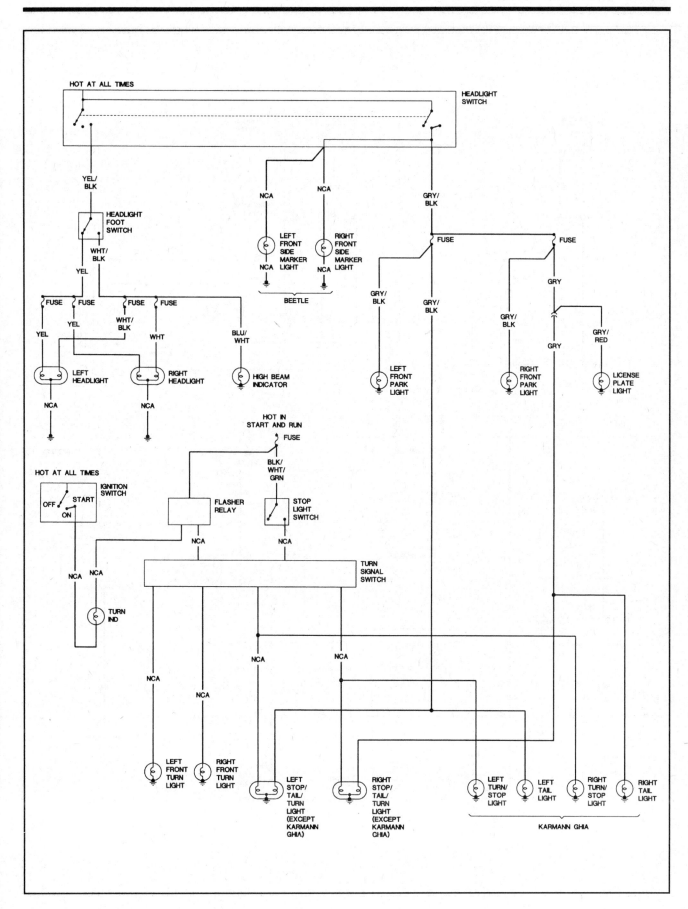

Chassis wiring schematic (continued) - 1958 - 65 models

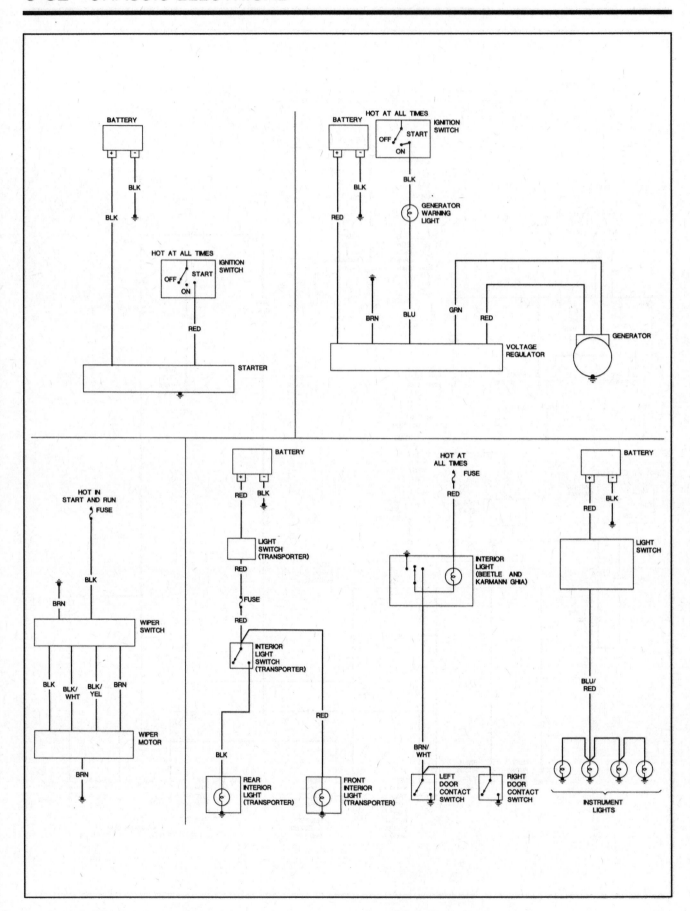

Chassis wiring schematic - 1966 - 69 models

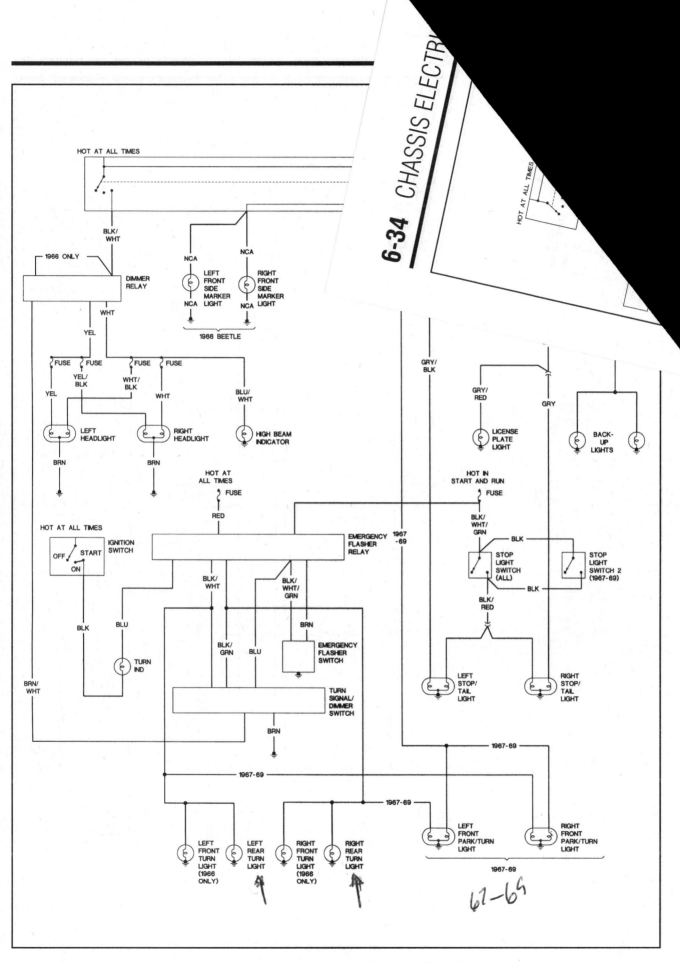

Chassis wiring schematic (continued) - 1966 - 69 type 1 and 3 models; 1966 - 67 type 2 models

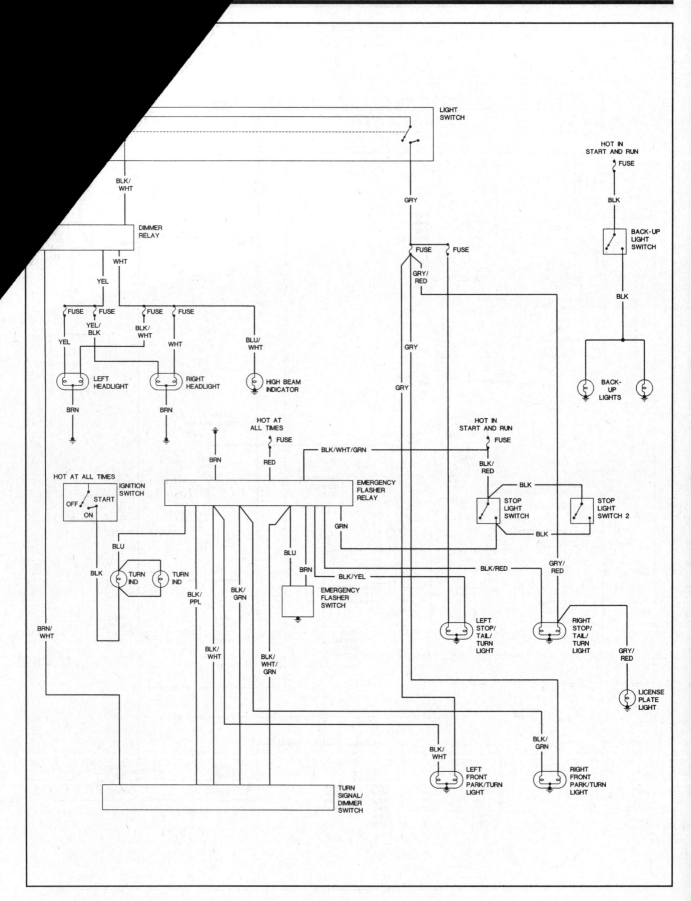

Chassis wiring schematic (continued) - 1968 - 69 type 2 models

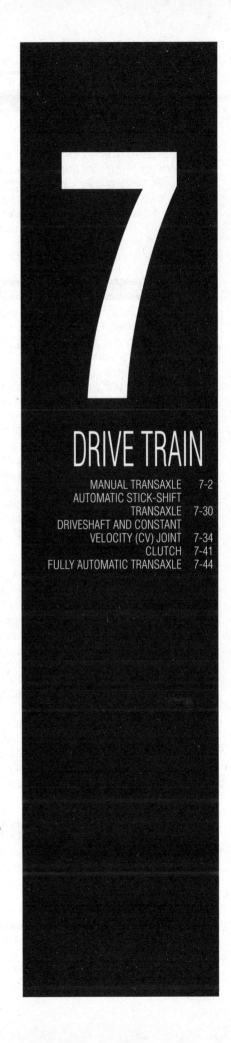

7

DRIVE TRAIN

MANUAL TRANSAXLE

All of the Volkswagens covered in this manual are equipped with transaxles, so named because the transmission gears and the axle gears are contained in the same housing. On manual and automatic stick shift VWs, the transmission part of the assembly shares the same hypoid gear oil as the rear axle part. Automatic transaxles use ATF Dexron in the transmission part, and hypoid gear oil in the rear axle.

All transaxles are mounted in a yoke at the rear of the car and bolt up to the front of the engine.

The transaxle case is constructed of aluminum alloy.

Understanding the Manual Transaxle

Because of the way an internal combustion engine breathes, it can produce torque, or twisting force, only within a narrow speed range. Most modern, overhead valve pushrod engines must turn at about 2500 rpm to produce their peak torque. By 4500 rpm they are producing so little torque that continued increases in engine speed produce no power increases. The torque peak on overhead camshaft engines is generally much higher, but within a much narrower speed range.

The manual transaxle and clutch are employed to vary the relationship between engine speed and the speed of the wheels so that adequate engine power can be produced under all circumstances. The clutch allows engine torque to be applied to the transaxle input shaft gradually, due to mechanical slippage. Consequently, the vehicle may be started smoothly from a full stop. The transaxle changes the ratio between the rotating speeds of the engine and wheels by the use of gears. The gear ratios allow full engine power to be applied to the wheels during acceleration at low speeds and at highway/passing speeds.

The power is usually transmitted from the input shaft to a mainshaft or output shaft. The gears of the mainshaft mesh with gears on the input shaft, allowing power to be carried from one to the other. All forward gears are in constant mesh and are free from rotating with the shaft unless the synchronizer and clutch are engaged. Shifting from one gear to the next causes one of the gears to be freed from rotating with the shaft and locks another to it. Gears are locked and unlocked by internal dog clutches which slide between the center of the gear and shaft. The forward gears employ synchronizers; friction members which smoothly bring gear and shaft to the same speed before the toothed dog clutches are engaged.

All manual transaxles (covered by this manual) employ four forward speeds and a reverse. All forward speeds have synchromesh engagement. The gears are helical and in constant mesh. Gear selection is accomplished by a floor-mounted lever working through a shift rod contained in the frame tunnel. The final drive pinion and ring gear are also helical cut.

General Information

The transaxle and engine are mounted as one unit at the rear of the car. The transaxle case is rubber-mounted and is supported at three points. The transaxle case contains the transmission, the differential and ring gear.

Recent transaxle cases are of one-piece, die-cast construction. Transaxles of 1960 and earlier models (36 hp with a nonsynchromesh first gear) are of a split-type construction. With the 40 hp engine introduced on the 1961 models, all transaxles have been of the one-piece type. In the case of the split-type cases, both halves must be replaced at the same time, since they are cast and machined in pairs.

The transaxle has four speeds forward and one reverse, with various ratios.

Selection of gears in the Volkswagen is by a floor-mounted lever working through a shift rod contained in the frame tunnel. The gears are helical, and are in constant mesh. In every speed, engine power is transmitted through a pair of gears. There is no direct drive in the Volkswagen transaxles.

The drive pinion and ring gear are helically-cut. These gears must be perfectly adjusted in order that long life and silent operation will be ensured.

Transaxles work of any kind requires removal of the engine.

Transaxle Assembly

REMOVAL & INSTALLATION

Swing Axle Models

1 With the engine removed from the car, remove the rear wheels, disconnect the brake lines at the rear wheels and plug the lines.
2 Disconnect the parking brake cables from the push bar at the frame and withdraw the cables from their conduit tubes.
3 Remove the bolts at the rear axle shaft bearing.
4 Disconnect the clutch release cable from the operating shaft lever and pull it from its guide plate.
5 From the access hole under the rear seat, disconnect the shift rod in back of the coupling.
6 Remove the nuts from the mounting studs at the front of the transmission.
7 Remove the lower shock absorber mounting bolts and mark the position of the rear torsion bar radius arm in relation to the rear axle bearing housing by using a chisel.
8 Disconnect the wires from the starter motor.
9 Disconnect the ground strap from the frame and remove the nuts from the auxiliary spring rods (1966 Squareback and 1967 - 68 beetles).
10 Place a suitable jack under the unit, and remove the two bolts at the transmission attachments with a 27mm wrench.
11 Withdraw the transaxle toward the rear of the car. Be sure that the

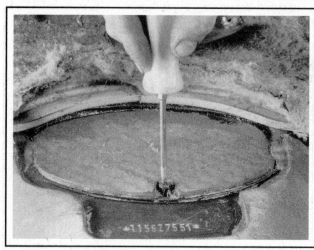

To access the shifter coupling, remove the cover plate retaining screw . . .

. . . and lift the cover plate off of the floor tunnel

Once the cover plate is removed, the coupling (arrow) can be accessed

main driveshaft is not damaged or bent when the unit is placed on the ground.

Installation of the transaxle unit is accomplished by reversing the removal procedure. The two bolts at the transaxle carrier should be greased before being tightened. When a new rear axle is being installed, it is advisable that the retaining nuts of the transaxle cradle be tightened fully only after the front mounting has been securely tightened. This tightening sequence is necessary to prevent distortion and premature wear of the rubber mountings.

When the shift rod coupling is reinstalled, the point of the coupling screw should be correctly engaged in the recess. The screw should be secured with a piece of wire. After replacing the ground strap, install the rear axle tubes in their correct positions. The mounting bolts on the sprig plate should be tightened to a torque of about 80 ft. lbs. Tighten the lower mounting bolts of the shock absorbers securely. Install the engine and adjust the clutch pedal free-play to 2/5 - 4/5 in. and tighten the rear axle shaft nuts to 217 ft. lbs. If the cotter pin cannot be lined up, turn further until it can be inserted. Bleed the brakes and adjust the hand brakes.

➡**When a new axle, frame, spring plate or front transmission mounting is installed, the rear wheels must be re-aligned.**

A special optical alignment gauge is necessary for this purpose. An accurate setting it not otherwise possible.

Independent Rear Suspension (IRS) Models

1   Disconnect the negative battery cable.
2   Remove the engine, as described in Section 3.
3   Remove the special 12-point socket head screws which secure the driveshafts to the transaxle. Remove the bolts from the transaxle end first, then remove the shafts.

➡**It is not necessary to remove the driveshafts entirely from the car if the car does not have to be moved while the transaxle is out.**

4   Disconnect the clutch cable from the clutch lever and remove the clutch cable and its guide tube from the transaxle. Loosen the square head bolt at the shift linkage coupling located near the rear of the transaxle. Slide the coupling off the inner shift lever. There is an access plate under the rear seat to reach the coupling on Type 1 and 3 models. It is necessary to work under the car to reach the coupling on Type 2 models.
5   Label and disconnect the starter wiring.
6   Label and disconnect the back-up light switch wiring.
7   Remove the front transaxle mounting bolts.
8   Support the transaxle with a floor jack and remove the transaxle carrier bolts.
9   Carefully lower the jack and remove the transaxle from the car.

Cut the safety wire . . .

. . . then loosen the retaining screw so that . . .

. . . the shift tube can be moved forward to separate the coupling from the transaxle shaft

To install:

10 Jack the transaxle into position and loosely install the bolts.

11 Tighten the transaxle carrier bolts first, then tighten the front mounting nuts.

12 Install the driveshaft bolts with new lockwashers. The lockwashers should be positioned on the bolt with the convex side toward the screw head.

13 Reconnect the wiring, the clutch cable, and the shift linkage.

➡It may be necessary to align the transaxle so that the driveshaft joints do not rub the frame.

14 Install the engine.

TRANSAXLE OVERHAUL (SPLIT-CASE TYPE)

Disassembly

1 Drain the transaxle lubricant (see Chapter 1).

2 Remove the transaxle from the vehicle.

3 Remove the front mount, the transaxle carrier and the rear mounts.

4 Remove the outer bearings and axle tubes (see Chapter 8).

➡Note: You can't remove the axleshafts until after the gear cases have been split.

5 Remove the clutch release bearing (see Chapter 8).

6 Remove the nuts holding the gear selector rod housing at the front of the case and remove the housing.

7 Unlock the two tab washers from the large nuts on the ends of the input and pinion shafts. To loosen these two nuts (do it now while it's easy), engage two gears simultaneously by pulling out the outer two selector fork rails. This locks the two shafts. Loosen the nuts.

8 Remove all through bolts and nuts that clamp the two halves of the case together. Don't forget the bolts inside the bellhousing or the long thin through bolt that goes right through the center of the case.

9 Once all the bolts are removed, the only thing preventing the two halves from falling apart is the tight fit of the two side bearings. A few gentle taps with a mallet or block of wood will separate the two halves.

☀☀ CAUTION:

Do not, under any circumstances, use force or leverage between the two mating faces or serious damage could result: The fit around the bearings could become too loose, resulting in oil leaks.

10 Pull one case half over the axleshaft and the two gearbox shafts can simply be lifted out of the other half.

11 Detach the axleshafts and differential assembly from the other case half.

12 Usually, the differential side bearings are left in place in each case half, but the spacer rings and shims fitted on the differential housing can be removed. Just make sure you don't switch them! As you remove each case half, clearly label the set of shims for each side and put them away (tape them into position on the differential, if you wish). The transaxle is now disassembled into the main sub-assemblies.

13 To disassemble the pinion shaft, remove the nut and washer. Remove the ball bearing - with the retaining ring fitted in its outer groove - by holding the bearing so that the shaft hangs down and then striking the end of the shaft with a soft faced hammer. If you have no one to support the shaft, hold it just above the bench surface over a small pile of rags.

14 Remove the shims, the thrust washer, the bushing, the fourth

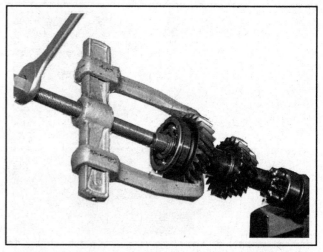

Remove fourth and third gears from the input shaft with a small puller - don't lose the keyways or the spacer sleeve between the gears

gear synchro ring and the third/fourth synchro hub. If the third/fourth synchro assembly is difficult to break loose from the splines, tap it carefully with a small soft mallet but don't let it fall apart when it slides free.

15 Remove the third gear synchro ring, third gear, the bushing, second gear and the second/first synchro assembly. Don't lose the three springs which will pop out of the center sleeve when the shaft comes out.

16 Finally remove any shims - note their number and position - and the outer race of the pinion roller bearing. Don't try to remove the inner race without expert assistance. It's a very tight press fit on the shaft and is difficult to remove without the proper tool and a press. You can damage the pinion if you're not extremely careful.

17 If third or fourth gear on the input shaft is badly worn or damaged, or if one of the other two gears - which are part of the shaft - is damaged, you'll have to disassemble the input shaft.

18 To disassemble the input shaft, remove the nut and the washer. Remove the ball bearing the same way you removed the bearing from the pinion shaft (see Step 13). Using a puller, remove fourth gear, the spacer sleeve and third gear. Don't lose the keyways for third and fourth gears. Remove the seal and roller bearing from the other end with a puller too.

19 The reverse gear pinion runs on a shaft which is locked in place in the case by a pin, the protruding end of which also locates the rear ball bearing of the input shaft. Remove the pin and the shaft can be pulled out. Note that the gear spins on a bushing - if it's worn, replace it. Any radial play between the gear and shaft can may allow the gear to rock, which can cause it to jump out of engagement in reverse, under a load.

20 To remove the selector forks, remove the two threaded plugs from the case and loosen the clamping screws. Don't remove the rails or selector forks unless they need to be replaced (see Inspection). The selector forks need not be removed unless inspection indicates that they are too slack a fit in the sleeve grooves.

Inspection

➡Note: The following inspection procedure applies to both split-case and single-piece case transaxles, unless noted otherwise.

21 The amount of wear determines the economics of repair vs. replacement. If, after inspecting the components, you calculate that a

Inspect the ring and pinion gear - if either of them looks like this badly damaged pinion gear, replace both as a matched set

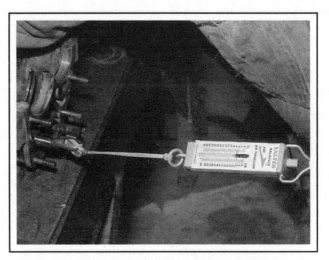

To check the pressure of the spring-loaded ball in the groove for each selector rail, attach a spring balance to the end of each selector fork - if the amount of pull required is significantly outside the specified pull, replace the spring(s)

rebuild will cost almost as much as a rebuilt transaxle, you may wish to consider whether to proceed with an overhaul or simply purchase a rebuilt unit.

22 It's not usually necessary to immerse the gearbox components in solvent for inspection purposes. Just wipe them off with a clean cloth. However, you should wash the case with solvent. Just be sure to remove the roller bearings.

23 Examine the case for signs of cracks or damage, particularly near the bearing housings and on the mating surfaces where the gear carrier and side bearing plates join.

24 Inspect the ring and pinion. If they're badly worn - chipped teeth, excessive backlash, etc. - replace them as a sub-assembly. The special tools needed to reassemble and readjust a rebuilt differential and ring and pinion assembly are difficult to obtain and expensive.

25 Some gears run on separate bushings on the shaft, so make sure there's no play between the gear, bushing and shaft. If there is, a new bushing will usually solve the problem. Don't forget to check the reverse gear bushing.

26 Inspect all gear teeth for signs of pitted mating surfaces, chips or scoring. If one gear is damaged, then its counterpart on the other shaft will probably be damaged too.

27 Two types of bearings - ball and needle roller - are used. Generally, needle rollers wear very little because they're not subject to axial thrust. But note carefully how they spin. If any bearing exhibits the slightest roughness, drag or play, replace it. Inspect the two tapered roller bearings for the differential too. If they need to be replaced, have a VW transaxle specialist do it. Also have him inspect and, if necessary, reset the ring and pinion as well.

28 Using a hydraulic press, remove all synchro rings for examination. The grooved taper face of the ring provides the braking action on the mating face of the gear wheel cone. If the ridges are worn, the braking or synchro action will be less effective. The only way to effectively determine the condition of the rings is by comparing them with new parts. New rings are relatively inexpensive, so it's a good idea to simply replace all of them. When fitting a synchro ring over its cone on the gear wheel, the gap between the synchro ring and the gear teeth should be between the normal and minimum dimensions listed in this Chapter's Specifications. If the gap is near the lower limit, get new rings.

29 The synchro hubs must be assembled for inspection. There must be no axial or radial play at the splines between the inner hub and outer sleeve. When replacing the synchro rings, it's a good idea to replace the sliding keys and their locating springs. The keys - which fit into the cut-outs in the synchro rings - are subject to wear, and the springs eventually weaken.

30 The selector forks are some of the most critical components in the transaxle. The two forks run in grooves in the outer sleeves of the synchro hubs. If the clearance of the forks in the grooves is excessive, the gears they control may jump out. The clearance of the fork in the groove should not exceed the maximum clearance listed in this Chapter's Specifications. Excessive clearance can be caused by wear on the fork, or the groove or both. Take the forks to the dealer parts department or a transaxle specialist and ask them to compare the thickness of the used forks with new ones. If the difference in thickness isn't enough to compensate for the excess gap between the fork and the hub groove, replace the hub assembly as well. It's an expensive part, but the gap is critical, so there's no alternative.

31 The selector rails on which the forks are mounted need not be removed from the case. Some force is needed to overcome the pressure of the spring-loaded ball in the groove. To check it, measure it with a spring balance hooked on to the end of each selector fork. If the required pull is significantly outside the range listed in this Chapter's Specifications, check the detent springs and balls. Push the selector rods out of the case to release the ball and spring plugs from their respective bores (on earlier, split-type case transaxles, the detent balls and springs are released inside the case when the rails are pulled out - keep a hand over the hole to prevent them flying out).

➡ Note: You'll need to obtain new plugs for reassembly.

32 Check the spring free length and compare your measure-

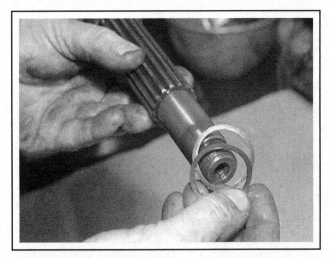

Install the same number of shims, in the same order, that you removed from the pinion shaft

Install the bearing on the pinion shaft

ments to the dimension listed in this Chapter's Specifications. If the springs are too short, replace them. Inspect the balls for pitting and grooves and make sure the selector rods themselves are a tight fit in their bores. Look at the detent grooves in the rails - they shouldn't be worn. While the rails are removed, don't lose the interlock plungers which fit between the selector rod grooves.

Reassembly

33 Prepare a clean space of adequate size on your work bench. Don't start until you've collected all the necessary parts and gaskets and have made sure that all of them fit.

➡**Note: It's a good idea to keep the old gaskets you remove until the job is done - gasket sets often contain items for a variety of models, so you need to pick the right gaskets.**

34 Reassembly of the split-case type transaxle is generally simpler than reassembly of the later single-piece unit, as long as the ring and pinion don't have to be reset. Side bearing adjustment involves reassembly of the complete transaxle, then - if the side bearing shims must be changed - disassembly again.

35 The mating surfaces of both case halves must be perfectly clean and unmarked by dents or burrs. Use solvent to remove any traces of old sealing compound.

36 Obtain good quality sealing compound suitable for prepping the mating surfaces.

37 Make sure that new gaskets are available. This is particularly important when refitting the gear change end cover because the thickness of the gaskets determines the pressure on the shaft bearings which eliminates axial movement.

38 Install the shims and bearing on the pinion shaft.

➡**Note: There shouldn't be any problems with shim settings - as long as you carefully noted their number and position during removal.**

39 If you're replacing the ring and pinion, assembly of the pinion shaft is a little more involved. You'll need to have access to an assortment of shims and be able to get the inner race of the pinion bearing heated and pressed off and onto the shaft. Be advised, however, that adjusting the ring gear, and side bearing pre-load, is more complex and requires a special gauge. It's best to leave this job to a specialist with the skills and tools.

40 To install the second gear synchronizer/first gear hub assembly, fit the single, square section key retaining ring into the groove in the center section of the hub, slide the hub onto the shaft with the retaining ring nearest the pinion gear, place the three key springs into the holes and hook the flat, stepped end of each sliding key under the retain-

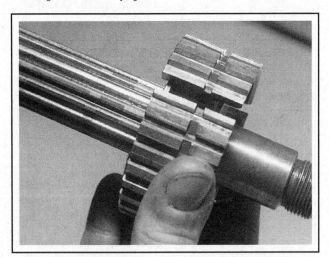

To install the second gear synchronizer/first gear hub on the pinion shaft, fit the single, square section key retaining ring into the groove in the center section of the hub, slide the hub onto the shaft with the retaining ring nearest the pinion gear . . .

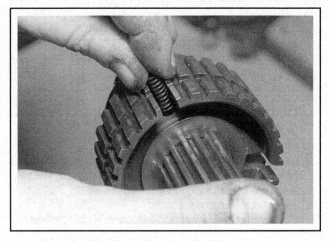

. . . place the three key springs into the holes . . .

. . . hook the flat, stepped end of each sliding key under the retaining ring so the raised dimple faces outward . . .

. . . look for marks inside the outer sleeve - make sure the depressions in three of the splines line up with the centers of the three sliding keys . . .

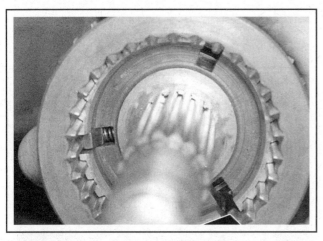

. . . slide the outer sleeve over the hub so the keys are held in place . . .

. . . install the second gear synchro ring . . .

ing ring so that the raised dimple faces outwards. Now slide the outer sleeve over the hub so that the keys are trapped and held in position. If marks exist or have been made on the inner and outer hubs, lining up the splines is no problem. If there aren't any marks, look inside the outer sleeve and make sure that the three depressions in three of the

splines line up with the centers of the three sliding keys. Now install the second gear synchro ring and second gear.

41 Install the splined, shouldered bushing.

42 Install third gear and the third gear synchro ring on the pinion shaft.

. . . and install second gear

Install the splined, shouldered bushing on the pinion shaft

Install third gear . . .

. . . and the third gear synchro ring on the pinion shaft

Install the third/fourth synchro assembly on the pinion shaft

43 Install the third/fourth synchronizer assembly. To verify that your reassembly is correct, when the third/fourth synchronizer hub has been fitted to the shaft the inner sleeve should line up with the end face of the splined part of the shaft. This alignment should not vary by more than 0.002 inch (0.05 mm). If it does, the assembly is wrong or the shim thickness next to the roller bearing is incorrect.

44 Install the fourth gear bushing.

45 Install the fourth gear synchro ring.
46 Install fourth gear.
47 Install the thrust washer. Note that the grooves in the washer face the gear.
48 Install the shims.

Install the fourth gear bushing on the pinion shaft

Install the fourth gear synchro ring on the pinion shaft

Install fourth gear on the pinion shaft

Install the thrust washer on the pinion shaft - note that the grooves in the thrust washer face the gear

Install the shims on the pinion shaft

Install the ball bearing on the end of the pinion shaft . . .

. . . and drive it on until it's fully seated against the shims

Install the bushing into reverse gear

Insert the reverse gear shaft through the case, plain end first, and align the cut-out with the hole in the bearing housing

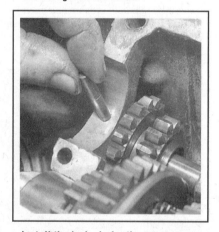

Install the lock pin for the reverse gear shaft

49 Install the ball bearing. Drive it on until it's fully seated against the shims. The lockwasher and shaft nut should be installed but not tightened fully at this stage.

50 Lining up the keyways to tight fitting gears can be tricky. Heat the gears to about 194 degrees F (90 degrees C) in an oil bath, then slide them onto the shaft and position them over the Woodruff keys. Make sure the keys are a snug fit and fully engaged in their slots or they might shift - and jam - before the gear is positioned. Install third (the smaller) gear first - it should butt right up to the second gear on the shaft. Then install the spacer and, finally, fourth gear which should butt up tight to the spacer.

51 You can tap the two bearings onto the shaft with a pipe of sufficient diameter or use the hot oil bath to heat them up and slide them into place. Don't heat the bearings any other way or you could damage them.

52 The bearing with the retaining circlip goes on the threaded end of the shaft with the circlip nearest to the threaded end. Inspect the transaxle case where the bearing fits. The circlip fits into a recess or groove in the front face. The bearing should not protrude more than a fraction of a millimeter in front of the case.

53 Replace, but do not fully tighten, the lockwasher and nut.

54 Fit the reverse gear to the case before installing the input shaft. Fit the sleeve into the gear, then hold the gear in position in the case with the smaller of the two rows of gear teeth towards the front.

55 Insert the reverse gear shaft through the case, plain end first, and align the cut-out with the hole in the bearing housing.

56 Install the lock pin.

57 Have an assistant handy for the next Steps. Place the assembled pinion shaft in position in the left half of the case and check the setting

To check the setting of the selector forks, temporarily place the assembled pinion shaft in position in the left case half (note the locating dowel (arrow) for the bearing) . . .

. . . verify that both synchro hub outer sleeves are in the central (neutral) position on their hubs and engage each gear to ensure that the sleeves mesh correctly

Install the input shaft assembly - make sure the hole in the rear bearing engages with the protruding end of the reverse shaft lock pin (arrows) - and, if everything is installed correctly . . .

. . . this is how it should look

Before lighting the case fasteners, apply RTV sealant to the outside of the input shaft seal and install it onto the rear end of the input shaft - make sure the seal lip faces into the case

of the selector forks. If new forks or rails have been fitted, put the rails in the neutral position and - with the forks engaged correctly with their respective hub grooves - verify that both synchro hub outer sleeves are in the neutral (central) position on their hubs. Then engage each gear to

ensure that the sleeves mesh correctly. At this stage, no further adjustment is possible. If there's trouble later, you can make further adjustments after the transaxle is installed. The reverse gear selector fork, however, can't be adjusted later, so install the input shaft temporarily and verify that the gears line up correctly when reverse gear is engaged. If necessary, move the selector fork along the rail until the small gear of the sliding pinion meshes fully with the gear teeth of the first/second

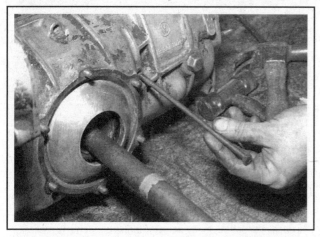

When bolting the case halves together, don't forget the long center bolt

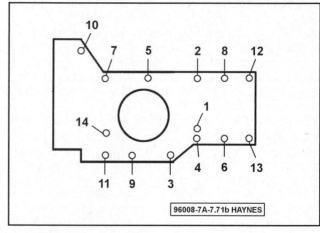

Bolt tightening sequence for split-case type housing

hub on the pinion shaft. The larger gear of the sliding pinion should be in mesh with the gear teeth on the input shaft at the same time. Then select neutral and first gear, in turn, to ensure that the sliding reverse gear pinion is well clear of engagement with anything else.

58 Determine the direction of rotation of the differential ring gear so that the axleshaft assembly turns in the right direction. The left case half carries the differential ring gear and the selector mechanism. So the axle/differential assembly must go in first.

59 Make sure the correct shims are in position on the ring gear side of the differential case.

60 Position the left half of the case in a suitable position. Bear in mind that the two axleshafts must be positioned - and supported - so that their weight doesn't upset the balance of the case.

61 Ensure that all parts are scrupulously clean and that the shims and spacers are correct for each side of the differential casing. Remember that the shims serve two functions - they pre-load the side bearings and they position the differential ring gear correctly in relation to the pinion.

62 You might argue that the shim combinations should be recalculated if new bearings are fitted. In practice, however, it's unnecessary as long as you're installing the same differential ring gear and pinion and have never altered the shim combinations.

63 When fitting new bearings, support the side cover evenly and securely and arrange the bearings so that the closed side of the ball race faces the outside of the case. The bore in the side cover must be scrupulously clean and free of any snags or burrs.

64 Tap the new bearing into place with a heavy mallet and a large socket or a piece of pipe with an outside diameter slightly smaller than the diameter of the outer race of the bearing. Make sure it doesn't cock in the bore when you start to drive it in. If it does, work it out and start again.

65 Make sure both mating surfaces are perfectly clean. Apply a thin even film of RTV sealant to the mating face of the case. Using a new O-ring, install the right side bearing and cover. Tighten the nuts evenly to the torque listed in this Chapter's Specifications.

66 Insert the axleshaft through the bearing and guide the differential into the case, ring gear side first (with the teeth visible). If necessary, tap the case so the bearing fully seats on the shoulder of the differential.

67 Install the pinion shaft assembly. The selector forks should be in the neutral position and they must engage in the grooves of the hub sleeves. At the same time the rear bearing outer race should be turned so that the peg in the case engages the hole.

68 Install the input shaft. Make sure the hole in the rear bearing engages with the protruding end of the reverse shaft lock pin.

69 Verify that the differential side bearing shims are in position on the differential. Install the right case over the shaft and against the differential so that the bearing locates on the shoulder. Simultaneously supporting the weight of the axles, holding the cases and aligning the bearings with the dowel pegs can be challenging. An assistant is helpful at this point. Or arrange the left shaft into a near vertical position by hanging it over the edge of the bench. Place two wooden boxes on end, side by side, on the floor; with the shaft hanging down between them. Tap the case half into position onto the shoulder of the differential. If you have difficulty getting the two halves to butt together, one of the bearing dowel pegs isn't properly located. Don't force anything. Take it off, have a look and try again.

70 Before reattaching the case halves, apply RTV sealant to the outside of the input shaft oil seal and install it onto the rear end of the input shaft. Make sure the seal lip faces into the case.

71 Install all new nuts, bolts and washers. Note that one or two are longer than the others. Don't forget the long center bolt. Tighten the case bolts evenly and gradually in the pattern shown to the initial torque listed in this Chapter's Specifications. Make sure both shafts revolve freely and each of the gears engage. If they don't, split the cases and have a look. If they do, tighten the case bolts in the sequence shown to the final torque listed in this Chapter's Specifications.

72 To tighten the input and pinion shaft nuts, engage two gears by pulling out the two outer selector rods. Tighten the larger, pinion shaft nut to the torque listed in this Chapter's Specifications. Bend up the block tabs against a flat on the nuts.

73 Fitting the gear change rod housing on the end of the case is critical because gasket thickness determines the pressure applied to the outer races of both ball bearings to prevent any movement when end thrust is applied. Use new gaskets and tighten the housing bolts securely.

74 When placing the gear shift cover in position, the selector rails should be in neutral and the change rod should fit into the cut-out slots in the ends of the rails. Replace the nuts and tighten them evenly to the torque listed in this Chapter's Specifications.

75 Install the mounting bracket and flexible mounting blocks, the clutch release thrust ring and the unit is ready for replacement in the car.

Selector forks - adjustment

1 You can make adjustments to the forward speed selector forks (not reverse) with the transaxle installed in the vehicle. Such adjustments, which prevent a gear from jumping out of mesh under power, are usually necessary just after the transaxle has been overhauled. Under any other circumstances, adjustment simply compensates for wear. The down side, however, is that adjusting a fork to prevent one gear from jumping out of mesh may very well cause another gear to jump instead. For example, if you adjust a fork to cure a third gear jump, you might well find that fourth gear then jumps out instead! The same applies to first and second, so before you start adjusting selector forks, decide which gear is going to bother you least if it jumps out!

2 On the lower forward end of the left side of the transaxle case, two large plugs cover holes through which you can access the clamp screws of the selector forks. The front one is for the third and fourth selector fork and the other for first/second.

3 To make an adjustment, select Neutral and remove the plug for the fork you wish to adjust.

4 If third gear jumps out, remove the front plug, loosen the fork set screw, slide the front selector fork backwards a fraction on its rail, retighten the set screw, install the plug and road test. If fourth gear

If third gear jumps out, remove the front plug from the transaxle . . .

. . . loosen the selector fork set screw, slide the fork to the rear on its rail, tighten the set screw, install the plug and road test the vehicle to check your work - you may have to repeat this process several times until the gear mesh feels right

jumps out, move the front selector fork forwards.

5 If first gear is jumping out, leave it alone - the fault is unlikely to be the selector fork setting. If second gear jumps out, slide the rear selector fork forward.

6 You may have to repeat this process several times for each fork until the mesh feels just right.

7 Sometimes, when the transaxle is badly worn, any adjustment results in all gears jumping out. You'll have to decide which ones cause the least inconvenience and take up the slack in the appropriate direction. Needless to say, jumping out of gear - particularly with the power on - can be dangerous, so don't be too casual about correcting this problem. If you get into the habit of holding a gear in mesh, you can expect accelerated wear of everything connected with the synchromesh mechanism.

8 There may also be wear in the shift lever mechanism. A certain amount of adjustment is possible at the shift lever. Loosen the two retaining bolts. The mounting bolt holes are elongated, so the shift lever assembly can be moved forward or backward a little. If you move the assembly forward, second and fourth gears will engage more positively; if you move it to the rear, first and third will be more positive. But remember: This adjustment is normally used only to seek the exact central position. Too much adjustment at the shift lever could have exactly the same results as too much adjustment at the selector forks.

TRANSAXLE OVERHAUL (SINGLE-PIECE CASE)

Disassembly

➡**Note: Gasket sets often contain items covering a variety of models. Save the old gaskets you remove during disassembly. You can use them to determine which gaskets in the new set are for your transaxle.**

1 Remove the transaxle from the vehicle.

2 Drain the oil, remove the front mount, transaxle carrier and rear mounts and clean the transaxle exterior thoroughly.

3 On swing axle models, remove the axleshafts and axle tubes (see Chapter 8).

4 Remove the nuts holding the gear selector lever housing and remove the housing together with the lever.

Remove the circlip which locks the reverse gear sleeve to the input shaft

5 Bend back the tabs of the lockwashers and remove the large nuts on the ends of the input and pinion shafts. To prevent the shafts from rotating, pull or push the two outer selector fork rails which protrude from the end of the case. This will lock the two shafts by engaging two gears at once.

➡**Note: On later models, circlips are used instead of these nuts. Remove the circlip on the input shaft end before attempting to withdraw the two shafts from the bearings in the gear carrier.**

✳✳ CAUTION:

Cover the end of the shaft with a shop rag when releasing this circlip. It's under tension from a dished thrust washer underneath, so it may fly off when released from its groove.

6 Remove the nuts from the studs which secure the gear carrier (end case) to the main case. Also remove the ground strap.

7 Turn the whole unit on its side so that the left side bearing cover is facing up (remember, the narrow end of the case is the front).

8 On driveaxle models, remove the sealing plugs from the centers of the drive flanges by punching the blade of a screwdriver through them and levering them out. Then remove the circlips from the grooves in the ends of the splined shafts and lever off the flanges. There's a spacer ring behind the flange. If you can dig it out now, remove it. If not, you can remove it after you pull off the side cover.

9 Remove the left side bearing cover retaining nuts and remove the cover. Give it a few taps with a soft face mallet if necessary - don't use force. When the cover comes off, the outer race of the tapered roller side bearing usually comes off with it. If the bearing comes off with the side cover, don't lose the shim(s) between the bearing inner race and the differential. These shims, which control the side bearing pre-load and ring and pinion backlash, are critical. Label them, tape them to the bearing to prevent mix-ups with the shims for the other side cover and set them aside. If the bearing stays on, leave it there for now. Note the paper gasket between the cover and case.

10 Turn the transaxle on its side with the opening for the left side cover facing up and carefully lift out the differential assembly.

11 If you can't lift it out, turn the transaxle over again, and, using a drift punch placed against the inner race of the right bearing, gently tap it out. Support the differential to prevent it from dropping under its own weight. If it's easier for you to tap out the differential with the bearing

To remove the gearbox assembly from the case, strike the
end of the pinion with a heavy soft-faced mallet . . .

. . . or place a small scissors-type jack inside the differential
housing and push the gearbox assembly loose

still in the side cover, by all means do it that way. Collect the shims
for the other side bearing, label them, tape them together and set them
aside.

12 Turn the transaxle over with the right side bearing cover facing
up. On driveaxle models, remove the drive flange (see Step 8). Remove
the right side bearing cover nuts and remove the cover. Again, note the
paper gasket.

13 Remove the circlip which locks the reverse gear sleeve to the
input shaft. Slide it back along the shaft and slide the sleeve along
behind it.

14 Unscrew the rear end of the input shaft from the front half. Take
off the gear/sleeve and remove the circlip from the shaft. Withdraw the
shaft from the rear through the oil seal. Remove the input shaft seal and
discard it.

➡Note: This seal can be replaced with the transaxle installed.

15 On earlier units, four bolts secure the pinion shaft bearing
retainer plate. Carefully pry up the lock tabs on each bolt. Don't let the
tool slip and strike the pinion gear. Carefully remove the bolts. Later
units use a locking castellated ring threaded onto the pinion bearing
instead of a four-bolt flange. On these models, simply unscrew the lock
ring. Again, make sure you don't damage the pinion teeth.

16 To remove the gearbox assembly from the case, use a heavy
copper faced mallet and strike the end of the pinion. Or insert a jack
small enough to fit between the pinion and the opposite side of the
case. Cushion the head of the jack touching the pinion and press it out.
Be sure to support the gear carrier when the gear shafts come free. As
soon as they're clear, collect the shims(s) from the pinion flange and
attach them to the flange or put them in a plastic bag to prevent loss.

17 To remove first gear and its shaft, remove the circlip. The gear is
a slide fit on a key. Pull it off. Pry it a little with a screwdriver if necessary. Remove the key from the shaft and remove the shaft from the
front.

18 To remove the needle roller bearings from the reverse shaft,
unscrew the locating screw (secures the spacer sleeve between the two
bearings) from the case. Use a drift of suitable diameter to drive the two
needle rollers and spacer out towards the rear of the case.

19 The other needle bearing outer race is also secured by a screw
in the case. Remove it too. Then tap out the needle roller bearing race.
(This is the bearing that supports the rear end of the forward half of the
input shaft.)

20 The large side bearings located in either the covers or on the
differential can remain in place unless inspection indicates that they're
worn. Knock them off the differential or out of the covers. If you're
removing them from the covers, make sure the covers are firmly
and evenly supported. Don't attempt to do it the other way round
- support the bearings and knock the covers out - or you may damage
the cover.

21 Separate the two shafts with their clusters of gears from the gear
carrier.

22 Remove the small sliding gear and the reverse fork from the pivot
on the reverse lever.

23 Loosen the clamping bolts which hold the two other selector
forks to their respective rails. Slide back the rail for the first/second
gear fork far enough to remove the fork. The other fork is trickier to
remove because the gear carrier is in the way. Drive the rail back far
enough to free it from the fork.

✳✳ CAUTION:

**DO NOT drive the rails out of the gear carrier. If you do, the
detent balls and springs will pop out and you will be looking at
a lot of extra work.**

To remove a differential side bearing from the differential,
tap it off with a drift and hammer

24 Remove the two gear shafts from the carrier. It's a good idea to tape both shafts together. Then, when you release the ends of the shafts, they won't fall apart. You'll need an assistant for this Step. Hold the carrier - with the shafts hanging down - while another person strikes the end of the input shaft with a soft faced mallet and supports the weight of the gear shafts as they are driven out. Do NOT let them drop down.

25 Remove the two bearings in the carrier. The needle roller bearing is located by a screw similar to that used on the needle roller bearings you just removed. Drive out the input shaft front bearing from inside the carrier. The outer race of this bearing is flanged. The bearing will only come out one way.

26 To dismantle the input shaft, remove the spacer ring, then fourth gear and the needle bearing cage on which it runs. Remove the synchro rings. Using a hydraulic press and V-blocks, press off the inner race from the shaft. Position the 'V' blocks so they provide support behind the third gear wheel to prevent damage to the shaft or gears and prevent the synchro hub assembly from coming apart. Make sure all parts are supported and held while under pressure.

27 Remove third gear and its needle roller bearing. It's not necessary to remove the third gear bearing inner race or the key which locates the synchro hub. Keep the synchro rings with their respective gears for future reference - fix them with adhesive tape to prevent mix-ups.

28 Disassemble the pinion shaft only far enough to remove the gears, synchro hub and synchro rings. The double-taper pinion roller bearing held by the notched locking nut can be left on the shaft. Its removal requires the use of special tools which most home mechanics probably don't have.

29 Using a hydraulic press, remove fourth gear, the inner race of the needle bearing spacer, the shim, the concave washer, third gear, the needle roller bearing, second gear and the first/second gear synchro hub. Don't use a hammer instead of a press! Repeatedly striking the threaded end of the shaft - even with a soft headed mallet - can distort the threads and ruin the shaft. Remove the synchro rings.

30 On later models with circlips instead of retaining nuts on the ends of the two shafts, remove the circlips. Then press off fourth gear, the inner race, the spring spacer, the second circlip and third gear.

31 Unless the transaxle has been abused or has very high mileage, the synchro hub assemblies shouldn't require service. Handle the synchro hub assemblies with care to prevent them from coming apart. If the center hub and outer sleeve are accidentally separated, they must be properly reassembled. If you wish to disassemble the hubs, remove the spring retaining clip on each side and slide the sleeve out of the hub. Don't drop or lose the three sliding keys. Put the parts for each hub assembly in a plastic bag and set it aside for inspection.

32 Don't remove the selector fork rails from the carrier unless inspection indicates that there's something wrong with the detent balls and springs.

Inspection

33 As we mentioned in Section 1, the degree of component wear determines whether you should repair or replace the transaxle. If the differential ring gear and pinion are badly worn - causing significant backlash and noise - they can be repaired for about half the cost of a new unit. Such work is beyond the scope of the average owner so this manual doesn't cover differential rebuilds. On the other hand, using no special tools aside from a hydraulic press, we fitted the transaxle in the accompanying illustrations with new ball bearings, synchro rings, synchro hub keys and retaining clips.

34 Normally, it shouldn't be necessary to immerse all the components in solvent. Wipe components with a clean cloth for examination. In this way the likelihood of dry spots during the first moments of use

Using a hydraulic press and V-blocks, press the inner race from the input shaft - support third gear with the V-blocks to prevent damage to the shaft or gears, and to prevent the synchro hub from coming apart

after reassembly are minimized. The case itself should be thoroughly washed out with solvent. Do not leave the needle roller bearings in position when doing this.

35 Thoroughly inspect all parts of the case for signs of cracks or damage, particularly near the bearing housings and on the mating surfaces where the gear carrier and side bearing plates join.

36 Using a small two or three-jaw puller, remove all synchro rings - if you haven't already done so - for inspection. The grooved taper face of each ring provides the braking action on the mating face of the gear wheel cone. If the ridges are worn, the braking or synchro action will be less effective. The only way to accurately assess the condition of this face is to compare it with a new part. As a rule of thumb, when a synchro ring is fitted over its cone on the gear wheel, there should be a minimum gap of 0.024 inch (0.6 mm) between the synchro ring and the gear teeth. The normal gap is 0.043 inch (1.1 mm), so it's obvious that, if the gap is near the lowest limit, new rings should be fitted. When buying new synchro rings, make sure the parts store identifies and marks each one to go with its respective gear. Modifications have taken place over the years, so although the new ones will still fit and may even work, they aren't necessarily identical to the ones you took off. If you mix them up, you could have problems. They're also not all the same in a set - for example, some have wider cut-outs. So carefully mark the new ones.

➡**Note: These parts are cheap, so it makes good sense to simply replace them while the transaxle is disassembled.**

37 Two types of bearings are uses - ball and needle roller. As a rule, needle roller bearings wear very little because they're not subjected to end thrust of any sort. The two large side bearings are ball bearings which carry the forward end of the input shaft. Inspect all bearings for noise and roughness. If they sound even slightly rough or if they drag when they turn, replace them. Check the double-taper roller bearing for roughness and excessive endplay. If it allows any endplay, carefully inspect the condition of the pinion gear and differential ring gear. If they need to be replaced, the setting of the whole box is altered and clearances and shims have to be re-calculated and changed. This is a job for a specialist.

38 Inspect the teeth of all gears for signs of pitted mating surfaces, chips and scoring. If one gear is damaged, its counterpart on the other shaft will usually be just as badly worn.

Measure the clearance between the selector fork and the groove of the synchro hub sleeve - if this clearance is excessive, the gears can jump out of mesh

Install three new sliding keys, or blocker bars . . .

. . . and new retainer spring clips when rebuilding the synchro hubs

39 Assemble the synchro hubs (see Step 43). With the keys removed, the inner and outer sections of the hub should slide easily, but there must be no axial play or backlash between the splines of the inner and outer parts. The actual amount of acceptable wear is difficult to describe. No play at all is ideal, but hardly likely. Ask someone with experience how much slop is acceptable.

40 Some of the most critical parts of the transaxle are the selector forks. The two forks run in grooves in the outer sleeves of the synchro hubs. If the clearance of the forks in the grooves is excessive, the gears will probably jump out. Measure the clearance between the fork and the groove. It shouldn't exceed 0.3 mm (0.012 inch). Excessive clearance could be caused by wear on the fork, or the groove, or both. So take the forks to the parts department and ask them if you can compare the thickness of new parts with your old ones. If the difference in thickness isn't enough to compensate for the excessive clearance between the fork and the hub groove, then replace the hub assembly as well. This is an expensive item, but this gap is critical, so there's no alternative.

41 The selector rails on which the forks are mounted need not be removed from the case. A certain force is required for them to overcome the pressure of the spring loaded ball in the groove. Measure this force with a spring balance hooked on the end of each selector fork. If the required pull is significantly outside the range of 33 to 44 lbs (15 to 20 kgs), it's advisable to check the detent springs and balls. Push the selector rod out of the case to release the ball and spring. To remove the springs, pry out the plastic plugs. Be sure to get some new plugs for reassembly.

42 Check the spring free length. It should be one inch. If it's less, replace the spring(s). The balls should be free from pitting and grooves and the selector rods themselves shouldn't be a sloppy fit in the bores. The detent grooves in the rails shouldn't be worn. If they are, replace the rail(s). If you have to remove the rails, don't lose the interlock plungers which fit between the selector rod grooves.

Reassembly

43 If you're rebuilding the synchro hubs, service them as a complete assembly. It isn't a good idea to fit an inner hub to an old outer sleeve, or vice versa. Keep in mind the following points when reassembling a synchro hub:

a) When the synchro rings are replaced, it's a good idea to replace the three sliding keys and their locating spring rings as well. The keys fit into the cut-outs in the synchro rings and are subject to wear, and the springs weaken over time.

b) Always use new blacker bars (sliding keys) and retaining spring clips in the hubs to take full advantage of the new, unworn cut-outs in the rings.

c) The splines of the inner hub and outer sleeve are matched - either by selection on assembly or by wear patterns during use. Those matched on assembly have marks etched on the inner hub and outer sleeve to facilitate alignment. If a hub has no marks, make some of your own with a small dab of paint to ensure reassembly in the same position. If a hub falls apart accidentally, you'll have to live with the fact that it may wear out more quickly.

d) Fit the retaining spring clips so the ends fit behind, but not into, the keys, and so that the clips overlap on each side, i.e. don't have more than two clip ends over one key.

44 Install the needle roller cage for third gear on the input shaft. Then install third gear with its matching synchro ring onto the roller bearings with the cone towards the front end of the shaft.

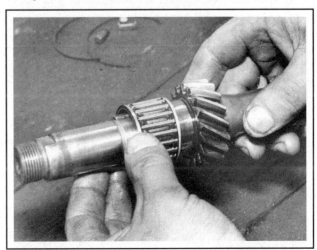

Install the needle roller cage for third gear on the input shaft . . .

. . . then install third gear with its matching synchro ring onto the roller bearings with the cone toward the front of the input shaft

Install the third/fourth gear synchro hub assembly on the input shaft . . .

. . . making sure it's lined up with the keyway . . .

. . . then drive on the hub with a suitable piece of pipe and a heavy hammer

Drive the inner race for the fourth gear needle bearing onto the input shaft

45 Install the third/fourth gear synchro hub assembly. It must line up with the key in the shaft. Once the keyway in the center part of the hub is lined up with the key in the shaft, drive on the hub with a suitable piece of pipe and a heavy hammer. Some later models have a groove in the outer sleeve 1 mm deep. Make sure the hub with this groove faces toward the front of the shaft. If there's no groove, you can install the hub facing either way. Drive the center part of the hub, or it could come

apart. Line up the slots in the synchro ring with the keys in the hub. Have someone hold the synchro ring in position with the keys in place while you drive the hub into place.

46 Drive the inner race for the fourth gear needle bearing onto the shaft the same way you installed the hub in the previous Step. Drive it right down to the hub. Then install the needle roller cage and the synchro ring and fourth gear. The synchro ring also has three cut-outs

Install the needle roller cage . . .

. . . and install the synchro ring and fourth gear

Install the thrust washer on the end of the input shaft with the V-cuts facing the front of the shaft

which engage with the sliding keys in the hub.

47 Install the thrust washer on the end of the shaft with the V cuts (if any) facing the front end of the shaft. Loosely install the locknut and lockwasher, or install the circlip, and lay the input shaft assembly aside.

48 As it was pointed out earlier, we disassembled the pinion shaft only as far as the pinion bearing. If you have replaced this bearing, the gearbox and final drive must be reshipped. This is a skilled job requiring special equipment and a selection of special shims.

49 Install the shim(s) that control first gear endplay. To measure the endplay after the first gear and hub are installed, measure the gap between the thrust washer (already locked in position behind the first gear needle bearing) and the face of the gear. If the gap is outside the limits of 0.004-0.010 inch (0.10-0.25 mm), you'll need different shims to correct it. In effect, the shims determine the position of the inner sleeve of the first/second gear synchro hub in relation to the captive thrust washer. First gear endplay is controlled between the thrust washer and center hub face.

50 Install the bearing retainer over the shaft and up to the pinion bearing with the smooth, machined face towards the pinion gear at the end of the shaft.

Loosely install the lockwasher and locknut and set the assembled input shaft aside

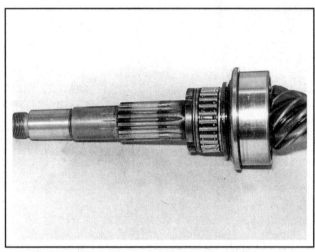

This is as far as you should disassemble the pinion shaft, unless you want to reshim the gearbox and final drive - a job that will take an expert with special tools

Install the thrust shim(s) on the pinion shaft that control first gear endplay

Install the bearing retainer over the shaft and up to the pinion bearing . . .

. . . with its smooth, machined side facing toward the pinion gear

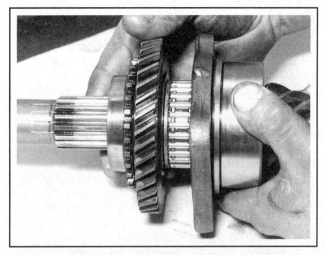

Install first gear (the big gear with the helically cut teeth) over the needle roller bearings with the cone side of the synchro facing away from the pinion gear

Install the first gear synchro ring over first gear, then the first and second gear hub over the splines of the shaft with the selector fork groove of the outer sleeve facing toward the front end of the shaft

51 Install first gear (the largest one with helically cut teeth) in position on the needle roller bearings with the cone face of the synchro pointing away from the pinion gear.

52 Install the first gear synchro ring over first gear and install the first and second gear hub over the splines of the shaft with the selector fork groove of the outer sleeve facing toward the front end of the shaft. Make sure that the three cut-outs in the synchro ring engage with the sliding keys in the hub before pushing the hub into place. Remember - the synchro rings for first and second gears are slightly different - first gear has narrower cut-outs than those in the second gear ring.

53 Check the first gear endplay as described in Step 49.

54 Place the second gear synchro ring in position in the hub so that the slots engage with the sliding keys.

55 Install second gear with the cone facing toward the hub.

56 Install third gear - and the needle roller bearing which fits together with it - inside second gear. Note the large bearing boss integral with third gear.

57 Install the dished washer onto the shaft with the raised inner circumference facing toward the end of the shaft. Install the shim. If the only changes made to the pinion shaft have been new synchro rings, the existing washer and shim can be reused. If, however, the synchro hub or any gears have been replaced, then the shim thickness will likely

Check first gear endplay again the same way you checked it in Step 49

need to be altered. The dished washer is designed to exert a pressure of about 220 pounds on third gear and the hub to eliminate sloppiness along the shaft. The critical dimension is the distance between the face

Place the second gear synchro ring in position in the hub so that the slots engage with the sliding keys

Install second gear with the cone facing toward the hub

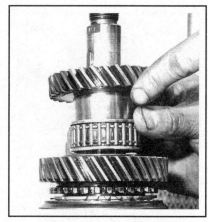

Install third gear - and the needle roller bearing which fits together with it - inside second gear

Install the dished washer on the shaft with its raised inner circumference facing toward the end of the shaft . . .

. . . install the shim . . .

. . . and install the spacer sleeve on top of the washer

of third gear and the shoulder on the shaft against which fourth gear will be installed. This length of shaft has a spacer collar which bears on the concave washer (and shim) when fourth gear is finally installed. Obviously a thicker shim will increase the pressure, and vice versa. If you have to recalculate the shim requirement, you'll need an accurate measuring device. The dished washer has a designed spring travel of 0.17 mm in order to exert its pressure and has a thickness of 1.04 mm. Thus the length of the distance collar plus the total concave washer dimensions (1.21 mm) should equal the shaft distance from the third gear face to the fourth gear shoulder. Select the appropriate shim sizes to make up the difference. Install the spacer sleeve on top of the washer and shim.

58 On later gearboxes, install a selective circlip in place of the concave washer. Measure the endplay of third gear between the gear and the circlip. It should be between 0.004 and 0.010 inch (0.10 and 0.25 mm). Later models also use a spring spacer after the circlip.

59 Heat fourth gear to at least 194-degrees F (90-degrees C) in a bath of hot oil. This will expand it so you can slide it onto the shaft and over the key. Grasp the hot gear firmly with a pair of pliers and install it with the wider, protruding face of its hub toward the spacer collar. Make sure it seats firmly against the shoulder on the shaft.

✳✳ CAUTION:

Don't try to press fourth gear on. Although it was pressed off, it's virtually impossible to press it on and align it with the keyway. Also, once you start it on, it can't be re-aligned.

60 Press, or drive, the inner race for the needle roller bearing onto the shaft.

61 On later models, press or drive on the gear against the spring spacer and install a circlip. Force the circlip down against the concave washer in order to seat it into its groove. If you don't have a press and jig, select a piece of tubing which will fit round the shaft, wrap the whole assembly with shop rags, have an assistant grip it firmly and drive on the circlip against spring pressure. Then press on the inner race for the needle bearing. Put the pinion shaft aside.

62 Two sets of needle roller bearings are installed at the rear end of the main case. The set for the reverse drive shaft consists of two roller cages and a spacer between them. Drive one cage into the case with a socket on an extension, or a suitable drift, so that it's flush with one end of the bore. The metal face of the end of the needle cage should face inward. Then insert the spacer with its slot aligned so it engages with

After heating fourth gear to over 194-degrees F in hot oil, slide it onto the pinion shaft with the wider, raised hub facing toward the spacer collar

Tap the inner race for the needle roller bearing onto the pinion shaft

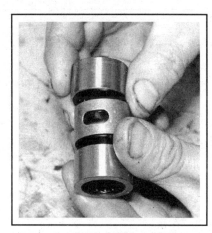

The needle roller bearings for the reverse drive shaft consists of two roller cages and a spacer between them

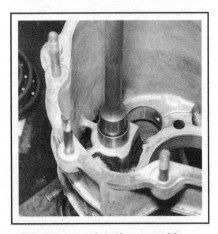

Drive one cage into the case with a socket on an extension so that it's flush with the one end of the bore - the metal face of the end of the needle should face in . . .

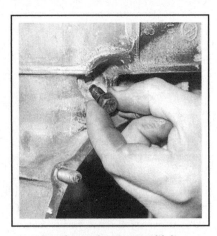

. . . then insert the spacer with its slot aligned so it engages with the lock bolt screwed into the side of the case

The other needle roller bearing supports the rear end of the front half of the input shaft - tap it into the larger bore (arrow) so that the circular recess in the outer race lines up with the lock screw hole in the case

the lock bolt screwed into the side of the case. Then drive the other needle roller bearing into the other end of the bore.

63 The other bearing supports the rear end of the front half of the input shaft. Tap the single needle roller cage into the larger bore so that the circular recess in the outer race lines up with the lock screw hole in the case. Install the lock screw and tighten it securely.

64 To install the reverse gear shaft, slide the spacer ring over the shaft so that it butts against the splined section, insert the shaft through the needle bearings from the front of the case, install the key into the keyway, support the front end of the shaft and push the gear onto the shaft. Make sure it engages the key and the projecting side of the gear hub faces out. Install the circlip. Make sure it's fully seated into the groove.

65 Line up the needle roller bearing for the forward end of the pinion shaft so that the hole for the locking screw corresponds with the recess in the bearing. Tap it into position and install the lock bolt.

66 Drive the special ball bearing (with the flange outer race) into position in the carrier case.

67 Before installing the input and pinion shafts in the gear carrier, place them side-by-side, bind them together with strong tape and place the third/fourth selector fork in position.

Slide the spacer ring over the shaft so that it butts against the splined section of the reverse gear shaft . . .

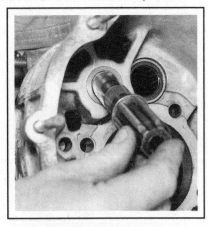

. . . insert the shaft through the needle bearing from the front of the case . . .

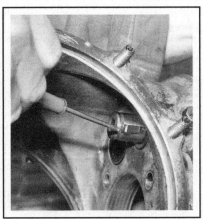

. . . fit the key into the keyway. . .

. . . support the front end of the shaft, push the gear onto the shaft - make sure it engages the key and the projecting side of the gear hub faces out

Install the clip - make sure it seats into the groove

Position the needle roller bearing for the front end of the pinion shaft so that the hole for the locking screw is lined up with the recess in the bearing . . .

. . . tap it into position. . .

. . . and install the lock bolt

Place the special ball bearing with the flanged outer race into position in the carrier with the flange facing up. . .

. . . and tap it into place in the carrier

Before you install the input and pinion shafts in the gear carrier, place them side-by-side, bind them together with strong tape and place the third/fourth selector fork in position

Position the taped shafts in the carrier, move the third/fourth selector fork into position in the synchro hub - and keep it there - as you push the shafts into position . . .

. . . then pull back the fork rail so it can be fitted on the fork as it's carried into place

This is how the third/fourth selector fork looks when it's properly positioned

68 You'll need an assistant for the next few Steps. Position the taped shafts in the carrier. Move the third/fourth selector fork into position in the synchro hub - and keep it there - as you push the shafts into position. Pull back the fork rail so it can be mated with the fork as it's carried in.

69 Once the selector fork for third/fourth gear is in position in its groove with the clamp lug facing out from the case - tap the two shafts into their respective bearings. Alternate taps between the two shafts and drive them into place as a single assembly. The ball bearing may come out of the carrier as you tap in the input shaft, so support it from behind to prevent it from falling out. As you tap the two shafts into the case, line up the selector fork with its appropriate rail. Make sure the fork doesn't jam. Once the fork's on the rail, move the rail back in line with the others.

70 Once both shafts are fully seated in the carrier bearings, install new lock washers and shaft nuts. Make sure the lock washer tangs engage the groove in each shaft. To hold the assembly while tightening the nuts, stand the main case on end and carefully place the gear carrier assembly onto the studs. Tighten both nuts to the initial torque listed in this Chapter's Specifications. Back them off and tighten them to the final torque listed in this Chapter's Specifications. Don't bend up the lock washers on to the nuts yet - if anything is amiss, you may have to remove them.

71 On later models with circlips instead of nuts, install a dished

Once the selector fork for third/fourth gear is in position in its groove - with the clamp lug facing out from the case - tap the two shafts into their respective bearings

Once both shafts are fully seated in the carrier bearings, install new lock washers - make sure the lock washer tangs engage the groove in each shaft . . .

. . . and install new shaft nuts

To hold the assembly while you tighten the nuts, stand the case on end and carefully lower the gear carrier assembly onto the studs

Use a socket to drive the circlip against the concave washer and pop it into the groove in the end of the input shaft on later units that don't use a nut

Install the selector pad and relay lever for reverse gear onto the rail . . .

washer and circlip on each shaft. The washer must be compressed to fit the circlip into its groove, so you'll need a press or a socket or pipe to do the job.

72 Once the shaft nuts have been tightened, remove the gear carrier from the case in preparation for setting the selector forks.

73 Setting the selector forks is critical. If the wear between the fork and groove is outside the limit, the likelihood of a gear not being fully engaged - and jumping out - is increased. Ideally, you should try to have the unit set up by a transaxle specialist for the next few Steps. If that isn't possible, lay the assembly on the bench and do it yourself, but work very carefully.

74 Install the selector pad and relay lever for reverse gear onto the rail, then install the selector fork for first/second gears into its groove and mount it on the selector rail. Set all three selector rails in the neutral position (cut-outs in their ends all line up) and set the synchro hub outer sleeves in neutral with the forks in position. Then tighten the fork clamp bolts sufficiently to prevent them slipping. Push each selector so that each gear is fully engaged. The outer sleeve of the appropriate synchro hub must move fully over the dogs of the synchro ring and gear.

The fork must not bind in the groove in any gear.

75 If you have trouble engaging a gear, loosen the fork clamp nut, slide the synchro hub sleeve on the shaft until it's fully meshed and retighten the fork clamp. Then move the selector back to neutral and into the opposite gear position. In all three positions there must be no pressure in either direction between the fork and the sides of the groove in which it runs. Don't forget that the synchro hub and second and third gears on the pinion shaft are preloaded because of the dished washers and will rotate stiffly. This can make it difficult to line up the dogs when engaging second gear. Once both forks have been correctly set, tighten the clamp bolts to the torque listed in this Chapter's Specifications.

76 Install the small reverse sliding gear and yoke on the reverse gear shaft. To position them correctly, engage second gear. The reverse sliding gear should be midway between the straight cut teeth on the synchro hub sleeve and the helical teeth of second gear on the input shaft. Then move out of second gear and shift into reverse and verify that the reverse gears mesh completely. If necessary, adjust the block clamped to the selector rail.

77 To help you line up the bolt holes in the pinion bearing flange

. . . then install the selector fork for first/second gear into its groove, mount it on the selector rail and lighten the clamp bolt to prevent slipping

Install the small reverse sliding gear and yoke on the reverse gear shaft - the gear should be midway between the straight cut teeth on the synchro hub sleeve and the helical teeth of the second gear on the input shaft

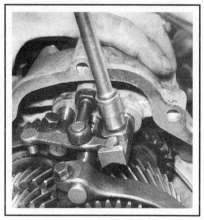

If it's necessary to reposition reverse gear, loosen and adjust the block clamped to the selector rail

Install a pair of three-inch long studs in the pinion bearing flange to help you line up the bolt holes (you can't move the flange when it's in position)

Install the pinion setting shims on the flange (early units with four bolt pinion flange)

Install the pinion setting shims on a later pinion shaft with castellated locking nut instead of flange

Place a new gasket over the studs on the case - make sure the gasket mating surface is immaculate

As you install the gear carrier on the case, just remember these three things - make sure the pinion flange lines up correctly, don't let the pinion shim fall out of place and make sure the splined reverse gear shaft lines up with the sliding reverse gear!

on earlier units (impossible to move when fully in position), install two three-inch-long studs in the flange. These studs are pilots for the holes in the case and will automatically line up the flange. Later units don't use this flange. Instead, they use a castellated lock ring that screws onto threads at the base of the pinion bearing.

78 Install the pinion setting shims in position on the face of the flange. Your two guide studs will help position them. If the flange has small bumps cast into the edge, line up the shim so that its shape matches the bumps. Put a dab of grease on the shim to prevent it falling off.

79 Place a new gasket over the studs on the case. Make sure no traces of old gasket remain on the mating surfaces, which must be perfectly clean and smooth.

80 Make sure the reverse sliding gear is still in place. To prevent it from sliding out of place, engage reverse gear.

81 Install the gear carrier to the case with the case standing upright. Watch three things as you install the carrier. First, as you guide the temporary studs into the bolt holes in the case, make sure the flange lines up properly. Second, don't let the pinion shim fall out of place. Third, make sure the splined reverse gear shaft lines up with - and goes into - the sliding reverse gear. If you take care of these three things, the whole unit will drop into place easily. Tap the carrier a few times with a

Using new lock plates, install the four pinion flange bolts and tighten them in a criss-cross pattern, evenly and gradually, to the specified torque

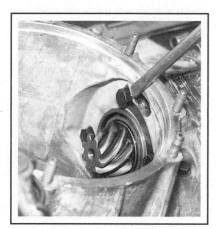

Bend up the lock plate tabs

Install the carrier nuts and tighten them in a criss-cross pattern, evenly and gradually, to the specified torque

If all the shafts rotate freely, bend up the lock tabs against the flats on the nuts for the input and pinion shaft nuts

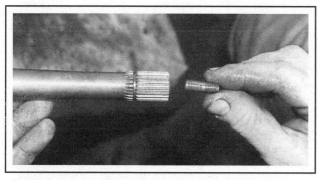

Install the small link stud into the end of the front shaft

soft mallet to butt the mating faces together. If for any reason something binds during this procedure, stop and have a look. Don't force anything. Check the three areas mentioned above and try again.

82 Once the gear carrier is installed, turn the case on its side and remove the guide studs from the pinion bearing flange. Using new lock plates (included in the gasket set) install the four pinion flange bolts and tighten them in a criss-cross fashion, evenly and gradually, to the torque listed in this Chapter's Specifications. Take care to avoid slipping and damaging the pinion while tightening these bolts. Turn the

bolt head between reverse gear and the pinion shaft so that a flat on the head faces the pinion to prevent the reverse gear sleeve from fouling the bolt head. Don't exceed the specified torque to do this - back off the bolt if necessary and retighten to a slightly lower torque. Bend up the lock plate tabs.

83 Install the carrier nuts. Tighten them in a criss-cross fashion, evenly and gradually, to the torque listed in this Chapter's Specifications. Don't forget that one nut secures the ground strap.

84 If all shafts rotate freely, bend up the lock tabs against flats on the nuts for the input and pinion shaft nuts.

85 Before installing the front section of the input shaft, lubricate the land in the center which will run in the oil seal and screw the small link stud into the end of the front shaft. Then carefully insert the shaft through the oil seal from the rear of the main case.

86 Install a new circlip over the splines and beyond the groove on the smooth part of the shaft.

87 Install the reverse gear/splined sleeve onto the shaft, plain end first. Screw the shaft stud into the end of the protruding input shaft. Screw it in as far as it will go, then back it off one turn to allow the splined collar to engage both halves of the shaft. DO NOT engage the sleeve with the ends of the shafts butted tightly together. Move the sleeve forward so that the gears engage, then move the circlip back along the shaft so that it engages fully into the groove. On later units,

Install a new circlip over the splines and beyond the groove on the smooth part of the shaft

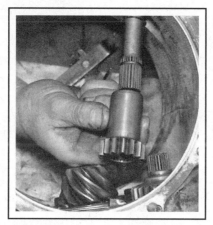

Install the reverse gear/splined sleeve onto the shaft, plain end first . . .

. . . screw the shaft stud into the end of the protruding input shaft . . .

. . . and move the sleeve forward so that the gears engage

On later units, install the sleeve over the input shaft extension

Clean the mating surfaces on the end of the gear carrier and shift housing and position a new gasket onto the gear carrier

When you install the shift housing, make sure the end of the gear change lever (arrow) seats in the cut-outs in the ends of the three selector rails

A close-up view of the relationship between the gear change lever and the cut-outs

To install new side bearings, support the side cover evenly and securely, then tap the new bearing into place with a wide, flat metal bar or a block of wood - the closed side of the ball race must face toward the outside of the case

install the sleeve over the input shaft extension.

88 Clean the mating surfaces on the end of the gear carrier and shift housing and position a new gasket over the gear carrier studs.

89 Verify that the transaxle is in neutral by checking the cut-outs in the ends of the three selector rods, which should be lined up. Install

Install a new O-ring on the side cover . . .

. . . make sure the gasket mating surfaces are perfectly clean, install a new gasket over the case studs (no sealing compound is necessary), place the bearing side cover in position and install it

Install the differential shims and hold them in position with a dab of grease

Carefully install the differential ring gear assembly

the gear change lever into the housing. It should easily slide into the housing, but there shouldn't be any sideplay. If the lever fits too loosely, it could cause jamming or other problems of changing gear.

90 Install the housing. Make sure the end of the gear change lever seats in the cut-outs in the ends of the three selector rails. Install the housing nuts and tighten them to the torque listed in this Chapter's Specifications.

91 Make sure all differential and side bearing parts are clean, and the shims and spacers are correct for each side of the differential casing. Remember that the shims have two functions, to put a pre-load on the side bearings, and to position the differential ring gear correctly in relation to the pinion gear.

92 In theory, you might think that if new bearings are installed, the shim requirements should be recalculated. In practice, this isn't necessary, provided that the same ring gear and pinion are installed and no shims have been previously altered in an attempt to improve some earlier malfunction.

93 To install new bearings, support the side cover evenly and securely and arrange the bearing so that the closed side of the ball race faces the outside of the case when the side cover is installed. The bore in the side cover must be scrupulously clean and free of any snags or burrs. Tap the new bearing into place with a heavy mallet and a wide, flat metal strap or wood block to evenly distribute the force. Make sure

the bearing doesn't cock in the bore as you start to drive it in. If it does, remove it and start again.

94 Make sure the gasket mating surfaces are perfectly clean, install a new gasket over the case studs (no sealant is necessary), install a new O-ring, place the side cover and bearing assembly in position (it will only fit one way) and install it. Tighten the nuts in a criss-cross fashion, gradually and evenly, to the torque listed in this Chapter's Specifications.

95 Install the differential shims. Hold them in position with a dab of grease. Make sure everything is perfectly clean.

➡**Note: If the shims are mixed up, you won't be able to set the pinion/ring gear backlash correctly. DON'T guess! Take the whole assembly to a transaxle specialist and have him reset it.**

96 If you know which shims came off each side, make sure they're arranged with the thicker spacer ring fitted first - with its chamfered side facing in - and the shims after that (so they'll be between the spacer ring and the bearing).

97 With the spacer and shims in place, install the differential assembly. Place the differential in the case very carefully and tap it into position. The shoulder must be fully seated against the inner race of the bearing in the cover.

98 Make sure the other set of shims is properly located on the ring gear end of the differential, place a new gasket in position and install the left bearing side cover. The cover has to fit down onto the differ-

Make sure the shims are properly located on the differential ring gear, place a new gasket in position and install the left bearing side cover

Carefully tap the left bearing side cover down onto the differential - don't use the retaining nuts to draw it down or you may crack the cover

Install the cover nuts only after you have driven it into place

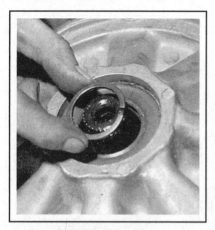

On later units with driveaxles, install the spacer ring into each side bearing cover . . .

. . . push the drive flange onto the shaft . . .

. . . install the circlip onto the shaft . . .

. . . tap it on the shaft with a socket until it pops into its groove . . .

. . . and install a new sealing plug

ential, so tap it into position until the nuts can be installed onto the studs. DO NOT use the cover retaining nuts to pull the cover and bearing down. This could easily crack or break it. Tighten the nuts to the same torque as the other side cover.

99 On swing axle models, install the axleshafts and tubes (see Chapter 8).

100 On driveaxle models, install the spacer ring over the shaft, push the drive flange onto the shaft, fit the circlip over the end of the shaft, tap it into the groove using a socket of suitable diameter and fit a new sealing plug. Repeat this procedure for the other side bearing cover.

101 Install the transaxle.

Shift Linkage

ADJUSTMENT

The Volkswagen shift linkage is not adjustable. When shifting becomes difficult or there is an excessive amount of play in the linkage, check the shifting mechanism for worn parts. Make sure the shift linkage coupling is tightly connected to the inner shift lever located at the rear of the transaxle under a plate below the rear seat on Types 1 and 3. On Type 2 models, Check the setscrew where the front shift rod connects to the center section below the passenger compartment, and the rear setscrew where the linkage goes into the transaxle. Worn parts may

be found in the shift lever mechanism and the supports for the linkage rod sometimes wear out.

Gear Shift Lever

SHIFT LEVER AND SHIFT ROD - REMOVAL AND INSTALLATION

Shift lever

1 If you're replacing the shift lever, make sure you obtain the correct replacement part. On vehicles produced before August 1967, the lever is straight; on later models, it's curved. Don't try to swap levers from one model to another unless they're identical. The lever on 1973 and later models is about 1-1/2 inches shorter than those on earlier models.

2 Pull back the floor mat, put the shift lever in Neutral and mark the position of the stop plate in relation to the ball housing flange to ensure proper alignment during installation.

❊❊ CAUTION:

Incorrect adjustment of the stop plate in the shift lever assembly can cause shifting problems.

Before you loosen the bolts on the ball housing flange, mark the position of the stop plate in relation to the flange (arrow) - the plate must be properly adjusted at installation, or you'll have shifting problems

Remove the shift lever, ball housing, rubber boot and spring as a unit

3   Remove the mounting bolts from the ball housing flange.

4   Remove the shift lever, ball housing, rubber boot and spring as a single unit.

5   Before removing the stop plate, note the orientation of the raised tab(s) on the stop plate. Some stop plates have a single tab on the right side of the hole which faces up; other plates have two tabs facing up, with the long, low, narrow tab near the driver and the shorter, higher tab on the right. Regardless of the design, the important thing to remember is that the stop plate must be reinstalled with the tab(s) oriented exactly the same way they were before removal.

6   Clean all parts thoroughly.

7   Inspect the shift lever collar, stop plate and shift lever ball socket in the shift rod for wear. Replace any worn parts.

8   Make sure the shift lever locating pin is secure. Check the spring in the steel ball for tension. Replace it if it's worn.

9   Install the stop plate. Make sure it's oriented with the tab(s) facing the same way as before removal.

10   Lubricate all moving parts with multi-purpose grease.

11   Inspect the condition of the rubber boot. Replace it if it's damaged.

12   Install the shift lever assembly (lever, ball housing and spring). Make sure the shift lever locating pin engages the slot in the ball socket and the stop plate seats in the hollow central part of the ball housing. If the lever is installed and seated properly, it will be vertical when its in Neutral.

13   Install the ball housing flange bolts loosely. Match up the alignment marks on the flange, stop plate and tunnel and tighten the bolts securely.

14   Recheck the position of the shift lever by engaging the gears. Readjust as necessary.

Shift rod

➡Note: If you're replacing a shift rod, make sure the replacement is the same length as the original - the rod on later models is shortened to fit the relocated mounting bracket for the guide bushing in the frame tunnel.

15   Remove the shift lever assembly (see Steps 1 through 5).

16   Remove the rear seat.

17   Remove the inspection cover on the frame tunnel.

18   Remove the fasteners from the shift rod coupling.

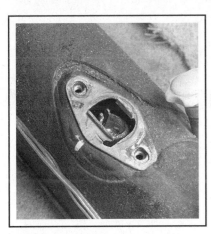

Make sure the stop plate is installed with the tab(s) facing the same way they were before removal

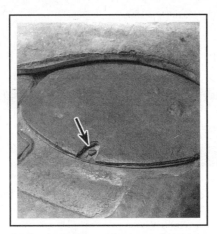

Remove the inspection cover from the frame tunnel

To disconnect the earlier type shift rod coupling, remove this bolt

To disconnect the later type shift rod coupling, remove this bolt and the self-tapping screw on the side, then knock out the spring pin with a hammer and punch

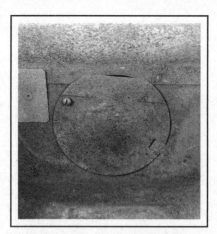

Remove the access cover from the frame head

Using a pair of pliers through the hole in the tunnel for the shift lever, work the shift rod out of the coupling and through the shift rod guide bushing - keep working it forward until it's free of the bushing

19 Remove the front bumper (see Chapter 11).

20 Remove the access cover in the frame head and in the front body apron.

21 Working through the hole in the frame tunnel, use a pair of pliers to separate the shift rod from the coupling and slide it through the shift rod guide bushing. If the grease on the shift rod - or the bushing itself - is dry, you may encounter some resistance.

22 Working through the hole in the frame head, pull the shift rod forward, through the tunnel and out the hole.

23 Inspect the shift rod for distortion. Replace it if it's warped or damaged (a bent shift rod can cause hard shifting and/or the loss of first and third gear).

24 Inspect the shift rod guide bushing for dryness, cracking or other damage. Replace it if necessary. To remove the old bushing, pull it - and the wire ring - out of the shift rod guide with a pair of pliers. To install a new bushing, slide a new wire ring onto the end of the bushing and install the bushing, slotted end first, into the shift rod guide.

25 Coat the entire shift rod with multi-purpose grease.

26 Insert the shift rod through the hole in the frame head, through the shift rod guide in the tunnel and push it all the way to the rear until it's fully engaged into the shift rod coupling. Install the frame head

cover, the access cover in the front apron and the bumper.

27 Install the shift rod coupling fasteners and tighten them securely. Install the inspection cover on the frame tunnel. Install the rear seat.

28 Install the shift lever assembly (see Steps 6 through 12).

29 Adjust the shift lever (see Step 13).

Main Driveshaft Oil Seal

REPLACEMENT

The main drive shaft oil seal can be replaced with the transaxle installed or removed. Remove the engine, clutch release bearing, and the seal from the transaxle case.

Before installing the new seal, lightly coat the outer edge of the seal with sealing compound, and lubricate the main driveshaft and the lip of the seal. Then, slide the oil seal onto the main driveshaft, and drive it into position with a suitable sleeve or pipe. The seal should be slid onto the shaft very carefully in order to avoid mis-positioning the spring around the lip.

AUTOMATIC STICK-SHIFT TRANSAXLE

Understanding the Automatic Stick-Shift Transaxle

An automatic clutch control three speed transaxle has been available on the Type 1. It is known as the Automatic Stick Shift.

It consists of a three speed gear box connected to the engine through a hydrodynamic torque converter. Between the converter and gearbox is a vacuum-operated clutch, which automatically separates the power flow from the torque converter while in the process of changing gear ratios.

While the torque converter components are illustrated here, the picture is for familiarization purposes only. The unit cannot be serviced. It

is a welded unit, and must be replaced as a complete assembly.

The power flow passes from the engine via converter, clutch and gearbox to the final drive, which, as with the conventional gearbox, is located in the center of the transaxle housing.

The converter functions as a conventional clutch for starting and stopping. The shift clutch serves only for engaging and changing the speed ranges. Friction-wise, it is very lightly loaded.

There is an independent oil supply for the converter provided by an engine driven pump and a reservoir. The converter oil pump, driven off the engine oil pump, draws fluid from the reservoir and drives it around a circuit leading through the converter and back to the reservoir.

This circuit also furnishes cooling for the converter fluid.

OPERATION

The control valve is activated by a very light touch to the top of the shift selector knob which, in turn, is connected to an electromagnet. It has two functions.

At the beginning of the selection process, it has to conduct the vacuum promptly from the intake manifold to the clutch servo, so that the shift clutch disengages at once, and thus interrupts the power flow between converter and transmission. At the end of the selection process, it must, according to driving conditions, automatically ensure that the shift clutch engages at the proper speed. It may neither slip nor engage too harshly. The control valve can be adjusted for this purpose.

As soon as the selector lever is moved to the engaged position, the two contacts in the lever close the circuit. The electromagnet is then under voltage and operates the main valve. By this means the clutch servo is connected to the engine intake manifold, and at the same time the connection to the atmosphere is closed. In the vacuum space of the servo system, a vacuum is built up, the diaphragm of the clutch servo is moved by the difference with atmospheric pressure and the shift clutch is disengaged via its linkage. The power flow to the gearbox is interrupted and the required speed range can be engaged. The process of declutching, from movement of the selector lever up to full separation of the clutch, lasts about 1/10 seconds. The automatic can, therefore, declutch faster than would be possible by means of a foot-operated clutch pedal.

When the selector lever is released after changing the speed range, the switch interrupts the current flow to the electromagnet, which then returns to its rest position and closes the main valve. The vacuum is reduced by the reducing valve and the shift clutch re-engages.

Clutch engagement takes place, quickly or slowly, according to engine loading. The clutch will engage suddenly, for example, at full throttle, and can transform the full drive moment into acceleration of the car. Or, this can be effected slowly and gently if the braking force of the engine is to be used on overrun. In the part-load range, too, the duration of clutch re-engagement depends on the throttle opening, and thus the vacuum in the carburetor venturi.

Vanes on the outside of the converter housing aid in cooling. In the case of abnormal prolonged loading, however (lugging a trailer over mountain roads in second or third speed), converter heat may exceed maximum permissible temperature. This condition will cause a red warning light to function in the speedometer.

After removing the engine, secure the torque converter (A/T) in place with wire ties (arrows)

There is also a starter locking switch. This, combined with a bridging switch, is operated by the inner transaxle shift lever. It performs two functions:

1 With a speed range engaged, the electrical connection to the starter is interrupted. The engine, therefore, can only be started in neutral.

2 The contacts in the selector lever are not closed in the neutral position. Instead, the bridging switch transmits a voltage to the electromagnets of the control valve. This ensures that the separator clutch is also disengaged in the neutral shifter position.

Transaxle Assembly

REMOVAL & INSTALLATION

1 Disconnect the negative battery cable.

2 Remove the engine.

3 Make a bracket to hold the torque converter in place. If a bracket is not used, the converter will slide off the transaxle input shaft.

4 Detach the gearshift rod coupling.

5 Disconnect the driveshafts at the transaxle end. If the driveshafts are not going to be repaired, it is not necessary to detach the wheel end.

6 Disconnect the drive ATF hoses from the transaxle. Seal the open ends. Disconnect the temperature switch, neutral safety switch, and the back-up light switch.

7 Pull off the vacuum servo hose.

8 Disconnect the starter wiring.

9 Remove the front transaxle mounting nuts.

10 Loosen the rear transaxle mounting bolts. Support the transaxle and remove the bolts.

11 Lower the transaxle and remove it from the car.

To install:

12 With the torque converter bracket still in place, raise the axle into the car.

13 Tighten the nuts for the front transaxle mounting. Insert the rear mounting bolts, but do not tighten them at this time.

14 Replace the vacuum servo hose.

15 Connect the ATF hoses, using new washers. The washers are seals.

16 Connect the temperature switch and starter cables.

17 Install the driveshafts, using new washers. Turn the convex sides of the washers toward the screw head.

18 Align the transaxle so that the inner driveshaft joints do not rub on the frame fork and then tighten the rear mounting bolts.

19 Insert the shift rod coupling, tighten the screw, and secure it with wire.

20 Remove the torque converter bracket, and install the engine.

21 After installing the engine, bleed the ATF lines if return flow has not started after 2 - 3 minutes.

OVERHAUL

Disassembly

1 Remove the gearshift housing with the inner transaxle shift lever.

2 Remove the hex nuts holding the gear carrier.

3 Remove the transaxle cover and gasket.

4 Take out the locking clip and loosen the roller bearing retaining ring at the pinion gear until it just contacts the ring gear. Special wrench VW 183 is normally used.

➥The transaxle can also be removed with the differential in place.

5 Press out the transaxle gear unit until the retaining ring touches the case. Alternately loosen the retaining ring and press out the transaxle gear unit until ring has been completely screwed clear of the bearing. Hinged lever VW 281 is required to press out the transaxle. Press out the bearing with the transaxle gear unit. Note the thickness and the number of the drive pinion adjusting shims.

6 Support the gear carrier in a vise. Remove the selector fork clamping screws and remove the first-reverse selector fork.

7 Remove the second-third selector shaft from the fork.

8 Remove the circlip and the dished washer from the main driveshaft. The washer is under tension.

9 Press the main driveshaft out of the gear carrier. Be careful not to damage the splines or the second-third selector fork.

Assembly

1 Check all parts; replace or repair as needed.

2 Engage the second-third selector fork in operating sleeve.

3 Position the pinion shaft and main driveshaft in press. Press the gear carrier onto the main driveshaft, being careful not to damage the splines or jam the second-third selector fork.

4 Install the dished washer and a new circlip on the main driveshaft. Press the circlip down until it snaps into the groove. Squeeze the circlip all round with water pump pliers until it bottoms in the groove.

5 Install the gear carrier and pinion shaft in the setting appliance VW 294b. The pinion adjusting shims, but not the paper gear carrier gasket, must also be installed in the appliance.

6 Screw the retaining ring on the pinion roller bearing and hand-tighten with C-wrench VW 183.

7 Push the selector shaft into the second third fork. Install the clamp screw. Install the first-reverse selector fork and clamp screw.

8 Move the first-reverse lower selector shaft into the first gear detent groove. Slide the operating sleeve and fork over the synchronizer teeth until it is against the first gear. Centralize the fork in the operating sleeve groove and tighten the clamp screw. The selector forks must not rub on the sides of the groove in the sleeve when in either Neutral or a gear position.

9 Select First, Neutral, and Reverse several times while turning the transaxle. Check for clearance between fork and sleeve groove in each position. In Reverse, the sleeve contacts a stop pressed into the hub. If necessary, alter the selector fork setting until there is the same clearance between the sleeve and the gear sleeve and the stop in both end positions. Tighten the clamp screw.

10 Move the upper selector shaft into the detent groove for Third. Adjust the fork as for First-Reverse. Tighten the clamp screw.

11 Check the interlock mechanism. It must not be possible to engage two gears at once. Resume transaxle assembly:

12 Insert the transaxle gear unit with the pinion shims and the gear carrier gasket into the transaxle case. Drive the pinion and mainshaft in with a rubber hammer. On transaxles with the locating screw for pinion shaft bearing, align bearing outer race hole with hole in housing.

13 If the differential is still in place, the pinion bearing retaining ring must be inserted and screwed on while the transaxle gear unit is driven in.

14 Tighten the retaining ring to 108 ft. lbs.

15 Tighten the gear carrier nuts diagonally. Insert the retaining ring locking clip and tighten the screw. On transaxles with the pinion shaft bearing locating screw, insert and align the locking clip so the screw can be installed when the cover is fitted.

16 Insert the gearshift housing and transaxle shift lever with the new gasket. Tighten the nuts.

17 Install the transaxle cover with a new gasket and tighten the screws diagonally. Coat the end of the bearing locating screw with sealing compound and insert the screw.

Gear Carrier Details

If difficult shifting was noted, check the selector shaft detent springs. To remove the plugs holding in the springs, cut a 6mm thread in each. Spring free length should be 0.9 - 1.0 in. The force required to overcome the grooves should be 33 - 44 lbs.

When using a replacement gear carrier from a four speed manual transmission, the holes for the reverse shift rod must be plugged. Only the old type of gear carrier with the long guide for the first-second shift rod is supplied as a replacement. When using this carrier for the Automatic Stick-shift, the hole for the first-second shift rod must be drilled about 16mm deep from inside with a 16mm dia. drill. If this is not done, the shift rod will probably jam.

Main Driveshaft Disassembly

1 Remove the thrust washer, third gear, needle bearing, and synchronizer stop ring.

2 Press off the needle bearing inner race, clutch gear with operating sleeve, and second gear.

3 Take out the shaft key.

4 Disassemble the clutch gear.

Main Driveshaft Assembly

1 Check the gears, synchronizer teeth, thrust washer, main driveshaft, and key for wear and damage.

2 Press the synchronizer stop-rings onto the gears and measure the clearance between synchronizer ring and gear with a feeler gauge.

- Gear - Installation Clearance - Wear Limit
- First - 0.043 - 0.070 in. - 0.023in.
- Second, Third - 0.040 - 0.075 in. - 0.023 in.

3 Install the second gear with the needle bearing and synchronizer stop-ring.

4 Install the key.

5 Fit the operating sleeve and clutch gear for the second and third gears together, aligning the marks. Sleeve and clutch gear may be replaced in matched sets only. Install springs with the ends overlapping 120-degrees. The angled spring ends must fully engage over the shift plates.

6 Seat the reassembled clutch gear. The 1mm deep groove on the operating sleeve must point toward third gear and the wide chamber on one side of the clutch gear must be toward the second gear.

7 Heat the inner race of the third gear needle bearing to about 212-degrees F and press it into position.

8 Install the needle bearing, gear with synchronizer stop-ring, and thrust washer for third gear.

Drive Pinion Shaft Disassembly

1 Remove the circlip, while holding third gear down with a press.

2 Press the third gear and needle bearing inner race off together.

3 Take off the spacer spring and remove the second gear circlip. Take off the second gear, first gear with synchronizer ring, first gear needle bearing, clutch gear with operating sleeve, and shim.

4 Unscrew the round nut. Tool VW 293 may be used.

5 Press off the bearing. Remove the operating sleeve, shift plates, and spring from clutch gear.

Drive Pinion Shaft Assembly

1 Check all parts for wear and damage. Second and third gears may be replaced only in pairs. Press the synchronizer ring over the cone on the gear and measure the clearance. Clearances and wear limits are as given in Step 2 under Main Driveshaft Disassembly.

2 Heat the inner races of the double taper roller bearing to about 212-degrees F and install the bearing on the shaft. Allow it to cool to room temperature and press it on with 3 tons pressure.

3 Screw on new round nut and tighten to 159 ft. lbs. Tool VW 293 should be used. Check the bearing turning torque. On used bearings, there should be no end-play. To check the turning torque, install the pinion shaft in the transaxle housing without the shim, fit the retaining ring and tighten it to 108 ft. lbs. (87 ft. lbs. when using VW 183). Turn the pinion with a torque gauge, oiling the bearings lightly with hypoid oil. Turn the pinion rapidly in each direction about 15 - 20 turns, then take the reading while turning. Turning torque should be 5 - 18 inch lbs. (0.6 - 2.0 Nm) for a new bearing or 3 - 6 inch lbs. (0.3 - 0.7 Nm) for a used bearing. Peen locking shoulder of round nut into pinion splines at three places 120-degrees apart, using a blunt chisel. Be careful not to crack or burr the shoulder.

4 Find the thickness of shim for round nut as follows: Measure from the end of the pinion gear to the base of the bearing race. This is dimension **a.** Measure from the end of the pinion gear to the top of the bearing inner race. This is **b.** Measure from the bearing contact shoulder on the pinion to the upper edge of the shim. This is **X. X** should be 44.40 - 44.50mm Shim thickness = **X x b - a.**

After removing the rubber boot, disconnect the wire (arrow) . . .

5 Assemble the pinion shaft up to the second gear. The clearance between the second gear and its circlip should be 0.0039 - 0.0098 in. (0.10 - 0.25mm). Circlips of various sizes are available.

6 Fit the spacer spring and third gear.

7 Heat the needle bearing inner race to about 212-degrees F and press it on with the third gear.

8 Install the circlip.

Differential Details

Before removing the differential, the transaxle gears must be removed. Replacing and adjusting the differential requires numerous special tools and procedures. For this reason, these operations are best left to an authorized repair facility.

Differential specifications are as follows:

- Backlash - 0.0059 - 0.0098 in. (0.15 - 0.25mm)
- Side bearing preload (new bearings) - 16 - 19 inch lbs. (1.8 - 2.1 Nm)
- Side bearing preload (used bearings) - 2.5 - 6.1 inch lbs. (0.28 - 0.68 Nm)

Shift Linkage

ADJUSTMENT

The Volkswagen shift linkage is not adjustable. When shifting becomes difficult or there is an excessive amount of play in the linkage, check the shifting mechanism for worn parts. Make sure the shift linkage coupling is tightly connected to the inner shift lever located at the rear of the transaxle under a plate below the rear seat on Types 1 and 3. On Type 2 models, Check the setscrew where the front shift rod connects to the center section below the passenger compartment, and the rear setscrew where the linkage goes into the transaxle. Worn parts may be found in the shift lever mechanism and the supports for the linkage rod sometimes wear out.

Gear Shift Lever

REMOVAL & INSTALLATION

The gear shift lever can be removed after the front floor mat has been lifted and the screws removed that attach the gear shift lever ball housing to the central frame tunnel. After the two retaining screws

. . . and remove the 13mm mounting bolts . . .

. . . then lift the shifter assembly up and off of the floor tunnel

When removing the stop plate, note its position for installation

have been removed, the gear shift lever, ball housing, rubber boot, and spring are removed as a unit. The spring will have to be turned in order to clear the pin. Remove the stop plate, clean all components, and check them for wear.

Installation of the gear shift lever is the reverse of the removal procedure. Replace any worn parts. Be sure that the locating pin is a firm fit, but not overly tight. The spring in the steel ball should be checked for tension and replaced if necessary. When installing the stop plate, be sure that the turned-up ramp is on the right-hand side. Lubricate all

parts generously with universal grease. After installation is completed, operate the various gears in order to check ease of movement.

✳✳ CAUTION:

Carefully mark the position of the stop plate and note the position of the turned up ramp at the side of the stop plate. Normally the ramp is turned up and on the right-hand side of the hole.

DRIVESHAFT AND CONSTANT VELOCITY (CV) JOINT

Driveshaft and CV-Joint Assembly

REMOVAL & INSTALLATION

Independent Rear Suspension (IRS)

▶ **See Figure 16**

1 Remove the bolts which secure the joints at each end of the shaft, tilt the shaft down and remove the shaft.

2 Loosen the clamps which secure the rubber boot to the axle and slide the boot back on the axle.

3 Drive the stamped steel cover off of the joint with a drift.

➡ **After the cover is removed, do not tilt the ball hub as the balls will fall out of the hub.**

4 Remove the circlip from the end of the axle and press the axle out of the joint.

5 Installation is the reverse of the removal procedure. The position of the dished washer is dependent on the type of transmission. On automatic transmissions, it is placed between the ball hub and the circlip. On manual transmissions, it is placed between the ball hub and the shoulder on the shaft. Be sure to pack the joint with grease.

➡ **The chamfer on the splined inside diameter of the ball hub faces the shoulder on the driveshaft.**

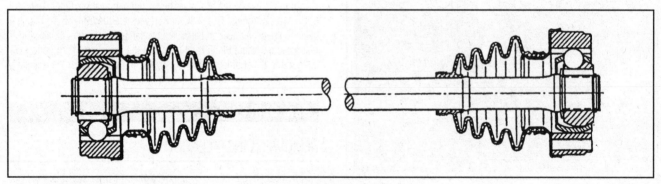

Cross-sectional view of a typical Independent Rear Suspension (IRS) halfshaft assembly

To remove an IRS halfshaft, remove the 6 outer halfshaft-to-wheel bearing flange bolts . . .

. . . then remove the 6 inner bolts

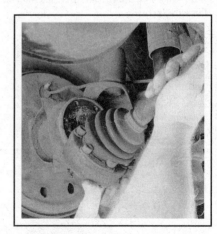

Drop the outer end of the halfshaft down to clear the flange . . .

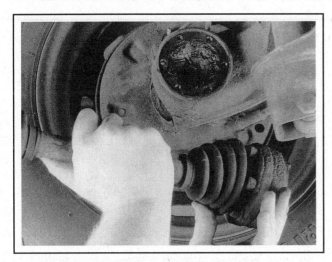

. . . then lower the entire assembly out of the vehicle

Remove the six nuts on the axle tube retainer

Swing Axle Rear Suspension

The rear axle tube and shaft can be removed while the transaxle is still in the car.

1   Remove the brake drum, bearing cover, back plate and rear wheel bearing.

2   Remove the nuts of the axle tube retainer and remove the axle tube and retainer.

3   Take off the gasket and plastic packing.

4   Remove the differential side gear lockring, the differential side gear thrust washer and the axle shaft.

5   After removing the differential side gear and fulcrum plates from the differential housing, knock the dowel pin from the bearing flange.

6   Remove the rear axle dust sleeve.

7   Press the axle tube out of its bearing flange.

Installation is mainly the reverse of the removal procedure. The rear axle boot should be checked for wear and replaced if necessary. The tube retainer and its seat should be cleaned thoroughly. The clearance between the flat end of the rear axle shaft and the inner diameter of the side gear should be 0.0012-0.004 in. (0.03 - 0.10mm). The axles and gears are coded according to color, and fall into four tolerance groups:

yellow, blue, pink and green. Only parts in the same size group should be mated.

Paint Mark	Inner Diameter Side Gear	Outer Diameter Axle Shaft
• Yellow	59.93 - 59.97mm (2.3200 - 2.3610 in.)	59.87 - 59.90mm (2.357 - 2.3582 in.)
• Blue	59.98 - 60.00mm (2.3610 - 2.3622 in.)	59.91 - 59.94mm (2.3583 - 2.3598 in.)
• Pink	60.01 - 60.04mm (2.3626 - 2.3638 in.)	59.95 - 59.97mm (2.3602 - 2.3610 in.)
• Green	60.05 - 60.07mm (2.3642 - 2.3650 in.)	59.98 - 60.00mm (2.3614 - 2.3622 in.)

The maximum allowable run-out for the rear axle is 0.002 in. (0.05mm). This measurement is taken at the seat of the ball bearing. Axles that are slightly bent can be straightened cold. A feeler gauge is used to measure the side clearance between the flat ends of the axle and the fulcrum plates. This clearance should be 0.0014 - 0.0096 in. (0.035-0.244mm). Excessive clearance can be taken care of by installing oversize fulcrum plates, which have a groove on the face.

Reach through the final drive cover with a pair of snap-ring pliers and remove the lock-ring (snap-ring) that secures the axleshaft and side gear in the differential

Using a feeler gauge of the correct thickness, measure the thickness between the rounded ends of the flat-bladed tip of the axleshaft and the inner diameter of the differential side gear

Install the old fulcrum plates between the flat sides of the axleshaft tip and the differential side gear . . .

. . . and, using a feeler gauge of the correct thickness, measure the clearance between the axleshaft and the fulcrum plates

The paper gaskets are identified by means of holes punched into them: one hole indicates a 0.004-inch thickness; two holes indicate an 0.008-inch thickness

Use a vernier caliper (or a micrometer) to measure the thickness of the original combination of paper gaskets or hard paper shims that you removed, then try to duplicate that same thickness with an assortment of new gaskets/shims

Insert the differential side gear and axleshaft through the final drive cover and into the differential - push them in until the side gear meshes with the spider gears in the differential . . .

. . . slide the thrust washer into place against the outer face of the side gear . . .

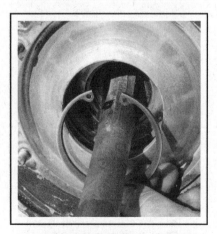

. . . and install the lock-ring (snap-ring) - make sure it seats properly into its groove in the axle bore of the differential

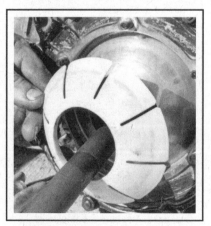

Install the plastic packing (older models)

Install the paper gaskets or hard paper shims

Slide the axle tube, boot and retainer onto the axleshaft

Apply a thin coat of sealing compound to the mating surfaces of the boot

Make sure the axle tube is installed with the notch in the bearing housing facing up and the boss for the shock absorber facing down

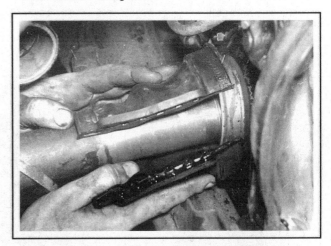

Don't get any oil on the sealing compound when you install the new boot

Install the differential side gear, axle and thrust washer in the differential housing and insert the lockring. Install the retainer gasket and the axle tube with the retainer. There should be no end-play between the axle tube and the axle tube retainer. This is accomplished by choosing a gasket of suitable thickness. The axle tube retainer nuts should be tightened to a torque of 14 ft. lbs. Over- or under-tightening should be avoided, for this will lead either to rapid wear or to leaks. Axle boots should not be tightened before the car is on the ground, axle intact. Otherwise, the boots may become twisted and damaged.

AXLE BOOT REPLACEMENT

The original rear axle boots (dust sleeves) are of a one-piece design and must be cut open in order to be removed for replacement. A split-type axle boot is available for replacement which can be installed and then tightened down. To remove the axle boot, take off the retaining clip at each end, and cut off the damaged boot. Clean both the axle tube and the axle tube retainer thoroughly so that the new boot will fit securely.

Upon installation, put a light coating of sealing compound on the joining faces of the boot and ensure that the smaller diameter of the

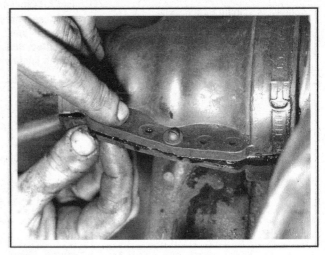

Pinch the mating surfaces along the seam together, then install the screws, washers and nuts - don't overtighten them or the boot will leak

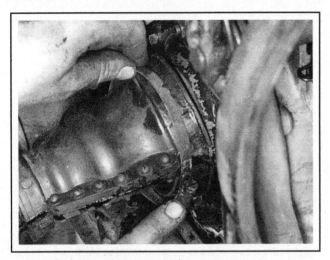

Seat the hose clamps and tighten them securely

boot is 89mm. When positioning the new boot, keep the joining faces in a horizontal plane and on the rear of the axle. Tighten the joining screws and the retaining clips (do not overtighten) only after the rear axle is in a loaded condition, and be sure that the boot is not twisted.

CONSTANT VELOCITY JOINT OVERHAUL

The Constant Velocity joint (CV-joint) must be disassembled to remove and replace old grease and to inspect. The individual pieces of the CV joint are machined matched; in the event that some part of the joint is bad, the entire joint (not including the axle shaft) must be replaced.

1 Remove the circlip and tap the axle shaft through the CV joint.
2 Pivot the ball hub and ball cage out of the joint until they are at a ninety degree angle to the case, and pull the ball hub and cage out as an assembly.
3 Press the balls out of the cage.
4 Align the two grooves and take the ball hub out of the cage.
5 Check the outer race, ball hub, ball cage and balls for wear and pitting. Check the ball cage for hairline cracks. Signs of polishing indicating the tracks of the ball bearings is no reason for replacement.
To assemble:
6 Fit the ball hub into the cage. It doesn't matter which way the hub is installed. Press in the ball bearings.
7 Fit the hub assembly into the outer race at a ninety degree angle to the outer race. When inserting, make sure that a wide separation between ball grooves on the outer race and a narrow separation between ball grooves on the hub are together when the hub and cage

. . . then tap the driveaxle out of the joint. If it won't come out of the joint easily, use a press. If you don't have access to a press, take the driveaxle to an automotive machine shop to have the joint removed

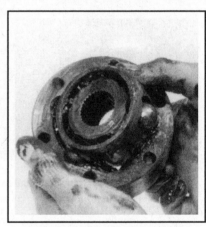

Tilt the inner race out of the outer race and separate them

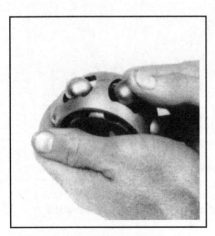

Remove the circlip from the end of the axle . . .

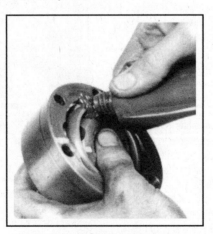

Press the bearings in until they snap into place

Pack the joint with CV joint grease (don't use any other kind of grease)

Apply CV joint grease to the inside of the boot, also

assembly is swung into the outer race (direction of arrow in illustration).

8   When pivoting the ball hub and cage assembly into the outer race, the hub should be pivoted out of the cage so that the balls spread apart enough to fit into the ball grooves.

9   Press the cage firmly down until the hub swings fully into position.

10 Pack the unit completely with axle grease. The joint is properly assembled when the ball hub can be moved over the full range of axial movement by hand.

Rear Wheel Bearing And Oil Seal

REPLACEMENT

1   Remove the brake drum and the brake shoes (see Section 9).

2   Remove the bearing cover bolts. Remove the cover, the paper gasket, the oil deflector and the seal.

3   Remove the spacer, the two sealing rings and the large washer.

4   Detach the brake line and remove the brake backing plate.

5   VW recommends that the rear wheel bearings be removed with a hydraulic press, but you can fabricate an inexpensive puller in less than an hour. Obtain a pair of 3/8-inch diameter bolts at least six inches long. Cut the heads off with a hacksaw and carve out notches near the unthreaded end of each bolt with a round file. Then, get a 3/16-inch thick steel plate, about six inches long by two inches wide. Insert the hooked ends of the bolts into position between the inner and outer races as shown, lay the plate across their opposite (threaded) ends and mark where they hit the plate. Drill out two holes for the bolts, add washers and nuts and your puller is ready! Hook it up as shown and remove the bearing. Remove the inner spacer and set it aside.

6   Install the inner spacer.

7   Install the new bearing with the sealed side facing the transaxle and the open side (numbers on the outer race) facing out. Use a brass drift to drive the new bearing into place. Start it onto the axleshaft by tapping all the way around the inner race. When the bearing reaches the axle housing, start tapping on the outer race as well. Alternate your taps between the inner and outer races until the bearing is fully seated.

8   Install the large O-ring, washer and small O-ring, then smear the O-rings with a film of oil.

➡Note: Make sure all the parts are absolutely clean. Always use new O-rings. You can re-use the large washer if it's clean

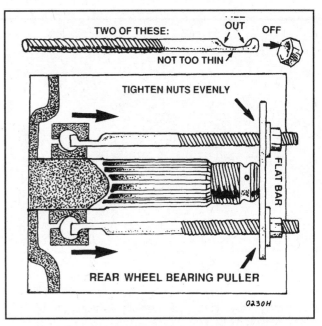

Take two 3/8-inch diameter bolts about six inches long, cut off the heads and notch the unthreaded ends as shown, then drill two holes in a six-inch by two-inch by 3/16-inch plate - insert the notched ends of the bolts between the races with the notches facing the outer race, install the plate, washers and nuts and pull off the rear wheel bearing

Install the inner spacer

Install the rear wheel bearing

Install the large O-ring onto the bearing

Install the washer

Install the small O-ring

Install the brake backing plate

and rust free. **Inspect the spacer carefully. It must not be scored, cracked or rusty.**

9   Install the brake backing plate, making sure the large O-ring doesn't slip off the bearing. Attach the brake line.

10   Place a new seal in position, square with the bore in the bearing cover, and drive it into place with a seal driver or a hammer and a flat piece of wood.

11   Slip the outer spacer onto the axleshaft. Push or tap it into place against the new bearing. Lubricate the outside of the spacer with a little oil to protect the sealing lip of the new bearing cover seal. Also lubricate the lip of the seal.

12   Place a new paper gasket in position and install the bearing

cover. Make sure the oil drain hole in the cover faces down. Tighten the bearing cover bolts to the torque listed in this Chapter's Specifications.

✷✷ CAUTION:

When you slip the bearing cover over the end of the axleshaft, make sure you don't damage the seal lip on the shaft splines.

13   Install the brake shoes and the brake drum (see Section 9).

14   Check the transaxle lubricant and refill if necessary (see Section 1).

15   Adjust and bleed the brakes (see Section 9).

Place the bearing cover on a block of wood, position the new seal - numbers facing up, open side facing down - square with the recessed bore in the cover and carefully tap the seal into place

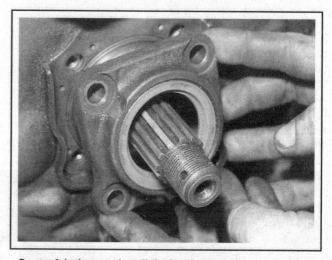

Be careful when you install the bearing cover, or you could easily damage the seal lip on the axleshaft splines

CLUTCH

Understanding the Clutch

The clutch used in all models is a single dry disc mounted on the flywheel with a diaphragm spring type pressure plate. The release bearing is the ball bearing type and does not require lubrication. On Types 1, 2 and 3, the clutch is engaged mechanically via a cable which attaches to the clutch pedal. On the Type 4, the clutch is engaged hydraulically, using a clutch pedal operated master cylinder and a bell housing mounted slave cylinder.

✳✳ CAUTION:

The clutch driven disc may contain asbestos, which has been determined to be a cancer causing agent. Never clean clutch surfaces with compressed air! Avoid inhaling any dust from any clutch surface! When cleaning clutch surfaces, use a commercially available brake cleaning fluid.

The purpose of the clutch is to disconnect and connect engine power at the transaxle. A vehicle at rest requires a lot of engine torque to get all that weight moving. An internal combustion engine does not develop a high starting torque (unlike steam engines) so it must be allowed to operate without any load until it builds up enough torque to move the vehicle. Torque increases with engine rpm. The clutch allows the engine to build up torque by physically disconnecting the engine from the transaxle, relieving the engine of any load or resistance.

The transfer of engine power to the transaxle (the load) must be smooth and gradual; if it weren't, drive line components would wear out or break quickly. This gradual power transfer is made possible by gradually releasing the clutch pedal. The clutch disc and pressure plate are the connecting link between the engine and transaxle. When the clutch pedal is released, the disc and plate contact each other (the clutch is engaged) physically joining the engine and transaxle. When the pedal is pushed inward, the disc and plate separate (the clutch is disengaged) disconnecting the engine from the transaxle.

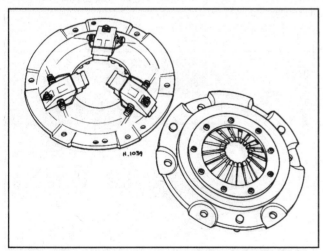

Typical early (left) and later (right) diaphragm spring clutch pressure plates: Early version uses release levers like older coil spring types - on later version, levers are eliminated and diaphragm spring is attached to plate (you can swap the earlier version for the later one at overhaul time)

Most clutches utilize a single plate, dry friction disc with a diaphragm-style spring pressure plate. The clutch disc has a splined hub which attaches the disc to the input shaft. The disc has friction material where it contacts the flywheel and pressure plate. Torsion springs on the disc help absorb engine torque pulses. The pressure plate applies pressure to the clutch disc, holding it tight against the surface of the flywheel. The clutch operating mechanism consists of a release bearing, fork and cylinder assembly.

The release fork and actuating linkage transfer pedal motion to the release bearing. In the engaged position (pedal released) the diaphragm spring holds the pressure plate against the clutch disc, so engine torque is transmitted to the input shaft. When the clutch pedal is depressed, the release bearing pushes the diaphragm spring center toward the flywheel. The diaphragm spring pivots the fulcrum, relieving the load on the pressure plate. Steel spring straps riveted to the clutch cover lift the pressure plate from the clutch disc, disengaging the engine drive from the transaxle and enabling the gears to be changed.

The clutch is operating properly if:

1 It will stall the engine when released with the vehicle held stationary.

2 The shift lever can be moved freely between 1st and reverse gears when the vehicle is stationary and the clutch disengaged.

Driven Disc and Pressure Plate

REMOVAL & INSTALLATION

Manual Transaxle

1 Remove the engine.

2 Remove the pressure plate securing bolts one turn at a time until all spring pressure is released.

3 Remove the bolts and remove the clutch assembly.

➡**Notice which side of the clutch disc faces the flywheel and install the new disc in the same direction.**

4 Before installing the new clutch, check the condition of the fly-

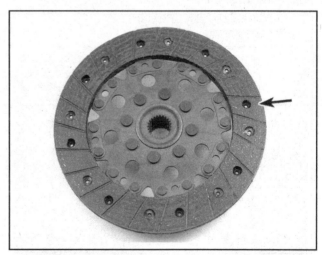

Inspect the clutch lining material (arrow) - there should be at least 1/16-inch of lining above the rivet heads - also look for loose rivets, distortion, cracks, broken springs and other damage

Inspect the friction surface of the pressure plate for wear, cracks and grooves - alternating bright and dull areas indicate a warped plate

On later pressure plates with diaphragm springs, inspect the spring fingers (arrow) for excessive wear and make sure they're not distorted - shake the pressure plate and make sure the diaphragm spring doesn't rattle

wheel. It should not have excessive heat cracks and the friction surface should not be scored or warped. Check the condition of the throwout bearing. If the bearing is worn, replace it.

5 Lubricate the pilot bearing in the end of the crankshaft with grease.

6 Insert a pilot shaft, used for centering the clutch disc, through the clutch disc and place the disc against the flywheel. The pilot shaft will hold the disc in place.

7 Place the pressure plate over the disc and loosely install the bolts.

➡**Make sure the correct side of the clutch disc is facing outward. The disc will rub the flywheel if it is incorrectly positioned.**

8 After making sure that the pressure plate aligning dowels will fit into the pressure plate, gradually tighten the bolts.

9 Remove the pilot shaft and reinstall the engine.

10 Adjust the clutch pedal free-play.

Automatic Stick-Shift

1 Disconnect the negative battery cable.
2 Remove the engine.

3 Remove the transaxle.

4 Remove the torque converter by sliding it off of the input shaft. Seal off the hub opening.

5 Mount the transaxle in a repair stand or on a suitable bench.

6 Loosen the clamp screw and pull off the clutch operating lever. Remove the transaxle cover.

7 Remove the hex nuts between the clutch housing and the transaxle case.

➡**Two nuts are located inside the differential housing.**

8 The oil need not be drained if the clutch is removed with the cover opening up and the gearshift housing breather blocked.

9 Pull the transaxle from the clutch housing studs.

10 Turn the clutch lever shaft to disengage the release bearing.

11 Remove both lower engine mounting bolts.

12 Loosen the clutch retaining bolts gradually and alternately to prevent distortion. Remove the bolts, pressure plate, clutch plate, and release bearing.

13 Do not wash the release bearing. Wipe it dry only.

Center the clutch disc with an alignment tool, then tighten the pressure plate bolts

Note how the clips on the release bearing engage the release forks (you'll need to remember this for reassembly), then pry the clips loose from the release forks with a screwdriver

14 Check the clutch plate, pressure plate, and release bearing for wear and damage. Check the clutch carrier plate, needle bearing, and seat for wear. Replace the necessary parts.

15 If the clutch is wet with ATF, replace the clutch carrier plate seal and the clutch disc. If the clutch is wet with transmission oil, replace the transaxle case seal and clutch disc.

16 Coat the release bearing guide on the transaxle case neck and both lugs on the release bearing with grease. Insert the bearing into the clutch.

17 Grease the carrier plate needle bearing. Install the clutch disc and pressure plate using a pilot shaft to center the disc on the flywheel.

18 Tighten the pressure plate retaining bolts evenly and alternately. Make sure that the release bearing is correctly located in the diaphragm spring.

19 Insert the lower engine mounting bolts from the front. Replace the sealing rings if necessary. Some units have aluminum sealing rings and cap nuts.

20 Push the transaxle onto the converter housing studs. Insert the clutch lever shaft behind the release bearing lugs. Push the release bearing onto the transaxle case neck. Tighten the bolts which hold the clutch housing to the transaxle case.

21 Install the clutch operating lever.

22 It is necessary to adjust the basic clutch setting. The clutch operating lever should contact the clutch housing. Tighten the lever clamp screw slightly.

23 First adjust dimension (a) to 0.335 in. Adjust dimension (b) to 3.03 in. Finally adjust dimension (c) to 1.6 in. by repositioning the clutch lever on the clutch shaft. Tighten the lever clamp screw.

24 Push the torque converter onto the support tube. Insert it into the turbine shaft by turning the converter.

25 Check the clutch play after installing the transaxle and engine.

Clutch Cable

ADJUSTMENT

Manual Transaxle

1 Check the clutch pedal travel by measuring the distance the pedal travels toward the floor until pressure is exerted against the clutch. The distance is 3/8 to 3/4 in.

2 To adjust the clutch, jack up the rear of the car and support it on jackstands.

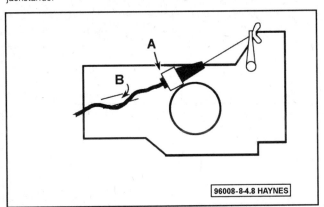

96008-8-4.8 HAYNES

For smooth clutch action, dimension (B) should equal 1.0 - 1.7 in. - to adjust the cable to provide the proper amount of sag at (B), install or remove washers from point (A)

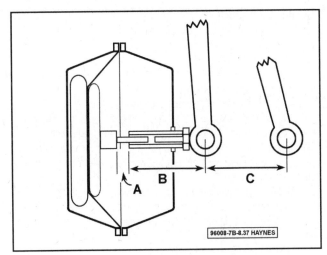

96008-7B-8.37 HAYNES

Adjust the automatic stick shift clutch to the three dimensions shown (A, B and C) - A should be equal 0.355 inch, B should equal 3.03 inch and C should be adjusted to 1.6 inch

3 Remove the left rear wheel.

4 Adjust the cable tension by turning the wing nut on the end of the clutch cable. Turning the wingnut counterclockwise decreases pedal free-play, turning it clockwise increases free-play.

5 When the adjustment is completed, the wings of the wingnut must be horizontal so that the lugs on the nut engage the recesses in the clutch lever.

6 Push on the clutch pedal several times and check the pedal free-play.

6 Install the wheel and lower the car.

Automatic Stick-Shift

The adjustment is made on the linkage between the clutch arm and the vacuum servo unit.

To check the clutch play:

1 Disconnect the servo vacuum hose.

2 Measure the clearance between the upper edge of the servo unit mounting bracket and the lower edge of the adjusting turnbuckle. If the clearance (e) is 0.16 in. or more, the clutch needs adjustment.

3 Reconnect the vacuum hose.

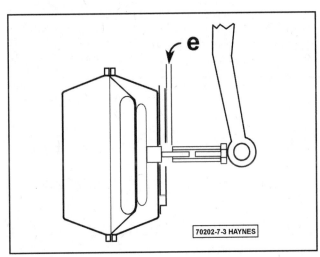

70202-7-3 HAYNES

When checking the clutch freeplay on automatic stick shift transaxles, "e" should be less than 0.16 inch (4 mm)

To adjust the clutch:

4 Disconnect the servo vacuum hose.

5 Loosen the turnbuckle locknut and back it off completely to the lever arm. Then turn the servo turnbuckle against the locknut. Now back off the turnbuckle 5 - 5 1/2 turns. The distance between the locknut and the turnbuckle should be 0.25 in.

6 Tighten the locknut against the adjusting sleeve.

7 Reconnect the vacuum hose and road test the vehicle. The clutch is properly adjusted when Reverse gear can be engaged silently and the clutch does not slip on acceleration. If the clutch arm contacts the clutch housing, there is no more adjustment possible and the clutch plate must be replaced.

The speed of engagement of the Automatic Stick Shift clutch is regulated by the vacuum operated valve, rather than by the driver's foot. The adjusting screw is on top of the valve under a small protective cap. Adjust the valve as follows:

8 Remove the cap.

9 To slow the engagement, turn the adjusting screw 1/4 - 1/2 turn clockwise. To speed engagement, turn the screw counterclockwise.

10 Replace the cap.

11 Test operation by shifting from second gear to first gear at 44 mph without depressing the accelerator. The shift should take exactly one second to occur.

REPLACEMENT

1 Jack up the car and remove the left rear wheel.

2 Disconnect the cable from the clutch operating lever.

3 Remove the rubber boot from the end of the guide tube and off the end of the cable.

4 On Type 1, unbolt the pedal cluster and remove it from the car. It will also be necessary to disconnect the brake master cylinder pushrod and throttle cable from the pedal cluster. On Type 2, remove the cover under the pedal cluster, then remove the pin from the clevis on the end of the clutch cable. On Type 3, remove the frame head cover and remove the pin from the clevis on the end of the clutch cable.

5 Pull the cable out of its guide tube from the pedal cluster end.

6 Installation is the reverse of the removal procedure.

➡**Grease the cable before installing it and readjust the clutch pedal free-play.**

FULLY AUTOMATIC TRANSAXLE

The fully automatic transaxle, consisting of an automatically shifted three speed planetary transaxle and a torque converter, was introduced in 1969.

The torque converter is a conventional three element design. The three elements are an impeller (driving member), a stator (reaction member), and the turbine (driven member). Maximum torque multiplication, with the vehicle starting from rest, is two and one-half to one. Maximum converter efficiency is about 96 per cent.

The automatic transaxle is a planetary unit with three forward speeds which engage automatically, depending on engine loading and road speed. The converter, planetary unit, and control system are incorporated together with the final drive in a single housing. The final drive is located between the converter and the planetary gearbox. Driving and driven shafts fit one inside the other in contrast to the manual transaxle in which they are located one below the other. The planetary gear unit is controlled by two multi-plate clutches which make up the third-reverse and forward clutch, a first gear band, a second gear band, and a roller clutch which permits the planetary ring gear to rotate only in the direction of drive.

The transaxle control system includes a gear type oil pump, a centrifugal governor which regulates shift points, a throttle modulator valve which evaluates engine loading according to the intake manifold pressure, and numerous other regulating components assembled in the transaxle valve body.

Power flow passes through the torque converter to the turbine shaft, then to the clutch drum attached to the turbine shaft, through a clutch to a sungear. The output planet carrier then drives the rear axle shafts via the final drive.

Transaxle ranges are Park, Reverse, Neutral, Drive (3), Second (2), and First (1).

Transaxle Assembly

REMOVAL & INSTALLATION

1 Remove the battery ground cable.

2 On the sedan, remove the cooling air intake duct with the heating fan and hoses. Remove the cooling air intake connection and bellows,

then detach the hoses to the air cleaner.

3 On station wagons, remove the warm air hoses and air cleaner. Remove the boot from between the dipstick tube and the body and the boot from between the oil filler neck and the body. Disconnect the cooling air bellows at the body.

4 Disconnect the wires at the regulator and the alternator wires at the snap connector located by the regulator. Disconnect the auxiliary air regulator and the oil pressure switch at the snap connectors located by the distributor.

5 Disconnect the fuel injection wiring. There are 12 connections and they are identifiable as follows:

a) Fuel injector cylinder 2: 2-pole, protective gray cap.

b) Fuel injector cylinder 1: 2-pole, protective black cap.

c) Starter: 1-pole, white.

d) Throttle valve switch: 4-pole.

e) Distributor: 3 pole.

f) Thermo switch: 1-pole, white.

g) Cold start valve: 3-pole.

h) Temperature sensor crankcase: 2-pole.

i) Ground connection: 3-pole, white wires.

j) Temperature sensor for the cylinder head: 1-pole.

k) Fuel injector cylinder 3: 2-pole, protective black cap.

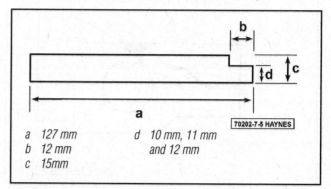

a	127 mm	d	10 mm, 11 mm
b	12 mm		and 12 mm
c	15mm		

70202-7-5 HAYNES

To correctly align the automatic transaxle during installation, three aligning tools must be fabricated to the specifications shown

l) Fuel injector cylinder 4: 2-pole, protective gray cap.

6 Disconnect the accelerator cable.

7 Disconnect the right fuel return line.

8 Raise the car.

9 Disconnect the warm hoses from the heat exchangers.

10 Disconnect the starter wires and push the engine wiring harness through the engine cover plate.

11 Disconnect the fuel supply line and plug it.

12 Remove the heater booster exhaust pipe.

13 Remove the rear axles and cover the ends to protect them from dirt.

14 Remove the selector cable by unscrewing the cable sleeve.

15 Remove the wire from the kickdown switch.

16 Remove the bolts from the rubber transaxle mountings, taking careful note of the position, number, and thickness of the spacers that are present.

✳✳ CAUTION:

These spacers must be reinstalled exactly as they were removed. Do not detach the transaxle carrier from the body.

17 Support the engine and transaxle assembly in such a way that it may be lowered and moved rearward at the same time.

18 Remove the engine carrier bolts and the engine and transaxle assembly from the car.

➡**The top carrier bolts on the Type 2 are the top engine-to-transaxle bolts. Be sure to support the engine/transaxle assembly before completely removing the bolts.**

19 Matchmark the flywheel to the torque converter and remove the three attaching bolts.

20 Remove the engine-to-transaxle bolts and separate the engine and transaxle.

✳✳ CAUTION:

Exercise care when separating the engine and transaxle, as the torque converter will easily slip off the input shaft if the transaxle is tilted downward.

To install:

21 Install and tighten the engine-to-transaxle bolts after aligning the matchmarks on the flywheel and converter.

22 Making sure the matchmarks are aligned, install the converter-to-flywheel bolts.

23 Make sure the rubber buffer is in place and the two securing studs do not project more than 0.7 in. from the transaxle case.

24 Tie a cord to the slot in the engine compartment seal. This will make positioning the seal easier.

25 Lift the assembly far enough to allow the accelerator cable to be pushed through the front engine cover.

26 Continue lifting the assembly into place. Slide the rubber buffer into the locating tube in the rear axle carrier.

27 Insert the engine carrier bolts and raise the engine until the bolts are at the top of their elongated slots. Tighten the bolts.

➡**A set of three gauges must be obtained to check the alignment of the rubber buffer in its locating tube. The dimensions are given in the illustration as is the measuring technique. The rubber buffer is centered horizontally when the 11mm gauge can be inserted on both sides. The buffer is located vertically when the 10mm gauge can be inserted on the bottom side and the 12mm gauge can be inserted on the top side. See Steps 28**

and 29 for adjustment procedures.

28 Install the rubber transaxle mount bolts with spacers of the correct thickness. The purpose of the spacers is to center the rubber buffer vertically in its support tube. The buffer is not supposed to carry any weight; it absorbs torsional forces only.

29 To locate the buffer horizontally in its locating tube, the engine carrier must be vertical and parallel to the fan housing. It is adjusted by moving the engine carrier bolts in elongated slots. Further travel may be obtained by moving the brackets attached to the body. It may be necessary to adjust the two rear suspension wishbones with the center of the transaxle after the rubber buffer is horizontally centered. Take the car to a dealer or alignment specialist to align the rear suspension.

30 Adjust the selector level cable.

31 Connect the wire to the kickdown switch.

32 Install the rear axles. Make sure the lockwashers are placed with the convex side out.

33 Reconnect the fuel hoses and heat exchanger hoses. Install the pipe for the heater booster.

34 Lower the car and pull the engine compartment seal into place with the cord.

35 Reconnect the fuel injection and engine wiring. Push the starter wires through the engine cover plate and connect the wires to the starter.

36 Install the intake duct with the fan and hoses, as well as the cooling air intake.

Fluid Pan

REMOVAL & INSTALLATION

1 Some models have a drain plug in the pan. Remove the plug and drain the transmission oil. On models without the plug, loosen the pan bolts 2 - 3 turns and lower one corner of the pan to drain the oil.

2 Remove the pan bolts and remove the pan from the transaxle.

➡**It may be necessary to tap the pan with a rubber hammer to loosen it.**

3 Use a new gasket and install the pan. Tighten the bolts loosely until the pan is properly in place, then tighten the bolts fully, moving in a diagonal pattern.

➡**Do not overtighten the bolts.**

4 Refill the transaxle with ATF.

5 At 5 minute intervals, retighten the pan bolts two or three times.

FILTER SERVICE

The Volkswagen automatic transaxle has a filter screen secured by a screw to the bottom of the valve body. Remove the pan and remove the filter screen from the valve body.

✳✳ CAUTION:

Never use a cloth that will leave the slightest bit of lint in the transaxle when cleaning transaxle parts. The lint will expand when exposed to transaxle fluid and clog the valve body and filter.

Clean the filter screen with compressed air. 1976 - 81 Type 2s have a non-cleanable filter which must be replaced with a new one if the ATF fluid is very dirty.

Kickdown Switch

ADJUSTMENT

1 Disconnect the accelerator cable return spring.

2 Move the throttle to the fully open position. Adjust the accelerator cable to give 0.02 - 0.04 in. clearance between the stop and the end of the throttle valve lever.

3 When the accelerator cable is adjusted and the throttle is moved to the fully open position, the kickdown switch should click. The ignition switch must be **ON** for this test.

4 To adjust the switch, loosen the switch securing screws and slide the switch back and forth until the test in Step 3 is satisfied.

5 Reconnect the accelerator cable return spring.

Shift Linkage

ADJUSTMENT

Make sure the shifting cable is not kinked or bent and that the linkage and cable are properly lubricated.

1 Move the gear shift lever to the Park position.

2 Loosen the clamp which holds the front and rear halves of the shifting rod together. Loosen the clamping bolts on the transaxle lever.

3 Press the lever on the transaxle rearward as far as possible. Spring pressure will be felt. The manual valve must be on the stop in the valve body.

4 Holding the transaxle lever against its stop, tighten the clamping bolt.

5 Holding the rear shifting rod half, push the front half forward to take up any clearance and tighten the clamp bolt.

6 Test the shift pattern.

Transmission Gear Ratios

Model	4th	3rd	2nd	1st	R	Final Drive	Reduction Gears or Torque Converter
1951-54 Type 1	.79	1.22	1.88	3.60	4.63	4.375 or 4.43	–
1954-60 Type 1	.82	1.23 ④	1.88 ③	3.60	4.63	4.375	–
1961-67 Type 1 and 3	.89	1.32	2.06	3.80	3.88	4.375 ①	–
1968-70 Type 1 and 3	.89	1.26	2.06	3.80	3.61	4.125	–
Automatic Stick-shift	–	.89	1.26	2.06	3.07	4.375	2.1
Fully Automatic	–	1.00	1.59	2.65	1.80	3.670	2.5
Type 2 1,500 cc.	.82	1.22	2.06	3.80	3.88	4.375	1.26 ②

① Type 3, 4.125

② 1,200cc. Type 2, 1.4 or 1.39

③ 1.94 also used.

④ 1.22 also used.

Additional final drive ratios available for special purposes: 3.875 - type 181; 5.375 - type 2 (1 ton); 5.857 - type 2 (1 ton).

Torque Specifications— Transmission and Rear Axle

Fastener	Thread Size	Torque (ft.lbs.)
Transmission and Rear Axle (Standard and Partly-synchronized) Transmission) Type 1 and 2		
Drive pinion nut (Partly-synchronized transmission) up to Chassis No. 1 454 550/238 499	M 22 x 1.5	80-87 ①
Drive pinion nut (Partly-synchronized transmission /new lockwasher) from Chassis No. 1 454 551/238 500	M 22 x 1.5	58-65 ①
Slotted nut for pinion (Standard transmission)	M 18 x 1.5	36 ②
Main drive shaft nut	M 16 x 1.5	30-36
Reverse selector fork screw	M 7 x 12	14
Ring gear screws	M 10 x 1.5	43
Selector fork clamp screw	M 8 x 1.25	18
Transmission housing nuts and bolts ③	M 8 x 1.25	14
Oil drain plug	M 18 x 1.5	22-29
Oil filter plug	M 24 x 1.5	14
Axle shaft nut	M 24 x 1.5	217
Transmission carrier to frame	M 18 x 1.5	166
Spring plate nuts/bolts	M 12 x 1.5	72
Transmission and Rear Axle (fully synchronized) all Types		
Drive pinion round nut: 1-for double ball bearing.	M 35 x 1.5	87
2-for double taper roller bearing	M 35 x 1.5	144
Pinion bearing retainer screws	M 10 x 1.5	36
Pinion nut	M 22 x 1.5	43 ④
Drive shaft nut	M 22 x 1.5	43 ④
Reverse lever guide screw	M 7 x 1	14
Selector fork screws	M 8 x 1.25	18
Nuts for gearshift housing	M 7 x 1	11
Ring gear screws	M 10 x 1.5	43
Final drive cover nuts	M 8 x 1.25	22
Axle tube retainer nuts	M 8 x 1.25	14
Rear wheel bearing retainer screws	M 10 x 1.5	43
Oil drain plug	M 24 x 1.5	14
Oil filter plug		
Rear axle shaft nut (Type 1 and 3)	M 24 x 1.5	217

Torque Specifications— Transmission and Rear Axle

Fastener	Thread Size	Torque (ft.lbs.)
Nut on driven shaft (Type 2 from August 1963)	M 30 x 1.5	108
Nut on rear axle driven shaft (Type 2) up to Chassis No. 1144302	M 24 x 1.5	217 ⑤
from Chassis No. 1144303	M 30 x 1.5	217 ⑤
Transmission carrier on frame	M 18 x 1.5	166
Spring plate/reduction gear housing screw (Type 2)	M 12 x 1.5	72-87
Additional torques for transmission and rear axle (Stickshift automatic)		
Temperature switch/ Selector switch/Starter inhibitor switch	M 14 x 1.5	18
Converter to drive plate screws	M 8 x 1.25	18
Retaining nut for taper roller bearing	M 80 x 1	159
Nut for converter housing	M 8 x 1.25	14
Screw for one-way clutch support	M 6 x 1	11 ⑥
Screw for clutch	M 6 x 1	11
Lock screw	M 8 x 1.25	7
Clamp screw for clutch lever	M 8 x 1.25	18
Screw for transmission oil pan and lock plate	M 7 x 1.25	7
Union for oil pressure line	M 12 x 1.5	25
Union for oil return line	M 14 x 1.5	25
Screw for drive shaft	M 8 x 1.25	25
Fitted screw in diagonal arm	M 14 x 1.5	87
Additional torques for transmission and rear axle (Type 3 Automatic)		
Screw for oil pump on transmission case	M 6 x 1	3
Screw for valve body on transmission case	M 6 x 1	3
Screw for transfer plate on valve body	M 5 x 0.8	2
Screw for oil strainer on valve body	M 6 x 1	2
Screw for oil pan on transmission case	M 8 x 1.25	7
Pin for operating lever on transmission case	M 10 x 1.5	4
Plug for pressure connections/transmission case	M 10 x 1	7

Torque Specifications— Transmission and Rear Axle

Fastener	Thread Size	Torque (ft.lbs.)
Vacuum unit/transmission case	M 14 x 1.5	18
Screw for bearing cap/ diff. carrier	M 10 x 1.5	40
Screw for ring gear/ differential housing	M 9 x 1	32
Screw for converter on drive plate	M 8 x 1.25	14
Screw for drive shaft on flange	M 8 x 1.25	25
Screw for front band	M 12 x 1.75	3.5 ⑦
Screw for rear band	M 12 x 1.75	3.5 ⑧
Lock nut for band adjusting screw	M 10 x 1.75	14
Nut for differential carrier on rear axle housing	M 6 x 1	6
Nut for side cover on rear axle housing	M 6 x 1	6
Nut for transmission/final drive housing	M 8 x 1.25	14
Nut and screw for spring plate	M 12 x 1.75	80
Screw for bearing cover	M 10 x 1.5	43
Fitted bolt for diagonal arm	M 10 x 1.5	87

Transmission and Rear Axle (fully synchronized) Type 2-from Chassis No. 218 000-001

Fastener	Thread Size	Torque (ft.lbs.)
Retaining ring for double taper roller bearing/ transmission case	M 80 x 1	109
Round nut/pinion	M 35 x 1.5	144
Union nut/clamp sleeve	M 14 x 1.5	18-22
Bracket/reverse shifter shaft on gear carrier	M 8 x 1.5	18
Support/rocket lever on on gear carrier	M 8 x 1.5	18
Shift fork on shift rod	M 8 x 1.25	18
Locking screw with dog point	M 8 x 1.25	11
Clamp sleeve on gear carrier	M 14 x 1.5	32
Shift housing on gear carrier	M 7 x 1	11
Nuts on gear carrier, transmission and clutch housing	M 8 x 1.25	68
Ring gear to differential housing	M 9 x 1	32
Double taper roller bearing retainer	M 9 x 1.25	22 ⑨
Final drive side covers	M 8 x 1.25	14
Brake back plate to housing	M 8	18
Brake back plate to housing	M 10	25
Slotted nut on rear wheel shaft	M 30 x 1.5	230-253 ⑩

Torque Specifications— Transmission and Rear Axle

Fastener	Thread Size	Torque (ft.lbs.)
Joint to flange (socket head screw)	M 8	25
Control arm to frame	M 12 x 1.5	58
Cover/spring plate mounting	M 10	32
Control arm to bearing housing	M 14 x 1.5	94
Shock absorber to frame and bearing housing	M 12 x 1.5	43

① The nut should be tightened and not backed off.

② First tighten to 108 ft. lbs., then back off and tighten to 36 ft. lbs.

③ Note tightening sequence, illustrated in Power Train Chapter.

④ Tighten first to 86 ft. lbs. then back off and finally tighten to 43 ft. lbs.

⑤ If cotter pin holes are not in line, tighten to a maximum of 250 ft. lbs. If hole is still not in line, fit a different nut.

⑥ Use new screws

⑦ Tighten to 7 ft. lbs. first, loosen and tighten again. Turn out 1 3/4 - 2 turns from this position.

⑧ Tighten to 7 ft. lbs. first, loosen and tighten again. Turn out 3 1/4 - 3 1/2 turns from this position.

⑨ Tighten to 32 ft.lbs. first, slacken off and tighten to 22 ft. lbs.

⑩ With reinforced spacer sleeve: at least 253 ft. lbs. then turn on to cotter pin hole.

Notes

8

SUSPENSION
AND STEERING

FRONT SUSPENSION

Each front wheel rotates on a ball joint mounted spindle (1966 - 69 models), or on a kingpin mounted spindle (1949 - 65 models). The spindle is suspended independently by a pair of torsion bars.

The principle of torsion bars is that of springing action taking place via twisting of the bars. When a front wheel goes up or down, the torsion bars are twisted, causing a downward or upward force in the opposite direction.

The supporting part of the Volkswagen front axle is the axle beam, which is two rigidly joined tubes attached to the frame with four screws. At each end of the tubes there is a side plate designed to provide additional strength and serve as the upper mounting point for the shock absorbers. Because the front axle is all-welded, it is replaced as a unit whenever damaged.

Torsion Bar

REMOVAL & INSTALLATION

1 Jack up the car and remove both wheels and brake drums.
2 On 1966 and later models, remove the ball joint nuts and remove the left and right steering knuckles. A forked ball joint removal tool is available at most auto parts stores. On 1965 and earlier models,

Use one of the torsion arms to pull the torsion bars out of the axle tube

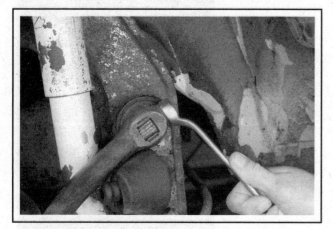

To detach a torsion arm from the torsion bar, loosen the locknut on the set screw on the inner end of the arm . . .

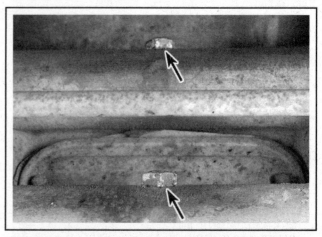

Remove the locknut which secures the torsion bar retaining bolt and remove the (8mm Allen) retaining bolt (if you're removing the upper bolt, you may find it necessary to grind down the short part of an L-shaped Allen wrench in order to get the wrench into the recessed head of the retaining bolt)

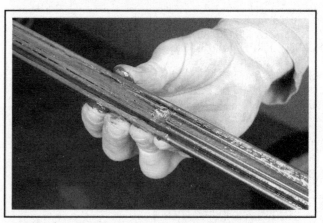

Before you insert the torsion bars through the axle tube, make sure they're aligned like this so that the recessed dimple is oriented toward the hole for the retaining bolt - when the bars are installed in the tube, the retaining bolt must seat into this dimple

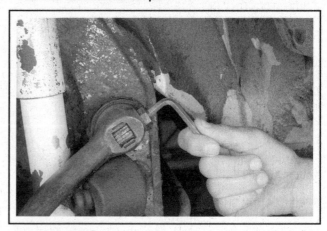

. . . loosen the set screw with an Allen wrench and pull the arm off

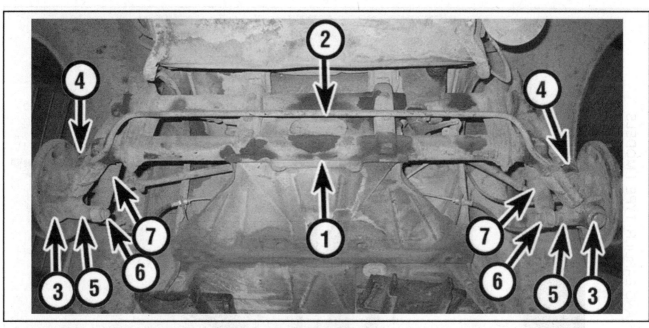

Component locations for a 1966 and later torsion bar front end assembly

1 Axle beam
2 Stabilizer bar
3 Lower balljoint
4 Upper balljoint
5 Steering knuckle
6 Shock absorber lower mounting nut
7 Shock absorber

1. Sway bar
2. Shock absorber mount
3. Lower torsion bar arm
4. Outer tie rod
5. Upper torsion bar arm
6. Mounting pin
7. Pinch pin
8. Kingpin bushing
9. Steering knuckle

Identification of front suspension components (1965 and earlier models)

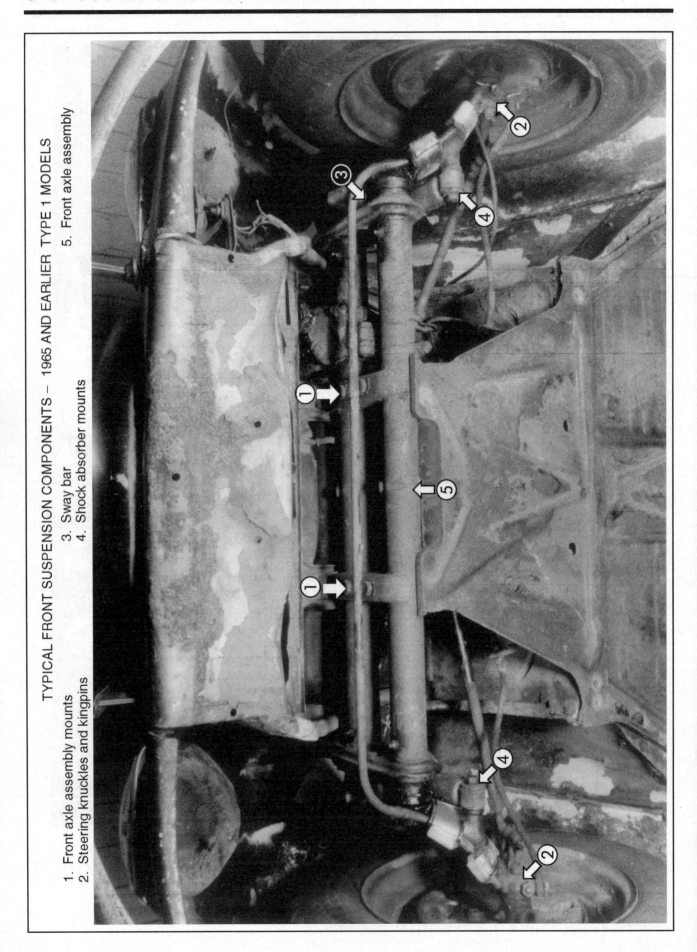

TYPICAL FRONT SUSPENSION COMPONENTS – 1965 AND EARLIER TYPE 1 MODELS

1. Front axle assembly mounts
2. Steering knuckles and kingpins
3. Sway bar
4. Shock absorber mounts
5. Front axle assembly

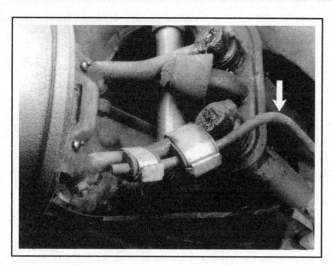

To remove the sway bar (arrow), first remove the wheel for added clearance . . .

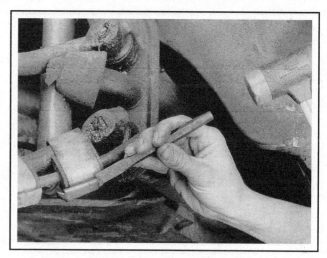

. . . then drive the clamp off of the bracket with a drift or chisel

remove the steering knuckles as described under King pin removal and installation later in this Section.

✳✳ WARNING:

Never strike the ball joint stud.

3 Remove the arms attached to the torsion bars on one side only. To remove the arms, loosen and remove the arm setscrew and pull the arm off the end of the torsion bar.

4 Loosen and remove the setscrew which secures the torsion bar to the torsion bar housing.

5 Pull the torsion bar out of its housing.

To install:

6 Carefully note the number of leaves and the position of the countersink marks for the torsion bar and the torsion arm.

7 Align the countersink mark in the center of the bar with the hole for the setscrew and insert the torsion bar into its housing. Install the setscrew. Install the torsion arm.

8 Reverse Steps 1 - 3 to complete.

Torsion Arm

REMOVAL & INSTALLATION

1 Jack up the car and remove the wheel and tire.

2 Remove the brake drum and the steering knuckle.

3 If the lower torsion arm is being removed, disconnect the stabilizer (sway) bar. To remove the stabilizer bar clamp, tap the wedge-shaped keeper toward the outside of the car or in the direction the narrow end of the keeper is pointing.

4 On Types 1 and 2, back off on the setscrew locknut and remove the setscrew. On Type 3's, remove the bolt and keeper from the end of the torsion bar.

5 Slide the torsion arm off the end of the torsion bar.

6 Installation is the reverse of the removal procedure. Check the camber and toe-in settings.

Hold onto the clamps for installation

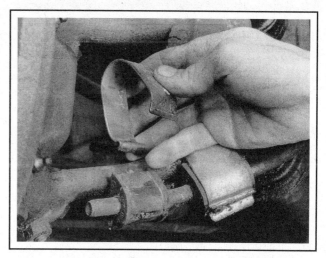

After removing both clamps, remove the two brackets . . .

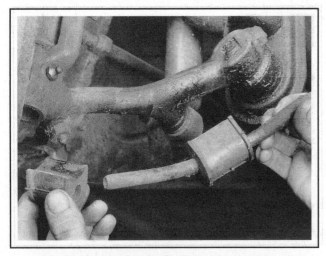

. . . and slide the rubber bushings off of the sway bar

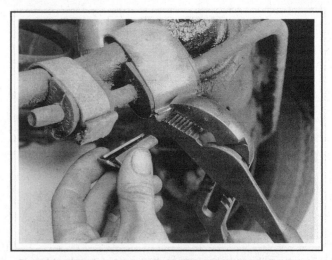

During installation, use a pair of pliers to compress the brackets enough to install the clamps

To remove the front shock absorber, first remove the lower mounting bolt . . .

. . . then loosen . . .

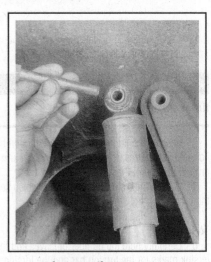

. . . and remove the upper mounting bolt

Shock Absorber

REMOVAL & INSTALLATION

1 Remove the wheel and tire.

2 Remove the nut from the torsion arm stud and slide the lower end of the shock off of the stud.

3 Remove the nut from the shock absorber shaft at the upper mounting and remove the shock from the vehicle.

4 The shock is tested by operating it by hand. As the shock is extended and compressed, it should operate smoothly over its entire stroke with an even pressure. Its damping action should be clearly felt at the end of each stroke. If the shock is leaking slightly, the shock need not be replaced. A shock that has had an excessive loss of fluid will have flat spots in the stroke as the shock is compressed and extended. That is, the pressure will feel as though it has been suddenly released for a short distance during the stroke.

5 Installation is the reverse of Steps 1-3.

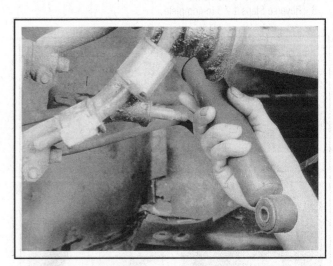

Remove the shock absorber from the vehicle

This illustration shows how much offset between the torsion arms can be created with various shim combinations: The letters "A", "B", "C" and "D" above each column on the chart refer to the four points - two inner and two outer - at which the linkpins can be shimmed (if you haven't lost any shims, and you put them all back on at the same locations, the camber should be the same as it was before you removed the steering knuckle)

1959 and earlier models (10 shims)

| | Washers installed on linkpins at: | | | |
	A	B	C	D
Offset (mm)				
5	3	7	7	3
5.5	3	6	7	3
6	4	6	6	4
6.5	5	5	6	4
7	5	5	5	5
7.5	6	4	5	5
8	6	4	4	6
8.5	7	3	4	6
9	7	3	3	7

1960 and later models (8 shims)

| | Washers installed on linkpins at: | | | |
	A	B	C	D
Offset (mm)				
5.5	2	6	5	3
6	2	6	4	4
6.5	3	5	4	4
7	3	5	3	5
7.5	4	4	3	5
8	4	4	2	6
8.5	5	3	2	6

King Pin

REMOVAL & INSTALLATION

➡**Only 1949 - 65 models are equipped with king pins. 1966 - 69 models are equipped with ball joints.**

1 Loosen the front wheel lug nuts and brake drum center nut while the vehicle rests on the ground.

2 Apply the parking brake, block the rear wheels, then raise and safely support the front of the vehicle on jackstands.

3 Remove the front wheel.

4 Remove the brake drum and brake components, including the backing plate.

5 Remove the two pinch bolts and nuts from the steering knuckle, then remove the two mounting pins. Drive the pin bushings out of their bosses with a hammer and drift.

6 If the pins are damaged while removing them, they must be replaced with new ones.

7 Remove the steering knuckle from the two torsion bar ends.

8 Position the steering knuckle in a padded vise and drive the king pin out of its boss.

9 Separate the spindle from the knuckle.

10 Installation is the reverse of the removal procedure. When installing the knuckle-to-torsion bar pin bushings, make certain that the grease holes in the pin bushings are aligned with the grease fittings in the knuckle housing.

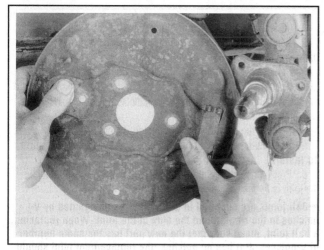

To remove the steering knuckle, remove the brake components and backing plate . . .

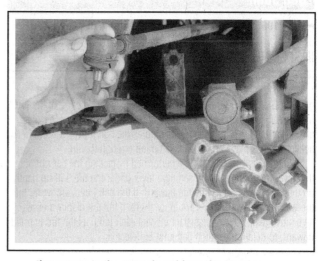

. . . then separate the outer tie rod from the steering knuckle arm

Remove the pinch bolts and nuts . . .

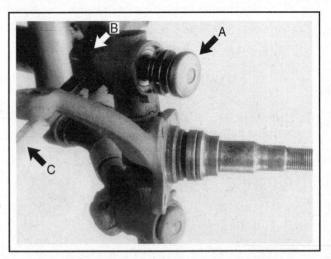

. . . then slide the mounting pins (A) out while opening the housing (B) with a prybar (C)

Remove the steering knuckle from the two torsion bars

When working on the steering knuckle and king pins, lay the parts out to prevent confusion

Ball Joint

➡Only 1966 - 69 models are equipped with ball joints.

INSPECTION

A quick initial inspection can be made with the vehicle on the ground. Grasp the top of the tire and vigorously pull the top of the tire in and out. Test both sides in this manner. If the ball joints are excessively worn, there will be an audible tap as the ball moves around in its socket. Excess play can sometimes be felt through the tire.

A more rigorous test may be performed by jacking the car under the lower torsion arm and inserting a lever under the tire. Lift up gently on the lever so as to pry the tire upward. If the ball joints are worn, the tire will move upward 1/8 - 1/4 in. or more. If the tire displays excessive movement, have an assistant inspect each joint, as the tire is pried upward, to determine which ball joint is defective.

REPLACEMENT

1 Jack up the car and remove the wheel and tire.
2 Remove the brake drum and disconnect the brake line from the backing plate.
3 Remove the nut from each ball joint stud and remove the ball joint stud from the steering knuckle. Remove the steering knuckle from the car. A ball joint removal tool is available at most auto parts stores. Do not strike the ball joint stud.
4 Remove the torsion arm from the torsion bar.
5 Remove the ball joint from the torsion arm by pressing it out.
To install:
6 Press a new ball joint in, making sure that the square notch in the joint is in line with the notch in the torsion arm eye.

➡Ball joints are supplied in different sizes designated by V-notches in the ring around the side of the joint. When replacing a ball joint, make sure that the new part has the same number of V-notches. If it has no notches, the replacement joint should have no notches.

7 Reverse Steps 1 - 4 to complete the installation.

Front Wheel Bearings

REMOVAL & INSTALLATION

1 Jack up the car and remove the wheel and tire.
2 Remove the caliper and disc (if equipped with disc brakes) or brake drum.
3 To remove the inside wheel bearing, pry the dust seal out of the hub with a prytool. Lift out the bearing and its inner race.
4 To remove the outer race for either the inner or outer wheel bearing, insert a long punch into the hub opposite the end from which the race is to be removed. The race rests against a shoulder in the hub. The shoulder has two notches cut into it so that it is possible to place the end of the punch directly against the back side of the race and drive it out of the hub.
5 Carefully clean the hub.
6 Install new races in the hub. Drive them in with a soft faced hammer or a large piece of pipe of the proper diameter. Lubricate the races with a light coating of wheel bearing grease.
7 Force wheel bearing grease into the sides of the tapered roller bearings so that all spaces are filled.
8 Place a small amount of grease inside the hub.
9 Place the inner wheel bearing into its race in the hub and tap a new seal into the hub. Lubricate the sealing surface of the seal with grease.
10 Install the hub on the spindle and install the outer wheel bearing.
11 Adjust the wheel bearing and install the dust cover.
12 Install the caliper (if equipped with disc brakes).

ADJUSTMENT

The bearing may be adjusted by feel or by a dial indicator.

To adjust the bearing by feel, tighten the adjusting nut so that all the play is taken up in the bearing. There will be a slight amount of drag on the wheel if it is hand spun. Back off fully on the adjusting nut and retighten very lightly. There should be no drag when the wheel is hand spun and there should be no perceptible play in the bearing when the wheel is grasped and wiggled from side to side.

To use a dial indicator, remove the dust cover and mount a dial indicator against the hub. Grasp the wheel at the side and pull the wheel in and out along the axis of the spindle. Read the axial play on the dial indicator. Screw the adjusting nut in or out to obtain 0.001 - 0.005 in. of axial play. Secure the adjusting nut and recheck the axial play.

Front End Alignment

GENERAL INFORMATION

The critical geometrical angles in the front end of the Volkswagen vary significantly from model to model and even change somewhat from early models to later models. Because of the importance of these angles to the safe operation of the car, it is suggested that adjustments be left to one's local VW workshop. However, for the enlightenment of technical-minded readers, a description of the relevant angles follows:

Camber is the angle, viewed from the front of the car, that the wheel is inclined from the vertical.

King pin inclination is the angle between a line perpendicular to the road and the pivot point of the steering knuckle.

Caster is the angle, viewed from the side, between the pivot point of

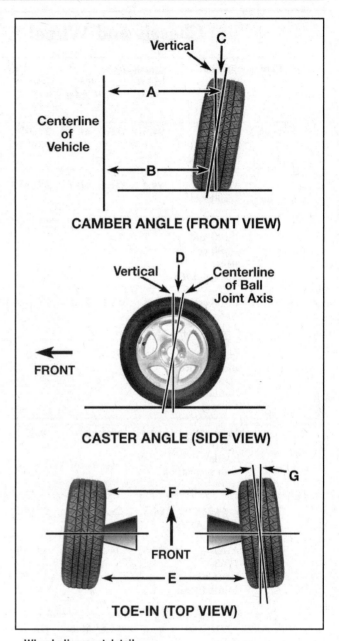

Wheel alignment details

A minus B = C (degrees camber)
D = degrees caster
E minus F = oe-in (measured in inches)
G = toe-in (expressed in degrees)

the steering knuckle and the vertical line through the wheel center.

Caster helps to bring the wheels back to the straight-ahead position after they have been turned. If the caster angle is too small, the result will be a tendency for the car to wander and be excessively influenced by cross winds and uneven road surfaces.

If the camber angle is too great, steering will be difficult, for the wheels will have a very strong tendency to remain in the straight-ahead position.

Toe-in is the difference in the distance between the rear of the front wheels and the front of the front wheels when the car is facing forward. Toe-in causes the front wheels to be "pigeon-toed" when the car is stationary. However, when the car is moving, the wheels move in parallel

Chassis and Wheel Alignment Specifications

Vehicle	Model	Chassis (in.)			Wheel Alignment					Wheel Pivot Ratio (deg.)	
		Wheel-base	Track Front	Track Rear	Caster (deg.) (or in.)	Camber (deg.)	Toe-in (in.) (or deg.) ④	King-Pin Inclination (deg.)	Rear Wheel Camber (deg.)	Inner Wheel	Outer Wheel
Type 1	25 hp. and 36 hp. 1,200cc.	94.5	51	49.2	2°30' ±30'	0°40' ±30'	.04-.12	4°20'	NA	NA	NA
	42 hp. 1,200cc.	94.5	51.4	50.7	2°±15'	0°40' ±30'	.08-.16	4°20'	3°±30'	34	28
	42hp. 1,200 and 1,300 cc.- after August, 1965	94.5	51.4	51.2	2°±15'	0°30' ±15'	.08-.18	4°20'	3°±30' ①	34	28
	1,500 cc. -Swing Axles	94.5	51.4	53.5	2°±15'	0°30' ±15'	.08 -.18	4°20'	① 1°±1°	34	28
	1,500cc. and 1,600cc - Double Jointed Rear Axles	94.5	51.57	NA	3°20' ±1°	30' ±20'	30'± 15	5°	-1°20' ±40'	34±2	28-1
	1971 Super Beetle with suspension struts	95.3	54.3	53.2	.008 in.	1°20' ±20'	20' ±15	NA	-1°20' ±40'	40	35
Type 2	Pre-1968 -Swing Axles	94.5	54.1	53.5	3°±40'	40 ±30'	±.04 (5'±10')	NA	3°±30' ②	NA	NA
	After 1968- Double Jointed Rear Axles	94.5	54.5	56.2	3°±40'	40'±15'	10' ±10'	5°	-50' ±30'	32	24
	1971 -Disc brakes	94.5	54.6	56.6	NA	NA	NA	NA	NA	NA	NA
Type 3	With Swing Axles	94.5	51.58	52.99	4°±40'	1°20' ±20'	40' ±5'	NA	2°30' ±1° ③	NA	NA
	With Double Jointed Rear Axles	94.5	51.58	53.14	4°±40'	1°20' ±20 '	40' ±15'	5°10'	-1°20' ±40'	30	27-1

NA - Information not available
① *1967 sedan: 1°±1°*
  1967 Karmann Ghia and VW convertible: 15'±1°
② *After chassis No. 117 901:*
  Van: 4°±30'
  Kombi: 3°30'±30'
  Bus: 3°±30'
③ *1967 and later Notchback and Type 3 Karmann Ghia: 1°45'±1°*
④

Size Wheel	10' toe-in equals :
14in.	.043 in.
15in.	.047 in.
16in.	.051 in.

due to being forced outward at the front by camber, rolling resistance, wheel bearing play and other factors. Toe-out occurs naturally when the wheel is turned in cornering so that there is a common center point around which all four wheels will turn when a curve is negotiated. If the critical angles are not what they should be, the result will be excessive tire scuffing and wear.

CASTER ADJUSTMENT

Caster is the forward or backward tilt of the spindle. Forward tilt is negative caster and backward tilt is positive caster. Caster is not adjustable on the torsion bar suspensions.

CAMBER ADJUSTMENT

Camber is the tilt of the top of the wheel, inward or outward, from true vertical. Outward tilt is positive, inward tilt is negative.

The upper ball joint on each side (on ball joint suspensions) is mounted in an eccentric bushing. The bushing has a hex head and it may be rotated in either direction using a wrench.

TOE-IN ADJUSTMENT

Toe-in is the adjustment made to make the front wheels point slightly into the front. Toe-in is adjusted on all types of front suspensions by adjusting the length of the tie-rod sleeves.

DIAGONAL ARM REAR SUSPENSION

The rear wheels of Types 1, 2, and 3 models are independently sprung by means of torsion bars. The inside ends of the torsion bars are anchored to a body crossmember via a splined tube which is welded to the frame. The torsion bar at each side of the rear suspension has a different number of splines at each end. This makes possible the adjustment of the rear suspension.

On Type 3 models and 1967 and later Type 1 models, an equalizer bar, located above the rear axle, is used to aid the handling qualities and lateral stability of the rear axle. This bar also acts progressively to soften bumps in proportion to their size.

Swing Axle Rear Suspension

The rear wheels of the Volkswagen are independently sprung by means of torsion bars. The inside ends of the torsion bars are anchored

to a body cross member via a splined tube which is welded to the frame. The torsion bar at each side of the rear suspension has a different number of splines at each end. This makes possible the adjustment of the rear suspension.

The torsion bars of different models may be slightly different in diameter, depending on the loads designed to be carried. For example, the torsion bars at the rear of the 1967 type 1 are 21mm. in diameter compared to 23mm. for the Squareback sedan. The length of the torsion bar also has an effect on its springing properties, and Volkswagens have, through the years and models, had torsion bars ranging in length from 21.7" (1967 type 1) to 24.7" (the first type 1 produced).

The suspension of the Squareback sedan is reinforced by a transverse torsion bar which is located above the rear axle. This bar acts progressively to soften the bumps in proportion to their size, and also to add to the handling qualities and lateral stability of the rear axle. This reinforcing spring is also present on all 1967 and 1968 models. For earlier models, there is available an accessory known as the "Camber Compensator."

This device is a transverse leaf spring which is installed below the rear axle. It reduces oversteer by resisting the tendency of the rear wheels to tuck under the body on hard cornering.

The rear shock absorbers of the Volkswagen are of the double-acting type which dampen the shocks of the road as well as prevent excessive rebound when the wheel(s) are in the unloaded position.

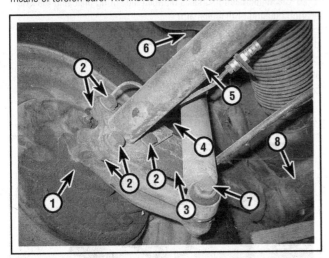

(8-15) Rear suspension details on a swing axle model

1   Bearing housing
2   Axle tube-to-spring plate fasteners
3   Spring plate
4   Bump stop
5   Axle tube
6   Shock absorber upper mounting bolt
7   Shock absorber lower mounting bolt
8   Torsion housing

Spring plates and rear torsion bars - removal, installation and adjustment

REMOVAL

1   Loosen the rear wheel lug bolts, raise the rear of the vehicle, place it securely on jackstands and remove the wheels.

2   On driveaxle models, remove the driveaxle (see Chapter 8).

3   Disconnect the parking brake cables at the parking brake lever (see Chapter 9).

4   On swing axle models, mark the relationship of the spring plate to the axle bearing housing with a chisel.

5   On driveaxle models, mark the relationship of the spring plate to the diagonal arm with a chisel.

6   Disconnect the lower end of the shock absorber (see Section 12).

7   On swing axle models, remove the bolts securing the spring plate

to the axle tube. Pull the axle tube to the rear, out of the spring plate. Suspend the axle tube with a piece of wire or support it on a jackstand.

8   On driveaxle models, remove the bolts securing the spring plate to the diagonal arm. Remove the diagonal arm pivot bolt and the diagonal arm (see Section 15).

9   Remove the bolts securing the spring plate hub cover and remove the cover. Also remove the rubber bushing (see illustration). Warning: The spring plate is under tremendous spring pressure. DO NOT place any part of your body under the spring plate while performing the next step, or anytime the spring plate hub cover is removed and the spring plate is resting on its stop.

10   Place a floor jack under the end of the spring plate and raise it just until it comes off the stop. Lever the spring plate out away from the vehicle using a prybar, while simultaneously lowering the jack until the spring plate has reached the end of its travel and the torsion bar is relaxed. Pull the spring plate off the torsion bar.

11   Remove the bolts that secure the forward and top part of the fender. Pull the front part of the fender to allow the torsion bar to come out.

12   Carefully slide the torsion bar out. Check it for nicks or cracks. Sometimes cracks may not be visible to the eye, so it's a good idea to have them checked by a dealer service department, automotive machine shop or other repair shop that is equipped to do the work.

INSTALLATION AND ADJUSTMENT

13   Grease the splines on the torsion bar and carefully guide it into the torsion housing until you feel the splines engage.
Note: Torsion bars are marked L (left) and R (right). If you have removed both torsion bars, make sure you install them on the correct side.

14   Coat the inner and outer rubber bushings with talcum powder to prevent the spring plate from turning them.

15   Install the inner bushing with the word "Oben" at the top. Note that the inner bushing is different from the outer bushing - don't mix them up.

16   Install the spring plate.

17   To ensure proper wheel alignment and sufficient spring travel under varying loads, the spring plate must be adjusted on the torsion bar. There are 40 splines on the inner end and 44 splines on the outer end of the torsion bar. If you rotate the inner end of the bar one spline, it alters the spring plate angle 9-degrees, 0-minutes; if you rotate the

spring plate one spline on the bar, it alters the angle 8-degrees, 10-minutes. So, you can set the spring plate at any multiple of 50-minutes by rotating the splines in opposite directions. VW has a special tool for this job, but it's expensive and hard to find. Using the following procedure, you can adjust the spring plate with easily obtainable tools. Note: Be sure to adjust both spring plates, even if only one has been removed, especially on a high mileage vehicle.

18   Measure the spring plate angle in relation to the bottom of the door opening or the frame tunnel. Of course, it's unlikely that either the door opening or the frame tunnel are level, since the rear of the vehicle is elevated. First, you need to determine the angle at which the vehicle is inclined from the horizontal.

19   Place a protractor (angle finder) on the frame tunnel (see illustration). Prop up the opposite end of the level until its bubble is centered. Note the angle of the tunnel and record this measurement.

20   Now place the protractor (angle finder) on top of the spring plate, lift the spring plate by hand slightly to remove any play, then measure the spring plate angle. Again, record your measurement.

21   Subtract the angle you measured in Step 19 from the angle you measured in Step 20. The difference should equal the spring plate angle listed in this Chapter's Specifications for model and year of the vehicle. If it doesn't, rotate the inner end of the torsion bar on its splines, or rotate the spring plate on the torsion bar, or both, until the correct angle is attained.

22   Coat the outer rubber bushing with talcum powder and install it with the word "oben" at the top.

23   Install the spring plate hub cover and loosely install the bolts.

24   Using a floor jack, lift the spring plate until its lower edge clears the lower stop.
Note: If the vehicle begins to raise up off the jackstand, it'll be necessary to secure the vehicle to the floor jack with a length of heavy-duty chain.

25   Tighten the spring plate hub cover bolts securely.

26   Clean the mating surfaces between the spring plate and the axle bearing housing or diagonal arm.

27   Install the spring plate-to-bearing housing or spring plate-to-diagonal arm bolts (and the diagonal arm pivot bolt), make sure the chisel marks on the spring plate and bearing housing or diagonal arm are aligned and tighten the bolts to the torque listed in this Chapter's Specifications.

28   On driveaxle models, install the driveaxle (see Chapter 8).

29   Reattach the parking brake cable and adjust it (see Chapter 9).

On swing axle models, mark the spring plate position in relation to the housing for the rear axle bearing

On driveaxle models, mark the spring plate position in relation to the diagonal arm

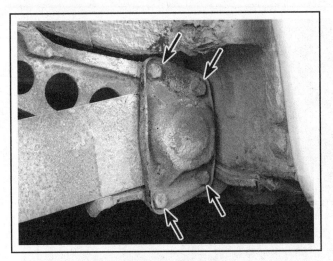

Remove the cover for the spring plate hub

Remove the rubber bushing from the hub

Place a protractor (angle finder) on the tunnel to measure the angle at which the vehicle is setting

Lift the spring plate slightly to remove any freeplay, place the protractor (angle finder) on top of the spring plate and record the indicated angle

30 Install the fender.

31 Install the wheel(s), lower the vehicle and tighten the wheel lug bolts to the torque listed in the Chapter 1 Specifications.

32 If you installed a new spring plate, have the wheel alignment checked and, if necessary, adjusted.

Double Jointed Axle Rear Suspension

This rear suspension system was first introduced on the 1968 type 2 and on the Automatic Stickshift type 1. The axle shafts each have two constant velocity joints. The rear wheels are located by trailing arms as on swing axle models, and by diagonal control arms from the rear crossmember. The axle shafts and final drive therefore do not absorb any thrust forces. In this design, there is only a very slight change in rear wheel track and camber during suspension travel. This results in more stable handling, since rear wheel traction remains constant regardless of the suspension position.

Shock Absorber

REMOVAL & INSTALLATION

The shock absorber is secured at the top and bottom by a through-bolt. Raise the car and remove the bolts. Remove the shock absorber from the car.

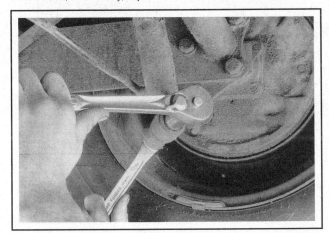

To remove the rear shock absorber, loosen the lower mounting bolt and nut . . .

COMMON REAR SWING AXLE SUSPENSION COMPONENTS

1. Trailing suspension arms
2. Upper shock absorber mounts
3. Lower shock absorber mounts
4. Halfshafts

. . . then slide the bolt out and
separate the shock from the
lower mount

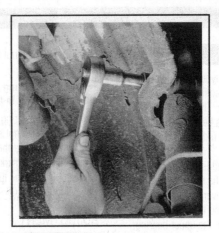

Remove the upper mounting bolt . . .

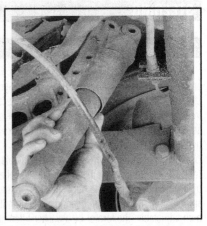

. . . and lower the shock absorber
from the vehicle

Diagonal Arm

REMOVAL & INSTALLATION

1   Remove the wheel shaft nuts.

✳✳ CAUTION:

**Do not raise the car to remove the nuts. They can be safely
removed only if the weight of the car is on its wheels.**

2   Disconnect the driveshaft on the side to be removed.

3   Remove the lower shock absorber mount. Raise the car and
remove the wheel and tire.

4   Remove the brake drum, disconnect the brake lines and emergency brake cable, and remove the backing plate.

5   Matchmark the torsion bar plate and the diagonal arm with a cold
chisel.

6   Remove the four bolts and nuts which secure the plate to the
diagonal arm.

7   Remove the pivot bolts for the diagonal arm and remove the arm
from the car.

➡**Take careful note of the washers at the pivot bolts. These
washers are used to determine alignment and they must be put
back in the same place.**

8   Remove the spring plate hub cover.

9   Using a steel bar, lift the spring plate off of the lower suspension
stop.

10   On Type 1 models, remove the five bolts at the front of the fender.
On all others, remove the cover in the side of the fender.

11   Remove the spring plate and pull the torsion bar out of its housing.

➡**There are left and right torsion bars designated by an (L) or
(R) on the end face. (Coat any rubber bushings with talcum powder upon installation. Do not use graphite, silicon, or grease.**

To install:

12   Insert the torsion bar, outer bushing, and spring plate. Make sure
that the marks you made earlier line up.

13   Using two bolts, loosely secure the spring plate hub cover. Place

a thick nut between the leaves of the spring plate.

14   Lift the spring plate up to the lower suspension stop and install
the remaining bolts into the hub cover. Tighten the hub cover bolts.

15   Install the diagonal arm pivot bolt and washers and peen it with a
chisel. There must always be at least one washer on the outside end of
the bolt.

16   Align the chisel marks and attach the diagonal arm to the spring
plate.

17   Install the backing plate, parking brake cable, and brake lines.

18   Reconnect the shock absorber. Install the brake drum and wheel
shaft nuts.

19   Reconnect the driveshaft. Bleed the brakes.

20   Install the wheel and tire.

21   Check the suspension alignment.

Adjustments

TYPE 1

The only adjustment possible is the toe-in adjustment. The adjustment is performed by varying the number of washers at the diagonal
arm pivot. There must always be one washer located on the outboard
side of the pivot.

TYPES 2 & 3

The transaxle and engine assembly position in the vehicle is adjustable. It is necessary that the assembly be correctly centered before the
suspension is aligned. It may be adjusted by moving the engine and
transaxle brackets in their elongated slots.

The distance between the diagonal arms may be adjusted by moving
the washers at the A-arm pivots. The washers may be positioned only
two ways. Either both washers on the outboard side of the pivot or a
single washer on each side of the pivot. To adjust the distance, position
the diagonal arms and move the washers in the same manner at both
pivots.

The wheel track angle may be adjusted by moving the diagonal arm
flange in the elongated slot in the spring plate.

The toe-in is adjusted by positioning the washers and the diagonal
arm pivot.

STEERING

General Information

Type 1 and 3 steering is of the roller type. The type 2 uses worm and peg steering. All models since 1968 have collapsible or breakaway steering column arrangements for crash protection. The movements of the steering wheel are transmitted to the wheels via tie rods which are adjustable and maintenance-free. Road shocks are reduced through a hydraulic steering damper.

The worm in the steering case is adjustable, and is engaged by a roller shaft with a needle bearing mounted roller. The roller shaft is held by bronze bushings in the housing and housing cover, while the worm spindle is mounted in ball bearings. The spindle and the roller shaft are both adjustable, the former by a washer fitted under the upper bearing, and the latter by a screw in the housing cover.

Steering Wheel

REMOVAL & INSTALLATION

1 Disconnect the negative battery cable.
2 Remove the center emblem. This emblem will gently pry off the wheel, or is attached by screws from the back of the steering wheel.

3 Remove the nut from the steering shaft. This is a right-hand thread.

➡**Mark the steering shaft and steering wheel so that the wheel may be installed in the same position on the shaft.**

4 Using a steering wheel puller, remove the wheel from the splined steering shaft. Do not strike the end of the steering shaft.
5 Installation is the reverse of the removal procedure. Make sure to align the matchmarks made on the steering wheel and steering shaft. The gap between the turn signal switch housing and the back of the wheel should be 0.08 - 0.12 in.

ADJUSTMENT

If the steering wheel spokes are not parallel to the floor of the car when the car is being driven in a straight line, it is necessary to reposition the wheel. This should never be carried out by simply altering the position of the wheel on the column. It requires that one tie rod be lengthened and the other shortened by the same amount. If the tie rod lengths are not changed by the same amount, the result will be a change in the toe-in of the car. The diagrams shown illustrate the direction in which to turn the two tie rods in case the steering wheel is slanted in either direction.

To remove the steering wheel, first remove the horn cover . . .

. . . then detach the horn wire

Remove the steering wheel mounting nut . . .

. . . and matchmark the wheel to the steering column

Remove the mounting nut washer . . .

. . . then slide the steering wheel off of the steering shaft

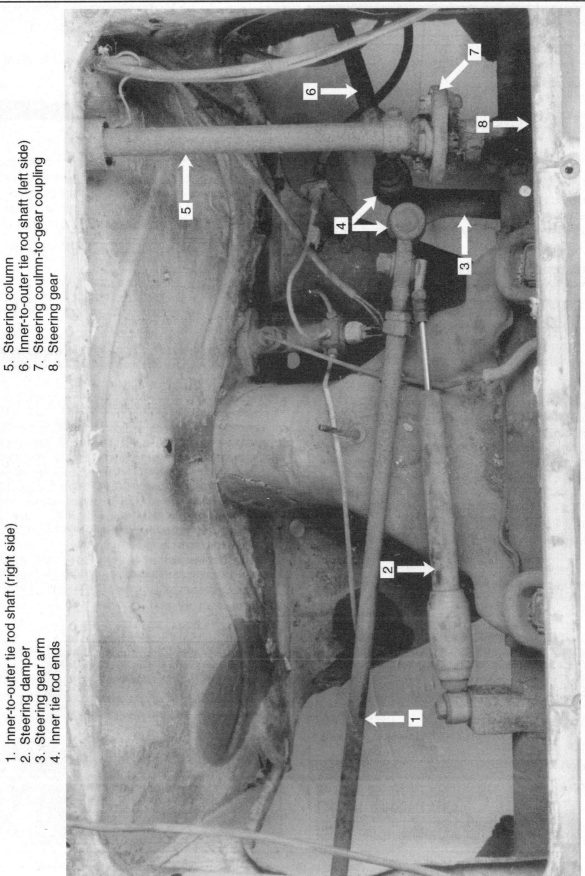

TYPICAL STEERING COMPONENTS – TYPE 1 MODELS

1. Inner-to-outer tie rod shaft (right side)
2. Steering damper
3. Steering gear arm
4. Inner tie rod ends
5. Steering column
6. Inner-to-outer tie rod shaft (left side)
7. Steering coulmn-to-gear coupling
8. Steering gear

Turn Signal Switch

REMOVAL & INSTALLATION

1 Disconnect the negative battery cable.
2 Remove the steering wheel.
3 Remove the four turn signal switch securing screws.
4 Disconnect the turn signal switch wiring plug under the steering column.
5 Pull the switch and wiring guide rail up and out of the steering column.
6 Installation is the reverse of the removal procedure. Make sure the spacers located behind the switch, if installed originally, are in position. The distance between the steering wheel and the steering column housing is 0.08 - 0.12 in. Install the switch with the lever in the central position.

Ignition Switch

REMOVAL & INSTALLATION

1 Disconnect the steering column wiring at the block located behind the instrument panel and pull the column wiring harness into the passenger compartment.
2 Remove the steering wheel.
3 Remove the circlip on the steering shaft.
4 Disconnect the negative battery cable.
5 Insert the key and turn the switch to the **ON** position. On Type 3 vehicles it is necessary to remove the fuse box.
6 Remove the three securing screws and slide the switch assembly from the steering column tube.

➡**It is not necessary to remove the turn signal switch at this time. If it is necessary to remove the switch from the housing, continue with the disassembly procedure.**

7 Remove the turn signal switch.
8 After removing the wiring retainer, press the ignition switch wiring block upward and out of the housing and disconnect the wiring.
9 Remove the lock cylinder and the steering lock mechanism.
10 Remove the ignition switch screw and pull the ignition switch rearward.

11 Installation is the reverse of the removal procedure. When reinstalling the turn signal switch, make sure the lever is in the center position.

➡**The distance between the steering wheel and the ignition switch housing should be 0.08 - 0.12 in. (2 - 3mm).**

Ignition Lock Cylinder

REMOVAL & INSTALLATION

1 Proceed with Steps 1 - 8 in the Ignition Switch procedure.
2 With the key in the cylinder and turned to the **ON** position, pull the lock cylinder out far enough so the securing pin can be depressed through a hole in the side of the lock cylinder housing. Use a steel wire to depress the pin.
3 As the pin is depressed, pull the lock cylinder out of its housing.
To install:
4 Gently push the cylinder into its housing. Make sure the pin engages correctly and that the retainer fits easily in place. Do not force any parts together; when they are correctly aligned, they will fit easily together.

Steering Linkage

REMOVAL & INSTALLATION

All tie-rod ends are secured by a nut which holds the tapered tie-rod end stud into a matching tapered hole. There are several ways to remove the tapered stud from its hole after the nut has been removed.

First, there are several types of removal tools available from auto parts stores. These tools include directions for their use. One of the most commonly available tools is the fork-shaped tool, which is a wedge that is forced under the tie-rod end. This tool should be used with caution because instead of removing the tie-rod end from its hole it may pull the ball out of its socket, ruining the tie-rod end.

It is also possible to remove the tie-rod end by holding a heavy hammer on one side of the tapered hole and striking the opposite side of the hole sharply with another hammer. The stud will pop out of its hole.

To remove the outer tie rod, first remove the cotter pin . . .

. . . then loosen the tie rod retaining nut

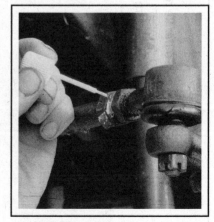
Matchmark the position of the tie rod in relation to the inner tie rod shaft . . .

. . . then loosen the inner-to-outer tie rod mounting nut

Remove the outer tie rod-to-knuckle retaining nut, then use a separator tool . . .

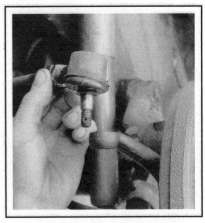

. . . and remove the tie rod from the steering knuckle

Use a large pair of pliers to turn the outer tie rod off of the inner tie rod shaft

✳✳ WARNING:

Never strike the end of the tie-rod end stud. It is impossible to remove the tie-rod end in this manner.

Once the tie-rod end stud has been removed, turn the tie-rod end out of the adjusting sleeve. On the pieces of the steering linkage that are not used to adjust the toe-in, the tie-rod end is welded in place and it will be necessary to replace the whole assembly.

When reassembling the steering linkage, never put lubricant in the tapered hole.

Manual Steering Gear

ADJUSTMENT

There are two types of adjustable steering gear units. The first type is the roller type, identified by the square housing cover secured by four screws, one at each corner. The second type is the worm and peg type, identified by an asymmetric housing cover with the adjusting screw located at one side of the housing cover.

Worm and Roller Type

To adjust axial play of the worm

1   From underneath the front of the vehicle, turn the steering column U-joint coupling back and forth from left to right and watch the section of the pinion between the U-joint flange and the steering gear.

2   Loosen the locknut for the steering worm adjuster.

3   Turn the steering worm back and forth at the steering coupling while simultaneously tightening the adjuster until all play in the worm is removed.

4   Hold the adjuster and tighten the locknut to the torque listed in this Chapter's Specifications.

5   Turn the steering worm from lock to lock. It should rotate smoothly, with no "tight spots." If there are, the adjuster is too tight. Loosen it a little and check again. If you can't eliminate play by adjusting the worm, try adjusting the play between the roller and the worm.

To adjust play between the roller and the worm

1   Turn the steering wheel 90-degrees to the left or right of its centered position.

2   Raise the luggage compartment hood, remove the spare tire and remove the access panel for the steering gear.

3   Loosen the locknut for the roller shaft adjustment screw. Loosen the adjustment screw about one turn.

4   Tighten the adjustment screw until you feel the roller touching the steering worm.

5   Hold the adjustment screw and tighten the locknut securely.

6   With the vehicle on the ground, check the adjustment with the wheel turned 90-degrees to each side. Play must not exceed one inch at the circumference of the steering wheel. If there's more play on one side than the other, readjust the roller to worm play for that side.

7   Road test the vehicle. Carefully negotiate a corner at 10 to 12 mph. The steering should return to within 45-degrees of its centered position after you exit the corner. If it doesn't, the roller is still too tight. Repeat the adjustment procedure or the worm and roller will be damaged.

8   If you can't get the steering to perform as specified after several attempts to readjust the play between the worm and roller, the axial play of the steering roller must be checked. This is a job for the dealer service department or other repair shop, because adjustment requires special tools and disassembly of the steering gear.

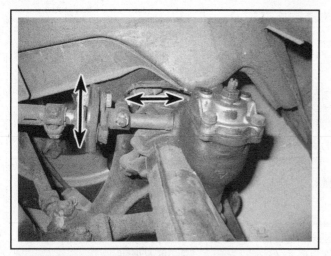

Turn the steering wheel column U-joint flange back and forth, from left to right, and watch the section of the pinion between the U-joint and the steering gear - if it moves up and down (arrow), adjust the axial play of the worm

Loosen the locknut (A) for the steering worm adjuster (B). A special tool is available to turn the adjuster, but an alternative can be made from a large bolt and two nuts tightened up against each other

Worm and Peg Type

Have an assistant turn the steering wheel back and forth through the center position several times. The steering wheel should turn through the center position without any noticeable binding.

To adjust, turn the adjusting screw inward while the assistant is turning the steering wheel. Turn the screw in until the steering begins to tighten up. Back out the adjusting screw until the steering no longer binds while turning through the center point, then tighten the adjusting screw locknut.

The adjustment is correct when there is no binding and no perceptible play.

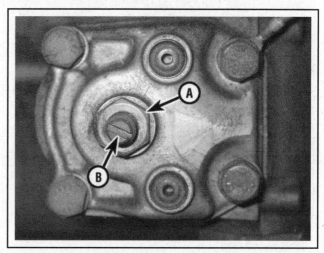

Loosen the locknut (A) for the roller shaft adjustment screw (B) and turn the screw out about one turn, then tighten the screw until you feel the roller touching the worm

Torque Specifications

Fastener	Thread Size	Torque (ft.lbs.)
Steering damper/frame bolt and nut (up to Chassis No. 851 389)	M 10 x 45	32
Steering damper/axle tube screw (from Chassis No. 851 390)	M 10 x 40	29-32
Steering damper/ swing lever screw	M 10 x 72	29-32
Setscrew for torsion bars	M 14 x 1.5	29
Lock nut for setscrew	M 14 x 1.5	29
Stabilizer to torsion arm	M 10	25-36
	M 8	18
Screw for brake back plate to steering knuckle	M 10	36-43
Clamping screw for link pins to torsion bar	M 10	29-36
Type 3 Front axle		
Front axle securing bolts		
a - upper and lower	M 10	22
b - center	M 10	
Grub screw securing torsion bars	M 14 x 1.	
Grub screw securing stabilizer	M 14 x 1.5	32-40
Lock nut for grub screw	M 14 x 1.5	29
Torsion bar to axle beam screws	M 10	29
Clamp screw stabilizer	M 10	29
Adjusting screw for stabilizer	M 8	7 ⑥
Shock absorber to axle beam screws	M 12 x 1.5	22-25
Shock absorber nut on torsion arm	M 10	22-25
Steering arm on steering knuckle	M 10 x 1	40
Nuts for upper and lower ball joints	M 20 x 1.5 or M 18 x 1.5	80

Fastener	Thread Size	Torque (ft.lbs.)
Clamp screws for upper and lower ball joints up to Chassis No. 0273513 (October 1963)	M 10x 40	40
	M 8 x 40	25
Socket head screw in split nut	M 7	7-max. 9
Inner wheel bearing nut up to Chassis No. 315 220 883	M 16 x 1.5	11 ②
Wheel bearing locknut	M 16 x 1.5	50 ②
Tie rod nuts	M 12 x 1.5	22 ④
	M 10 x 1	18 ④
Steering damper screw on axle	M 10	29-32
Steering damper nut on drop arm	M 10	18

① Tighten inner nut to 29 ft. lbs. first, fit new lock plate and slacken nut 72° (distance from one wheel bolt hole in drum to next). Then tighten outer nut to 50 ft. lbs.

② Tighten nut while turning wheel. Then slacken nut off until the specified axial play of .03 - .12 mm (.001 - .005 in.) is obtained. If front axle tends to be noisy, keep play to lower limit (.03 - .06 mm.) When play is correct, tighten socket head screw to the correct torque.

③ Turn on to cotter pin hole.

④ Tighten inner nut to 25 ft. lbs. first while turning wheel. Then fit new lock plate and slacken nut off until specified axial play of .03 - .12 mm. (.001 - .005 in.) is obtained. If front axle tends to be noisy, keep play to lower limit (.03 - .06 mm.) When play is correct, tighten outer locknut to 50 ft. lbs.

⑤ Always use new self-locking nuts after removal.

⑥ Tighten clamp screw to 29 ft. lbs. first, then tighten adjusting screw to 7 ft. lbs. and lock it.

Torque Specifications

Fastener	Thread Size	Torque (ft. lbs.)
Steering damper/frame bolt and nut (up to Chassis No. 851 389)	M 10 x 45	32
Steering damper/axle tube screw (from Chassis No. 851 390)	M 10 x 40	29-32
Steering damper/ swing lever screw	M 10 x 72	29-32
Setscrew for torsion bars	M 14 x 1.5	29
Lock nut for setscrew	M 14 x 1.5	29
Stabilizer to torsion arm	M 10	25-36
	M 8	18
Screw for brake back plate to steering knuckle	M 10	36-43
Clamping screw for link pins to torsion bar	M 10	29-36

Type 3 Front axle

Fastener	Thread Size	Torque (ft. lbs.)
Front axle securing bolts		
a - upper and lower	M 10	22
b - center	M 10	
Grub screw securing torsion bars	M 14 x 1.	
Grub screw securing stabilizer	M 14 x 1.5	32-40
Lock nut for grub screw	M 14 x 1.5	29
Torsion bar to axle beam screws	M 10	29
Clamp screw stabilizer	M 10	29
Adjusting screw for stabilizer	M 8	7 ⑥
Shock absorber to axle beam screws	M 12 x 1.5	22-25
Shock absorber nut on torsion arm	M 10	22-25
Steering arm on steering knuckle	M 10 x 1	40
Nuts for upper and lower ball joints	M 20 x 1.5 or M 18 x 1.5	80

Fastener	Thread Size	Torque (ft. lbs.)
Clamp screws for upper and lower ball joints up to Chassis No. 0273513 (October 1963)	M 10 x 40	40
	M 8 x 40	25
Socket head screw in split nut	M 7	7-max. 9
Inner wheel bearing nut up to Chassis No. 315 220 883	M 16 x 1.5	11 ②
Wheel bearing locknut	M 16 x 1.5	50 ②
Tie rod nuts	M 12 x 1.5	22 ④
	M 10 x 1	18 ④
Steering damper screw on axle	M 10	29-32
Steering damper nut on drop arm	M 10	18

① Tighten inner nut to 29 ft. lbs. first, fit new lock plate and slacken nut 72° (distance from one wheel bolt hole in drum to next). Then tighten outer nut to 50 ft. lbs.

② Tighten nut while turning wheel. Then slacken nut off until the specified axial play of .03 - .12 mm (.001 - .005 in.) is obtained. If front axle tends to be noisy, keep play to lower limit (.03 - .06 mm.) When play is correct, tighten socket head screw to the correct torque.

③ Turn on to cotter pin hole.

④ Tighten inner nut to 25 ft. lbs. first while turning wheel. Then fit new lock plate and slacken nut off until specified axial play of .03 - .12 mm. (.001 - .005 in.) is obtained. If front axle tends to be noisy, keep play to lower limit (.03 - .06 mm.) When play is correct, tighten outer locknut to 50 ft. lbs.

⑤ Always use new self-locking nuts after removal.

⑥ Tighten clamp screw to 29 ft. lbs. first, then tighten adjusting screw to 7 ft. lbs. and lock it.

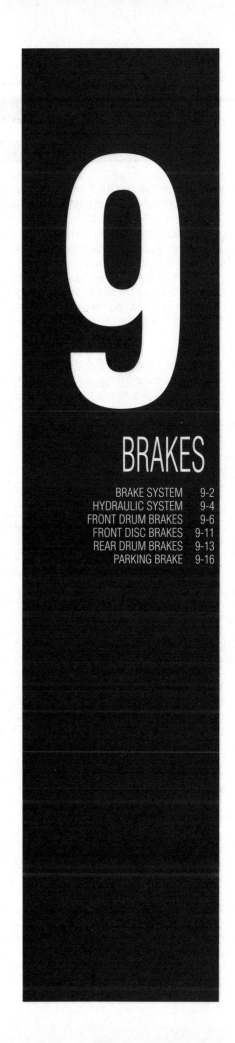

9

BRAKES

BRAKE SYSTEM

Basic Operating Principles

Hydraulic systems are used to actuate the brakes of all modern automobiles. The system transports the power required to force the frictional surfaces of the braking system together from the pedal to the individual brake units at each wheel. A hydraulic system is used for two reasons.

First, fluid under pressure can be carried to all parts of an automobile by small pipes and flexible hoses without taking up a significant amount of room or posing routing problems.

Second, a great mechanical advantage can be given to the brake pedal end of the system, and the foot pressure required to actuate the brakes can be reduced by making the surface area of the master cylinder pistons smaller than that of any of the pistons in the wheel cylinders or calipers.

The master cylinder consists of a fluid reservoir along with a double cylinder and piston assembly. Double type master cylinders are designed to separate the front and rear braking systems hydraulically in case of a leak. The master cylinder coverts mechanical motion from the pedal into hydraulic pressure within the lines. This pressure is translated back into mechanical motion at the wheels by either the wheel cylinder (drum brakes) or the caliper (disc brakes).

Steel lines carry the brake fluid to a point on the vehicle's frame near each of the vehicle's wheels. The fluid is then carried to the calipers and wheel cylinders by flexible tubes in order to allow for suspension and steering movements.

In drum brake systems, each wheel cylinder contains two pistons, one at either end, which push outward in opposite directions and force the brake shoe into contact with the drum.

In disc brake systems, the cylinders are part of the calipers. At least one cylinder in each caliper is used to force the brake pads against the disc.

All pistons employ some type of seal, usually made of rubber, to minimize fluid leakage. A rubber dust boot seals the outer end of the cylinder against dust and dirt. The boot fits around the outer end of the piston on disc brake calipers, and around the brake actuating rod on wheel cylinders.

The hydraulic system operates as follows: When at rest, the entire system, from the piston(s) in the master cylinder to those in the wheel cylinders or calipers, is full of brake fluid. Upon application of the brake pedal, fluid trapped in front of the master cylinder piston(s) is forced through the lines to the wheel cylinders. Here, it forces the pistons outward, in the case of drum brakes, and inward toward the disc, in the case of disc brakes. The motion of the pistons is opposed by return springs mounted outside the cylinders in drum brakes, and by spring seals, in disc brakes.

Upon release of the brake pedal, a spring located inside the master cylinder immediately returns the master cylinder pistons to the normal position. The pistons contain check valves and the master cylinder has compensating ports drilled in it. These are uncovered as the pistons reach their normal position. The piston check valves allow fluid to flow toward the wheel cylinders or calipers as the pistons withdraw. Then, as the return springs force the brake pads or shoes into the released position, the excess fluid reservoir through the compensating ports. It is during the time the pedal is in the released position that any fluid that has leaked out of the system will be replaced through the compensating ports.

Dual circuit master cylinders employ two pistons, located one behind the other, in the same cylinder. The primary piston is actuated directly by mechanical linkage from the brake pedal through the power booster. The secondary piston is actuated by fluid trapped between the two pistons. If a leak develops in front of the secondary piston, it moves forward until it bottoms against the front of the master cylinder, and the fluid trapped between the pistons will operate the rear brakes. If the rear brakes develop a leak, the primary piston will move forward until direct contact with the secondary piston takes place, and it will force the secondary piston to actuate the front brakes. In either case, the brake pedal moves farther when the brakes are applied, and less braking power is available.

All dual circuit systems use a switch to warn the driver when only half of the brake system is operational. This switch is usually located in a valve body which is mounted on the firewall or the frame below the master cylinder. A hydraulic piston receives pressure from both circuits, each circuit's pressure being applied to one end of the piston. When the pressures are in balance, the piston remains stationary. When one circuit has a leak, however, the greater pressure in that circuit during application of the brakes will push the piston to one side, closing the switch and activating the brake warning light.

In disc brake systems, this valve body also contains a metering valve and, in some cases, a proportioning valve. The metering valve keeps pressure from traveling to the disc brakes on the front wheels until the brake shoes on the rear wheels have contacted the drums, ensuring that the front brakes will never be used alone. The proportioning valve controls the pressure to the rear brakes to lessen the chance of rear wheel lock-up during very hard braking.

Warning lights may be tested by depressing the brake pedal and holding it while opening one of the wheel cylinder bleeder screws. If this does not cause the light to go on, substitute a new lamp, make continuity checks, and, finally, replace the switch as necessary.

The hydraulic system may be checked for leaks by applying pressure to the pedal gradually and steadily. If the pedal sinks very slowly to the floor, the system has a leak. This is not to be confused with a springy or spongy feel due to the compression of air within the lines. If the system leaks, there will be a gradual change in the position of the pedal with a constant pressure.

Check for leaks along all lines and at wheel cylinders. If no external leaks are apparent, the problem is inside the master cylinder.

DISC BRAKES

Instead of the traditional expanding brakes that press outward against a circular drum, disc brake systems utilize a disc (rotor) with brake pads positioned on either side of it. An easily-seen analogy is the hand brake arrangement on a bicycle. The pads squeeze onto the rim of the bike wheel, slowing its motion. Automobile disc brakes use the identical principle but apply the braking effort to a separate disc instead of the wheel.

The disc (rotor) is a casting, usually equipped with cooling fins between the two braking surfaces. This enables air to circulate between the braking surfaces making them less sensitive to heat buildup and more resistant to fade. Dirt and water do not drastically affect braking action since contaminants are thrown off by the centrifugal action of the rotor or scraped off the by the pads. Also, the equal clamping action of the two brake pads tends to ensure uniform, straight line stops. Disc brakes are inherently self-adjusting. There are three general types of disc brake:

1 A fixed caliper.
2 A floating caliper.
3 A sliding caliper.

The fixed caliper design uses two pistons mounted on either side of the rotor (in each side of the caliper). The caliper is mounted rigidly and does not move.

The sliding and floating designs are quite similar. In fact, these two types are often lumped together. In both designs, the pad on the inside of the rotor is moved into contact with the rotor by hydraulic force. The caliper, which is not held in a fixed position, moves slightly, bringing the outside pad into contact with the rotor. There are various methods of attaching floating calipers. Some pivot at the bottom or top, and some slide on mounting bolts. In any event, the end result is the same.

DRUM BRAKES

Drum brakes employ two brake shoes mounted on a stationary backing plate. These shoes are positioned inside a circular drum which rotates with the wheel assembly. The shoes are held in place by springs. This allows them to slide toward the drums (when they are applied) while keeping the linings and drums in alignment. The shoes are actuated by a wheel cylinder which is mounted at the top of the backing plate. When the brakes are applied, hydraulic pressure forces the wheel cylinder's actuating links outward. Since these links bear directly against the top of the brake shoes, the tops of the shoes are then forced against the inner side of the drum. This action forces the bottoms of the two shoes to contact the brake drum by rotating the entire assembly slightly (known as servo action). When pressure within the wheel cylinder is relaxed, return springs pull the shoes back away from the drum.

Most modern drum brakes are designed to self-adjust themselves during application when the vehicle is moving in reverse. This motion causes both shoes to rotate very slightly with the drum, rocking an adjusting lever, thereby causing rotation of the adjusting screw. Some drum brake systems are designed to self-adjust during application whenever the brakes are applied. This on-board adjustment system reduces the need for maintenance adjustments and keeps both the brake function and pedal feel satisfactory.

POWER BOOSTERS

Virtually all modern vehicles use a vacuum assisted power brake system to multiply the braking force and reduce pedal effort. Since vacuum is always available when the engine is operating, the system is simple and efficient. A vacuum diaphragm is located on the front of the master cylinder and assists the driver in applying the brakes, reducing both the effort and travel he must put into moving the brake pedal.

The vacuum diaphragm housing is normally connected to the intake manifold by a vacuum hose. A check valve is placed at the point where the hose enters the diaphragm housing, so that during periods of low manifold vacuum brakes assist will not be lost.

Depressing the brake pedal closes off the vacuum source and allows atmospheric pressure to enter on one side of the diaphragm. This causes the master cylinder pistons to move and apply the brakes. When the brake pedal is released, vacuum is applied to both sides of the diaphragm and springs return the diaphragm and master cylinder pistons to the released position.

If the vacuum supply fails, the brake pedal rod will contact the end of the master cylinder actuator rod and the system will apply the brakes without any power assistance. The driver will notice that much higher pedal effort is needed to stop the car and that the pedal feels harder than usual.

Vacuum Leak Test

1   Operate the engine at idle without touching the brake pedal for at least one minute.
2   Turn off the engine and wait one minute.
3   Test for the presence of assist vacuum by depressing the brake pedal and releasing it several times. If vacuum is present in the system, light application will produce less and less pedal travel. If there is no vacuum, air is leaking into the system.

System Operation Test

1   With the engine OFF , pump the brake pedal until the supply vacuum is entirely gone.
2   Put light, steady pressure on the brake pedal.
3   Start the engine and let it idle. If the system is operating correctly, the brake pedal should fall toward the floor if the constant pressure is maintained.

Power brake systems may be tested for hydraulic leaks just as ordinary systems are tested.

Brake Adjustments

All type 1 models (except the Karmann Ghia), and type 2 models are equipped with front drum brakes. Discs are used at the front of 1967 - 69 type 1 Karmann Ghias and all type 3 models. All models use rear drum brakes.

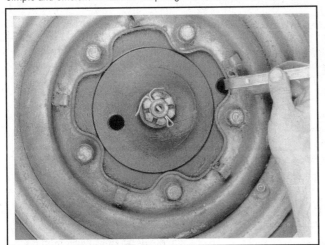

On models with 5 lug hubs, the brakes are adjusted through the brake drum . . .

. . . whereas, on vehicles with 4 lug wheels, the brakes are adjusted from the backing plate

Disc brakes are self-adjusting and cannot be adjusted by hand. As the pads wear, they will automatically compensate for the wear by moving closer to the disc, maintaining the proper operating clearance.

Drum brakes, however, must be manually adjusted to take up excess clearance as the shoes wear. To adjust drum brakes, both front and rear, it is necessary to jack up the car and support it on jackstands. The wheel must spin freely. On the backing plate there are four inspection holes with a rubber plug in each hole. Two of the holes are for checking the thickness of the brake lining and the other two are used for adjustment.

➡**There is an adjustment for each brake shoe. That means that on each wheel it is necessary to make two adjustments: one for each shoe on that wheel.**

The only equipment needed to adjust the drum brakes of the Volkswagen is a screwdriver. Pre-1966 Volkswagens have an adjuster hole in the outside of the brake drum for the purpose of adjustment. Models of 1966 and later have adjustment holes in the back plate.

Before adjusting the brakes press the pedal down several times to centralize the shoes in the drums. Turn the wheel so that an adjusting nut is visible through the adjustment hole. Using the screwdriver, turn the adjustment nut until a slight drag is felt when the wheel is rotated by hand. At this point, back off the adjusting nut until the wheel turns freely (about 3 or 4 teeth of the adjusting nut will pass the adjustment hole). Move on to the other adjusting nut of the wheel. The adjustment nuts on each wheel turn in opposite directions, so whichever direction of rotation was needed to tighten one shoe will loosen the adjustment of the other shoe. The handbrake is adjusted by means of adjusting nuts at the rear of the control lever inside the car. However, when the rear brakes are adjusted, the handbrake is automatically adjusted also. If this is not enough to hold the rear wheels at 4 notches, the hand brake should be adjusted by means of the adjusting nuts. When the brake lever is applied by 2 notches, both rear wheels should resist turning by an equal amount of force. If for some reason, it were necessary to use the handbrake to stop in an emergency, it could be dangerous if both rear wheels did not tend to lock equally.

➡**One of the star wheels in each wheel has left-hand threads and the other star wheel has right-hand threads.**

Repeat the above procedure on each wheel equipped with drum brakes.

HYDRAULIC SYSTEM

Master Cylinder

REMOVAL & INSTALLATION

✳✳ CAUTION:

Clean, high quality brake fluid is essential to the safe and proper operation of the brake system. You should always buy the highest quality brake fluid that is available. If the brake fluid becomes contaminated, drain and flush the system, then refill the master cylinder with new fluid. Never reuse any brake fluid. Any brake fluid that is removed from the system should be discarded.

1 Drain the brake fluid from the master cylinder reservoir.

✳✳ WARNING:

Do not get any brake fluid on the paint, as it will dissolve the paint.

2 On Type 3 models, remove the master cylinder cover plate.

3 Pull the plastic elbows out of the rubber sealing rings on the top of the master cylinder, if equipped, or unfasten the fluid pipe seat nuts.

4 Remove the two bolts which secure the master cylinder to the frame and remove the cylinder. Note the spacers on Type 1 models between the frame and the master cylinder.

To install:

5 Bolt the master cylinder to the frame. Do not forget the spacers on Type 1 models.

6 Lubricate the elbows with brake fluid and insert them into the rubber seals.

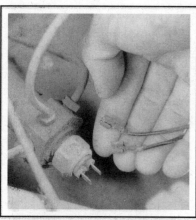

To remove the master cylinder, detach the electrical wires from the warning lamp switch . . .

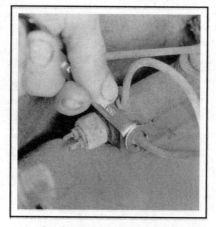

. . . then loosen the brake line fittings . . .

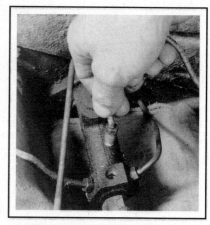

. . . and pull the lines away from the master cylinder

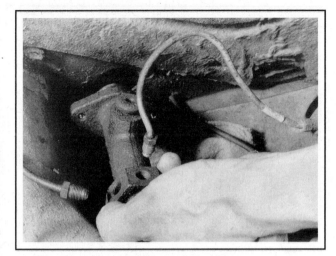

After removing the mounting bolts from inside the vehicle, pull the cylinder away from the firewall

7   If necessary, adjust the brake pedal free travel. On Type 1, 3, and 4 models, adjust the length of the master cylinder pushrod so that there is 5 - 7mm of brake pedal free-play before the pushrod contacts the master cylinder piston. On Type 2 models, the free-play is properly adjusted when the length of the pushrod, measured between the ball end and the center of the clevis pin hole, is 4.17 in.

8   Refill the master cylinder reservoir and bleed the brakes.

OVERHAUL

1   Remove the master cylinder from the car.

2   Remove the rubber sealing boot.

3   Remove the stop screw and sealing ring on the top of the unit.

4   Insert a small prytool in the master cylinder piston, exert inward pressure, and remove the snapring from its groove in the end of the unit. The internal parts are spring loaded and must be kept from flying out when the snapring is removed.

5   Carefully remove the internal parts of the unit and make note of their order and the orientation of the internal parts. If parts remain in the cylinder bore, they may be removed with a wire hook or very gentle application of low pressure air to the stop screw hole. Cover the end of the cylinder bore with a rag and stand away from the open end of the bore when using compressed air.

6   Use alcohol or brake fluid to clean the master cylinder and its parts.

7   It may be necessary to hone the cylinder bore, or clean it by lightly sanding it with emery cloth. Clean thoroughly after honing or sanding. Lubricate the bore with brake fluid before reassembly.

To assemble:

8   Holding the master cylinder with the open end downward, place the cup washer, primary cup, support washer, spring retainer, and spring onto the front brake circuit piston and insert the piston vertically into the master cylinder bore.

9   Assemble the rear brake circuit piston, cup washer, primary cup, support washer, spring retainer, stop sleeve, spring, and stroke limiting screw and insert the assembly into the master cylinder.

10 Install the stop washer and snapring.

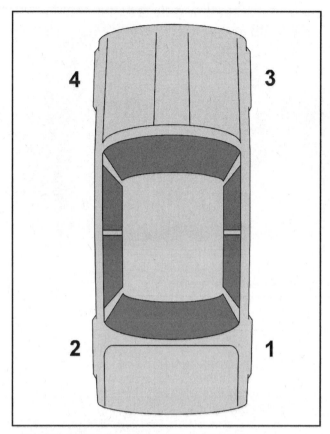

Bleed the brakes on all Volkswagen models in the sequence shown

11 Install the stop screw and seal, making sure the hole for the screw is not blocked by the piston. If the hole is blocked, it will be necessary to push the piston further in until the screw can be turned in.

12 Install the master cylinder and bleed the brakes.

Hydraulic System Bleeding

The hydraulic brake system must be bled any time one of the lines is disconnected or air enters the system. This may be done manually or by the pressure method.

PRESSURE BLEEDING

1   Clean the top of the master cylinder, remove the caps, and attach the pressure bleeding adapter.

2   Check the pressure bleeder reservoir for correct pressure and fluid level, then open the release valve.

3   Fasten a bleeder hose to the wheel cylinder bleeder nipple and submerge the free end of the hose in a transparent receptacle. The receptacle should contain enough brake fluid to cover the open end of the hose.

4   Open the wheel cylinder bleeder nipple and allow the fluid to flow until all bubbles disappear and an uncontaminated flow of fluid exists.

5   Close the nipple, remove the bleeder hose, and repeat the procedure on the other wheel cylinders or brake calipers.

Use a plastic hose and bottle filled with clean brake fluid to assist with rear brake bleeding . . .

MANUAL BLEEDING

This method requires two people: one to depress the brake pedal and the other to open the bleeder nipples.

1 Remove the reservoir caps and fill the reservoir.

2 Attach a bleeder hose and a clear container as outlined in the pressure bleeding procedure.

3 Have the assistant depress the brake pedal to the floor several times and then have him hold the pedal to the floor. With the pedal to the floor, open the bleeder nipple until the fluid flow ceases and then close the nipple. Repeat this sequence until there are no more air bubbles in the fluid.

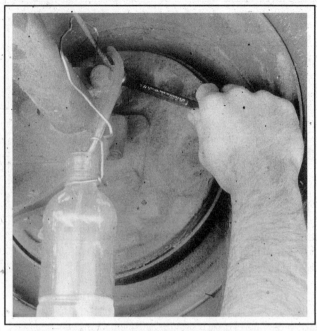

. . . then bleed the front brakes in the same manner

➡As the air is gradually forced out of the system, it will no longer be possible to force the brake pedal to the floor.

Periodically check the master cylinder for an adequate supply of fluid. Keep the master cylinder reservoir full of fluid to prevent air from entering the system. If the reservoir does run dry during bleeding, it will be necessary to rebleed the entire system.

FRONT DRUM BRAKES

Brake Drum

REMOVAL & INSTALLATION

1 Jack up the car and remove the wheel and tire.

2 On the left side, remove the clip which secures the speedometer cable to the wheel bearing dust cover. Remove the dust cover.

3 Loosen the nut clamp, remove the wheel bearing adjusting nut and slide the brake drum off of the spindle. It may be necessary to back off on the brake shoe star wheels so that there is enough clearance to remove the drum.

To remove the front brake drum, remove the wheel . . .

. . . then loosen the shoe adjustment to ease brake drum removal

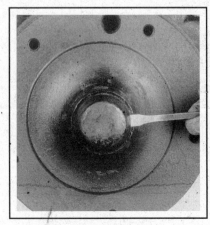

Pry on the dust cover lip . . .

. . . and remove the dust cap from the brake drum

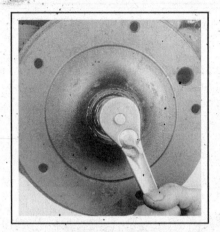

Remove the wheel bearing retaining nut . . .

. . . then remove the washer

Remove and bearing and race . . .

. . . then slide the drum off of the spindle

At this time the inner bearing race can be removed from the spindle

4 Installation is the reverse of removal. Adjust the wheel bearings after installing the drum.

INSPECTION

If the brake drums are scored or cracked, they must be replaced or machined. If the vehicle pulls to one side or exhibits a pulsating braking action, the drum is probably out of round and should be checked at a machine shop. The drum may have a smooth even surface and still be out of round. The drum should be free of surface cracks and dark spots.

Brake Shoes

REMOVAL & INSTALLATION

Type 1

1 Jack up the car and remove the wheel and tire.
2 Remove the brake drum.
3 Remove the small disc and spring which secure each shoe to the

After the brake drum is removed, the brake shoes can be replaced

backing plate.
4 Remove the two long springs between the two shoes.
5 Remove the shoes from the backing plate.
6 If new shoes are being installed, remove the adjusters in the end of each wheel cylinder and screw the star wheel up against the head of the adjuster. When inserting the adjusters back in the wheel cylinders,

FRONT DRUM BRAKE COMPONENTS – TYPE 1 VEHICLES

1. Brake shoes
2. Brake shoe retaining springs
3. Brake shoe retaining pins
4. Brake shoe retaining cups

5. Front brake shoe return spring
   (away from wheel cylinder)
6. Rear brake shoe return spring
   (near wheel cylinder)

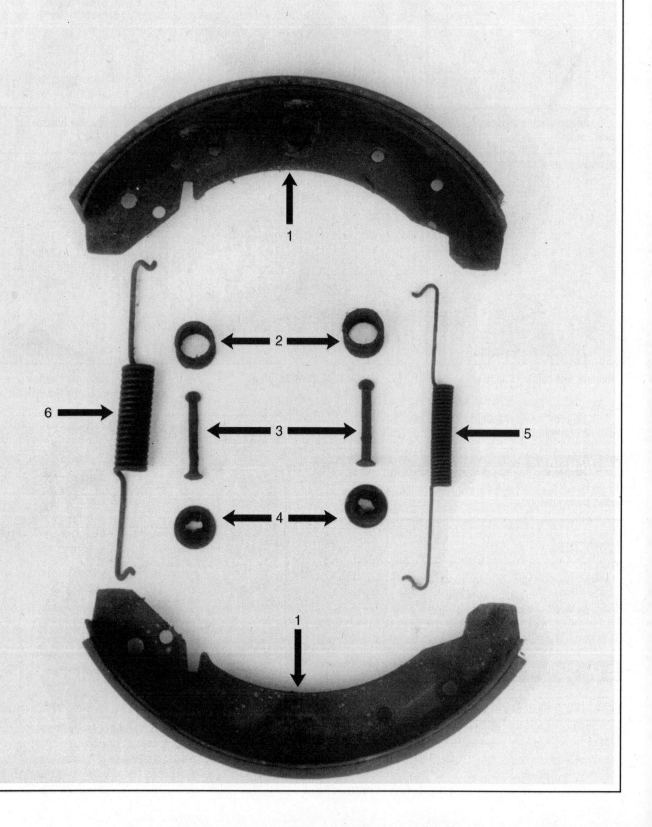

Clean all of the brake parts with an approved brake cleaner

. . . then remove the front return spring

notice that the slot in the adjuster is angled and must be positioned as illustrated.

7   Position new shoes on the backing plate. The slot in the shoes and the stronger return spring must be at the wheel cylinder end.

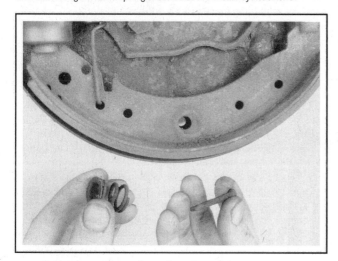

. . . then remove the spring, pin and retaining cup from both shoes

If not already done, adjust the brake shoes to relieve the tension on the return springs . . .

Depress the brake shoe retaining springs . . .

8   Install the disc and spring which secure the shoe to the backing plate.

9   Install the brake drum and adjust the wheel bearing.

Remove the two brake shoes and rear return spring together . . .

. . . then unhook the return spring from the brake shoes

At this point, the adjusters can be removed for service

Type 2

1 Remove the brake drum.

2 Pry the rear brake shoe out of the adjuster, as illustrated, and detach the return springs. Remove the forward shoe.

3 If new shoes are to be installed, screw the star wheel up against the head of the adjuster.

4 Install the rear brake shoe.

5 Attach the return spring to the front brake shoe and then to the rear shoe.

6 Position the front brake shoe in the slot of the adjusting screw and lever it into position in the same manner as it was removed. Make sure that the return springs do not touch the brake line between the upper and lower wheel cylinders.

7 Install the brake-drum and adjust the wheel bearings.

Wheel Cylinder

REMOVAL & INSTALLATION

❊❊ CAUTION:

Clean, high quality brake fluid is essential to the safe and proper operation of the brake system. You should always buy the highest quality brake fluid that is available. If the brake fluid becomes contaminated, drain and flush the system, then refill the master cylinder with new fluid. Never reuse any brake fluid. Any brake fluid that is removed from the system should be discarded.

1 Remove the brake shoes.

2 On Type 1 models, disconnect the brake line from the rear of the cylinder. On Type 2 models, disconnect the brake line from the rear of the cylinder and transfer line from the front of the cylinder.

3 Remove the bolts which secure the cylinder to the backing plate and remove the cylinder from the vehicle.

4 Installation is the reverse of the removal procedure. Bleed the brakes.

OVERHAUL

1 Remove the wheel cylinder.

Prior to installation, apply grease to the adjuster where indicated (arrow)

2 Remove the brake adjusters and remove the rubber boot from each end.

➡The Type 2 cylinder has only one rubber boot, piston, and cup. The rebuilding procedures are the same.

3 On Type 1 models, push in on one of the pistons to force out the opposite piston and rubber cup. On Type 2 models, remove the piston and cup by blowing compressed air into the brake hose hole.

4 Wash the pistons and cylinder in clean brake fluid or alcohol.

5 Inspect the cylinder bore for signs of pitting, scoring, and excessive wear. If it is badly scored or pitted, the whole cylinder should be replaced. It is possible to remove the glaze and light scores with crocus cloth or a brake cylinder hone. Before rebuilding the cylinder, make sure the bleeder screw is free. If the bleeder is rusted shut or broken off, replace the entire cylinder.

6 Dip the new pistons and rubber cups in brake fluid. Place the spring in the bore and insert the rubber cups into the bore against the spring. The concave side of the rubber cup should face inward.

7 Place the pistons in the bore and install the rubber boot.

8 Install the cylinder and bleed the brakes after the shoes and drum are in place. Make sure that the brakes are adjusted.

FRONT DISC BRAKES

Brake Pad

REMOVAL & INSTALLATION

1 Loosen, but do not remove the reservoir cover.
2 Jack up the car and remove the wheel and tire.
3 Using a punch, remove the two pins which retain the disc brake pads in the caliper.

➡ **If the pads are to be reused, mark the pads to insure that they are reinstalled in the same caliper and on the same side of the disc. Do not invert the pads. Changing pads from one location to another can cause uneven braking.**

4 If the pads are not going to be reused, force a wedge between the disc and the pad and pry the piston back into the caliper as far as possible.
5 Using a suitable brake parts cleaner, rinse away the brake dust. Pull the old pad out of the caliper and insert a new one, taking care to note the position of the retaining plate.

➡ **On ATE and many Teves disc brakes, before inserting the brake pads, make sure the relieved part of the piston is in the correct position to accept the retaining plate. The sides of the retaining plate fit into the relieved area while the circular part of the plate fits in the piston's center. On some Type 2's and other models, the retaining plate is simply a flat piece of metal with two notches which fit into the relieved areas in the piston. The relieved side of the piston should face against (away from) the rotation direction of the wheel when the car is going forward.**

6 Now insert the wedge between the disc and pad on the opposite side and force that piston into the caliper. Remove the old pad and insert a new one.
7 If the old pads are to be reused, it is not necessary to push the piston into the caliper. Pull the pads from the caliper and reinstall the pads when necessary.
8 pin. Insert the pin from the inside of the caliper and drive it to the outside.
9 Pump the brake pedal several times to take up the clearance between the pads and the disc before driving the car.
10 Install the wheel and tire and carefully road test the car. Apply the brakes gently for first 500 to 1,000 miles to properly break in the pads and prevent glazing.

Brake Caliper

REMOVAL & INSTALLATION

✳✳ CAUTION:

Clean, high quality brake fluid is essential to the safe and proper operation of the brake system. You should always buy the highest quality brake fluid that is available. If the brake fluid becomes contaminated, drain and flush the system, then refill the master cylinder with new fluid. Never reuse any brake fluid. Any brake fluid that is removed from the system should be discarded.

1 Jack up the car and remove the wheel and tire.
2 Remove the brake pads.
3 Disconnect and plug the brake line from the caliper.

Knock the pad retaining pin(s) out with a hammer and drift, then pull them out of the caliper housing - be careful not to let the pad spreader spring fly out

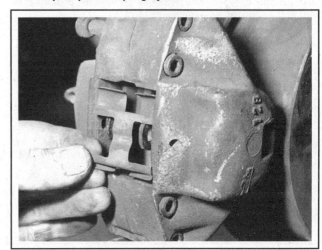

Before you remove the pad spreader spring, make sure you note how it's installed

Note how the brake pads are oriented in the caliper, then you remove each of them, depress its respective piston into the caliper to make room for the new pad

4   Remove the two bolts which secure the caliper to the steering knuckle and remove the caliper from the vehicle.

5   Installation is the reverse of the removal procedure. Bleed the brakes after the caliper is installed.

OVERHAUL

➡**Clean all parts in brake system cleaner, alcohol or brake fluid.**

1   Remove the caliper from the vehicle.

2   Remove the piston retaining plates.

3   Pry out the seal spring ring using a small prytool. Do not damage the seal beneath the ring.

4   Remove the seal with a plastic or hard rubber rod. Do not use sharp-edged or metal tools.

5   Rebuild one piston at a time. Securely clamp one piston in place so that it cannot come out of its bore. Place a block of wood between the two pistons and apply air pressure to the brake fluid port.

✳✳ CAUTION:

Use extreme care with this technique because the piston can fly out of the caliper with tremendous force.

The brake pads on this vehicle were obviously neglected, as they wore deep grooves into the disc - wear this severe will require replacement of the disc

6   Remove the rubber seal at the bottom of the piston bore using a rubber or plastic tool.

7   Check the bore and piston for wear, rust, and pitting.

8   Install a new seal in the bottom of the bore and lubricate the bore and seal with brake fluid.

9   Gently insert the piston, making sure it does not cock and jamb in the bore.

➡**When installing pistons on ATE and Teves calipers, make sure the relieved part of the piston is in the correct position to accept the retaining plate for the brake pads. See brake pad removal and installation for more information and illustration.**

10   Install the new outer seal and new spring ring.

11   Install the piston retaining plate.

12   Repeat the procedure on the other piston. Never rebuild only one side of a caliper.

Brake Rotor (Disc)

REMOVAL & INSTALLATION

1   Jack up the car and remove the wheel and tire.

2   Remove the caliper.

3   On Type 2 models, remove the three socket head bolts which secure the disc to the hub, and remove the disc from the hub. Sometimes the disc is rusted to the hub. Spray penetrating oil on the seam and tap the disc with a lead or brass hammer. If it still does not come off, screw three 8 x 40mm screws into the socket head holes. Tighten the screws evenly and pull the disc from the hub.

4   Type 1, 3, and 4 models, remove the wheel bearing cover. On the left side it will be necessary to remove the small clip which secures the end of the speedometer cable to the cover.

5   Loosen the nut clamp, unscrew the wheel bearing nut and remove the nut and outer wheel bearing.

6   Pull the disc off of the spindle.

7   To remove the wheel bearing races, see the "Wheel Bearing Removal and Installation" procedure.

8   Installation is the reverse of the removal procedure. Make sure the wheel bearing is properly adjusted.

to check disc

If you decide to skip machining, be sure to break the glaze on the disc surface with emery cloth or sandpaper

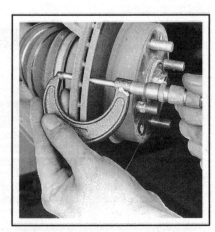

Check the thickness of the disc with a micrometer at several points (typical)

9-19 A Once the brake drum is removed, use a seal puller to remove the old inner bearing grease seal

9-19 B A correct-sized driver must be used to install the new inner bearing grease seal into the brake drum

INSPECTION

Visually check the rotor for excessive scoring. Minor scores will not affect performance; however, if the scores are over 1/32 in., it is necessary to replace the disc or have it resurfaced. The disc must be 0.02 in. over the wear limit to be resurfaced. The disc must be free of surface cracks and discoloration (heat bluing). Hand spin the disc and make sure that it does not wobble from side to side. Also check the disc for runout using a dial indicator.

Front Wheel Bearings

REMOVAL & INSTALLATION

1   Jack up the car and remove the wheel and tire.
2   Remove the caliper and disc (if equipped with disc brakes) or brake drum.
3   To remove the inside wheel bearing, pry the dust seal out of the hub with a prytool. Lift out the bearing and its inner race.
4   To remove the outer race for either the inner or outer wheel bearing, insert a long punch into the hub opposite the end from which the race is to be removed. The race rests against a shoulder in the hub. The shoulder has two notches cut into it so that it is possible to place the end of the punch directly against the back side of the race and drive it out of the hub.
5   Carefully clean the hub.

6   Install new races in the hub. Drive them in with a soft faced hammer or a large piece of pipe of the proper diameter. Lubricate the races with a light coating of wheel bearing grease.
7   Force wheel bearing grease into the sides of the tapered roller bearings so that all spaces are filled.
8   Place a small amount of grease inside the hub.
9   Place the inner wheel bearing into its race in the hub and tap a new seal into the hub. Lubricate the sealing surface of the seal with grease.
10 Install the hub on the spindle and install the outer wheel bearing.
11 Adjust the wheel bearing and install the dust cover.
12 Install the caliper (if equipped with disc brakes).

ADJUSTMENT

1   The bearing may be adjusted by feel or by a dial indicator.
2   To adjust the bearing by feel, tighten the adjusting nut so that all the play is taken up in the bearing. There will be a slight amount of drag on the wheel if it is hand spun. Back off fully on the adjusting nut and retighten very lightly. There should be no drag when the wheel is hand spun and there should be no perceptible play in the bearing when the wheel is grasped and wiggled from side to side.
3   To use a dial indicator, remove the dust cover and mount a dial indicator against the hub. Grasp the wheel at the side and pull the wheel in and out along the axis of the spindle. Read the axial play on the dial indicator. Screw the adjusting nut in or out to obtain 0.001 to 0.005 in. of axial play. Secure the adjusting nut and recheck the axial play.

REAR DRUM BRAKES

Brake Drum

REMOVAL & INSTALLATION

1   With the wheels still on the ground, remove the cotter pin from the slotted nut on the rear axle and remove the nut from the axle. This isn't as easy as it sounds. You'll need a very long breaker bar or metal pipe for this operation.

➥**Make sure the parking brake is now released.**

2   Jack up the car and remove the wheel and tire.
3   The brake drum is splined to the rear axle and the drum shou'' slip off the axle. However, the drum sometimes rusts on the splines it is necessary to remove the drum using a puller.
4   Before installing the drum, lubricate the splines. Install the on the axle and tighten the nut on the axle to 217 ft. lbs. Line u' in the nut with a hole in the axle and insert a cotter pin. Never the nut to align the slot and hole.

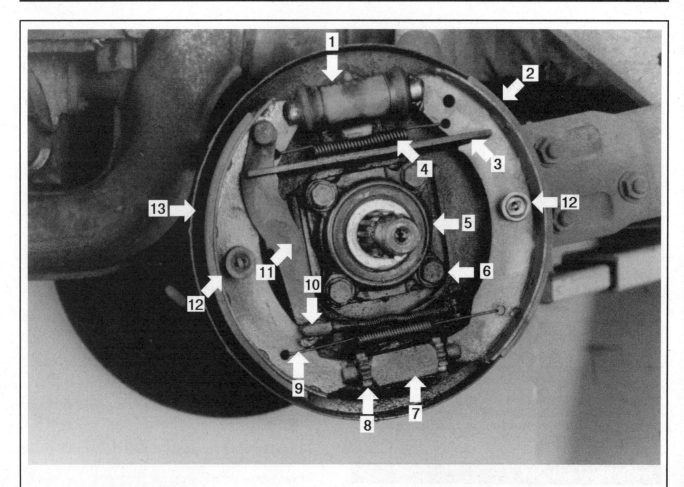

1. Wheel cylinder
2. Backing plate
3. Connecting link
4. Upper return spring
5. Rear axle shaft bearings
   (under cap)
6. Backing plate/Bearing cap
   mounting bolts
7. Anchor block
8. Star adjuster wheel (1 of 2)
9. Lower return spring
10. Parking brake cable
11. Parking brake lever
12. Hold-down spring
    with cup and pin

Identification of the typical rear drum brake components

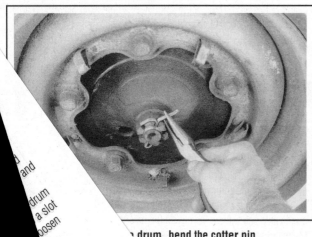

. . . drum, bend the cotter pin

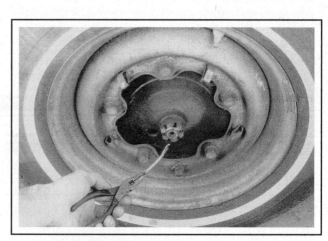

. . . then remove the cotter pin from the castle nut

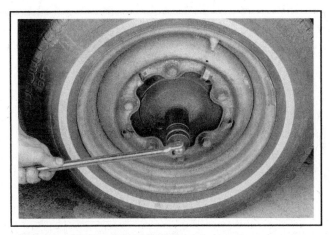

With the vehicle weight on the wheel, loosen the mounting nut

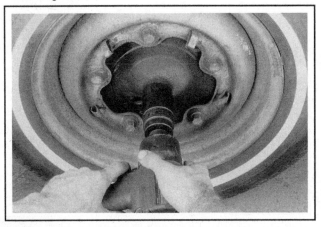

A pneumatic impact gun makes loosening the nut much easier

Brake Shoes

REMOVAL & INSTALLATION

1 Remove the brake drum.
2 Remove both shoe retaining springs.

Slide the brake drum off of the axle stub

3 Disconnect the lower return spring.
4 Disconnect the hand brake cable from the lever attached to the rear shoe.
5 Remove the upper return spring and clip.
6 Remove the brake shoes and connecting link.
7 Remove the parking brake lever from the rear shoe.
8 Lubricate the adjusting screws and the star wheel against the head of the adjusting screw.
9 Reverse Steps 1 - 7 to install the shoes.
10 Adjust the brakes.

After the brake drum is removed, the brake shoes can be replaced

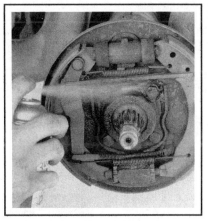

Use a brake cleaning solution to remove all brake dust from the components

Depress the brake shoe retaining spring . . .

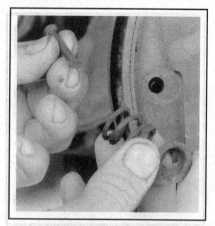

. . . and remove the spring, pin and retainer cup from both shoes

Detach the lower return spring from both shoes . . .

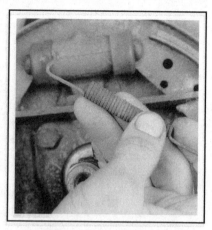

. . . then remove the upper return spring

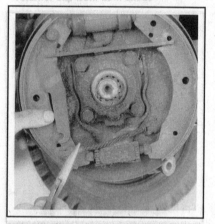

Detach the cable from the parking brake lever . . .

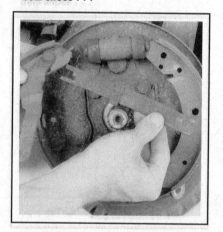

. . . then remove the rear shoe, guide strut . . .

. . . and the front shoe

Wheel Cylinder

REMOVAL & INSTALLATION

✳✳ CAUTION:

Clean, high quality brake fluid is essential to the safe and proper operation of the brake system. You should always buy the highest quality brake fluid that is available. If the brake fluid becomes contaminated, drain and flush the system, then refill the master cylinder with new fluid. Never reuse any brake fluid. Any brake fluid that is removed from the system should be discarded.

Remove the brake drum and brake shoes. Disconnect the brake line from the cylinder and remove the bolts which secure the cylinder to the backing plate. Remove the cylinder from the vehicle.

OVERHAUL

Overhaul is the same as given in the Front Drum Brake portion of this section.

PARKING BRAKE

Cable

ADJUSTMENT

Brake cable adjustment is performed at the handbrake lever in the passenger compartment on all vehicles except Type 2 models. There is a cable for each rear wheel and there are two adjusting nuts at the lever. On Type 2 models, adjust from below the vehicle.

To adjust the cable, loosen the locknut. Jack up the rear wheel to be adjusted so that it can be hand spun. Turn the adjusting nut until a very slight drag is felt as the wheel is spun. Then back off on the adjusting nut until the lever can be pulled up three notches on all models except Type 2's, six notches on Type 2 models.

✳✳ WARNING:

Never pull up on the handbrake lever with the cables disconnected.

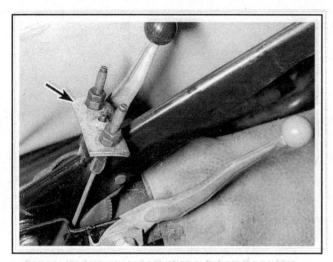

Remove the locknuts and adjusting nuts from the parking brake cables and remove the compensating lever

REMOVAL & INSTALLATION

1 Disconnect the cables at the handbrake lever by removing the two nuts which secure the cables to the lever. Pull the cables rearward to remove that end from the lever bracket.

2 Remove the brake drums and detach the cable end from the lever attached to the rear brake shoe.

3 Remove the brake cable bracket from the backing plate and remove the cable from the vehicle.

4 Reverse the removal procedure for installation. Adjust the cable.

Brake Specifications

Vehicle	Model	Type		Brake Cylinder Bore (in.)			Brake Drum or Disc Diameter (in.)	
		Front	Rear	Master Cylinder	Wheel Cylinder		Front	Rear
					Front	Rear		
Type 1	25 hp., 36 hp. 1,200cc.	Drum ①	Drum	.750	.750	.690	9.05 +.008	9.05 +.008
	40hp. 1,200 and 1,300cc.	Drum	Drum	.687	.874	.750	9.059 +.008	9.055 +.008
	1,500 and 1,600cc. Single Master Cylinder	Drum	Drum	.687	.875	.687	9.059 +.008	9.055 +.008
	1,500 and 1,600cc.– Tandem Master Cylinder	Drum	Drum	.750	.875	.687	9.059 +.008	9.055 +.008
	Karmann Ghia	Disc	Drum	NA	1.574	.687	10.9	NA
Type 2	Tandem Master Cylinder	Drum	Drum	.875	1.00	.875	9.843 +.008	9.843 +.008
Type 3	Tandem Master Cylinder	Disc	Drum	.750	1.653	.875	10.9	9.768 +.008

Torque Specifications— Brakes and Wheels

Fastener	Thread Size	Torque (ft.lbs.)
Brakes Type 1		
Master cylinder to frame	M 8	14-22
Screws for bearing cover/ back plate/bearing flange.	M 10	40-47
Back plate/steering knuckle screws	M 10	36
Brake hose unions	M 10 x 1	11-14
Brake pipe unions	M 10 x 1	11-14
Stop light switch	M 10 x 1	11-14
Wheel cylinder to back plate	M 8	14-22
Caliper to steering knuckle	M 10	36
Residual pressure valve in tandem master cylinder	M 12 x 1	14
Brakes Type 2		
Screws for bearing cover to rear brake back plate	M 10	40-43
Brake back plate/wheel cylinder front	M 10	40-43
Brake hose unions	M 10 x 1	11-14
Brake pipe unions	M 10 x 1	11-14
Stop light switch	M 10 x 1	11-14
Tandem master cylinder to brake servo	M 8	9
Brake servo to retaining retaining plate/front axle	M 8	9
Brakes Type 3		
Master cylinder to frame	M 8	14-22
Screws for bearing cover/ back plate rear	M 10 x 1.5	40-47
Wheel cylinders		
a - rear on back plate	M 8	18
b - front on back plate/steering knuckle	M 10 x 1	32
Disc brake caliper housing to steering knuckle	M 10	43
Brake hose at		
a - brake pipe	M 10 x 1	11-14
b - wheel cylinder	M 10 x 1	11-14
c - disc brake caliper housing	M 10 x 1	11
Stop light switch	M 10 x 1	11-14
Wheels		
Wheel bolts		
Type 1	M 12 x 1.5	72
from August 1965 (four hole wheel) ①	M 14 x 1.5	108
Type 2	M 14 x 1.5	94
Type 3	M 12 x 1.5	72
from August 1965 (four hole wheel)	M 14 x 1.5	108

① Only on vehicle with disc brakes. For all from Chassis No. 118 000 001.

10

BODY

EXTERIOR

Front Doors

REMOVAL & INSTALLATION

Types 1 and 3 Models

If the original door is going to be reinstalled, it is easier to press out the hinge pins rather than remove the hinges from the car body; this will avoid the need to align the door later. If you do decide to remove the hinges, carefully matchmark the hinges to the vehicle body to ease aligning the door during installation.

> ※※ **WARNING:**
>
> **Never leave a door unsupported while one of the hinges is unscrewed, or while its hinge pin is out; doing so could bend or break the other hinge.**

1 Open the door and position a padded floor jack under the door for support.

2 Remove the circlip from the lower end of the pin that holds the door check strap to the body, then remove the door check strap.

3 If the original door is to be reinstalled, perform the following:

a) *Remove the plastic caps from the tops of the hinge pins.*

b) *Press out the hinge pins with a special press-out tool.*

> ※※ **WARNING:**
>
> **Do not attempt to hammer the pins out of the hinges; the hinges will be damaged.**

c) *With the help of an assistant, remove the door from the vehicle.*

4 If the hinge pins are going to be left in place, perform the following:

a) *Pry the plastic caps (that are adjacent to the hinges) out of the body's hinge pillar (except on Karmann Ghias).*

b) *Using an impact driver, loosen the Phillips head screws holding the hinges to the body.*

c) *Taking care not to scratch the door, body, or fender, remove the door (together with its hinges) from the body.*

To install:

5 If the original door is being installed on the vehicle, the installation procedure is the reverse of the removal procedure. Make certain to check the weatherseal; if it is cracked, torn, or otherwise damaged, replace it.

6 If a replacement door is being installed, perform the following:

a) *Remove the lock striker plate from the lock pillar on the body.*

b) *Install the new door, together with its hinges, but do not fully tighten the Phillips head screws.*

➡**The hinges are screwed to movable threaded plates. This makes it possible to shift the position of the door in its opening for alignment purposes.**

c) *Align the door in the door opening so that it contacts the weatherstrip evenly all around and the door's trim molding is in line with the trim molding on the side of the body.*

d) *After the door is aligned, tighten the Phillips head screws, then set them firmly with an impact driver.*

e) *Install the door check strap with the pin and circlip. Install the lock striker plate and adjust it as described later in this section.*

Type 2 Models

If the same door is to be reinstalled, matchmark the location of the hinges on your body. this will prevent your having to align the door later.

1 Remove the circlip off the pin for the door check strap. Remove the pin and disconnect the strap.

2 With the door solidly supported so that the upper hinge will not bend or break by the door's weight, remove the 2 Phillips head (or socket head) screws that hold the lower hinge to the hinge pillar. If the screws are rusted tight, loosen them with an impact driver.

3 With the door supported, remove the 2 Phillips head (or socket head) screws from the upper hinge and remove the door together with its hinges.

To install:

4 Inspect the rubber weatherstrip around the door. If it is cracked or deformed, replace it.

➡**Before replacing the weatherstripping, clean all of the old adhesive off of the door with solvent. Install the new weatherstripping with trim adhesive.**

5 If a new door is being installed, remove the lock striker plate from the lock pillar.

6 If the original door is being installed, mount the hinges with the matchmarks correctly aligned. If a new door is being installed, do not fully tighten the hinge mounting screws.

➡**The hinges are screwed to movable threaded plates. This makes it possible to shift the position of the door in its opening for alignment purposes.**

7 To align a new door, position the door in the door opening so that it contacts the weatherstripping evenly all around and the door's trim molding is aligned with the trim molding on the side of the body.

8 After the door is properly aligned, tighten the hinge mounting screws. Set the Phillips head screws firmly with an impact driver.

9 Attach the door check strap to its bracket with the pin and circlip.

10 Install the door lock striker plate and adjust it as described later in this section.

STRIKER PLATE ADJUSTMENT

All Models

After installing a replacement door, adjust the striker plate so that the rear edge of the door aligns with the body. The striker plate should also be adjusted if the door rattles or requires excessive force to close and lock.

Because of body flexion, the door lock striker plate cannot be accurately adjusted while the car is raised on jackstands or a lift.

A door rattle that persists even after all possible adjustments have been made indicates a worn rubber wedge.

1 Remove the striker plate mounting screws and remove the striker plate from the body. Close the door and check its alignment. Adjust the door if it is out of adjustment.

2 Insert the striker plate, bottom first, in the latch. Press the latch down into its fully locked position. Turn the striker plate until it is in its

The striker plate can be adjusted horizontally and vertically to bring the door into proper alignment (1966 and earlier Type 1 models shown)

You may need an impact screwdriver to remove the four Phillips head screws that retain the striker plate (1967 and later Type 1 models shown)

normal upright (vertical) position.

3   If the striker plate exhibits vertical (up and down) free-play, the rubber wedge is worn. Either add shims or replace the wedge with a new one.

➡**To correct either a misalignment between the door and front body, or a lack of uniformity in the gap between the door and body, adjust the hinges and not the striker plate. Only misalignment (vertical or horizontal) between the door and rear body should be corrected by adjusting the striker plate.**

4   After correcting any excessive wedge play, correct any misalignment between the door and rear body. Center the striker plat on the lock pillar by aligning the marks on the striker plate with those on the pillar.

5   Close the door. Check if the door aligns with the rear body. If necessary, adjust the position of the striker plate on the lock pillar.

➡**The striker plate screws onto the movable threaded plate. By moving the plate up or down, you can correct any misalignment of the ridge in the body where the door and the rear body meet. Moving the plate in or out corrects the position of the door so that it will be flush with the side of the car when the door is closed.**

6   After aligning the door, feel for play between the lock and the striker plate. If there is play, or if the door will not latch, rotate the top of the striker plate toward the outside of the vehicle. If the door is too difficult or hard to close, or if the handle works stiffly, rotate the top of the striker plate toward the inside of the vehicle. Only rotate the striker plate a little at a time, then recheck the alignment. Once the proper alignment is found, tighten the striker plate screws securely.

Side Sliding Door

REMOVAL & INSTALLATION

Type 2 Models

➡**An assistant will be necessary to safely perform this procedure.**

1   Remove the outside runner cover as follows:

a) *Remove the 3 Phillips head screws, located at the front of the outside runner cover, that hold the cover on the body.*

b) *Remove the cover securing nut and bolt from inside the passenger compartment.*

c) *Fully open the sliding door.*

d) *Loosen the Phillips head screw on the retaining strip by about 15 revolutions.*

e) *Place a punch against the head of the Phillips head screw, then, using a hammer, tap the punch sharply to drive the retaining strip toward the rear of the body.*

f) *Starting at the rear of the sliding door, lift the outside runner cover up and out of the retaining strip.*

g) *After taking the cover off, fully remove the Phillips head screws from the ends of the retaining strip and remove the retaining strip from the body.*

2   Push the door far enough to the rear so that the guide piece and the roller on the hinge link can be lifted sideways out of the recess in the center runner.

3   Push the door completely to the rear and lift it until the upper roller can be lifted out of the top runner.

4   Swing the door slightly outward and pull the lower rollers out of the break in the bottom runner and remove the door.

To install:

5   Inspect the runners and, if necessary, straighten them. Check the guide and support rollers on the door. Replace damaged rollers. Lubricate the rollers with multipurpose grease if they turn stiffly.

6   Inspect the rubber weatherstripping around the door opening in the body. If necessary, remove the old weatherstripping, using solvent to remove any residual traces of the weatherstripping. Use a weatherstripping adhesive to glue the new weatherstripping in place.

7   Insert the door first into the bottom runner, then into the top runner.

8   Push the door forward until the roller and guide can be inserted in the break in the center runner.

9   Loosely install the retaining strip. Press the cover into the gap between the body and the retaining strip from above, then insert the beading.

➡**Place a small amount of plastic sealing compound ("dumdum") between the retaining strip and the body to maintain a gap while the cover and beading are being installed.**

10   Install the 2 Phillips head screws which screw in from below.

11   By turning the Phillips head screw in the front end of the retain-

These photos illustrate a method of repairing simple dents. They are intended to supplement Body repair this Chapter and should not be used as the sole instructions for body repair on these vehicles.

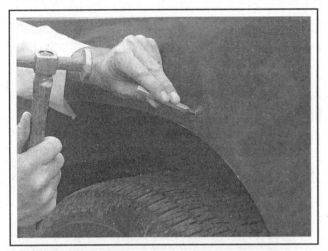

1   If you can't access the backside of the body panel to hammer out the dent, pull it out with a slide-hammer-type dent puller. In the deepest portion of the dent or along the crease line, drill or punch hole(s) at least one inch apart . . .

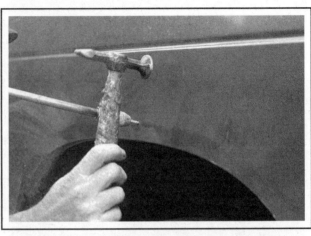

2   . . . then screw the slide-hammer into the hole and operate it. Tap with a hammer near the edge of the dent to help 'pop' the metal back to its original shape. When you're finished, the dent area should be close to its original contour and about 1/8-inch below the surface of the surrounding metal

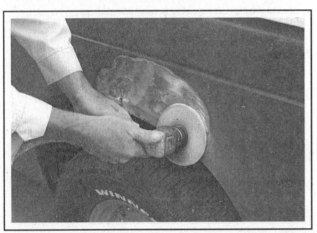

3   Using coarse-grit sandpaper, remove the paint down to the bare metal. Hand sanding works fine, but the disc sander shown here makes the job faster. Use finer (about 320-grit) sandpaper to feather-edge the paint at least one inch around the dent area

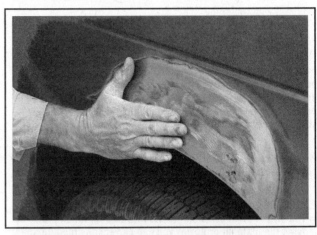

4   When the paint is removed, touch will probably be more helpful than sight for telling if the metal is straight. Hammer down the high spots or raise the low spots as necessary. Clean the repair area with wax/silicone remover

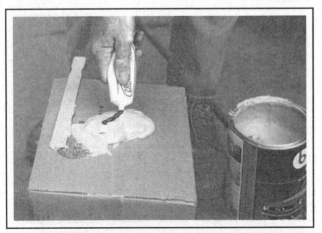

5   Following label instructions, mix up a batch of plastic filler and hardener. The ratio of filler to hardener is critical, and, if you mix it incorrectly, it will either not cure properly or cure too quickly (you won't have time to file and sand it into shape)

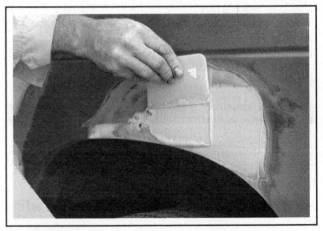

6   Working quickly so the filler doesn't harden, use a plastic applicator to press the body filler firmly into the metal, assuring it bonds completely. Work the filler until it matches the original contour and is slightly above the surrounding metal

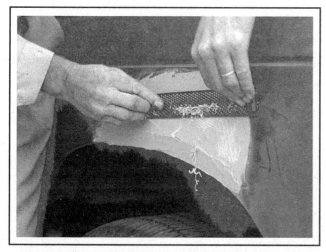

7   Let the filler harden until you can just dent it with your fingernail. Use a body file or Surform tool (shown here) to rough-shape the filler

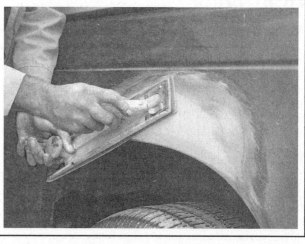

8   Use coarse-grit sandpaper and a sanding board or block to work the filler down until it's smooth and even. Work down to finer grits of sandpaper - always using a board or block - ending up with 360 or 400 grit

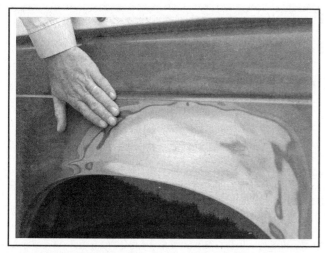

9   You shouldn't be able to feel any ridge at the transition from the filler to the bare metal or from the bare metal to the old paint. As soon as the repair is flat and uniform, remove the dust and mask off the adjacent panels or trim pieces

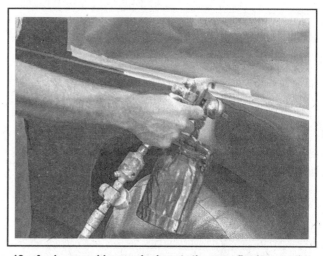

10   Apply several layers of primer to the area. Don't spray the primer on too heavy, so it sags or runs, and make sure each coat is dry before you spray on the next one. A professional-type spray gun is being used here, but aerosol spray primer is available inexpensively from auto parts stores

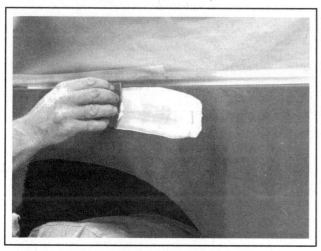

11   The primer will help reveal imperfections or scratches. Fill these with glazing compound. Follow the label instructions and sand it with 360 or 400-grit sandpaper until it's smooth. Repeat the glazing, sanding and respraying until the primer reveals a perfectly smooth surface

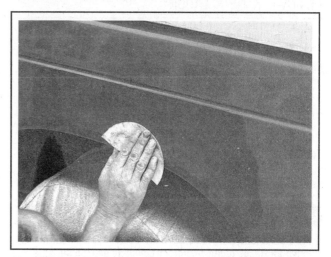

12   Finish sand the primer with very fine sandpaper (400 or 600-grit) to remove the primer overspray. Clean the area with water and allow it to dry. Use a tack rag to remove any dust, then apply the finish coat. Don't attempt to rub out or wax the repair area until the paint has dried completely (at least two weeks)

ing strip, tension the retaining strip while making sure that the beading is correctly positioned.

12 Secure the cover at the lock pillar end with the remaining Phillips head screw. Install the nut and bolt from inside the passenger compartment.

13 Align the side sliding door, as described later in this section.

ALIGNMENT

The sliding door is properly adjusted if the gap between the door and the door opening is even all around. The trim or waistline on the door must align with the trim or waistline on the body and the door surface must be flush with the surface of the body.

• If the door is not aligned at the bottom, adjust the lower roller. To do this, loosen the Phillips head screw and the 2 socket head screws which hold the lower roller bracket. Insert or remove shims to adjust the height of the roller; the roller can also be moved forward or rearward.

• If the door is not flush with the body at the top, loosen the nut on the top roller shaft. Adjust the roller in or out until the top of the door is flush.

• To prevent excessive vertical door movement, loosen the 3 Phillips head screws that hold the top roller bracket. Raise the bracket until the clearance between the roller and the runner is as small as possible.

• To adjust the door gap to a uniform width, close the door. Loosen the 4 bolts on the hinge housing and adjust the angle of the hinge link.

• To check excessive latch play, press the door firmly near the hinge link. If there is any detectable play, adjust the striker plate (as described earlier in this section).

• To align the door retainer with the rear bracket, loosen the Phillips head screws and shift the position of the retainer up or down.

• To adjust the locking plate for the remote control lock, slightly loosen the 2 locking plate bolts and close the door to center the locking plate. Open the door and tighten the bolts securely. If necessary, up to 2 spacer shims can be placed behind the locking plate.

Front Hood

REMOVAL & INSTALLATION

To avoid damaging the finish, cover the cowl panel with a protective cloth. To save installation time, matchmark the hinge positions before removing the hood. An assistant is needed for this procedure:

1 Matchmark the hinges to the underside of the hood.

2 Remove the 2 hood bolts from one of the hinges.

3 Have an assistant hold the unbolted side of the hood while you remove the 2 hood bolts from the other side.

4 Together, lift the hood up and off toward the front of the car.

To install:

5 Before installing the hood, check the condition of the rubber weatherstripping. If necessary, reglue or replace it.

✳✳ WARNING:

If the weatherstripping is going to be replaced, make certain to remove all traces of old weatherstripping by using a suitable solvent. Otherwise the new weatherstripping may not install evenly or may fail to adhere properly to the body.

6 Attach the hood loosely. Move the hood in the elongated bolt

holes until it contacts the weatherstripping evenly all around. Then tighten the bolts securely.

7 On type 3 models, align the hood with the fenders by screwing the adjustable rubber bumpers in or out. To prevent vibrations, be sure the bumpers contact the body.

8 Check the lock operation by opening and closing the hood several times. If necessary, adjust the lock.

➡**If it is necessary to lower the hinges after the hood has been removed, use a lever bolted to the hinge.**

To remove the hinge from the body, remove the dashboard access panel from the rear of the luggage compartment by removing the 2 knurled nuts. Also remove the front luggage compartment load liner. Pry the E-clip off the bottom pivot pin for the spring mount. Then press out the pin and swing the spring toward the front of the car until it is no longer compressed. unbolt the hinge from the bracket under the dashboard.

Rear Hood

REMOVAL & INSTALLATION

Type 1 Models

1 Open the rear hood, then remove the air cleaner assembly.

2 Matchmark the hinge position on the rear hood.

3 Disconnect the negative battery cable.

4 Cover the carburetor intake to prevent the entry of dirt.

5 Disconnect the license plate light wire and unfasten it from the hood so that it will not be damaged as the hood is removed.

6 Remove the 4 bolts that hold the hood hinges to the curved hinge brackets on the body.

7 Pull the hood out and upward against spring pressure and unhook the load spring from the bracket on the vehicle's roof panel. The spring will stay with the hood when the hood is removed.

8 If necessary, remove the curved hinge brackets from the car body by removing the 3 bolts at each bracket.

To install:

9 Before installing the hood, check the condition of the rubber weatherstripping. If necessary, reglue or replace the weatherstripping.

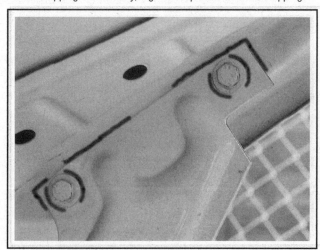

Draw or scribe around each washer to ensure correct hood alignment with the hinges during reattachment - to adjust the hood, make alignment marks along the edge of each hinge so you can judge how much you're moving the hood relative to the hinge

To remove the rear deck lid from a Type 1 model, first remove the air cleaner assembly (A), then separate the hinges (B) from the hinge supports (C) by removing the mounting bolts (D)

If the weatherstripping is going to be replaced, make certain to remove all traces of old weatherstripping by using a suitable solvent. Otherwise, the new weatherstripping may not install evenly or may fail to adhere properly to the body.

10 Loosely install one hood hinge on the curved bracket on the car body.

11 Holding the hood at an angle so that you can reach behind it, engage the spring in the bracket on the car roof panel.

12 Push the hood upward and toward the car. Loosely install the remaining hinge.

13 Move the hood in the elongated bolt holes until it contacts the weatherstripping evenly all around, then tighten the hinge bolts securely.

Types 2 and 3 Models

Some Type 2 models are equipped with an upper luggage compartment hood and a lower engine access hood, whereas the Type 3 models are equipped with one rear hood which supplies access to the luggage compartment and engine bay - all rear hoods on these models are removed in the same manner.

1 Before removing the rear luggage compartment hood or the rear engine access hood, matchmark its position on the hinges for easier alignment during installation.

2 Disconnect the negative battery wire.

3 Cut the license plate light wire in the middle so that it can later be rejoined with a splice or butt-end connector.

4 Remove the hinge-to-hood bolts on one side of the hood. Have an assistant support the unbolted side of the hood while you remove the hinge-to-hood bolts on the other side of the hood.

5 Lift off the rear hood together.

To install:

6 Installation is the reverse of the removal procedure. Make sure that the hinge-to-hood matchmarks are properly aligned and make certain that the latch works correctly.

7 Once the hood is properly aligned and the hinge-to-hood bolts and tightened securely, splice the two ends of the license plate light wire back together.

8 Connect the negative battery cable.

Bumpers

REMOVAL & INSTALLATION

Type 1 Models

Only the bumper itself can be removed by taking off the nuts on the back of the bumper. The brackets and reinforcement strap can stay on the car.

FRONT BUMPER

1 Using a 13mm wrench, remove all bumper bracket-to-body bolts.

2 Pull the bumper, together with the brackets and reinforcement strap or the damping elements, out of the slots in the front fenders.

3 Remove the 3 nuts from each bracket. Separate the reinforcement strap from the bumper and the brackets.

4 Remove the 3 nuts from each bumper bracket. Remove the brackets from the bumper.

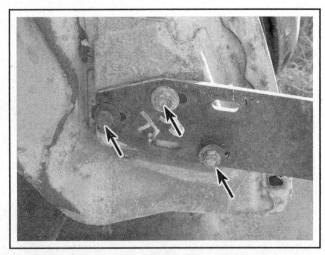

Typical bumper assembly on a 1967 or earlier Beetle - to remove the bumper, simply unbolt the brackets

5 Installation is the reverse of the removal procedure. Replace the rubber grommets in the front fenders if they are weathered or damaged. Lubricate the threads on the nuts and bolts before installing them.

When installing the bumper and the brackets on the car, install the bolts, but do not tighten them. Adjust the bumper to a uniform gap with the body before tightening the bolts to 14 ft. lbs.

REAR BUMPER

1 Using a 13mm wrench, remove all bumper bracket-to-body bolts.

2 Pull the bumper, together with the brackets and reinforcement strap or the damping elements, out of the slots in the front fenders.

3 Remove the 3 nuts from each bumper bracket or damping element. remove the brackets or damping elements from the bumper.

4 Installation is the reverse of the removal procedure. Replace the rubber grommets in the front fenders if they are weathered or damaged. Lubricate the threads on the nuts and bolts before installing them.

When installing the bumper and the brackets on the car, install the bolts, but do not tighten them. Adjust the bumper to a uniform gap with the body before tightening the bolts to 14 ft. lbs.

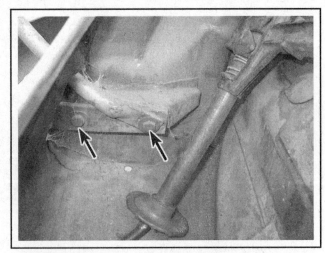

To get at the bumper bracket bolts on 1967 and earlier Beetles and Karmann Ghias, open the hood and remove the spare tire

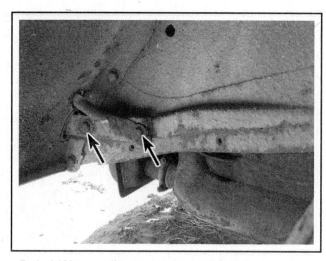

Typical 1967 or earlier rear bumper bracket bolts

Type 2 Models

FRONT BUMPER

1 Thoroughly clean the exposed threads on all bumper mounting bolts before you attempt to remove them. If corrosion is evident, or if the nuts or bolts are difficult to turn, apply penetrating oil to the threads.

2 Remove the 2 side support bolts located just ahead of each front wheel.

3 Remove the 2 bumper bracket-to-frame rail bolts from one end of the bumper.

4 Place a support under the unbolted end of the bumper, or have someone hold it. Then remove the 2 bolts from the other end of the bumper and remove the bumper from the vehicle.

5 To remove the bumper bracket, remove the nuts and bolts attaching the bracket to the bumper.

6 To remove the end pieces, take out the 3 nuts and bolts that hold them on the bumper. Be careful not to damage the rubber seal.

7 Installation is the reverse of the removal procedure. Loosely install the assembled bumper and brackets on the vehicle. Then, by sliding the brackets and side supports on their elongated bolt holes,

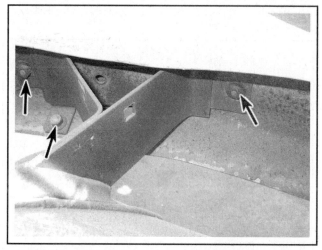

Bumper mounting fasteners - 1968 and later Beetles (Karmann Ghias similar)

obtain a uniform gap between the bumper and the body. When the bumper is properly aligned, tighten the bolts to 25 ft. lbs.

REAR BUMPER

1 Remove the bolts and nuts at both sides of the vehicle that hold the cover plate to the body.

2 Remove the 2 bolts that hold one of the bumper brackets to the frame sidemember.

3 Place a support under the unbolted end of the bumper, or have someone hold it. Then remove the 2 bolts from the other bracket and remove the bumper from the vehicle.

4 The brackets and cover plate can be unbolted at this time.

➡**Thoroughly clean the exposed threads. if corrosion is evident, or if the nuts are hard to turn, apply penetrating oil.**

5 Installation is the reverse of the removal procedure. Be careful not to damage the rubber spacers by overtightening the bolt on the cover plate. Loosely install the assembled bumper and brackets on the vehicle. Then, by sliding the brackets and cover plate on their elongated bolt holes, obtain a uniform gap between the bumper and the body. When the bumper is properly aligned, tighten the bracket bolts to 25 ft. lbs. Do not overtighten the bolts that hold the cover plates on the body.

Type 3 Models

FRONT BUMPER

1 Disconnect the negative battery cable.

2 Disconnect the horn wire. the horn may be left attached to the bumper until the bumper is removed from the car.

3 Remove the 2 screws securing the reinforcement bar inside the bumper.

4 Remove the 3 bolts under each front fender that hold the bumper brackets onto the body.

5 Pull the bumper forward and off the car, complete with brackets and reinforcement bar.

6 Lift out the reinforcement bar. Remove the nuts from the carriage bolts that hold the brackets to the bumper, then remove the brackets. Unbolt the horn and remove it.

7 Installation is the reverse of the removal procedure. When installing the bumper assembly, make certain that the gap between the bumper and the body is uniform. When bolting the bumper brackets to the body, remember to install the washers.

REAR BUMPER

The brackets used to mount the rear bumper are different from those used to mount the front bumper.

1 Remove the 2 bumper bracket-to-body bolts on each end of the bumper.

2 Pull the bumper rearward and off the vehicle, complete with brackets.

3 Unbolt the brackets and back-up lights, if applicable.

4 Installation is the reverse of the removal procedure.

Fenders

REMOVAL & INSTALLATION

Karmann Ghia fenders are welded to the body and require special tools and skills for replacement. Fenders on other models can be replaced by any car owner.

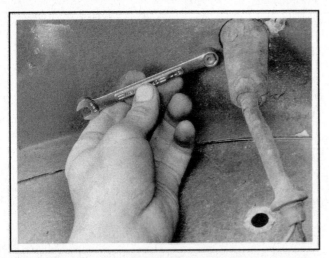

To remove the front fender, detach the turn signal wiring and remove the signal's mounting nuts . . .

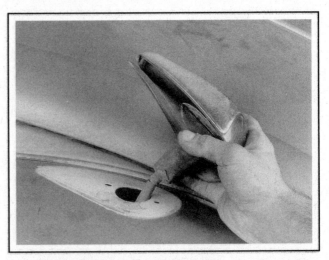

. . . then lift the turn signal off of the fender

Type 1 Models

FRONT FENDERS

1 Disconnect the negative battery cable.

2 Use an 8mm wrench to remove the 2 nuts under the fender. Remove the turn signal/side-marker light assembly from the fender, then disconnect the light from its wires. Label the wires to ensure correct installation.

3 Pull the gasket for the turn signal/side-marker light assembly down through the fender.

5 Remove the headlight, as described in Section 6.

6 Insert a small flat-bladed prytool into the small slot below each terminal in the sealed beam connector. Then pull the wire and terminal out of the rear of the connector.

7 Pull the wires and their protective hose back and out of the fender's headlight housing.

8 Remove the front bumper, as described earlier in this section.

9 On left fenders, disconnect the wires from the horn, then remove the horn.

10 Remove the nut, bolt and washers that hold the fender to the running board. Then remove the 10 fender bolts and washers and remove the fender and beading.

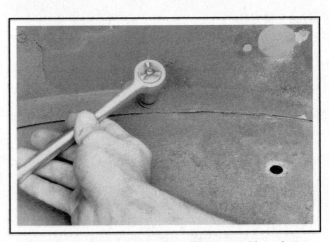

After removing the bumper and headlight assembly, unfasten the fender mounting bolts

To install:

11 Position the fender against the car body without the beading. Loosely install a bolt at the top of the fender in order to support it.

12 Start the remaining 7 bolts in their threads so that the fender hangs loosely on the car.

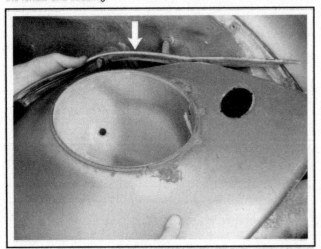

Pull the fender away from the vehicle and remove the plastic beading (arrow) . . .

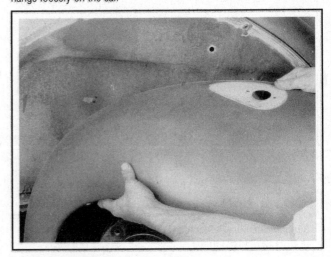

. . . then remove the fender from the vehicle

13 Install a new rubber spacer washer between the fender and the running board. Install, but do not tighten the nut, bolt and washers.

14 Using your hand, press the beading into the space between the fender and the body. Make sure the beading is even and that the notches have all slipped over the bolts.

15 Gradually tighten the bolts to 11 ft. lbs., checking constantly to see that the beading remains in place.

16 Tighten the bolt that holds the fender to the running board to 11 ft. lbs.

17 The remainder of installation is the reverse of the removal procedure. When installing the sealed beam terminals in their connector, the yellow wire goes in the top center slot, the white wire in the left slot and the brown wire in the right slot (as seen from the front of the car, looking into the headlight).

REAR FENDERS

1 Working under the fender, use an 8mm wrench to remove the tail light nuts, then remove the tail light assembly.

2 Disconnect the wires from the tail light assembly and label them for correct reinstallation. Pull the wires and the rubber grommet down and out of the fender.

3 Remove the rear bumper, as described earlier in this section.

4 Remove the nut, bolt and washers that hold the fender to the running board. Then remove the 9 bolts and washers which hold the fender to the car body. Remove the old beading.

To install:

5 Position the fender against the car body without the beading. Loosely install a bolt at the top of the fender in order to support it.

6 Start the remaining 8 bolts in their threads so that the fender hangs loosely on the car.

7 Install a new rubber spacer washer between the fender and the running board. Install, but do not tighten the nut, bolt and washers.

8 Using your hand, press the beading into the space between the fender and the body. Make sure the beading is even and that the notches have all slipped over the bolts.

9 Gradually tighten the bolts to 11 ft. lbs., checking constantly to see that the beading remains in place.

10 Tighten the bolt that holds the fender to the running board to 11 ft. lbs.

11 The remainder of installation is the reverse of the removal procedure. Make certain that the tail lights, stop lights and turn signals all work properly.

RUNNING BOARD

To remove the running board, remove the nuts, bolts and washers that hold the running board to the front and rear fenders. remove the two rubber spacer washers from between the fenders and the running board. Then loosen, but do not remove, the 4 bolts that hold the running board to the body.

Installation is the reverse of the removal procedure. Use new rubber spacer washers at the front and rear of the running board. Tighten the bolts that fasten the running board to the fenders to 11 ft. lbs. Tighten the bolts which hold the running board to the body to 7 ft. lbs.

Type 2 Models

The fenders on Type 2 models are not removable. If the fenders are damaged and need replacement, have the fenders repaired by someone qualified to do automotive body work.

Type 3 Models

The fenders can be removed and installed on the body without any cutting or welding. All fenders are held in place by bolts. Plastic beading forms a gasket between the individual fenders and the body itself.

FRONT FENDERS

The bumper brackets pass through the front fenders. The front bumper and reinforcement bar must therefore be removed prior to removing the front fender.

1 Disconnect the negative battery cable.

2 Disconnect the horn wire (left fender only).

3 Remove the tank filler flap lock and cable (right fender only).

4 Remove the hexagon head sheet metal screw, located under the edge of the fender just ahead of the door.

5 With the car door open, remove the single bolt from the door hinge pillar.

6 Carefully pull the front side panel trim off the body interior, then remove the bolts behind the front side panel trim.

7 Remove the 4th bolt underneath the instrument panel. You must take the fuse box out first when working on the left side of the car.

8 Remove the 9 sheet metal screws together with the flat washers and rubber washers.

To install:

9 Apply new D 19 sealing tape on the hinge pillar.

10 Install the fender loosely, using all of the bolts.

11 Insert the plastic beading between the fender and the body.

12 Align the fender properly with the body and tighten all of the bolts.

13 Glue the front panel trim back with D 12 trim cement.

REAR FENDERS

The rear fenders of the Fastback, Notchback, and Squareback sedans differ, but the mounting fastener locations are identical. The main difference in removal procedures is that all 8 upper mounting screws of the Squareback are removed from the rear luggage area. On the Fastback and Notchback models, 5 screws are removed from inside the luggage area and 3 are removed from the car's interior. On all models, the rear bumper must be removed to get working clearance.

1 Using a wooden wedge, pry the trim molding off the lower front area of the rear fender.

2 Remove the rear seat.

3 Pull the beading off of the door pillar.

4 Remove the side trim panel from the car's interior.

➡**The side trim panel is different in Fastback, Notchback, and Squareback models. The number of spring clips that hold the side trim panel to the inner body panel also differs. However, removal is essentially the same for both models.**

5 Remove the 2 bolts that hold the fender to the side member. The bolts are located under the front forward edge of the fender.

6 Remove the rear light lens, then remove the entire rear light assembly. Disconnect the wires and pull them free of the fender, being careful not to damage the rubber grommets.

7 Remove the single bolt in the rear light assembly hole.

8 Remove the 2 sheet metal screws located under the rear lower edge of the fender.

9 Partially remove the luggage compartment lid seal from the metal band that is beside the rear light opening.

10 Remove the 2 fasteners located next to the rear light assembly opening.

11 For Squareback models, support the fender. Working from inside the rear load area, remove the 8 hexagon head sheet metal screws along the upper fender edge. Take the fender off the car.

12 For Fastback and Notchback models, support the fender to avoid buckling it when the bolts are removed. Then remove the 3 hexagon head sheet metal screws from inside the car, next to the rear seat.

13 For Fastback and Notchback models, remove the 5 hexagon head sheet metal screws from inside the luggage compartment, then remove the fender from the vehicle.

To install:

14 Check the fender seals and replace them if damaged.

15 Check the condition and mounting of the rubber seal around the lower part of the wheel housing. if it is damaged, replace it before installing the fender.

16 Attach the fender to the body loosely and insert the plastic beading between them.

17 Align the fender with the door and body. Tighten the bolts securely.

18 Install the exterior trim strip. glue the interior trim panels in position with D 12 trim cement.

AUTO BODY REPAIR

You can repair most minor auto body damage yourself. Minor damage usually falls into one of several categories: (1) small scratches and dings in the paint that can be repaired without the use of body filler, (2) deep scratches and dents that require body filler, but do not require pulling, or hammering metal back into shape and (3) rust-out repairs. The repair sequences illustrated in this section are typical of these types of repairs. If you want to get involved in more complicated repairs including pulling or hammering sheet metal back into shape, you will probably need more detailed instructions. Chilton's **Minor Auto Body Repair, 2nd Edition** is a comprehensive guide to repairing auto body damage yourself.

Tools and Supplies

The list of tools and equipment you may need to fix minor body damage ranges from very basic hand tools to a wide assortment of specialized body tools. Most minor scratches, dings and rust holes can be fixed using an electric drill, wire wheel or grinder attachment, half-round plastic file, sanding block, various grades of sandpaper (#36, which is coarse through #600, which is fine) in both wet and dry types, auto body plastic, primer, touch-up paint, spreaders, newspaper and masking tape.

Most manufacturers of auto body repair products began supplying materials to professionals. Their knowledge of the best, most-used products has been translated into body repair kits for the do-it-yourselfer. Kits are available from a number of manufacturers and contain the necessary materials in the required amounts for the repair identified on the package.

Kits are available for a wide variety of uses, including:

- Rusted out metal
- All purpose kit for dents and holes
- Dents and deep scratches
- Fiberglass repair kit
- Epoxy kit for restyling.

Kits offer the advantage of buying what you need for the job. There is little waste and little chance of materials going bad from not being used. The same manufacturers also merchandise all of the individual products used - spreaders, dent pullers, fiberglass cloth, polyester resin, cream hardener, body filler, body files, sandpaper, sanding discs and holders, primer, spray paint, etc.

✳✳ CAUTION:

Most of the products you will be using contain harmful chemicals, so be extremely careful. Always read the complete label before opening the containers. When you put them away for future use, be sure they are out of children's reach!

Most auto body repair kits contain all the materials you need to do the job right in the kit. So, if you have a small rust spot or dent you want to fix, check the contents of the kit before you run out and buy any additional tools.

Rust, Undercoating, and Rustproofing

GENERAL INFORMATION

Rust is an electrochemical process. It works on ferrous metals (iron and steel) from the inside out due to exposure of unprotected surfaces to air and moisture. The possibility of rust exists practically nationwide - anywhere humidity, industrial pollution or chemical salts are present, rust can form. In coastal areas, the problem is high humidity and salt air; in snowy areas, the problem is chemical salt (de-icer) used to keep the roads clear, and in industrial areas, sulfur dioxide is present in the air from industrial pollution and is changed to sulfuric acid when it rains. The rusting process is accelerated by high temperatures, especially in snowy areas, when vehicles are driven over slushy roads and then left overnight in a heated garage.

Automotive styling also can be a contributor to rust formation. Spot welding of panels creates small pockets that trap moisture and form an environment for rust formation. Fortunately, auto manufacturers have been working hard to increase the corrosion protection of their products. Galvanized sheet metal enjoys much wider use, along with the increased use of plastic and various rust retardant coatings. Manufacturers are also phasing out areas in automotive bodies where rust-forming moisture can collect.

To prevent rust, you must stop it before it gets started. On new vehicles, there are two ways to accomplish this.

First, the car should be treated with a commercial rustproofing compound. There are many different brands of franchised rustproofers, but most processes involve spraying a waxy "self-healing" compound under the chassis, inside rocker panels, inside doors and fender liners and similar places where rust is likely to form. Prices for a quality rustproofing job range from $100 - $250, depending on the area, the brand name and the size of the vehicle.

Ideally, the vehicle should be rustproofed as soon as possible following the purchase. The surfaces of the car have begun to oxidize and deteriorate during shipping. In addition, the car may have sat on a dealer's lot or on a lot at the factory, and once the rust has progressed past the stage of light, powdery surface oxidation rustproofing is not likely to be worthwhile. Professional rustproofers feel that once rust has formed, rustproofing will simply seal in moisture already present. Most franchised rustproofing operations offer a 3 - 5 year warranty against rust-through, but will not support that warranty if the rustproofing is not applied within three months of the date of manufacture.

Undercoating should not be mistaken for rustproofing. Undercoating is a black, tar-like substance that is applied to the underside of a vehicle. Its basic function is to deaden noises that are transmitted from under the car. It simply cannot get into the crevices and seams where moisture tends to collect. In fact, it may clog up drainage holes and ventilation passages. Some undercoatings also tend to crack or peel with age and only create more moisture and corrosion attracting pockets.

The second thing you should do immediately after purchasing the car is apply a paint sealant. A sealant is a petroleum based product marketed under a wide variety of brand names. It has the same protective properties as a good wax, but bonds to the paint with a chemically inert layer that seals it from the air. If air can't get at the surface, oxidation cannot start.

The paint sealant kit consists of a base coat and a conditioning coat that should be applied every 6 - 8 months, depending on the manufacturer. The base coat must be applied before waxing, or the wax must first be removed.

Third, keep a garden hose handy for your car in winter. Use it a few times on nice days during the winter for underneath areas, and it will pay big dividends when spring arrives. Spraying under the fenders and other areas which even car washes don't reach will help remove road salt, dirt and other build-ups which help breed rust. Adjust the nozzle to a high-force spray. An old brush will help break up residue, permitting it to be washed away more easily.

It's a somewhat messy job, but worth it in the long run because rust often starts in those hidden areas.

At the same time, wash grime off the door sills and, more importantly, the under portions of the doors, plus the tailgate if you have a station wagon. Applying a coat of wax to those areas at least once before and once during winter will help fend off rust.

When applying the wax to the under parts of the doors, you will note small drain holes. These holes often are plugged with undercoating or dirt. Make sure they are cleaned out to prevent water build-up inside the doors. A small punch or penknife will do the job.

Water from the high-pressure sprays in car washes sometimes can get into the housings for parking and taillights, so take a close look. If they contain water merely loosen the retaining screws and the water should run out.

One thing you have to remember about rust: even if you grind away all the rusted metal in a panel, and repair the area with any of the kits available, **eventually** the rust will return. There are two reasons for this. One, rust is a chemical reaction that causes pressure under the repair from the inside out. That's how the blisters form. Two, the back side of the panel (and the repair) is wide open to moisture, and unpainted body filler acts like a sponge. That's why the best solution to rust problems is to remove the rusted panel and install a new one or have the rusted area cut out and a new piece of sheet metal welded in its place. The trouble with welding is the expense; sometimes it will cost more than the car is worth.

One of the better solutions to do-it-yourself rust repair is the process using a fiberglass cloth repair kit. This will give a strong repair that resists cracking and moisture and is relatively easy to use. It can be used on large or small holes and also can be applied over contoured surfaces.

GLOSSARY

AIR/FUEL RATIO: The ratio of air-to-gasoline by weight in the fuel mixture drawn into the engine.

AIR INJECTION: One method of reducing harmful exhaust emissions by injecting air into each of the exhaust ports of an engine. The fresh air entering the hot exhaust manifold causes any remaining fuel to be burned before it can exit the tailpipe.

ALTERNATOR: A device used for converting mechanical energy into electrical energy.

AMMETER: An instrument, calibrated in amperes, used to measure the flow of an electrical current in a circuit. Ammeters are always connected in series with the circuit being tested.

AMPERE: The rate of flow of electrical current present when one volt of electrical pressure is applied against one ohm of electrical resistance.

ANALOG COMPUTER: Any microprocessor that uses similar (analogous) electrical signals to make its calculations.

ARMATURE: A laminated, soft iron core wrapped by a wire that converts electrical energy to mechanical energy as in a motor or relay. When rotated in a magnetic field, it changes mechanical energy into electrical energy as in a generator.

ATMOSPHERIC PRESSURE: The pressure on the Earth's surface caused by the weight of the air in the atmosphere. At sea level, this pressure is 14.7 psi at 32-degrees F (101 kPa at 0-degrees C).

ATOMIZATION: The breaking down of a liquid into a fine mist that can be suspended in air.

AXIAL PLAY: Movement parallel to a shaft or bearing bore.

BACKFIRE: The sudden combustion of gases in the intake or exhaust system that results in a loud explosion.

BACKLASH: The clearance or play between two parts, such as meshed gears.

BACKPRESSURE: Restrictions in the exhaust system that slow the exit of exhaust gases from the combustion chamber.

BAKELITE: A heat resistant, plastic insulator material commonly used in printed circuit boards and transistorized components.

BALL BEARING: A bearing made up of hardened inner and outer races between which hardened steel balls roll.

BALLAST RESISTOR: A resistor in the primary ignition circuit that lowers voltage after the engine is started to reduce wear on ignition components.

BEARING: A friction reducing, supportive device usually located between a stationary part and a moving part.

BIMETAL TEMPERATURE SENSOR: Any sensor or switch made of two dissimilar types of metal that bend when heated or cooled due to the different expansion rates of the alloys. These types of sensors usually function as an on/off switch.

BLOWBY: Combustion gases, composed of water vapor and unburned fuel, that leak past the piston rings into the crankcase during normal engine operation. These gases are removed by the PCV system to prevent the buildup of harmful acids in the crankcase.

BRAKE PAD: A brake shoe and lining assembly used with disc brakes.

BRAKE SHOE: The backing for the brake lining. The term is, however, usually applied to the assembly of the brake backing and lining.

BUSHING: A liner, usually removable, for a bearing; an anti-friction liner used in place of a bearing.

CALIPER: A hydraulically activated device in a disc brake system, which is mounted straddling the brake rotor (disc). The caliper contains at least one piston and two brake pads. Hydraulic pressure on the piston(s) forces the pads against the rotor.

CAMSHAFT: A shaft in the engine on which are the lobes (cams) which operate the valves. The camshaft is driven by the crankshaft, via a belt, chain or gears, at one half the crankshaft speed.

CAPACITOR: A device which stores an electrical charge.

CARBON MONOXIDE (CO): A colorless, odorless gas given off as a normal byproduct of combustion. It is poisonous and extremely dangerous in confined areas, building up slowly to toxic levels without warning if adequate ventilation is not available.

CARBURETOR: A device, usually mounted on the intake manifold of an engine, which mixes the air and fuel in the proper proportion to allow even combustion.

CATALYTIC CONVERTER: A device installed in the exhaust system, like a muffler, that converts harmful byproducts of combustion into carbon dioxide and water vapor by means of a heat-producing chemical reaction.

CENTRIFUGAL ADVANCE: A mechanical method of advancing the spark timing by using flyweights in the distributor that react to centrifugal force generated by the distributor shaft rotation.

CHECK VALVE: Any one-way valve installed to permit the flow of air, fuel or vacuum in one direction only.

CHOKE: A device, usually a moveable valve, placed in the intake path of a carburetor to restrict the flow of air.

CIRCUIT: Any unbroken path through which an electrical current can flow. Also used to describe fuel flow in some instances.

CIRCUIT BREAKER: A switch which protects an electrical circuit from overload by opening the circuit when the current flow exceeds a predetermined level. Some circuit breakers must be reset manually, while most reset automatically.

COIL (IGNITION): A transformer in the ignition circuit which steps up the voltage provided to the spark plugs.

COMBINATION MANIFOLD: An assembly which includes both the intake and exhaust manifolds in one casting.

COMBINATION VALVE: A device used in some fuel systems that routes fuel vapors to a charcoal storage canister instead of venting them into the atmosphere. The valve relieves fuel tank pressure and allows fresh air into the tank as the fuel level drops to prevent a vapor lock situation.

COMPRESSION RATIO: The comparison of the total volume of the cylinder and combustion chamber with the piston at BDC and the piston at TDC.

CONDENSER: 1. An electrical device which acts to store an electrical charge, preventing voltage surges. 2. A radiator-like device in the air conditioning system in which refrigerant gas condenses into a liquid, giving off heat.

CONDUCTOR: Any material through which an electrical current can be transmitted easily.

CONTINUITY: Continuous or complete circuit. Can be checked with an ohmmeter.

COUNTERSHAFT: An intermediate shaft which is rotated by a mainshaft and transmits, in turn, that rotation to a working part.

CRANKCASE: The lower part of an engine in which the crankshaft and related parts operate.

CRANKSHAFT: The main driving shaft of an engine which receives reciprocating motion from the pistons and converts it to rotary motion.

CYLINDER: In an engine, the round hole in the engine block in which the piston(s) ride.

CYLINDER BLOCK: The main structural member of an engine in which is found the cylinders, crankshaft and other principal parts.

CYLINDER HEAD: The detachable portion of the engine, usually fastened to the top of the cylinder block and containing all or most of the combustion chambers. On overhead valve engines, it contains the valves and their operating parts. On overhead cam engines, it contains the camshaft as well.

DEAD CENTER: The extreme top or bottom of the piston stroke.

DETONATION: An unwanted explosion of the air/fuel mixture in the combustion chamber caused by excess heat and compression, advanced timing, or an overly lean mixture. Also referred to as "ping".

DIAPHRAGM: A thin, flexible wall separating two cavities, such as in a vacuum advance unit.

DIESELING: A condition in which hot spots in the combustion chamber cause the engine to run on after the key is turned off.

DIFFERENTIAL: A geared assembly which allows the transmission of motion between drive axles, giving one axle the ability to turn faster than the other.

DIODE: An electrical device that will allow current to flow in one direction only.

DISC BRAKE: A hydraulic braking assembly consisting of a brake disc, or rotor, mounted on an axle, and a caliper assembly containing, usually two brake pads which are activated by hydraulic pressure. The pads are forced against the sides of the disc, creating friction which slows the vehicle.

DISTRIBUTOR: A mechanically driven device on an engine which is responsible for electrically firing the spark plug at a predetermined point of the piston stroke.

DOWEL PIN: A pin, inserted in mating holes in two different parts allowing those parts to maintain a fixed relationship.

DRUM BRAKE: A braking system which consists of two brake shoes and one or two wheel cylinders, mounted on a fixed backing plate, and a brake drum, mounted on an axle, which revolves around the assembly.

DWELL: The rate, measured in degrees of shaft rotation, at which an electrical circuit cycles on and off.

ELECTRONIC CONTROL UNIT (ECU): Ignition module, module, amplifier or igniter. See Module for definition.

ELECTRONIC IGNITION: A system in which the timing and firing of the spark plugs is controlled by an electronic control unit, usually called a module. These systems have no points or condenser.

END-PLAY: The measured amount of axial movement in a shaft.

ENGINE: A device that converts heat into mechanical energy.

EXHAUST MANIFOLD: A set of cast passages or pipes which conduct exhaust gases from the engine.

FEELER GAUGE: A blade, usually metal, of precisely predetermined thickness, used to measure the clearance between two parts.

FIRING ORDER: The order in which combustion occurs in the cylinders of an engine. Also the order in which spark is distributed to the plugs by the distributor.

FLOODING: The presence of too much fuel in the intake manifold and combustion chamber which prevents the air/fuel mixture from firing, thereby causing a no-start situation.

FLYWHEEL: A disc shaped part bolted to the rear end of the crankshaft. Around the outer perimeter is affixed the ring gear. The starter drive engages the ring gear, turning the flywheel, which rotates the crankshaft, imparting the initial starting motion to the engine.

FOOT POUND (ft. lbs. or sometimes, ft.lb.): The amount of energy or work needed to raise an item weighing one pound, a distance of one foot.

FUSE: A protective device in a circuit which prevents circuit overload by breaking the circuit when a specific amperage is present. The device is constructed around a strip or wire of a lower amperage rating than the circuit it is designed to protect. When an amperage higher than that stamped on the fuse is present in the circuit, the strip or wire melts, opening the circuit.

GEAR RATIO: The ratio between the number of teeth on meshing gears.

GENERATOR: A device which converts mechanical energy into electrical energy.

HEAT RANGE: The measure of a spark plug's ability to dissipate heat from its firing end. The higher the heat range, the hotter the plug fires.

HUB: The center part of a wheel or gear.

HYDROCARBON (HC): Any chemical compound made up of hydrogen and carbon. A major pollutant formed by the engine as a byproduct of combustion.

HYDROMETER: An instrument used to measure the specific gravity of a solution.

INCH POUND (inch lbs.; sometimes in.lb. or in. lbs.): One twelfth of a foot pound.

INDUCTION: A means of transferring electrical energy in the form of a magnetic field. Principle used in the ignition coil to increase voltage.

INJECTOR: A device which receives metered fuel under relatively low pressure and is activated to inject the fuel into the engine under relatively high pressure at a predetermined time.

INPUT SHAFT: The shaft to which torque is applied, usually carrying the driving gear or gears.

INTAKE MANIFOLD: A casting of passages or pipes used to conduct air or a fuel/air mixture to the cylinders.

JOURNAL: The bearing surface within which a shaft operates.

KEY: A small block usually fitted in a notch between a shaft and a hub to prevent slippage of the two parts.

MANIFOLD: A casting of passages or set of pipes which connect the cylinders to an inlet or outlet source.

MANIFOLD VACUUM: Low pressure in an engine intake manifold formed just below the throttle plates. Manifold vacuum is highest at idle and drops under acceleration.

MASTER CYLINDER: The primary fluid pressurizing device in a hydraulic system. In automotive use, it is found in brake and hydraulic clutch systems and is pedal activated, either directly or, in a power brake system, through the power booster.

MODULE: Electronic control unit, amplifier or igniter of solid state or integrated design which controls the current flow in the ignition primary circuit based on input from the pick-up coil. When the module opens the primary circuit, high secondary voltage is induced in the coil.

NEEDLE BEARING: A bearing which consists of a number (usually a large number) of long, thin rollers.

OHM: The unit used to measure the resistance of conductor-to-electrical flow. One ohm is the amount of resistance that limits current flow to one ampere in a circuit with one volt of pressure.

OHMMETER: An instrument used for measuring the resistance, in ohms, in an electrical circuit.

OUTPUT SHAFT: The shaft which transmits torque from a device, such as a transmission.

OVERDRIVE: A gear assembly which produces more shaft revolutions than that transmitted to it.

OVERHEAD CAMSHAFT (OHC): An engine configuration in which the camshaft is mounted on top of the cylinder head and operates the valve either directly or by means of rocker arms.

OVERHEAD VALVE (OHV): An engine configuration in which all of the valves are located in the cylinder head and the camshaft is located in the cylinder block. The camshaft operates the valves via lifters and pushrods.

OXIDES OF NITROGEN (NOx): Chemical compounds of nitrogen produced as a byproduct of combustion. They combine with hydrocarbons to produce smog.

OXYGEN SENSOR: Used with the feedback system to sense the presence of oxygen in the exhaust gas and signal the computer which can reference the voltage signal to an air/fuel ratio.

PINION: The smaller of two meshing gears.

PISTON RING: An open-ended ring which fits into a groove on the outer diameter of the piston. Its chief function is to form a seal between the piston and cylinder wall. Most automotive pistons have three rings: two for compression sealing; one for oil sealing.

PRELOAD: A predetermined load placed on a bearing during assembly or by adjustment.

PRIMARY CIRCUIT: The low voltage side of the ignition system which consists of the ignition switch, ballast resistor or resistance wire, bypass, coil, electronic control unit and pick-up coil as well as the connecting wires and harnesses.

PRESS FIT: The mating of two parts under pressure, due to the inner diameter of one being smaller than the outer diameter of the other, or vice versa; an interference fit.

RACE: The surface on the inner or outer ring of a bearing on which the balls, needles or rollers move.

REGULATOR: A device which maintains the amperage and/or voltage levels of a circuit at predetermined values.

RELAY: A switch which automatically opens and/or closes a circuit.

RESISTANCE: The opposition to the flow of current through a circuit or electrical device, and is measured in ohms. Resistance is equal to the voltage divided by the amperage.

RESISTOR: A device, usually made of wire, which offers a preset amount of resistance in an electrical circuit.

RING GEAR: The name given to a ring-shaped gear attached to a differential case, or affixed to a flywheel or as part of a planetary gear set.

ROLLER BEARING: A bearing made up of hardened inner and outer races between which hardened steel rollers move.

ROTOR: 1. The disc-shaped part of a disc brake assembly, upon which the brake pads bear; also called, brake disc. 2. The device mounted atop the distributor shaft, which passes current to the distributor cap tower contacts.

SECONDARY CIRCUIT: The high voltage side of the ignition system, usually above 20,000 volts. The secondary includes the ignition coil, coil wire, distributor cap and rotor, spark plug wires and spark plugs.

SENDING UNIT: A mechanical, electrical, hydraulic or electromagnetic device which transmits information to a gauge.

SENSOR: Any device designed to measure engine operating conditions or ambient pressures and temperatures. Usually electronic in nature and designed to send a voltage signal to an on-board computer, some sensors may operate as a simple on/off switch or they may provide a variable voltage signal (like a potentiometer) as conditions or measured parameters change.

SHIM: Spacers of precise, predetermined thickness used between parts to establish a proper working relationship.

SLAVE CYLINDER: In automotive use, a device in the hydraulic clutch system which is activated by hydraulic force, disengaging the clutch.

SOLENOID: A coil used to produce a magnetic field, the effect of which is to produce work.

SPARK PLUG: A device screwed into the combustion chamber of a spark ignition engine. The basic construction is a conductive core inside of a ceramic insulator, mounted in an outer conductive base. An electrical charge from the spark plug wire travels along the conductive core and jumps a preset air gap to a grounding point or points at the end of the conductive base. The resultant spark ignites the fuel/air mixture in the combustion chamber.

SPLINES: Ridges machined or cast onto the outer diameter of a shaft or inner diameter of a bore to enable parts to mate without rotation.

TACHOMETER: A device used to measure the rotary speed of an engine, shaft, gear, etc., usually in rotations per minute.

THERMOSTAT: A valve, located in the cooling system of an engine, which is closed when cold and opens gradually in response to engine heating, controlling the temperature of the coolant and rate of coolant flow.

TOP DEAD CENTER (TDC): The point at which the piston reaches the top of its travel on the compression stroke.

TORQUE: The twisting force applied to an object.

TORQUE CONVERTER: A turbine used to transmit power from a driving member to a driven member via hydraulic action, providing changes in drive ratio and torque. In automotive use, it links the driveplate at the rear of the engine to the automatic transmission.

TRANSDUCER: A device used to change a force into an electrical signal.

TRANSISTOR: A semi-conductor component which can be actuated by a small voltage to perform an electrical switching function.

TUNE-UP: A regular maintenance function, usually associated with the replacement and adjustment of parts and components in the electrical and fuel systems of a vehicle for the purpose of attaining optimum performance.

TURBOCHARGER: An exhaust driven pump which compresses intake air and forces it into the combustion chambers at higher than atmospheric pressures. The increased air pressure allows more fuel to be burned and results in increased horsepower being produced.

VACUUM ADVANCE: A device which advances the ignition timing in response to increased engine vacuum.

VACUUM GAUGE: An instrument used to measure the presence of vacuum in a chamber.

VALVE: A device which control the pressure, direction of flow or rate of flow of a liquid or gas.

VALVE CLEARANCE: The measured gap between the end of the valve stem and the rocker arm, cam lobe or follower that activates the valve.

VISCOSITY: The rating of a liquid's internal resistance to flow.

VOLTMETER: An instrument used for measuring electrical force in units called volts. Voltmeters are always connected parallel with the circuit being tested.

WHEEL CYLINDER: Found in the automotive drum brake assembly, it is a device, actuated by hydraulic pressure, which, through internal pistons, pushes the brake shoes outward against the drums.

NOTES

MASTER INDEX

NOTES